European Integration in
Constitutional Borderla

European Integration in the Constitutional Borderlands

The NextGenerationEU Model and the Struggle for Europe's Future

Päivi Leino-Sandberg and Peter L. Lindseth

OXFORD
UNIVERSITY PRESS

OXFORD
UNIVERSITY PRESS

Great Clarendon Street, Oxford, OX2 6DP,
United Kingdom

Oxford University Press is a department of the University of Oxford.
It furthers the University's objective of excellence in research, scholarship,
and education by publishing worldwide. Oxford is a registered trade mark of
Oxford University Press in the UK and in certain other countries.

Published in the United States of America by Oxford University Press
198 Madison Avenue, New York, NY 10016, United States of America.

British Library Cataloguing in Publication Data
Data available

Library of Congress Control Number: 2026937255

ISBN 978–0–19–894952–7

DOI: 10.1093/oso/9780198949527.001.0001

Printed and bound by
CPI Group (UK) Ltd., Croydon, CR0 4YY

The manufacturer's authorized representative in the EU for product safety is
Oxford University Press España S.A. of Parque Empresarial San Fernando de Henares,
Avenida de Castilla, 2 – 28830 Madrid (www.oup.es/en or product.safety@oup.com).
OUP España S.A. also acts as importer into Spain of products made by the manufacturer.

MIX
Paper | Supporting
responsible forestry
FSC® C013604
FSC
www.fsc.org

To our families

Preface and Acknowledgements

We began this joint project in earnest in early 2023, which was, in retrospect, an oddly hopeful time. Despite the dislocations of Covid as well as the Russian invasion of Ukraine, the still-emerging NextGenerationEU (NGEU) programme and related initiatives suggested potentially promising possibilities for the future of European governance. Although we did not share the exuberance of many other legal scholars towards what NGEU might achieve, we recognised the functional pressures to which it responded, which were both acute and intense. But we also recognised that the broader ambition of NGEU was to address deeper and more chronic challenges relating to the construction of the Economic and Monetary Union (EMU). This, in turn, gave rise to the question at the heart of this book: whether and how forms of governance contemplated by NGEU—particularly its revenue, borrowing, planning, and spending dimensions (which this book calls 'the NGEU model')—might become permanent in the EU over time.

This more gradualist perspective, if we can call it that, was almost completely overtaken by the very changed political environment of the first half of 2025, precisely the time when the manuscript was being completed. The return of Donald Trump to the US presidency in January 2025, as well as the dramatic (and, following his own characterisation, dictatorial)[1] mode in which he preferred operating, radically altered US economic and security policy in the coming weeks and months and hence also the macroeconomic and geopolitical environment for Europeans. The jolt, in its historically pivotal implications, was arguably greater than the rise of China over the prior decades or even the advent of the Russian war on Ukraine in 2022. Mario Draghi, in a speech before a gathering of European and national parliamentarians in February 2025,[2] noted the dramatic changes that had taken place since he presented his report on the future of European competitiveness in September 2024:[3]

> Now the EU will face tariffs by the new US administration ... hindering our access to our largest export market ... [W]e can [also] expect to be left largely alone to guarantee security in Ukraine and in Europe itself ... The complexity of the policy response ... will require an unprecedented degree of coordination between all actors, national governments and parliaments, the Commission and the European

[1] AP News (2023), Popli (2025).
[2] Draghi (2025a).
[3] Draghi (2024a), (2024b).

> Parliament. The response must be fast, because time is not on our side ... The response must be commensurate with the size of the challenges ... Speed, scale and intensity will be essential.[4]

As the title to this book suggests, in the midst of these crises, Europe is necessarily struggling to cross what we are calling a 'constitutional borderlands'. We recognise that for certain readers, the idea of borderlands resonates with historical dynamics involving the *physical* extension of political power into new spaces and the peoples who occupy them—processes that have often involved violence and conquest, as well as difficult political-cultural adjustments to legalise and institutionalise those extensions of power.[5] We are using the idea of borderlands in a different and more metaphorical sense. Here it refers to the dynamics that have taken hold when an existing polity of ambiguous constitutional character—the EU—has sought to expand its authority not spatially (though that is part of the story) but through internal legal and political change. The principal aim has been to meet pressing macroeconomic and geopolitical demands, although one might fairly add that another key aim—at least on the part of the European Commission—has been to achieve long cherished institutional ambitions to consolidate its leadership of the integration process (a theme to which we will return at multiple junctures throughout this book).

For the EU writ large, the transformation that is our focus here has involved moving away from exercising primarily regulatory power towards developing new but still incomplete fiscal capacities, that is, dramatically increased levels of collective borrowing and spending to steer policymaking on the national level. Whether and to what extent this 'phase transition'[6] in the nature of EU governance comes to fruition remains an open question. But as this book seeks to show, this transition has also required—and continues to require—difficult adjustments of a political-cultural as well as legal-institutional nature. The process points toward the possible emergence of an EU that could lay claim to having a robustly 'constitutional' character in its own right, whose identifying characteristic would be the capacity to mobilise fiscal resources in a legitimate and compulsory fashion separate and apart from the Member States.[7] The EU is not there yet, and hence the description of the topography, obstacles, and opportunities that mark these metaphorical 'constitutional borderlands' is a central purpose of this book.

To understand the struggle that Europe is now facing, one must recognise this key fact: what we might call the 'old EU' was simply 'not built to operate in this environment'.[8] No doubt, 'the adoption of NextGenerationEU sharply increased the central level and brought under collective control a number of policy initiatives' that

[4] Draghi (2025a, min 04:54–07:08).

[5] See, eg, Blackhawk (2023, p 11, nn 36–37 and accompanying text), providing a brief overview of borderlands legal-historiography in the US case, citing, eg, Dudziak and Volpp (2006).

[6] See, eg, Lindseth (2023, p 207), (2021a, p 1028), (2017, p 61).

[7] See Chapter One, Section B.

[8] Wyplosz (2024, p 9).

had previously been understood to be 'the exclusive responsibility of national governments'.[9] As we completed the book over the course of the first half of 2025, it was increasingly clear that there were dramatically heightened functional pressures to go still further in this centralisation and supranationalisation process. To quote another line of Mario Draghi from his February 2025 speech that we intentionally omitted from the block quotation above: 'To cope with these challenges, *it is increasingly clear that we need to act more and more as if we were one state*' (emphasis added). As the Introduction and Chapter One describe in greater detail, the operative term in this sentence is 'as if'. Despite a dominant discourse in the EU that describes the integration project as *already* of an autonomously constitutional character, supranational governance in Europe has nonetheless remained heavily dependent on the constitutional power and legitimacy flowing from the Member States severally rather than possessing that power and legitimacy in its own right.

In the interest of completeness, this book has obviously needed to grapple with the implications of the dramatically changed environment post-January 2025, as well as whether and to what extent NGEU provides a model that will help the EU meet those challenges. The book certainly still reflects the more gradualist ('muddling through'-type) sensibility of the pre-January 2025 era. But in thinking of the ways that Europe might continue to evolve from here (especially in the book's later chapters), we also needed to recognise the acute transformation of the geopolitical, macroeconomic, and hence legal situation, and how that impacts the EU's navigation through the constitutional borderlands in which it finds itself. The analysis follows developments through (and a few months beyond) the publication in July 2025 of the Commission's package of proposals for the new Multiannual Financial Framework (MFF) for 2028–2034—which, as we shall see, demonstrates quite clearly how several dimensions of the NGEU model may be emerging as a new normal for European governance.

The analysis is both descriptive and normative. Embedded within the historical developments are numerous normative questions about the sort of integration project the EU may, could, or should become in the future. Our analysis attempts to address these normative dimensions head on, most importantly with regard to the growing institutional ambitions of the European Commission. As the chapters below will demonstrate, the Commission has worked assiduously over the life of the NGEU programme—and indeed well before it—to control not only outcomes but also access to information about the process leading to those outcomes. A key element of this story is how the Commission has sought to obscure the law as a realm of political contestation, involving critical questions that, in normal circumstances, should be the subject of robust democratic and constitutional debate. One of the central aims of this book is to return those obscured legal questions to the political foreground and hopefully prompt the sort of debate needed for the integration project

9 Ibid.

to navigate its way successfully through these complex and difficult constitutional borderlands.

* * *

It is of course impossible to undertake a project of this magnitude without accumulating some serious debts of gratitude. Special thanks go to the Helsinki Institute for Social Sciences and Humanities for supporting our research through a visiting professorship that allowed us to deepen our collaboration over the course of writing this book. Special thanks also go the University of Connecticut School of Law and its Dean, Eboni Nelson, along with a succession of research deans, Richard Wilson (now of Princeton University) and Anne Dailey, for supporting the work of this book through funding a sabbatical leave and various other research stipends.

As always, the authors are solely responsible for the arguments and assertions in this volume. Nonetheless, we would like to thank colleagues (listed here alphabetically) who generously commented on excerpts of earlier chapters in progress or related texts, or engaged in conversations about the central ideas of this book: Anya Bernstein, Gráinne de Búrca, Richard Crowe, Armin Cuyvers, Marco Dani, Paul Dermine, Aaron Dhir, Tim Ellemann, Joyce Esser, Miguel de Figueiredo, Berina Fischinger-Corbo, Cristina Fasone, Susi Forderer, Daniel Francis, Alberto de Gregorio Merino, Friedrich Heinemann, Tamara Hervey, Louis Honée, Bogdan Iancu, Jasper Kamradt, Maciej Kisilowski, Martti Koskenniemi, Mattias Kumm, Mattis Leson, Nicola Lupo, John Morijn, Gaurav Mukherjee, Ingolf Pernice, Ángel Oquendo, Maria Patrin, Giovanni Piccirilli, Emanuele Rebasti, Amnon Reichman, Antti Ronkainen, Matthias Ruffert, Lukas Schaupp, Joep Schoenmakers, Moritz Schramm, Marta Simoncini, Luke Dimitrios Spieker, Marc Steiert, Francesca Strumia, Vesa Vihriälä, Wim Voermans, and Ruth Weber. We have also benefited from the work of a number of investigative journalists covering the RRF, including Jean Comte, Staffan Dahllöf, Alexander Fanta, Jarno Liski, and, last but certainly not least, Peter Teffer. We would also like to extend special thanks to Tuomas Saarenheimo, who generously read all draft chapters and offered numerous critical comments, pushing back on both tone and substance. The authors also wish to thank Marius Berbier, Juan Manuel Klein, and Emily Lemke for their helpful research assistance. We thank also our editors at OUP, Peter Daniell, Kezia Johnson, David Lipp, Reyman Joseph, and Fiona Tatham for shepherding this project from the original book proposal through production and publication.

In addition, the authors are grateful for the opportunity to discuss and/or present earlier drafts of portions of this book in the following venues: the Jean Monnet Center for International and Regional Economic Law & Justice at NYU School of Law; the Global Constitutionalism Colloquium at the Wissenschaftszentrum Berlin für Sozialforschung (WZB); the Institute for the Study of European Laws at City Law School University of London; the High-Level Roundtable on Recovery and Resilience Facility organised by the Cabinet of President Ursula van der Leyen, European Commission; the EU Law Scholars Workshop at Berkeley Law School;

the Informal Expert Dialogue on EU Cohesion Policy organised by Clingendael - Netherlands Institute of International Relations; the Center for Parliamentary Studies at LUISS Guido Carli University of Rome; the publication event 'The Future of Cohesion Policy 2028–2034 from a Fiscal Policy Perspective' organised by the Centre for European Economic Research (ZEW) and the German Federal Ministry of Finance; the Conference 'The EU (Re)Turn to Economic Activism' at the Faculty of Law, University of Trento; the Emmy Noether Junior Research Group, Walter Hallstein Institut für Europäisches Verfassungsrecht der Humboldt-Universität zu Berlin; the Doctoral Seminar, Department of Legal Studies, Central European University, Vienna; the Department of Constitutional and Administrative Law, the University of Leiden Faculty of Law; the 'Numeric Constitutionalism' workshop organised at the Department of Legal Studies, University of Bologna; the Constitutional Law and Politics Working Group at the European University Institute Department of Law; the faculty workshop at the University of Connecticut School of Law, and the inaugural conference of the European Law Unbound Society in Prague.

We have chosen a cover picture meant to align with the title and central animating metaphor of this book. The photo is of Scandes seen from atop Halti close to the Three-Country Cairn where the international borders of Finland, Sweden, and Norway meet. The photo is taken by Mikko Karjalainen, and we are grateful for the permission to use it.

Portions of this book draw on publications that have appeared previously: Leino-Sandberg, P and Lindseth, P, How Cohesion Became the EU's Vehicle for Economic Policy: Tracing the Hidden History of Article 175(3) TFEU. Verfassungsblog (14 August 2023), https://verfassungsblog.de/how-cohesion-became-the-eus-vehicle-for-economic-policy/; Leino-Sandberg, P, In the Dark: How the Commission Deals with Access to Documents Requests relating to Europe's Recovery Transformation. Verfassungsblog (15 April 2024), https://verfassungsblog.de/in-the-dark/; Leino-Sandberg, P, 'Very Tight Control': On (the Absence of) Member State Scrutiny of the EU's Recovery Spending. Verfassungsblog (22 April 2024), https://verfassungsblog.de/very-tight-control/; Lindseth, PL and Leino-Sandberg, P, Crisis, Reinterpretation, and the Rule of Law: Repurposing 'Cohesion' as a General EU Spending Power. *Hague Journal on the Rule of Law* 16, 587–610 (2024); Lindseth, PL and Leino-Sandberg, P, Democratizing Draghi: Why the 'Competitiveness Report' Demands Treaty Reform. Verfassungsblog (12 September 2024), https://verfassungsblog.de/draghi-report-investment-eu-competition-treaty-reform/; Leino-Sandberg, P, Cohesion Policy and Subsidiarity: A Legal Analysis, in L Feld, F Heinemann, and Z Asatryan (eds), *The Future of EU Cohesion* (pp 75–122), Mohr Siebeck 2025; Leino-Sandberg, P '70 Years of EU Law'—The Politics of a Professional Language', *Zeitschrift für ausländisches öffentliches Recht und Völkerrecht* (2026); Leino-Sandberg, P, 'The Secret Life of EU Treaties. The Politics of the EU's 'Living Constitutionalism', *European Law Open* (2026).

We dedicate this book to our families. Special thanks belong to Lise Martina for her steadfast support throughout the project, including willingness to listen to Peter's karaoke in Helsinki while immersing herself in the art of Helene Schjerfbeck.

Finally, at numerous junctures in the book, we qualify our statements with the phrase 'as of this writing'. This should be taken to mean through the end September 2025, although at points during the final editing of the manuscript we were also able to take note of certain sources or events after that date.

Päivi Leino-Sandberg
Helsinki

Peter L. Lindseth
New York

15 October 2025

Contents

PART TWO: THE EMERGENCE AND DEVELOPMENT OF THE NGEU MODEL

Abbreviations

BICC	Budgetary Instrument for Convergence and Competitiveness
BoP	Balance of Payments
BVerfG	Bundesverfassungsgericht
CAP	Common Agricultural Policy
CBAM	Carbon Border Adjustment Mechanism
CCI	Convergence and Competitiveness Instrument
CCT	Competitiveness Coordination Tool
CEE countries	Central and Eastern European countries
CFR	Charter of Fundamental Rights
CFSP	Common Foreign and Security Policy
CJEU	Court of Justice of the European Union
CLM	Community Loan Mechanism
CORE	Corporate Resource for Europe
COSAC	Conference of Parliamentary Committees for Union Affairs of Parliaments of the European Union
CPF	Common Provisioning Fund
CPR	Common Provision Regulation
CRA	credit-rating agency
CRO	Chief Risk Officer
CSR	Country-specific recommendation
DFS	Diversified Funding Strategy
DG BUDG	Directorate-General for Budget
DG ECFIN	Directorate-General for Economic and Financial Affairs
DG EMPL	Directorate-General for Employment, Social Affairs and Inclusion
DG REGIO	Directorate-General for Regional and Urban Policy
EAG	External Action Guarantee
EAGGF	European Agricultural Guidance and Guarantee Fund
EAR	external assigned revenue
EC	European Community
ECA	European Court of Auditors
ECB	European Central Bank
ECF	European Competitiveness Fund
EDF	European Defence Fund
EDP	Excessive Deficit Procedure
EEA	European Economic Area
EFB	European Fiscal Board
EFC	Economic and Financial Committee
EFSF	European Financial Stability Facility
EFSM	European Financial Stabilisation Mechanism
EFTA	European Free Trade Association

EGBs	European Government Bonds
EGF	Economic Governance Framework
EGTS	European groupings of territorial cooperation
EIB	European Investment Bank
EISF	European Investment Stabilisation Function
ELM	External Lending Mandate
EMU	Economic and Monetary Union
EP	European Parliament
EPC	Economic Policy Committee
EPF	European Peace Facility
EPP	European People's Party
EPPO	European Public Prosecutor's Office
ERA	Extraordinary Revenue Acceleration Loans
ERDF	European Regional Development Fund
ERM II	European Exchange Rate Mechanism
ESA	European System of Accounts
ESBs	European Safe Bonds
ESF	European Social Fund
ESI	European structural and investment funds
ESM	European Stability Mechanism
ESRB	European Systemic Risk Board
ETS	Emissions Trading System
ETS2	expanded Emissions Trading System
EU	European Union
EURI	European Union Recovery Instrument
FCC	German Federal Constitutional Court
FNLC	financing not linked to costs
GDP	Gross Domestic Product
GG	Grundgesetz
GNI	Gross National Income
IFI	International Fund for Ireland
IFIs	independent fiscal institutions
IIA	Interinstitutional Agreement
IMF	International Monetary Fund
IPCEI	Important Projects of Common European Interest
JURI	Committee on Legal Affairs of the European Parliament
MDB	multilateral development bank
MFA	macro-financial assistance
MFF	Multiannual Financial Framework
MLI	multilateral lending institution
MOU	Memorandum of Understanding
MTFSP	medium-term fiscal-structural plan
NGEU	NextGenerationEU
NGO	non-governmental organisation
NP	National Parliament
NRPP	National and Regional Partnership Plan

NRRP	National Recovery and Resilience Plan
OA	Operational Arrangement
OBF	off-budget fund
OECD	Organization for Economic Cooperation and Development
OLAF	European Anti-Fraud Office
OMT	Outright Monetary Transactions
ORD	Own Resources Decision
PCS	Pandemic Crisis Support
PEPP	Pandemic Emergency Purchase Programme
PSPP	Public Sector Purchase Programme
RDT	Reform Delivery Tool
RECOVER	Recovery and Resilience Task Force
RRF	Recovery and Resilience Facility
RRP	Recovery and Resilience Plan
RSP	Reform Support Programme
S&D	Socialists and Democrats
SAFE	Security Action for Europe
SBBS	Sovereign Bond-Backed Securities
SCF	Social Climate Fund
SGP	Stability and Growth Pact
SME	small and medium-sized enterprise
SMP	Securities Market Programme
SPV	special purpose vehicle
SRM	Single Resolution Mechanism
SRSP	Structural Reform Support Programme
SSAs	Supranationals, Sub-Sovereigns, and Agencies
SSM	Single Supervisory Mechanism
STEP	Strategic Technologies for Europe Platform
SURE	Support to mitigate Unemployment Risks in an Emergency
SWD	Staff Working Document
TEC	Treaty Establishing the European Community
TFEU	Treaty on the Functioning of the European Union
UFA	Unified Funding Approach
ULCM	Ukraine Loan Cooperation Mechanism
VAT	Value-Added Tax

Introduction

NextGenerationEU as a Programme and Model for the Future

A. The Contours of a Constitutional Experiment

As of the date of publication of this book in 2026, the European Union will be in the sixth and final year of the NextGenerationEU (NGEU) programme, adopted in the midst of the Covid crisis in 2020. As this book shows, NGEU has been a legal, political, and ultimately constitutional experiment of considerable proportions. The programme itself was understood initially as 'an exceptional response to exceptional circumstances',[1] emerging in a moment of deep empathy generated by the first pandemic pictures coming from Bergamo, Italy, in early 2020 and then broadcast throughout Europe. In that atmosphere, the need for heightened forms of solidarity seemed broadly apparent.[2] Nonetheless, the adoption and subsequent implementation of NGEU has led to a fundamental transformation in the nature of the integration project, involving an effort to establish a quasi-autonomous EU borrowing and spending power of an unprecedented scale and scope. The programme further envisioned backing that power with new revenue to help service the dramatically increased levels of EU debt. And it further sought to use the new revenue, borrowing, and spending powers to support a national-supranational planning process designed to address not only immediate macroeconomic and geopolitical crises but also longer-term environmental and climate challenges.

The purpose of this book is to assess the historical origins, current trajectories, and future implications of the NGEU experiment by foregrounding the legal debate and its political implications. To understand the experiment's various dimensions, however, it is impossible to look at the NextGenerationEU programme in isolation. The reason, quite simply, is that NGEU is *not just a programme but also a model.*[3] Elements of this 'NGEU model' are visible today in numerous other initiatives known under a

[1] Wyplosz (2024, p 9).

[2] See Chapter Three, nn 199–200 and accompanying text.

[3] See, eg, Mario Draghi, then-Prime Minister of Italy, speaking before the European Parliament in May 2022: 'For long-term investments in areas such as defence, energy, food and industrial security, the model is NextGenerationEU'. European Parliament (2022a) ('*Per quanto riguarda gli investimenti di lungo periodo in aree come la difesa, l'energia, la sicurezza alimentare e industriale, il modello è quello del Next Generation EU*').

European Integration in the Constitutional Borderlands. Päivi Leino-Sandberg and Peter L. Lindseth, Oxford University Press.
DOI: 10.1093/oso/9780198949527.003.0001

collection of EU labels and acronyms such as SURE, REPowerEU, the Social Climate Fund, STEP, the reformed Economic Governance Framework, the Competitiveness Fund, the Ukraine Facility and the ReArmEurope—Readiness 2030 plan, among many others,[4] not to mention the Commission's package of proposals for the new Multiannual Financial Framework (MFF) for 2028–2034 in July 2025.[5] This book initially focuses on NextGenerationEU itself because that is where we see most clearly the emergence of the revenue, borrowing, planning, and spending powers upon which the new model of integration has been built.[6]

As this book argues, the emergence of the NGEU model has been marked by deep contradictions suggestive of a difficult struggle that Europe is enduring as it attempts to traverse the borderlands between the old regime of 'integration through law' to a new regime that aspires to be one of 'integration through funding'.[7] The book assesses this new regime critically, questioning whether it in fact entails a real advance in the integration process. The NGEU model has evolved under the intense geopolitical pressures brought on by the Russian war on Ukraine and the return of Donald Trump to the US presidency, pushing it in new directions. What this book shows is that, in terms of revenues, borrowing, planning, and spending, key components of NGEU were the product of ideas that had been gestating in the institutional background for nearly a decade if not more. Those ideas were far too ambitious to implement outside the context of crisis (at least without Treaty change); hence the importance of the ongoing atmosphere of upheaval that has beset the EU over the last decade and a half or more. At the time of finalising the manuscript in the first half of 2025—and more particularly with the announcement of the Commission's MFF proposals in July of that year—we can now see quite clearly how the NGEU model has shaped a new vision of a permanently transformed system of EU governance.[8]

NextGenerationEU—both as a programme and a model for the future—has been an ongoing experiment taking place in real time. The ideas undergirding the model find their origins in functionalist problem-solving and legal reinterpretation and re-engineering of the existing Treaties that, in their essential details, have taken place almost entirely outside of public view, much less debate. This is in keeping with a standard imperative in crisis management, in which—according to two political scientists studying the origins of the NGEU model—the group of key players must 'be kept informal, arguably even "unrepresentative" or "undemocratic"'.[9] In a parallel fashion, on the planning and spending side, the NGEU model has involved a relatively small cadre of officials at the national and supranational levels whose interactions were often barely visible to politically responsible actors or the broader public.[10]

[4] For more detailed discussion of this model beyond the confines of NGEU strictly speaking, see generally Chapter Five.
[5] See Chapter Six, Section B.
[6] See especially Chapters Three and Four.
[7] de Witte (2023); see also Patrin (2023a).
[8] See generally Chapter Six.
[9] Smeets and Beach (2023, p 392).
[10] See Chapter Four, Sections A and B.

As for key components of the NGEU model, such as 'financing not linked to costs',[11] or 'cash for reforms',[12] the Commission had essentially zero experience, certainly not at scale, thus reinforcing the truly unprecedented and experimental character of the programme. The transformative effects of the NGEU model are thus an object lesson in how non-transparent legal reinterpretations and technocratic practices can gain permanence through continuing functional demand as well as path-dependency and institutional and political lock-in over time. The problems that the NGEU model were designed to address were indisputably real. Nonetheless, the means used—stealth re-engineering of the existing Treaties, the development of executive-technocratic means of implementation, the magnification of the Commission's role combined with the systematic exclusion of parliamentary debate and scrutiny, both European and national—are profoundly concerning, particularly if extended into the future.

No doubt, the EU Treaties may present a classic case of the 'trade-off between interpretation and amendment',[13] in which texts that are formally difficult to amend are often forced to evolve informally by way of interpretation.[14] Our main concern here is not based on some theoretical objection derived from our understanding of the proper boundary between interpretation and amendment, a challenging question to be sure.[15] Nor is it primarily based, from a substantive legal perspective, on the questionable nature of those reinterpretations—there is a considerable historical pedigree to using legally doubtful means to effectuate constitutional change (a point to which we return in the Conclusion).[16] Our main concern, rather, relates to the consequences of those reinterpretations for the functioning of democratic procedures and accountability at both EU and national level, as well as the political economy and distributive impact of the resulting transformation. The extension of powers of EU institutions, in particular those of the Commission, into areas of national competence without engaging in Treaty reform has resulted in modes of operation that are at once both highly inefficient while also difficult to justify, much less explain. The core changes repeatedly strain what this book calls the 'power-legitimacy nexus',[17] referring to the essential connection between the scope of the powers that the EU purports to exercise and the extent of the autonomous legitimacy it possesses. This strain is one symptom of the ultimate fragility of the NGEU model, whose complex design and operation has flowed from the EU's need to draw on democratic and constitutional legitimacy of the Member States at repeated junctures. This has meant that the model has been much better at funding ultimately national projects rather than developing genuinely European public goods.[18]

[11] See Chapter Two, nn 263–73 and accompanying text.

[12] See chapter Three, nn 123–25 and accompanying text.

[13] Hirschl and Shachar (2018, p 431).

[14] Though that claim is empirically doubtful given the number of times Treaties have been successfully amended, or even largely rewritten, over the course of integration history stretching back three quarters of a century.

[15] Cf Levinson (1991), Kay (2019).

[16] See, eg, Ackerman (1991) and Kay (2014); see also Lindseth (2021b).

[17] For background on this nexus, see, eg, Lindseth (2023), (2020a), (2016a).

[18] For further discussion, see Chapter Four, Section E.

This fragility and distributive inefficiency leads us to call for a more overt and political process of constitutional reflection about the foundations, design, and operation of the NGEU model going forward, including Treaty change if necessary. An overtly political process of reassessment—and, if needed, possible course correction—will be essential to shore up the model's legitimacy, effectiveness, and durability. The purpose of this book is to contribute to that process even as the integration project continues to navigate its way through uncharted borderlands of profound constitutional change.

B. Merging the Perspectives of Two Scholars

This is a co-authored book. We list our names alphabetically, not as an indicator the amount of work that each of us did but as a sign that our contributions were quite even and complementary over the three and half years of research and writing. In the end, our shared efforts are quite difficult to disaggregate.

The analysis that follows explicitly seeks to merge the perspectives of two different scholars. Before this project, we did not actually even know each other personally. Both our friendship and our scholarly collaboration have grown together as this project has unfolded. We met only because one of us (Päivi) decided to email the other (Peter) to ask whether he might be willing to offer comments on a chapter she was then writing that drew on some of his ideas in further developing her own views on NGEU.[19] Multiple emails and Zoom conversations followed, from which it became quickly apparent that we were like-minded on many dimensions of European integration—sympathetically supportive but also deeply critical on crucial points. A collaborative project on the implications of NGEU seemed in order. But it also soon became clear that the initial plan—a law review article of some kind, either a more focused one in a European journal or a more extended one in a US journal—would be inadequate to match the scope of the topic or the numerable issues it raised. What was needed was a more comprehensive account that only a book could provide. Fortunately, along the way, we also learned that we very much enjoyed the back-and-forth in terms of research and writing together and that our skill-sets were complementary. More importantly, as the collaboration deepened, we came to appreciate that our ideas and prior work synergised in very productive ways.

This book reflects that synergy. Chapter One will give a deeper sense of the elements of our thinking that this work seeks to pull together, along with a more detailed overview of the argument of the book. Suffice it to say here that Päivi's prior work—beyond her service as a legal advisor on many of the governance processes described in the book—has critically examined key aspects of the Economic and Monetary Union (EMU),[20] as well as the legal dimensions of NGEU more specifically.[21] Perhaps

[19] The chapter has now appeared as Leino-Sandberg (2023a).
[20] See, eg, Leino-Sandberg and Saarenheimo (2018), (2017).
[21] Leino-Sandberg and Ruffert (2022).

more importantly for our purposes, her work has also focused scholarly attention on 'the politics of legal expertise in EU policy-making'.[22] This second line of analysis has brought to the surface the crucial but often hidden roles of institutional EU lawyers in navigating around the limits and gaps in EU powers in order to expand supranational authority. This mode of operation is made all the more problematic by the EU's characteristic lack of transparency—another longstanding research interest of Päivi's—which has been particularly important in the development of the NGEU model.

Peter's body of work directly complements this second line of analysis, raising questions about the ideological presuppositions that those very same EU lawyers (along with EU judges and supportive legal academics) have used to justify many of these expansions.[23] The most important has been to treat the EU *as if* it were already robustly constitutional rather than an extension of executive-technocratic (ie 'administrative') governance from the national to the supranational level.[24] The key distinguishing characteristic between a merely administrative versus a genuinely constitutional level of governance is that the latter possesses the power and legitimacy to extract and redirect ('mobilise') fiscal and human resources from society in a compulsory fashion in its own right.[25] The analytical problem at the core of this book is that the EU has lacked (and, indeed, still lacks) the robust legitimacy, and hence the power, to exercise this defining characteristic of autonomous constitutional authority on its own. This explains why the EU remains ultimately dependent, 'parasitically' as Kaarlo Tuori has put it,[26] on the intermediation of the Member States for the legitimate-compulsory mobilisation of fiscal resources. The academic terminology we use to capture this reality is 'polycentric' and '*demoi*-cratic', in which integration is forced to coordinate among multiple constitutional polities representing still distinct 'peoples'.[27] The lack of legitimate-compulsory mobilisation of fiscal resources at the EU level is a reflection of the persistently polycentric and *demoi*-cratic character of the integration project.

Despite the advent of common borrowing for spending on a large scale, the emergence of the NGEU model has not changed this basic polycentric and *demoi*-cratic reality in any fundamental sense. What the development of the NGEU model *has* done, however, is to bring the integration project right up to the edge of a genuinely constitutional transformation, through a process of reinterpreting an array of Treaty provisions (albeit in deeply tenuous and often hidden ways).[28] The EU is now struggling to find a way to cross the Rubicon that lies at the heart of these constitutional borderlands—that is, it is trying to develop some form of fiscal mobilisation powers to help it address a range of pressing macroeconomic, geopolitical, and environmental demands—or at least to buy some measure of legitimacy by associating itself with the

22 Leino-Sandberg (2021a); see also Leino-Sandberg (2023a), (2022).
23 See, eg, Lindseth (2023); see also Lindseth (2017).
24 See generally Lindseth (2010). For the ultimate roots of this view, see Lindseth (1999).
25 See, eg, Lindseth (2023), (2017), (2016a).
26 Tuori (2015). For a review, critique, and further development of that thesis, see Lindseth (2016a).
27 See Chapter One, n 43 and accompanying text.
28 See especially Chapters Three, Four, and Five.

national public goods (say, in health care or education) that NGEU has been quite adept at producing.[29] Compulsory mobilisation of fiscal resources requires a deeper kind of *demos* legitimacy—what Lincoln called government *of* a people, understood as the historically legitimate basis for such mobilisation.[30] If the EU lacks the legitimacy to cross the constitutional Rubicon in this most robust sense—attaining a fully autonomous power to mobilise fiscal resources in its own right, notably through its own powers of taxation—then it can still seek to find a way at least to make the more limited NGEU model permanent (and, as such, perhaps wade into the constitutional Rubicon a few metres, rather than just 'dipping its toes').[31] That is the challenge of constitutional transition that the EU is struggling to overcome today.

The seeming success of the 'as if'-constitutional approach to Treaty interpretation in getting the EU to this point might suggest that Treaty change is unnecessary to go still further along the path of developing the EU's fiscal capacities.[32] From this view, reinterpreting the Treaties will get the EU everywhere it needs to go,[33] because all the important questions have already been decided, and the need for additional democratic-constitutional politics (instead of mere constitutional reinterpretation) is limited.[34] But as the subsequent chapters explain in detail, the legal underpinnings of the NGEU model remain quite precarious despite the heroic interpretative efforts of these same institutional lawyers. Moreover, the highly technocratic and non-transparent way in which the NGEU model has been implemented over the last half decade raises serious concerns of accountability and democratic oversight. The increasingly prevalent mode of integration—one that is inserting the EU into areas where it enjoys, at best, only supportive competence (if that)—depends on nationally-prepared but supranationally-steered and supranationally-approved spending plans. The result of this process has been to shift quite significant areas of heretofore national policymaking into an opaque process of negotiation between small groups of national executive-technocratic actors and supranational officials in the European Commission.[35] National parliaments, much less the European Parliament (EP), play little or no role in this process.

A key flaw in this process, however, has been the over-production of national rather than European public goods—that is, goods with clear European added value which will be under-produced without the intervention of EU spending.[36] This must change. Moreover, any future programmes (eg the massive planning, spending, and budget reform process contemplated by the report of Mario Draghi on 'The Future of European Competitiveness' in September 2024,[37] which the Commission sought to

[29] See Chapter Four, Section E.
[30] See Lindseth (2012a, p 6).
[31] See Chapter One, Section B.
[32] See, eg, Spieker (2024, pp 745–46); de Witte (2022, p 17).
[33] See Chapter One, nn 81–87 and accompanying text.
[34] See Conclusion, Section B.
[35] See Leino-Sandberg (2024a). For further detail, see Chapter Four, Sections A and B.
[36] For further details, see Chapter Four, Section E; and more generally Conclusion.
[37] Draghi Report (2024a), (2024b).

implement with its proposals for the new MFF for 2028–2034)[38] require much more open and transparent democratic and constitutional deliberation for their adoption and implementation.[39] Only then, in our view, would such a transformation in the nature of the integration process have any hope of gaining the necessary socio-political and socio-legal underpinnings to endure over time.

C. Methods, Sources, and Access to Documents

The methodology we use in this work is empirical, legal, and historical, though with an eye clearly trained on the future. This work places the development of the NGEU model in the context of an ongoing effort to shift the focus of integration away from its traditional legal and regulatory orientation ('integration through law') to one that uses revenue, borrowing, planning, and spending ('integration through funding') as a means of achieving a range of more ambitious goals, both internal and external.[40]

Our historical methodology thus leads us to view the NGEU model as part of the development of the Economic and Monetary Union extending back over multiple decades and persisting through and including the series of crises that have buffeted the integration project over the last decade and a half.[41] Most importantly, the NGEU model must be understood in the confines of the long-established, if much criticised, Treaty-based choice to build the EMU on an 'asymmetrical' basis. This refers to the centralisation of monetary policy at the EU level but the continued decentralisation of fiscal and economic policy in the Member States, subject only to coordination at the EU level. To paraphrase the words of one EU institutional lawyer (a member of the Commission Legal Service, writing in a personal capacity in 2019),[42] the aspiration of what would become the NGEU model was explicitly to find a way to circumvent this Treaty-based choice. The aim, from this perspective, has been to fill the 'gaps' in the 'famously incomplete' and asymmetrical EMU,[43] offering 'another route' around the limitations in the Treaties that have restricted EU economic-policy competence to coordination of Member State policies.[44]

Given the empirical, legal, and historical methodology of this work, the analysis depends considerably on access to documentary evidence coming from the EU institutions themselves.[45] Some of that evidence is public (Commission communications and proposals; legal acts as actually adopted; a limited number of court decisions, etc). But before one places too much stock in currently available documentary record, one

[38] See Chapter Six, Section B.
[39] Lindseth and Leino-Sandberg (2024a); see Conclusion, Section D.
[40] See Chapter One, n 23 and accompanying text, citing de Witte (2023).
[41] See generally Chapter Two; see also Chapters Three and Five.
[42] Flynn (2019).
[43] Ibid, p 60.
[44] Ibid, p 48. For further discussion, see Chapter Three, Section A.3.
[45] For more on this methodology, see generally Leino-Sandberg (2025a).

must engage in a bit of *Quellenkritik*, or 'source criticism'. This is cornerstone of classical historical-critical methodology, which, despite the high-sounding label, simply asks us to use a bit of common sense in examining the documentary record. We must ask ourselves who produced the document, when, and with what motivation, in order to assess its reliability or probative value.

In the case of NGEU, we are often prevented from asking these questions at the level of the individual, though sometimes fair inferences can be drawn. For example, writings 'in a personal capacity' from an official of a European institution go through an authorisation procedure. Even with this standard disclaimer, any such writings must still comply with the obligation under the Staff Regulations that the writer 'conduct himself solely with the interests of the Union in mind ... objectively, impartially and in keeping with his duty of loyalty to the Union'.[46] This obligation is especially important to keep in mind when the writer is suggesting interpretations to expand the scope of EU authority that are unprecedented or operate in the face of seeming restrictions in the Treaties. Moreover, such writings 'in a personal capacity' are frequently used to influence academic scholarship, explain institutional choices, or pave the way for new interpretations—often before a highly receptive audience. There are multiple examples of such interventions by officials serving EU institutions cited throughout this book.[47]

We also can certainly engage in *Quellenkritik* at the level of the institution and its component parts, a particularly useful exercise when examining documents produced (or *not* produced) by the institution at the heart of the NGEU model: the European Commission. One striking feature of NGEU has been the Commission's consistent effort to curate NGEU's public image, a theme to which we return at several points throughout this book. Taking advantage of programme features it played a central role in designing, the Commission was able to exploit the inevitable information asymmetries that arose in a planning and spending process spread across twenty-seven Member States, controlling what information to make available and when. In our research, we have sought to move beyond this curated picture. Sometimes this involved merely asking pointed questions to the Europe Direct Contact Centre, 'the European Union's helpline when you want to know something about the EU'.[48] More

[46] Regulation No 31 (EEC), 11 (EAEC), art 11 [Staff Regulations].

[47] See, eg, Calleja et al (2024) (then-Director-General of the Commission Legal Service; see Chapter Six, nn 78–92 and accompanying text); Crowe (2024) (European Parliament Legal Service, working on the EU budget; see Chapter One, nn 86–87 and accompanying text, and Chapter Five, nn 317–18 and accompanying text); de Gregorio Merino (2024) (previously director for EMU in the Legal Service of the Council and now Director-General in the Commission Legal Service; see Chapter One, n 82 and accompanying text, and Conclusion, n 31 and accompanying text); Ioannidis (2020) (Legal Counsel, European Central Bank; see Chapter One, n 17 and accompanying text); Keppenne (2020a) (Director at the Commission Legal Service; see Chapter Three, nn 100, 110 and accompanying text) and Lindner and Nguyen (2024) (Lindner is Head of the Division for EU Institutions & Fora at the European Central Bank; see Chapter Five, n 321).

[48] Europe Direct (2025a). See, eg, Chapter Four, n 27 (re composition of Commission units dealing with RRF relevant matters); Chapter Four, n 552 (re cost of the Commission advertising campaign celebrating the achievements of the RRF).

often it has entailed making requests under Regulation (EC) No 1049/2001 (or, more simply, 'Regulation 1049/2001'), the EU's general law on public access to documents and the legal framework for requesting documents from the Commission and the Council. Regulation 1049/2001 covers all documents 'held by an institution, that is to say, documents drawn up or received by it and in its possession, in all areas of activity of the European Union.'[49] Regulation 1049/2001 requires that all access requests be handled 'promptly', within fifteen working days, though that time limit can be extended by an additional fifteen working days in exceptional circumstances.[50] If there is a denial of the initial request, the party may make a confirmatory application, which is again subject to the same fifteen-day response requirement.[51]

As detailed in Chapters Three and Four, document requests as part of the research for this book yielded important information, to which we will turn in a moment.[52] On a more general level, however, it is worth reflecting first on how our requests fit into the broader information-brokering process in the EU.[53] The von der Leyen Commission, in particular, has proven to be a deeply resistant broker of information, to put it mildly. The European Ombudsman found in a special report to the European Parliament in 2023 that Commission delays in responding to document requests under Regulation 1049/2001 were 'systemic' across all subject-matter areas and hence 'amount[ed] to maladministration'.[54] As we discuss in Chapter Four, these problems would be especially acute in the context of NGEU. This behaviour would lead one of us to conclude, contra the 'old adage in the world of official transparency that "sunlight is the best disinfectant"', that 'when it comes to Europe's recovery transformation ... the Commission insists on conducting as much of it as possible in the dark'.[55]

The Commission's deficient transparency practices, always a source of frustration, gained new prominence in the context of the Pfizergate ruling of the General Court in May 2025,[56] which in turn, in July 2025, contributed directly to the first motion of censure in eleven years against a Commission.[57] The Commission survived the motion,[58] with Ursula von der Leyen dismissing it as the product of far-right and hard-right extremist parties.[59] But as noted by the former Irish Minister for European Affairs, Dick Roche, 'there was no sign of introspection, no admission of any error' in the speech of the Commission President in opposition to the motion, nor any indication that she 'or those around her either recognise or are willing to address the transparency and accountability problems that exist in the EU institutional structure'.[60] These concerns

[49] Regulation (EC) No 1049/2001, art 2(3).
[50] Ibid, art 7.
[51] Ibid, art 8.
[52] See this Introduction below, nn 63–95 and accompanying text.
[53] Walby and Larsen (2012, p 32).
[54] European Ombudsman (2023a, paras 12–13).
[55] Leino-Sandberg (2024a).
[56] Case T-36/23, *Stevi and The New York Times v Commission* (2025).
[57] European Parliament (2025a, point E).
[58] European Parliament (2025b).
[59] von der Leyen (2025a).
[60] Roche (2025).

have been characteristic of the implementation of the NGEU, and more particularly its major planning and spending component, the Recovery and Resilience Facility (RRF). Faced with numerous complaints directed at the Commission, in February 2022 the European Ombudsman opened an own-initiative strategic investigation on the transparency and accountability of the RRF, which found numerous faults in the Commission's approach.[61] The Ombudsman's basic message was, in effect, that transparency delayed is transparency denied. We have benefited from the efforts of the Ombudsman as well as those of investigative journalists who have sought to gain access to information on how particular National Recovery and Resilience Plans under the RRF were formulated, assessed, and implemented, which we detail in Chapter Four. Despite the Commission's efforts to maintain a largely opaque policy and planning process relating to NGEU, this experience, difficult as it no doubt was, has also demonstrated that it was still possible to 'work around barriers to access and produce an anthology of data for collaborative exploration and circulation to interested parties'.[62]

Much information, unfortunately, still remains concealed. An illuminating case of problematic non-transparency involves the dramatic reinterpretation of the so-called 'cohesion flexibility clause' in Article 175(3) TFEU,[63] which we explore in detail in the opening section of Chapter Three. This reinterpretation has served, via the RRF, as a cornerstone for the entire NextGenerationEU edifice, effectively turning an obscure (and previously little used) provision into a general EU spending power in the 'general Welfare'—that is, for the general public good—akin to Article I, Section 8, Clause 1 of the United States Constitution.[64] And yet puzzlingly (to put it mildly), the legal reasoning of the Commission and Council accompanying the proposals for NGEU—strategically published to aid the process of adoption in 2020—ignored Article 175(3) TFEU entirely, despite its central importance to NGEU's spending dimension.[65]

The Court of Justice of the European Union (CJEU) has made it quite clear that opinions of the legal services relating to legislative matters should, as the main rule, be disclosed;[66] nonetheless, key legal advice relating to the reinterpretation of Article 175(3) TFEU remained entirely out of the public eye. Consequently, in March 2023, as a part of the empirical work for this book, one of us made two separate requests addressed to the Council and the Commission asking for public access to legal advice on legislative measures from the years preceding the Covid crisis that had been

[61] European Ombudsman (2023b). For further discussion, see Chapter Four, nn 92–99 and accompanying text.

[62] Walby and Larsen (2012, p 39).

[63] Article 175 TFEU is actually unnumbered, so technically the cohesion flexibility clause is properly cited as art 175, third paragraph. However, many official EU documents refer to it as art 175(3) TFEU and we thus adopt this more streamlined citation form throughout this book.

[64] For an earlier statement of this argument, see Lindseth and Leino-Sandberg (2024b). For further discussion, see Chapter Three, Section A.

[65] See European Commission (2020a) and Council Legal Service (2020a). For further discussion, see Chapter Three, nn 16–20 and accompanying text.

[66] Joined Cases C-39/05 P and C-52/05 P, *Sweden and Turco* v *Council* (2008); Case C-408/21 P *Council v Laurent Pech* (2023).

grounded, in whole or in part, in Article 175(3) TFEU. We have summarised the subsequent developments to these requests elsewhere,[67] but given their importance to the writing of this book, a more detailed description is merited here.

The bottom line is that the Council proved to be considerably more forthcoming to our requests than the Commission. This is fortunate, given that the cross-institutional collaboration between the legal services of the Commission and the Council was at the heart of the NGEU model's development.[68] The Council, after initial hesitation, produced the key opinions of its legal service from 2019 and early 2020 that have been essential to understanding the problematic nature of the reinterpretation of Article 175(3) TFEU on which the NGEU model would be ultimately based.[69] These opinions suggested that the Council was largely willing to accept the constitutional transformation of Article 175(3) TFEU that the Commission had initiated with its prior proposals (albeit on grounds that the Commission itself refused to disclose). By contrast, the initial stance of the Commission's legal service, where most of the reinterpretation took place in the first instance, was to claim implausibly that it had little in its possession aside from a few documents involving minor technical amendments to draft proposals preceding their formal approval, none of them illuminating.

From the beginning, the Commission justified its resistance to disclosure by arguing, in effect, that the increase in spending pursuant to a legislative measure was telling enough and that the legal interpretation of the Treaty provision on which that increase was based was therefore irrelevant:

> It is true, and cannot be disputed, that the public should be informed about how public money is spent. Such information made available to citizens reinforces public control of the use to which that money is put and contributes to the best use of public funds. Nevertheless, please note that this objective is already achieved by publishing comprehensive information on the EU budget, as well as the amounts allocated to the various areas with supporting explanations, which contributes to transparency in the use of public funds. No such link can be established regarding the full disclosure of the legal advice to which you are seeking access.[70]

Our initial request was written in intentionally broad terms, to encompass '*any legal advice in the possession of the European Commission relating to*' the specified legislative proposals (our emphasis). Nonetheless, the Commission only disclosed documents relating to the final interservice consultation that takes place prior to the final approval of the proposal in the College of Commissioners. Thus, the Commission either misunderstood our request or intentionally excluded legal advice on the earlier

[67] See generally Leino-Sandberg and Lindseth (2023), Lindseth and Leino-Sandberg (2024b), and Leino-Sandberg (2025b).

[68] Smeets and Beach (2023).

[69] See Chapter Three, Section A.2.

[70] European Commission (2023a, p 3).

development of the proposals when the crucial analysis of the adequacy of the legal basis would have been undertaken. This is an issue we clearly pointed out in our confirmatory application, which simply led the Commission to insist it had no other legal advice in its possession.

We thus asked the European Ombudsman to investigate what we saw as clear evidence of maladministration. The Ombudsman's office, however, suggested that a new request would be 'the more appropriate course of action. We have asked the Commission to treat any such follow-up public access request promptly'.[71] We thus resubmitted the request on 6 September 2023, specifying that we sought access to:

> advice provided by the Commission legal service at the stage when [the proposals in question] were prepared in the relevant Commission DGs. This request relates to all stages of preparatory work preceding the respective Inter-Service Consultations and also covers informal advice offered in the form of e-mail messages or other informal correspondence between the Legal Service and the DGs that were in charge of preparing the proposals and that may have influenced how the proposals were formulated.

On 16 October 2023 the Commission replied, informing us that 'the Legal Service has not identified any document matching the terms of [our] request' and that, 'in line with the applicable rules, the Legal Service and the competent directorate generals of the Commission have carried out a thorough search in their corporate document management systems'.[72]

This response again struck us as highly implausible, even a bit astounding. We had since learned of the article published by the member of the Commission Legal Service noted above,[73] which was written at precisely the time the proposals in questions were being discussed. This intervention suggested that at least one member of the Service had highly developed views on the topic, which presumably were formulated in providing legal advice internally within the Commission. This member of the Commission Legal Service looked to Article 175(3) TFEU specifically as means—*without Treaty change*—to fill 'gaps' in the EMU,[74] offering a way to navigate around the Treaty-based limitations on EU competence to the 'coordination' of national policies.[75] A confirmatory application was thus submitted referring directly to this published article, and the matter was raised again with the Ombudsman.[76]

71 European Ombudsman (2023c).
72 European Commission (2023b).
73 Flynn (2019). See this Introduction above, nn 42–44 and accompanying text.
74 Ibid, p 60.
75 Ibid, p 48. For further discussion, see Chapter Three, nn 171–75 and accompanying text.
76 Unbeknownst to us at the time but not long after the publication of Flynn (2019), another member of the Commission Legal Service acknowledged in an OUP legal commentary that there were 'links between [these proposals] and economic policy' but that, because they 'develop[ed] a concept of cohesion as embracing real convergence between the Member States and of augmenting the resilience of their economies', they should not be regarded as exercises of economic policy. See Keppenne (2020a, p 875). For further discussion, see Chapter Three, nn 100, 110 and accompanying text.

The final decision on our application did not come until June 2024, a full sixteen months after our initial access request.[77] In the end, the Commission did manage to identify a small number of more informal documents in its registers from the relevant time period (twelve in total). But while the Commission did disclose some of the queries from the DGs to which its lawyers had been reacting, it blanked out all the actual legal advice. The Commission claimed the advice need not be disclosed because it 'concern[ed] purely internal exchanges related not even to any draft versions of future proposals (and therefore not part of [any] legislative file) and thus should be as a rule protected as part of the institution's "space to think"'.[78] This claim is at best highly formalistic and at worst disingenuous, designed to obscure the clear factual context.

The context was this: from spring 2017 onwards, the Commission was developing legislative proposals regarding what would come to be known as the 'euro-area budget', including, most importantly, a macroeconomic 'stabilisation function' based in whole or in part on Article 175(3) TFEU. This stabilisation function was the key antecedent to NGEU and, more particularly, the RRF, which was based exclusively on Article 175(3) TFEU.[79] The Commission's White Paper on the Future of Europe in March 2017,[80] along with the Reflection Paper on the Future of EU Finances of 28 June 2017,[81] contemplated such a stabilisation function. In his State of the Union Address of 13 September 2017,[82] together with the accompanying Letter of Intent,[83] Commission President Jean-Claude Juncker provided a clear schedule for the introduction of the necessary proposals 'by end 2018'.[84] The Commission Work Programme for 2018, published on 24 October 2017,[85] did the same. The Commission then approved the two initial proposals on 31 May 2018.[86] By December 2018, the Euro Summit mandated the Commission to start work on a more comprehensive proposal for a Budgetary Instrument for Convergence and Competitiveness (BICC) as part of the then-upcoming MFF.[87] The Commission approved its formal proposal for the BICC on 25 July 2019,[88] which remained under consideration until formally withdrawn and replaced by the RRF Proposal in May 2020.[89]

In short, as we shall explore in much greater detail in Chapter Three, for much of the three years preceding the RRF, the Commission was working on multiple, closely

[77] See European Commission (2024a).
[78] Ibid, p 11.
[79] See Chapter Three, Section A.2.
[80] European Commission (2017a, pp 25 and 29) (foreseeing that 'a euro area fiscal stabilisation function is operational' by 2025).
[81] European Commission (2017b, pp 22–23).
[82] Juncker (2017).
[83] Juncker and Timmermans (2017).
[84] Ibid, p 7.
[85] European Commission (2017c).
[86] European Commission (2018a), (2018b).
[87] Euro Summit (2018).
[88] European Commission (2019a).
[89] European Commission (2020b).

intertwined legislative processes that encompassed or touched on a macroeconomic stabilisation function that would be based, in whole or in part, on Article 175(3) TFEU. Consequently, it strains credulity to claim, as the Commission now does, that the documents it identified in response to our public access request 'do not form part of any legislative process' and hence should not be disclosed.[90] The European Ombudsman, after inspecting the documents, expressed little doubt that the documents in question related to a legislative process and that, as such, the Commission should, in principle, 'grant[] the widest possible access'.[91] The CJEU has made clear that even 'early stage' legal opinions are integral to the 'institution in its legislative capacity' and presumptively subject to disclosure.[92] The Court also rejected a distinction between 'political decision-makers' and the legal services of an institution; to do so, the Court held, would call into question 'entirely the particular status conferred by the case-law on legal opinions drawn up by the legal services of the institutions and relating to a legislative procedure'.[93]

Nonetheless, in the end—despite two public access requests, two confirmatory applications, as well as the initiation of two Ombudsman investigations—the Commission resolutely refused to reveal anything that would give the European public a better understanding of (or, perhaps more importantly, the ability to hold the Commission accountable for) its revolutionary reinterpretation of the EU's spending powers under Article 175(3) TFEU.[94] The parts of the documents that were disclosed, however, do reveal some of the questions that were debated within the Commission, while also illustrating the role of the Commission Legal Service in debates within the Council. The Commission's final refusal, moreover, repeatedly acknowledged that, whatever its legal advice was, it could not be disclosed because it was 'relevant [not just] for current, but also future instruments'. Among those specifically mentioned were the RFF, that is, the NGEU's main planning and spending vehicle, as well as unspecified defence spending programmes and preparations for the next MFF.[95]

We may be reading too much importance into the access requests submitted as part of the research for this book. However, not long after definitively rejecting the final confirmatory application, the Commission updated its Rules of Procedure in December 2024 to establish a blanket presumption that opinions of the Commission Legal Service should not be disclosed.[96] This was without regard to whether the

[90] See European Commission (2024a, p 13).
[91] European Ombudsman (2024a).
[92] Case C-408/21 P *Council v Laurent Pech* (2023), paras 87–88.
[93] Ibid, paras 92–93.
[94] In her decision closing the case following the Commission's production of documents, the European Ombudsman found 'nothing that could justify … what is manifestly a significant delay in replying to the complainant's request', seeing the case as 'another example of the significant delays encountered by the Commission in processing public access requests, which the Ombudsman found to amount to maladministration in her own-initiative inquiry into the matter'. European Ombudsman (2025, paras 24–25), citing European Ombudsman (2023a). See also Chapter Four, Section A.
[95] European Commission (2024a, pp 13–15).
[96] Under the new rules: 'There is a presumption that access to the following documents … undermines interests protected by Article 4(1) to (3) of Regulation (EC) No 1049/2001: . . (c) opinions of the Legal

opinions relate to legislative matters and hence are *presumptively disclosable* under prevailing case law, with the burden on the Commission to show otherwise.[97] Our experience serves to demonstrate that the Commission is unlikely to ever find its new, inverted presumption overridden (and for this reason, among others, one of us has brought a legal challenge to the Commission decision adopting the new rules before the General Court).[98] As a consequence, under those rules any legal reinterpretation by the Commission Legal Service, no matter how significant it proves to be, should always be kept secret. Indeed, when responding to the requests for access related to this book, the Commission confirmed the transformative character of the NGEU model going forward, cutting across the RRF, defence spending, and the upcoming Multiannual Financial Framework. Moreover, it also pointed out, even if inadvertently, that the stakes are commensurately high in ensuring that we find the most secure legal basis for the NGEU model as possible, one that goes beyond the strained reinterpretation of the various Treaty provisions on which the NGEU model has to date been based.

In this regard, in other words, the Commission—despite its declared intention to be maximally non-transparent—has at least confirmed why the aims of this book, as spelled out in the chapters that follow, are so important.

D. Plan of the Book: Synthesising Past, Present, and Future

Whether and how the EU traverses the constitutional borderlands in which it finds itself, this book seeks to show, has necessarily involved the complex interplay of past and present in the face of an uncertain future. For this reason, this book seeks to approach that interplay synthetically, in order to capture '*where* we are, and *whither* we are tending', and hence 'better judge *what* to do, and *how* to do it' (emphasis in original).[99]

Part One of the book, entitled 'Situating the Argument', is comprised of Chapters One and Two.

Chapter One, entitled 'Entering the Constitutional Borderlands: the NGEU Model in the Law and History of European Integration', provides a general overview of the argument of the book as a whole. It begins with a description of the basic elements of the NGEU model, notably the issuance of debt to fund a range of spending programmes, the most important being the RRF with its exclusive legal basis in Article

Service … No access to those documents shall therefore be granted, unless the applicant demonstrates an overriding public interest …'. Commission Decision (EU) 2024/3080, art 4(2)(c).

97 See this Introduction above, n 66 and accompanying text.

98 Case T-146/25, *De Capitani and Others v Commission* (2025).

99 Lincoln (1953) [1858].

175(3) TFEU. It also introduces the reader to the key enabling feature of NGEU—the Own Resources Decision (ORD) of December 2020—and more particularly its increased 'headroom', which serves as the binding commitment on the part of the Member States to cover the resulting additional liabilities under NGEU beyond the EU's regular budget. While NGEU would not have been possible without this national backing, this crucial foundation has often been obscured behind an 'as if'-constitutional approach adopted by institutional lawyers in re-engineering several key Treaty provisions, not least Article 175(3) TFEU as well as several others. The interpretive approach, while driven by a desire to achieve broader political ends, is ultimately 'reductionist'; that is, it looks at words in isolation without regard to the emergent systemic or institutional effects of these reinterpretations on the system as a whole. The aim of this book is precisely to describe those broader systemic and institutional effects.

Chapter Two is entitled 'Past as Prologue: Integration from the Inception of EMU to the Eve of the Covid Crisis'. It reviews the transformations of the integration project from the initial conception of the EMU in the late 1980s through the multiple crises of the last decade and a half. It focuses in particular on how the differential legitimacy between the EU and the Member States—again, the power-legitimacy nexus—shaped the transformations on which NGEU would eventually build. The power-legitimacy nexus helps us better understand, for example, both the asymmetry of the EMU (with its centralised monetary policy at the EU level, on the one hand, without any commensurate centralised EU fiscal capacity, on the other) as well as the failure of the Commission's surveillance role under the European Semester as initially constructed. The chapter closes with an overview of the efforts to construct a financial model for the EU built around three pillars: revenue (to align own resources to EU policies); borrowing (to mobilise resources and develop a so-called European safe asset); and spending (to develop 'performance-based' incentives to buy greater Member State compliance with broad EU objectives). Cutting across all these elements were pressures on cohesion funding to move away from its original regional-developmental aims to become the primary vehicle for 'positive' incentives to the Member States—in effect, money for reforms. The general goals of economic policy were thus conflated with, or ratcheted into, the realm of cohesion policy, so that the latter could serve the purposes of the former. We call this the 'ratcheting strategy' for cohesion.

Part Two, entitled 'The Emergence and Development of the NGEU Model', brings us to the heart of the book, comprising Chapters Three, Four, and Five.

Chapter Three is entitled 'Assembling the Components: The Legal Engineering of NGEU'. It begins not with NGEU itself but with crucial developments in the years immediately preceding the Covid crisis that are inextricably tied to NGEU. These years saw a series of legislative efforts (culminating with proposals to develop a so-called euro-area budget) that depended on the re-engineering of cohesion policy into a tool of general EU economic policy making.[100] The chapter then turns to the development

[100] This analysis builds on Leino-Sandberg and Lindseth (2023).

of NGEU in the context of the Covid emergency in the second half of 2020, drawing on the ideas for an integration-reinforcing financing model of the prior decade. The chapter demonstrates that, as a consequence of careful legal preparatory work over a period of several years, the NGEU, and more particularly the RRF, were able to draw on an expansive reinterpretation of the cohesion flexibility clause of Article 175(3) TFEU as a way of compensating for the EU's lack of competence in economic and fiscal policy. Despite the absence of Treaty change, in other words, the effect was to claim that the EU already possessed such a constitutional spending power with considerable regulatory effects beyond the competence of the EU strictly speaking. The chapter concludes with an overview of the legal design of the RRF, in which the ratcheting strategy for cohesion that first appeared in Chapter Two was taken to a whole new level. It was combined with a vague and ultimately boundless conception of 'resilience' to inaugurate a system of, in effect, 'cohesion without limits', reaching effectively any policy domain, whether national or supranational, available for deployment with little regard to other competence limitations in the EU Treaties.

Chapter Four, entitled 'NGEU in Action: Planning and Spending under the Recovery and Resilience Facility', telescopes in on the operation of the NGEU's most important component: the RRF. It begins by exploring the RRF's governance dimension, in which key decisions were vested in small group of executive and technocratic officials at the national and supranational levels. At the heart of that governance is the insistence of the Commission to limit transparency and accountability for the RRF planning and spending process to a highly curated image that the Commission itself tightly controls. The chapter then turns to the spending side of the RRF in more detail, exploring ways in which implementation and disbursement, particularly in relation to RRF's 'performance-based' model, further illuminates persistent challenges regarding democratic legitimacy, performance measurement, and cross-national scrutiny. The chapter also delves into the question of audit and control of RRF funding, with a particular eye on its necessarily diffuse character (heavily reliant on national compliance) as well as the challenges flowing from the shift to a 'financing not linked to costs' (FNLC) model. The chapter concludes with an extended examination of the renegotiation of the limits of EU competence under the RRF's 'six pillars', leading, in effect, to a new competence system built on supportive EU funding for matters otherwise primarily within national competence. However, the ultimately national character of EU spending under the RRF raises serious questions about both value for money and impact on the future, in which the debt overhang from NGEU may impose significant constraints on the EU's ability to pursue genuinely European public goods in the future.

Chapter Five, entitled 'The Emergence of the NGEU Model: Extensions and Deviations', examines changes to the original NGEU programme as well as the establishment of new programmes drawing on NGEU elements. The extended NGEU model took shape initially through two amendments of the RRF Regulation (for REPowerEU and STEP), which recycled NGEU funding towards new geopolitical and macroeconomic needs, demonstrating the incremental transformation of the programme into a general crisis management instrument. The second element of the emergent model was the extension (and modification) of the planning model and the 'performance-based' incentives system to various other domains. These included macro-financial assistance and other foreign aid programmes extending support to partner countries (the Ukraine Facility and the Reform and Growth Facility for the Western Balkans); EU intervention into social policy (the Social Climate Fund); and, perhaps most importantly, coordination of national economic and fiscal policies under the Stability and Growth Pact and European Semester (the new Economic Governance Framework). The chapter concludes with an extended analysis of the evolution of the EU's financial model since the inception of NGEU, focusing first on the stalled quest for new own resources (the 'Fit for 55' saga); the need for budgetary workarounds (the Social Climate Fund revisited); and the continued dependence of the EU on the Member States to support any new collective borrowing (the demand for which dramatically increased following the Russian war on Ukraine). The chapter concludes by examining the EU's aspiration to be seen by investors as a 'sovereign-style issuer' of debt, a goal made difficult by the EU's lack of autonomous powers of taxation, unmediated through the Member States. This concluding section allows us to take stock of the limitations of 'as if' constitutionalism in understanding the nature and limitations of the integration project under the NGEU model and beyond.

Part Three of the book, entitled 'Taking Stock of "Where We Are and Whither We Are Tending"', is comprised of Chapter Six and the Conclusion.

Chapter Six is entitled 'The NGEU Model Made Permanent?' In terms of chronology, the focus shifts to the very recent past—in effect, between the Draghi Report of September 2024 and the announcement of the Commission's new MFF and ORD proposals in July 2025 and the early debate concerning these proposals during the first two months after they were issued. The chapter begins with an examination of proposals to use 'targeted' changes in EU law as a way of responding to intensifying functional demands, not least in the areas of defence, security, and competitiveness. The chapter then turns to examining the extent to which the new MFF and ORD proposals of July 2025 might be seen as new extensions of the NGEU model, looking to planning and spending as the means of solidifying what has been a deep transformation in EU governance. At the time of this writing, the new MFF and ORD proposals suggested a consolidation of the planning and performance-based funding models; nonetheless, they remained ambiguous regarding collective borrowing, looking to debt-financing primarily to support loans to Member States rather than further expenditure (the most ambitious feature of the NGEU model).

The Conclusion, entitled 'Democratic Politics and the Fate of the NGEU Model', offers a set of reflections about EU governance in the constitutional borderlands. The NGEU model has undoubtedly helped the EU identify new ways of spending money, although these were often targeted at national rather than European public goods. Financing the new spending has proved much more difficult, primarily because of the EU's lack of autonomous fiscal mobilisation capacities—the Rubicon at the heart of the constitutional borderlands which the EU has yet to cross. To continue navigating its way through these borderlands, the EU has instead relied heavily on executive and technocratic modes of governance, actively avoiding parliaments or the broader public in the political task of constitutional transformation. The legal background work supporting this effort, under the guise of so-called 'living constitutionalism', has had massive distributive consequences as well as a significant (and arguably adverse) impact on the functioning of European democracy. In this sense, the chosen approach has been fundamentally an elite project, amounting to little more than a variant of 'as if' constitutionalism destined to fall short of what is needed for the EU to transition to autonomous fiscal mobilisation capacities in a robustly constitutional sense.

PART ONE
SITUATING THE ARGUMENT

Chapter One
Entering the Constitutional Borderlands

The NGEU Model in the Law and History of European Integration

A. Basic Elements of the Model

The NextGenerationEU programme was adopted in the midst of the Covid crisis in 2020.[1] It authorised the European Commission to issue debt on a massive scale (€750 billion at 2018 prices) to fund a range of spending programmes under the EU's cohesion, environmental and agricultural policies.[2] The largest programme by far is the Recovery and Resilience Facility, valued at €672.5 billion at 2018 prices.[3] The RRF is based on an expansive reading of the flexibility clause for cohesion funding in Article 175(3) TFEU,[4] a provision whose purpose had been understood primarily as a means of channelling investment financing for specific projects in underdeveloped and 'least favoured' regions in the EU.[5] Through the RRF, the Commission was empowered to redistribute borrowed funds to all Member States, regardless of development status, up to the shares pre-allocated by the European Council, as either grants (up to a total of €312.5 billion in 2018 prices) or as loans (up to a total of €360 billion in 2018 prices) to support not just investments but also a broad range of national legislative and regulatory reforms under the NGEU programme.[6]

The basic political agreement and core features of NGEU were decided by the European Council in a special summit in July 2020, as part of the compromise on

[1] The legal foundations of NGEU were laid between December 2020 and February 2021 in four pieces of legislation: the Multiannual Financial Framework (MFF) for 2021–2027, Council Regulation (EU, Euratom) 2020/2093; the 2020 Own Resources Decision, Council Decision 2020/2053; the European Union Recovery Instrument (EURI), Council Regulation 2020/2094; and the Recovery and Resilience Facility (RRF), Regulation (EU) 2021/241.

[2] Council Decision 2020/2053 [ORD], recital (14) and art 5(1)(a); Council Regulation 2020/2094 [EURI], art 2(2).

[3] Beyond the RRF, the disbursal of the remainder of NGEU funds is through a range of other programmes, such as the Recovery Assistance for Cohesion and the Territories of Europe (REACT-EU), Horizon Europe, InvestEU, European Agricultural Fund for Rural Development or the Just Transition Fund (JTF). The focus of this book will be primarily on disbursal through the RRF.

[4] See Regulation (EU) 2021/241 [RRF], recital (2) (asserting that Article 175 TFEU broadly permits the Member States 'to coordinate their economic policies in such a way as to attain the objectives on economic, social and territorial cohesion set out in Article 174 TFEU'). For further details on the RRF's legal basis and design, see Chapter Three, Section D.

[5] See Regulation (EU) 2021/241 [RRF], recital (3). For a discussion of the longer term developments in cohesion policy, see Chapter Two, Section C.3; see also Díez Sánchez (2025).

[6] Regulation (EU) 2021/241 [RRF], art 6(1); Council Regulation 2020/2094 [EURI], art 2(2).

European Integration in the Constitutional Borderlands. Päivi Leino-Sandberg and Peter L. Lindseth,
Oxford University Press.
DOI: 10.1093/oso/9780198949527.003.0002

the new Multiannual Financial Framework 2021–2027.[7] The programme was formalised in law over the subsequent five months as a time-limited, emergency measure outside the EU's regular budget, with major components adopted in December 2020 and the RRF adopted in February 2021.[8] The new NGEU programme authorised the Commission to issue debt over a six-year period between 2021 and 2026, which it then obligated the EU to repay over a thirty-year period, up to the end of 2058. To enable the EU to undertake this borrowing and repayment, the programme 'temporarily' increased (again through 2058) the so-called 'headroom' in the Own Resources Decision of December 2020 (the '2020 ORD').

An ORD is the legal instrument that binds Member States to finance the EU and acts as the ultimate guarantee of the EU's creditworthiness. The 'headroom' in an ORD is the difference between the maximum amount that the Member States are legally bound to cover (the 'own resources ceiling') and the own resources actually necessary to finance the EU budget itself.[9] The 2020 ORD expanded its 'headroom' by an additional 0.6% of the aggregated gross national income (GNI) of the Member States to serve as a binding commitment to cover the resulting additional liabilities under the NGEU programme beyond the EU's regular budget.[10] Whatever creditworthiness the EU derives from an ORD, however, is ultimately dependent on national tax collection,[11] as well as on national creditworthiness, especially that of the strongest, AAA-rated Member States.[12] An ORD thus only gains effect, constitutionally speaking, when approved by the Member States in accordance with their respective constitutional requirements.[13]

Even with this crucial dependence on the Member States via the 2020 ORD, NGEU has still been a transformative programme. It built, in particular, on several reform initiatives and lines of thinking that developed over prior years and decades which we will also review in detail in this book.[14] The immediate purpose of NGEU was to raise and redistribute funds to address the economic dislocations of the Covid crisis while also promoting the political priorities of the von der Leyen Commission relating to digitalisation, climate change, and energy transition. Beyond these stated purposes, however, NGEU built upon, but also sought to transcend, the effort to 'complete' the Economic and Monetary Union while enhancing supranational involvement in national economic policymaking.[15] Although the roots of these two latter dimensions

[7] European Council (2020).

[8] See generally Council Regulation (EU, Euratom) 2020/2093 [MFF 2021–2027]; Council Decision 2020/2053 [ORD]; Council Regulation 2020/2094 [EURI]; and Regulation (EU) 2021/241 [RRF].

[9] The 2020 ORD defines this latter number as 1.4% of the aggregated GNI of the Member States for 'appropriations for payments', or as 1.46% of their aggregated GNI for 'appropriations for commitments'. Council Decision 2020/2053 [ORD], arts 3(1) and (2).

[10] Council Decision 2020/2053 [ORD], art 6 (raising the relevant ceilings in arts 3(1) and (2) by 0.6%).

[11] See this chapter below, nn 30–39 and accompanying text.

[12] See this chapter below, nn 47–54 and accompanying text.

[13] Article 311 TFEU.

[14] See generally Chapters Two and Three.

[15] See Leino-Sandberg and Saarenheimo (2018), (2017). For further discussion, see Chapter Two, Sections A and B.

can be traced back to the inception of EMU in the 1980s and 1990s, these aspirations became even more pressing during what was often called the 'polycrisis'[16]—the intensifying and overlapping series of challenges that have afflicted the EU since the onset of the global financial crisis of 2008–2009 (and which, indeed, are still continuing, with the ongoing effects of Russia's war on Ukraine, continuing geopolitical and macroeconomic pressures on the EU's overall competitiveness, and the return of Donald Trump to the US presidency). With Covid, this persistent atmosphere of crisis led EU institutions to a shift in emphasis away from merely completing the EMU (with a primary focus on the 'responsibility' of Member States in the euro area) to constructing a new form of 'solidarity' among all EU Member States,[17] reflected not just in NGEU but also the other programmes that the NGEU model would come to encompass.[18]

More prosaically, the adoption of NGEU might be characterised as simply an 'economic policy shift', one 'legal[ly] engineer[ed]' within the confines of the existing Treaties by the legal services of the Council and Commission at the behest of their political leadership.[19] For its legal basis, NGEU built on the reinterpretation of several Treaty provisions. These included not just the flexibility clause relating to cohesion funding in Article 175(3) TFEU (on the spending side),[20] but also the emergency assistance rules contained in Article 122 TFEU[21] combined with the general financial and budgetary rules in Articles 310–311 TFEU (on the revenue and borrowing side).[22] From this perspective, the effort at legal engineering marked an important further step in reorientating the integration project away from a regime of 'integration through law' to one of 'integration through funding'.[23]

The emergence of the NGEU model suggests that this new regime could come to enjoy a power that the old regime notably lacked: a capacity of the EU to leverage revenue commitments of the Member State (in the ORD) into a programme of borrowing at a macroeconomically and geopolitically salient scale,[24] creating a pool of new funds that can then be redirected back to Member States through EU-level spending programmes built not just on loans but also outright grants to fund a range

[16] Former European Commission President Jean-Claude Juncker introduced the term 'polycrisis' into EU discourse in 2016, See Juncker (2016). He borrowed the term from the French complexity theorist Edgar Morin, who first used it in the 1990s.

[17] For a sympathetic overview of this shift, see Ioannidis (2020). This shift has also been noteworthy in the language of the CJEU. For a critique, see Leino-Sandberg (2023a).

[18] See, eg, SURE, REPowerEU, the Social Climate Fund, STEP, as well as the European Peace Facility, the European Defence Fund, the Ukraine Facility, and SAFE. For further detail, see Chapters Five and Six.

[19] See de Witte (2021).

[20] See above nn 4–5 and accompanying text; see also Chapters Three and Four. Article 175(3) TFEU would be supplemented on the spending side by Article 197(2) TFEU for technical and administrative support to the Member States.

[21] Council Regulation 2020/2094 [EURI], preamble.

[22] See Council Decision 2020/2053 [ORD], preamble. Commentators have pointed out that only Article 122 TFEU is explicitly an emergency legal basis, whereas Article 175(3) TFEU is not. See, eg, de Witte (2021, p 658) For additional analysis, see Leino-Sandberg and Ruffert (2022) and Dermine (2020). For an argument that dispenses with Article 122 TFEU and asserts that NGEU could be independently grounded in the other provisions of the Treaty, see Panascì (2024, p 45, n 95).

[23] de Witte (2023).

[24] For a sense of the scale, see, eg, Buettner (2023, p 164).

of investments and reforms at the national level. An integral part of the NGEU model is another potential polity-building feature: a planning process for those investments and reforms involving intensified information flows and coordination between executive and technocratic actors in Brussels and national capitals, via the Commission's ongoing oversight of Member States' implementation of their National Recovery and Resilience Plans (NRRPs) under the RRF.[25] Further framing this information exchange and coordination are new regulations on spending conditionality to protect the EU budget as it is deployed to—or withheld from—the Member States out of 'rule of law' concerns.[26]

To describe the NGEU, however, as simply an 'economic policy shift' does not really do justice to the deeper constitutionalising potential of the new model. Extracting resources from society and then redirecting them towards public ends through spending programmes is at the heart of genuine constitutional power.[27] Thus, it might be said that NGEU marked an effort to transcend a type of integration that the dominant discourse in EU public law had for too long—mistakenly in our view—described *as if* it were already robustly constitutional.[28] The category mistake of this 'as if' constitutionalism has been in how it ignores the core function of a genuine constitution, which is not simply to *constrain* power—something that all public law does, not just constitutional law—but rather actually to *constitute* it.[29] By initiating a longer-term process of establishing a borrowing and spending power at the supranational level, as well as by modifying the revenue streams from the Member States under the ORD to support it, the integration project has now taken small steps to move beyond the EU's traditional 'as if' constitutionalism towards something coming closer to the real thing.

In this sense, the emergent new regime of integration is at a place in between—what we are calling in this book 'constitutional borderlands'—in which the EU is seeking to use its nascent borrowing and spending capacity towards collective polity-building goals. This book aims to describe how the integration project reached this point in its political and legal trajectory, how it developed and has exercised these new 'borderlands' powers, and how the resulting transformation in the nature of EU governance might be made more efficient and more accountable, both nationally and supranationally, as a step towards further development in the future.

[25] Regulation (EU) 2021/241 [RRF], arts 17–21. For further discussion on this overall process of exchange and interaction, see Chapter Three, Section D; and Chapter Four, Sections A and B.

[26] See Regulation (EU, Euratom) 2020/2092 [Conditionality Regulation]. Also of pervasive and perhaps even greater significance is the 'horizontal' conditionality mechanism established under Articles 9 and 15(1) as well as Annex III of the Common Provisions Regulation of 2021. See Regulation (EU) 2021/1060 [2021 CPR]. For further discussion, see Scheppele and Morijn (2023a), (2023b). See also Chapter Four, Section C.2.

[27] See generally Lindseth (2021a), (2017). For the application of this claim more specifically to the EU, see also Lindseth (2023), (2018), (2016a).

[28] See generally Lindseth (2023), (2018), (2016a).

[29] Lindseth (2018). Contemporary constitutional theory is only beginning to come to terms with this more fundamental feature of constitutionalism. See, eg, Khosla and Tushnet (2022). However, as we will argue in this book, the constraint function of the EU Treaties, as the purported constitution for the integration project, is increasingly breaking down. See Conclusion, Sections A and B; see also Leino-Sandberg (2025c).

B. Dipping into, but not Crossing, the Constitutional Rubicon (of Autonomous EU Fiscal Capacity)

The robust constitutional extraction of fiscal resources from society is normally accomplished through taxation. This, however, is a power that the EU notably lacks and the NGEU programme did little to change. The EU is instead the beneficiary of the aforementioned 'own resources' collected by the Member States. To a relatively small and diminishing extent, these revenues consist of so-called traditional own resources such as customs and sugar duties. However, to a much larger extent, own resources consist of transfers from Member States' budgets linked either to the value-added tax (VAT) base or to GNI. The Treaties require an ORD instituting or modifying the EU's own resources to be grounded in a collective decision of Member State executives at the EU level, thus giving it a supranational character.[30] But, as noted above, an ORD only gains effect, constitutionally speaking, when approved by the Member States in accordance with their respective constitutional requirements;[31] the EU has no power of adoption in its own right. For this reason, the European Commission has stressed that Member State approval of an ORD is of a '*quasi-constitutional* nature' (emphasis in original),[32] thus acknowledging national institutions as the crucial mechanisms of democratic and constitutional legitimation in this key respect.

Moreover, as a practical matter, any own resources contemplated by an ORD must first be collected by Member State administrations; the EU has traditionally lacked that power too, not to mention the administrative capacity to actually exercise it. As a high-level report put it in 2016, in terms still true post-NGEU: 'Member States are the only taxpayers to the EU budget, not the 510 million EU citizens who only contribute indirectly'.[33] The 2020 ORD, adopted together with the NGEU,[34] was innovative in how it more clearly aligned the one new own resource it established (relating to unrecycled plastic waste) with new EU policy initiatives.[35] In line with the European Council Conclusions of July 2020 that established the overall political agreement for NGEU,[36] the recitals to the 2020 ORD further contemplated additional own resources (eg a carbon border adjustment mechanism, a digital levy, revenues from the EU Emissions Trading System, as well as, potentially, a Financial Transaction Tax) which could be adopted in the future.[37] In this regard, the 2020 ORD pointed towards

[30] See Article 311 TFEU.
[31] See this chapter above n 12 and accompanying text.
[32] European Commission (2020a).
[33] Monti Report (2016, p 7). This inter-institutional group included members designated by the European Commission, Parliament, and Council.
[34] Council Decision 2020/2053 [ORD].
[35] See generally Neumeier (2023); for earlier developments, see Chapter Two, Section C.1.
[36] European Council (2020).
[37] Council Decision 2020/2053 [ORD], recital (8). For discussion of later developments, see Chapter Five, Section C.1.

an expansion in the supranational character of those resources. As the European Commission put it, this was an effort 'to further embed EU policy priorities in the revenue side of the EU budget'.[38] Nonetheless, the actual power to collect the revenues in question, even post-NGEU, has remained firmly with the Member States, precisely because that is where the robust state capacity and democratic and constitutional legitimacy needed to support this form of extraction power actually resides.[39] As one commentator has observed, 'the creation of new own resources may be associated with the hope of promoting a political process toward the creation of an EU tax. But the constitutional requirements for true tax autonomy are lacking'.[40]

This relationship between resource extraction and the locus of robust power and legitimacy is a specific manifestation of the more general 'power-legitimacy nexus' that has long deeply shaped the process of European integration.[41] As we argue in this book, this nexus—between the powers the EU can reasonably exercise and the nature and depth of the legitimacy it possesses—has shaped and will continue to shape the integration project under NGEU and beyond. As we will see at repeated junctures in this book, the NGEU model, particularly in terms of resource mobilisation, has necessarily depended on highly complex mechanisms designed to draw, 'parasitically', on the power and legitimacy of national institutions in order to advance its supranational goals.[42] This need for ultimately national forms of legitimation is evidence of the persistently polycentric and *demoi*-cratic character of the integration project even under the NGEU.[43]

Mobilising resources from society can of course take forms other than taxation, most importantly through borrowing, the mechanism at the heart of the NGEU model. Borrowing involves the strategic use of leverage and repayment over time, which can thus accelerate short-term mobilisation capacity well beyond what taxation alone would permit. This tool is especially useful in moments of crisis and intense financial need, as NGEU itself has shown. However, when undertaken at a lesser scale—as has long been the case with the EU and its predecessors and affiliates—borrowing is typically unremarkable in terms of public law. Such borrowing has often been used to acquire an asset on the EU's balance sheet (such as a building or a

[38] European Commission (2020a).

[39] This of course raises delicate issues when a national parliament, for democratic or constitutional considerations of its own, engages in a critical debate in which rejection of the ORD appears as a serious option, an issue that arose regarding Finland in its approval of the NGEU. See Hakahuhta (2021) and Liski (2021). As this episode suggests, however, unlike in the traditional domain of 'legal integration', see Chapter Two, nn 4–5 and accompanying text, the EU lacks tools in the context of the adoption of the ORD apart from imposing political pressure and reputational consequences to bring the Member State into line.

[40] Buettner (2023, p 171).

[41] See Chapter Two, Section A. For further background on the concept, see generally Lindseth (2023), (2020a), (2020b), (2018), (2016a).

[42] On the nature and implications of the EU's 'parasitic legitimacy' drawn from the Member States, see Lindseth (2016a), reviewing Tuori (2015).

[43] On the polycentric character of the EU, see, eg, Lindseth (2010, p 53), Majone (2005, p 173); see also Bartolini (2005). On the concept of *demoi*-cracy in European integration, see, eg, Nicolaïdis (2004), (2011), (2012), (2013). For a survey of Nicolaïdis's crucial work on *demoi*-cracy as it relates to the ongoing crisis in the EU, see Lindseth (2014). For a critical overview of the literature, see Schutze (2020).

back-to-back loan to a Member State or third-party). In those circumstances, the EU is simply engaged in financial operations that many sub-constitutional supranational entities have often undertaken; moreover, the resulting economic or political impact on spending is typically marginal.[44]

When, however, this borrowing and spending reaches a macroeconomically or geopolitically salient scale, as has been the case with the NGEU experiment of the last several years—and, more importantly, when that borrowing feeds into spending programmes built on outright grants to the Member States, thus *not* yielding a corresponding asset on the EU's balance sheet—then, as the saying goes, 'size matters'.[45] The operation might thus give the impression of something approaching quasi-autonomous constitutional power in its own right, although on closer inspection that impression is mistaken. The reason is that EU borrowing remains anchored in constitutional extraction power on the national level, via the 2020 ORD. Moreover, as this book will explore in detail, the objects of spending often still remain focused on national rather than European projects.[46]

This point is brought home to us by the way in which the EU's creditworthiness is actually calculated. The NGEU bonds have been consistently rated AAA/Aaa/AAA (outlook stable) by most leading credit-rating agencies (CRAs)—Fitch, Moody's, and DBRS—and as AA+ (outlook stable) by S&P (this slightly lower rating results from a pre-NGEU downgrade for the EU flowing from Brexit). To achieve that rating, however, the CRAs do not look to the EU as an autonomous constitutional entity with its own extraction powers and creditworthiness; rather they look to the Member States via the 2020 ORD.[47]

The crucial feature of the 2020 ORD, in this regard, is Article 9. This provision makes the Member States' obligations 'callable' up to the new own resources ceiling; that is, it empowers the Commission to demand that Member States provide additional funds, up to their legally defined share of the new ceiling in case the EU cannot, through own resources or financial operations, generate sufficient funds to honour the NGEU debt obligations.[48] However, a Member State's liability for this 'callable

[44] Leino-Sandberg and Ruffert (2022, p 452) (text accompanying nn 97–98).

[45] See generally Wutscher (2023). On the question of size and its impact on broader questions of the legal basis of NGEU, see this chapter below, nn 63–67 and accompanying text.

[46] See especially Chapter Four, Section E.

[47] DBRS (2022) ('The EU's AAA rating is primarily underpinned by the Support Assessment which reflects the creditworthiness of its core member states'); Fitch (2022a) (the EU's AAA rating is 'primarily based on the capacity and propensity of "AAA" rated MS ... to provide additional funding to the EU budget, if needed to repay debt'); Moody's (2022) ('The Aaa rating of the EU ... is particularly based on the creditworthiness of large and highly rated member states'); S&P (2022, pp 119–20) ('we apply two notches of uplift to reach a final issuer credit rating at "AA+"... [based on] our view that highly rated member states would be willing to provide support over and above budgetary contributions if needed'). For further discussions of the implications of this dimension of the EU's creditworthiness on its borrowing costs, see Chapter Five, Section C.4.

[48] Council Decision 2020/2053 [ORD], arts 9(4)–(6); see also recital (23). Further backing up this specific commitment are two additional general commitments, one in secondary EU legislation, the other Treaty-based. Article 14 of the so-called Making Available Regulation provides that the Commission has the legal right to draw on all Member States in the event a borrowing country fails to repay its loan to the EU on time. See Council Regulation (EU, Euratom) No 609/2014. Article 323 TFEU also states that the EU

headroom' (as it is sometimes called)[49] is *not* joint and several; rather, the liability is limited to the Member State's *pro rata share* of the 0.6% of the EU's aggregated GNI.[50] In order to get the highest possible credit rating from the CRAs, the NGEU caps common borrowing at an amount to ensure that the callable pro rata shares of the most creditworthy Member States, aggregated together, will always be adequate to cover the service obligations on the EU's full debt.[51] In other words, without the strongest Member States ultimately backing up the Union's finances in a constitutional sense, the credit rating of NGEU bonds would have been much lower, thus impairing the common borrowing at the heart of the NGEU model.

Given this ultimate dependence of common EU borrowing on the Member States, the EU is still navigating its way through the constitutional borderlands but by no means has it exited them as a robustly constitutional entity in its own right. At most, it has dipped its toes in the Rubicon of autonomous fiscal mobilisation powers, but it certainly has not yet crossed that barrier in anything approaching the fullest sense.[52] The ultimately national foundations of the supranational creditworthiness under the NGEU model are just one reminder that the integration project still remains much closer to the non-constitutional (or sub-constitutional) side of the borderlands that it is otherwise struggling to traverse.[53]

This reality is in fact made explicit in the analytical category that one credit-rating agency (Fitch) has developed to evaluate the EU. It is, according to Fitch, best seen as a 'supranational administrative body',[54] a label that aligns with critical scholarship on the actual legal character of the integration phenomenon to date.[55] From this perspective, common borrowing under the NGEU model becomes a mechanism whereby the strongest Member States lend their creditworthiness—derived from their robustly constitutional capacity to mobilise fiscal resources—to weaker Member States via the administrative conduit of the EU and more particularly that of the European Commission. As we will explore more fully in Chapter Three, however, 'the Union is [undoubtedly] the real, final debtor, rather than merely a clearing house for affordable financing for Member States in trouble'.[56] The common borrowing under the NGEU,

institutions 'shall ensure that the financial means are made available to allow the Union to fulfil its legal obligations in respect of third parties'. The 2020 ORD actually only established one new own resource, a levy on Member States related to the amount non-recycled plastic packaging waste. Council Decision 2020/2053 [ORD], art 2(1); see also recital (7). However, it further contemplated additional own resources (eg a carbon border adjustment mechanism, a digital levy, revenues from the EU Emissions Trading System, as well as, potentially, a Financial Transaction Tax), Council Decision 2020/2053 [ORD], recital (8). See this chapter below, nn 36–37 and accompanying text.

[49] See, eg, Christie et al (2021, p 2), Claeys et al (2023), and European Commission (2023c, p 140 n 177).

[50] Council Decision 2020/2053 [ORD], art 9(5).

[51] Fitch (2021).

[52] For a similar view, see Mayer (2024).

[53] For further discussion, see Chapter Five, Section C.4.

[54] Fitch (2022b, pp 3, 18).

[55] See Lindseth (2010) (detailing the EU's 'administrative, not constitutional' legitimacy); see also Lindseth (1999) (on the 'administrative character of supranationalism').

[56] Leino-Sandberg and Ruffert (2022, p 452). See Chapter Three, n 267 and accompanying text.

in other words, is just another manifestation—undoubtedly an ingenious one—of the strategy of the still-sub-constitutional EU to draw on the constitutional power and legitimacy of the Member States to achieve goals it cannot achieve on its own.

C. The Struggle—and Need—to Move Beyond 'As If' Constitutionalism in the EU

These ultimately national foundations of the NGEU model lead us to one of the core problems that this book seeks to highlight. Even as the integration project, post-NGEU, remains closer to the non-constitutional (or sub-constitutional) side of the borderlands it is seeking to cross, the NGEU model itself has nonetheless built upon problematic features of the old 'as if'-constitutional mindset to short-circuit broad-based democratic and constitutional deliberation. This resort to 'as if' constitutionalism is thus, in our view, a threat to the legitimacy, effectiveness, and durability of the transition that the EU is otherwise rightly attempting to undertake.

The fundamental problem with the 'as if'-constitutional mindset is that it assumes that the EU's development is simply a matter of top-down legal and institutional engineering of an apparatus *already* assumed to be robustly constitutional.[57] From this perspective, all the important questions have been asked and answered, and the aim of interpretation is simply to let the already established constitution 'live' and 'breathe'.[58] This leads lawyers, judges, and legal scholars inclined to this view to discount or even ignore the limits imposed not merely by the Treaties but also by the underlying socio-political realities (notably the power-legitimacy nexus).[59] By this, we mean the necessary connection between the EU's delegated power and the nature of its legitimacy to actually exercise that power. The 'as if'-constitutional mindset leads, in our view, to legal interpretations that disregard the constraints of that nexus and instead pursue a political-purposive exercise used primarily to support the EU's institutional agenda. In that pursuit, as long as the interpretation can be functionally justified as necessary to achieve that agenda, consistency with earlier interpretations—usually considered important for doctrinal change—disappears, as do connections with broader socio-political realities.

The legal construct on which NGEU has been built[60] is a great example of the flaws of this approach. Regardless of how one regards NGEU as an emergency response to Covid (and considerable doubts exist on that point),[61] the legal flimsiness of the

[57] The 'constitutional' literature on the EU is vast, but for a recent example, see, eg, Bast and Bogdandy (2024).

[58] See, eg, this chapter below, nn 82–87 and accompanying text.

[59] See this chapter above, n 41 and accompanying text. See also Chapter Two, Section A; and Chapter Five, Section C.

[60] See this chapter above, nn 20-22 and accompanying text; see also Chapter Three.

[61] For a sense of the debate on this point, see this chapter above, n 22 and accompanying text. See also Chapters Three and Four.

NGEU model flows not just from questionable reinterpretations of several Treaty provisions.[62] Perhaps even more importantly, it also flows from the massive scale of money—and the broader institutional consequences flowing from that radical scaling up—that these questionable interpretations are now meant to support.[63] Size does indeed matter not just to the legality of NGEU *ab initio*[64]—though that is no longer our primary concern here[65]—but also to how the integration project is expected to operate under the NGEU model going forward, which is the focus of this book.

The question of size brings to mind a lesson that physicists long ago recognized, that 'more is different'.[66] Reductionist scientific methods can obscure the impact of scaling on emergent properties that can only be understood at the level of the system as a whole. Analogously reductionist methods in legal interpretation, no matter how functionally necessary to meet their defined political ends, operate to the same effect. They obscure emergent properties in legal and political systems that are then built on those reinterpretations. Reducing legality to the creative interpretation of isolated words found in the Treaties (like 'other revenue' in Article 311 TFEU or 'cohesion' in Articles 174–175 TFEU—crucial terms, as we will see, in the construction of the NGEU)[67] ignores the impact of those interpretations on the integration project as a whole; that is, its behaviour *in action* and *at scale*.[68] The core aim of this book is to understand that impact through a thorough-going analysis of the resulting institutional system.

The negative impact of this reductionist approach starts with the supranational actors who are called upon to do the necessary reinterpretation, as well as what that assignment suggests about the nature of the integration process more broadly. Even as the ultimate decisions remained matters for political leadership (*Chefsache*), evidence suggests that the actual proposals were developed by 'Commission officials ... collaborating with their counterparts in the Council Legal Service' in which 'only a very small number of people were involved'.[69] By relying on EU institutional lawyers reinterpreting or re-engineering the existing Treaties in often strained and opaque ways,[70] the development of the NGEU model extended on what Giandomenico Majone famously derided as 'integration by stealth'.[71] Increasingly, fundamental legal changes were hidden behind phrasings like 'targeted adjustments',[72] specifically to imply something focused and limited rather than transformational.[73] This sort of stealth

62 See generally Chapter Three.
63 See generally Chapter Four.
64 Wutscher (2023),
65 Cf Leino-Sandberg and Lindseth (2023).
66 Anderson (1972).
67 See Chapter Three.
68 See generally Chapters Four and Five.
69 Smeets and Beach (2023, p 386); see also (2023, pp 281–83).
70 See generally Leino-Sandberg and Ruffert (2022). For the potential unconstrained consequences of such reinterpretation, see, eg, Panascì (2024).
71 Majone (2005).
72 See, eg, Draghi Report (2024b, p 307).
73 See Chapter Six, Section A.1.

approach has a long tradition but also an equally long record of undermining popular confidence in the integration project. In such an approach, the Commission and Council legal services (supported ultimately by broad sections of the legal academy) take on central justificatory roles,[74] eventually subject to much delayed and inevitably deferential review by judges on the Court of Justice of the European Union.[75] The effect is to circumvent the democratic process normally required to amend the Treaties in favour of technocratic and juristocratic reconfiguration of the integration project.

Such an approach may have been acceptable in a world of integration through law (in, say, the legal construction of the internal market), though even there it was questionable.[76] However, in circumstances where the genuine 'constitution' of an EU resource-mobilisation power is at stake,[77] this approach entails significantly greater risks of backlash.[78] This is particularly so in an environment of underdeveloped monitoring of ever-more-opaque exchanges between national and supranational administrative actors in the planning process at the heart of the NGEU model.[79] While the NGEU model was supposed to augment EU power, it may have done the opposite by leaving individual Member States in a central position to determine the national policy measures on which EU funding would be spent—and in ways that are often difficult for their fellow Member States to monitor and trace.[80]

Advocates of elite-driven Treaty reinterpretation or other forms of subordinate legal or administrative re-engineering tend to rely on two main rationales for their approach. The first is less an argument than simply an article of faith, in which whatever advances supranational authority is, ipso facto, a good thing.[81] The second is, in effect, an argument of necessity, in which the accumulating demands of multiple crises require the sort of flexibility and quick response that only behind-the-scenes reinterpretation/re-engineering can provide. One advocate of the reinterpretation approach—Alberto de Gregorio Merino, formerly a Director in the Council Legal Service, and now the newly appointed Director-General of the Commission Legal Service—captured both rationales well in an academic article in 2024, arguing for the need to think of the Treaties as a 'living constitution': 'In the absence of revisions, an evolutive reading of the treaties is necessary to avoid a stasis that could compromise the very future of the EU project. This has led to an overall teleological reading of the

[74] See generally Leino-Sandberg (2023a). See, eg, Introduction, n 47 and sources cited. For more on the role of institutional lawyers, see Leino-Sandberg (2021a). For more on the symbiotic relationship with the legal academy, see Leino-Sandberg (2022).

[75] On the inevitability of delayed but deferential review, see Leino-Sandberg (2021b).

[76] See generally Lindseth (2016a).

[77] Lindseth and Fasone (2020).

[78] Cf. Lindseth (2020b).

[79] See Chapter Four, Sections A and B. Cf also Majone (1996, p 13) ('decisions to redistribute resources from one group of individuals, regions, or countries to another group, cannot be taken by independent experts, but only by elected politicians'); cf additionally Dawson and de Witte (2013, p 826) (making a similar argument).

[80] See generally Leino-Sandberg (2023b); see also Leino-Sandberg (2024b) (report commissioned by German Federal Ministry of Finance). For further discussion, see Chapter Four, Section B.2.

[81] See generally Leino-Sandberg (2025d), reviewing European Commission Legal Service (2022).

treaties. The response to the crisis has consisted in a continuous exercise of constitutional audacity'.[82]

This is 'as if' constitutionalism in action. During the research for this book, we have seen similar thinking in arguments regarding each of the legal components of the NGEU model, as, for example, in the 'more flexible interpretation' of the emergency assistance powers in Article 122 TFEU: 'After all, the [European Treaties] constitute a constitutional charter intended to endure for ages to come, and consequently to be adapted to the various crises of human affairs'.[83] Or the expansive reading of the flexibility clause for cohesion funding in Article 175(3) TFEU:[84] 'the EU Treaties are a living instrument, whose interpretation can be adjusted in light of changing circumstances ... [O]ne could conceive of Article 175 TFEU as a self-standing legal basis to enact another fiscal stimulus programme at EU level'.[85] Or, finally, the budgetary rules in Articles 310–311 TFEU, in which, despite the well-established balanced budget demands of Article 310 TFEU, common borrowing could become, as some argue, an 'own resource' under the Treaties.[86] This last step towards 'budgetary autonomy' would be justified because it would 'complement the autonomy of [the EU] legal order'.[87] What is notable in these characterisations is the lack of concern about how or by whom these reinterpretations happen; the main point is to get them done.

This privileging of perceived necessity as a driver of legal or institutional change may have a venerable history in theories of European integration, tracing back to their early development in the postwar decades or even more deeply to the tumult of the interwar years.[88] But the approach also empowers lawyers and judges in providing the legal foundations of new initiatives without the need for broader democratic scrutiny, particularly through the vehicle of Treaty change.[89] In our view, this approach poorly fits what the EU needs today, whether in providing a foundation for making the NGEU model permanent or, more ambitiously, in developing the integration project into a robustly democratic and constitutional system in its own right. Regardless of how one views elite-driven legal re-engineering in the context of the Covid emergency, its more permanent use would simply further 'expose the limits

[82] de Gregorio Merino (2024, p 162). See also de Gregorio Merino (2021) (describing NGEU as part of the EU's 'living constitution'): and Goldmann (2023, pp 791, 793, 795) (specifically using the English term 'living constitution'). For further critique of the concept of the 'living constitution' as it applies to the EU, see Conclusion, Section B.

[83] Chamon (2023a). For further elaboration of the argument, see Chamon (2023b), (2024). See also Chapter Three, n 228 and accompanying text; and Chapter Six, n 78 and accompanying text.

[84] See Chapter Three, Section A.

[85] Fabbrini (2022a, p 61); see also Panascì (2024, p 45, n 95).

[86] Crowe (2024, p 65), Grund and Steinbach (2024, pp 1008–16). For further discussion, see Chapter Five, nn 347–48, 527–28 and accompanying text.

[87] Crowe (2024, pp 70–71).

[88] See generally Lindseth (2015).

[89] This arguably points to why EU lawyers and judges have long been regarded as the greatest adherents (and exemplars) of functionalist theories of integration, given how those theories maximise the legal and judicial role. See Lindseth (2012, p 462) (drawing, for this argument, from the work of Morten Rasmussen and Antoine Vauchez). See also Burley and Mattli (1993), Isiksel (2015). For a further exploration of the implications of Europe's ultimately 'functional constitutionalism', see Isiksel (2016).

of the law's malleability towards politics, and the risks that interpretative stretching and legal acrobatics imply for the integrity of primary law, the power balance between Member States and the Union, and the EU rule of law'.[90] Any legal proposals to make the NGEU model more durable (including those advanced in this book)[91] should be tested in the realm of democratic politics, most importantly on the national level via debates over Treaty change if needed.[92] Only then will the emergent properties of revenue, borrowing, planning, and spending gain the necessary legitimation to secure a durable institutionalisation in the integration project going forward.

One may readily acknowledge that there are moments in history—'critical junctures' to use the language of historical-institutionalist theory[93]—where pressing needs (functional demands) seem to overwhelm resistant political interests or the alternative cultural conceptions of legitimacy they might deploy.[94] This functionalist dynamic is often invoked to justify a particular conception of the integration process, articulated most famously by Jean Monnet, who argued that 'the Union would be "forged in crisis", and would be "the sum of the solutions adopted for those crises." '[95] The polycrisis facing Europe over the last nearly two decades may well be another such critical juncture in the forging of Europe.[96] Upon closer examination, however, the institutional and legal effects of such critical junctures typically have proven to be much more complex than simplistic legal-functionalist arguments might suggest.[97] Functional demands, derived from crisis or otherwise, have never been sufficient, in themselves, to explain legal or institutional outcomes. New and durable constitutional settlements have always been the product of a complex reconciliation of functional claims of necessity, political contestation and push-back, as well as cultural debates over competing conceptions of legitimate governance.[98]

[90] Dermine (2020, p 347).
[91] See Conclusion, Section D.
[92] For a similar perspective, see Dawson (2023).
[93] See, eg, Capoccia (2015). For an exploration of this concept in connection with European integration, see Lindseth (2020a).
[94] In this history of European state-formation, the functional demands of war and security threats have been particularly crucial drivers of the processes of fiscal extraction (taxation) and centralised capacity-building. For a review of the literature and effort to analyse European integration from the perspective of state-formation, see Kelemen and McNamara (2022); see also Lindseth (2020a).
[95] See, eg, Delhomme and Hervey (2022, p 81) (quoting and translating Jean Monnet, *Mémoires* (1976)).
[96] Draghi (2023). For a robust defence of functionalist incrementalism in the face of the demands of the polycrisis, combined with a particular understanding of the possibilities of supranational democratic constitutionalism, see Goldmann (2023, p 798).
[97] The origins and subsequent trajectory of European integration demonstrate this point quite well. The catastrophic events of 1914–1945 out of which the integration project emerged can be understood as its own kind of polycrisis. It certainly opened the way for new structures of public governance beyond the state in the immediate postwar years. But even that process, it should be remembered, turned out to be as much about the 'rescue of the nation-state' as its transcendence (Milward, 2000). For this reason, any effort to dismiss such complexity in favour of a straightforwardly functionalist account, see, eg, Panascì (2024, p 54) (characterising more complex interpretation as 'a reactionary attempt to oppose the trajectory of history'), would seem rather outlandish, not to say historiographically naïve. For further discussion, see Chapter Five, Section C.4.
[98] Lindseth (2010, pp 13–14). For more detail, see also Lindseth (2023), (2017). Cf, from a social-science perspective on the interplay of 'Identity, Interest, and Public Support for the Integration of Core State Powers', Bremer et al (2020).

The historical process of European integration as a whole, *contra* Monnet's famous dictum of a Europe 'forged in crisis', in fact well exemplifies the complex interplay between the functional needs of integration and the continuing (if evolving) political and cultural claims of Member States. This interplay has had a deep impact on the evolution of EU governance over time, inhibiting integration's ability to achieve an autonomously constitutional character in its own right.[99] The multiple crises of the last several decades have seemed to suggest that the situation might be changing,[100] albeit to a more limited extent than the most hopeful advocates of an emergent EU fiscal capacity acknowledged.[101] As of this writing—including the Commission's MFF proposals in July 2025—it was still unclear the extent to which this situation might change in the future.[102] To this point, the EU has continued to exist in a world constrained by the polycentric realities of European *demoi*-cracy, 'operat[ing] in the shadow of national representative democracy, with indirect accountability as its primary focus'.[103] We fully acknowledge that augmented accountability mechanisms at the EU level will be instrumentally important in any future settlement, not least via the European Parliament acting as a co-legislator with the Council and as a check on the Commission's role in the actual operation of the new regime.[104] But the new regime should also respect the principles of conferral and subsidiarity in the Treaties and hence also maintain the nexus between the *actual* locus of mobilisation power in European integration (the Member States) and their corresponding processes of democratic and constitutional legitimation (eg in the approval of an ORD instituting or modifying the EU's own resources).[105]

We will elaborate on these points in the Conclusion. At this stage, it is sufficient to say that, based on the analysis set forth in the chapters below, it is difficult to view the NGEU model as necessarily a step towards deeper fiscal integration. To borrow a phrase again from Mario Draghi, one might say that NGEU (both as a programme and a model) could turn out to be just another 'of the many examples where the European Union is less than the sum of its parts'.[106]

[99] See generally Lindseth (2023), (2017), (2010); see also Lindseth (2020a).
[100] Lindseth and Fasone (2020); see also Crowe (2024).
[101] See, eg, Fabbrini (2022b, p 156) ('[b]y endowing the EU with brand new borrowing, spending, and taxing [*sic*] powers ... the NGEU establishes a fiscal capacity in the EU and leads to the emergence in Europe of governance arrangements in economic affairs resembling those of mature federal systems'). See also Panascì (2024). But see Albuquerque Matos (2025, pp 47, 61–62, 64) (stressing the 'mismatch' between national revenue sources on which common borrowing currently depends and what is supposed to be a strong supranational role in determining spending priorities).
[102] See Chapter Six, Section B.
[103] Nicolaïdis (2013).
[104] See Conclusion, Section D.
[105] See this chapter above, nn 30–32 and accompanying text.
[106] Draghi (2025a, min 16:12).

Chapter Two
Past as Prologue
Integration from the Inception of EMU to the Eve of the Covid Crisis

The centre of gravity of European integration, as traditionally pursued, has always been more legal and regulatory than fiscal. Over the course of its history, the integration project has operated primarily through norm-production and enforcement powers delegated to a set of supranational 'pre-commitment' institutions[1]—so-called because their core function has been to ensure the credibility of the Member States' mutual legal commitments to each other, whether in the EU Treaties or their predecessors, or in subordinate European law.[2] In this way, these institutions—originally, primarily the European Commission and the Court of Justice, later joined by the European Central Bank (ECB)—have served as technocratic and juristocratic agents to help overcome the inevitable challenges of cooperation and coordination across multiple constitutional principals, the Member States.[3]

This norm-production and enforcement apparatus was quite successful in advancing what came to be known as 'legal integration',[4] also often called 'integration through law'.[5] These terms refer to the accumulation of laws and doctrines produced and enforced by the EU's pre-commitment institutions to facilitate the integration project in all its forms, whether in terms of free movement of goods, labour, and capital or the construction of the internal market and related regulatory goals. While there were evident strains on that system even before the advent of the multiple crises of the last decade and a half,[6] the pressures flowing from these crises would eventually reveal even more fundamental limitations. These related primarily to an important shift in the EU's pre-commitment function out of the strictly legal and regulatory domains into the realm of economic governance[7]—a shift that once again revealed how

[1] On the notion of a 'pre-commitment' institution in supranational delegation, see, eg, Lindseth (2016b); see also Lindseth (2020b).

[2] For a discussion of the so-called 'commitment problem' and its relation to delegation of power to supranational institutions in the EU, see Majone (2001); see also Majone (1996).

[3] In this task, the EU's pre-commitment institutions are aided by representative-political institutions in the Council and the European Parliament.

[4] The literature on this phenomenon is vast; for an overview, see Dyevre (2022).

[5] See, eg, Augenstein (2012).

[6] See, eg, Kelemen and Pavone (2023).

[7] See generally Leino-Sandberg and Saarenheimo (2017), (2019), and Leino-Sandberg and Losada Fraga (2020).

European Integration in the Constitutional Borderlands. Päivi Leino-Sandberg and Peter L. Lindseth, Oxford University Press.
DOI: 10.1093/oso/9780198949527.003.0003

important the power-legitimacy nexus has been and will continue to be in European integration.[8]

A. The EU's Evolving Pre-Commitment Function: Economic Governance and the Power-Legitimacy Nexus

The roots of the transformation of the EU's pre-commitment function can be traced, at least in part, to core design features of Economic and Monetary Union as envisioned in the late 1980s. The Treaty-based structure of EMU was (and still is) 'asymmetric': monetary policy was supranationalised in the European Central Bank, but economic policy was to remain, for better or worse, at the national level. Even as monetary policy might successfully be delegated to a technocratic central bank, this asymmetric structure in EMU in effect recognized that the necessary democratic and constitutional legitimacy to make economic and related fiscal policies continued to reside overwhelmingly at the national level.[9]

This asymmetric structure, however, would not be without risks, something understood even before the EMU's formal establishment in the Treaty of Maastricht in 1993. The 1989 report by a high-level study group exploring the future EMU, chaired by then-European Commission President Jacques Delors (the Delors Report), noted how undisciplined national economic and fiscal policies could 'put an increasing and undue burden on monetary policy' as carried out by the future ECB.[10] The integration process, the Delors Report thus concluded, 'requires more intensive and effective policy coordination' to act as a check on this possibility.[11] 'Hence countries would have to accept that sharing a common market and a single currency area imposed policy constraints', which would include 'effective upper limits on budget deficits of individual member countries',[12] even as the competence for making substantive economic and fiscal policy remained with the Member States.[13]

The European Treaties post-Maastricht enshrined the main elements of this asymmetric framework, tempered by the need for coordination at the EU level. On the one hand, Article 125 TFEU expressly prohibited assumption of liability for another Member State's commitments; each Member State would therefore remain, in principle, responsible for its own finances and be subject to market discipline as a consequence. On the other hand, Articles 121 and 126 TFEU (on the multilateral

[8] On the power-legitimacy nexus generally, see Chapter One, nn 41–43 and accompanying text. On its effects on the shift in the EU's pre-commitment function specifically, see this chapter below, nn 31–80 and accompanying text.

[9] See this chapter below, nn 82–84 and accompanying text.

[10] Delors Report (1989, p 11 para 12).

[11] Ibid (emphasis in original omitted).

[12] Ibid, p 20 para 30.

[13] Ibid, p 14 para 20.

surveillance procedure and the excessive deficit procedure, respectively) set out the provisions on the coordination of economic policies, implementing the obligation set forth in Article 2(3) TFEU: 'The Member States shall coordinate their economic and employment policies within arrangements as determined by this Treaty, which the Union shall have competence to provide'. Building on these provisions, secondary law established a series of successively more demanding regimes of coordination and surveillance under the rubric of the Stability and Growth Pact (SGP), beginning in 1998 and culminating in the 'European Semester' as it came to be known in the early 2010s.[14] The shift in the EU's pre-commitment role into the realm of economic governance thus can be traced to the establishment of these successively more demanding regimes of coordination and surveillance as a means of tempering Treaty-based EMU asymmetry.

The roots of that shift, however, can also be traced more specifically to the two-pronged response to the sovereign-debt crisis in the euro area that grew out of the global financial crisis beginning in 2007–2008: assistance programmes of various kinds as well as increased supervision over national economic policy.[15] The fundamental driver of each was that certain Member States lost access to the credit markets, either due to their unsustainably high levels of sovereign debt (Greece, Portugal) or to acute borrowing needs to bail out vulnerable domestic banks when the credit-driven boom collapsed, along with domestic demand and tax receipts (Ireland, Spain, Cyprus). Because these countries issued debt in a currency they did not control (the euro), none possessed tools otherwise available to a sovereign borrower (currency devaluation, debt monetisation).[16] In these circumstances, maintaining market access was crucial. If they could not, they needed recourse to a politically supported lending mechanism, subject to conditionality and oversight of the borrower's economic policies.

At the international level, the International Monetary Fund (IMF) has traditionally served as that mechanism. At the outset of the sovereign-debt crisis in the EU, however, there was no European-level mechanism playing a similar role. Eventually, by 2012, the EU would establish the European Stability Mechanism (ESM) as a permanent collective borrowing and lending vehicle akin to the IMF but working within the euro area. But in the interim between the advent of the crisis and the establishment of the ESM, Member States in distress received financial assistance through either ad hoc programmes (as in the case of the initial aid to Greece in May 2010) or programmes under two more hastily created vehicles, the European Financial Stabilisation Mechanism (EFSM) and the European Financial Stability Facility (EFSF). The EU established the EFSM under the emergency assistance provisions of Article 122(2) TFEU, with borrowing backed by the then-available €60 billion fiscal headroom in the

14 The literature tracing these developments is vast. See, eg, Ioannidis (2016), Hinarejos (2015), Tuori and Tuori (2014), and Snyder (1999).

15 Craig (2013, p 3); see also Ioannidis (2016).

16 de Grauwe (2011), Buiter and Rahbari (2012), and de Grauwe and Ji (2013).

EU budget.[17] The EFSF was, by contrast, organised by euro area Member States as a special-purpose vehicle under Luxembourg law to collectively borrow up to €440 billion, backed by guarantees of those Member States in accordance with their share in the paid-in capital of the ECB.[18]

In addition to loans to distressed Member States from these vehicles, assistance also took other, more indirect forms, most importantly as purchases of euro area sovereign bonds on secondary markets by the ECB and national central banks in the Eurosystem.[19] Additionally, as part of the regulatory effort to break the 'doom loop' between a Member State's public finances and domestic banks holding its bonds, the EU established a banking union with a single supervisory mechanism (SSM) and a single resolution mechanism (SRM) for the largest and most systemically important institutions.[20] Regardless of the form of assistance, the EU's response led to a form of risk mutualisation, even if in limited and often quite indirect ways to avoid the seeming no-bailout strictures of Article 125 TFEU.

In the course of the crisis, Article 125 TFEU effectively received a new meaning, no longer so much prohibiting financial assistance as requiring conditionality to ensure that the distressed Member State followed a sound budgetary policy.[21] This was made clear, in particular, in the CJEU's *Pringle* judgment in 2012, in which it held that emergency lending to a Member State via the new ESM was compatible with Article 125 TFEU as long as 'the conditions attached to such assistance are such as to prompt that Member State to implement a sound budgetary policy'.[22] In forcing a clarification of the meaning of Article 125 TFEU along these lines, the euro crisis also clarified the emergency assistance rules of Article 122 TFEU, which had been little used in the integration process before the crisis.[23]

Article 122 TFEU has two subparagraphs. Article 122(1) TFEU only applies in the limited circumstances of 'severe difficulties ... in the supply of certain products, notably in the area of energy' and thus played little role in the euro area crisis.[24] The more

[17] Council Regulation (EU) 407/2010 [EFSM].

[18] While the EFSM continues to exist, the activities of the EFSF are now carried out by the ESM and EFSF Consolidated Articles of Association and the EFSF Framework Agreement can be found on the ESM website. See European Stability Mechanism (2025a).

[19] The purchases were made on the secondary market because of the prohibition on direct monetary financing in Article 123 TFEU. As a consequence of asset-purchase programmes, the size of the Eurosystem's consolidated balance sheet reached its peak in mid-2022 at around €8.8 trillion (8.8 thousand billion). Much of the growth was due to Eurosystem purchases of bonds issued by euro area governments, as part of its quantitative easing programme, the combined amount of which stood still at the end of 2022 at nearly €5 trillion. For an overview, see European Central Bank (2023); see also Fruzzetti et al (2021).

[20] For an overview of the elements of the banking union, including SSM, the SRM, the proposal for a European deposit insurance scheme (EDIS), and the quest for a European 'safe asset' via sovereign bond-backed securities (SBBS), see European Commission (2025a).

[21] Case C-370/12, *Pringle* (2012), paras 131, 135–37.

[22] Ibid, para 137.

[23] Eur-lex identifies only one pre-Lisbon instrument approved on the basis of Article 122 TFEU's predecessor provision: a Council directive imposing an obligation on Member States to maintain minimum stocks of crude oil and/or petroleum products; a matter also addressed later in a 2015 decision. See Council Directive 2009/119/EC, and Council Decision (EU) 2015/632.

[24] However, it would play a role in the Covid crisis. See, eg, Council Regulation (EU) 2020/521; Council Regulation (EU) 2022/2372; see also European Commission (2021a). It would also play a role in the

general emergency provision is Article 122(2) TFEU, which authorizes assistance to a Member State 'in difficulties or ... seriously threatened with severe difficulties caused by natural disasters or exceptional occurrences beyond its control'. As noted above, this provision served as the legal basis for the EFSM lending vehicle.[25] Article 122(2) TFEU authorises the Council, on a Commission proposal, to 'grant, under certain conditions, Union financial assistance to the Member State concerned'. This provision is thus a direct empowerment of national executives in the Council, and, because it is not technically a legislative procedure, it does not directly involve parliaments apart from an obligation to inform the European Parliament of the measures taken.

In its *Pringle* judgment in 2012, the CJEU made clear that Article 122(2) TFEU only provided a legal basis for non-permanent, ad hoc measures in situations of severe difficulties, thus holding it could not be used to set up a permanent mechanism.[26] In this sense, Article 122(2) TFEU should not be able to serve as a general-purpose basis to bypass inconvenient legal and procedural requirements.[27] Moreover, the language referring to assistance only 'under certain conditions' would also play a crucial role; on this basis, macroeconomic conditionality came to be understood in the euro crisis as an essential element of any such assistance, aimed at restoring the ability of the Member State to finance itself, subject to market discipline.[28]

To enforce the credibility of these heightened mutual commitments to fiscal discipline—whether, for distressed Member States, via conditionality in emergency financial assistance programmes, or, for all Member States, in the general obligations under the SGP and the European Semester—the Member States looked to the Commission to serve as their key pre-commitment agent. But the euro crisis had now deeply transformed the Commission's function in that regard. Now the oversight would focus on whether the Member States were exercising their 'core state powers'[29] in fiscal and economic policy in compliance with rules and standards defined in various executive processes at the supranational level.[30]

As we shall see later, however, there is a distinction to be drawn between Commission oversight as part of an emergency lending programme and the more general Commission oversight envisioned as part of the SGP and the European Semester. In the former, the Commission's technocratic legitimacy was reinforced by the functional demands of lost market access, whereas in the latter, it was not, or at least

energy crisis following the Russian invasion of Ukraine. See, eg, Council Regulation 2022/1369; Council Regulation 2022/1854; and Council Regulation (EU) 2022/257. For further discussion, see Chapter Five, Section A.1.

25 See this chapter above, n 17 and accompanying text.

26 Case C-370/12, *Pringle* (2012), para 65 and paras 105 et seq.

27 But see Chamon (2023b); see also Chamon (2023a). For further discussion of this purportedly 'flexible' use of Article 122 TFEU under NGEU, see Chapter Three, n 228 and accompanying text; and Chapter Six, n 78 and accompanying text.

28 Council Regulation (EU) 407/2010 [EFSM], art 3(3)(b). See in particular Borger (2020); see also de Witte (2021, p 649).

29 Genschel and Jachtenfuchs (2014), (2016), (2018).

30 See generally Leino-Sandberg and Saarenheimo (2019) See also Ioannidis (2016).

certainly not directly. But in both contexts the Commission's technocratic legitimacy alone would be insufficient to sustain the scope of the power that the Commission was being asked to exercise, thus showing the importance of the power-legitimacy nexus in defining the limits EU governance.[31]

We begin with the context of emergency lending. The long experience of the IMF had made clear that a technocratic agency, even one operating beyond the confines of the state, could be empowered to supervise conditionality attached to such lending programmes. But this empowerment came with an important qualification. The IMF was forced, over time, to recognise that, even in the context of emergency lending, the success of a programme depended importantly on a sense of 'national ownership' of the promised reforms on which the lending was conditioned.[32] The IMF defined national ownership as 'a willing assumption of responsibility for an agreed program of policies, by officials in a borrowing country who have the responsibility to formulate and carry out those policies, based on an understanding that the program is achievable and is in the country's own interest'. The IMF's definition of ownership did not, however, imply a one-way obligation on the part of the borrowing country's officials; rather, the quest for ownership demanded a 'flexible and responsive' approach on the part of the lender to the full range of 'institutional, administrative, and political factors' that would contribute to such ownership.[33] Reinforcing the IMF's role here was always the functional demands of lost market access, which left the recipient country with few other financing options. The borrowing countries may not have liked the IMF's interference—and, more often than not, they did not—but the needs of public finance left them little choice. But the quest for greater national ownership nonetheless reflected a recognition that, even in the context of the extreme functional demands of lost market access, technocratic legitimacy alone could not guarantee success without drawing on the more robust political and cultural legitimacy of national officials and institutions.

This is a lesson that the EU would need to (re-)learn in the context of the emergency lending programmes in the early phase of the euro crisis in the first half of the 2010s. The manager of these programmes—the Troika (the Commission and the ECB together with the IMF)—possessed little more legitimacy than the technocratic IMF itself alone possessed. While other EU actors (the European Council, the Council, and the Eurogroup) also played key roles in designing and managing the programmes, they were formally run through intergovernmental arrangements, supported by the Troika, rather than the EU 'constitutional' framework. Furthermore, in formal terms the crisis programmes and their associated conditionality were ultimately based on agreements—concessional loans in exchange for reforms—into which each party entered voluntarily. The power balance in the negotiations may have been extremely asymmetric, but the crisis countries always had the full legal option to decline the

[31] See Chapter One, nn 41–43 and accompanying text.
[32] International Monetary Fund (2001a), (2001b).
[33] Boughton (2003, pp 8–9).

agreement. What they lacked, of course, were the economic incentives (indeed, even ability) to do so given the lack of access to the credit markets.

What followed with these programmes provides a telling insight into the difficulty of using technocratic institutions to impose economic policies on a Member State from the outside, even under the extreme functional pressures of lost market access. Greece's first programme, for example, was prepared in Brussels and was quite demanding; the result was little national ownership, poor implementation, an undermining of faith in domestic democratic institutions, even apathy, nihilism, radicalisation, and a risk of serious unrest. The experience with subsequent programmes in Greece and elsewhere was directionally similar, if perhaps (though not always) less extreme: a poor record of implementation, frequent standoffs, alienated citizens and the emergence of reactive political movements seeking to capitalise on the situation through anti-European platforms.[34]

All of this helps to explain the extreme wariness—which persists to this day, particularly in southern Member States—towards any lending model based on traditional conditionality, for example, via the ESM.[35] This wariness would also deeply shape both the design and implementation of NGEU and more particularly its most important component, the Recovery and Resilience Facility.[36] This negative experience also points to a deeper weakness in the primarily technocratic approach, what we might call 'the paradox of conditionality as a mode of supranational governance'.[37] Whether creditor-imposed conditionality can induce reforms on the national level has typically depended on whether national institutions and actors believed in, and were able to sell, the reform programme to the electorate and thus create broad ownership for it. Where such national ownership was absent, implementation faltered. Further, any perception that a national government was being reduced to subservience to creditors or the Troika was typically badly received by the electorate and punished at the polls, or it triggered other forms of resistance.[38]

In other words, even as the intergovernmental actors in the Council or Eurogroup, supported by the technocratic Troika, ultimately held the purse-strings and could impose conditionality, they could not actually *displace* national institutions or officials and implement reforms directly—a sign of their ultimate weakness, at least in a democratic and constitutional sense. This was not just a formal distinction. The national level remained the locus of the necessary democratic and constitutional legitimacy to

[34] Indeed, even where reforms were 'successfully' implemented, there were other downside risks for Europe's reputation. Spain, for example, adopted several labour market and social reforms under pressure from the Troika that did not exist in the electoral platforms of the governing parties. The reforms soon proved to be a failure, achieving the opposite of what, in theory, they were designed to achieve. See generally Navarro (2014).

[35] This attitude has been particularly pronounced in Italy, the only country whose parliament has not ratified the reform of the ESM Treaty. For a brief overview, see Beraldo (2024). For more detailed analysis of Italy's longstanding resistance, see Galli (2020).

[36] See Chapters Three and Four; see also Smeet and Beach (2023, p 386).

[37] Lindseth (2020a, p 519).

[38] See, eg, Hadoulis (2017).

ensure the adoption and implementation of the demanded reforms; the technocratic Troika or the broader EU could not do it on its own. In short, even in the euro crisis, supranational governance still depended on the power and legitimacy of the *demoi*-cratic Member States.

Turning now to the Commission's role in the European Semester process, we can see the ultimate weakness of supranational technocracy at play in an arguably even more pronounced fashion. This context typically lacked the direct threat of lost access to the credit markets, even as markets could sometimes be sensitive to Commission assessments. Instead, oversight was primarily designed to enforce Treaty commitments to coordination of economic and fiscal policies among the Member States. In that regard, the Commission's leverage was even weaker than the Troika's in the emergency lending context. And yet, in the context of the European Semester, the Commission in principle had a much broader range of oversight powers to interfere, potentially, throughout the national fiscal policy cycle of all Member States—whether through recommendations, instructions and, potentially, even outright sanctions.

In this sense, the European Semester contemplated a generalised system of customised, or tailored, policy steering led by the Commission. The original framework—which consisted of common benchmarks set out in the Treaties (3% annual deficits and 60% total debt as a percentage of GDP)[39] accompanied by very general broad economic policy and employment guidelines—were now operationalised as a comprehensive fiscal framework and much more detailed country-specific recommendations (CSRs). What was thus initially established as an emergency brake to be invoked when a Member State's policies posed a direct threat to the stability of the single currency, over the course of the crisis decade turned into a broad vehicle for the Commission to guide the Member States towards policies deemed adequate along multiple dimensions, not just limited to the economic and fiscal domains but also encompassing social and growth policies.[40]

Researchers in particular perceived a progressive effort to 'socialise' the European Semester, 'both in terms of its substantive content and its governance procedures'.[41] Significant impetus for this effort would come with the declaration of the European Pillar of Social Rights in 2017, covering various questions falling under national competence ranging from equal access to labour markets (such as skills, education, equal opportunities, active promotion of employment); fair working conditions (including flexible employment, salaries, working conditions, dialogue between labour market parties); and social protection and participation (including childcare, minimum wage, unemployment benefits, access to basic social and health services, and long-term care).[42] The later-adopted European Pillar of Social Rights Action Plan would

[39] See Article 126(2) TFEU, incorporating by reference Article 1 of Protocol (No 12) on the Excessive Deficit Procedure.

[40] The procedure is described in detail in Leino-Sandberg and Saarenheimo (2019) and Leino-Sandberg and Losada Fraga (2020).

[41] Zeitlin and Vanhercke (2018, p 152).

[42] European Commission (2017d).

specifically identify the European Semester as the key tool to monitor and steer national actions 'in a way to further the implementation of the principles of the Social Pillar'.[43]

As this process developed, however, the focus remained on 'compliance'—essentially the polar opposite of 'ownership'—in which success was defined as transferring ideas from the supranational to the national level instead of allowing national institutions to determine their own priorities. Exemplifying this focus were two reports from the Presidents of leading European institutions: the so-called Four Presidents' Report in 2012 (authored by the President of the Council, together the Presidents of the Commission, the Eurogroup, and the ECB),[44] and the Five Presidents' Report in 2015 (authored by the President of the Commission, together with the Presidents of the Council, the Eurogroup, the ECB and the EP).[45] The Four Presidents' Report contemplated the creation of 'an EMU fiscal capacity' to serve a 'shock absorption function' but also '[l]inking it tightly to compliance with the broad EU governance framework, including possible arrangements of a contractual nature'.[46] In a similar vein, the Five Presidents' Report suggested that a Member State's right to benefit from certain Union programmes should be 'tightly linked to [its] compliance with the broad EU governance framework and to progress in converging towards ... common standards'.[47]

A key aim of that heightened compliance was stronger traction for demands for 'structural reforms'—a category that had dominated EU economic discussions at least since the adoption of the Lisbon strategy in 2000,[48] even as its precise meaning was often vague.[49] A standard definition (this one, in fact, from the Five Presidents' Report) defined them as 'reforms geared at modernising economies to achieve more growth and jobs', including 'both more efficient labour and product markets and stronger public institutions'.[50] This definition was sufficiently capacious to leave a great deal of room for debate over which reforms would fit within this broad category, or how to assess their impact.[51] One detailed study of the term's usage in the EU during the crisis decade, for example, went so far as to call the phrase an 'empty signifier' without real substantive content.[52] Moreover, the Commission's own internal manual on the implementation of the Stability and Growth Pact (including the European Semester) noted the multiple challenges of assessing structural reforms, from 'direct positive budgetary impact, as for instance is the case of pension reforms, health care reforms

43 European Commission (2021b).
44 Four Presidents' Report (2012).
45 Five Presidents' Report (2015).
46 Four Presidents' Report (2012, p 12). For further discussion of the 'contractual' dimension of the Four Presidents' Report, see this chapter below, nn 58, 236 and accompanying text.
47 Five Presidents' Report (2015, p 15).
48 European Council (2000).
49 See generally Crespy and Vanheuverzwijn (2016).
50 Five Presidents' Report (2015, p 7).
51 See, eg, Tsoukala (2020).
52 Crespy and Vanheuverzwijn (2016, pp 10 and 28).

or reforms to public administration', to 'indirect sustainability-enhancing effect, in cases where they result in higher potential output and, therefore, lead to higher future revenues', to outright 'budgetary costs, particularly in the short run'.[53]

Despite the 'uncertainties associated' with defining and assessing structural reforms,[54] the pressure for intensified enforcement of national promises along these lines increased as the pace of economic growth and innovation in Europe continued to lag. In line with the aspirations of the Lisbon strategy's own efforts to promote greater economic efficiency and competitiveness[55]—but also following that strategy's failure to reach its goals (often attributed to its non-binding character)[56]—structural reforms increasingly became associated with monitoring and promotion under a system of top-down governance by experts armed with real enforcement authority and the possibility to impose sanctions.[57] The Four Presidents' Report in 2012 envisioned 'setting up of a mechanism for stronger coordination, convergence and enforcement of structural policies based on arrangements of a contractual nature between Member States and EU institutions on the policies countries commit to undertake and on their implementation'.[58] The Five Presidents' Report contemplated an even 'more binding' process based 'on a set of common high-level standards that would be defined in EU legislation' for 'labour markets, competitiveness, business environment and public administrations, as well as certain aspects of tax policy'.[59]

The quest for a more binding approach, however, was also in tension with the constraints of the power-legitimacy nexus in the most fundamental sense.[60] The Five Presidents' Report depended on a notion of EU 'sovereignty over policies of common concern' that necessarily presupposed a more robust democratic and constitutional legitimacy than the EU actually possessed.[61] The EU at that point enjoyed, at best, executive and technocratic legitimacy that was insufficient to support the sort of 'strong decision-making at [the supranational] level' that the Five Presidents' Report suggested was needed.[62] There were also legal obstacles, as Jean-Paul Keppenne, Director for EMU matters in the Commission Legal Service, later pointed out in a published legal commentary.[63] The objective of a more integrated economic policy at EU level that involved 'a centralized budget with redistributive features and some fiscal power' would 'require deep and major Treaty changes, in order to allow some form of debt mutualisation' as well as 'veto power on national budgets; a sizeable euro area budget; and integration of the ESM in the EU'.[64]

[53] European Commission (2019b, p 20).
[54] Ibid. On these difficulties, see also Chapter Four, Section B.
[55] European Council (2000). The same tendencies would also manifest itself in transformation of cohesion policy, discussed in more detail in Section C.3.
[56] See, eg, Deutsche Welle (2010). But see also Wyplosz (2010).
[57] Leino-Sandberg and Saarenheimo (2019); see also Tsoukala (2020).
[58] Four Presidents' Report (2012, p 4).
[59] Five Presidents' Report (2015, p 9).
[60] See Chapter One, nn 41–43 and accompanying text.
[61] Five Presidents' Report (2015, p 9).
[62] Ibid.
[63] Keppenne (2020b).
[64] Ibid, p 810.

For all these reasons, it should hardly surprise us that this top-down, compliance-oriented system in the European Semester ultimately proved unsatisfactory—indeed, largely unworkable[65]—thus necessitating reform.[66] The framework that began as a relatively clear, rules-based system (and thus better suited to the Commission's executive and technocratic legitimacy) ultimately evolved into an increasingly complex, discretionary system where a wide variety of exceptional circumstances, temporary factors, and measurement issues came into play.[67] The failure of the system, however, was not just, or even primarily, a consequence of its technical complexity. Instead, it was a consequence of the deeply political character of oversight, which often prompted 'genuine and legitimate disagreement' on the part of Member State governments about what they were being asked to do.[68] The actions that fell under the banner of structural reforms tended to target policies that were often popular among the electorate (or were backed by politically powerful interests with sway over public opinion). Consequently, these policies were often politically difficult to modify—in particular if they required the adoption of legislation—serving as a further reminder of weakness at the heart of technocratic conditionality as a mode of governance.[69] The former president of the European Commission, Jean-Claude Juncker, captured that weakness succinctly by his description of the infamous 'curse' afflicting European politicians at this time: 'We all know what to do, but we don't know how to get re-elected once we have done it'.[70]

The sort of authority needed in such circumstances—cutting close to the most robust forms of democratic and constitutional legitimacy[71]—was well beyond what the Commission was able to muster given its primarily technocratic and administrative 'legitimacy resources'.[72] The result was a disconnect between seemingly demanding (albeit complex) rules and ultimately lax enforcement. This eventually led to calls for greater 'national ownership', seen as a vehicle 'to better enforcement of commonly agreed rules' by 'remov[ing] the perception that [the] rules are hierarchically imposed'.[73] But rather than strengthening the role of national actors, the aspiration behind such calls was 'internalisation of the spirit of EU's fiscal rules into the national budgetary process'[74]—in short, a still top-down acceptance of EU rules

[65] Leino-Sandberg and Saarenheimo (2017) and Leino-Sandberg and Losada Fraga (2020); see also Tesche (2023).

[66] On 5 February 2020, on the eve of the coronavirus pandemic, the Commission launched an assessment and revision of the system of fiscal oversight. See European Commission (2020c). That process took over four years and resulted in a reform that would rely on key elements of the planning model of NGEU and more particularly the RRF. See European Commission (2023d) as well as Regulation (EU) 2024/1263 [Economic Governance Framework]. For more detail, see Chapter Five, Section B.3.

[67] See also the European Commission (2020c, p 10).

[68] Bokhorst (2022, p 112).

[69] See this chapter above, n 37 and accompanying text.

[70] Buti et al (2008), quoting *The Economist*, 'Special Report: The Quest for Prosperity', 15 March 2007; see also Charlemagne (2010), Bremer et al (2020).

[71] Leino-Sandberg and Saarenheimo (2019, pp 146–47).

[72] On the concept of legitimacy resources and its impact on European integration, see Lindseth (2010, pp 11, 52–53, 186, 224, 227–28, 249, 265, 275); see also Leino-Sandberg and Saarenheimo (2018, p 645).

[73] Alcidi and Gros (2017).

[74] Schlosser (2018, p 53).

and recommendations by national governments and parliaments and, ultimately, the voters to whom they are accountable.

The Commission's inability to play the sort of command-and-control role that the European Semester effectively envisioned for it taught an important lesson in what can occur when there is a break in the power-legitimacy nexus (again, the necessary connection between an institution's delegated power and the nature of its underlying legitimacy).[75] The risk of such a break is why, in European integration, one must never lose sight of one key question: 'legitimate for what?'[76] The EU's core legitimacy—variously technocratic, juristocratic, and therefore primarily 'administrative'[77]—ultimately defines what roles its component institutions can realistically undertake (at least until the EU is able to attain robust democratic and constitutional legitimacy of its own).[78] It is one thing to ask the Commission to serve a pre-commitment function in the traditional realm of legal or regulatory integration (though, again, even there, that role was arguably breaking down even before the polycrisis).[79] But it is quite another to do so in the area of fiscal and economic policy where the legitimacy demands are so much greater.

In a still polycentric and *demoi*-cratic EU, where robust governing legitimacy remains, for better or worse, distributed among the Member States as ultimate constitutional principals in the system, special care should be taken not to ask the Commission (or any other European institution for that matter) to undertake roles that it cannot successfully fulfil. This was ultimately the problem in the shift of the Commission's pre-commitment function out of the strictly legal and regulatory domains into the realm of economic governance: it asked the Commission to attempt, across the full range of countries, a 'principal-agent inversion'.[80] In that situation, the erstwhile supranational pre-commitment agent was asked to take on, in effect, the role of the principal in the system, albeit without the necessary socio-political, socio-cultural legitimacy to support it. As the experience of the European Semester demonstrated over the course of the 2010s, that was a recipe for failure.

B. Overcoming Asymmetry, Completing EMU: The Quest for a Supranational Fiscal Dimension

The risk of an unsupported principal–agent inversion is especially acute in the context of what we might call the 'metabolic' function of a constitution; that is, in the

[75] See generally Chapter One, nn 41–43 and accompanying text.
[76] Lindseth (2012b).
[77] See generally Lindseth (2010); see also Lindseth (1999).
[78] Cf Majone (1993); see also Leino-Sandberg and Saarenheimo (2019, p 145).
[79] See Kelemen and Pavone (2023).
[80] For more on the risks of such a principal–agent inversion, see Lindseth (2017, p 87); see also Lindseth (2020b, p 45). For a contribution that argues in a similar direction, see Bradford et al (2018).

extraction of fiscal or human resources from society and their conversion into work towards public ends—arguably the *sine qua non* of genuine constitutionalism.[81] When the EU tries to give instructions to an individual Member State on how it should, within its national scope of competence, do this extraction/conversion, the legitimacy demands on the governance structure are at their highest.[82] In fact, the Treaty-based choice in favour of an 'asymmetric' EMU,[83] with policy coordination and oversight at the EU level but fiscal and economic policy at the national level, reflected the basic understanding that the EU lacked the robust fiscal (much less human) mobilisation capacity of its own, thus requiring it to rely on the Member States to fulfil this essential constitutional function. The EU remained, for this reason, primarily a producer and enforcer of norms but otherwise 'parasitically' dependent on the Member States for this 'metabolic' constitutional power.[84]

Just as in the context of Commission oversight of national fiscal discipline,[85] the power-legitimacy nexus also played an important role in shaping the fiscal/economic versus monetary policy dimensions of supranational authority. At various junctures of the crisis decade, the ECB and Eurosystem were undoubtedly called upon to play an outsized role in providing liquidity to the sovereign bond markets.[86] Despite the obvious economic-political import of these monetary interventions, they nonetheless fell well within accepted (if still debatable) understandings of what a technocratic central bank can and should legitimately be able to do in such circumstances. Regardless of whether one traced the origins of these understandings to the German Bundesbank or to the US Federal Reserve, it was clear that, by the 1990s, the model of a technocratic, independent central bank had gained broad acceptance throughout developed countries, including in Europe.[87]

This acceptance of the technocratic power and legitimacy of central banks meant that, over the course of the crisis decade, the ECB's monetary interventions became (economically speaking) 'the only game in town', as the saying went. The ECB was compelled to take on a central role at various stages of the crisis decade because only it had the tools to intervene at scale, supported by the requisite legitimacy (in this case, technocratic).[88] In a direct and powerful manifestation of the power-legitimacy nexus at work, the EU otherwise lacked any comparable authority of its own in the fiscal or economic domain, apart from the system of constraining

[81] Lindseth (2016a), (2017), (2018), (2023).

[82] See this chapter above, nn 71–78 and accompanying text.

[83] See this chapter above, nn 11–14 and accompanying text.

[84] See generally Lindseth (2016a), reviewing Tuori (2015), which coins the notion of 'parasitic legitimacy' to describe the EU. See also Chapter One, n 42 and accompanying text.

[85] See this chapter above, nn 29–80 and accompanying text.

[86] See this chapter above, n 19 and accompanying text.

[87] See, eg, the German *Bundesverfassungsgericht*'s discussion (and acceptance) of the constitutionality of ECB independence in its ruling on the constitutionality of the Treaty of Maastricht of 1992. *Brunner v European Union Treaty* (1993), translated at 33 ILM 388, 439 (1994) (justifying such independence on the basis of technocratic expertise, as well as on the political incapacities of parliaments under electoral and interest group pressures).

[88] Cf Tooze (2020).

oversight under the European Semester. This brought to the fore a central contradiction in the way the system of economic governance under the old regime of European integration operated. Stated in constitutional terms: 'National institutions [were] increasingly constrained in the exercise of their [own fiscal] constitutional authority', but the EU lacked both the power and legitimacy to 'fill the void' because it did not possess the essential attribute of 'genuine constitutionalism': the autonomous capacity to mobilise fiscal resources at the EU level in a legitimate and compulsory manner.[89]

From the early to middle part of the 2010s, the EU's lack of an autonomous fiscal capacity became a point of intensified political discussion. The Four Presidents' Report had, as early as 2012, contemplated a 'common but limited shock absorption function' built around a supranational fiscal capacity, which could 'contribute to cushioning the impact of country-specific shocks and help prevent contagion across the euro area and beyond'.[90] The Commission's 'Blueprint for a deep and genuine economic and monetary union'[91] also called for a supranational fiscal capacity and stabilisation function, anticipating many of the features of its later proposal for a so-called 'Convergence and Competitiveness Instrument' (CCI) in 2013—discussed in more detail later.[92] However, the Commission's 'Blueprint' was quite frank that the more ambitious dimensions of its proposals, such as an EU power 'to raise revenue by indebting itself on the markets (presently barred by Articles 310 and 311 TFEU)', would require Treaty change.[93]

As the euro crisis started to fade, so too did political momentum towards deeper integration. Plans for expanding the EU's role in the fiscal sphere were placed on the backburner but were not forgotten. As low inflation and lagging growth persisted in the euro area into the middle part of the decade, fears increased about the re-emergence of the euro crisis, giving urgency to advocacy of an EU fiscal capacity, in effect, to navigate around what observers framed as a flaw (or 'incompleteness') in the EMU's original Treaty-based design. At the forefront of these discussions would be the Five Presidents' Report in 2015,[94] which helped to prompt broader reflection on how to 'complete' the EMU by giving it, in effect, some form of a more centralised fiscal component. These calls, however, often lacked specificity, were contradictory, or were simply contestable about what an EU fiscal capacity could or should do.[95] Moreover, as always in the fiscal context, any move towards developing an EU fiscal capacity needed to avoid 'overload[ing] the EU's modest legitimacy

[89] Lindseth (2016a, p 701).
[90] Four Presidents' Report (2012, p 10).
[91] European Commission (2012).
[92] See this chapter below, nn 232–45 and accompanying text.
[93] European Commission (2012, p 33).
[94] Five Presidents' Report (2015). For an overview and analysis of the literature on 'completing' the EMU in the 2010s, with special emphasis on the Five Presidents' Report, see Leino-Sandberg and Saarenheimo (2018).
[95] See generally Leino-Sandberg and Saarenheimo (2018).

resources', which might then 'result in ... highly visible and embarrassing clash[es] of authority'.[96]

The response of the ECB and the Eurosystem in these circumstances, consistent with their technocratic legitimacy as central bankers, was to begin quantitative easing in March 2015 via its third sovereign bond-buying programme of the half-decade.[97] But additionally, in response to what many saw as overly cautious fiscal policies in the northern euro-area countries (in particular in Germany), there were calls for greater focus on euro-area aggregate fiscal stance to counterbalance the restrictive effects of the one-sided discipline of the SGP. In June 2016, for example, the ECB itself cautioned that, by leaving fiscal policy entirely decentralised, there was 'no guarantee that the coordination of national fiscal policies through the SGP results in an appropriate aggregate euro area fiscal stance'.[98]

Of course, guarantees of this type have very rarely existed for any monetary arrangement. A country's ability to exercise countercyclical fiscal policy has always been dependent on the interplay of a complex array of political and economic factors, which cannot be straightforwardly reduced to whether there exists fiscal space to engage in further public borrowing (which is itself a complex political and economic calculation).[99] Indeed, very few countries—mostly concentrated at the highest echelons of the income scale—have had the ability to exercise countercyclical fiscal policies in any regular way.[100] The problem in Europe was, in any case, never really the aggregate fiscal stance of the euro area; it was the unsustainable level of debt in many Member States. This meant that, however one calculated it, the space for outright fiscal stimulus was quite unevenly distributed in the euro area (some Member States had a great deal of space, others none at all). This factor would eventually play a key role in driving support for collective borrowing under NGEU five years later.[101]

The fire-power in the EU budget, without that collective borrowing, was small. Under the then-prevailing Own Resources Decision, the budget was just slightly over 1% of the EU GNI, and the vast bulk of EU spending went to the Common Agricultural Policy (CAP) and cohesion funding traditionally conceived.[102] With these relatively

[96] Ibid, p 645. On the concept of 'legitimacy resources', see also the discussion in this chapter above, n 72 and accompanying text.

[97] The Public Sector Purchase Programme (PSPP) followed the Securities Market Programme (SMP) in 2010 and the Outright Monetary Transactions Programme (OMT) in 2012 (announced but never implemented). See European Central Bank (2025a).

[98] European Central Bank (2016, p 69). For a view from high-level staff on the Commission, see, eg, Rodríguez Muñoz and Buti (2016).

[99] International Monetary Fund (2018).

[100] There exists a robust debate among economists about why this is so. For a recent review of the literature and a reassertion of a particularly influential hypothesis, see Eichengreen et al (2023).

[101] See Chapter Three, nn 195–97 and accompanying text.

[102] During the 2014–2020 programming period, 39% of the budget went to 'sustainable growth/natural resources', a category dominated by the CAP and related programmes, and 34% went to 'economic, social, and territorial cohesion'. See European Commission (2023e). For further discussion of the evolution of the EU budget and dominant place of CAP and cohesion funding in it, this chapter below, nn 185–96 and accompanying text.

meagre resources, the Commission needed to be creative in finding ways to use its then-existing funding streams to steer the Member States towards what it viewed as better fiscal and economic policies or, even more ambitiously, to stabilise economic cycles within the euro area. The fact that much of this initial steering involved considerable political uncertainties and trade-offs, or fell outside the EU's areas of competence entirely, was a matter of constitutional importance that at the time garnered little commentary.

A first step by the Commission to use its then-existing funding streams to steer the Member States, for example, was its effort to generalise the use of conditionalities in European structural and investment (ESI) funds.[103] Conditionalities on EU funding had been integral to the Copenhagen accession criteria, and the Commission then introduced them in EU budgeting more generally as part of the establishment of the Cohesion Fund in 2006.[104] But EU legislation substantially widened their use in the aftermath of the euro area crisis and extended them to all ESI funds in the Common Provisions Regulation of 2013.[105] These early efforts, however, were still very much anchored in the original, sanctions-based philosophy that also guided the SGP and the European Semester, in the sense that they were nearly all stick and no carrot.[106] Additionally, they were also indicative, after the failure of the Lisbon strategy, of the increasing interest in legally binding, but still ultimately technocratic, compliance mechanisms.[107] These measures, however, were often limited in scope to the protection of the EU budget; bad macroeconomic policies were not a basis, in themselves, for suspension of funds (though both the Four Presidents' Report in 2012, and the Five Presidents' Report in 2015 had contemplated sanctions along these lines).[108] This made the macroeconomic conditionality mostly a theoretical consideration and not a truly effective tool to promote better national policies. As for the more ambitious goal of countercyclical stabilisation, the small size of the EU budget made it a poor candidate for that role. A 2016 report on Future Financing of the EU, authored by a high-level inter-institutional group chaired by former Italian Prime Minister and EU Commissioner Mario Monti (hence commonly known as the Monti Report),[109] made this point quite clearly: 'The budget is too small for real anti-cyclical economic stabilisation and substantive redistribution ... or for what orthodox wisdom would require of a "federal-level" budget'.[110]

'Orthodox wisdom' might also include another purpose in a federal-level budget: spending on European public goods, that is, for projects that benefit

[103] The following discussion draws on Núñez Ferrer et al (2018).

[104] See Article 4 of Council Regulation (EC) No 1084/2006.

[105] Regulation (EU) No 1303/2013 [2013 CPR].

[106] For a sense of this philosophy, see, eg, the discussion of the Five Presidents Report in this chapter above, nn 47–59 and accompanying text.

[107] See this chapter above, nn 47–59 and accompanying text.

[108] See this chapter above, nn 58–59 and accompanying text.

[109] Monti Report (2016).

[110] Ibid, p 6.

European citizens broadly and can be more effectively supplied at the supranational rather than national level. But given the historical political economy of EU spending, it was extraordinarily difficult to reorient spending in this direction. The budget's primary function, historically, was to compensate those sectors (eg French agriculture from the 1960s onward) or regions (eg the less developed parts of Central and Eastern Europe after accession in 2004) that were either most sceptical of, or least positioned to benefit from, the benefits of freer trade in an internal market, that is, integration's core historical function. Outside of those sectors, the Member States remained laser-focused on *juste retour*; that is, on what each of them got from the EU budget as opposed to what they paid into it.[111] As the Monti Report lamented:

> Member States' prime objective is to maximise the returns from the EU budget, preferably by means of 'pre-allocated envelopes', and to minimise their respective share of national contributions going into the EU budget. Member States consider this to be in their best interest.
>
> The struggle to maximise [national] envelopes, to improve the endowment of those programmes with traditionally high reflows to one's own economic actors and strong sectors or the fervour with which budgetary corrections are pursued may seem rational in a traditional context of negotiators seeking to maximise benefits and minimise costs.
>
> It reveals however, the lack—or the lack of recognition—of the added value that comes with spending programmes which are designed to underpin common European objectives and bring advantages, at least indirectly, to the entire single market.[112]

Apart from the national envelopes of agriculture and cohesion policies, the relevant elements of budget negotiations thus focused on own resources, associated rebates, and other special burden-sharing arrangements for individual Member States. The result was a calculation of the national net return with a precision that was ultimately spurious, given that it ignored beneficial effects of genuinely European action. In this environment, the first programmes to be squeezed in any negotiation involved funding that may have brought European added value but did not create calculable pay-outs to individual Member States. Member States tended to treat these 'as "other programmes"' deserving only of 'whatever [was] left under [the budget's] artificial overall limit (the infamous 1%)'.[113] As the Monti Report concluded in 2016: 'Budget lines under these headings present "soft targets" for budget cuts, despite their often

[111] See generally Becker (2012) and Laffan and de Feo (2020).
[112] Monti Report (2016, p 60).
[113] Lehner (2020, pp 22–23).

manifest added value—while agriculture and cohesion programmes are often ring-fenced and shielded from reductions . . .'[114]

C. Inching Towards an Integration-Reinforcing Financial Model for the EU

It was also in 2016 that then-Commission President Jean-Claude Juncker introduced the term 'polycrisis' into European discourse.[115] He used the new label as a way of crystallising awareness of the multiple, mutually reinforcing challenges facing Europe, from 'the worst economic, financial and social crisis since World War II' through 'the security threats in our neighbourhood and at home, to the refugee crisis, and to the UK referendum'[116]—and one might add also, of course, climate change and the challenge of energy transition. Juncker argued that these interlocking crises all 'feed each other, creating a sense of doubt and uncertainty in the minds of our people'.[117]

As the decade of the 2010s continued, few could predict that, by its end, the overlapping crises would take on a whole new dimension, in the form of a pandemic whose demographic, social, and economic impacts would transcend even the very worst of what the polycrisis had served to date.[118] But NGEU, as a model for action in the face of that pandemic, did not emerge out of whole cloth. Instead, it depended on various strands of thinking that developed in earlier stages of the polycrisis, each the product of deepening examination of the limits of the existing regime of integration and how to transcend them.

This section looks at three products of that examination, which taken together pointed towards the elements of what might become a new, more integration-reinforcing financing model for the EU. The first related to the revenue side: the reform of the own-resources system, most importantly by aligning it more directly to corresponding policies at the EU level while also reducing the share taken up by GNI-based Member-State contributions. The second focused on the borrowing side, in particular the possibility of EU-issued 'Eurobonds' or the like, to mobilise the collective creditworthiness of the Member States to address macroeconomic challenges, while also perhaps developing a European 'safe asset' to help deepen the EU's financial system. The third was anchored on the spending side: the use of cohesion funding to provide Member States with 'positive' incentives to comply with EU policy preferences and thus reduce dependency on any sort of command-and-control system of the type that had so clearly failed in the European Semester.

114 Monti Report (2016, p 60).
115 See Juncker (2016).
116 Ibid.
117 Ibid.
118 Or indeed, if we stretch our perspective just a few years further into the 2020s, we can also add the impact of war in Europe, a topic to which we return in Chapter Five, et seq.

1. Revenue: Aligning Own Resources to EU Policies

Reforming the own-resources system had long been a topic of discussion in the EU. But it gained further momentum with the publication of the Monti Report, whose principal purpose was to undertake a comprehensive analysis of the own-resources system.[119] The report engaged at both a conceptual and policy level, the former in some sense shaping the concrete options considered at the latter level.

We touched in the prior section of this chapter on one of the main conceptual difficulties: the Member States' expectation of *juste retour* as an impediment to broader thinking about the EU budget as a vehicle for European added value.[120] That challenge in turn reflected a deeper 'conceptual bias where some own resources [were] in fact considered a national transfer or "cost" item, and not a resource "owned" by the EU'.[121] It was, in other words, one thing for positive law (via an Own Resources Decision) to declare the EU's 'ownership' of a particular resource; but it is quite another for the political class or electorate in a Member State to internalise that ownership as a matter of embedded political culture, particularly given that an Own Resources Decision depends on both national approval and national collection of the resources in question, which reinforces their seemingly national character.[122]

To address this challenge, the Monti Report argued from the perspective of European added value, hoping to make that value more apparent in the own-resources system. EU ownership of a resource depended not simply on its legal definition in an ORD; it also depended on its linkage to an identifiable policy at the EU level, whose benefits accrued Union-wide and hence should be calculated on that basis. The classic example—indeed, the most 'traditional' of traditional own resources—were customs duties and levies, whose linkage to the Customs Union and Common Commercial Policy were long established and quite well settled in the political culture of European integration.[123] By contrast, own resources calculated as a percentage of the VAT base or, more broadly, Gross National Income, were merely 'statistical aggregate[s]' lacking 'any link with an EU policy and [thus] the resulting amounts ha[d] to be carved out of the body of general income in national budgets . . .'.[124]

For this reason, the Monti Report 'strongly argu[ed] in favour of new own resources which would help enforce some EU policies and support EU policy objectives, in

[119] Monti Report (2016). For another discussion of the developments discussed in this subsection, see Neumeier (2023, pp 324–26).

[120] See this chapter above, nn 111–14 and accompanying text. See also Marján (2009, p 301).

[121] Monti Report (2016, p 7; see also pp 21–22).

[122] See Chapter One, nn 30–32 and accompanying text.

[123] Monti Report (2016, pp 22–23).

[124] Ibid, p 23. In addition to own resources, the Union also has competence to collect levies that regulate private-party conduct under the EU's general regulatory competence in that space. See C-265/87, *Schräder v Hauptzollamt Gronau* (1989), para 11. These levies are treated as 'other revenue' within the meaning of Article 311 TFEU. See Neumeier (2023, p 336).

particular economic, social and environmental sustainability'.[125] The hope was that, 'if a coordinated tax [eg targeted to fight climate change or promote energy efficiency] were to be introduced in Member States, and some of its proceeds attributed to the EU budget', then that nationally imposed tax would 'participate in an EU policy'.[126] Moreover, this alignment of own resources towards identifiable EU policies and away from the statistical aggregates like VAT or GNI 'would help refocus budget negotiations on the quality of expenditure and rationale of EU policies, instead of being exclusively focused on net returns and on a vacuous zero-sum game which fuels the perception that some Member States are winners and other losers'.[127] One commentator saw in this dimension of the Monti Report the potential for a 'Copernican shift in perspective from the dominant state-centric' own-resources system that had determined the EU's revenues and budget to date.[128]

The European Commission, in its initial 2018 proposal for a new MFF for 2021–2027,[129] adopted this shift in perspective but only in part. The proposal would not fundamentally alter the existing own-resources system derived from customs and sugar duties, a statistical portion of the VAT base, and Member-State contributions proportional to Gross National Income. Nonetheless, the Commission proposed 'to forge a stronger link between the financing of the budget and the Union's policies by introducing a basket of new Own Resources'.[130] These would include a share of Emissions Trading System (ETS) revenues and a national contribution calculated on the amount of non-recycled plastic packaging waste. The Commission hoped that these new own resources would contribute to financing the new priorities in the budget, while also allowing national contributions based on GNI to be reduced.[131]

These and other aspects of the Commission's 2018 proposal framed the ensuing negotiations of the MFF up to the eve of the Covid pandemic in February 2020.[132] As an indicator of the MFF's importance to the Member States, the European Council included it on the agenda of six of their nine intervening meetings, culminating in a special meeting solely devoted to MFF on 20–21 February 2020. Although that meeting did not yield a final agreement, Commission President von der Leyen indicated in the post-meeting press conference that many Member States were in favour of introducing new forms of own resources but still needed more discussions to agree on the specific type.[133] As we shall see, however, even in the hot-house environment of addressing the Covid crisis in the coming months, those discussions would drag on. Indeed, aside from the levy on Member States calculated on their amount of

125 Monti Report (2016, p 8).
126 Ibid.
127 Ibid, p 4.
128 Crowe (2017, p 451).
129 European Commission (2018c).
130 Ibid, p 27 (emphasis in original omitted).
131 Ibid.
132 For a succinct summary of these intervening negotiations, see Drachenberg (2020a).
133 Drachenberg (2020b, p 3).

non-recycled plastic packaging waste,[134] they would not find a satisfactory conclusion over the course of the 2021–2027 MFF.[135]

2. Borrowing: Debating Eurobonds, Developing a 'Safe Asset'

The core of what would become NGEU, however, involved not revenue but borrowing, and more particularly borrowing backed by the EU budget. This idea—in effect, leveraging the Union budget to raise money for other ends—had a long (if 'forgotten') history,[136] which began with the Community Loan Mechanism (CLM) of 1975 offering back-to-back loans to Member States experiencing acute balance-of-payments difficulties tied to the oil crisis. The CLM eventually evolved, by 1988, into the EU's more general Balance of Payments (BoP) Assistance Facility, which continues to exist to this day for non-euro area Member States.[137] Driving the creation of the CLM, however, was an entirely recognisable concern from a more contemporary perspective: the extent to which the asymmetric impact of an economic shock on 'weaker' Member States (ie those whose financial situation raised a serious risk of losing access to credit on reasonable terms) might deeply disrupt the integration process. In the 1970s, these countries still had the option of devaluing their own currency, which 'would have jeopardized the plan to progressively stabilize EC currencies'.[138] Hence the pressure for the Community to act via the CLM.

Fast forward, then, to the sovereign-debt crisis in the euro area of 2009–2010 and after. No longer did the euro area member governments have the ability to devalue their currency or monetise their debt (and in that regard, they were not unlike sovereigns in emerging markets borrowing in a currency they do not control, hence vulnerable to runs and panics).[139] But their financial instability, most often derived from concerns about unsustainability of their sovereign debt, still posed an existential threat to the survival of the common currency. That threat was, of course, the main driver for establishing the ESM as a collective borrowing and lending mechanism in 2012, as well as for laying the foundations of a banking union through single supervisory and resolution mechanisms for Europe's largest banks.[140] Over the course of the decade, there would be efforts to interlink these two tools, reforming the ESM Treaty, inter alia, to allow the mechanism to serve as the 'backstop' for the SRM through a credit line if member-bank contributions to the resolution fund proved inadequate

[134] Council Decision 2020/2053 [ORD], art 2(1)I; see also recital (7).
[135] See Chapter Five, Section C.1.
[136] Horn et al (2020). See also Meyer et al (2020).
[137] European Commission (2025b).
[138] Horn et al (2020, p 4).
[139] See above n 16 and accompanying text.
[140] See this chapter above, n 20 and accompanying text.

at acute moments.[141] Italy, however, has refused to ratify the Treaty change. Rather, populist parties, in a show of their increasing dominance in Italian politics over the last decade, have 'managed, with considerable skill, to exploit the criticisms of' the ESM more generally[142]—the stringent conditionality in lending programmes, as well as features of the reform that seemingly raised the prospects of an eventual restructuring of Italy's massive sovereign debt—to block the reform.[143]

In many ways, Italian resistance to ESM reform simply serves as a reminder that unsustainable levels of sovereign debt in key Member States have ultimately been at the core of the political and financial challenges facing Europe. In these circumstances, it was only natural that economists and policy makers would start to look for other, more structural solutions to the problem. In the early years of the euro crisis, much of the discussion focused on the joint issuance of public debt—so-called 'Eurobonds'.[144] This option had been debated at least since the late 1990s, originally as a way to create a larger and more liquid market for government debt and thereby achieve somewhat lower costs of funding.[145] It was the euro crisis, however, that led various think tanks and academic economists to revisit the question, this time as a means of stabilising the euro area through either debt mutualisation[146] or some kind of debt redemption mechanism (hence to reduce the overall stock of debt to more sustainable levels)[147]—this latter idea gaining a nod from the Commission its 2012 'Blueprint' on strategies to deepen the EMU.[148] At least as a solution to the euro crisis, the proposals ultimately failed to gain much additional traction, but their very existence suggested how intense the functional pressures were towards some kind of collective borrowing in the euro area.[149]

Collective borrowing via the EU itself (as opposed to via a multilateral lending institution like the ESM) differed not only in whether the former might avoid the conditionality that had made the latter anathema in countries like Italy. There were also differences in the methodology that credit-rating agencies would use to determine creditworthiness of the borrower.[150] The ratings category of 'supranationals' primarily includes multilateral development banks (MDBs) and multilateral lending institutions (MLIs)—the largest example in fact being the EU's own European Investment Bank (EIB).[151] But it also includes more general regional integration entities like the EU itself. The key distinguishing characteristic between MDBs/MLIs and regional

[141] See Five Presidents' Report (2015, p 11); see also European Stability Mechanism (2025b).
[142] Galli (2020).
[143] Fonte and Amante (2023); see also Beraldo (2024).
[144] See, eg, Moesen and de Grauwe (2009); see also Frankel (2012) and Mody et al (2012).
[145] Giovannini Group (2000).
[146] See, eg, Delpla and von Weizsäcker (2010).
[147] See, eg, Bofinger et al (2011).
[148] European Commission (2012, pp 28–29).
[149] These pressures would continue and indeed further intensify through the Covid crisis and the establishment of EU borrowing under NGEU. See, eg, Eisl and Tomay (2020); see also Chapter Three.
[150] This analysis draws from the methodology used by CRAs in the mid-2010s (with the exception of S&P, where the earliest publicly available information was from 2019). See DBRS (2015), Fitch (2015), Moody's (2013), and S&P (2019).
[151] Craviotto et al (2023) and Demertzis et al (2023).

integration entities like the EU is that the former are structured as separate corporations (with state shareholders supporting the entity through paid-in as well as callable capital), while regional integration entities are creatures of public international law comprised of 'member states' (which, rather than capital, have other kinds of financial support obligations for the entity). Most importantly, the state shareholders of MDBs/MLIs are subject to capital calls to shore up the entity's creditworthiness in extraordinary circumstances, whereas a regional integration entity is not, or at least not formally or in the same way.

For a regional integration entity like the EU, therefore, the challenge is to create binding obligations on the part of the Member States to support the EU's borrowing and lending operations in ways analogous to 'callable capital' in the case of MDBs/MLIs.[152] This brings us to the crucial point: regardless of the specific type of supranational entity, CRAs focus squarely on the financial support the entity can expect, both legally and politically, from the states that own or comprise it. Indeed, for regional integration entities without a capital base (like the EU) the assessment of ongoing support obligations by Member States dominates the analysis.[153] Moreover, within that support assessment, CRAs typically give special (often decisive) weight to the extent of support from the very highest rated Member States, particularly if that support is adequate, in itself, to cover the entity's outstanding obligations.[154] The typical result is 'high ratings' but only if 'the [entity] has a few strongly committed AAA-rated or AA-rated [members]'.[155] The key phrase in this last sentence, however, is 'strongly committed'. The credit analysis turns not merely on the members' *capacity* to pay but also, importantly, on their *willingness* or *propensity* to pay, that is, the overall *credibility* of their commitments.[156] This aspect of the analysis has typically

152 As stressed by Moody's, for example, just because regional integration entities do not 'have capital and therefore do not have callable capital ... does not mean that other forms of contractual support cannot exist. We use explicit guarantees or legally-binding grant payments, for example, in place of callable capital in the calculation of Contractual Support'. Moody's (2013, p 20). As discussed in Chapter One, a key design feature of the 2020 ORD supporting NGEU was the 'callable headroom' obligations of the Member States. See Chapter One, nn 48–51 and accompanying text.

153 DBRS (2015, p 13) ('for institutions that lack their own capital base (eg, the EU ...), ... [t]heir ratings are normally entirely dependent on the support assessment'); Fitch (2015, p 3) ('the rating is predominantly, if not entirely, driven by the support from member states'); Moody's (2013, p 20) ('the creditworthiness of [a regional integration entity] is less dependent on intrinsic financial strength and more dependent on actual or potential funding from their sovereign members'); S&P (2019, p 114) (describing the bespoke methodology for the EU, based on 'the capacity and willingness of its 12 wealthiest members [to contribute] to the EU budget').

154 Fitch (2015, p 4) ('Fitch's approach is to determine the rating of the lowest-rated [member state] whose [contribution], when added to that of the higher-rated shareholders, ensures *full* coverage of outstanding net debt') (emphasis in original); Moody's (2013, p 20) (methodology '[p]lace[s] more emphasis on the Strength of Member Support than on Intrinsic Financial Strength such that the former is the driver of the scorecard-implied rating range'); S&P (2019, p 114); see also S&P (2019, p 115) ('the EU has a contingent claim ("fiscal headroom") on its members, [and] EU members have made this pledge for the express purpose of backing the union's financial obligations. EU members are jointly obliged to honor both this pledge and any budgetary payments').

155 DBRS (2015, p 2).

156 Ibid, p 5 ('the analysis then centers on the strength of each [member]'s commitment to lend support'); Fitch (2015, p 4) ('[t]o assess support, Fitch determines [members'] capacity and propensity to provide support in case of need'); Moody's (2013, p 21) (indicating, under 'Extraordinary Support', two

focused on several factors, including the extent and legal enforceability of 'callable' support obligations (or their equivalent),[157] as well as the functional 'importance' of the supranational entity to its members.[158] As one CRA (Fitch) put it, the analysis ultimately demanded 'a qualitative judgement', which 'largely depends upon political considerations'.[159]

Those political considerations can be quite difficult to assess, at least outside the context of acute crisis. In the interim beyond the UK's Brexit vote in 2016 and the onset of the Covid crisis in 2020, for example, there were real questions about the political condition of the EU, which led one leading CRA (S&P) to wonder publicly about 'the willingness of sovereigns ... at or above the level of the rating on the EU to fulfill [their] pledges'.[160] S&P thought this willingness 'might be tested if some other members [proved] unwilling to contribute' as they had previously committed.[161] S&P noted that 'the EU has a contingent claim ("fiscal headroom") on its members, which we expect will average 0.25% of GNI (or about €30 billion annually) over the 2014-2020 MFF. EU members have made this pledge for the express purpose of backing the union's financial obligations'.[162] This pledge also served as an important reminder that, legally and politically speaking, Member States are the EU's only taxpayers.[163] For this reason the credit-rating methodology of CRAs necessarily focused on the Member States' capacity and willingness to support the supranational entity, unclouded by any inquiry into their purported (ie 'as if') constitutional features, as the dominant legal discourse in the EU would have it.[164] Those features were ultimately irrelevant to the question of supranational creditworthiness, which instead remained entirely 'reliant on regular cash inflow from members, guarantees by members, grants from members, taxes levied on sovereign members' economies and other forms of member support'.[165]

Nonetheless, even with the headroom mechanism potentially available to back heightened borrowing by the EU, a seemingly insurmountable legal obstacle remained. The third paragraph of Article 310(1) TFEU provides: 'The revenue and expenditure shown in the budget shall be in balance'. As the Commission itself acknowledged in response to a parliamentary question in 2015: 'The Treaty establishes the principle of a balanced budget for the EU. Filling a gap between revenue and expenditure by issuing public debt is therefore not possible'.[166] To establish common

factors: 'Ability' and 'Willingness', with the latter further broken down into 'Propensity to Support' and 'Priority of Support').

157 Fitch (2015, p 4); Moody's (2013, pp 20–21).
158 DBRS (2015, pp 5–6); Fitch (2015, p 4).
159 Fitch (2015, p 4).
160 S&P (2019, p 115).
161 Ibid.
162 Ibid.
163 Monti Report (2016, p 7). See also Chapter One, n 33 and accompanying text.
164 See Chapter One, nn 47–55 and accompanying text.
165 Moody's (2013, p 20).
166 European Commission (2015).

borrowing directly based on the EU budget, the Commission recognised that this would require 'submitting proposals to modify the Treaty', which the Commission was 'at this stage not envisaging'.[167] Unless the debt was counterbalanced by an asset on the EU's balance sheet (such as a debt-financed building or the receivables in a back-to-back loan to a Member State), the requirement of a balanced budget Article 310(1) TFEU was understood to preclude debt-financing for regular operations and programmes. For this reason, at least prior to NGEU (whose workarounds in this regard are taken up in Chapter Three),[168] programmes such as the Investment Plan for Europe of 2015–2017 (the so-called 'Juncker Plan')[169] needed to be financially structured to operate through implementing partners like the EIB to avoid this budgetary stricture.[170]

Related to, but distinct from, the question of collective borrowing was the question of developing a euro-denominated 'safe asset' for the European financial system, akin to the role that US Treasuries play in the US (and global) financial system. This would involve creating a new instrument that, while not necessarily mutualising risks, would nonetheless pool (and hence diversify) those risks in a way designed to counter the 'doom loop' between banks and the debt of their home-sovereigns, a particularly troubling dimension of the euro crisis.[171] A euro-denominated safe asset would need to meet three basic criteria: 'low default risk, or high asset "quality"'; retention of 'value during bad times ("robustness")'; and the ability to be resold 'at or near current (robust) market prices in most market conditions ("liquidity")'.[172]

Think tanks and academic economists were at the forefront of the discussions about a euro-denominated safe asset, the core proposal of which revolved around the idea of 'European Safe Bonds' (ESBies).[173] These instruments would be formed from the senior tranche of a diversified portfolio of euro area sovereign bonds into a new instrument that could then be held by European banks (hence the idea of 'safety in tranches').[174] The design was intended to meet the three criteria of quality, robustness, and liquidity, but considerable work would be required to bring such an instrument to fruition, not least in terms of establishing the right regulatory environment to allow a market in these securities to develop. Unlike Eurobonds, the proposals for ESBies gained slightly more traction in official EU circles over the course of the 2010s, eventually proceeding under the name 'Sovereign Bond-Backed Securities' (SBBS). In 2016, the European Systemic Risk Board (ESRB) commissioned a High-Level Task

167 Georgieva (2015).
168 See Chapter Three, nn 249–74 and accompanying text.
169 For an overview, see Council of the European Union (2017).
170 As the Commission acknowledged, in response to a parliamentary question on this point: 'The Investment Plan can therefore not serve to finance EU budget expenditure by issuing public debt'. See European Commission (2015).
171 See European Commission (2019c).
172 Bletzinger et al (2023a).
173 See, eg, Brunnermeier et al (2011), (2016a).
174 Brunnermeier et al (2016b).

Force on Safe Assets to examine their feasibility.[175] The ESRB Task Force published its main findings in January 2018,[176] determining that SBBS might indeed be feasible under certain circumstances if the regulatory environment became conducive. The European Commission adopted a legislative proposal in May 2018 for that purpose.[177] The European Parliament endorsed the idea in April 2019 as part of final agreement on the comprehensive set of reforms proposed by the Commission that included SBBS.[178]

By the onset of the Covid crisis, however, the SBBS idea had essentially died. Even as the Commission has kept it on its website as one potential future element of the Banking Union,[179] '[p]olicymakers and public debt management agencies in many euro-area countries [were] afraid of the unintended consequences that such a drastic change could entail for the sovereign bond markets of the eurozone'.[180] From this perspective, the SBBS proposal was seen as a 'distraction' from the primary task of 'making all euro-area sovereign bonds safe again, and for good', through effective macroprudential policies and a completed Banking Union.[181] But these elements would also need to be accompanied by a euro-area stabilisation instrument to deal with large asymmetric shocks.[182] And this would require either a reformed ESM—towards which, as noted above, there was extreme wariness in many countries (notably Italy)[183]—or it would require developing some other kind of avenue to provide support on a more solidaristic basis.

3. Spending: Repurposing Cohesion as an Instrument of 'Positive Incentives' in EU Economic Governance

This brings us then to the final element of a potentially integration-reinforcing financing model—one that would be of overwhelming importance to NGEU, and especially the RRF. This final element looked to spending under the rubric of cohesion policy as a vehicle for 'positive incentives' under the European Semester (though eventually, as we shall see in Chapter Three, it would morph into an instrument of attempted fiscal stabilisation as well).[184] However, to appreciate the extent to which this change constituted a break with established practice, a bit of history on the evolution of cohesion funding within the overall EU budget is needed.

[175] European Systemic Risk Board (2016).
[176] ESRB High-Level Task Force on Safe Assets (2018).
[177] European Commission (2018d).
[178] See European Parliament (2021).
[179] See this chapter above, n 20.
[180] Claeys (2018a).
[181] Claeys (2018b).
[182] Ibid.
[183] See this chapter above, n 35 and accompanying text, and nn 141–43 and accompanying text.
[184] See especially Chapter Three, nn 82–95 and accompanying text.

a. Cohesion Within the Historical Political Economy of the EU Budget

The political economy of the EU budget has, from its beginnings, evolved primarily as a tool for facilitating trade and economic integration.[185] The benefits of free trade have never been shared equally, however, and free movement in all its forms (goods, labour, and capital) can lead to the agglomeration of economic activity in some geographic areas while leaving others at the margins. Even with its historically small size, the EU budget (including cohesion policy within it) has been used as a tool to diffuse political resistance to these tendencies, partly by supporting vulnerable regions and partly by compensating those Member States that feel threatened by free trade. As such, the EU budget has been instrumental in securing political support for the integration project.[186]

In the early days of European integration, the Common Agricultural Policy was the principal mechanism to perform this political-economic task. Introduced in 1962, the CAP served to facilitate agreement on the removal of internal tariffs on agricultural products while also providing a mechanism to rebalance the perceived asymmetric benefits of trade in manufactured goods. From the CAP's inception, and indeed preceding it, there existed other, smaller mechanisms with a similar aim, notably the European Social Fund (ESF) and the European Agricultural Guidance and Guarantee Fund (EAGGF), both created in 1957. Later, in 1975, the European Regional Development Fund (ERDF) was created to complement these earlier mechanisms, with a specific focus on supporting regional development efforts in the Member States.[187] At a general level, the ERDF was justified by reference to how an effective policy on regional structures was an essential prerequisite to the realisation of the EMU.[188] It was designed to operate in conjunction with national aids in heavily agricultural areas or those affected by industrial change and structural unemployment, allocating funding according to the relative severity of regional imbalances.[189] The ERDF thus introduced programming by objectives, geographical prioritisation, and additionality to national investments, all intended 'to foster good governance in the beneficiary regions'.[190]

From the 1980s onward, with both the creation of the ambitious single market agenda and then the successive accession of relatively less developed new Member States, cohesion policy began to rival the CAP as the EU's largest redistributive mechanism, serving as the umbrella for funding across a range of domains, albeit all with a regional development focus.[191] Under Article 130a of the Single European Act (1986),

185 See this chapter above, nn 110–11 and accompanying text.
186 Again, see this chapter above, nn 110–11 and accompanying text.
187 Regulation (EEC) No 724/75 [ERDF].
188 Regulation (EEC) No 724/75 [ERDF], preamble.
189 Regulation (EEC) No 724/75 [ERDF], preamble.
190 Cipriani (2017, p 143).
191 This and the subsequent two paragraphs draw from Leino-Sandberg (2024b).

economic and social cohesion became an explicit competence of the Community, with the aim, in particular, of 'reducing disparities between the various regions and the backwardness of the least-favoured regions'. In 1994, the EU created the Cohesion Fund to provide a financial contribution to projects in the fields of the environment and trans-European networks.[192] The importance of cohesion and structural funds further increased with the 2004 enlargement to Central and Eastern European (CEE) countries.[193]

In 2009, the Treaty of Lisbon added cohesion to the list of EU objectives in Article 3 TEU, specifying that its focus was not merely economic and social but also, importantly, *territorial* cohesion.[194] This clarification reflected how the policy had long been traditionally understood. As Dirk Ahnert, Director General for Regional and Urban Policy (DG REGIO) in the Commission, wrote in a piece for the Institut Jacques Delors in 2009: 'Cohesion policy is different from general development policies in that it *adopts a territorial approach to reach EU citizens* ... EU countries rarely correspond to such territories' (emphasis in original).[195] Hence: 'Cohesion Policy is a *development policy* aiming at ... EU *regions* and at strengthening the integration of *regional economies* ... This overall objective is served mainly by promoting investments ... which help mobilizing resources in *regions* ...' (emphasis added).[196]

Cohesion policy has been geared towards providing supranational support to national efforts addressing regional development challenges within their borders.[197] The umbrella of regional development has been broad enough to reach a large variety of areas such as transportation, energy, environment, and digitalisation, but also including non-physical investments in education and culture.[198] Over the years, a great part of environmental funding has been channelled either through agriculture and cohesion policy; funds specifically based on environmental policy remained scarce.[199] Moreover, the possibility of using the Cohesion Fund to finance specific projects in Member States in the area of transport infrastructure is also specifically mentioned in Article 171(1) TFEU on trans-European networks.

From a competence perspective, this raises no particular issues, as both environmental policies and trans-European networks are a shared EU competence. However, by opting for funding under the rubric of cohesion, certain other features of that

[192] Council Regulation (EC) No 1164/94.
[193] Cipriani (2017, p 144).
[194] According to Article 3(2) TEU, the EU 'shall promote economic, social and territorial cohesion, and solidarity among Member States'.
[195] Ahner (2009, p 4).
[196] Ibid, pp 1–2.
[197] Sometimes regional development needs transcend national borders. See, eg, the International Fund for Ireland, addressing regional development across the Ireland–Northern Ireland border, among other goals. This fund gave rise to an important decision of the European Court of Justice on the limits of cohesion policy relative to those other policy goals. See Case C-166/07, *Parliament v Council (International Fund for Ireland)* (2009). We take up this case in Chapter Three, Section A.
[198] See generally Bachtler et al (2013).
[199] This situation has changed more recently. See, eg, Regulation (EU) 2021/783, which is based on Article 192(1) TFEU.

policy domain were also generally understood to be essential, notably co-financing by Member States (to incentivise only the most worthwhile projects); multilevel governance (empowerment of sub-national, regional, and local actors); as well as use of funding only to cover the actual costs of investments. As described by a leading expert in this domain:

> Cohesion policy is more than a 'side-payment' to buy support for other EU programmes and agendas. In public finance terms, Cohesion policy has an 'allocative' rationale. The aim is to raise the welfare and well-being of the territories and people of the EU through growth-enhancing investment strategies and projects. Accordingly, its means and methods differ from unconditional transfer payments that lie within the policy toolkit of national social policies or, in the case of the EU, income support to farmers under the CAP. Indeed, there are many strings attached to the use of Cohesion policy resources to ensure that it is used effectively towards meeting its developmental objectives, even if the effects are disputed ... In short, Cohesion policy is anything but a 'blank cheque'.[200]

As this quotation implies, however, the pursuit of cohesion policy has not been without criticism for much of its existence.[201] These criticisms only intensified with the 2004 enlargement to CEE countries, as well as continuing pressures to align cohesion policy with the growth and competitiveness priorities of the Lisbon strategy of 2000, which some commentators at the time dubbed the 'Lisbonisation' of cohesion policy, to problematise the shift away from the policy's traditional focus on regional development.[202]

In legal terms, this shift was made explicit in 2006, with the adoption of a new general provisions regulation for structural and cohesion funds that stated '[c]ohesion policy should contribute to increasing growth, competitiveness and employment by incorporating the Community's priorities for sustainable development as defined at the Lisbon European Council of 23 and 24 March 2000 ... '.[203] This was the beginning of a longer-term process that would, in some sense, reach full fruition under the RRF Regulation of 2021—what can be called a *ratcheting strategy*[204]—in which general goals of economic policy (indeed, eventually, of any policy domain) get conflated with, or ratcheted into, the realm of cohesion policy, so that the latter could serve the purposes of the former.[205]

[200] Bachtler et al (2013, pp 12–13).

[201] See this chapter above, nn 110–14 and accompanying text.

[202] See generally Marján (2009). The term became common in the academic literature to describe this linkage to the Lisbon strategy. See, eg, Jouen (2009) and Mendez (2011); see also Molica et al (2024).

[203] Council Regulation (EC) No 1083/2006 [General Provisions], recital (2); see also art 3. See also Díez Sánchez (2025, p 22).

[204] See Chapter Three, nn 321–27 and accompanying text.

[205] See, eg, Council Regulation (EC) No 1083/2006 [General Provisions], recital (3).

At least initially, this shift in cohesion policy was 'done softly'[206]—that is, in a hybrid fashion—with significant flows continuing to CEE countries according to the old redistributive logic. But the continuing redistribution coincided with increasing calls to promote growth efficiently, which meant funding 'should be allocated where the productivity of capital is highest and to projects with clear spillovers'[207] (ie it should go where the money would produce 'the biggest benefit' in efficiency terms).[208] This meant shifting more funding towards wealthier areas and away from the disadvantaged, rural, or deindustrialised regions that were traditionally understood to be the focus of cohesion policy under the Treaties.[209] Pressures for such reallocations under the guise of cohesion, which have operated in modest ways at least since the mid-nineties, have strongly intensified over the last two decades.[210]

As a consequence of these developments, Leticia Díez Sánchez has aptly (and provocatively) entitled a recent analysis of cohesion's evolution over this period as 'Why cohesion policy is not about cohesion'.[211] We thoroughly agree with this characterisation, but we would push back on one point in Díez Sánchez's analysis: this evolution should not be ascribed to the 'inner logic of cohesion policy itself', as she has claimed.[212] Rather, it is better seen as the product of classically functionalist dynamics, in which political actors have strategically sought to redefine cohesion because it was the only available mechanism (short of Treaty change) to distribute money to meet pressing financial, economic, and political needs.[213] Most importantly, as we shall see in the remaining subsections of this chapter as well as Chapters Three and Four, this process has been aimed at ratcheting all manner of policy goals into the realm of cohesion, with little regard for the objectives and limits of cohesion traditionally conceived.

b. Cohesion, Conditionality, and 'Positive Incentives'

It was in this context of flux between traditional cohesion policy and pressures towards meeting the general economic goals of the Lisbon strategy that, in 2008, the then-Commissioner for Regional Policy, Danuta Hübner, asked for a comprehensive report on reforming cohesion policy. The Barca Report, as it was known, issued in April 2009,[214] made a robust defence of the traditional territorial orientation of cohesion policy (under the label of 'place-based'), while also questioning the idea that

[206] Marján (2009, p 301).
[207] Santos (2009, p 7).
[208] Marján (2009, p 297).
[209] Díez Sánchez (2025, pp 22–23).
[210] For a succinct overview of these developments from a legal perspective, see Díez Sánchez (2025, pp 19–26, but esp 22–26 for developments since 2007 '[i]nfluenced by the Lisbon agenda for growth and jobs').
[211] Díez Sánchez (2025, p 15).
[212] Ibid. Indeed, this article, in its admirably detailed analysis of the evolution of cohesion policy over many decades, provides support to the functionalist explanation of cohesion policy, without Treaty change, offered in this volume. We otherwise fully agree with ibid, p 15 that 'recent crisis-response instruments are not the origin but the *manifestation* of th[is] shifting logic of cohesion' (emphasis in original).
[213] See, eg, this chapter below, nn 257–62 and accompanying text.
[214] Barca Report (2009). The author was the former Director-General of Italy's Ministry of the Economy.

overall economic 'convergence ... captures the aim of cohesion policy'.[215] This later view strongly contradicted the premise of aligning cohesion policy with the Lisbon strategy (which would eventually provide inspiration for the NGEU, and more particularly the RRF as well).[216]

The Barca Report made its argument by drawing on comparative history (particularly the US case) as well as social theory.[217] But most importantly, it set out a detailed economic rationale for the placed-based approach, while also offering policy recommendations designed to appeal to the efficiency mindset of those seeking a more Lisbon-grounded cohesion policy. The Barca Report thus found 'severe limits of the quantitative evidence available on policy performance' and strongly urged creating performance-based incentives linking financing to verifiable results.[218] The proposals for reform were built around several pillars, including 'a European Strategic Development Framework, setting out [inter alia] indicators for assessing performance'; a 'new type of contractual agreement (a National Strategic Development Contract) ... specifying verifiable commitments'; 'establishment of a set of ex-ante conditionalities [and] a system for assessing progress in meeting targets'; and 'linkage to the Stability and Growth Pact, plus a contractual commitment and an assessment of how the policy is delivering the value added for which it is justified'.[219] The Barca Report recognised that reforms of this nature 'would require a strong political compromise'.[220]

What followed was in fact a several-year process of negotiation that would not be finalised until the end of 2013, with the adoption of the new Common Provision Regulation (CPR) for all ESI funds under the MFF for 2014–2020.[221] The 2013 CPR marked the introduction into cohesion discourse of a key concept—'resilience'[222]—that, over time, would serve as the major rhetorical driver for the transformed vision of cohesion upon which the NGEU would eventually be based.[223] One of the key sticking points in the negotiations, however, were different perspectives on conditionalities.[224] Member States pushed back hard on 'the idea of linking disbursements to country-specific recommendations and to the annual cycle of the European semester'.[225] Member State representatives were concerned that this linkage could

215 Ibid, p xiv.
216 See generally Chapter Three.
217 For an overview, see Jouen (2009).
218 Barca Report (2009, p viii).
219 Ibid, pp viii–ix (italics omitted).
220 Ibid, p ix.
221 See Regulation (EU) No 1303/2013 [2013 CPR]. For a detailed overview of the results the negotiations, see European Commission (2014 Chapter 8, pp 235 et seq.).
222 The starting point, at least in the 2013 CPR, was disaster and climate resilience. Regulation (EU) No 1303/2013 [2013 CPR], arts 8, 96(7)(a), 101(f), and Annex I sec 5.2(2).
223 See this chapter below, n 247 and accompanying text. But more importantly see Chapter Three, nn 321–27 and accompanying text; and Chapter Four, nn 496–99 and accompanying text. For a general discussion of the emergence of 'resilience' in EU policy discussions over the course of the 2010s, culminating in the RRF under NGEU, see Joseph and Juncos (2019) and (2024).
224 See this chapter above, n 105 and accompanying text.
225 European Parliament (2011, p 91); see also Bachtler and Mendez (2020, p 7).

'breach the principle of subsidiarity with respect to member state competences over structural reform'.[226] A contemporaneous study conducted by the European Parliament noted that there was a clear preference among many Member States for incentives over sanctions.[227]

The 2013 CPR, in the end, did authorise *ex ante* conditionalities in the use of ESI funds, as well as the possibility of suspension for non-fulfilment,[228] but such conditionalities would cover only issues strictly related to the implementation of the Cohesion Policy.[229] While Member States were asked to make an effort to ensure consistency with European Semester priorities, the CPR gave them discretion to take into account those CSRs most relevant to their use of the funding.[230] The 2013 CPR otherwise specifically excluded from the scope of any possible suspension anything related to the implementation of European Semester recommendations and aimed at structural reforms.[231]

In view of this resistance to what was perceived as a punitive approach, the focus of enforcing conditionalities did indeed shift, over time, towards more positive incentives—in effect, money for reforms. But the initial steps in this direction were cautious and started with a set of trial balloons from the Commission in 2013 on creating 'Ex ante coordination of plans for major economic policy reforms' as well as a Convergence and Competitiveness Instrument (CCI) to help finance them.[232] Importantly, the Commission left the legal bases for these two initiatives decidedly vague. It saw *ex-ante* coordination compatible with 'the spirit of Article 121(1) of the Treaty', which includes a commitment by Member States to 'regard their economic policies as a matter of common concern'.[233] The discussion document for the CCI made no reference to any legal basis at all. Instead, the Commission spoke, in classically functionalist terms, solely in terms of 'need':

> As part of the new economic governance of the Euro area and of the EU, there is a *need* to ensure that the structural reforms which are *needed* to remove key weaknesses in some economies take place and take place earlier than has recently been the case. The Commission sees it as an instrument designed to meet the specific *needs* that arise from Euro area membership. Being bound together in a single currency area implies the *need* for timely and targeted reforms. Therefore, an additional instrument is *needed* to promote and support reforms that can also have a positive impact on others when individual Member States are under stress [emphasis added].[234]

[226] Bachtler and Mendez (2020, pp 7–8).
[227] European Parliament (2011, p 92).
[228] Regulation (EU) No 1303/2013 [2013 CPR], art 23.
[229] European Court of Auditors (2017, p 14).
[230] Regulation (EU) No 1303/2013 [2013 CPR], Annex I, sec 2(3).
[231] Regulation (EU) No 1303/2013 [2013 CPR], Annex III, sec 2(iv).
[232] European Commission (2013a), (2013b).
[233] European Commission (2013a, p 2).
[234] European Commission (2013b, p 3).

Beyond functional need, the Commission placed great weight on the 'contractual' nature of the proposed instrument, whose legal force derived not from competences in the Treaties but from the 'measures a Member State commits to put in place, with agreed timelines'.[235] The Four Presidents' Report (which had prompted the Commission to develop the CCI in the first place) had also envisioned a 'contractual arrangement' to create a binding national commitment to 'successfully implement reforms', which would then 'also serve as a criterion for participating in the [contemplated] asymmetric shock absorption'.[236] Under the CCI, the Commission would 'monitor implementation of the arrangement on an annual basis as part the European Semester'.[237] However, the Commission was careful to stress that ultimate responsibility for structural reforms belonged to the Member States, and that the purpose of the instrument was simply 'to support Member States in the sometimes difficult process of implementing [those] reforms'.[238]

In line with the Four Presidents' Report, the CCI also acknowledged democratic legitimacy concerns by calling for the 'timely and active involvement of national parliaments and other relevant national stakeholders'.[239] One might question, however—as an advisory opinion of the Economic and Social Committee later did—whether 'this nod to democratic legitimacy' by the CCI was 'more apparent than real', given that the proposed instrument was embedded in a technocratic surveillance system ultimately backed by threats of sanctions.[240] As the Commission itself put it, the instrument 'would build on the existing EU surveillance framework ... link[ing] the policy guidance resulting from the Country Specific Recommendations in the European Semester and the national process of structural reform implementation'.[241] The document contemplated a range of enforcement options for further discussion, from voluntary participation to displacement of the contractual arrangements by 'the (mandatory) Corrective Action Plan [under] Regulation (EU) No 1176/2011 on the prevention and correction of macroeconomic imbalances'.[242]

But even if embedded within the compliance-focused mindset of the European Semester, the key innovation of the proposed CCI was its reliance on 'solidarity in the form of financial help to support increased economic responsibility and fiscal discipline ... set out clearly and with conditions through "contractual arrangements"'.[243] Moreover, the CCI mentioned that this financial support could be treated as 'external

[235] Ibid, p 2.
[236] Four Presidents' Report (2012, p 10).
[237] European Commission (2013b, p 6).
[238] Ibid, p 6. This same rationale would live on in the Commission's proposal for a 'Budgetary Instrument for Convergence and Competitiveness' (BICC) in 2019, part of the collection of initiatives as part of the so-called 'euro area budget' that would the model on which the NGEU, and more particularly the RRF, would build. See Chapter Three, nn 141–45 and accompanying text.
[239] European Commission (2013b, p 6).
[240] European Economic and Social Committee (2013, para 3.4).
[241] European Commission (2013b, p 4).
[242] Ibid, p 5.
[243] Ibid, p 2.

assigned revenues' from a budgetary perspective,[244] a technique that would be later used as the foundations for deficit spending under NGEU.[245] In these crucial respects, the Commission's outline for a Convergence and Competitiveness Instrument anticipated a model for 'money for reforms' that would only be fully realised just under a decade later.

Nonetheless, in 2013, the CCI remained a model in search of a legal basis. Over the remaining years of the decade, an expanded and transformed understanding of cohesion policy, away from its origins as primarily an instrument of regional development, would emerge as the prime candidate to serve as that basis. The Council, over the course of the decade, made a series of exhortations (eg this one in 2016)[246] underlining 'cohesion policy [as] the main investment policy at the EU level', stressing its value 'in providing a stable long-term EU framework and financial means for investment in jobs and growth and the delivery of structural reforms' and 'in providing positive incentives for many Member States and subnational actors to implement structural reforms'. The Commission, in its 'Reflection Paper on the Future of EU Finances' in 2017, echoed this view, asserting that '[f]ostering lasting economic convergence and resilience is the main objective of EU cohesion policy', and that its 'link with the economic governance and the European Semester may need to be strengthened'.[247]

The first concrete step in this direction—the creation of the Structural Reform Support Programme (SRSP) for the period 2017–2020[248]—was in fact quite modest. Modelled after a similar instrument in the IMF toolbox,[249] the SRSP was primarily a technical assistance tool whose legal basis was the cohesion flexibility clause of Article 175(3) TFEU, combined with Article 197(2) TFEU, which authorised support to the Member States to improve their administrative capacity to implement Union law. The SRSP had a limited budget of €142.8 million, raised by an additional €80 million in 2018,[250] which was designed to help Member States design and implement institutional, administrative, and structural reforms.[251]

As we shall see in Chapter Three, however, this legal formula—giving Article 175(3) TFEU the leading role, supported by Article 197(2) TFEU—would be foundational to the emergence of the NGEU model.[252] Even if the Commission refused to explain its reasoning, the import for cohesion policy was there for all to see. The incipient

[244] Ibid, p 7.

[245] See Chapter Three, nn 251–74 and accompanying text.

[246] Council of the European Union (2016).

[247] European Commission (2017e, pp 16–17). See also ISMERI Europa and WIIW (2018). The reference to resilience here may be understood as part of the 'resilience turn' in EU political discourse, See Joseph and Juncos (2019), (2024).

[248] Regulation (EU) 2017/825 [SRSP].

[249] See International Monetary Fund (2024).

[250] See Regulation (EU) 2018/1671.

[251] The successor to the SRSP would be the Technical Support Instrument (TSI). See Regulation (EU) 2021/240 [TSI], which would play a supportive role in the implementation of the NGEU programme under the RRF. The legal basis of the TSI Regulation, like the SRSP Regulation before it, is Articles 175 and 197(2) TFEU.

[252] See Chapter Three, nn 126–37 and accompanying text.

repurposing of cohesion into a more general spending power suggested how '[t]he old redistributive task of structural funds and the objective of reducing regional disparities with the help of European funds [was] replaced by a new focus on growth and investment combined with enhanced efficiency and effectiveness of the policy'.[253] Or at least that was the aspiration; during the second half of the 2010s the progress was in fact quite halting,[254] even as the political momentum began to accelerate. But what is clear is that, over the course of the second half of the decade, cohesion policy was increasingly part of 'the increased politicisation of the EU budget', reflected most prominently in 'the alignment between Cohesion Policy and economic governance'.[255] In turn, cohesion policy became 'more detached from lagging-behind regions', even as it still 'brand[ed] itself as a tool for social inclusion'.[256]

Meeting the needs of economic governance, of course, was not the only dynamic pushing cohesion policy away from its focus on regional development and towards a repurposing as a general spending power writ large.[257] In the absence of other available EU funding, cohesion also offered one of the few available means for quickly redirecting money to Member States in need, whether due to the continuing demands of the financial crisis,[258] natural disasters,[259] or, as we would see, in the early stages of the Covid crisis.[260] The money was available because many Member States, in practice, often struggled to use their full share of cohesion funds in their EU budget envelopes,[261] thus leaving the excess to be redeployed in crisis circumstances. But as the European Court of Auditors would later point out, repeatedly using cohesion policy as a crisis response mechanism risked diverting it from its primary strategic purpose of regional development.[262]

c. 'Milestones' and 'Targets': Towards a 'Performance-Based' System 'Not Linked to Costs'

As we shall see in Chapters Three and Four, the use of cohesion policy as a tool both of economic governance and crisis response—breaking with its traditional regional-developmental focus—would come to full fruition in the emergence and development of the NGEU model. But this transformation ultimately depended on one more (at the time) little-noticed but fundamental change in the Financial Regulation in 2018.[263] Under Article 125(1) of the Financial Regulation (FR), a new subsection (a)

[253] Becker (2019, p 153).
[254] For an overview, see European Court of Auditors (2021); see also European Court of Auditors (2017).
[255] Bachtler and Mendez (2020, p 10).
[256] Díez Sánchez (2025, p 23).
[257] This repurposing is a core topic discussed in Chapters Three and Four. See also Lindseth and Leino-Sandberg (2024b).
[258] See Regulation (EU) 2016/2135; Regulation (EU) 2015/1839.
[259] Regulation (EU) 2017/1199.
[260] Regulation (EU) 2020/460; Regulation (EU) 2020/558; and Regulation (EU) 2020/2221.
[261] See this chapter above, n 112 and accompanying text.
[262] European Court of Auditors (2023a, p 42).
[263] Regulation (EU, Euratom) 2018/1046 [FR].

was added, specifying that EU funding 'under direct, shared and indirect management'—a category including cohesion funding—could now take the form of 'financing not linked to the costs [FNLC] of the relevant operations based on ... the achievement of results measured by reference to previously set milestones or through performance indicators [ie 'targets']'. As the recitals to the new FR explained:

> More emphasis should be put on performance and results. It is thus appropriate to define an additional form of financing not linked to costs of the relevant operations in addition to the forms of Union contribution already well established (reimbursement of the eligible costs actually incurred, unit cost, lump sums and flat-rate financing). This form of financing should be either based on the fulfilment of certain conditions ex ante or the achievement of results measured by reference to the previously set milestones or [targets].[264]

The Commission's discussion document on the Convergence and Competitiveness Instrument in 2013 had anticipated this approach. It was already then envisioning a system in which 'financial support would be committed up front at the moment of approval of the contractual arrangement and paid in regular instalments or instalments otherwise linked to the agreed timetable for reforms'.[265] This long-sought shift was also intimately bound up with the desire to augment 'national ownership' through intensified information exchange and coordination between administrative actors in Brussels and national capitals. What this addition to the FR ultimately allowed was the provision of EU financing to Member States as a *pure incentive, irrespective of the actual cost of the underlying measures*—a core requirement of cohesion funding as traditionally conceived. The change attracted little attention and no doubt appeared technical and inconsequential to all but those few policy makers who paid attention. Yet it created a whole new way for the EU to project its power irrespective of competence limitations or the structural constraints of the Treaty-based choice for an asymmetric EMU. The change in the FR would thus help to pave the way for a profound transformation in the use EU funds under the NGEU model.[266]

The FNLC model could be used from 2019 onwards for European Regional Development Fund (ERDF) investments in the areas of energy efficiency and energy from renewable sources.[267] It also became an option for the use of cohesion policy funds and mandatory for certain actions designed to reinforce Member States' administrative capacity.[268] However, in the 2014–2020 period, only Austria piloted the FNLC model for one ERDF project with an EU contribution of around €36 million.[269]

264 Ibid, recital (56).
265 European Commission (2013b, p 8). See also this chapter above, n 236 and accompanying text.
266 See also Leino-Sandberg, (2023b).
267 Commission Delegated Regulation (EU) 2019/694 [FNLC].
268 European Court of Auditors (2021, p 57).
269 Ibid, p 53.

There have been experiments with different kinds of results-based initiatives elsewhere in the world, often with mixed results.[270] The EU thus had little experience with its difficulties and pitfalls (certainly not at scale) before using FNLC as the foundation for the 'performance-based' milestones and targets under NGEU and more particularly the RRF.[271] Some of the standard challenges earlier experiences had uncovered—and which the EU would face in building its own performance-based system—included capacity constraints, data quality, performance measurement (including defining meaningful performance indicators), and contextual variability.[272]

This latter factor was particularly important because, in the face of high contextual variability, one study urged that pilot programmes 'be used to fine-tune ... implementation strategies before they are rolled out on a larger scale'.[273] This is obviously something the EU was unable to do before attempting to roll out a performance-based system under the NGEU and RRF, involving complex (and often highly discretionary) issues of planning, monitoring, implementation, and disbursement across twenty-seven very different Member States.

[270] Abbasov (2025) ('the effectiveness of [performance-based initiatives] remains a contested issue ... the magnitude of efficiency gains varies widely'); Schick (2014, p 50) (these initiatives are '[o]ften tried but rarely successful (in terms of their lofty objectives').

[271] See Chapter Four, nn 63–67 and accompanying text.

[272] See Abbasov (2025); see also Moynihan and Beazley (2016).

[273] Abbasov (2025).

PART TWO

THE EMERGENCE AND DEVELOPMENT OF THE NGEU MODEL

Chapter Three
Assembling the Components
The Legal Engineering of NGEU

NextGenerationEU undoubtedly is, as several early observers suggested, 'a skilful legal construction',[1] one reflecting the 'ingenuity'[2] and 'craftsmanship [of] the legal services of the EU institutions'.[3] Others went further, calling the elements of NGEU 'masterpieces of high-tech legal engineering', involving 'incremental development of the Treaties in line with fundamentally changing contexts'.[4] The programme's major legal components—the new Own Resources Decision (the 2020 ORD),[5] the European Union Recovery Instrument (EURI) Regulation,[6] along with the Recovery and Resilience Facility Regulation,[7]—all required significant reinterpretations of key Treaty provisions to meet 'the political needs of the moment'.[8] These involved, most importantly, the general financial and budgetary rules in Articles 310–311 TFEU (for the 2020 ORD), the emergency assistance rules in Article 122 TFEU (for the EURI), and the flexibility clause for cohesion policy in Article 175(3) TFEU (for the RRF).

It was difficult not to admire the audacity and speed with which the components of NGEU were assembled. But its legal foundations also raise legal and political questions about the future, many of which this and subsequent chapters seek to explore. The reinterpretation of the Treaties at the heart of NGEU was a classically legal-functionalist exercise very much in keeping with the 'as if' constitutional mindset we introduced in Chapter One.[9] It was, moreover, not solely focused on addressing the demands of the Covid crisis. As Ursula von der Leyen made clear from the moment she announced the Commission's various proposals for NGEU at the end of May 2020: 'The recovery plan turns the immense challenge we face into an opportunity, not only by supporting the recovery but also by investing in our future: the European Green Deal and digitalization will boost jobs and growth, the resilience of our societies and the health of our environment'.[10] The acute functional pressures driving this broad policy experiment, however, meant that there was little time for—as well as,

1 Leino-Sandberg and Ruffert (2022, p 437).
2 Dermine (2020, p 347).
3 de Witte (2021, p 638).
4 Constamagna and Goldmann (2020).
5 Council Decision 2020/2053 [2020 ORD].
6 Council Regulation 2020/2094 [EURI].
7 Regulation (EU) 2021/241 [RRF].
8 Dermine (2020, p 347).
9 See Chapter One, nn 28–29, 57–105 and accompanying text.
10 European Commission (2020d).

European Integration in the Constitutional Borderlands. Päivi Leino-Sandberg and Peter L. Lindseth,
Oxford University Press. © Päivi Leino-Sandberg and Peter L. Lindseth 2026.
DOI: 10.1093/oso/9780198949527.003.0004

perhaps, little interest in—any 'deeper reflection' about the impact of these emergency efforts on 'the sustainability of the EU's and the Eurozone's order of competences'.[11] This was particularly the case for the division of competences between national and supranational levels over the longer term.

In this chapter, we focus on the legal design of NGEU at its inception, though our aim is not to revisit the question of the NGEU's legality per se. That ship sailed long ago—at the publication date of this book, nearly all the funding under NGEU will have been borrowed, disbursed, and spent, and there will be little chance that they would, could, or even should be clawed back (except perhaps in the cases of outright fraud under investigation).[12] Rather, what we seek to do here is critically assess how the legal design of the NGEU—largely driven by the desire to avoid Treaty change—defined the programme's operation and impacted its ability to achieve its objectives. To get to that point, we must undertake the further examination of the implementation of NGEU in Chapter Four as well as the extension of the model to other domains in Chapter Five.

The present chapter will begin, in Section A, by examining the reinterpretation of Article 175(3) TFEU as a foundation for what would become the RRF. Starting here is justified for several reasons. NGEU comprises other spending instruments aside from the RRF (ReactEU, the Just Transition Fund, the Rural Development Fund, InvestEU, Horizon Europe, RescEU); however, the RRF—whose sole basis is the cohesion flexibility clause of Article 175(3) TFEU—is by far the largest and most significant of those instruments and hence worthy of our focused attention for that reason alone.[13] Moreover the RRF, like other important NGEU spending initiatives—notably, the Rural Development Fund and the Just Transition Fund—uses an allocation formula that includes, in significant part, national financial envelopes with pre-assigned amounts.[14] Consequently, in this crucial respect, spending under the RRF reflects the persistence of a '*juste retour*' logic even as the overall programme seeks to redistribute funding to address broader issues at a European scale.[15]

The main reason for beginning with Article 175(3) TFEU, however, lies elsewhere. Most importantly, opening with that provision allows us to address a puzzling gap in the discussions of the legal foundations of the NGEU programme that emerged from the very outset of the legislative process in the spring and summer of 2020. It was at that time that the Commission and Council both published analyses of selected aspects of the legal underpinnings of the new emergency programme. The

[11] Dermine (2020, p 8).

[12] See, eg, EPPO (2024a), Stamouli (2024), and Tamma (2023). For further discussion, see Chapter Four, Section C.1.

[13] In 2018 prices, the RRF's allocation is €672.5 billion, whereas ReactEU is €47.5 billion, the Just Transition Fund €10 billion, Rural Development €7.5 billion, InvestEU €5.6 billion, Horizon Europe €5 billion, and RescEU €2 billion.

[14] See Regulation (EU) 2021/241 [RRF], Annex IV.

[15] On the legally problematic nature of that logic, see this chapter below, nn 153–55 and accompanying text. On the role of *juste retour* in the allocation formula used in the RRF, see this chapter below, nn 285–87 and accompanying text.

Commission's analysis was quite limited and sparse, in the form of a press release in June 2020 of just under 2,000 words in length, entitled 'Q&A: Next Generation—Legal Construction'.[16] We will have more to say about this 'Q&A' below.[17] The Council was more forthcoming, strategically deciding to publish in full, in the face of public debate and pressure from hesitant national governments, the normally highly confidential and lengthy legal opinion of the Council Legal Service, also in June 2020.[18]

Conspicuously absent from both analyses, however, was any discussion of Article 175(3) TFEU or how it could serve as the legal basis for the spending under what would become the RRF. Article 175(3) TFEU includes a narrow authorisation for the adoption of 'necessary' and 'specific actions' within the framework of cohesion policy but otherwise 'outside the Funds', that is, those traditional regional-development tools contemplated or specifically mentioned in Articles 174, 175(1) TFEU and/or 177(1) and (2) TFEU. Given that this provision's prior use had been quite limited (both in scope of coverage and scale of spending),[19] one would think that any reinterpretation of Article 175(3) TFEU to support the much larger amounts of spending in the RRF—across numerous domains with little or no connection to cohesion traditionally conceived—would have called for detailed legal justification. And yet there was none, or at least none that the EU institutions made public in the spring of 2020.

So the obvious question is: why the silence? Why, for example, did the otherwise detailed opinion of the Council Legal Service of June 2020 not mention Article 175(3) TFEU at all, much less analyse how it could serve the sole legal basis of the RRF? The opinion's discussion of the RRF focused only on whether it fell 'within the scope of the Recovery Instrument' and whether its method of allocating funds 'correspond[ed] to the rationale of Article 122 TFEU',[20] that is, the legal basis for the EURI Regulation rather than the RRF's own legal basis, Article 175(3) TFEU.

As we shall see later, in order to support the hundreds of billions of euros of spending under the RRF, Article 175(3) TFEU did indeed require a quite significant reinterpretation—coming close, as we shall see, to transforming that heretofore marginal provision into a general spending clause in the 'general Welfare' of the EU, akin to the general spending clause that appears in the United States Constitution.[21] The potential import of that reinterpretation is extensive, not least because, in practice, it opened up an avenue for the EU to free itself from competence restrictions in the Treaties, seeking to achieve goals indirectly through funding that it could not achieve directly by regulation (a topic we take up at the close of Chapter Four).[22]

Our intuition was that the foundations for this reinterpretation of the EU's spending power first occurred not in the formulation of NGEU in 2020 but in fact several years

[16] European Commission (2020a) [Q&A].
[17] See this chapter below, nn 257–70 and accompanying text.
[18] Council Legal Service (2020a). For further details, see Leino-Sandberg (2021a, p 299).
[19] See this chapter below, nn 61–67 and accompanying text.
[20] Council Legal Service (2020a), para 143.
[21] See Lindseth and Leino-Sandberg (2024b).
[22] See Chapter Four, Section D.6.

earlier, outside public scrutiny, in relation to proposals (never in fact adopted) to establish a so-called 'euro-area budget' that were formulated between 2017 and 2019. They built on a capacious reinterpretation of the EU's authority under Article 175(3) TFEU, which raised evident concerns about the boundary between cohesion and other policy domains.[23] On the basis of this 'hidden history' of Article 175(3) TFEU—greatly extending the 'ratcheting strategy' begun in earlier efforts to harness cohesion as a tool of economic governance[24]—institutional lawyers in the EU apparently believed there was no need to address the adequacy of Article 175(3) TFEU in the spring of 2020, or in the actual design of the RRF.[25]

One of us submitted applications both to the Commission and Council to make the legal advice on the euro-area budget proposals publicly available. As we describe in the Introduction to this volume,[26] the Commission's initial response to the request was implausibly small, identifying just a few documents involving minor technical amendments to draft proposals just prior to their formal approval, none of them illuminating. After two appeals to the European Ombudsman, the Commission eventually identified twelve additional documents containing legal advice, none of which were disclosed without heavy redactions, blocking out the entirety of that advice. The Council Legal Service's response to our request was also initially reluctant but, in the end, stood in contrast to the Commission Legal Service's near-total refusal to disclose. After initially denying access, the Council Legal Service, in response to a confirmatory application, produced a series of detailed legal opinions on the earlier euro-area budget proposals,[27] which we examine in Section A of this chapter.[28] From there we turn to a discussion of the legal basis for the other NGEU components: the emergency assistance rules in Article 122 TFEU for the EURI (Section B) and the general financial and budgetary rules in Articles 310–311 TFEU for the 2020 ORD (Section C). We then return to the legal design of the RRF in the final section of the chapter (Section D) to demonstrate how it inaugurated a system of, in effect, 'cohesion without limits', greatly expanding on the ratcheting strategy we introduced in Chapter Two.[29] The RRF built not merely on the questionable reinterpretation of

[23] See this chapter below, nn 40–42 and accompanying text, discussing Leino-Sandberg and Saarenheimo (2018, p 639) One can understand these reinterpretations in terms of the concept of 'sedimentation' as articulated in Tuori (2013).

[24] See Chapter Two, nn 204–62 and accompanying text; see also this chapter below, nn 321–29 and accompanying text.

[25] Leino-Sandberg and Lindseth (2023); See also Lindseth and Leino-Sandberg (2024b).

[26] See Introduction, nn 70–95 and accompanying text. For further discussion of our public access requests, see Leino-Sandberg and Lindseth (2023); See also Lindseth and Leino-Sandberg (2024b). Section A of this chapter draws on, but further develops, the discussion in both of these prior publications.

[27] The documents produced were Council Legal Service (2019a), (2019b), and (2020b) (copies now available *erga omnes* in the Council's public register). The Council Secretariat's initial decision was to grant only partial access to Council Legal Service (2019b), and (2020b), but in response to a confirmatory application, it granted full access. A final set of documents (13116/19 + REV1) did not involve the scope of authority under Article 175(3) TFEU and hence are not discussed below.

[28] See this chapter below, nn 75–155 and accompanying text.

[29] See Chapter Two, nn 204–62 and accompanying text. See also this chapter below, nn 321–29 and accompanying text.

Article 175(3) TFEU noted above, but also inaugurated an opaque and highly technocratic process of national–supranational negotiation that we explore in much greater detail in Chapter Four.

A. Conducting Economic Policy through Article 175(3) TFEU: From the Euro-Area Budget Proposals to NGEU

In his 'State of the Union' message of September 2017, then-Commission President Jean-Claude Juncker called for the creation of 'a strong Euro area budget line within the EU budget'.[30] This initiative built on ideas for an EU-level macroeconomic stabilisation function first advanced in the Commission's White Paper on the Future of Europe in March 2017,[31] along with the Reflection Paper on the Future of EU Finances of 28 June 2017.[32] The aim of this initiative was not, however, merely macroeconomic stabilisation. Rather, it also sought to incentivise structural reforms in the Member States as discussed in Chapter Two—an idea that stretched at least back to the Convergence and Competitiveness Instrument in 2013.[33] To that end, the drafting process for what would become the euro-area budget proposals began at least as early as spring 2017, and it culminated in the proposals formally advanced by the Commission in 2018 and 2019. While these proposals were much smaller than what would eventually become NGEU, they were, like the eventual RRF, based on Article 175(3) TFEU in whole or in important part.

The Commission formally advanced its first two euro-area budget proposals in May 2018. The first was the €25 billion Reform Support Programme (RSP), of which €22 billion was to finance a reform delivery tool (RDT) to incentivise structural reforms.[34] The second was the European Investment Stabilisation Function (EISF),[35] which was intended to complement the RSP/RDT by introducing an element of macroeconomic stabilisation into the mix. The EISF would guarantee back-to-back loans of up to €30 billion to countries in the euro area and countries participating in the European Exchange Rate Mechanism (ERM II). Non-euro area Member States wishing to join the euro would be covered by a similarly designed Convergence Facility also under the RSP.[36] In 2019, however, the Commission, after extensive discussions in the Euro Group under a mandate from the Euro Summit, effectively folded these two instruments into a third proposal called the Budgetary Instrument for Convergence and

[30] Juncker (2017).
[31] European Commission (2017a, pp 25 and 29) (foreseeing that 'a euro area fiscal stabilisation function is operational' by 2025).
[32] European Commission (2017e).
[33] See Chapter Two, nn 232–45 and accompanying text, discussing European Commission (2013b) [Convergence and Competitiveness Instrument proposal].
[34] European Commission (2018a) [RSP Proposal].
[35] European Commission (2018b) [EISF Proposal].
[36] For a description of both instruments, see European Commission (2018e).

Competitiveness (BICC), which encompassed similar elements.[37] But while the first two proposals were based, in whole or in (overwhelming) part, on Article 175(3) TFEU, the BICC proposal was framed as a measure of economic governance, limited to the euro area states and based on Article 136(1)(b) TFEU in combination with Article 121(6) TFEU.[38] Nonetheless, as we shall see later,[39] the BICC envisaged a substantial component related to the distribution of funds to the Member States, which was also to be based on Article 175(3) TFEU.

For those paying close attention (and few were), the reliance of these earlier proposals on the cohesion flexibility clause of Article 175(3) TFEU raised an important issue of boundary drawing. The proposed instruments were based on an implicit reading of Article 175(3) TFEU that seemed to suggest that literally *any* EU economic intervention could 'also contribute to economic and social cohesion'.[40] This would be possible only if one ignored the historically more narrow focus of cohesion policy—'reducing disparities between the levels of development of the various regions and the backwardness of the least favoured regions' (Article 174 TFEU, second paragraph).[41] The boundary problem was that, if Article 175(3) TFEU were read expansively in the way these proposals suggested, very few economic policy measures would not come within the scope of this provision, thus 'rais[ing] the question of how to draw the border between economic policies and cohesion policies'.[42]

Subsequent research—particularly as to the existing case law on policing the boundaries of the cohesion flexibility clause in Article 175(3) TFEU[43]—has only deepened this boundary-drawing concern. Once we gained public access to, and were able to analyse, the opinions of the Council Legal Service on these various proposals, it became clear that limits of the cohesion flexibility clause in the case law were in fact almost completely ignored.[44] The practical result of these re-readings was to ratchet Article 175(3) TFEU into a nearly unfettered tool of economic governance, thereby constituting a major step in the process begun earlier, as described in Chapter Two.[45] Indeed, the purpose was to convert cohesion into a general spending power that could be deployed with little regard to other competence limitations in the EU Treaties.[46]

37 European Commission (2019a) [BICC Proposal].

38 The BICC was also to be accompanied by a Convergence and Reform Instrument (CRI), which was nearly identical to the BICC but aimed at the non-euro area countries, together with other ancillary arrangements to compensate non-euro area countries for their part in financing the BICC.

39 See this chapter below, nn 148–50 and accompanying text.

40 Leino-Sandberg and Saarenheimo (2018, p 639).

41 For further discussion, see Lindseth and Leino-Sandberg (2024b).

42 Leino-Sandberg and Saarenheimo (2018, p 639).

43 See this chapter below, nn 48–60 and accompanying text.

44 See this chapter below, nn 72–154 and accompanying text.

45 ...

46 See this chapter below, nn 180–81 and accompanying text. Cf Case C-376/98, *Germany v Parliament and Council* (Tobacco Advertising) (2000), para 79 ('Other articles of the Treaty may not ... be used as a legal basis in order to circumvent the express exclusion of' competence elsewhere in the Treaty); cf also Case C-19/23, *Denmark v Parliament and Council* (Alternative Minimum Wages) (2025), Opinion of Advocate General Emiliou, paras 133–34.

1. Policing the Limits of Cohesion: The Existing Case Law

Article 175(3) TFEU, as noted above, authorises the adoption of 'necessary' and 'specific actions' within the framework of cohesion policy but otherwise 'outside the Funds'. Based on that language, the function of Article 175(3) TFEU appeared to be rather limited, tied to supplementing EU action under the existing structural and cohesion funds, whose regional-developmental purposes traced back decades.[47] In fact, this is how the prior case law viewed this provision. The CJEU's 2009 judgment in *International Fund for Ireland (IFI)* is to our knowledge the only extant ruling interpreting the cohesion flexibility clause as a legal basis.[48]

The *IFI* judgment arose from an action by the European Parliament (EP) to annul a Council regulation authorising the EU to contribute to an international fund supporting the peace process in Northern Ireland. This regulation was adopted on the basis of the Treaty's general flexibility clause (in ex-Article 308 TEC). The EP, in its challenge, asserted that the cohesion flexibility clause provided a fully adequate legal basis upon which to adopt the spending regulation. In the EP's view, the aims of the fund were coterminous with cohesion in that both were 'directed towards the strengthening of social cohesion and solidarity between the populations of Northern Ireland and the border areas of Ireland'.[49] The Advocate General agreed with the EP. He stressed that cohesion was 'a broad overall concept with imprecise contours'.[50] He further argued that:

> the policy of cohesion may be defined as a device for restoring a balance and for redistribution among the Member States. It is also an expression of solidarity between them and their peoples. In so far as the Community's financial contributions to the IFI are intended ... to bring about sustainable economic and social improvement in the areas concerned, in my view they fully form part of a redistribution policy seeking to correct economic and social imbalances ...[51]

The Court, however, *did not adopt* this expansive interpretation of cohesion policy. It ruled, instead, that the cohesion flexibility clause could only *in part* provide a legal basis,[52] thus also requiring reliance on ex-Article 308 TEC. In this regard, the Court

[47] The two oldest funds—the European Agricultural Guidance and Guarantee Fund (EAGGF) and the European Social Fund (ESF)—can be traced all the way back to the Treaty of Rome in 1957 (Articles 40 and 123–28 respectively). The European Regional Development Fund (ERDF) was created in 1975, and the Cohesion Fund in 1994.

[48] Case C-166/07, *Parliament v Council* (*International Fund for Ireland*) (2009) [hereinafter *IFI*]. The case involved the substantively identical predecessor clause in Article 159(3) TEC, but its reasoning would apply with equal force to Article 175(3) TFEU.

[49] Case C-166/07, *IFI* (2009), para 24.

[50] Opinion of Advocate General Bot, Case C-166/07, *IFI* (2009), para 82.

[51] Ibid, para 85.

[52] Case C-166/07, *IFI* (2009), para 69.

agreed with the more limited interpretation advanced by the then-Commission, that 'the range of activities financed by the contested regulation'—given its broader focus on reconciliation between long antagonistic populations—'would extend beyond the scope of the Community's policy on economic and social cohesion' strictly speaking.[53] In short, cohesion could not, and did not, mean anything conducive to the overall goals of European integration but rather it referred to a subset of policy goals distinct from those general aims.

The Court specifically held that the cohesion flexibility clause 'covers only independent action [that] does not extend beyond the scope of the ... policy on economic and social cohesion'.[54] As Leticia Díez Sánchez has characterised this judgment (correctly in our view), the Court held that the flexibility clause is an inappropriate legal basis where 'cohesion is *only the by-product* of another objective' (emphasis in original).[55] This points to why the 'ratcheting strategy'—or what she calls the intensifying 'transformation of cohesion policy' over the last several decades—'is problematic'.[56] As she elaborates:

> There is nothing inherently wrong with using the EU budget for competitiveness-oriented investments that are predominantly decided and executed by national governments bearing national interests in mind (although it appears odd to do so while defending fiscal restraint). It is just that this is not the *particular* goal of cohesion policy [emphasis in original], conceived as a redistributive tool with a specific geographical dimension [ie among disadvantaged regions].[57]

Indeed, in articulating this holding, the Court established a legal framework that suggests a strict policing of the boundary between cohesion and other purported EU competences (or lack thereof). The Court grounded its more restrictive approach on the phrase 'specific actions' in the cohesion flexibility clause. This meant that the provision could only serve as the appropriate legal basis when the legislator could '*guarantee* that all of the interventions' of the programme adopted under this provision 'will in fact address the objectives that are *specific to the [EU]'s policy on economic and social cohesion*' (emphasis added).[58] This 'guarantee' obligation of the Union legislator, in turn, created a related obligation on the part of European institutions implementing any such programme to '*prevent* the use [of funds] to cover actions which, while complying with the objectives of [that programme], *extend beyond the scope of the [Union]'s policy on economic and social cohesion*' (emphasis added).[59]

[53] Ibid, para 63.
[54] Ibid, para 64.
[55] Díez Sánchez (2025, p 46), citing Case C-166/07, *IFI* (2009), paras 64–64. This interpretation of *IFI* resonates with the position taken by the Council Legal Service in early March 2020; see this chapter below, nn 165–66 and accompanying text, discussing Council Legal Service (2020c, p 10, para 28).
[56] Díez Sánchez (2025, p 46).
[57] Ibid.
[58] Case C-166/07, *IFI* (2009), para 62.
[59] Ibid, para 59.

The Court's combination of the 'guarantee' and 'prevention' obligations under the cohesion flexibility clause clearly constrained the discretion of the Union legislator as well as that of implementing administrative actors (both supranational and national). In reaching this conclusion, the Court specifically did not adopt the idea, advanced by the Advocate General, that cohesion could open-endedly serve 'as a device for restoring a balance and for redistribution among the Member States' or as 'an expression of solidarity between them and their peoples'.[60] The cohesion flexibility clause had a much more 'specific' purpose than that. The Court's reasoning thus directly supports the point—logically necessary by the terms of the cohesion flexibility clause itself—that not every policy measure with economic implications could be redefined as 'cohesion' policy as that term is understood under the Treaties.

Given the Court's restrictive interpretation, neither Article 159(3) TEC nor its successor, Article 175(3) TFEU, saw extensive use as a legal basis over the subsequent decade. Prior to 2009, Article 159(3) TEC had served as the legal basis for three programmes: a fund to assist Member States confronting natural disasters[61] (since modified, post-Covid, to extend to public health emergencies);[62] a fund to assist workers made redundant by globalisation;[63] and a technical instrument to enable and regulate so-called 'European groupings of territorial cooperation' (EGTC).[64] Later, in 2014, Article 175(3) TFEU would serve as the legal basis to create a fund to provide food and/or basic material assistance to marginalised members of society, often through non-governmental organisations (NGOs) or other partner organisations.[65] Otherwise, Article 175(3) TFEU provided the legal basis for certain limited aspects of external action,[66] and for regulating actions relating to EU funds.[67]

For scholars, cohesion policy has remained 'one of the most difficult EU policies to define and categorise'.[68] And as Chapter Two discussed in detail, the functional pressure on cohesion policy to serve broader purposes increased considerably over the course of the 2010s, with the political aspiration that it might serve as 'a stable long-term EU framework and financial means for investment in jobs and growth and the delivery of structural reforms'.[69] It was bound up with what we are calling a

[60] Opinion of Advocate General Bot, Case C-166/07, *IFI* (2009), para 85.

[61] Council Regulation (EC) No 2012/2002. See also Regulation (EU) 661/2014 (clarifying eligibility criteria, including, inter alia, required advanced risk-mitigation measures, as well as enhanced measures for protection of Union financial interests).

[62] Regulation (EU) 2020/461.

[63] See Regulation (EC) No 1927/2006; Regulation (EU) No 1309/2013; Regulation (EU) 2021/691.

[64] Regulation (EC) No 1082/2006; Regulation (EU) No 1302/2013.

[65] Regulation (EU) No 223/2014.

[66] There are three instruments falling into this category, one related to the withdrawal of the United Kingdom from the EU (Brexit), and the other three related to the European Economic Area (EEA), which includes all EU Member States plus Iceland, Liechtenstein, and Norway. See Regulation (EU) 2021/1755; Council Decision (EU) 2022/1026; Council Decision (EU) 2015/900; Council Decision 2014/348/EU.

[67] Regulation (EU) 2019/1796; Regulation (EU) 2018/1671; Regulation (EU) 2017/2396; Regulation (EU) 2015/1017.

[68] Bachtler et al (2013, p 11).

[69] Council of the European Union (2016).

'ratcheting strategy',[70] designed to blur the boundaries of cohesion away from its original regional-developmental purposes and towards the broader task of '[f]ostering lasting economic convergence and resilience' with a strong 'link with the economic governance and the European Semester'.[71]

Pre-Covid and pre-NGEU, no initiative better exemplified these aspirations than the Commission's three euro-area budget proposals.[72] Even though the Commission has refused to disclose the legal interpretation on which these proposals were grounded, the unredacted portions of the documents they have produced are still illuminating. For example, on the front end, there was an email exchange dated 10–14 July 2017 between the Directorate-General for Budget and the Commission Legal Service. This exchange provided legal advice—still undisclosed—about whether and on what legal basis the EU might adopt an instrument in which country-specific recommendations under the European Semester 'could be "incentivized" rather than "imposed" through perceived "sanctions" such as suspension of European and Structural and Investment Funds'.[73] The Legal Service later distributed this advice internally during the same time period when the Commission was finalising the Reform Support Programme, the Reform Delivery Tool, and the European Investment Stabilisation Function proposals in the winter and spring of 2018. Just over a year later, as part of the drafting of the Budgetary Instrument for Convergence and Competitiveness, the Commission Legal Service was working on an 'Issues note' as a follow-up to a recent meeting of the Eurogroup, addressing, inter alia, ways to strengthen country-specific recommendations in the euro area through a regulation under Article 175(3) TFEU.[74]

These documents are undoubtedly just a fraction of the legal advice the Commission Legal Service provided during this crucial period of legislative drafting. What the Commission has chosen to disclose nonetheless demonstrates that the euro-area budget proposals built on legal analyses specifically focused on the boundary between cohesion and economic policy. Because of the Commission's unwillingness to give public access, however, we must rely on the legal opinions produced by the Council Legal Service to gain a better sense of how these debates played out.[75] And as the discussion in the next subsection makes clear, the legal interpretation underlying

[70] See Chapter Two, nn 204–62 and accompanying text. See also this chapter below, nn 321–29 and accompanying text, and Chapter Four, Section D.4.

[71] European Commission (2017e, pp 16–17). On the 'resilience turn' in EU political discourse, see Joseph and Juncos (2019), (2024). For more on resilience in the development of the NGEU model, see this chapter, nn 97–112 and nn 322–27 and accompanying text and Chapter Four, Section D.5.

[72] See this chapter above, nn 34–37 and accompanying text.

[73] Ares(2018)649814, Document 7 attached to European Commission (2024a), email exchange dated 10–14 July 2018 between [name redacted] (BUDG) and Jean-Paul Keppenne (SJ), subject: 'Instrument for incentivising Structural Reforms in Member States'.

[74] Ares(2019)2908188, Document 2b attached to European Commission (2024a), 'Budgetary Instrument for Convergence and Competitiveness: Issues note for internal discussion' (24 April 2019); Ares(2019)2908188, Document 2c to European Commission (2024a), 'Budgetary Instrument for Convergence and Competitiveness: Issues note for internal discussion' (26 April 2019).

[75] See this chapter above, n 27.

the euro-area budget proposals effectively sought to eliminate the distinction between cohesion and economic policy entirely, accomplishing a fundamental transformation in supranational authority without Treaty change.

2. Dissolving the Boundary Between Cohesion and Economic Policy

By way of preliminary observation to the discussion of the Council Legal Service opinions in this subsection, it is important to note the differences in the institutional context between the Council Legal Service and that of its counterpart in the Commission.[76] The Council Legal Service is the main source of legal advice to the Council and the European Council, and it is always present in Council decision making. The Legal Service of the Commission—in line with the task of the master that it serves—remains more integrationist in its approach, focused on removing obstacles that the law might pose. The Council Legal Service, by contrast, is generally believed to be more concerned with preserving Member State interests. Nonetheless, the Council Legal Service also enjoys strategic room for manoeuvre on this point.[77] The 'will' of the Council is often difficult to discern, given the great variety of views among the Member States. As matter of political reality, that 'will' is often based on the views of the dominant or a few strong Member States that have reached an agreement on a particular issue sufficient to push it through. Identifying compromises and providing the legal language for realising those agreements is where the Council Legal Service derives much of its power,[78] even as it seeks to hold itself out as an apolitical broker among all the Member States.

In its various opinions on the Commission's euro-area budget proposals discussed below, the Council Legal Service exploited this strategic room for manoeuvre. Rather than operating within the confines of the 'guarantee' and 'prevention' obligations articulated by the CJEU in *IFI*,[79] the Council Legal Service seized on the more forgiving logic of the AG's opinion.[80] This selective reading resulted in a significantly more expansive interpretation of Article 175(3) TFEU, one that is arguably in deep tension with what the Court actually held in *IFI*.[81] Typically, it is the Commission Legal Service whose legal analysis is more heavily constrained by the imperative of a narrow political landing zone. In this instance, the analysis of the Council Legal Service seemed to be operating within equally narrow limits.

[76] Leino-Sandberg (2021a, chs 5–6).
[77] Cf Eckes and Leino-Sandberg (2022).
[78] Leino-Sandberg (2021a, ch 6).
[79] See this chapter above, nn 58–59 and accompanying text.
[80] See this chapter below, n 87 and accompanying text.
[81] See this chapter above, nn 52–59 and accompanying text.

a. The European Investment Stabilisation Function (EISF)

As proposed by the Commission, the EISF would introduce an element of macroeconomic stabilisation into the new euro-area budget by guaranteeing back-to-back loans of up to €30 billion to euro-area Member States. The sole legal basis identified by the Commission was Article 175(3) TFEU. The Commission's Explanatory Memorandum accompanying the proposal claimed recourse to Article 175(3) TFEU was justified—that is, made 'necessary outside the Structural Funds'—because those funds 'do not [otherwise] provide for a specific instrument to support macro-economic stabilisation by preserving public investment in case of large asymmetric shocks'.[82]

One might suggest that cohesion policy had not provided for such an instrument because cohesion competence was previously not understood to extend to such a broad-based macroeconomic function. In effect, the Commission was arguing that it was something of a 'sleeping competence', which the EU always purportedly possessed but simply had not exercised. Elaborating further, the Commission's Explanatory Memorandum argued that the EISF would:

> help beneficiary Member States [in] preserving growth-friendly public investment in case of macroeconomic instability. This in turns helps easing the economic adjustment in the euro area Member State or Member States concerned and helps returning them to a sustainable growth path rather than deepening and lengthening the recession which negatively impacts their economic and social cohesion.[83]

The Commission's EISF proposal thus undertook to blur the line between general economic policies and cohesion policies, effectively subsuming economic policy into a sub-category of cohesion policy, to justify the use of Article 175(3) TFEU as the legal basis. When responding to our public access request, the Commission Legal Service produced no documents containing legal advice on this or any other dimension of the European Investment Stabilisation Function. We find it implausible, however, that the Commission lawyers never advised on the EISF. Fortunately, however, we have the Council Legal Service's first euro-area budget opinion, issued on 15 January 2019,[84] which also dealt with that proposal.[85]

In its opinion on the EISF, the Council Legal Service correctly acknowledged that, per the existing case law, 'cohesion cannot be used as an instrument to achieve the Union aims in other policy areas, such as economic policy'.[86] But the opinion then, consistent with the proposal itself, went on to blur this distinction so as to avoid the

[82] European Commission (2018b) [EISF Proposal], Explanatory Memorandum, sec 1, first bullet point ('Reasons for and objectives of the proposal').
[83] Ibid, Explanatory Memorandum, sec 2, first bullet point ('Legal basis').
[84] Council Legal Service (2019a).
[85] European Commission (2018b) [EISF Proposal].
[86] Council Legal Service (2019a, para 28), quoting Case C-166/07, *IFI* (2009), para 46.

implications of this prohibition. The opinion stressed that the 'notion of cohesion policy is particularly broad and inclusive', citing for this proposition language in the Advocate General's opinion that the Court in *IFI* did not adopt.[87] Furthermore, instead of considering the actual wording of Article 174 TFEU (particularly its clear emphasis on regional development), the Council Legal Service argued that the 'scope of Article 174 TFEU is not limited to specific sectors and is defined functionally—on the basis of its objectives—rather than organically'.[88] From this, the opinion concluded that the Treaty 'leaves a large margin of discretion to the legislator as to how the cohesion aims should be achieved'.[89] This conclusion, however, simply ignored the constraints on that discretion derived from the 'guarantee' and 'prevention' obligations that the CJEU had defined in *IFI*.[90]

To get around these requirements, the Council Legal Service advanced a more forgiving analytical framework, grounded in a discretion-enhancing 'preponderant aim' test. To quote the opinion, the violation of the boundaries of Article 175(3) TFEU as a legal basis should turn on whether cohesion was 'be[ing] used with the preponderant aim' either 'to enhance the economic coordination between Member States' or 'of ensuring the stability of the euro area'.[91] To avoid the conclusion that this was precisely how the EISF was being used, the Council Legal Service then engaged in a rhetorical and analytical sleight of hand. Over a series of rather elliptical paragraphs,[92] it found in effect that the Treaty-based asymmetry in the EMU between centralised monetary policy and decentralised fiscal policy, along with derivative risks of 'asymmetric shocks' across the Member States which that structural and economic asymmetry created,[93] gave rise to 'vulnerabilities' that the Union legislator was empowered to address as a matter of cohesion under Article 175(3) TFEU.[94]

The fact that the Treaties themselves created the EMU's asymmetry—eminently a choice of economic and fiscal policy of the most fundamental sort—while Article 175(3) TFEU was merely a back-up flexibility provision for a policy domain with 'specific' regional-developmental purposes, was the 'elephant in the room' that the Council Legal Service's opinion did not address. Instead, the opinion simply concluded 'that the overall economic rationale of the [EISF] constitutes a plausible element of justification to allow the legislator to exercise the large margin of discretion that it holds in this area of Union competence'.[95] In short, the Council Legal Service found that the Union had the tools to address the constitutional design flaws in the EMU's asymmetry not through the difficult process of Treaty change, as one might

[87] Council Legal Service (2019a, para 35), citing Opinion of Advocate General Bot, Case C-166/07, *IFI* (2009), para 90.

[88] Council Legal Service (2019a, para 35).

[89] Ibid.

[90] See this chapter above, nn 58–59 and accompanying text.

[91] Council Legal Service (2019a, paras 29 and 31).

[92] Ibid, paras 12, 40–41, and 54–57.

[93] Ibid, paras 3, 11–13, 38–41, 44, 54–56.

[94] Ibid, paras 39 and 48.

[95] Ibid, para 57.

suppose, but through a process of legally re-engineering the concept of cohesion to extend it to 'vulnerabilities' of a fundamentally macroeconomic type.

b. The Reform Support Programme (RSP) and Reform Delivery Tool (RDT)

This effort at legally re-engineering cohesion continued in the €22 billion Reform Delivery Tool based on the cohesion flexibility clause of Article 175(3) TFEU.[96] This use of Article 175(3) TFEU was justified, according to the Commission's Explanatory Memorandum, because the instrument was designed to support 'the completion of reforms of a structural nature aimed at improving the performance of the national economies and at promoting resilient economic and social structures in the Member States'.[97] This justification was a good example of the increasing importance of 'resilience thinking' in a crisis-addled EU, which sociologists have seen as part of the EU's 'resilience turn' in the second half of the 2010s.[98] Reforms eligible for funding under the RDT were those that aimed at addressing challenges identified in the context of the European Semester.[99] The advice of the Commission Legal Service on the RDT remains undisclosed, but Jean-Paul Keppenne, the Director in the Commission Legal Service whose team was in charge of that file, later explained in a published legal commentary: 'The justification for the RDT as an instrument of cohesion policy is that the completion of reforms of a structural nature improves the performance of the national economies, thereby promoting resilient economic and social structures in the Member States'.[100] Again, the blurring of the line between cohesion and general economic policy was unmistakable.

The Council Legal Service's opinion on the Reform Support Programme identified a problem with that attempted blurring: '[N]ot all of the actions required under the Semester framework are susceptible of having [the requisite] direct cohesion impact' to come within Article 175(3) TFEU.[101] Nonetheless, the Council Legal Service maintained that, '[e]conomic and monetary policy being a common policy of the EU, convergence efforts within that policy cannot be regarded as detached from the overall cohesion objectives of the Union because, ultimately, all Member States (with the exceptions laid down in primary law) are called to have the euro as their currency'.[102] The Council Legal Service made no distinction here between monetary policy (as an EU exclusive competence) and economic policy (where the EU merely enjoys powers of coordination). Instead, its inquiry focused on whether 'the reform delivery tool constitutes a genuine instrument of cohesion, or whether its content rather consists of a mechanism of coordination of the economic policies of Member States'.[103] To find

[96] European Commission (2018a) [RSP Proposal].
[97] Ibid, Explanatory Memorandum, sec 2, first bullet point ('Legal basis').
[98] Joseph and Juncos (2019), (2024).
[99] European Commission (2018a) [RSP Proposal], art 8.
[100] Keppenne (2020a, p 875).
[101] Council Legal Service (2019b, para 31).
[102] Ibid, para 46.
[103] Ibid, para 27.

that the RDT fell into the former rather the latter category, the Council Legal Service said the question turned on whether the RDT 'promot[ed] resilient economic and social structures in the Member States'.[104] Promoting 'resilience' thus became the analytical hook on which the cohesion legal basis of Article 175(3) TFEU ultimately hung, purportedly distinguishing the RDT from other hypothetical programmes whose preponderant aim was, say, coordination of economic policies or the stability of the euro.[105] While approving the legal basis, the Council Legal Service moreover made its use 'subject to a number of adaptations of provisions relating to i) the eligibility of reforms, ii) the assessment and allocation criteria for funding, iii) the governance and decision making, so that they constitute a genuine instrument of cohesion', understood now in terms of resilience.[106]

The reasoning of the Council Legal Service here was an example of how resilience, as 'a wide and vague' concept—which does not appear anywhere in the Treaties—could be deployed to 'deliberately blur contested issues',[107] in this case the scope of authority under Article 175(3) TFEU. It is genuinely difficult to think of an economic policy measure that could not be argued to contribute, through some route, to economic or social resilience. Specifically, this is what coordination of economic policies under Article 121 TFEU was supposed to achieve; moreover, the stability of the euro was and is a more general prerequisite to resilient economic and social structures. Nonetheless, the Council Legal Service opinion found that the aim of the RSP was 'not to create the conditions for the optimal and proper functioning of the euro, thus its stability'.[108] Rather, it was 'to underpin the economic resilience of Member States' and hence was an exercise of cohesion policy as now expansively reinterpreted.[109] As Keppenne of the Commission Legal Service later argued in his published legal commentary: 'There are links between such actions and economic policy, but the RDT does not make use of the Title VIII ('Economic and Monetary Policy') as a legal basis. Instead, it develops a concept of cohesion as embracing real convergence between the Member States and of augmenting the resilience of their economies'.[110]

This formalistic distinction borders on the absurd. These two aims are really one and the same and trying to differentiate between them is rather nonsensical. Yet, these are the sort of mental gymnastics that the Reform Support Programme and its Reform Delivery Tool forced on the lawyers in both the Council and the Commission legal services. Cohesion became the overarching label for a basket of broad economic aims that now all purportedly fit under Article 175(3) TFEU, including 'competitiveness,

[104] Ibid, para 8.
[105] Ibid, paras 12, 23–24, 44–48.
[106] Ibid, para 64).
[107] Joseph and Juncos (2024, p 377; see also pp 380–82), as well as Rega and Bonifazi (2020) ('resilience entails value judgments about achievements which are "internally complex, constitutively ambiguous and inherently open (and hence, persistently vague)"') and Grove (2018, p 49) ('[t]he meaning of resilience is thus neither transparent nor objectively determined').
[108] Council Legal Service (2019b, para 48).
[109] Ibid, para 48.
[110] Keppenne (2020a, p 875).

productivity, research and innovation, smart, sustainable and inclusive growth, jobs and investment'.[111] Indeed, the Council Legal Service opinion claimed that, if the moneys spent under the RSP and RDT advanced any of these aims, they should '[i]n principle' be seen as 'earmarked for policies which are identified as cohesion'.[112] The seemingly elastic category of cohesion was thus blown wide open to include essentially any goal of general economic policy, forgetting that cohesion was supposed to be geared to a subset of policies primarily about regions, not entire states or even the EU as a whole.

Even under this expansive understanding of cohesion, however, the Council Legal Service opinion still expressed concerns as it moved from an abstract analysis '[i]n principle' to one focused on the RSP's operation '*in concreto*' (italics in original).[113] The former analysis, given the expansive re-engineering of cohesion described above, found 'plausible economic reasoning … to establish the proposal's general objectives, bearing in mind the large margin of discretion that the Council holds in this area of Union competence'.[114] In the latter context, however, the question was more difficult: it required a determination of 'whether the particular reforms that may be the object of funding under the Reform Delivery Tool are *in concreto* cohesion relevant'.[115] This concern recalled the interplay of the 'guarantee' and 'prevention' obligations articulated by the CJEU in *IFI* in the application of the flexibility clause for cohesion policy.[116] Whereas the former obligation applied to the Union legislator in the adoption of the programme, the later applied in particular to the Commission in the implementation of the programme. The Council Legal Service's reasoning here suggested that, even under its generous interpretation of the scope of EU legislative discretion under Article 175(3) TFEU, Commission implementation could still breach those limits or simply pursue other goals, implicitly including goals outside EU competence entirely.[117]

In raising this issue, the Council Legal Service focused on a concern that it had touched on only obliquely in its EISF opinion:[118] the Commission's large power of discretion when taking its decisions under the programme.[119] The Council Legal Service's main worry here was not the possibility that the EU might exceed its conferred powers, but rather that the *Commission* could invade the province of the *Council*. This 'may lead to situations whereby decisions by the Commission under the Reform Delivery Tool overlap with the process of economic policy coordination'

[111] Council Legal Service (2019b, paras 10 and 28).
[112] Ibid, para 28.
[113] Ibid, para 26.
[114] Ibid, para 26.
[115] Ibid, para 26.
[116] See this chapter above, nn 58–59 and accompanying text, discussing Case C-166/07, *IFI* (2009), paras 59 and 62.
[117] For a further discussion of the use of spending power to reach regulatory domains outside of EU competence, see Chapter Four, Section D.6.
[118] Council Legal Service (2019a, paras 55–56).
[119] Council Legal Service (2019b, para 35).

under the ultimate authority of the Council under Article 121 TFEU.[120] Given the potential scope of the Commission's discretion escaping effective Council oversight, 'the Reform Delivery Tool [c]ould *constitute an autonomous procedure of economic coordination*' (emphasis added).[121] That would violate not just the requirements of Article 121 TFEU but would also transgress the limits of Article 175(3) TFEU, which states that any actions under the cohesion flexibility clause must be 'without prejudice to the measures decided upon within the framework of the other Union policies'.[122]

This points us towards a difficult challenge of ongoing compliance not just by the Commission but all administrative actors (both supranational and national) involved in the process of implementing a programme based on Article 175(3) TFEU. It anticipates similar concerns with the NGEU in action, and more particularly with the RRF and the Commission's role in approving and overseeing the implementation of the National Recovery and Resilience Plans (a topic we introduce in Section D of this chapter below and explore in much greater detail in Chapter Four). The challenge would become all the more difficult when one considers the scale of the money—and the broader institutional consequences flowing from scaling up—that this re-engineering of cohesion would eventually be asked to support under NGEU.[123] What is striking is that the EU went forward with this massive scaling without any experience of how the 'cash for reforms' model actually operated in practice, and more particular how it interfaced (or not) with cohesion. According to Keppenne, '[t]he Commission had intended to carry out a "test run" for the RDT by putting in place a pilot phase of the programme' but the necessary regulation failed to make it out of the European Parliament.[124] Thus, as we shall see when we reach Chapter Four, when it came to actually standing up such a programme under the RRF, the Commission would necessarily be 'learning on the job',[125] albeit at a scale that involved massively larger amounts of money.

c. The Important Supporting Role of Article 197(2) TFEU

Perhaps cognisant of concerns over whether Article 175(3) TFEU alone could sustain the weight being placed on it, the Commission advanced a second legal basis to support the €25 billion Reform Support Programme: Article 197(2) TFEU. Like its much more modest predecessor—the €142.8 million Structural Reform Support Programme (SRSP) of 2017[126]—the portions of the RSP not allocated specifically to the RDT (€22 billion) also relied on Article 197(2) TFEU as a legal basis. This

[120] Ibid, para 36.
[121] Ibid.
[122] Thus, as the Council Legal Service itself recognised in both the RSP *and* EISF opinions: '*cohesion instruments cannot contain autonomous measures and procedures of economic coordination independent and separated from those laid down under the relevant provisions of economic policy under the Treaties and secondary legislation*' (emphasis in original). Ibid, para 34, quoting Council Legal Service (2019a, para 30).
[123] See Chapter One, nn 63–68 and accompanying text.
[124] Keppenne (2020a, pp 875–76).
[125] Schramm et al (2022, p 121). See Chapter Four, Section B.1.
[126] See Chapter Two, nn 248–50 and accompanying text.

provision authorised '[t]he Union [to] support the efforts of Member States to improve their administrative capacity to implement Union law'; but it further stressed that '[n]o Member State shall be obliged to avail itself of such support', giving it a seemingly transactional quality ultimately grounded in the Member States own competences.[127] Administrative cooperation is a competence that the EU can use to support, coordinate, or supplement the actions of the Member States (Article 6 TFEU) 'without thereby superseding their competence' (Article 2(5) TFEU). This Union competence is thus weaker than the shared competence that the EU enjoys in cohesion policy; hence the need to support it through the Member States' own authority, via seemingly voluntary requests, for example.

Despite this weakness, in the emails produced by the Commission in response to our public-access request, Article 197(2) TFEU was seen as important in supporting the Reform Support Programme, either alone or jointly with Article 175(3) TFEU. The emails show that discussions on using Article 197(2) TFEU for the RSP and RDT took place in February 2018 between the Commission Legal Service and the Structural Reform Support Service, the Secretariat-General, the Directorate-General for Budget, and the Directorate-General for Economic and Financial Affairs, building on earlier discussions of the same issues in connection with the SRSP in January 2016.[128] In 2018, the Legal Service had received requests for advice concerning the scope of Article 197(2) TFEU as a legal base where '[o]ne important area of difference between the options concerns the actions of the Member States that would be supported'.[129] These questions, however, had already surfaced during the negotiations for the SRSP in 2016, as the attachment to the 2018 email indicated. In an illuminating passage from that earlier email, the Commission official posing the question to the Legal Service recounted:

> [T]he Dutch Presidency ... asked us two prepare one or two slides with the justification (why is Article 175 chosen and not Article 174 of the TFEU, which is the legal basis of the for the (*sic*) Structural Fund Regulation, and why do we need to add Article 197 of the TFEU) and explain it in the meeting of the ECON/FIN Committee on 29 January. On this date the Committee will proceed to the Article-by-Article analysis of the Commission proposal.

[127] This is not unlike the 'contractual' nature to the support contemplated in the Commission's proposal for a Convergence and Competitiveness Instrument in 2013. See Chapter Two, nn 235–36 and accompanying text.

[128] Ares(2019)804472, Document 5a attached to European Commission (2024a) [on file with authors], email from [redacted] to [redacted], dated 11 February 2019, subject line 'FW: Structural Reform Delivery Tool: Scope of Article 197(2) TFEU as a legal base', forwarding emails between named and redacted recipients in SJ, SRSS, ECFIN, SG and BUDG, dated 5–6 February 2018, subject line 'Structural Reform Delivery Tool: Scope of Article 197(2) TFEU as a legal base' and attaching a further email exchange dated 22 January 2016 between named and redacted members of SRSS and SJ with the subject line 'FW: Legal basis of the Commission proposal for a Regulation on the creation of the SRSP'.

[129] Ares(2019)804472, Document 5a attached to European Commission (2024a), email exchange of 5 February 2018.

> The objective of the Dutch Presidency is to have a convincing justification in order to avoid asking the Commission to produce a written opinion of its Legal Service, (which could also lead to a written opinion of the Legal Service of the Council) and prevent complications on the legal basis, especially if the Member States that have raised the question of the legal basis are not happy with the Commission opinion.[130]

This exchange is suggestive of how a momentous change in the legal interpretation of the Treaties was buried in an entirely secret negotiating process, reduced, as it were, to 'one or two [PowerPoint] slides'.[131] The advice of the Legal Service (much less the slides that it presumably produced in response to this query)—which clearly concerned questions that had emerged during legislative negotiations between the Commission and the Council—were nonetheless not disclosed. In its decision justifying that non-disclosure, the Commission acknowledged that its communications contained 'detailed and general statements about the scope and the possibilities offered by [Article 197(2) TFEU], and its relationship to other legal bases, in particular on cohesion policy [ie Article 175(3) TFEU]' in a way that is 'relevant for many pending and future proposals, in particular in the context of the future MFF preparations'.[132] The Commission or its Legal Service have never since seen fit to reveal, much less publicly defend, these fundamental legal reinterpretations in a detailed legal opinion.

Consistent with the repurposing of cohesion as a vehicle for advancing general economic-policy goals, the Commission sought to repurpose administrative support under Article 197(2) TFEU in a similar way: 'One reason for the slow implementation of reforms', the Commission explained in its Explanatory Memorandum, 'is low administrative capacity'.[133] Thus, the Commission relied on the combination of Articles 175(3) and 197(2) TFEU as a means of supporting 'cohesion, competitiveness, productivity, growth, and employment'.[134] The Commission would do the same in the successor instrument under NGEU, known as the Technical Support Instrument (TSI), adopted in February 2021 in conjunction with the RRF to support the implementation of NRRPs in the Member States.[135] But in doing so, the TSI, like the RSP before it, would depend on a sort of inverted subsidiarity logic. Matters falling under national competence (structural reforms, or the lack thereof) are used to *justify*, rather than constrain, EU intervention.[136] The logic of 'positive incentives'[137] is not just to support

[130] Ares(2019)804472, Document 5a attached to European Commission (2024a), email exchange of 22 January 2016.

[131] We return to this point in the Conclusion, nn 91–92 and accompanying text.

[132] European Commission (2024a, p 14).

[133] European Commission (2018a) [RSP Proposal], Explanatory Memorandum, sec 1, first bullet point ('Reasons for and objectives of the proposal').

[134] Ibid, Explanatory Memorandum, sec 2, first bullet point ('Legal basis').

[135] See Regulation (EU) 2021/240. In its proposal for the TSI in 2020, the Commission justified the combined legal basis under Articles 175(3) and 197(2) TFEU as a means of 'enhancing cohesion, through measures that allow recovery, resilience and convergence in/of the Member States concerned'. See European Commission (2020e) [TSI Proposal].

[136] European Commission (2020e) [TSI Proposal].

[137] See Chapter Two, nn 214–47 and accompanying text.

national competences but in fact to give the EU a leading role in steering their exercise towards ends that Union institutions deemed appropriate.

d. The Budgetary Instrument for Convergence and Competitiveness (BICC)

There is one final episode in the euro-area budget saga that we need to explore. While the RSP and EISF proposals were making little progress in the Union legislature, the Eurogroup and, bilaterally, France and Germany, continued to discuss ways to unify these two elements into a single programme. In November 2018, the two countries issued a joint declaration (the 'Meseberg Declaration'),[138] which endorsed the idea of a euro-area budget line. The Eurogroup included the idea in its report to the December 2018 Euro Summit, asking for and receiving a mandate to begin working on a broader Budgetary Instrument for Convergence and Competitiveness, along with a parallel 'voluntary' instrument for ERM II Member States. The Euro Summit envisaged the BICC as:

> part of the EU budget, coherent with other EU policies, and subject to criteria and strategic guidance from the euro area Member States. We will determine its size in the context of the MFF. The features of the budgetary instrument will be agreed in June 2019. The instrument will be adopted in accordance with the legislative procedure, as foreseen by the Treaties, on the basis of the relevant Commission proposal to be amended if necessary.[139]

Accordingly, in June 2019, after the Eurogroup had converged on a term sheet,[140] the Commission advanced the proposal for the BICC.[141] The BICC was to serve as a comprehensive vehicle for the euro-area budget, providing its Member States with financial grants, not only as reward for reforms as in the RDT, but—as a modest nod to the EISF—also to finance public investments. It envisaged a process whereby Member States would submit projects for reforms and investments, linked to National Reform Programmes.[142] Like the Convergence and Competitiveness Instrument of 2013 before it,[143] the BICC also relied on seemingly contractual features to justify its broad reach into domains of national competence.[144] In this sense, the BICC took cognisance of the limitations of a top-down, command-and-control approach in the

[138] Meseberg Declaration (2018).
[139] Euro Summit (2018).
[140] Eurogroup (2019).
[141] European Commission (2019a) [BICC Proposal].
[142] Council of the European Union (2019a).
[143] See Chapter Two, nn 235–36 and accompanying text.
[144] As the Commission explained in the 'Subsidiarity (non-exclusive competence)' section of its Explanatory Memorandum accompanying European Commission (2019a) [BICC Proposal]: 'The strategic orientations and country-specific guidance to be adopted under this proposal are limited to providing guidance to the euro-area Member States, while the choice of actual reforms and investment remains with the Member State concerned. As a result, the proposed Regulation does not prejudice the right of each Member State to decide what action is necessary or opportune to be undertaken at national, regional or

European Semester in favour of more bottom-up initiative from the Member States, and in so doing promoting greater national political ownership and legitimacy. In turn, the BICC would also stress the seemingly transactional character of the programme, arguably trying to shore up its tenuous legal underpinnings.[145]

The redacted documents disclosed by the Commission in response to our public access requests show that legal discussions surrounding the BICC between December 2018 and June 2019 also examined the appropriate legal basis for the new instrument. According to the Commission's own characterisation, those documents included 'correspondence regarding the limits of the use of a legal basis that was not eventually used in the legislative proposals tabled by the Commission',[146] as well as 'preliminary legal advice—not validated by the Legal Service hierarchy—regarding the possibility to combine different legal bases'.[147] The BICC's specified legal bases were ultimately Articles 121(6) and 136 TFEU, authorising establishment of multilateral surveillance procedures to coordinate budgetary and economic policies. However, spending under the BICC would also require '[a]n enabling clause to be included in the Regulation based on Art[icle] 175 [TFEU]'.[148] The disclosures in response to our public-access request further confirm that the BICC envisioned an accompanying regulation based on Article 175(3) TFEU.[149] Moreover, the subject line of the legal opinion of the Council Legal Service on the BICC acknowledged the same need, referring to the 'compatibility of the [BICC's] proposed allocation method with the cohesion legal basis (article 175, 3rd paragraph, TFEU)'.[150]

This allocation method, however, presented a legal challenge that implicated the classic obstacle in the political economy of the EU budget—*juste retour*—or what each Member State would receive from the instrument relative to their contributions to the general EU budget.[151] Relying on the approach created for the RSP, the BICC would allocate the funding based on a complex formula tied, inter alia, to relative population and the inverse of GDP per capita of each Member State.[152] Several Member States

local level; the proposed Regulation respects the principle that the implementation of reforms and investment remains a national competence and the Member States are responsible for it at the appropriate level of government'.

[145] See this chapter above, n 127 and accompanying text. See also this chapter below, nn 282–83 and 291–94 and accompanying text.

[146] European Commission (2024a, p 14), characterising Document 1c, Ares(2019)2779415, 'E-mail exchange regarding BICC financing—bullet points for future note'.

[147] Ibid, characterising Document 2a, Ares(2019)2908188, 'BICC—Exchange of e-mails of 30 April 2019'.

[148] Council of the European Union (2019b).

[149] See this chapter above, n 74 and accompanying text, discussing Ares(2019)2908188, Document 2b attached to European Commission (2024a), 'Budgetary Instrument for Convergence and Competitiveness: Issues note for internal discussion' (24 April 2019); Ares(2019)2908188, Document 2c to European Commission (2024a), 'Budgetary Instrument for Convergence and Competitiveness: Issues note for internal discussion' (26 April 2019).

[150] Council Legal Service (2020b).

[151] See Chapter Two, nn 111–14 and accompanying text.

[152] Council Legal Service (2020b, paras 12–14, 22–23). The insertion into the calculation of inverse GDP per capita responded directly to a concern raised by Council Legal Service in its RSP opinion that the allocation key must, to serve the purposes of cohesion, include 'parameters linked to the relative degree of

were concerned that this allocation method would thus 'incorporate a refunding or "*juste retour*" logic' that 'would put at jeopardy the cohesion objectives of the instrument' (italics in original).[153] The concern was entirely understandable in view of established understandings of the limits of the cohesion flexibility clause in the existing case law.[154]

Specifically regarding the dimensions of the allocation criteria that suggested reliance on a *juste retour* logic, the Council Legal Service in the end concluded that those dimensions were unproblematic, in ways that are illuminating for our purposes. According to the opinion, the allocation method:

> can be reconciled with the cohesion purposes of the proposal, bearing in mind the very specific nature of this cohesion instrument which aims at bringing convergence and competitiveness within the euro area through the implementation of reforms and investments. Actually, in an area so economically integrated as the one of the monetary union, the implementation of eligible reforms and investments by bigger economies (i.e., those with the higher share of [Gross National Incomes]) may have a more significant impact in bringing about the overall convergence and competitiveness of the euro area as a whole.[155]

Thus, by rationalising sending money to the centre—that is, 'bigger economies (i.e., those with the higher share of [Gross National Incomes])'—the transformation of cohesion policy was now essentially complete. It turned into a tool to pursue general economic policy goals like 'convergence and competitiveness' across the EU as a whole, without any regard for the particular needs of disadvantaged regions.[156]

This is where the matter stood when, in spring 2020, the demands of the Covid crisis led to the withdrawal of the BICC (and hence the euro-area budget proposals) in favour of the NGEU package. But the proposals for a euro-area budget lived on as the foundations for the new crisis instruments. As the Commission specified in its proposal for the RRF in May 2020, the new spending programme took 'as a basis the latest text discussed by the co-legislators on the proposal establishing a Reform Support Programme ... and makes appropriate changes to it to reflect the revised objectives, and the adjusted delivery mode of the new instrument'.[157] And undoubtedly

prosperity of Member States'. Council Legal Service (2019b, para 33). For further discussion of the role of this factor in the allocation key under the REPowerEU Regulation of 2023, see Chapter Five, nn 63–65 and accompanying text.

[153] Council Legal Service (2020b, para 25).

[154] Case C-166/07, *IFI* (2009).

[155] Council Legal Service (2020b, para 27).

[156] This shift in funding towards wealthier areas was not without precedent, stretching back to the reorientation of cohesion policy in 2006 in line with the goals of the Lisbon strategy in 2000. See Chapter Two, nn 209–10 and accompanying text. See also Díez Sánchez (2025, pp 22–23) (discussing developments after 2007 '[i]nfluenced by the Lisbon agenda for growth and jobs').

[157] European Commission (2020b, pp 1–2) [RRF Proposal].

the still-secret analysis of Article 175(3) TFEU as both the legal basis for these earlier measures as well as the sole legal basis of the RRF lived on as well.[158]

3. Article 175(3) TFEU Transformed: Completing EMU Without Treaty Change?

When we think back to the puzzle with which we began this chapter—why did the legal analyses published by the Commission and Council in the lead up to NGEU in the spring of 2020 not address Article 175(3) TFEU as a legal basis of the RRF?[159]—the answer to that question should now be clear. The legal services of both institutions apparently believed, on the basis of the analyses undertaken in connection with the euro-area budget proposals, that the question had already been answered and did not need to be revisited in the context of NGEU. This transformation was accomplished without any public debate about whether Article 175(3) TFEU could sustain the weight now being placed on it. From the comparatively meagre €25 billion in grants for the RSP or €30 billion in loans and interest-rate subsidies for the EISF, the RRF would up the ante twelvefold to a total of €672.5 billion (at 2018 prices), distributed to all Member States, as either grants (up to a total of €312.5 billion in 2018 prices) or loans (up to a total of €360 billion in 2018 prices).

What is strange, however, is that in the interim between euro-area budget proposals and the advent of the Covid crisis giving rise to NGEU, the Council Legal Service issued another (much overlooked) opinion of 2 March 2020; that is, on the cusp of, but still before, the full-blown Covid crisis. The March 2020 opinion took a much stricter line in policing the limits of Article 175(3) TFEU, albeit completely outside the economic policy context.[160] That opinion dealt with a 2018 Commission proposal to set up a legal framework to resolve disputes between Member States regarding cohesion projects of a cross-border character, in which the legal basis was Article 175(3) TFEU.[161] In this context (obviously less weighty than the euro-area budget proposals or those coming under NGEU), the Council Legal Service addressed a question on which it had remained silent in all the preceding opinions: 'the extent to which an act based on the cohesion legal basis can affect national institutional and procedural autonomy' as well as also possibly 'conflict with other policies laid down in the Treaties'.[162] As the opinion noted, the mechanism in question could 'apply to any field or subject in an unqualified manner', which potentially opened 'its scope to remits other than cohesion for which the Treaties may establish specific EU competences and procedures, or for which the Union would hold no competence at all'.[163] In view

[158] See this chapter below, nn 321–29 and accompanying text.
[159] See this chapter above, nn 16–21 and accompanying text.
[160] See Council Legal Service (2020c).
[161] European Commission (2018f).
[162] Council Legal Service (2020c, p 7, para 20).
[163] Ibid, p 16, para 47.

of these risks, Article 175(3) could not serve as the legal basis without 'a number of significant adaptations' in the proposal.[164]

Aside from its restrictive conclusion, the reasoning of the March 2020 opinion was also pertinent. The Council Legal Service determined that the flexibility clause in Article 175(3) TFEU had 'a subsidiary character with respect to other legal bases in the Treaties and the measures decided under other such Union policies'.[165] This character was an extension of the 'one way relationship between cohesion and other Union policies', in which other policies are required to take the developmental needs of cohesion into account, but cohesion could not be used as a stand-alone basis with the 'aim of achieving the Union objectives in other policy areas'.[166] This opinion was exceptional also because the Council Legal Service does not typically go out of its way to address whether the EU is potentially reaching beyond its competence. This opinion is equally interesting because the same unit within the CLS—on 'Economic and Financial Affairs, Budget, Structural Funds'—likely had opined on this instrument as well as the euro-area budget proposals, and its opinions would have been carefully coordinated in the Legal Service.[167] The stakes of openly engaging with competence questions were significantly lower in a technical file involving cross-border administrative cooperation.

As we shall see later in this chapter and discuss further in the Conclusion, the legal design of NGEU (and more particularly the RRF) ignored several pertinent legal bases that could have supported at least some of the RRF spending (though most of that spending would be nakedly dependent on the expansive reinterpretation of the cohesion as their sole means of support).[168] Moreover, the opinion of March 2020 also suggested that much deeper scrutiny of the legal effects and scope of application of any mechanism adopted under Article 175(3) TFEU (as compared to the euro-budget proposals) would be required.[169] Finally, as noted above, even in its earlier opinions on both the RSP and EISF, the Council Legal Service expressed some concerns that Article 175(3) TFEU could be misused to support 'autonomous measures and procedures of economic coordination', not just in the formulation of a programme but also its implementation over time.[170]

Leo Flynn, a member of the Commission Legal Service, writing in a personal capacity in an academic working paper in 2019, presented cohesion policy as a way to fill the 'gaps' in the 'famously incomplete' and asymmetrical EMU.[171] The timing of

164 Ibid, p 22, para 63.
165 Ibid, p 10, para 28.
166 Ibid.
167 For further details on this coordination, see Leino-Sandberg (2021a, pp 212–13).
168 See this chapter below, n 316 and accompanying text, and Conclusion, Section D.
169 See Council Legal Service (2020c, p 10, paras 44–50) accessed. In this regard, the March 2020 opinion explicitly sought to follow the approach defined by the CJEU in *IFI*. See, eg, Council Legal Service (2020c, p 10, para 29), quoting case C-166/07, *IFI*, para 46. In response, the European Commission submitted a new proposal to address these concerns by narrowing its legal effects and scope of application in order to retain Article 175(3) TFEU as its legal basis. See European Commission (2023f).
170 See this chapter above, nn 119–22 and accompanying text. See also, regarding the design of the RRF specifically, this chapter below, n 303 and accompanying text.
171 Flynn (2019, p 60).

that public intervention was likely not coincidental. It was consistent, rather, with a strategy of the Commission Legal Service to float, before a favourable academic audience, its new reading regarding the dramatically expanded scope (and potential) of the cohesion flexibility clause in Article 175(3) TFEU. Cohesion, in his reading, offered a means of transcending limitations in the Treaties (notably Article 121 TFEU) that restricted EU economic-policy competence to 'coordination' of Member State policies only.[172] He argued that 'Union institutions [could] take another route' to making economic policy in their own right, via cohesion. 'The fact that the effects of the [cohesion] measure will have an impact on economic policy does not mean that the use of [cohesion policy] constitutes a circumvention of the limitations associated with Article 121 TFEU', he reasoned.[173] He based this argument on the fact that the CJEU, in the context of reviewing the legality of ECB monetary policy measures, had ruled that these did 'not fall into the sphere of economic policy for the sole reason that they may have indirect [economic-policy] effects'.[174] He argued, therefore, that cohesion policy should enjoy the benefit of the same logic, regardless of the fact that its purportedly 'indirect' economic-policy effects were 'foreseeable' (or, frankly, intended) and thus obviously quite 'direct'.[175]

Such reasoning would effectively allow cohesion to overtake economic policy without limit. In doing so, it ignored the strictures of the CJEU in *IFI* on the limits of using 'specific measures' under the cohesion flexibility clause for these sorts of ancillary general economic purposes[176] (a view that would later be echoed by the Council Legal Service in March 2020).[177] There was a deeper risk to this approach, however, which derived from reliance on the open-ended reasoning of the Advocate General in *IFI* that the Court itself did not adopt.[178] According to the Advocate General, the cohesion flexibility clause should be teleologically interpreted 'as a device for restoring a balance and for redistribution among the Member States' and as 'an expression of solidarity between them and their peoples'.[179]

This approach ignored, however, the constraints that the Treaties impose on the exercise of EU power at the level of *actual actions*.[180] Instead, the open-ended teleological approach takes the authorisation of 'necessary' and 'specific' actions 'outside the Funds' under Article 175(3) TFEU and ratchets them into a *general* spending

[172] Ibid, p 48.
[173] Ibid.
[174] Ibid, citing Case C-62/14 *Gauweiler and others* (2015), and Case C-493/17 *Weiss and others* (2018).
[175] Flynn (2019, p 49).
[176] See this chapter above, nn 58–59 and accompanying text, discussing Case C-166/07, *IFI* (2009), paras 59 and 62. Flynn was aware of *IFI* but characterised its holding at the highest level of generality, glossing over its more demanding features. He thus asserted that the Court found that '[m]easures contributing to economic cohesion in Ireland and Northern-Ireland [could] contribute to the peace process and thus to the overall development of the Union as a whole'. Flynn (2019, p 31). He failed to note that the Court had in fact found that 'the range of activities financed by the contested regulation would extend beyond the scope of [cohesion policy]'. Case C-166/07, *IFI* (2009), para 63.
[177] See this chapter above, nn 165–68 and accompanying text.
[178] See this chapter above, nn 51–54 and 87 and accompanying text.
[179] Opinion of Advocate General Bot, Case C-166/07, *IFI* (2009), para 85.
[180] See Lindseth and Leino-Sandberg (2024b).

clause to do, in effect, anything *desirable* in the interest of European integration *writ large*.[181] Specificity and necessity, and the implied limits on supranational authority that comes with them, were effectively jettisoned. What emerged was, in effect, a system of 'cohesion without limits'.[182]

B. Emergency Foundations: Stretching (and Straining) Article 122 TFEU

As discussed in Chapter Two, the emergency powers of Article 122 TFEU played an important, but ultimately secondary, role in the context of the euro crisis at the outset of the 2010s. This more limited role flowed both from the peculiar features of the two subsections of Article 122 TFEU (which we will revisit later), as well as from the restrictive interpretation of Article 122 TFEU in *Pringle* in 2012 that limited its utility in that particular emergency context.[183] Article 122 TFEU played, however, an even more significant (and expanding) role in the response to the Covid crisis in the spring of 2020 and, thereafter, in the construction of NGEU—serving, most prominently, as the legal basis for the European Union Recovery Instrument and indeed beyond.

Recourse to Article 122 TFEU was not only legally but also symbolically important. The use of the phrase 'in a spirit of solidarity between Member States' in Article 122(1) TFEU contributed to what some observers saw as the emergence of a second EU 'solidarity clause',[184] an economic counterpart to the more well known solidarity provision in Article 222 TFEU in the context of terrorism or natural as well as man-made disasters. This new appreciation of Article 122(1) TFEU was part of an important discursive shift in EU economic governance away from an emphasis on the 'responsibility' of Member States (as in the euro crisis) towards a new form of 'solidarity' among all Member States (as in the Covid crisis).[185] This discursive shift contributed to the speed with which the crisis response was constructed in the spring of 2020 (no doubt building on models developed over the prior ten years).

The euro crisis also required rapid and sometimes improvised action ('whatever it takes', in the famous words of then-ECB President Draghi in July 2012).[186] But the institutional and policy response to the euro crisis was assembled largely over a period of two years, between 2010 and 2012. By contrast, the elements of what would become NGEU took recognisable shape over a period of just two months between mid-March and late-May 2020,[187] emerging quite rapidly after lockdowns had become

[181] See this chapter below, nn 326–27 and accompanying text.
[182] See this chapter below, nn 324–30 and accompanying text.
[183] See Chapter Two, nn 22–28 and accompanying text, discussing Case C-370/12, *Pringle v Government of Ireland and others* (2012).
[184] Ioannidis (2020, p 5).
[185] Ibid, p 1.
[186] Draghi (2012).
[187] See European Commission (2020d).

widespread and Angela Merkel had famously declared Covid to be 'the biggest challenge since the second world war'.[188] In that two-month interim, there were a series of emergency measures that, while clearly justified by the immediate circumstances of the Covid crisis, also clearly linked back to debates and tensions that emerged over the prior decade. These included both the response to the euro crisis as well as, more deeply, the construction of EMU and the European Semester under the Stability and Growth Pact.[189] The most obvious example was the activation of the general 'escape clause' in the SGP on March 2020.[190] This certainly reflected 'lessons from the sovereign debt crisis' about 'the importance of counter-cyclicality and coordinated fiscal stimuli in times of economic downturn'.[191] But it also came on the heels of the decision at the beginning of February 2020—that is, before the onset of the Covid crisis—to launch an overall reassessment and revision of European economic governance because of its widely recognised dysfunctionality.[192]

The activation of the SGP escape clause, together with the dramatic relaxation of the EU's state aids rules on the same day in March 2020,[193] had the effect of addressing the first half of the constitutional contradiction that had become apparent in the EU over the course of the polycrisis: the legal limits imposed on national institutions 'in the exercise of their [own fiscal] constitutional authority'.[194] However, by lifting those limits and thus looking to the Member States as the initial sources of fiscal stimulus to address the crisis, the approach necessarily triggered two additional side effects. The first was the usual reliance on the ECB to support public and private sector bond markets, this time through the new Pandemic Emergency Purchase Programme (PEPP), which by the end of 2020 would reach an envelope of €1,850 billion.[195] The second was the intensifying frustration of many less financially secure Member States with the unevenly distributed fiscal space in the EU to take advantage of either the relaxed state-aid/fiscal constraints or the monetary-policy support from the ECB in response to the crisis.[196] Even as both these steps allowed the Member States to pump nearly €2 trillion into the economy by early May 2020, *The Economist* reported that '[h]alf of

[188] Henley and Oltermann (2020).

[189] The scholarly literature has covered these events in detail, generally adopting the emergency-response framing, albeit with varying degrees of nuance about linkages to the past. See, eg, Dermine (2020, pp 2–5), de Witte (2021, pp 638–42), Fabbrini (2022c, p 189); Leino-Sandberg and Ruffert (2022, pp 435–36); and Delhomme and Hervey (2022, pp 13–26). Along the latter dimension, see especially Dermine (2020) (analysing these developments, as well as those of the NGEU more generally, in terms of 'continuity and rupture').

[190] European Commission (2020f); Council of the European Union (2020).

[191] Dermine (2020, p 339).

[192] See Chapter Two, nn 65–66 and accompanying text.

[193] European Commission (2020g).

[194] See Chapter Two, n 89 and accompanying text, quoting Lindseth (2016a, p 701).

[195] See Chapter Two, n 19 and accompanying text; see also European Central Bank (2025b). The amount of the PEPP was initially set at €750 billion but was expanded by an additional €600 billion in June 2020 and a further €500 billion in December 2020, for a total of €1,850 billion.

[196] See Chapter Two, nn 97–101 and accompanying text. See also Leino-Sandberg and Ruffert (2022, p 443).

this was in Germany: a problem if you are a producer based in a country that cannot afford to be so generous, but which must accept German-made goods'.[197]

Consequently, there was increasing pressure building within European politics to address the EU's inability to 'fill the void' left by the fiscally constrained Member States due to the EU's lack of any autonomous capacity to mobilise fiscal resources on its own.[198] Soon after the crisis exploded in the first half of March 2020—with the first pandemic pictures coming from Bergamo followed by the beginning of shutdowns—the normally apolitical and soft-spoken President of Italy, Sergio Matterella, quickly called for *iniziative di solidarietà* ('initiatives of solidarity') from Italy's European partners.[199] The need for solidarity became a major theme in the discourse of many EU Member States as the Covid crisis spread, feeding directly into the political environment from which the proposal for NGEU, with its recovery fund based in part on grants, would emerge two months later.[200]

One early initiative along these lines—the Pandemic Crisis Support (PCS) credit line from the European Stability Mechanism —helped (together with ECB action) to keep lending conditions in the financial markets relatively calm. PCS was ultimately never intended to serve as a front-line source of financing, but its secondary role was nonetheless illuminating of the pressures towards new forms of solidarity. On 9 April 2020, the Eurogroup announced the establishment of this new ESM credit line,[201] which would make loans available to Member States up to two per cent of their 2019 GDP.[202] As a way to get around the legal requirement of 'strict conditionality' in ESM support (explicitly mentioned in Article 136(3) TFEU and confirmed by the CJEU in *Pringle)*,[203] access to the new credit line was conditioned solely on a commitment by the Member State 'to use this credit line to support domestic financing of direct and indirect healthcare, cure and prevention related costs due to the COVID 19'.[204] This initiative, however, was met by considerable scepticism on a broad range of grounds, not just economic and financial,[205] but also legal and constitutional.[206] Ultimately, no Member State applied for loans under the facility, which was available until the end of 2022. This was primarily because financial market conditions remained benign and thus the need for PCS support may have been unnecessary. But it was also likely because of the stigma still attached to entering into an ESM programme of any kind.[207] More solidaristic instruments were preferred.

[197] The Economist (2020).
[198] See Chapter Two, n 89 and accompanying text, quoting Lindseth (2016a, p 701).
[199] Mattarella (2020).
[200] For a contemporaneous overview of these developments, see Brunsden et al (2020).
[201] Eurogroup (2020).
[202] ESM (2022).
[203] See Chapter Two, nn 21–22 and accompanying text.
[204] Eurogroup (2020).
[205] See, eg, Erce and Corsetti (2020).
[206] See, eg, Leino-Sandberg (2020).
[207] Smeets and Beach (2023, p 386). Nonetheless, the ESM claimed that 'Pandemic Crisis Support played a useful role during the pandemic crisis by calming and reassuring financial markets that euro area countries could quickly gain access to emergency financing if needed'. ESM (2022).

It was thus no coincidence that, during this period, Article 122 TFEU would emerge as the EU's economic 'solidarity clause',[208] thus breaking with the conditionality associated with ESM funding. The Commission announced a set of initiatives in mid-March 2020 to redirect existing budgetary resources towards the crisis response.[209] These included the activation of emergency support to Member States for purchasing pandemic-responsive goods and services under Article 122(1) TFEU.[210] However, the most important early step under Article 122 TFEU—one that would come to be seen as an integral part of the NGEU model going forward—was the adoption of a €100 billion lending instrument, Support to mitigate Unemployment Risks in an Emergency (SURE).[211] Backed by guarantees from the EU budget that were in turn backed by counter-guarantees from the Member States, SURE was designed to support unemployment insurance schemes at the national level that had been depleted by the pandemic.

President von der Leyen would later call SURE 'real European solidarity in action'.[212] But SURE expressed that solidarity *legally* by almost completely collapsing the distinction between Articles 122(1) and (2) TFEU as the legal basis for the instrument.[213] Article 122(1) TFEU allows the Council, on a proposal by the Commission, to 'decide, in a spirit of solidarity between Member States' to adopt 'measures appropriate to the economic situation' in cases of 'severe difficulties arise in the supply of certain products, notably in the area of energy'. Article 122(2) TFEU is the more general emergency provision; it authorises assistance to a Member State 'in difficulties or ... seriously threatened with severe difficulties caused by natural disasters or exceptional occurrences beyond its control'. The failure to distinguish these two paragraphs in the SURE programme ran directly contrary to what the case law on Article 122 TFEU required.[214] However, even critical commentators recognised that SURE at least involved 'the type of assistance that Article 122(2) TFEU was designed for ... in the face of unexpected events' and hence could be justified.[215] More forgiving commentators argued that the justification could be 'easily found in the need to mitigate the effects of the COVID-19 crisis on public expenditures by the Member States, and in the fact that the instrument is temporary'.[216]

Such a forgiving approach became much more difficult to sustain when it came to the 'very extensive' and 'quite remarkable' reading of Article 122 on which the EURI

208 Ioannidis (2020, p 4).
209 European Commission (2020h).
210 See Council Regulation (EU) 2020/521.
211 Council Regulation (EU) 2020/672 [SURE].
212 von der Leyen (2020).
213 Council Regulation (EU) 2020/672 [SURE], preamble.
214 See Chapter Two, nn 22–28 and accompanying text, discussing the CJEU's judgment in *Pringle*. The Commission claimed in its explanatory memorandum that Article 122(1) TFEU served as the basis for 'the construction of the guarantee system' in the proposal, whereas Article 122(2) TFEU served as the basis for the 'organisation and management of the loan scheme'. See European Commission (2020i) (Explanatory Memorandum, sec 2, first bullet point 'Legal Basis').
215 Leino-Sandberg and Ruffert (2022, p 436).
216 de Witte (2021, p 654).

Regulation, as a cornerstone of NGEU, would be based.[217] There was one obvious difference between SURE and NGEU: the former relied on Article 122 TFEU 'to set up an emergency mechanism designed to finance contingency measures directly related to a crisis situation', whereas NGEU 'serves to finance a long-term strategic plan for economic recovery through structural reforms and investments'.[218] As such, NGEU 'had less to do with addressing the immediate consequences of the Covid crisis, and instead reflected Commission priorities and programs about the post-crisis ("Next Generation") EU'.[219]

The ultimate legal foundation for that long-term strategic plan is the EURI Regulation.[220] Adopted under Article 122 TFEU (again, undifferentiated), the EURI Regulation was 'a bit of an empty shell',[221] six very brief articles that served as 'the container instrument in which the total sum of €750 billion is embedded and assigned to various spending programmes'.[222] Presented as a response to the immediate emergency, the scope of the measures to which funding is allocated through the EURI Regulation—not to mention the timing of the spending extending through 2026—went well beyond the effects of the pandemic, involving amounts of money far too large to be disbursed during the acute phase of the crisis. Consequently, Article 122 TFEU was not considered a suitable basis for those spending programmes, most importantly RRF, which in the case of the latter would instead be based on Article 175(3) TFEU.[223]

This two-tiered structure of the NGEU—the EURI based on Article 122 TFEU and the RRF based on Article 175(3) TFEU—was the NGEU's most ingenious but also perhaps most legally fragile feature. The RRF's aims, based on Article 175(3) TFEU, were radically different from anything for which Article 122 TFEU had heretofore served as the basis. As Section D below will describe in greater detail, the RRF was designed as a large-scale, multi-year, redistributive programme with varying purposes, whether to stabilise markets, advance broad political goals, or catalyse action in virtually all government sectors. Indeed, its first euro would not be disbursed until the last days of 2021, shortly before the acute phase of the pandemic was about to peter out.

How could such long-term action conceivably be justified on the basis of Article 122 TFEU? One can get a sense of the reasoning of the EU institutions by looking at the legal advice of the Council Legal Service in June 2020.[224] To us, that advice is rather unpersuasive.[225] Even as it would rely primarily on Article 122(1) TFEU to support the EURI, the advice eclectically relies on both subsections. Its animating claim is that the 'two paragraphs [of Article 122 TFEU] need to be read jointly and on the

[217] Dermine (2020, p 345).
[218] Ibid.
[219] Smeets and Beach (2023, p 390).
[220] Council Regulation 2020/2094 [EURI].
[221] Dermine (2020, p 343).
[222] de Witte (2021, p 636).
[223] See Regulation (EU) 2021/241 [RRF], recital (2).
[224] Council Legal Service (2020a).
[225] For an overview and critique, see Leino-Sandberg and Ruffert (2022, pp 445–46).

basis of the specific purpose of Article 122 in the system of the Treaty'.[226] That claim, however, is in defiance of the CJEU's established interpretation in *Pringle*.[227] The legal problems go much deeper, however, to the establishment of a long-term instrument (the RRF) by way of the EURI, the operation of which goes far beyond addressing the immediate effects of the Covid crisis. There are contributions in the scholarly literature suggesting that Article 122 TFEU might be sufficiently flexible to make the NGEU model a permanent feature of European economic and fiscal governance, without further Treaty change.[228] To the extent that the principle of conferral should still matter today, however, there is considerable room for scepticism on that point. The Council Legal Service, in its legal opinion on the EISF proposal in 2019, specifically acknowledged that Article 122 TFEU could not be used to establish a permanent mechanism.[229] Indeed, the EISF opinion went further, rejecting the use of 'cohesion policy … to support the achievement of objectives for which economic policy lays down specific instruments of financial assistance [such as] Article 122(2) TFEU'.[230] This would logically also seem to cast doubt on the use of EURI as an 'empty shell' based on Article 122 TFEU to be filled by, inter alia, the RRF based on Article 175(3) TFEU.[231]

The judgment of the German Federal Constitutional Court (FCC) in December 2022 strengthens this impression.[232] The FCC's ruling arose out of a challenge to the implementation of the 2020 ORD in Germany to which Article 122 TFEU was directly relevant.[233] The FCC stressed that Article 122 TFEU 'must generally be interpreted narrowly',[234] not least 'to avoid turning [it] into a general blanket clause with hardly any restrictions that could be invoked to authorise virtually any type of measure … '.[235] This conclusion was directly contrary to the hopes of those who see an expansive reading of Article 122 TFEU as key to building a new EU 'constitutional charter intended to endure for ages to come, and consequently to be adapted to the various crises of human affairs'.[236]

Even as the FCC ultimately accepted Article 122 TFEU as an emergency legal basis in the Covid context, it nonetheless gave credence to concerns that it was being misused to establish a 'general stimulus package',[237] and that 'the connection between the EURI Regulation and the [effort] to counter the effects of the pandemic appears tenuous'.[238] The Court deferred to the emergency programme primarily on

226 Council Legal Service (2020a, p 49 n.68).
227 Again, see Chapter Two, nn 22–28 and accompanying text, discussing the CJEU's judgment in *Pringle*.
228 See, eg, Chamon (2023b), (2023a), (2024).
229 Council Legal Service (2019a, para 42).
230 Ibid, para 32.
231 See this chapter above, nn 221–22 and accompanying text.
232 BVerfG (2022).
233 See this chapter below, nn 268–70 and accompanying text.
234 BVerfG (2022), para 174.
235 Ibid, para 176.
236 See Chamon (2023a). For further discussion, see Chapter One, n 83 and accompanying text.
237 BVerfG (2022), para 177.
238 Ibid, para 176.

the assurance of the German government and Bundestag that 'NGEU was meant to be a one-time instrument' and that it 'did not constitute a step towards a "transfer union" [marked by institutionalised financial equalisation]' (bracketed insertion in the official English translation).[239] This reasoning suggested that the FCC would not be 'equally lenient in its findings the next time'—that is, when an instrument came before it that was purportedly based on NGEU but insufficiently connected to the pandemic.[240] If true, that would pose a significant obstacle to the NGEU model becoming permanent without finding some alternative to Article 122 TFEU as a legal basis.[241]

C. The Budgetary Dimension: Reinterpreting Articles 310–311 TFEU as the Foundation for the 2020 Own Resources Decision

Understanding the budgetary dimension of NGEU requires a grasp of the complex mechanics of the 2020 ORD as well as some basic background regarding EU budgetary law under Articles 310–311 TFEU. We begin with certain basic features of the 2020 ORD we introduced in Chapter One.

The key articles of the 2020 ORD for our purposes are Articles 5, 6, and 9. Article 5 authorised the Commission to issue debt of €750 billion (at 2018 prices) over a six-year period between 2021 and 2026, which Article 5 then obligated the EU to repay over a thirty-year period, up to the end of 2058.[242] Article 6 defined the foundational commitment of the Member States to support the EU in covering the NGEU debt through an extraordinary and temporary increase in the own resources ceilings for the allocation of the resources necessary for addressing the consequences of the Covid-19 crisis, applicable until all such liabilities have ceased to exist, and at the latest by 31 December 2058. 'Headroom' is the colloquial term to refer to the difference between the maximum amount the Member States are legally obligated to provide under the 'own resources ceiling', and the lesser amount needed to cover standard budgetary appropriations or commitments over the life of the MFF. Unlike the normal 'headroom', this special increase in the own resources ceilings in the 2020 ORD cannot be used to cover any other liabilities of the Union.[243] To service these ongoing obligations

[239] Ibid, para 187.

[240] Nguyen and van den Brink (2022). The authors focused on the so-called REPowerEU programme, but one could just as easily apply their reasoning to other elements of the NGEU model which will be discussed in Chapter Five.

[241] The FCC's reasoning regarding Article 122 TFEU could also have broader implications, not least for the use of Article 175(3) TFEU as an additional legal basis for a permanent version of the NGEU model (a question admittedly not before the Court). Borrowing the language of the FCC, the expansive reading of Article 175(3) TFEU on which the RRF is based would turn that provision into precisely the sort of 'general blanket clause ... to authorise virtually any type of [spending] measure'—something the Court refused to accept with regard to the proffered expansive reading of Article 122 TFEU. See generally this chapter below, Section D.

[242] Council Decision 2020/2053 [2020 ORD], art 5.

[243] Ibid, art 6. Article 6 specified that the increased headroom of the 2020 ORD is to be used 'for the sole purpose of covering all liabilities of the Union resulting from the borrowing' authorised in Article 5.

in the first instance, the 2020 ORD added to EU own resources with a levy payable by the Member States calculated on their amount of non-recycled plastic packaging waste.[244] Additionally, the preamble to the 2020 ORD contemplated a range of potential new own resources to be instituted in the future.[245] But as an ultimate backstop, Article 9 of the 2020 ORD made the Member States' special headroom obligations 'callable';[246] that is, the Commission is legally empowered to demand that Member States provide additional funds, up to their pro rata share of the new maximum own resources ceiling, in case the EU cannot, through own resources or financial operations, generate sufficient funds to honour its obligations.[247]

The design of the 2020 ORD, particularly as it relates to common borrowing, is no doubt impressive. But how does it conform to the budgetary rules set out in the Treaty? The answer advanced by European institutions at the time of the adoption of NGEU was hardly straightforward and was, in fact, in deep tension with how those budgetary rules had been traditionally understood.[248] As we discussed in Chapter Two,[249] it had long been well-settled in EU budgetary law that the third paragraph of Article 310(1) TFEU actually means what it says: 'The revenue and expenditure shown in the budget shall be in balance'. The requirement of a balanced budget had been universally understood as precluding debt-financing for regular operations and programmes (unless, of course, the debt is counterbalanced by an asset on the EU's balance sheet, such as a debt-financed building or the receivables in a back-to-back loan to a Member State). Moreover, it had also been well-settled that the first paragraph of Article 310(1) TFEU actually means that '[a]ll items of revenue and expenditure of the Union … shall be shown in the budget'. This is known as the principle of universality. It 'reflects the long-standing belief that making all public expenditures and revenues visible, rather than hiding them in an extra-budgetary fund, is essential for good fiscal stewardship and democratic control of public spending'.[250]

These two principles—balance and universality—are foundational to EU budgetary law. So, how was it possible that the debt-financed revenues supporting

[244] Ibid, art 2(1)(c); see also recital (7).

[245] These include eg, a carbon border adjustment mechanism, a digital levy, revenues from the EU Emissions Trading System as well as, potentially, a Financial Transaction Tax. Ibid, recital (8). For discussion of the 'Fit for 55' legislative package, see Chapter Five, Section C.1.

[246] On the idea of 'callable headroom', see Chapter One, nn 48–51 and accompanying text, citing Christie et al (2021, p 2), Claeys et al (2023), European Commission (2023c, p 140 n 177).

[247] Council Decision 2020/2053 [2020 ORD], arts 9(4)–(6); see also recital (23). Further backing up this specific commitment are two additional general commitments, one in secondary EU legislation, the other Treaty-based. Article 14 of the so-called Making Available Regulation provides that the Commission has the legal right to draw on all Member States in the event a borrowing country fails to repay its loan to the EU on time. See Council Regulation (EU, Euratom) No 609/2014. Article 323 TFEU also states that the EU institutions 'shall ensure that the financial means are made available to allow the Union to fulfil its legal obligations in respect of third parties'.

[248] See, eg, European Commission (2015) ('[t]he Treaty establishes the principle of a balanced budget for the EU. Filling a gap between revenue and expenditure by issuing public debt is therefore not possible … The Commission is at this stage not envisaging submitting proposals to modify the Treaty [to overcome this limitation]').

[249] See Chapter Two, nn 166–67 and accompanying text, discussing European Commission (2015).

[250] Leino-Sandberg and Ruffert (2022, p 453).

grants under the NGEU ('borrowing for spending'), which have no counterbalancing asset on the EU's balance sheet, have not appeared on the EU's budget, throwing it wildly out of balance? This answer exploits a heretofore marginally used exception to the universality principle in Article 311(2) TFEU (involving so-called 'other revenue'), combined with 'external assigned revenue' (EAR) defined in Article 21 of the EU's Financial Regulation.[251]

Article 311(2) TFEU states: 'Without prejudice to *other revenue*, the budget shall be financed wholly from own resources' (emphasis added). The provision is generally understood to mean that certain categories of 'other revenue' or the payments made from them are neither revenues nor expenditures within the meaning of Article 310(1) and are thus not subject to the principle of budgetary balance or universality. One such off-budget category is 'external assigned revenue', which includes many subcategories under Article 21 FR but typically refers to money collected from external sources for particular programmes; for example, contributions to EU programmes from participating third countries (eg EFTA countries), contributions from candidate countries (eg to the EU Neighbourhood Policy), or from Member States voluntarily contributing to certain other actions (eg to the Facility for Refugees in Turkey).[252]

Before the adoption of NGEU, 'EAR [was] an accepted and arguably necessary component of EU budgetary arrangements'.[253] It was also miniscule relative to the overall budget, amounting to €2.2 billion in 2019 and €4.4 billion in 2020.[254] With the coming into effect of NGEU in 2021, however, this category was massively expanded. The EURI Regulation, adopted pursuant to Article 122 TFEU, formally specified that the €384.4 billion raised from bond sales under the 2020 ORD earmarked for grants to the Member States under the RRF 'shall constitute external assigned revenue'.[255] While Article 21(5) FR technically authorises a 'basic act' like the EURI to make such a designation, the scale here was unprecedented and destabilising from the standpoint of budgetary integrity.

To justify this 'accounting trick of gigantic proportions',[256] both the Commission and the Council Legal Service floated a range of arguments that were questioned both inside and outside EU institutions.[257] At the most basic level, the proffered justification was highly formalistic: because external assigned revenues, by definition, 'do not form part of the appropriations "provided" in the budget', then 'by [their] very nature [they] cannot jeopardize the budgetary balance'.[258] While such formalistic

[251] Regulation (EU, Euratom) 2018/1046 [Financial Regulation].

[252] See Begg, et al (2022, p 29).

[253] Ibid, p 65.

[254] Ibid, p 10.

[255] Council Regulation 2020/2094 [EURI], art 3(1). This was also, it should be noted, the budgetary technique that the Commission envisioned using in its 2013 proposal for a 'Convergence and Competitiveness Instrument' to finance incentives to the Member States to adopt structural reforms. See Chapter Two, nn 244–45 and accompanying text.

[256] Dermine (2020, p 349).

[257] Leino-Sandberg and Ruffert (2022, pp 452–55) provides a detailed overview. Much of the subsequent discussion draws from this source.

[258] Council Legal Service (2020a, p 20, paras 33–34).

reasoning did indeed address concerns over balance, albeit tenuously, it did so 'at the expense of increasing the tension with the principle of universality ... which requires that all revenue and expenditure be shown in the budget'.[259] There is a clear difference between the historical practice of designating small revenue streams as external assigned revenues and channelling a massive borrowing and spending programme amounting to hundreds of billions of euros under the same rubric. Common borrowing under NGEU has created huge contingent liabilities—interest and repayment obligations—that the regular EU budget needs to bear going forward (a topic of major importance when we reach the Commission's 2028–2034 MFF proposals in Chapter Six).[260] Unless and until the EU, together with the Member States, adopts the additional new own resources to cover these obligations—or invokes, as a last resort, the Member States' callable headroom obligations—those interest and repayment liabilities exert massive downward pressure on the EU's regular budget.[261] Consequently, formalistically taking refuge behind external assigned revenues for balance purposes was arguably reckless and directly undermined the aims of good fiscal stewardship and democratic control at the heart of the universality principle.[262]

Given the weakness of this formalistic justification, the institutions advanced a more substantive claim: that, in effect, the legally binding character of the Member States' commitments under the 2020 ORD meant the contingent liabilities really ultimately belonged to the Member States. The Commission, for example, argued that the Member States' approval of the 2020 ORD 'will constitute [their] clear commitment to bear the liability from the borrowing'.[263] The Council Legal Service, for its part, claimed that the dedicated increase in the own resources ceiling in the 2020 ORD earmarked for servicing NGEU borrowing 'becomes an *irrevocable, definitive and enforceable guarantee of payment* that is given upfront by the Member States' and therefore constitutes 'a *credible and solid asset*, thereby *ensuring the budget neutrality*' (emphasis in original).[264] The obvious retort, however, was that, 'if the ORD constitutes a claim on Member States, and hence an asset for the Union, it would seem logical that it also constitutes a liability for the Member States'.[265] When asked to consider the claim, Eurostat, the EU's statistical agency, rejected it, concluding: 'The EU itself will absorb the liability, such that the financing ... is to be considered at present as a liability of the EU Budget and a contingent liability for the Union budgetary planning'.[266] It is hard to escape the conclusion that 'the Union is the real, final debtor, rather than merely a clearing house for affordable financing for Member States in

[259] Leino-Sandberg and Ruffert (2022, pp 452–53).
[260] See Chapter Six, Section B.
[261] See Draghi Report (2024b, p 289).
[262] Leino-Sandberg and Ruffert (2022, p 454).
[263] European Commission (2020a) [Q&A].
[264] Council Legal Service (2020a, p 20, paras 43–44).
[265] Leino-Sandberg and Ruffert (2022, p 454).
[266] Eurostat (2021, para 42) (original from 17 November 2020 is no longer available online).

trouble.'[267] Indeed, that is the very purpose of the common borrowing at the heart of the NGEU model.

The only argument left to the institutions in these circumstances was one grounded in an expansive reading of Article 122 TFEU's emergency powers in light of the demands of the Covid crisis. Despite the fact that Article 122 TFEU specifically opens with the proviso '[w]ithout prejudice to any other procedures provided for in the Treaties', the Commission nonetheless argued:

> Article 122 TFEU allows for targeted derogations from standard [budgetary] rules in exceptional crisis situations. On that basis, the [EURI Regulation] will provide for the financing, by reference to the authorisation to borrow provided by the [2020 ORD], and will assign those funds to the various spending programmes, as so-called 'external assigned revenues' [pursuant to Article 21(5) FR], for the purposes of recovery and resilience...
>
> The [EURI Regulation] is based on Article 122 TFEU [because it] allows for extraordinary measures in situations of crisis as an expression of solidarity among Member States.
>
> Recourse to that legal basis is necessary for derogating from standard Treaty rules, which would not allow the financing of such large amounts in addition to the Union's budget and outside of the annual budgetary procedure. This is justified only in the circumstances of the current crisis.[268]

The Commission also noted elsewhere in the Q&A that, with regard to the role of the 2020 ORD, it 'is of *quasi-constitutional* nature' (emphasis in original) because it 'only enters into force after approval by all Member States in accordance with their national constitutional requirements'.[269] This allowed the Commission to suggest more generally: 'This provides for the necessary democratic legitimacy ... necessary to fulfil the Union's objectives'.[270]

The Council Legal Service largely concurred that the crisis justified bending the budgetary rules, but only on a temporary and exceptional basis. It noted: 'The proposed volume of external assigned revenue for the NGEU is unprecedented and substantial'.[271] Therefore, safeguards were needed to ensure that borrowing for spending under the rubric of external assigned revenue 'cannot become a permanent mechanism or constitute a shift of paradigm in the EU budget processes and methods which would put at jeopardy the system of own resources as established by the Treaties'.[272] The Council Legal Service concluded: 'The substantial amount of external assigned revenue may, therefore, exceptionally be considered justified insofar as it is strictly

267 Leino-Sandberg and Ruffert (2022, p 452).
268 European Commission (2020a) [Q&A].
269 Ibid.
270 Ibid.
271 Council Legal Service (2020a, p 26, para 63).
272 Ibid.

circumscribed to cover measures linked to the COVID-19 pandemic and limited, in size and duration, to what is necessary to that end'.[273] Given the far-ranging nature of the spending contemplated under the RRF—extended well beyond 'measures linked to the COVID-19 pandemic'—that spending was, *by design*, not 'limited, in size and duration, to what is necessary to that end' as the Council Legal Service demanded.[274]

When we turn back to the ruling of the Federal Constitutional Court in the challenge to Germany's ratification of the 2020 ORD,[275] we find a number of concerns and a great deal of scepticism about the budgetary mechanics underlying NGEU, even as the Court decided to waive the programme through in a deferential manner. In particular, the FCC expressed deep reservations about the 'extraordinary large volume' of the borrowing.[276] Indeed, it questioned 'whether borrowing in such an amount and timeframe can still be considered an exceptional measure in relation to the EU budget'.[277] The Court followed (but also extended on) the logic of the Council Legal Service to suggest that, '[w]hen the [volume of] borrow[ing] exceeds the annual total budget of the European Union', as was the case in 2021 and 2022, 'that would certainly suggest that the authorisation violates [Article] 311(2) [TFEU]'.[278]

Nonetheless, the FCC chose to defer to the programme because the volume of borrowing did not exceed the aggregate EU budget over the full life of the Multiannual Financial Framework (MFF) for 2021–2027.[279] But in doing so, the Court added a particularly German emphasis to its (reluctant and sceptical) deference, stressing that 'the European Union is bound by the principle of conferral' under Articles 5(1) and 5(2) TEU.[280] The Court thus conditioned its deference on the expectation that the proceeds of borrowing as 'other revenue' (ie outside the budget) will only be:

> *used for the exercise of competences conferred upon the European Union* and, to that end, are from the outset *strictly assigned to such specific purposes*. The requirement that other revenue within the meaning of Art. 311(2) TFEU be assigned to specific purposes . . . *prevents the European Union from borrowing funds for tasks for which it lacks competence under the principle of conferral* in [Articles 5(1) and 5(2) TEU] (emphasis added).[281]

This suggests that mobilisation of resources as 'other revenue' outside the EU budget cannot then be turned around and given to the Member States for policy purposes falling under national competence, even as a 'positive incentive', simply to accomplish purely national ends.[282]

[273] Ibid, p 27, para 67 (citation omitted).
[274] See, eg, this chapter below, n 290 and accompanying text.
[275] BVerfG (2022).
[276] Ibid, para 190.
[277] Ibid, para 194.
[278] Ibid, para 196, citing Council Legal Service (2020a, pp 24–25, para 57).
[279] BVerfG (2022), paras 199–202.
[280] Ibid, para 126; see also para 132.
[281] Ibid, para 171.
[282] See this chapter above, nn 136–37 and accompanying text.

In other words, on the basis of the Treaties as they exist today, the EU cannot rely on the transactional character of the programme and thus claim that the tenuous legal bases for EU competence—for example, Articles 122 or 175(3) TFEU—are somehow reinforced through a voluntary request of the Member State for funding to support reforms that are ultimately within national competence to pursue.[283] The reasoning of the FCC on this point, just like the 'guarantee' and 'prevention' obligations articulated by the CJEU in *IFI*,[284] poses a significant challenge for both the design and the actual implementation of the RRF. We take up the initial design of the RRF in the section that follows, whereas the actual implementation of the RRF will be a central focus of the analysis in Chapter Four.

D. Spending Unbound: The Legal Design of the RRF

In its legal design, the RRF is a massively discretion-enhancing programme, whose main beneficiaries are the Commission, national executives, and subordinate administrators. The aim of the following three subsections is to introduce the main elements of that legal design, laying the groundwork for a much more detailed examination in Chapter Four. We begin with the RRF's effort to bring together planning and spending as a tool of European power, after which we turn to the scope of Commission discretion in the negotiation and implementation of national plans. We then conclude with an overview of the RRF's most important substantive feature: ratcheting other policy domains into the realm of cohesion, in order to inaugurate a system of, in effect, 'cohesion without limits'.

1. Planning and Spending

The RRF is a system of 'positive incentives' on steroids, using EU funding well beyond promoting structural reforms, with the effect being to augment supranational influence across a variety of regulatory domains. The RRF Regulation authorised what was, in 2021, an unprecedented increase in the scale of EU spending: an extra-budgetary fund totalling €672.5 billion at 2018 prices, distributed to all Member States across six years (2021–2026) regardless of developmental status, as either grants (up to a total of €312.5 billion at 2018 prices) or loans (up to a total of €360 billion at 2018 prices).

On the grants side, the RRF pre-defined the amounts each Member State was to receive under an allocation formula that, for the most part, paid little heed to the effects of the Covid crisis.[285] It allocated 70% of its funding according to factors unrelated to

[283] See this chapter above, nn 127 and 144–45 and accompanying text. See also Chapter Four, Section D.6.
[284] See this chapter above, nn 58–59 and accompanying text.
[285] Regulation (EU) 2021/241 [RRF], art 11 and Annexes I–IV.

Covid: the Member State's population, its inverse GDP per capita, and its average unemployment rate between 2015–2019.[286] Additionally, '[t]o avoid the concentration of resources'—that is, to ensure that each Member State gets something approaching its *juste retour*—the RRF capped the redistributive effect of these factors at certain fixed percentages of the EU average.[287] Only 30% of the funding depends on a factor that was at all Covid-dependent—'the aggregated change in real GDP for the period 2020-2021'—incorporated into the allocation formula in the year following the programme's formal adoption in 2021, in a planned updating solely to calculate that final 30% allocation to each Member State.[288]

Even though the RRF purports to be based on the cohesion flexibility clause, it neither requires national co-financing nor targets spending at deprived regions or populations—two core features of cohesion funding traditionally conceived. Rather, the RRF has operated at the level of the Member State, serving as a political deal which—outside of rule-of-law concerns particular to Hungary and Poland[289]—effectively promised *each Member State* a pre-defined share of the proceeds of the common borrowing under the 2020 ORD. The Member State could then, under Commission supervision, allocate the funding to an agreed set of projects, subject only to meeting certain overarching spending percentages defined in the RRF Regulation itself (37% for green transition/combatting climate change, and 20% for digitalisation).[290]

The specific projects—the reforms and investments incentivised by the RRF—were initially chosen by the Member State through a confidential process of negotiation with the Commission and then memorialised as milestones and targets in the Member State's National Recovery and Resilience Plan. The NRRP was the vehicle to promote national ownership of reforms and investments; indeed, the NRRP has formally operated as a voluntary mechanism through which Member States seek funding from the EU, under the administrative oversight of the Commission. In this way, like earlier proposals stretching back to the Convergence and Competitiveness Instrument of 2013,[291] through the BICC in 2019,[292] the underlying premise of the RRF was that the EU can, through spending, steer the exercise of national competences even without having supranational competence in those domains (cohesion or otherwise).[293] RRF payments were to be 'performance based'; that is, they 'depend[ed] on the delivery of the pre-agreed investments and reforms rather than the final costs incurred'.[294] RRF funding has thus operated within the framework of Article 125(1) of the Financial

[286] Ibid, art 11(1)(a) and Annexes I and II.
[287] Ibid, Annex I. Thus, one might question the assertion that NGEU enabled the EU 'to move past the recurrent logic of *juste retour* underlying EU finances'. Albuquerque Matos (2025, p 46).
[288] Regulation (EU) 2021/241 [RRF], art 11(1)(b) and Annexes I and III.
[289] See Chapter Four, Section C.2.
[290] Regulation (EU) 2021/241 [RRF], art 16(2)(b)(i) and (ii).
[291] See Chapter Two, nn 232–45 and accompanying text.
[292] See this chapter above, n 144 and accompanying text.
[293] For further discussion, see Chapter Four, Section D.6.
[294] European Commission (2023g).

Regulation,[295] discussed at the close of Chapter Two, which authorises 'financing not linked to the costs of the relevant operations'.[296] Payments under the RRF are offered purely as an incentive, to reward Member States for achieving 'previously set milestones or ... performance indicators [ie targets]'.[297]

By breaking the connection to actual costs this mode of financing opened the way for highly subjective (and potentially quite variable) determinations by the Commission as to what any particular milestone or target might actually be worth, or by what metrics the Commission could determine whether a milestone or target has actually been achieved.[298] This brings us to the second major feature on which we need to focus: the scope of Commission discretion in administering the RRF.

2. Commission Discretion

The intended scope of the Commission's discretion in the RRF, and over the NRRP process more particularly, was quite significant. It was built into the RRF's legal structure in three broad ways. The first was through the Commission's power to assess the Member State's proposed NRRP, including any subsequent amendments, subject to final approval by the Council.[299] The second was grounded in the Commission's power to monitor the Member State's implementation of its NRRP and its progress towards achieving the plan's various milestones and targets regarding investments and reforms.[300] The third was the Commission's power to authorise disbursement or suspension of payments to the Member State under the NRRP over time (though disbursement, at least, was also subject to 'tak[ing] into account' the opinion of the Economic and Financial Committee).[301]

In the drafting and assessment of the NRRPs, the RRF Regulation constrained the Commission's discretion primarily through hierarchical oversight and control by the Council, via its ultimate power to approve the implementing decision proposed by the Commission.[302] That reservation was arguably meant to address the concern raised by the Council Legal Service in connection with the euro-area budget proposals: that the Commission's 'large power of discretion' over funding decisions in these sorts of programmes might risk converting it into a 'an autonomous procedure of economic coordination' in violation of Article 121 TFEU.[303] As Chapter Four will elaborate in

[295] Regulation (EU, Euratom) 2018/1046 [Financial Regulation], art 125(1).
[296] Ibid. See also Regulation (EU) 2021/241 [RRF], recital (18).
[297] Regulation (EU, Euratom) 2018/1046 [Financial Regulation], art 125(1).
[298] This subjectivity and lack of metrics raised serious concerns for the European Court of Auditors about the exercise of the Commission's authority under the RRF. See European Court of Auditors (2022a).
[299] Chapter Four, Section A.
[300] Chapter Four, Section B.1.
[301] Regulation (EU) 2021/241 [RRF], art 24(4); see Chapter Four, Section B.2.
[302] Regulation (EU) 2021/241 [RRF], arts 20 and 21(2).
[303] Council Legal Service (2019b, paras 35–36).

much more detail, the Council's oversight, however, was heavily constrained by tight time limits (four weeks).[304] Moreover, the Commission was empowered to develop its proposed implementing decision through a largely opaque process of technocratic information and data exchange with the Member State,[305] which created major information asymmetries for the Council.[306]

During the implementation phase—that is, in monitoring the Member State's progress towards meeting the agreed milestones and targets—the RRF Regulation empowered the Commission to operate with even greater autonomy. Following the Council's adoption of the implementing decision, the Commission and Member State would then enter into 'Operational Arrangements' (OAs), 'detailing aspects of the implementation with respect to timelines, indicators for the milestones and targets, and [Commission] access to underlying [Member State] data'.[307] Where the rubber would meet the road in this system, however, would be in the actual disbursement of money to the Member State. The disbursement profile for each Member State would be set forth in the implementing decision; however, in reality it was the product of non-transparent negotiation, which in turn led to considerable variations in disbursement profiles among the Member States.[308]

Once a Member State concluded—presumably, again, after receiving informal green light from the Commission—that it had achieved an agreed milestone or target under the NRRP, it needed to make 'a duly justified request for payment' to the Commission.[309] The Commission then had up to two months to decide 'whether the relevant milestones and targets ... have been satisfactorily fulfilled'.[310] This decision belongs to the Commission; the RRF Regulation did not subject it to approval by the Council.[311] The RRF Regulation instead required the Commission to submit its preliminary assessment to the Economic and Financial Committee for an opinion on the satisfactory fulfilment of the relevant milestones and targets, to be taken into account in the Commission final assessment.[312] This process was also intended to serve, in extremis, as an informal escalation mechanism: 'If, exceptionally, one or more Member States consider that there are serious deviations from the satisfactory fulfilment of the relevant milestones and targets, they may request the President of the European Council to refer the matter to the next European Council'.[313]

304 Regulation (EU) 2021/241 [RRF], arts 20(7) and 21(2).
305 Regulation (EU) 2021/241 [RRF], arts 18–19.
306 Chapter Four, Section A.1.
307 Regulation (EU) 2021/241 [RRF], recital (70) and art 20(6).
308 See Chapter Four, Sections A.1 and B.1.
309 Regulation (EU) 2021/241 [RRF], art 24(2).
310 Ibid, art 24(3).
311 There is one exception. There are detailed rules for suspension of funding under the RRF where 'a Member State has not taken effective action to correct its excessive deficit'. Ibid, art 10(1). Formally speaking, the power of suspension in these circumstances is reserved to the Council under art 10(3).
312 Ibid, art 24(4).
313 Ibid, recital (52).

3. Ratcheting Cohesion into a Domain Without Limits

Our final point relating to the legal design goes to the substantive scope of the RRF Regulation. Here a more detailed discussion is called for, as a way of framing the subsequent analysis in Chapter Four.

The overall substantive objectives of the RRF—defined in the 'six pillars' of Article 3 of the Regulation—actually mention cohesion in only two of the pillars.[314] The real focus of Article 3 is more abstract—'policy areas of European relevance'—hence the copious references to other, more prominent goals of the first van der Leyen Commission: green transition, digital transformation, smart and inclusive growth, productivity, competitiveness, health, resilience, policies for the next generation, and so on.[315] These areas were wide enough to encompass almost any public policy field, some of which fall under EU competence while others are under national competence.[316] Indeed, some of these domains could have relied on other, more specific legal bases—for example, for green investments, Articles 191–193 TFEU; for digital transformation (at least in the public sector), Article 197(2) TFEU; for the coordination of economic policies, Article 121 TFEU. Many other policy domains covered by Article 3, however—particularly those spilling over into traditionally national domains of competence—stood nakedly dependent on the expansive reinterpretation of the cohesion flexibility clause in Article 175(3) TFEU as their sole legal basis.

And yet, as we shall see in this subsection, 'cohesion' as both a word and a concept was strikingly peripheral in the programme's substantive design. This suggests that the purpose of the RRF was not to advance common European policies (cohesion-related or otherwise) but simply to identify certain broad—and predetermined—priorities for EU funding.[317] As two commentators would later ask, was the RRF really just 'an economic stimulus at the expense of territorial cohesion?'[318] Reinforcing this impression was the fact that references to cohesion were almost completely absent from the political discourse around the RRF from its inception.[319] The programme was typically celebrated as a means, for example, to 'invest in making Europe greener, more digital, more resilient, for everyone's long term benefit', or as 'a unique chance to rebuild and revamp [European] economies for the post-COVID world'.[320]

[314] Ibid, arts 3(c)–(d).
[315] Ibid, recital (10) and art 3.
[316] See arts 4–6 TFEU.
[317] Smeets and Beach (2023, p 390).
[318] Bachtler and Dozhdeva (2021).
[319] This point was driven home for one of us when presenting at a symposium in Brussels in July 2024 (ZEW, 2024). In comments on the presentation, the then-Commissioner for Cohesion and Reforms, Elisa Ferreira, bluntly stated: The RRF is not about cohesion policy'. We agree, but this blunt acknowledgement must have come as a nasty shock to the Commission lawyers who had spent years trying to create a legal model that would support the exact opposite conclusion.
[320] European Commission (2021c) (statements by von der Leyen and Dombrovskis).

The RRF Regulation justified this broad substantive focus through what we have called the 'ratcheting strategy', under which distinct policy domains were conflated with, and hence drawn into, the realm of cohesion policy.[321] The RRF Regulation took this strategy to a new level, in which these other domains, in effect, *became* cohesion by legal fiat. Cohesion was transformed, in effect, into a policy domain without substantive limits of any kind. We see this strategy operating throughout the Regulation, whether in the recitals (eg recital (6)), in the definition of the RRF's 'general objective' (Article 4(1)), in the substantive standards governing the NRRPs (Article 18(4)(c)), or in the substantive standards governing their assessment by the Commission (Article 19(3)(c) and Annex V(2.3)).

To demonstrate how the strategy worked in the RRF Regulation, we focus here on two particularly illuminating examples. According to Article 4(1), the RRF's 'general objective' was:

> to promote the Union's economic, social and territorial cohesion *by* improving the resilience, crisis preparedness, adjustment capacity and growth potential of the Member States, *by* mitigating the social and economic impact of that crisis, in particular on women, *by* contributing to the implementation of the European Pillar of Social Rights, *by* supporting the green transition, *by* contributing to the achievement of the Union's 2030 climate targets ... and *by* complying with the objective of EU climate neutrality by 2050 and of the digital transition, *thereby* contributing to the upward economic and social convergence, restoring and promoting sustainable growth and the integration of the economies of the Union, fostering high quality employment creation, and contributing to the strategic autonomy of the Union alongside an open economy and generating European added value [emphasis added].

The word 'by' (or its variant 'thereby')[322] is doing a lot of work in this provision, converting such goals as 'improving the resilience, crisis preparedness, adjustment capacity and growth potential of the Member States', 'supporting the green transition', or 'digital transition' into instruments of cohesion writ large. The term 'thereby' then extended these disparate domains still further, into 'contributing to the upward

[321] See Chapter Two, nn 204–62 and accompanying text; see also Chapter Four, Section D.4.

[322] The three examples on which we do not go deeper here—Article 18(4)(c), Article 19(3)(c), and Annex V(2.3)—all use 'thereby' as their rhetorical instrument of ratcheting. It is also worth mentioning how otherwise isolated the mentions of cohesion actually are in the Regulation. Take, for example, the substantive standards for the NRRPs in Article 18(4). Beyond the sole element that actually mentions cohesion—Article 18(4)(c)—there are nineteen other specified elements for an NRRP, none of which mention cohesion at all, though Article 18(4)(a) requires the NRRP to 'contribut[e] appropriately to all pillars referred to in Article 3', thereby implicitly encompassing the cohesion in two out of the six pillars. Otherwise, the requirements of Article 18(4) range across, inter alia, country-specific recommendations under the European Semester, environmental policy, digitalisation, and cybersecurity. In other words, there is no effort to keep cohesion distinct from other policies; rather, the assumption is that cohesion subsumes all other policy areas in which spending is authorised under the RRF.

economic and social convergence, restoring and promoting sustainable growth and the integration of the economies of the Union, [or] fostering high quality employment creation'; indeed, cohesion even extended to 'contributing to the strategic autonomy of the Union alongside an open economy and generating European added value'. Article 4(1), moreover, spoke only at the level of the full Union or of particular Member States; it thus depended upon, and fully bought into, the dissolution of any distinction between cohesion policy and other policies geared towards improving the overall well-being of the Union or particular Member States (regardless of where they fall on the Union's developmental scale).[323]

Our second example is found in the recitals in the RRF Regulation, and more particularly recital (6), which explains how a 'lack of resilience' creates 'negative spill-over effects of shocks between Member States or within the Union as a whole, *thereby posing challenges to convergence and cohesion in the Union*' (emphasis added).[324] The idea of 'resilience'—which, as we saw earlier in this chapter, is 'a wide and vague' concept that could be strategically deployed to 'deliberately blur[] contested issues'[325]—is serving exactly that function here. By conflating resilience with the pursuit of cohesion, recital (6) effectively claimed that Article 175(3) TFEU could now serve as the legal basis for addressing, inter alia, '[r]eductions in spending on sectors, such as the education sector, cultural sector and creative sector, and on healthcare'; the lack of 'available fiscal space of Member States to take measures to mitigate the social and economic impact of the crisis'; or the need for '[s]ustainable and growth-enhancing reforms and investments that address structural weaknesses of Member State economies, and that strengthen the resilience, increase productivity and lead to higher competitiveness of Member States'.[326] Article 175(3) TFEU could thus provide the legal basis to take any action the EU deems *functionally or normatively desirable* across *any* sector).[327]

All that was left to justify the RRF from a cohesion standpoint was that the programme, at a macro level, tried to allocate funding in ways that took account of the different economic situations of the various Member States.[328] This was the justification advanced by the Council Legal Service in its opinion in support of NGEU in June 2020:

> The criteria proposed by the Commission are indicators of the difference in prosperity among the Member States and of their underpinning economic weaknesses. By allocating greater resources to Member States which are less prosperous and which have to tackle higher structural unemployment, the methodology targets

[323] Cf this chapter above, nn 101–12 and accompanying text.

[324] Regulation (EU) 2021/241 [RRF], recital (6).

[325] See this chapter above, n 107 and accompanying text, quoting Joseph and Juncos (2024, p 377; see also pp 380–82).

[326] Regulation (EU) 2021/241 [RRF], recital (6).

[327] Lindseth and Leino-Sandberg (2024b).

[328] See this chapter above, nn 286–88 and accompanying text.

> resources to the Member States which are more in need of investment and economic reforms.[329]

This justification transforms cohesion from a policy field focusing on disparities among regions or social groups *within* Member States to disparities *among* Member States—in effect, convergence—which again conflated cohesion with the integration process writ large.

Despite its tenuousness, this rationale has resonated with many advocates of the NGEU as a fundamental transformation in the nature of integration, albeit without Treaty change. As one academic favourable to this expansive reading of Article 175(3) TFEU has argued:

> A meaningful commitment to solidarity should aim at income equalization between Member States, with structural transfers from richer to poorer countries. Considering that this redistributive logic imbues cohesion policy and constitutes the rationale of Article 175(3) TFEU, which has been employed for the disbursement of NGEU funds, NGEU has become a genuinely transformative moment.[330]

The EU may well need such a transformative moment. It is doubtful, however, that a reinterpretation of Article 175(3) TFEU, without Treaty change, is the way to achieve it, certainly not on a permanent and enduring basis. Equally concerning, however, was how this approach disregards the necessary connection between the EU's delegated power and the nature of its underlying legitimacy, implicit in the principle of conferral but essential to the power-legitimacy nexus.[331] Respecting the constraints of this nexus has been key to the stability of integration over the long term. The NRRPs, as the key vehicle for national ownership in the RRF process, may have helped to mute, at least in the emergency context, some of the power-legitimacy tensions that the Commission's outsized discretion might otherwise raise. In this sense, the NRRPs may be understood as another instance in which the EU seeks to draw on the power and legitimacy of the Member States, in a *demoi*-cratic fashion, to make up for EU's own shortfalls along these crucial dimensions.[332] We turn to this and related questions in Chapter Four.

[329] Council Legal Service (2020a, p 59, para 144).

[330] Panascì (2024, p 42).

[331] See generally Chapter One, nn 41–43 and accompanying text. See also, for some of the historic effects of this nexus, Chapter Two, nn 31–80 and accompanying text.

[332] See Chapter One, n 43 and accompanying text; see also Lindseth (2016a).

Chapter Four
NGEU in Action
Planning and Spending under the Recovery and Resilience Facility

The task before us in this and the next chapter is to examine the NGEU model in action, first in terms of its own operation and then in its extension and modification in other contexts. This brings us to an important pivot point in our overall analysis. In Chapter Three, we focused on the legal engineering of NGEU in a narrow sense; that is, on how the programme was built on the expansive reinterpretation of several key Treaty provisions. In Chapters Four and Five, we turn to the broader systemic effects that flow from those reinterpretations. This is essential to understanding the NGEU model as the basis for a permanent transformation of European governance. Bruno de Witte—a scholar otherwise supportive of that Treaty re-engineering approach[1]—has rightly cautioned that we cannot simply assume a positive 'integration effect' from the NGEU; rather, we must examine the programme's operation empirically to make that determination.[2] We fully agree. Consequently, the task of this and the next chapter is to undertake such an empirical examination, with particular focus on emergent institutional and systemic dynamics.

In this chapter, we examine NGEU's dominant component—the Recovery and Resilience Facility—and more particularly the planning and spending model it establishes. This model has proven to be extraordinarily influential, as Chapters Five and Six will show, extending outward from the RRF into several other programmes, not just in traditional policy domains (eg Common Agricultural Policy) but also into those intended to address new dimensions of the ongoing set of crises: military threats, energy supply challenges, as well as economic, geopolitical, and strategic issues that raise questions about the robustness of European competitiveness in the most comprehensive sense. The planning and spending model that was first tried in the RRF has become the baseline for more general reform thinking that could eventually redefine the nature of EU governance as we have come to know it.[3] For this reason alone it is essential to examine the operation of the RRF on its

[1] de Witte (2021).
[2] de Witte (2023, pp 233–34).
[3] See, especially, the Draghi Report (2024a, 2024b), which contemplates a potentially dramatic expansion of the planning and spending model in order to address European competitiveness. See also Dermine (2024) and Lindseth and Leino-Sandberg (2024a). For further discussion, see Chapter Six, Section A.1.

European Integration in the Constitutional Borderlands. Päivi Leino-Sandberg and Peter L. Lindseth,
Oxford University Press.
DOI: 10.1093/oso/9780198949527.003.0005

own terms, in order to distil out its basic features and then subject them to critical analysis.

Cristina Fasone and Nicola Lupo have helpfully already attempted just such a distillation.[4] They suggest that the RRF marks the emergence of a new 'Euro-national' 'method of government' with three main elements: 'the setting of EU-wide priorities, their articulation in national medium-term and performance-based plans, and a continuous monitoring process carried out by the Commission to ascertain the compliance with multiple conditionality regimes'.[5] Any general distillation of this type will necessarily mask layers of complexity, and it is one of the purposes of this chapter to explore those layers in greater detail.[6] Nonetheless, the distillation advanced by Fasone and Lupo, and more particularly their general rubric—arguing in terms of a new method of *government*, not merely of *governance*—is still directionally helpful because it suggests the depth of the transformation that the RRF model may portend.

As Fasone and Lupo's terminology implies, the RRF's planning and spending model implicates a core capacity of constitutional government, that is, the mobilisation and distribution of fiscal resources.[7] The extent of that mobilisation and distribution, both as a percentage of national GDP and in the absolute amounts of RRF outlays (grants and loans), has varied across the EU. Moreover, those percentages and amounts have fluctuated as economic conditions have evolved and the implementation of the NRRPs has proceeded over time. Nonetheless, the relative hierarchy among high- and low-beneficiary Member States has remained reasonably stable. Greece has generally topped the list in terms of its allocation as a percentage of GDP, with combined grants and loans initially expected to reach 16.68%,[8] a number that has only gone up over time. In terms of absolute amounts, Italy has held steady as the largest overall recipient, with the combined grants and loans initially envisioned to be €191 billion (10.79% of GDP), or nearly a third of the total RRF outlays. At the opposite end of the spectrum are lower-beneficiary countries, including the lowest of them all, Ireland, which was allocated only a relatively small grant of €1.15 billion, amounting to just 0.23% of GDP.[9]

As the RRF has turned the EU into an increasingly important funding source (at least in high-beneficiary Member States), its potential leverage in national politics, in terms of both economic and policy impact, has potentially grown.[10] Researchers have

[4] Fasone and Lupo (2024).

[5] Ibid, p 884.

[6] For an alternative framework involving five elements (definition of EU priorities, design of national plans, EU assessment of national plans, national implementation of the plans, and EU monitoring), see Fabbrini (2025).

[7] Lindseth (2023), (2016a).

[8] For a helpful compendium of European Commission data at the time of approval in 2021, see Deloitte (2022).

[9] This number was drawn from the Recovery and Resilience Scoreboard on 18 April 2025. See European Commission (2025c).

[10] Darvas and Weslau (2023, p 29).

argued that the RRF gave 'new capacities' to the Commission, which 'in extremis' could be used as 'leverage [in national politics] in an overtly partisan way' (referring to interventions by Commissioner Gentiloni in both Italian and Spanish politics in the process of negotiating their NRRPs).[11] Others have found, at a more prosaic level, that 'negotiations with the Commission ... involved [not merely] qualitative discussions on the overall level of ambition of reforms, but also on issues of policy design, reform direction, coherence and timing'.[12] Another spoke of 'a cooperative bilateral approach to the drafting of the plans', in which the Commission nonetheless enjoyed 'an ample margin of manoeuvre to push forward its agenda and to align policy priorities at the national level'.[13]

Given this direct involvement in Member State politics and policy-making, Fasone and Lupo's rubric—emphasising a new method of Euro-national 'government'—would appear justified, especially in high-beneficiary Member States.[14] Their otherwise helpful terminology, however, nonetheless risks obscuring an important aspect of the RRF: its dependence on executive and technocratic officials, both national and supranational, as the primary actors in this 'new method'. By giving central roles to precisely the sort of actors we typically associate with the rise of administrative 'governance', the new method may not be so new at all. Rather, it appears as the extension of Europeanised administrative governance, something that has characterised the integration project since its inception.[15] And as Fasone and Lupo rightly acknowledge, the new method's 'mechanisms of democratic control and oversight ... have not [yet] been devised'.[16]

This is a major gap in the RRF model. As Paul Dermine has further described: 'the institutional underpinnings of the planning method reveal a managerial and technocratic approach ... under which direct democratic legitimacy and accountability remain limited'.[17] Equally troubling, as Dermine argues, this new method has added layers of 'constitutional uncertainty' to European integration flowing from the lack of clarity around both 'authorship' of the NRRPs (national or supranational?) as well as their 'effects' (merely political or enforceably legal?). And these uncertainties, in turn, undermine 'legal accountability and access to external review' while also creating opportunities for 'credit/blame-shifting and responsibility-diffusion'.[18] The dominance of this opaque, diffuse, technocratic, and managerial approach has undermined the RRF's capacity to achieve its own self-defined planning and

11 Miró et al (2024, p 1624).
12 Bokhorst and Corti (2024, p 727).
13 Patrin (2023b, p 249).
14 However, national governments retained powers to resist. See this chapter below, nn 445–55 and accompanying text.
15 Lindseth (2010), (1999).
16 Fasone and Lupo (2024, p 904).
17 Dermine (2024, p 985), citing Sacriste and Vauchez (2023).
18 Dermine (2024, pp 980–82). See, eg, this chapter below, nn 90–91, 102–03, 123–26, 150–60, 165–70 and accompanying text.

spending ambitions,[19] while also obscuring the many ways that the RRF process is transforming the balance between national and supranational competences.[20] It is by no means clear that the cooperative bilateralism of this 'new method' is conducive to the pursuit of European interest; indeed, as this and subsequent chapters show, it arguably is not.[21]

The analysis that follows is divided into five sections. It begins, in Section A, by examining the opaque character of the planning dimension of the RRF, in which key decisions were vested in a relatively small group of executive and technocratic officials at the national and supranational levels. The analysis then turns, in Section B, to questions of implementation and disbursement under the RRF, exploring the ways in which the spending dimension of the programme, and more particularly its performance-based model, illuminates persistent challenges regarding democratic legitimacy, performance measurement, and cross-national scrutiny. Section C examines the question of audit and control of RRF grant funding in light of the limited capacities of the Commission, with a particular eye to the challenges of implementing the 'financing not linked to costs' (FNLC) model as well as enforcing rule-of-law conditionality in the special cases of Poland and Hungary.

Section D then undertakes a detailed examination of the substantive outcomes of the RRF in action, illuminating multiple issues about its 'integration effect', including: the pursuit of green transition through national siloes in which the risks of 'greenwashing' were high and the lack of cross-border projects most strikingly visible; the questionable additionality of much EU funding under the digital pillar and beyond, often amounting to little more than (lightly) disguised budgetary support; the difficulties in incentivising reforms (structural or otherwise) through EU spending; the continuation of the ratcheting strategy, which has almost completely eclipsed traditional cohesion policy; the use of 'resilience' as a catch-all justification for spending in areas of national competence; and finally, whether and to what extent the EU may accomplish policy steering in the Member States through funding which, in view of competence limitations, it could not achieve directly by regulation. Section E then concludes by asking, among many other open questions (both substantive and institutional), whether the bottom-line yield of the RRF is ultimately a constraining debt overhang that financed a large number of primarily national projects of limited European added value.

[19] See Dermine (2024, p 987).

[20] Ibid, p 979.

[21] Among the many examples, see, eg, Chapter Five, nn 230–31 and accompanying text, discussing the European Fiscal Board's critique of the 'drift towards bilateralism' in the new Economic Governance Frameworks. See European Fiscal Board (2025, p 36).

A. Drafting and Approving the Plans: An Opaque, Technocratic Process

1. Centralised Decision-Making, National and Supranational

The purpose of using a centralised model to draft and approve the NRRPs, dominated by a small number executive and technocratic officials in the Commission and the Member States, was straightforwardly functionalist. The model was designed 'to enhance the efficiency of public policymaking through overcoming domestic obstacles and hurdles'.[22]

On the national side, the 'most visible and widespread effect [of the RRF] has been reinforcing the centralisation of authority and decision-making within national governments'.[23] The drafting and negotiation of the NRRPs were typically handled by a limited group of national officials either in the prime minister's office or the finance or economic ministries.[24] Keeping the group of national negotiators small and centralised was one means to ensure coherence, a key assessment criterion.[25] But it was also essential to ensuring that the national negotiators possessed the necessary power to respond to Commission demands, so that these could be quickly incorporated into the plans and thus raise the likelihood of a positive Commission assessment as well as quick disbursements in the future.

Authority within the Commission, at least formally, was similarly constrained, ultimately concentrated at the highest levels of the institution. As the European Court of Auditors described in a special report:

> The political governance of the RRF [took] the form of a high-level steering board, chaired by the President of the European Commission and composed of the three Executive Vice-Presidents, the Commissioner for Economy, the Secretary-General, the Head of the new Recovery and Resilience Task Force (RECOVER) and the Director-General for Economic and Financial Affairs (DG ECFIN). The steering board [has] over[seen] all steps, from early engagement with Member States on draft RRPs to implementation of the final RRPs and fulfilment of their milestones and targets.[26]

Apart from maybe a handful of high-profile cases, however, it is difficult to believe that members of this steering board could have familiarised themselves with even a

22 Bokhorst (2023, p 29); see also Vanhercke and Verdun (2022).
23 Zeitlin et al (2023, p 7; see also p 42).
24 Ibid; see further Zeitlin et al (2024, p 12).
25 Regulation (EU) 2021/241 [RRF], arts 18(4)(n) and 19(3)(k), and Annex V(2.11).
26 European Court of Auditors (2022a, p 16).

tiny fraction of the thousands of measures involved in the planning process. At an operational level, the key units were instead RECOVER and DG ECFIN. RECOVER was a surprisingly small group of officials—numbering only in the low- to mid-100s of members at any given time[27]—whose head reported directly to the Commission President. RECOVER and DG ECFIN were then charged with assembling a core country team for each NRRP to handle the 'daily exchange with Member State authorities and experts from across the Commission' that were at the heart of the negotiation process. Those country teams 'buil[t] on existing European Semester teams, but also include[d] specialists from all relevant DGs to provide the required expertise on the different policy areas covered by RRPs'.[28] But however comprised, the country teams were small. This suggests that the key actors in proposing milestones and targets under the plans were in the first instance national officials, interacting with their counterparts in the Commission.

In principle, the Commission's management of the RRF (and European Semester) was under the further oversight of the Council, which had ultimate authority to adopt the Implementing Decisions on the approval of the plans.[29] This oversight feature was not in the Commission's original RRF proposal, but the European Council demanded it as a way of introducing an important element of collective national-executive oversight and accountability into the planning model.[30] As the RRF process unfolded, however, it became clear that 'assigning the Council a prominent role in monitoring [was] in practice [going to] be very difficult'.[31] The Council's authority under the RRF Regulation was subject to tight time limits (four weeks to act on the Commission's proposed Implementing Decision) as compared to the two months allotted to the Commission from the formal submission of a plan (and prior to that, effectively unrestricted time for negotiations before the Commission green-lit the submission). Apart from the short time frame, the information received by the Council was also a tiny fraction of the interaction between the Commission and the national authorities. But more information would not have made much difference, given that the Council was hardly in a position to devote the resources even remotely sufficient to properly evaluate each Member State's performance.[32] These 'information asymmetries … ma[d]e it difficult for the Council to act as a credible counterweight', forcing it 'rather mechanically [to] follow the direction of the Commission'.[33] Consequently,

[27] As of 1 April 2024, RECOVER had 119 employees spanning 24 nationalities. The largest representations were Italian (21), French (14), and German (10), while Cyprus, Finland and Luxembourg each had zero. Additionally, 51 European Semester Officers also gave 50% of their time to RECOVER in Member States (the other 50% were given to communication activities for the Directorate-General for Communication). See Europe Direct (2024).

[28] European Court of Auditors (2022a, p 16).

[29] Regulation (EU) 2021/241 [RRF], art 20(1). See Chapter Three, nn 302–06 and accompanying text.

[30] Indeed, there were reports that Mark Rutte, the Dutch prime minister, demanded that the implementing decisions be subject to unanimity (Körner, 2020, p 3), but the European Council ultimately settled for approvals by qualified majority.

[31] Bokhorst (2023, p 29).

[32] See this chapter below, nn 200–30 and accompanying text.

[33] Dermine (2024, p 983).

RRF management was 'very much driven by the Commission, the only player able to absorb and process the plans in all their dimensions'.[34]

To appreciate those many dimensions, we should begin with the Commission's own description of the 'large and complex' character of the NRRP planning process.[35] Negotiations of the initial NRRPs in 2021–2022 usually required 'several months', 'carried out in conditions of strict confidentiality … to make progress on a document of technical and political complexity'.[36] The negotiations took place almost entirely out of the public eye, typically entailing 'thousands of documents and exchanges' starting well before the formal submission of the plan, followed by a two-month formal assessment period, which could be extended if necessary.[37]

It is here that the narrow group of Commission and Member State officials negotiated over the specific milestones and targets in the NRRPs. The Commission has argued that one of the great virtues of the planning model is how it identified 'the specific investments and reforms the Member States commit to implement', which then gave 'them full ownership to ensure a successful delivery'.[38] At the same time, this meant that there were rarely any common European projects proposed or pursued; instead, each Member State advanced its own priorities in its own national silo. Commission guidance on the preparation of the plans stated: 'Member States should describe the main challenges that they are facing under the pillars [of the RRF Regulation] and how the plan represents a comprehensive and adequately balanced response to the economic and social situation of the Member State'.[39] Given this national rather than transboundary or even European focus, the level of ambition of the chosen milestones and targets, as well as the metrics for performance among similar milestones and targets across Member States, varied considerably among the NRRPs.[40]

The typical plan involved, on average, ninety distinct reforms and investments,[41] broken down into many more specific milestones and targets.[42] Particular NRRPs, however, could include many more or significantly fewer. The Italian plan, for example, ultimately included a total of 614 milestones and targets across 67 reforms and 150 investments.[43] The Irish plan, by contrast, included only 118 milestones and targets across 11 reforms and 19 investments.[44] These components were the object of

[34] Bokhorst (2023, p 29); see also Dermine (2024, p 983). See also this chapter below, nn 247–54 and accompanying text.

[35] European Commission (2022a, p 4).

[36] European Commission (2022b).

[37] European Commission (2022a, p 4).

[38] European Commission (2023g).

[39] European Commission (2021d, p 4).

[40] European Court of Auditors (2023b, p 14, para 27, Box 1).

[41] European Commission (2022a, p 4); see also Rubio (2022, p 5) (the number of milestones and targets 'range[d] from 70-100 for the smallest NRRPs to 300-500 for the largest ones (the Spanish, Greek and Italian NRRPs)').

[42] According to Commission guidance: 'Investments and reforms [were to be] structured into a series of related milestones and targets spanning over multiple payment requests, in order to track progress with the delivery'. European Commission (2023g).

[43] European Commission (2025d).

[44] Government of Ireland (2025).

regular national-supranational and intra-Commission discussions at every stage of the decision-making process.[45] The Commission characterised the overall process as 'dynamic', involving regular requests for additional information, in response to which the Member State could revise its plan if needed.[46] Each of the national proposals could also require the involvement of different Commission experts in order to negotiate and assess the plan.[47]

An investment was defined as 'an expenditure on an activity, project, or other action ... that is expected to bring beneficial results to society, the economy and/or the environment'.[48] They could be 'direct (e.g. financing a project with public money) or indirect (e.g. public schemes to incentivise private investments, such as for example building renovations to improve energy and resource efficiency or digitalisation of small businesses)'.[49] While investments were reasonably easy to define and verify, reforms were much more difficult to pin down in measurable quantitative terms. As Commission guidance elaborated:

> A reform is an action or process of making changes and improvements with significant impact and long-lasting effects on the functioning of a market or policy, the functioning or structures of an institution or administration, or on progress to relevant policy objectives, such as growth and jobs, resilience and the twin transitions [green and digital].
>
> The aim of a reform is to structurally change parameters, address necessary drivers, or remove obstacles or other hindrances to the proper performance or to the fundamentals of fair and sustainable growth, quality employment and well-being. Reforms should also improve the framework conditions in areas such as quality of public institutions and services, as well as the business environment, research and innovation, education or social protection.[50]

Beyond certain broad parameters defined in the RRF Regulation itself (the maximum financial contribution to each Member State as well as the 13% pre-financing each Member State would receive upon approval of their plan),[51] the RRF Regulation left the Commission free, in its proposed Implementing Decision, to determine the actual amount and timing of the instalments that the Member State would receive for the completion of various investments or reforms.[52] As the Commission stressed, 'the

45 European Commission (2022a, p 4).
46 Ibid.
47 Ibid.
48 European Commission (2021d, p 16).
49 Ibid, p 17.
50 Ibid, p 14.
51 Regulation (EU) 2021/241 [RRF], arts 11 and 13. Under Article 13 of the RRF Regulation, the approval of the plan enables the Commission to 'make a pre-financing payment of an amount of up to 13 % of the financial contribution and, where applicable, of up to 13 % of the loan as set out in Article 20(2) and (3)'. This is not conditional on any of the milestones and targets actually being met.
52 Regulation (EU) 2021/241 [RRF], Annex V, sec 3.

RRF Regulation [did] not provide a methodology to set the [Member State's] specific disbursement profile',[53] though it did obligate the Commission to act 'in close cooperation with the Member State concerned'.[54] Thus, the RRF Regulation (which obviously the Commission played the central role in designing) gave it wide discretion to consider 'several factors, including the national financing needs and budgetary planning, and the proportion of milestones and targets in each instalment as well as their relative importance'.[55]

As a first step in setting the disbursement profile, the Member State provided an estimate of the total costs of the reforms and investments, which formed the basis of the Commission's determination of the overall 'efficiency' of the plan.[56] This seems to have proved a difficult task given that the Commission chose to give a uniform grade of 'B' to all plans on this criterion.[57] From there, the Commission was to determine 'the financial contribution to be paid in instalments once the Member State ha[d] satisfactorily fulfilled the relevant milestones and targets'.[58] On both of these crucial questions (along with the analysis of all other criteria for assessment), the details of the Commission's position was set forth in a Staff Working Document that accompanied the proposed Implementing Decision submitted to the Council.[59]

The determination of the amount and number of instalments, however, was by design delinked from costs. Instead, the ultimate assessment was based on the FNLC ('financing not linked to costs') model,[60] which served as the foundation of the RRF's incentive system 'based on the achievement of results'.[61] The total cost of reforms and investments only played a role in the initial phase, to ensure that the there was a correspondence between the total cost of the plan and the financial envelope allocated for it. From there on, the link to costs was cut, and no such correspondence existed between individual disbursements and the targets and milestones linked to it. This gave the Commission significant discretion to decide how much each milestone or target was worth, as measured against the total size of the financial envelope (including whether it consisted of grants or loans) as well as the total number of milestones and targets, and the nature of the reforms or investments to which the Member State committed. Moreover, much of this analysis was in fact the product of non-transparent negotiation with each Member State, which in turn led to considerable variations in disbursement profiles among the Member States as defined in the Council Implementing Decisions.[62]

[53] European Commission (2022a, p 7).
[54] Regulation (EU) 2021/241 [RRF], art 19(1).
[55] European Commission (2022a, p 7).
[56] Regulation (EU) 2021/241 [RRF], arts 18(4)(k), 19(3)(i), 20(4)–(5)(c), and Annex V, sec 2.9.
[57] For a discussion, see European Court of Auditors (2022a, pp 30–31, para 69).
[58] Regulation (EU) 2021/241 [RRF], art 20(5)(a).
[59] The SWDs for each NRRP can be found on the country pages of the Recovery and Resilience Scoreboard. See European Commission (2025c).
[60] Regulation (EU, Euratom) 2018/1046 [FR], art 125(1). See Chapter Two, nn 263–73 and accompanying text. See also this chapter above, nn 332–33 and accompanying text.
[61] Regulation (EU) 2021/241 [RRF], recital (18).
[62] European Court of Auditors (2022a, p 32, para 76).

The Commission's methods for determining the amount and timing of instalments, along with the variable disbursement profiles, would later raise concerns with the European Court of Auditors (ECA), as it spelled out in a 2022 report examining the NRRP assessment process in detail.[63] ECA noted that 'the methodology used [by the Commission] to determine the amount to be paid in a specific instalment', rather than being based on an objective metric like costs, was 'based on negotiated terms with Member States' in the NRRPs and hence 'lack[ed] transparency'.[64] ECA also found 'a significant heterogeneity in disbursement profiles' across the sampled Member States 'in terms of both the proportion of total funding in each instalment and the number of milestones and targets to be achieved for each instalment'.[65] The European Parliament's Committee on Budgetary Control would later echo ECA's critique, noting how the Commission's heterogeneous approach to defining disbursement profiles created distorted incentives for similarly situated Member States that had, for whatever undisclosed reason, negotiated their disbursement profiles differently.[66] The Commission's response to the Court of Auditors (and by extension to the EP as well) was brief and not particularly illuminating: it simply reiterated that its methodology was 'in line with the performance-based nature of the RRF' as well as the requirements of the Regulation.[67]

After the adoption of the Council Implementing Decision and the signing of the Financing Agreement between the Commission and the Member State,[68] Operational Arrangements were concluded to provide details on 'aspects of the [plan's] implementation with respect to timelines, indicators for the milestones and targets, and [Commission] access to underlying [Member State] data'.[69] While the OAs had a technical function, they were of political importance.[70] As the Staff Working Document on the Commission's mid-term evaluation put it, the OAs defined the modalities for monitoring and cooperation between the Commission and the Member State, including the verification mechanism for each milestone and target.[71] According to another description, the OAs 'establish[ed] the indicative timetable for payments and specif[ied] the type of documents or data (i.e., the verification mechanism) required to certify the fulfilment of each milestone or target'.[72] In short, the OAs defined the pathway from plan to disbursement, serving as a pre-requisite for submitting a payment request.[73]

[63] Ibid. See also this chapter above, nn 118–22 and accompanying text.
[64] European Court of Auditors (2022a, p 51, para 118; see also pp 31–32, paras 73–75).
[65] Ibid, p 32, para 76.
[66] European Parliament (2022b, p 9).
[67] European Commission (2022a, p 7).
[68] For further details on the Financing Agreement, see this chapter, n 269 and accompanying text.
[69] Regulation (EU) 2021/241 [RRF], recital (70) and art 20(6).
[70] Cf Rubio (2022, p 14) ('Contrary to popular wisdom, technocratic governance does not mean depolitisation').
[71] European Commission (2024b, p 19).
[72] Rubio (2022, p 5).
[73] European Commission (2024b, p 19).

Building on the Commission template, the OAs set forth standard provisions regarding the continued flow of information between the national and supranational levels (including regular meetings, both in person and virtual) to 'facilitate the smooth cooperation and effective implementation of the RRP'.[74] This meant that information relating to the OAs and disbursement requests were subject to same confidentiality requirements that the Commission imposed at the drafting and approval stage.[75] We examine the Commission's approach to RRF transparency—both in terms of proactive consultations and reactive access to documents—in the following two subsections.

2. Proactive Transparency: Limited and Curated

Keeping the negotiations confidential and limited to a small number of national and supranational negotiators—whether at the drafting and approval stage, or the implementation and disbursement stage—meant that outside participation and transparency, in a proactive sense, was quite limited. Our focus in this subsection is on the drafting and approval stage; we will turn to the implementation and disbursement stage below.[76]

Given the confidentiality surrounding drafting and approval of the plans, there was little public discussion reflecting broader stakeholder participation about the milestones and targets before the plans were finalised.[77] Most importantly, national parliaments were marginalised in the planning process, making it difficult for them to hold their governments politically accountable for investments and reforms included in their country's NRRP.[78] While the execution of the plan's elements would often later require legislative action, their inclusion in the plan would give them the character of a fait accompli (a topic we also consider when we get to the implementation and disbursement stage of RRF governance).[79]

Across the Member States, the space for national-parliamentary involvement at the drafting stage ranged from effectively non-existent to quite limited—in no country did the national parliament play a central or decisive role. The Bi-Annual Report of COSAC (the Conference of Parliamentary Committees for Union Affairs of Parliaments of the European Union) for mid-2021—that is, when the drafting of NRRPs was at its height—found that,

[74] See, eg, the OA for Poland, sec 1.1, set out on the Poland country page of the Recovery and Resilience Scoreboard. European Commission (2025c).
[75] See this chapter above, nn 173–77 and accompanying text.
[76] See this chapter below, nn 182–230 and accompanying text.
[77] For a rare discussion concerning football stadiums in Florence, see Kazmin (2023).
[78] Leino-Sandberg and Raunio (2023).
[79] See this chapter below, nn 188–95 and accompanying text.

> out of 33 respondents, five Parliaments/Chambers reported that the plan was presented by the government before the adoption of its draft, while another five Parliaments/Chambers reported that the draft plan was presented after the submission to the EU institutions. Four Parliaments/Chambers said it was presented after its adoption by the government but before the submission to the EU institutions ... Nine Parliaments/Chambers stated that the draft plan had not yet been presented or that it was still being drafted.[80]

As for actual national-parliamentary involvement in the drafting of the plans, COSAC's survey said it was even more 'sparse, with 31 out of 34 Parliaments/Chambers stating that they had not been involved'.[81] Self-initiated scrutiny remained possible (sixteen out of twenty-eight of the responding parliaments/chambers said they had undertaken such scrutiny at the drafting stage). However, this resulted in only six responding chambers adopting formal resolutions or opinions.[82] Moreover, there was no indication that these efforts had an impact on the planning process in any meaningful sense.

The centralised and opaque nature of the drafting and approval process also meant that other domestic stakeholders often had very little opportunity to voice their concerns,[83] even if the RRF Regulation contemplated—though did not actually require—broader consultations.[84] This lack of bottom-up participation was exceptional for a programme based on a cohesion legal basis, which was a domain with a well-established norm of multilevel governance.[85] However, it was only in a small group of countries that regional and/or local governments were given the opportunity to actively participate in the development of NRRPs.[86] Despite 'formal expressions of good intentions' in the RRF Regulation, one detailed study concluded that 'there were serious structural obstacles to deep consultation of domestic stakeholders in the drafting of the NRRPs', notably time constraints and the demands of centralisation.[87] The Commission nonetheless claimed that 'social partners, civil society organisations, local and regional authorities, NGOs and other stakeholders ... contributed to the design of the plans'.[88] 'Unfortunately', the same study found 'there [was] virtually no support' for this claim 'from other EU-level assessments', citing findings of the European Parliament, the Committee of the Regions, the EU Employment and Social Protection Committees, Eurofound, and the European Economic and Social Committee, which all contradicted the Commission's more favourable assessment.[89]

80 COSAC (2021).
81 Ibid, p 13.
82 Ibid.
83 Miró et al (2024, pp 1625–26).
84 Regulation (EU) 2021/241 [RRF], art 18(4)(q).
85 See also this chapter below, n 482 and accompanying text.
86 Ferry and Kah (2021, p 35). See also Committee of the Regions (2024).
87 Zeitlin et al (2023, p 27).
88 European Commission (2022c, p 4).
89 Zeitlin et al (2023, p 28); see also Munta et al (2024).

The Commission in fact later proved to be defensive on this point, with the head of RECOVER stating in an interview: 'It is absolutely not [our] fault. We called upon people to be inclusive and open, as we always do. It is up to each Member State to decide how they want to arrange matters and what their national rules are'.[90] In this way, 'blame-shifting and responsibility-diffusion' and unclear 'authorship' could be strategically deployed to limit or even undermine accountability in the planning process.[91] While the Commission formally called for inclusivity and openness, they designed a model that made both impossible. A part of this may flow from ignorance: many Commission officials have never worked in national administrations and thus have a very thin understanding about the intricacies and complexities of national law-making, including public consultations and parliamentary committee preparations.

Exacerbating the limited external participation at the drafting and approval stage were linguistic barriers across Member States, which derived from the central role given to national governments in generating the NRRPs in the first instance. As the European Ombudsman later noted (as part of a strategic investigation into RRF transparency that she initiated in 2022), the publication of the national plans remained the responsibility of Member State authorities, and thus the final plans were typically only available in the official language(s) of the Member State.[92] This made cross-national learning and peer-review—'pan-European scrutiny' in the words of the Ombudsman[93]—quite difficult at the drafting and approval stage (and even more pronounced at the implementation and disbursement stage).[94] The Commission produced machine-translations of NRRPs for the Council and EP; however, at the time of her report, the Ombudsman's recommendation to make machine translations more publicly available, even with appropriate disclaimers, had gone unheeded.[95]

The Ombudsman's strategic investigation of RRF transparency had much broader concerns than just these linguistic barriers. Most importantly, she found it 'regrettable that proactive transparency mainly happen[ed] only after the RRF national plans have already been approved, meaning it has been difficult for the public to follow the negotiations'.[96] The RRF Regulation included no specific requirement that any of the documents produced in the negotiation and assessment process be made public, apart from the final plans actually submitted by the Member States and the Commission's proposals for Council implementing decisions[97] (subject to any confidentiality and redaction requests from the Member States concerned).[98]

90 Pinster and Witteman (2022).
91 Dermine (2024, pp 980–82). See this chapter above, n 18 and accompanying text.
92 European Ombudsman (2023b).
93 Ibid.
94 See this chapter below, nn 231–55 and accompanying text.
95 European Ombudsman (2023b).
96 Ibid.
97 Regulation (EU) 2021/241 [RRF], art 25(1).
98 Ibid, art 25(2).

The Commission's response to the Ombudsman's strategic investigation was, in effect, to politely thank her for her efforts but then to recapitulate the limited transparency requirements that were specifically included in the RRF Regulation.[99] These limited transparency requirements allowed the Commission to present a highly curated picture of the planning and spending model in action. The Commission President set that framing early in her correspondence with the Ombudsman: 'the Commission has already made extensive material about the RRF proactively available', notably 'the Recovery and Resilience Plans by Member States ... the Commission proposals for the Council Implementing Decisions and ... the Staff Working Documents covering the Commission's analysis of the Recovery and Resilience Plans'.[100] The Commission otherwise took refuge in the national-supranational character of the planning process. This meant that, prior to the actual adoption of an Implementing Decision by the Council, the plans (and anything relating to their negotiation) could be treated as national documents.[101] It was only from the moment of their inclusion in the Council Implementing Decisions that they 'become a Union budget implementation matter'.[102] At that point, the Commission was willing to produce the Staff Working Documents or, later, the Operational Arrangements between the Commission and the Member State because both were intimately bound up with the approval and implementation of the NRRPs. Otherwise, proactive disclosure was limited to the curated set of documents that the RRF Regulation explicitly required to be disclosed. This, too, was another instance of how 'blame-shifting and responsibility diffusion' and unclear 'authorship' limited or undermined accountability in the planning process.[103]

Two other institutions—the European Parliament and the European Court of Auditors—were perhaps better positioned to push past that curated picture but only as needed to fulfil their particular oversight functions (rather than to increase transparency for the public generally).[104] The RRF Regulation requires information transmitted by the Commission to the Council to be made simultaneously available to the European Parliament, subject to confidentiality and redaction if needed.[105] The EP demanded this right of equal access during the drafting of the RRF Regulation,[106] largely to make up for its otherwise marginal role in the overall RRF decision-making process relative to the Commission and Council. This informational channel operated in parallel with, and was arguably reinforced by, the special informational rights the EP demanded and received under the Interinstitutional Agreement on budgetary matters of December 2020, which was concluded to account for EP's exclusion from any meaningful role in the adoption of the European Union Recovery Instrument

[99] See, eg, European Commission (2022d), (2023h).
[100] von der Leyen (2021).
[101] European Commission (2023h, p 3).
[102] Ibid.
[103] See Dermine (2024, pp 980–82). See this chapter above, n 18 and accompanying text.
[104] However, serious gaps existed, given that the debt part of the RRF were not audited at all.
[105] Regulation (EU) 2021/241 [RRF], art 25(2) and (3).
[106] European Parliament (2020).

(EURI) under Article 122 TFEU.[107] The EP's informational rights under the RRF Regulation were designed to support its role in 'ensur[ing] greater transparency and accountability' via the Recovery and Resilience Dialogue, also established by the RRF Regulation.[108] That Dialogue entailed a bi-monthly set of meetings (some public, some *in camera*)[109] between Commission representatives and members of the EP's competent oversight committees.

The importance of these informational channels via the EP should not be underestimated. But nor should they be exaggerated. In the best case, they have served as 'an effective instrument for information exchange and debate' but otherwise were 'a weak instrument of political accountability'.[110] They no doubt did lead to several meetings in camera with the heads of RECOVER and DG ECFIN, which could perhaps be used to probe issues relating to the planning process in ways not otherwise public.[111] MEPs also possessed additional, non-curated information through their national channels, which they could use to question the Commission's assessment.

Certainly as evidenced by its budgetary discharge resolutions, the EP was not reticent about critiquing various perceived failings in the Commission's management of the RRF as well as offering recommendations for improvement.[112] On the other hand, the documentary information available to the EP replicated what the Commission had made available to the general public on its own website or via the Recovery and Resilience Scoreboard that the RRF Regulation requires it to maintain,[113] much of which had the character of PR materials lacking detailed or illuminating analyses of strengths and weaknesses.[114] MEPs were aware that these limited informational rights constrained the scope of the EP's oversight role under the RRF, a point made specifically in an EP briefing prior to one of the RRF: 'as we do not have access to more detailed information than what is publicly available, our comments are selective and might not give credit to the full picture'.[115] In that regard, the EP's scrutiny ultimately depended, at least in an official documentary sense, on the Commission's curated picture of the RRF in action.

The European Court of Auditors, for its part, produced a crucial series of critical audit reports and reviews that pushed beyond that curated picture in important ways,[116] but only as far as the grants under the RRF were concerned. The ECA enjoyed broader access to documents and could also undertake site visits and conduct

[107] Interinstitutional Agreement (2020). For a detailed overview of the EP's understanding of its scrutiny rights under both the RRF Regulation and the Interinstitutional Agreement, see Dias (2022).
[108] Regulation (EU) 2021/241 [RRF], art 26.
[109] A pdf of these meetings (by event, date, topic, speakers, and whether public or *in camera*) is available on the EP website; see European Parliament (2024a).
[110] Bressanelli et al (2023, p 297).
[111] European Parliament (2024a).
[112] See European Parliament (2023a, para 205) [discharge of the 2021 budget], (2024b, para 286) [discharge of the 2022 budget].
[113] Regulation (EU) 2021/241 [RRF], art 30.
[114] European Commission (2025e).
[115] Magnus et al (2024, p 2).
[116] See, eg, European Court of Auditors (2022a), (2023c), (2023d), (2023e), (2023b), (2024a), (2024b), (2025a), (2025b), (2025c).

interviews, thus providing a limited but important window on the operation of the RRF model in a more granular way. Contemporaneous with the drafting and approval of the NRRPs, the most relevant was the 2022 report already discussed above,[117] which undertook an examination of the Commission's assessment of six NRRPs to better understand (and potentially improve upon) the assessment process overall.[118] As part of the underlying audit, the ECA gained access to the relevant correspondence with six Member States during the assessment process of their plans, and it interviewed staff from the Commission and the relevant national authorities.[119]

A key finding of that 2022 report was also suggestive of the opaque nature of the drafting and approval process as well as the numerous policy-political decisions embedded within it. The ECA found 'key documents ... supporting [the Commission's] final assessments were available and recorded', but that 'the documentation leading to the conclusions in the Staff Working Documents (SWDs)'—the detailed analyses accompanying the Commission's proposed Implementing Decision setting forth the Commission's overall evaluation of the plans—'was not always easily traceable'.[120] In other words, the ultimate policy decisions in the plans were disclosed but 'the reasons leading to' those policy decisions were not, or at least not necessarily.[121] ECA's resulting recommendation was that any 'key document'—including those containing the underlying reasoning– should be 'easily traceable to increase the transparency and efficiency of the process'.[122]

Given the strong emphasis of the RRF on the promotion of reforms, every step of the planning process potentially entailed important policy-political choices. In higher-beneficiary countries, for example, the drafting and approval process often involved difficult negotiations over 'politically sensitive reforms' not merely in areas 'like pensions [and the] labour market, but also justice and public administration, which require broad political support'.[123] And yet, the Commission insisted on treating the NRRPs as if they were 'a non-political, technical exercise of priority-setting and resource-allocation, guided by expertise and objective economic variables'.[124] Without disclosure or other forms of transparency, the policy-political choices inevitably embedded in the plans were buried in a process of executive and technocratic negotiation involving a very limited number of officials in the Commission and the Member State.[125] Here, too, one sees the potential of unclear authorship undermining

[117] See this chapter above, nn 62–65 and accompanying text.

[118] European Court of Auditors (2022a). The six NRRPS were those of the four Member States with the largest grant allocation in absolute terms (Germany, Spain, France, and Italy) and the two with the largest grant allocation relative to their 2020 gross domestic product (Greece and Croatia). European Court of Auditors (2022a, p 15). The audit predated the addition of REPowerEU chapters into the NRRPs. European Court of Auditors (2022a, p 14). For further details on that addition, see Chapter Five, Section A.1.

[119] European Court of Auditors (2022a, p 15).

[120] Ibid, p 18. On the role of the SWDs in the Commission assessment, see this chapter above, nn 52–59 and accompanying text.

[121] European Court of Auditors (2022a, p 48).

[122] Ibid.

[123] Bokhorst and Corti (2024, p 727).

[124] Dermine (2024, p 986).

[125] Again, see this chapter above, nn 62–65 and accompanying text.

accountability in the planning process overall.[126] ECA's criticism was effectively that, unless the underlying reasoning for those choices was traceable in the documentary record, those choices and their authors would effectively remain hidden. This, in turn, would impede accountability under the RRF's designated oversight mechanisms (the Council when adopting Implementing Decisions, or the EP in the Recovery and Resilience Dialogue) or, perhaps more importantly, by national parliaments, key stakeholders, and the general public.

The Commission formally accepted the criticism in ECA's 2022 report and promised to do better going forward.[127] But it also argued that the inevitable information asymmetries were a function of the complexity and dynamism of a negotiating process that stretched over months and involved thousands of documents and exchanges.[128] From a purely functionalist perspective, given the magnitude of the task assigned to the Commission and the time constraints under which it was forced to operate, the point was no doubt well taken. But it should again be remembered the Commission played a key role in designing the governance system of the RRF, in which it then served as both a negotiator and overseer. This made the process both more complex as well as (technocratically) opaque, rendering it essentially untraceable for the general public or national parliaments, not to mention supranational accountability bodies like ECA or oversight bodies like the Council or the EP.

This invisibility was a fundamental feature of the system and hence not just a result of its poor implementation. As the European Ombudsman had earlier noted in a 2021 letter to the Commission President, drafting documents were 'of significant public interest, relating to unprecedented measures the EU is taking in the context of a global crisis', in which case transparency should have been the rule in 'the Commission's negotiations with Member State authorities on their recovery and resilience plans'.[129] The Commission's functionalist defence of these inevitable information asymmetries was an implicit admission of the extent to which that RRF planning process, at least with regard to the matters covered by the NRRPs, had deviated from the traditional aspiration of open, representative government.[130]

3. Reactive Transparency: Delayed and Denied

We turn now from so-called proactive transparency (disclosure occurring while the decision-making process is taking place), to reactive transparency (disclosure after the fact, particularly as to the public access to documents).

[126] Dermine (2024, pp 980–82). See this chapter above, n 18 and accompanying text.
[127] European Commission (2022a, p 10).
[128] Ibid, p 4.
[129] European Ombudsman (2021).
[130] For further development of this point at the implementation and disbursement stage of the process, see this chapter below, nn 226–30 and accompanying text.

Regulation 1049/2001, the EU's general law on public access, involves reasonably tight time limits (fifteen working days to respond to an application or a confirmatory application after initial denial, with the possibility of fifteen-day extensions in exceptional circumstances).[131] Regulation 1049/2001 also spells out several grounds for refusing access in whole or in part, including two that have figured prominently in the Commission's responses under the RRF: that is, 'where disclosure would undermine protection of... the financial, monetary or economic policy of the Community or a Member State' or where disclosure 'would seriously undermine the institution's decision-making process, unless there is an overriding public interest in disclosure'.[132] As we shall see later, Ombudsman investigations of the many denied RRF access requests revealed how tenuous and conclusory the Commission's invocations of these exceptions often were.[133]

The Commission established its restrictive line on access requests from the very earliest stage of the NRRP process. In response to the Ombudsman's 2021 letter noted above,[134] President von der Leyen stressed that the time limits under Regulation 1049/2001 imposed heavy burdens in the context of the RRF, whether in 'defining the perimeter of documents concerned', 'identify[ing] and go[ing] through several hundred documents representing more than a thousand pages', and 'coordinat[ing] within and among services of the Commission'.[135] This was no doubt true, but it was also a reflection of the reluctance of the Commission to plan its processes and document management systems in a way that would makes transparency obligations manageable. The Commission's subsequent track record in responding to RRF-related access requests remained problematic. Its responses were regularly marked by delays of many months and sometimes even years before making a final decision,[136] followed by broad denials of access. This performance raised serious doubts about the assurance from President von der Leyen that the Commission 'remain[ed] fully committed to ensuring the access to documents rights of EU citizens' and 'endeavour[ed] to safeguard [those] rights ... within the strict deadlines provided by Regulation (EC) No 1049/2001'.[137]

We begin with the problem of delay, which under the first von der Leyen Commission was not in fact limited to RRF-related requests though it was particularly acute in that context. In a special report to the European Parliament in 2023, the Ombudsman described the delays as 'systemic'.[138] At the head of the list of the

[131] Regulation (EC) No 1049/2001, arts 2(3), 7, and 8. For further discussion, see Introduction, nn 49–51 and accompanying text.

[132] Regulation (EC) No 1049/2001, art 4.

[133] See this chapter below, nn 149–70 and accompanying text.

[134] European Ombudsman (2021); see this chapter above, n 129 and accompanying text.

[135] von der Leyen (2021).

[136] In relation to a request concerning the French NRRP, for example, the Commission took more than thirteen months to make a confirmatory decision on the request (from May 2021 to June 2022). European Ombudsman (2023d).

[137] von der Leyen (2021).

[138] European Ombudsman (2023a, paras 12–13).

Ombudsman's examples of the most egregious delays, however, were those drawn from the RRF. The report's summary on this point is worth quoting in full (all emphasis in original):

> *Recovery and Resilience Facility:* A journalist sought public access to documents concerning the national plans of Poland and the Netherlands under the Recovery and Resilience Facility (RRF). For the documents related to the Polish plan, the Commission granted partial access *nine months* after the complainant's initial request. The complainant considered that the Commission had failed to identify all documents falling within the scope of his request. The Commission replied that two additional documents exist but did not fall within the scope of the request. The Ombudsman considered that the Commission had defined the scope of the request very literally and found it regrettable that the Commission had not engaged with the complainant to *clarify the request*. She urged the Commission to register a new request for these two documents and deal with this request immediately. For the documents related to the Dutch plan, *in September 2023, the Commission had still not taken a final decision even though the complainant first asked for access in June 2022*. The Commission informed the Ombudsman that *external consultations were still ongoing nine months after receiving the confirmatory application*.[139]

The final decision in the referenced Dutch case would not ultimately come until July 2024, a full two years after the initial request. The Ombudsman found 'the egregious delay … constitute[d] maladministration'.[140] This experience was consistent with the Commission's handling of our own public-access requests, which we described in the Introduction, where the Commission took sixteen months from the date of the initial access request to make its final decision denying access in whole or in part.[141]

Regulation 1049/2001 is built on the assumption that a reasonably clear distinction can be made between documents originating from the EU institution and those originating from the Member State.[142] The 'large and complex' NRRP process described above placed this assumption under considerable strain, given that the process involved 'thousands of documents and exchanges' between the Commission and the Member States over an intensive period of several months[143] (or indeed years, if you extend the period forward into the implementation and disbursement stage, as the Commission claimed was appropriate).[144] In normal circumstances, the nature of the legal assessment of a request would differ depending on whether the requested document originated from an EU institution or the Member State. In the

[139] Ibid, para 23, first bullet point, citing European Ombudsman (2023e), (2024b).

[140] European Ombudsman (2024c, paras 33 and 39).

[141] See Introduction, nn 70–95 and accompanying text.

[142] The discussion that follows provides just the highlights of the Commission approach. For a more detailed analysis of the legal-technical dimensions of its argumentation, see Leino-Sandberg (2024a).

[143] European Commission (2022a, p 4).

[144] See this chapter below, nn 155–60 and accompanying text.

latter case, the institution would first consult with the Member State.[145] Given that it is the institution's responsibility to defend the decision in case of an appeal, it needs to verify whether the Member State has provided proper reasons for nondisclosure,[146] but this inquiry is limited to determining only whether those reasons are *prima facie* well founded.[147] By contrast, if the document originates from the EU institution itself, the institution should carry out a specific and individual examination of each document to determine whether it falls under one of Regulation 1049/2001's disclosure exceptions.[148]

Given these differences in assessment and procedure, the Commission has had an incentive, in effect, to expand the category of Member State-originating documents to reduce its own procedural and justificatory burden. A good example could be seen in the Commission's denial of access to documents relating to the French NRRP.[149] The nondisclosed documents originated from both the Member State (on which the Commission consulted France and then undertook the required *prima facie* verification) as well as the Commission itself (on which it was supposed to undertake a specific and individual examination of each document). But as to the latter category of documents, the Commission simply attempted to claim that nondisclosure was generally warranted on the same basis. It asserted that 'documents originating from the European Commission would reveal sensitive information about financial and fiscal reforms in France and the Commission's feedback on the proposed reforms expressed during the negotiations of the plan, which could negatively impact the economic policy of France'.[150] This is another example of the Commission's effort, in effect, to blur 'authorship' in order to undermine accountability in the planning process.[151]

The Commission buttressed this position by invoking the functional demands of the decision-making process itself, stressing that 'the exceptions relating to the protection of the financial, monetary or economic policy and the decision-making process are … closely connected'.[152] The Commission then advanced several general assertions about how disclosure would 'undermine the climate of mutual trust with the Member State', 'strain the working relations between the European Commission and … national authorities', and 'lead to speculations, premature conclusions and serious interference with the Commission decision-making process'.[153] In sum, the Commission argued that its own documents should not be disclosed because they 'reflect[ed] the discussions on specific issues related to the plan' and 'contain[ed]

[145] Regulation (EC) No 1049/2001, art 4(4)–(5).
[146] Case C-135/11 P, *IFAW Internationaler Tierschutz-Fonds* (2012), paras 61–62, and Case T-669/11, *Spirlea* (2014), paras 52–53.
[147] Case T-77/22, *Asesores Comunitarios* (2023), para 38.
[148] Case T-669/11, *Spirlea* (2014), paras 80–84.
[149] European Ombudsman (2023d).
[150] European Commission (2022e, p 8).
[151] See this chapter above, n 18 and accompanying text.
[152] European Commission (2022e, p 4).
[153] Ibid, p 14. For quite similar arguments, see the Commission's decision regarding access to documents relating to the negotiations of the Dutch NRRP. European Commission (2022b, pp 20–21).

detailed preliminary information on the planned reforms and investment projects . . . and on other specific details about financial planning and policies'.[154]

The same line of reasoning would also allow the Commission to expansively interpret the time period over which the decision-making must be protected. The Commission characterised the NRRP process as 'a continuum of discussions and exchanges . . . that does not end with the approval of the plan but continues during the implementation phase'.[155] As such, the process would only end only 'with the adoption of the Commission's decision authorising the disbursement of the relative financial contribution' on each milestone and target.[156] But as the Ombudsman later pointed out, this meant nontransparency through 'the deadline for the adoption of payment decisions by the Commission' in 2026.[157] The protections of the drafting and approval stage thus carried over to the implementation and disbursement stage, and vice versa, each purporting to reinforce each other.

The Ombudsman understandably found this latter proposition to be questionable both in logic and effect: '[I]t is difficult to understand', she wrote, 'how documents pertaining to the *closed* negotiations of an RRP "transform" into documents in an *ongoing* decision-making process on complying with the RRP' (emphasis in original).[158] From her perspective, the Commission failed to offer 'any argument showing how precisely the disclosure of the documents, which are related to the setting of milestones, could seriously undermine its future evaluation of whether these milestones have been achieved'.[159] The Commission's overall approach, she concluded, was 'not what citizens are entitled to expect from an open, modern and service-minded EU administration'.[160]

The most problematic of the Commission justifications of non-disclosure, however, was also the one most reflective of the Commission's deeply technocratic and administrative mindset. Access to NRRP documents should be denied, the Commission argued, because their disclosure would 'open the door to undue external pressure' on the decision-makers.[161] In a system 'founded on the values of . . . democracy',[162] one would think that openness to such pressure would be seen as a feature and not a bug. But from the technocratic perspective dominant within the Commission, insulation from democratic pressures helped to ensure 'the independence and objectivity' of supranational decision-making.[163] This is classic technocratic functionalism.[164]

[154] European Commission (2023i, pp 6–7).
[155] European Commission (2022e, p 12).
[156] Ibid.
[157] European Ombudsman (2023d, para 17).
[158] Ibid, para 32.
[159] Ibid.
[160] Ibid, para 36.
[161] European Commission (2022e, p 14).
[162] Article 2 TEU.
[163] European Commission (2022e, p 14). For a critique of such claims in the EU, particularly under conditions of seemingly perpetual crisis, see Vauchez and White (2025).
[164] Lindseth (2010, p 256; see also pp 95–96, 98). See additionally Majone (1994).

The challenges flowing from intensified national-supranational cooperation (and blurred authorship)[165] have certainly help strengthen this claim.[166] However, the Commission advanced much the same set of arguments even where there was no indication that the Member State concerned was actually consulted on the disclosure (as, eg, in a request for documents related to the Finnish NRRP),[167] or where the Member States concerned *did not oppose disclosure* (as in requests related to the Swedish and Danish NRRPs).[168]

The Commission's arguments in this latter case were particularly revealing. The Ombudsman found them not only 'vague and general' but also questionable in terms of the Commission's own self-conception as an independent expert body superior to the Member States. 'While the Commission may, *as a matter of law*, take a different view' from a Member State not opposing disclosure, 'it is [still] very difficult to understand, *as a matter of fact*, what insight the Commission has into the financial, monetary or economic policy of the two Member States that should prevail over their own views on what risks the disclosure of the documents would entail' (emphasis in original).[169] The Commission, in denying disclosure of these documents, set itself up as the independent expert of the policy interests *of the two Member States*. As the Ombudsman cogently concluded:

> The RRF forms part of an unprecedented stimulus package, financed by the EU, for the economies of the Member States ... The importance of the RRF must be matched with high transparency standards, and it is understandable that there is considerable public interest in knowing how the two RRPs in this case came into being ... The Commission has not disputed that citizens' interest in this is of a public nature. Still it has found that the interest of citizens cannot prevail over the interest in keeping its talks with the two Member States secret, at the cost of accountability.[170]

[165] Dermine (2024, pp 980–82). See this chapter above, n 18 and accompanying text.

[166] This was especially true in requests for documents relating to national applications for support under the Technical Support Instrument (TSI). In that context, part of the Commission's standard boilerplate for denying access was to state that TSI requests 'feed into [a] political process that belongs solely to [national] institutions'. See, eg, regarding the Italian TSI request (European Commission, 2022f); regarding the Dutch TSI request (European Commission, 2023j, p 2); and the Finnish TSI request (European Commission, 2024c, p 2).

[167] European Commission (2022g).

[168] European Ombudsman (2022).

[169] Ibid, para 18.

[170] Ibid, para 24 (internal citation omitted). Another problematic dimension of this and other cases is related to access to 'environmental information' that is presumptively disclosable under the Aarhus Regulation, which implements the Aarhus Convention on Access to Information, Public Participation in Decision-making and Access to Justice in Environmental Matters. See Regulation (EC) No 1367/2006 [Aarhus]. The Aarhus Regulation specifies that, where environmental information is sought pursuant to Regulation 1049/2001, the Commission's 'grounds for refusal shall be interpreted in a restrictive way, taking into account the public interest served by disclosure and whether the information requested relates to emissions into the environment'. Regulation (EC) No 1367/2006 [Aarhus], art 6(1). When the applicants complained to the European Ombudsman, she found the Commission's position contrary to the obligation under the Aarhus Regulation to invoke disclosure exceptions 'restrictively'. European Ombudsman (2023d,

In its effort to limit disclosure, the Commission received support from a traditional ally in the expansive interpretation of supranational prerogatives—the European judiciary.[171] In this case, the support came in the form of a judgment of the General Court relating to the Spanish NRRP,[172] which unfortunately was not subsequently appealed. The specific holding of the judgment was limited to nondisclosure of a small number of documents based on protecting Spanish financial and economic policy. The logic of the judgment, however, was more sweeping, adopting the rationale for nondisclosure advanced by the Commission in its argumentation. The judgment focused on generalised risks of 'undermining the progress of the forthcoming negotiations on the various stages of implementation of the RRP',[173] 'open[ing] the way to speculation or interference',[174] or 'subjecting [Spain] to external pressure',[175] all points urged on the Court by the Commission.[176] As a consequence, the Court wholly and without question supported the need to maintain the confidentiality 'at each stage of the negotiation process concerning the implementation of the RRP', in effect through 2026.[177]

The judgment's logic effectively presumed—contrary to the premise of Regulation 1049/2001—that confidentiality should be the default status of RRF-related documents. The Court did not make an independent examination of the requested documents, instead deferring to a set of conclusory assertions about what was 'reasonably foreseeable and not purely hypothetical' if the disclosure went forward.[178] The Court did not consider that it was at least equally, if not logically more 'foreseeable and not hypothetical' that any ensuing 'external pressure'—that is, democratic debate within the Member State—might operate not to interfere with NRRP commitments but rather to improve the seriousness of those commitments and the chances of delivering on them. The motivating concern behind the General Court's approach was, consistent with the Commission's position across numerous NRRP public access requests, fear of publicity and democratic process, particularly within the Member States.

The sedimentation of these more restrictive ideas into the existing case law has aided the Commission in its ongoing efforts to resist disclosure beyond the curated set of documents contemplated by the RRF Regulation.[179] Certainly this sedimentation will help drag out the processing of future requests, allowing the Commission to

para 33), (2022, para 23). This led her to conclude that the Commission should have granted significantly wider access to the requested documents. European Ombudsman (2023d, para 34), (2022, para 24).

[171] Lindseth (2010, pp 147–48); Ronkainen et al (2024).

[172] Case T-77/22, *Asesores Comunitarios* (2023).

[173] Ibid, para 64.

[174] Ibid, para 68.

[175] Ibid, para 66.

[176] Ibid, para 52.

[177] Ibid, para 65.

[178] Ibid, paras 52 and 63.

[179] See this chapter below, n 236, describing the Commission's objections to producing documents of the Economic and Financial Committee relating to the procedures it uses to produce opinions on Commission assessments of disbursement requests.

invoke the reasoning endorsed by the General Court to force future applicants into further rounds of initial denials, and confirmatory applications. These will then be followed by complaints to the Ombudsman, who will find that the Commission has been excessively restrictive, albeit with little effect of the Commission's actual approach to access. This strategy, as we have seen, often involved a deliberate blurring of 'authorship' to undermine accountability.[180] The more likely effect, however, was only to increase the political responsibility of the Commission itself. The NRRPs were never properly debated on either the national or supranational levels, so the 'ownership' of the milestones and targets belongs as much to the Commission as to the narrow band of national executive and technocratic officials who acted as its prime interlocutors. Moreover, the lack of broad knowledge about what the plans actually entailed increased the risk that the money would be poorly spent.[181]

B. Implementation and Disbursement: the Vicissitudes of a 'Performance-Based Instrument'

We turn now from drafting and approval to the implementation and disbursement stage of the planning process. In its communications, the Commission has always been careful to stress the character of the RRF as 'an innovative, performance-based instrument'.[182] This meant that, under the RRF, payments were to be 'made to Member States, as beneficiaries, upon delivering reforms and investments pre-agreed in national recovery and resilience plans'.[183] The 'performance logic of the RRF', moreover, made 'payments conditional on concrete outcomes', that is, 'on the delivery of the pre-agreed investments and reforms rather than the final costs incurred'.[184]

In other words, the EU disbursed funds not to cover the costs of a milestone or target but rather as a *reward to Member States for completing it*, which can in fact relate to a very early step in the investment or reform process. And the RRF Regulation designated the Commission as, effectively, the sole judge of whether completion had taken place and the reward should issue. The only check on the Commission's discretion was its obligation to 'take into account' the opinion of the Economic and Financial Committee,[185] the body also tasked with elevating any concerns to the European Council (which, to date, it has never done).[186] Otherwise, at the implementation and disbursement stage the Commission operated with very little direct

180 Dermine (2024, pp 980–82). See this chapter above, nn 18, 91, 103, 126, 151, 165 and accompanying text.
181 See generally Section D of this chapter below.
182 See, eg, European Commission (2023g, p 1).
183 Ibid.
184 Ibid.
185 Regulation (EU) 2021/241 [RRF], art 24(4). See this chapter below, nn 232–35 and accompanying text.
186 Regulation (EU) 2021/241 [RRF], recital (52).

oversight and even less transparency, whether proactive or reactive, as compared to the drafting and approval stage.[187]

Just as we saw in our discussion of the drafting of the NRRPs, the implementation of the RRF also raises significant democratic legitimacy and accountability concerns. As David Bokhorst has noted, a principal source of democratic tensions flowed from the fact that national governments proposed the plans and the Commission judged whether milestones were met and outcomes were in line with their initial plans.[188] As he continued:

> [M]oney will only be disbursed once parliament adopts the reform, meaning the milestone is met. This is the core rationale of the RRF, but it will also put pressure on democratic institutions. If parliamentarians have concerns, the bills might have to be settled by national, rather than European funds. In certain reform areas this might not be controversial and EU funds could be helpful. But [in others], reform conditionality will also be a factor in more sensitive domains [particularly those involving structural reforms demanded under CSRs].[189]

As the head of the RECOVER task force in the Commission, Céline Gauer, stressed in an interview in 2022, the agreements made by national governments with the Commission (the NRRPs and OAs) were 'not [just] on behalf of [themselves] but on behalf of their country'.[190] If a Member State government cannot get parliamentary approval for an NRRP-promised reform, then the Member State would not be in compliance 'with the milestone and cannot receive the payment corresponding to that milestone'.[191] This logic would also extend to presidential vetoes of legislation,[192] as well as to changes in government as a result of new elections, and constitutional challenges that have halted the completion of a milestone.[193] When the new Meloni government sought to revise Italy's NRRP after it was elected in 2022, the Commission refused, citing Article 21(1) of the RRF Regulation, which only allowed a plan to be amended where 'objective circumstances' justified it.[194] This logic could have the effect of turning the NRRP into 'a rigid government program, which practically reduce[d] the autonomy of whatever political majority may emerge victorious from the next parliamentary elections'.[195]

[187] On non-transparency regarding the implementation of the NRRPs after their approval, see especially this chapter above, nn 156–57 and 173–77, discussing European Ombudsman (2023d, para 17) and Case T-77/22, *Asesores Comunitarios* (2023), para 65.
[188] Bokhorst (2022, p 114).
[189] Ibid.
[190] Pinster and Witteman (2022).
[191] Ibid.
[192] Portugal.gov.pt (2023).
[193] Fasone (2024).
[194] Dermine (2024, p 986); Lupo (2023). For further details, see Chapter Five, nn 176–77 and accompanying text.
[195] Fabbrini (2022d, p 672).

Our discussion in this section will focus on RRF grants rather than loans, and more particularly on the Commission's discretion in assessing a Member State's requests for a disbursement of funds, followed by an analysis of the role of the opinion of the Economic and Financial Committee (EFC) as a way of checking that. These steps, we shall see, are indicative of broader challenges—both in measuring performance as well as in peer review and mutual accountability among the Member States—which help to illuminate the nature and effectiveness of the RRF's performance-based model as it has actually operated.

1. Disbursement Requests and the Challenge of Measuring Performance

As a planning and spending programme, the RRF was unprecedented in both scale and scope; consequently, there was no prior 'blueprint for delivering on [its] milestones and targets'.[196] This was true for the Commission throughout the process but not least in its central role assessing 'satisfactory fulfilment of milestones and targets', which the RRF Regulation left almost entirely to the judgment of the Commission.[197] This discretion was also intimately bound up with definition of the milestones and targets in each NRRP, as well as with 'the verification mechanism for each milestone and target' as defined in the OAs,[198] which served as the 'gateway' to assessing performance under the NRRPs.[199]

Lurking in the background was a more fundamental question: what did it mean for the RRF to be a 'performance-based instrument' in the first place? The label presupposed that the EU had a coherent conception of 'performance' but the RRF Regulation did not offer any definition apart from conclusory reference to 'satisfactory fulfilment' of milestones and targets. In a report published in 2023, the European Court of Auditors asserted that the RRF in fact was confused on this point in a quite fundamental way, mistaking 'outputs' for 'results' or 'performance'.[200]

An output, according to the ECA, was '[s]omething produced or achieved by a project, such as delivery of a training course or construction of a road'. A result was '[t]he immediate effect of a project or programme upon its completion, such as the improved employability of course participants or improved accessibility following the construction of a new road'. Performance was '[a] measure of how well an EU-funded action, project or programme has met its objectives and provides value for money'.[201] As to both the RRF's overall progress as well as the fulfilment of milestones and targets,

196 Schramm et al (2022, p 121).
197 Regulation (EU) 2021/241 [RRF], art 24(3)–(6).
198 European Commission (2024b, p 19).
199 Orefice (2022, p 100).
200 European Court of Auditors (2023b).
201 Ibid, p 55.

the RRF was almost exclusively focused on outputs, with little effort to measure results, much less performance. In fact, many milestones did not even involve 'outputs' but rather antecedent 'inputs'—such as producing a study, or recruiting temporary employees to process judicial backlogs—all in the hope of yielding some hoped-for output in the future.[202]

The overall progress of the RRF was supposed to be measured through 'common indicators' set by the Commission,[203] which were then incorporated into the Recovery and Resilience Scoreboard to display the progress of the implementation of the NRRPs.[204] The problem, according to ECA, was that '[m]ost common indicators [did] not go beyond measuring output'.[205] They were also marked by significant gaps, not least as 'to major structural reforms (economic, labour market and judicial reforms)', which 'could not be linked to any common indicator'.[206] The Scoreboard incorporated these shortcomings but also had several of its own. Most importantly, ECA found the Scoreboard was 'misleading' by giving the same value to 'a target relating to a large and costly investment' as to 'a milestone relating to a reform with no cost, or a target for an investment with a low cost'.[207] This echoed a similar critique of the European Ombudsman that, because 'milestones and targets [had] no attributed cost', the Scoreboard did 'not reflect Member States' actual expenditure' and thus undermined 'the ability of stakeholders to monitor the impact of projects and to protect the financial interests of the EU'.[208]

The problem of measuring performance extended to the fulfilment of milestones and targets under the NRRPs. ECA found that milestones and targets were 'mainly output-oriented', which meant 'they only assess[ed] the achievement of a specific measure and generally [did] not provide sufficient information on its contribution' to the RRF's overall economic or policy aims.[209] Consider, for example, the Portuguese NRRP, which included measures on 'completion of the design and implementation of new procurement models for the national central public procurement system', 'entry into force of the legislation underpinning the State Accounting Entity', or 'entry into force of a legal act modifying the legal framework of selected tax benefits'.[210] The entry into force of a legal act is of course easy to prove, if there is no expectation of also demonstrating that it has had positive effects or outcomes. Such effects could only be

[202] For some concrete examples, see this chapter below, n 508 and accompanying text, discussing European Commission (2023k, pp 60–61).
[203] Regulation (EU) 2021/241 [RRF], art 29(4)(a); see also Commission Delegated Regulation (EU) 2021/2106 [Common Indicators].
[204] Regulation (EU) 2021/241 [RRF], arts 30(1)–(3).
[205] European Court of Auditors (2023b, p 25, para 48).
[206] Ibid, p 24, para 45. For specific examples of the difficulty of measuring reforms, see this chapter below, nn 433–34 and accompanying text.
[207] European Court of Auditors (2023b, p 37, paras 79–80). In response to ECA's recommendation, 'the Commission now discloses on the Scoreboard the methodology used for reporting on disbursements per pillar'. See European Court of Auditors (2025b, p 21, para 40).
[208] European Ombudsman (2023b).
[209] European Court of Auditors (2023b, p 19, para 36).
[210] European Commission (2023l), pp 4–5, 7, recitals (25)–(26), (42)).

demonstrated over time, but the RRF did not require such demonstration—it simply assumed 'performance' on the basis of the 'output' alone. As two commentators put it: 'If we want the RRF to really make a difference, the formal box-ticking of performance targets is simply not enough'.[211]

The problem of measuring performance had a direct bearing on the Commission's handling of the disbursement requests under the NRRPs.[212] The most difficult problem arose in the context of partial payments; that is, when the Commission determined that the Member State had *not* satisfactorily fulfilled all the relevant milestones and targets covered by the payment request, in which case the RRF Regulation authorised the Commission to withhold 'all or part' of the instalment.[213] This required the Commission to decide what payment was appropriate in the face of a purportedly partial 'performance'. This was a largely qualitative judgement in which non-transparent negotiations with the Member State again loomed large. '[G]iven that any partial achievement of milestones and targets would need to be reflected in the payment', ECA found in its 2022 report on the assessment process, negotiations between the Commission and the Member State 'rather than [the] underlying costs' would be determinative of the payment.[214] It was not helpful, ECA further noted, that '[a]t the time of the audit, the Commission had not yet defined a methodology for calculating' partial payments.[215]

The Commission's attempt to develop a more transparent methodology, not merely in terms of partial payments but also through a general framework for interpreting milestones and targets in the NRRPs, came in two annexes attached to a 2023 Commission communication.[216] Both annexes were suggestive of the difficulties associated with Commission assessments of disbursement requests. Annex I (on the interpretation of milestones and targets) pointed to how, with the amounts of money at issue, clarifying what actually constituted 'requirements' of particular milestones and targets was in fact a high-stakes game.[217] For its part, Annex II (on partial payments methodology) tried to give the semblance of rigour to a process that was inherently riddled with judgement calls—using various 'coefficients' (5, 2, 1, 0.5) to calculate the partial payment depending on whether the non-fulfilment involved a

[211] Corti and Ruiz de la Ossa (2023, p 7).
[212] Regulation (EU) 2021/241 [RRF], art 24(2).
[213] Ibid, art 24(6).
[214] European Court of Auditors (2022a, p 32, para 75).
[215] Ibid.
[216] European Commission (2023g, pp 13–17) (Annex I—Framework for assessing milestones and targets under the RRF Regulation; and Annex II—Commission methodology for the determination of payment suspension under the Recovery and Resilience Facility Regulation).
[217] Ibid, p 13 (Annex I—Framework for assessing milestones and targets under the RRF Regulation). This annex also specified the sources that could be used to aid this interpretive process, some of which are part of the curated picture available to the public (the NRRPS, recitals to Council Implementing Decisions, associated Staff Working Documents and CSRs). But some are not ('notes to the file during the assessment, records of exchanges with the national authorities'), which arguably only raised the tensions over nontransparency. Ibid, p 13 (Annex I—Framework for assessing milestones and targets under the RRF Regulation).

'large' investment, a 'small' investment, a 'final step' reform, or an 'intermediate step' reform, etc.[218] The result was a document that, perhaps inadvertently, simply reinforced the view conveyed by ECA in its 2022 audit that once a cost-based approach had been abandoned, calculating partial payments became, in fact, an unmoored and free-floating exercise. Lithuania, in later exchanges with the Commission challenging a partial payment regarding a tax reform milestone, called this methodology 'highly subjective', allowing it 'to set disproportionately high financial sanctions for the underachievement of one milestone' in a manner violating 'the principles of legitimate expectations, proportionality and transparency'.[219]

A useful further example can be seen in how the Commission handled Portugal's October 2023 requests for the third and fourth grant and loan instalments (€1.8 billion and €0.8 billion, and €0.4 billion and €0.2 billion, respectively), relating to fourty-seven milestones and targets under its NRRP. The Commission's preliminary assessment found that forty-four out of the forty-seven milestones and targets had been achieved, which then triggered the procedure to determine a partial payment,[220] using the methodology it outlined in Annex II of its 2023 Communication.[221] But as a briefing in the Recovery and Resilience Dialogue in the European Parliament later described, the process was inscrutable:

> The exact amount withheld [was] not set out in the Commission's related press release (nor the Q&A). According to our calculation (comparing the amounts stipulated in the Operational Arrangements with the payments made), the amount withheld [was] approximately equal to 31% of the amount otherwise due . . . [222]

In such a situation, there was no realistic way for the Member State to perform an independent analysis of whether the Commission had properly calculated the partial payment. After some disagreement with the Commission, the Portuguese Prime Minister announced that the unmet measures were 'about to be met'[223] (referring to a parliamentary override of the presidential veto),[224] which would then lead to the release of the funds. Another example of partial fulfilment would be Bulgaria, which submitted its second payment request for an anticipated €653 million on 7 October

[218] Ibid, pp 15–17 (Annex II—Commission methodology for the determination of payment suspension under the Recovery and Resilience Facility Regulation).

[219] See European Commission (2024s, pp 20–21), recital 67 (quoting the Lithuanian objections). On the basis of these and a further violation of 'the principle of fiscal autonomy of Member States', Lithuania challenged the Commission's implementing decision before the General Court. See Case T-356/24, *Lithuania v Commission* (2024), although that action was apparently withdrawn in February 2025 following a change in government in Lithuania. See Lamer (2026). For a detailed timeline of Commission partial payments to Lithuania and other Member States, see Lilyanova and Schollaert (2024).

[220] Regulation (EU) 2021/241 [RRF], art 24(6).

[221] European Commission (2023g, pp 15–17) (Annex II—Commission methodology for the determination of payment suspension under the Recovery and Resilience Facility Regulation); see this chapter above, nn 218–19 and accompanying text.

[222] Magnus, et al (2024, p 4).

[223] Portugal.gov.pt (2023).

[224] See this chapter above, n 192 and accompanying text.

2023. After a great deal of wrangling, it was informed on 29 November 2024 that the Commission had made a positive preliminary assessment of the satisfactory fulfilment of fifty-three out of sixty-two milestones and targets. However, the suspension for the non-fulfilled nine milestones and targets in the areas of energy, anti-corruption, and public procurement reforms was greater than the reward for the fifty-three fulfilled ones, leading to the suspension of the entire payment.[225]

If the RRF sought, as we noted at the outset of this chapter, 'to enhance the efficiency of public policymaking through overcoming domestic obstacles and hurdles',[226] then among the most important obstacles was the limitation of parliamentary democracy itself.[227] Aside from playing no role in the drafting or adoption of the OAs, the marginalisation of national parliaments manifested itself throughout the implementation process, up to and including disbursement requests from national governments to the Commission. A survey undertaken for the European Parliament showed that, out of twenty-four responding national parliaments, twenty-one reported that their government had no legal obligation to submit to the national parliament the disbursement requests or the Commission's assessments.[228] Only thirteen had established practices for the government to present progress updates (including risks) on the implementation of the NRRPs.[229] Only five responding reported that their national government provided information on the implementation of NRRPs in other Member States. Moreover, fifteen parliaments indicated they did not intend to scrutinise the financing and realisation of specific projects under their NRRP.[230]

2. EFC Opinions and the Formalities of Cross-National Scrutiny

From the very inception of the NGEU in the spring and summer of 2020, the need to ensure some form of cross-national scrutiny of RRF spending—in effect, peer review—was a central aim of several national governments, particularly in the 'frugal' north.[231] As the then-Prime Minister of the Netherlands, Mark Rutte, explained to his Parliament in July 2020: 'If we in the Netherlands cannot immediately have full trust in the Brussels system not saying "well, the reform hasn't really happened, but here's your money anyway", then we need something in the governance to ensure the Netherlands has very tight control over the process'.[232] Rutte's position was in line with

[225] Nikolov (2024), Karagyozov (2025).
[226] Bokhorst (2023, p 29); see also Vanhercke and Verdun (2022). See this chapter above, n 22 and accompanying text.
[227] As for national constitutional courts in the NRRP process, Fasone (2024) found them to be even more marginalized, indeed passive.
[228] Binder et al (2022, p 5).
[229] Ibid.
[230] Ibid, p 6.
[231] This section further develops the argument in Leino-Sandberg (2024c).
[232] Rutte (2020), quoted in Bokhorst (2023, p 28).

those of other 'frugal' leaders, expressed both before and after the July 2020 European summit announced that NGEU would go forward.[233] The need for such 'very tight control'—in effect, an 'emergency brake'—meant that the Commission would be required, before disbursement, to seek the opinion of the Economic and Financial Committee, which was also empowered to elevate any disputes to the European Council.[234] The RRF Regulation incorporated this mechanism into the procedures of Article 24 on payments.[235]

How effective has the EFC opinion process been as a means of promoting on cross-national scrutiny and as a check on Commission discretion? As part of the research for this book, one of us sought, under Regulation 1049/2001, access to documents relating to the procedures and standards used by the EFC in formulating its RRF opinions. This led to the production of three documents,[236] which taken together suggest that cross-national scrutiny through the EFC was very time constrained and often highly general. On the basis of the documents produced, it would be difficult to characterise the EFC opinion process as the 'very tight control' described by Mark Rutte in July 2020.[237]

The first problem is limited personnel. As noted in Chapter Three, the EFC is a body comprised of senior Member State, Commission, and ECB representatives, whose main function is to advise the Council on economic and financial matters. It operates pursuant to Article 134(2) and (4) TFEU and its tasks are varied. They include 'assessments of the economic and financial situation, the coordination of economic and fiscal policies, contributions on financial market matters, exchange rate policies and relations with third countries and international institutions' as well as 'preparing and pursuing the dialogue between the Council and the European Central Bank'.[238] The EFC is not an audit body and lacks the staff to undertake such a function. It is, however, supported by the Economic Policy Committee (EPC), a body comprised of members nominated by the Member States, the Commission, and the ECB (two members each). Otherwise, the EFC has a small secretariat of roughly twenty-five members, who also support the EPC, the Eurogroup, the Eurogroup Working Group, as well as a number of EFC subcommittees.

[233] Löfven (2020) (Prime Minister of Sweden: 'money should be used carefully and only where we know it will make a real difference'), Marin (2020) (Prime Minister of Finland: 'The negotiations also agreed on an emergency brake mechanism … The matter can be brought to the European Council at the request of any member state').

[234] European Council (2020, p 6, sec A19).

[235] Regulation (EU) 2021/241 [RRF], art 24(4) and recital (52).

[236] See Council of the European Union (2024a), enclosing Economic and Financial Committee (2021), (2023a), (2023b). As the Council's reply indicated, they did so despite the Commission initially arguing for a refusal 'on the basis of protection of the financial and economic policy of the European Union and its Member States (Article 4(1)(a), fourth indent, of Regulation No 1049/2001) and of the decision-making process (Article 4(3), first subparagraph, of Regulation No 1049/2001)'. It was only after a confirmatory applications plus further interinstitutional consultations that the Commission agreed the documents should be produced. See Reply to Confirmatory Application No 07/c/01/24 annexed to Council of the European Union (2024a).

[237] See this chapter above, n 232 and accompanying text.

[238] Economic and Financial Committee (2025).

The next problem was limitations of time. Given that the RRF Regulation did not specify any time limits for the delivery of EFC opinions (in contrast to the four weeks specified for the Council on Implementing Decisions), the EFC gave itself the same deadline: 'four weeks after the Commission positive preliminary assessment, [so] the Commission [can] take [the opinion] into account in the final assessment'.[239] The EFC also delegated significant preparatory work on the opinion to the EPC, whose first meeting, according to the disclosed procedures, 'should be organised as soon as possible ... but not earlier than five working days after the Commission has provided to the EFC its findings related to its positive preliminary assessment. The EPC should have sufficient time to prepare each EFC opinion, possibly about 1.5 hours discussion for each opinion'.[240] The EFC stressed in the earliest document (from 2021) that the opinion should 'contribute to the effective implementation of the Recovery and Resilience Facility, by providing a (consensual—to the extent possible) view of Member States on the fulfilment of the relevant milestones and targets'.[241] The aim should be an opinion that would be 'standardised but flexible', 'giv[ing] an overall view' without necessarily 'present[ing] the EFC position on each relevant milestone and target. It should briefly summarise the discussions of the EFC and EPC' and strive to be '1-1.5 pages per payment request, dependent on the discussion'.[242]

Subsequent documents (from early and late 2023) indicated that the process remained, over the coming years, 'broadly consensual, facilitating the preparation of the EFC opinions. So far, only one opinion required a second EPC meeting, to adjust the wording related to a possible payment suspension'.[243] The overall trend was towards simplification and streamlining, as long as certain criteria were met:

- There is an agreement of the EPC on the text and no square brackets are left open;
- No member in the EPC discussion has asked for a discussion in the EFC;
- The payment request is not subject to a possible payment suspension;
- And the positive preliminary assessment is not on milestones and targets previously assessed as not achieved (in a payment suspension).[244]

The only exception would be for requests involving 'an audit-and-control-related milestone', in which case they would be 'handled through the standard procedure in the EFC'.[245] By the end of 2023, 'eight opinions [had] been successfully adopted via

[239] See, eg, Economic and Financial Committee (2021, p 3).
[240] Ibid.
[241] Ibid, p 2.
[242] Ibid.
[243] Economic and Financial Committee (2023b, p 2).
[244] Economic and Financial Committee (2023a, p 2).
[245] Ibid. For more on the special status of 'audit-and-control-related milestone[s]', see this chapter below, nn 259–60 and accompanying text.

the simplified procedure' which was 'expected to be used continuously over the next months, given the high volume of anticipated payment requests . . . '[246]

From the beginning, however, the 'imperative of a swift implementation' and 'additional workload' were major concerns of the EFC and appeared to be the drivers in the decision to delegate significant preparatory responsibilities to the EPC.[247] It was also the reason that the EFC recognised that it would need to 'rely on the . . . information [provided by the Commission] on the fulfilment of the relevant milestones and targets':[248]

> Neither the EFC nor the EPC will have the capacity to produce a separate assessment of the fulfilment of milestones and targets. The Regulation on the Facility provides that the Commission shall provide to the EFC its findings related to its positive preliminary assessment. The Commission preliminary assessment will therefore be the main basis for the EFC and EPC discussions and the subsequent EFC opinion.[249]

Over subsequent years, the EFC came to rely heavily on the Commission's findings. To justify the use of simplified procedures, for example, the EFC cited 'the highly comprehensive presentations and clarifications presented both by the Commission and Member States at the EPC.'[250] This suggests that the same sort of 'information asymmetries'—which as we saw earlier in this chapter,[251] 'ma[d]e it difficult for the Council to act as a credible counterweight' to the Commission on the approval of the NRRPs—also operated in the context of disbursement requests, similarly forcing the EFC (like the Council before it) to 'rather mechanically follow the direction of the Commission.'[252]

Following this, EFC has endorsed the opinions without changes in the text. The sole exception mentioned concerns the payment request of Lithuania, which was the first case of payment suspension.[253]

Thus, if we return to the question we posed at the outset of this subsection—how effective has this EFC opinion procedure been? —it is difficult to say, but the evidence points to a process that has served only as a loose constraint on Commission autonomy. Viewed most favourably, the process created an important informational channel, reflecting a lack of complete confidence in the Commission's ability to remain a neutral arbiter of Member State disbursement requests. In difficult cases, the

246 Economic and Financial Committee (2023b, p 2).

247 Economic and Financial Committee (2021, p 9) (Annex 2. Extract of the minutes of the EFC of 25 January 2021. Follow-up discussion on the role of the EFC in the implementation of the Recovery and Resilience Facility).

248 Ibid, p 2.

249 Ibid.

250 Economic and Financial Committee (2023b, p 2).

251 See this chapter above, nn 29–34 and accompanying text.

252 Dermine (2024, p 983).

253 Economic and Financial Committee (2023a, p 1).

Commission has needed to justify its findings for the EFC. But in this regard, the EFC's acknowledged reliance on Commission findings would seem troubling. The picture that emerges from the EFC documentation is that the Commission was left in near total control of all RRF-related information. One would think that the Commission is smart enough not to reveal information that could be used to challenge its own position. Moreover, the fact that the EFC has never seemed even close to considering elevating a question to the European Council might further reinforce the impression that this oversight mechanism has become something of a formality.

Regardless, the functional pressure on the EFC to move quickly has remained intense, particularly after the mid-term review in 2024 found disbursements lagging behind schedule.[254] Moreover, the functional constraints on the EFC have been considerable as well. Even if it had access to information beyond what the Commission chose to provide, the EFC would still have lacked the practical capacity to properly assess the enormous scope of issues covered by the twenty-seven national plans and the thousands of milestones and targets they contain. There is no doubt that the time frame in which the EFC is expected to deliver its opinions is objectively tight. However, it is unlikely that a lengthier process would have led to different outcomes.

In the end, it may well be that the Member States simply did not really want to scrutinise each other's performance with any great vigour. From a cost–benefit perspective, there may well have been little to gain but much to lose (particularly in heightened political tensions with fellow Member States). It is one thing to advocate for tougher controls in general; it is quite another to argue for rejecting or delaying a disbursement in a particular case. For that reason, it is understandable why Member States may have preferred to concentrate on their own milestones and targets rather than to worry (via their representatives on the EFC) about the thousands of others included in other countries' plans. That said, these disincentives to deeper scrutiny do suggest potentially concerning dynamics that could take hold in an integration project that remains, in crucial ways, still polycentric and *demoi*-cratic.[255]

C. Control and Audit: the Mechanics—and Politics—of Protecting EU Financial Interests

Once the Commission authorised a disbursement and the money was paid out, the RRF funding became general budgetary support for the Member State. The 'financing not linked to costs' model effectively relieved the Member State of the need to provide proof of payments for costs on a particular supported project, which had typically been required for EU funding in the past (eg under traditional cohesion). Alongside national co-financing (which the RRF also did not require), the FNLC

254 See European Commission (2024d, p 8, sec 1.4).
255 Cf Gambetta and Origgi (2013).

model dispensed with one of the key safeguards that had served as a mainstay in ensuring prudent use of EU money at the national level. Under the RRF, it is the Member State who benefits directly instead of a private entity or natural person, as is usual under direct management.[256] While the amended RRF Regulation now—after a great deal of pressure from the European Parliament—requires the 100 largest recipients to be published, often those named are actors at ministry level.[257] But as far as senior leaders in the Commission were concerned, they apparently had difficulty seeing 'how having a list of all the people who are renovating houses would benefit anyone'.[258]

The move away from cost-based funding and national co-financing did not mean that the RRF dispensed with financial controls. Rather, the RRF relied on a different model of financial assurance, which we might call the 'compliance' model. As is quite typical in financial and banking regulation in certain domains (eg anti-money laundering), regulatory schemes often mandate that the regulated entity create a compliance function within their organisation, encompassing both the hiring of compliance professionals and the implementation of controls. The compliance function may be understood, above all, as an informational plumbing system designed to facilitate the movement of risk-relevant information up and down the organizational hierarchy as well as to the regulator and, in that regard, reduce information asymmetries. Moreover, the failure to maintain a proper compliance function often becomes, in itself, a regulatory violation that can subject the regulated entity to sanctions.

As we shall see in this section, the RRF Regulation adopted features of this model. It mandated that the Member States, in effect, maintain a compliance function—an adequate control and audit infrastructure—to protect EU financial interests and prevent fraud. Aside from serving as a core condition of funding, it was designed to facilitate the flow of control and audit information from the Member States to the Commission. The sanction for failing to maintain such an infrastructure was, in principle, a *complete* suspension of RRF funding itself—partial performance (and hence partial payment) were, again in principle, categorically out of the question.[259] The threat of a complete suspension thus operated as a very direct and immediate incentive towards compliance.[260]

1. Control and Audit at the Limits of the Commission's Capacities

Fraud may not be the main concern for the European taxpayer with the RRF. Rather, it is the questionable selection of projects together with the Commission's eagerness to disburse the money before time runs out on the NGEU programme in 2026.

[256] Lilyanova (2023a, p 3).
[257] European Parliament (2024b, para 280); see also Lilyanova (2024a, p 7).
[258] Pinster and Witteman (2022) (interview with Céline Gauer).
[259] European Commission (2023g, p 10).
[260] There was thus, in principle, no room for the sort of 'hyperbolic time discounting' that one sees in the typical compliance context, in which a regulated entity might dismiss the possibility of a future regulatory enforcement action or sanction. See Langevoort (2018).

Nonetheless, the question of the prevention of fraud, as we will see in this subsection, is nonetheless revealing of some of the Commission's limited capacities under the RRF's planning and spending model. These limited capacities in turn raise questions about the advisability of extending that model to new domains, a topic we take up in Chapter Five.

The key provision in the RRF Regulation on protecting the Union's financial interests is Article 22. As a quid pro quo for receiving 'funds under the [RRF]', Article 22(1) obligated the Member States, inter alia, to 'provide an effective and efficient internal control system'.[261] This did not need to be a new system—'Member States [could] rely on their regular national budget management systems'—but whether new or existing, the system needed to meet the standard of 'effective and efficient'. The Commission thus established the FENIX tool for information sharing and reporting and ARACHNE tool for data-mining and risk-scoring, as a means of supporting the Member States' control and audit compliance obligations.[262]

As one of the assessment criteria for the NRRPs, the RRF Regulation required the Commission to consider whether the Member State had, or planned to establish, control systems and arrangements to prevent, detect, and correct corruption, fraud, irregularities, conflicts of interest, and double funding.[263] This criterion was to be judged on a binary basis ('A—adequate arrangements' or 'C—insufficient arrangements'), with the 'A' grade being required for successful assessment of the NRRP as a whole. The Commission chose to give all NRRPs an 'A' rating on this criterion, which would later puzzle the European Court of Auditors. Certain plans actually included milestones on internal control mechanisms, which meant that the needed controls were 'not yet in place'.[264] For the ECA, not having a fully functional control system in place implied the risk that the financial interests of the EU were not sufficiently protected until these milestones were fulfilled.[265]

The Commission responded by arguing, in effect, that the ECA confused drafting and approval with the implementation of the NRRPs.[266] The failure to have the controls in place at the time of the NRRP's adoption did not detract from the quality of the *plan*'s *commitments*; rather, the control-related milestones 'must be fulfilled for the first payment' to issue, which meant the plan's commitments served as 'an additional guarantee for proper implementation of the control systems'.[267] Under Article 22(2) of the RRF Regulation, any disbursement request from a Member State must include:

> a management declaration that the funds were used for its intended purpose, that the information submitted with the request for payment is complete, accurate and

[261] Regulation (EU) 2021/241 [RRF], art 22(1).
[262] See ibid, art 22(4).
[263] Ibid, art 20(e) and Annex V, sec 2.10.
[264] European Court of Auditors (2022a, p 47, para 111); see also European Court of Auditors (2023f, pp 15–16, paras 25–27).
[265] European Court of Auditors (2022a, p 47, para 111).
[266] European Commission (2022a, p 9).
[267] Ibid.

> reliable and that the control systems put in place give the necessary assurances that the funds were managed in accordance with all applicable rules, in particular rules on avoidance of conflicts of interests, fraud prevention, corruption and double funding from the Facility and other Union programmes in accordance with the principle of sound financial management; and ... a summary of the audits carried out, including weaknesses identified and any corrective actions taken.[268]

These additional guarantees found further expression in the Financing Agreement between the Commission and the Member State, a contract typically executed soon after the adoption of the Council Implementation Decision,[269] and including a comprehensive set of commitments to maintain a compliance function to control risks and ensure the flow of risk-salient information to regulatory, audit, and enforcement bodies at the supranational level.

The bottom line effect of these requirements was to externalise the cost of control and audit onto the Member States themselves, using mandates and potential suspension of disbursements, along with required information channels, to keep the Commission's own control and audit costs to a minimum.[270] In 2023, the President of the European Court of Auditors, Tony Murphy, expressed deep concerns about this strategy.[271] Murphy thought the system, in practice, proceeded on the wrong premise, in which 'the funds paid to the member states [were] national money', and it 'should therefore be the responsibility of each individual country' to control and audit the use of that funding.[272] This premise led the Commission, in Murphy's view, to believe it need not check whether member states' payment claims complied with national and EU rules; rather, it was 'actually up to the member states to check'.[273]

Murphy felt the Commission's implementation of the control system 'pose[d] a serious risk to the financial interests of the European Union, and a danger to the EU's very reputation'.[274] The EP's Committee on Budgetary Control echoed this concern that the EU's financial interests were 'not robustly protected in the RRF', inter alia, 'due to flaws in member states' reporting and control systems'.[275] Similarly, the European Ombudsman, in her strategic report on the RRF transparency and accountability discussed earlier in this chapter,[276] concurred that 'an assurance and accountability

[268] Regulation (EU) 2021/241 [RRF], art 22(2)(c).
[269] These agreements are generally not found on the RRF Scoreboard maintained by the Commission; rather, they are typically posted on the Member State's own RRF or NGEU website. See, eg, RRF Financing Agreement [Bulgaria] (2022), [Greece] (2021), [Spain] (2021).
[270] As Céline Gauer, then the head of SG RECOVER, put it in 2022: 'everything has a limit and our resources are what they are. We are trying to make the most of them ... Could I do with a doubling of my staff? Absolutely. [laughing] But you can't give me that, can you?' Pinster and Witteman (2022).
[271] Murphy (2023a).
[272] Ibid.
[273] Ibid; for further details, see European Court of Auditors (2023f, pp 17–18, paras 32–36).
[274] Murphy (2023a).
[275] European Parliament (2023b).
[276] European Ombudsman (2023b).

gap remain[ed] at EU level in protecting the financial interests of the Union'. She expressed 'regret' that, in her strategic investigation,

> the Commission's replies lack[ed] concrete details that would reassure an independent observer as to how it [would] safeguard the spending of these funds. For instance, the Commission [did] not specify when or how its *ex post* and system audits [would] be carried out and what procedures ha[d] been put in place to recover funds.[277]

The European Parliament in 2024, in its discharge of the 2022 budget, highlighted a concrete consequence of these failings. After making 'an on-the-spot check', ECA had found that the planting of certain trees, which had already been rewarded under an RRF payment, had not actually happened. The EP described itself as 'astonished' and called for 'a compulsory check on the reliability and accuracy of the data on milestones and targets before those milestones and targets are included in a payment request'.[278]

By 2024, the ECA President, among others, found little apparent improvement in the Commission's approach: 'There is less control and self-policing, so there is a higher risk of irregularity or even corruption ... Our reports show we cannot yet fully rely on the work of national bodies when it comes to control of EU funds. We therefore have serious reservations'.[279] A year later, ECA still found that the RRF control framework was not robust enough to guarantee EU financial interests. In particular, the Commission's '*ex ante* verifications do not systematically cover horizontal eligibility conditions, such as compliance with the eligibility period and the principles of not substituting recurring national budgetary expenditure, avoiding double funding and not reversing measures already completed'.[280] Moreover, its 'ex post audits ... had weaknesses in relation to checks on the reversal of measures for which payments have already been made, on compliance with the eligibility period and on the substitution of recurring national budgetary expenditure'.[281] But most fundamentally, 'the efficiency of resource use, and therefore value for money, cannot be assessed given that the Commission does not collect or use information on actual costs'.[282]

The European Anti-Fraud Office (OLAF) has been investigating instances of fraud since the inception of the RRF in 2021, with a particular focus initially on green projects as well as funding for digitalisation, the RRF's first two 'pillars', accounting for a minimum of 37% and 20% of funding respectively.[283] The Commission charged OLAF with undertaking the system audits of the Member States' internal controls,

[277] Ibid.
[278] European Parliament (2024b, para 278).
[279] Moller-Nielsen (2024).
[280] European Court of Auditors (2025b, p 25, para 48).
[281] Ibid, p 25, para 49.
[282] Ibid, p 7, para 11.
[283] OLAF (2022).

and, by 2023, OLAF reported that 'all Member States had been audited at least once'.[284] Another important entity in this regard, the European Public Prosecutor's Office, is also tasked to protect the EU budget and investigate crimes against its financial interests.[285] It has served a crucial role in the RRF control infrastructure, though in a reactive rather than proactive way, restricted to investigation and prosecution rather than audit.

EPPO's Annual Reports for 2023 and 2024 (the last available as of this writing)[286] show considerable activity fighting corruption in connection with NGEU funding, the overwhelming portion of which related to the RRF. In its 2023 report, EPPO indicated there were '206 active investigations ... with an estimated damage of over €1.8 billion', which represented 'approximately 15% of all the cases of expenditure fraud ... but in terms of estimated damage, it corresponds to almost 25%'.[287] A year later those numbers had risen to '311 active cases ... out of which 307 stemmed from the [RRF], corresponding to approximately 17% of all active expenditure fraud investigations' with 'estimated damage to the EU's financial interests [of] €2.8 billion [or] 30% of the overall estimated damage for expenditure fraud'.[288]

As with much else in European integration, the nature and scope of EPPO's role were shaped by the persistently polycentric and *demoi*-cratic character of the integration project as a whole, with impacts both obvious and more subtle. The decentralised structure of EPPO as well as the fact that all its prosecutions take place in national courts were the most obvious. But more subtly, there was also the 'minimal' role that EU bodies played in actually triggering EPPO investigations.[289] In 2024, for example, 90% of actionable reports leading to an EPPO investigation came from the national level, whereas tips from private parties triggered 6% and 'reports from EU institutions, bodies, offices and agencies for not even 3%'.[290] This minimal role suggests a lack of the sort of local, on-the-ground knowledge to oversee the spending process in the granular way it requires, either proactively or reactively. If that is true, it raises questions about the overall lack of transparency as well as the scope and effectiveness of the Commission's outsized role in the planning process described above. More broadly, it also raises questions about the advisability of extending the planning and spending model of the RRF beyond the confines of NGEU into any other domains where such local, on-the-ground knowledge would be important to effective governance.[291]

[284] European Commission (2024e, p 10).
[285] Council Regulation (EU) 2017/1939 [EPPO]. The only Member State within the AFSJ not to participate in EPPO is Hungary (Denmark and Ireland, which had earlier opted out of the AFSJ, also do not participate).
[286] EPPO (2024b), (2025).
[287] EPPO (2024b, p 68).
[288] EPPO (2025, p 71).
[289] EPPO (2024b, p 69) ('Reporting from EU institutions, bodies, offices and agencies has been minimal').
[290] EPPO (2025, p 71).
[291] See Chapter Five, nn 209–11 and accompanying text.

2. Rule of Law Conditionality and 'Super Milestones': Towards a Europe that Can Enforce Its Values

The audit and control system under Article 22 of the RRF Regulation has operated symbiotically with the EU's general Conditionality Regulation.[292] The latter was adopted in December 2020 in conjunction with several of the key elements of NGEU: the 2020 ORD, 2021–2027 MFF, and the EURI Regulation (the RRF Regulation would be formally adopted two months later, in February 2021).[293] In that regard, the Conditionality Regulation is typically associated with, and could indeed be regarded as part of, the overall NGEU model.[294]

The Conditionality Regulation has often been called the 'Rule of Law' Conditionality Regulation, which is not inaccurate but still something of a misnomer. Its purpose is to 'establish the rules necessary for the protection of the Union budget in the case of breaches of the principles of the rule of law in the Member State'.[295] As this phrasing suggests, the focus is only indirectly on the rule of law. It is more directly focused on the protection of the Union budget, which is the hook on which the EU's general regime of rule-of-law compliance, such as it is, now hangs. In that respect, the focus of the Conditionality Regulation is not far from the focus of Article 22 of the RRF Regulation on the protection of the financial interests of the Union.[296] And indeed, the two regulations overlap in the type of compliance functions each has incentivised and/or mandated at the Member State level (under threat, of course, of the suspension of payments to the Member State).

Article 4 of the Conditionality Regulation identified among potential breaches of the rule of law, for example, several that were entirely recognisable from the perspective of Article 22 of the RRF Regulation as well as Annex I of the Financing Agreements: absence of adequate 'financial control, monitoring and audit' functions, failure to undertake 'recovery of funds unduly paid', and lack of 'effective and timely cooperation' with OLAF and EPPO 'in accordance with the principle of sincere cooperation'.[297] What the Conditionality Regulation added, however, was opening the compliance aperture to a broader array of potential functions to support the rule of law more generally, relating to 'investigation and prosecution of fraud' or 'prevention and sanctioning of fraud' as well as, perhaps most importantly, 'the effective judicial review by independent courts'.[298] This broader array of potential deficiencies, in

[292] Regulation (EU, Euratom) 2020/2092 [Conditionality Regulation].

[293] See, in order of adoption between 14–17 December 2020, Council Decision 2020/2053 [ORD], Council Regulation 2020/2094 [EURI], Regulation (EU, Euratom) 2020/2092 [Conditionality Regulation], and Council Regulation (EU, Euratom) 2020/2093 [2021–2027 MFF]. See also Regulation (EU) 2021/241 [RRF] adopted in February 2021.

[294] See Chapter One, n 26 and accompanying text.

[295] Regulation (EU, Euratom) 2020/2092 [Conditionality Regulation], art 1.

[296] Regulation (EU) 2021/241 [RRF], art 22.

[297] Regulation (EU, Euratom) 2020/2092 [Conditionality Regulation], art 4(2).

[298] Ibid.

effect, established a general regime of rule-of-law protection applicable to any instrument (including the RRF) involving the transfer of funds from the EU to the Member States.[299] The ultimate focus on protection of the Union budget, however, raised concerns among certain observers that the Conditionality Regulation was 'unlikely to be a game changer in the EU enforcement of the rule of law' given the difficulty of proving a connection to the EU's financial interests.[300] To have any traction at all, it would need to be 'combined with other available instruments'.[301]

Such combinations in fact followed rather quickly. Due to its broader reach and general applicability, the Conditionality Regulation, in combination with the RRF, gave the Commission a legal basis to insist on broader rule-of-law compliance in two countries— Poland and Hungary. The concern with each country was not about the substance of their draft NRRPs. In the case of Poland, for example, its NRRP included commitments to the 'decarbonisation of the Polish economy by increasing the share of renewable energy in the energy mix, the energy efficiency of the economy and the independence of Poland's energy supply'.[302] Rather, the problem was that, prior to the negotiation of the NRRPs, both Poland and Hungary had been subject to a rule-of-law procedure under Article 7 TEU, had received several rule-of-law CSRs under the European Semester, and were the subject of critical Rule of Law Reports from the Commission.[303]

To address these issues beyond the Conditionality Regulation, the Commission also had at its disposal the 2021 Common Provisions Regulation governing traditional cohesion and related funding.[304] In both Poland and Hungary, funding under the 2021 CPR was quite substantial in its own right. The 2021 CPR included a horizontal principle (or enabling clause) in Article 9(1), which required Member States to comply with the Charter of Fundamental Rights (CFR) in the implementation of the wide array of funds covered by the CPR.[305] It was through the general applicability of the Conditionality Regulation that the concept of super milestones under the RRF was born— two in the Polish NRRP, twenty-seven in the Hungarian NRRP—which would need to be fulfilled before any funding could be disbursed to these Member States under the RRF.[306] The two super milestones in the Polish NRRP were quite general and dealt primarily with restoring the independence of the Polish judiciary. The super milestones in the Hungarian NRRP were more detailed but were also 'mostly the initial steps' towards combatting broader problems not just in the area of corruption but also concerns regarding 'public procurement, judicial independence and

299 Ibid, recital (7).
300 CMLR Editorial Comments (2021, p 282).
301 Ibid.
302 European Commission (2022h).
303 The Commission needed, however, to wait to apply the Conditionality Regulation until the resolution of court challenges by both Hungary and Poland. See Case C-156/21, *Hungary v Parliament and Council* (2022); Case C-157/21, *Poland v Parliament and Council* (2022).
304 Regulation (EU) 2021/1060 [2021 CPR].
305 See generally Scheppele and Morijn (2023a), (2023b).
306 For an overview, see generally Schwarcz (2023).

decision-making, most of which featured in the Article 7 procedure and one or more rule of law reports on Hungary'.[307]

Differences in the EU's approach to Poland and Hungary extended beyond the number of super milestones to significant differences over geopolitics, particularly in response to Russia's war on Ukraine (a topic that figures prominently in Chapter Five). In particular, Hungary isolated itself in the EU by remaining sympathetic to Putin's Russia, whereas Poland played a central role in operationalising the EU's response to the conflict, for example in managing refugee flows.[308] While the Commission was divided over the approval of the Polish NRRP,[309] the imperatives of the conflict weighed heavily on its internal discussions.[310] The minutes of the decisive Commission meeting quote Paolo Gentiloni as saying: 'The situation was currently highly unusual, with Russia's war of aggression against Ukraine, and it was very important for trust to remain between the Commission and Poland'.[311] The Commission agreed to send the proposed Implementing Decision for the Polish NRRP to the Council in June 2022, which adopted it quickly. Outside commentators, particularly members of the EP,[312] as well as academics,[313] were critical about the leverage lost in approving the NRRP. But the Commission could note that, in view of the super milestones, there were few 'risks, since no payments would be made if the established milestones were not fulfilled'.[314] Moreover, the Commission also retained considerable leverage by withholding other funding (most importantly traditional cohesion and like support) on the basis of the 2021 CPR.[315]

The Commission used the same double-barrelled approach in dealing with Hungary, withholding funds under both the 2021 CPR and the RRF, even as it approved the Hungarian NRRP itself.[316] As of this writing, Hungary had failed to fulfil its super milestones satisfactorily and thus no payments from the RRF have been made, with the exception of two smaller pre-financing disbursements.[317] However, in December 2023, as part of a deal to soften Hungarian opposition on support to Ukraine, the Commission partially unblocked cohesion funds for Hungary up to €10.2 billion.[318] In exchange, Viktor Orbán, 'in a pre-agreed and constructive manner', temporarily absented himself from the meeting of the European Council precisely as the vote was taken 'on the EU's €50 billion financial aid package to keep Ukraine's war-torn economy afloat and the political decision to open formal accession talks with the country'.[319] It was 'a highly unusual way to approve a decision—especially such a

307 Ibid, p 2.
308 Bonelli et al (2022, pp 643–44).
309 Wanat et al (2022).
310 European Commission (2022i).
311 Ibid, pp 18–19.
312 European Parliament (2022c).
313 See, eg, Sadurski (2022).
314 European Commission (2022i, p 19).
315 See, eg, European Commission (2022j, recital (4)).
316 European Commission (2022k, pp 23–32).
317 See 'timeline' for Hungary on the RRF Scoreboard. European Commission (2025c).
318 Hegedus (2023).
319 Brzozowski (2023).

major one'—but as one official later was quoted as saying, '[i]f someone is absent, they are absent. Legally, it is totally valid'.[320]

It was not merely legal (though also a bit venal). Rather, it could be taken as a potentially promising indication of how 'integration by funding' could be used to advance the EU's overall strategic interests as well as its values in the face of Russian aggression in Ukraine. Nearly simultaneous with this deal, the pro-European coalition government of Donald Tusk returned to power in Poland. Two days after being sworn in (on 13 December 2024), the Tusk government submitted a payment request for the first instalment of grant and loan support under the RRF, which the Commission positively assessed just over two months later.[321] In its accompanying press release, the Commission announced: 'Poland's efforts to restore rule of law [have] pave[d] the way for accessing up to €137 billion in EU funds'.[322] The reality was that many of Poland's rule-of-law problems did not disappear just with the change of government; 'many years could pass before the legal landscape of Poland is restored to pre-2015 conditions'.[323] But for the Commission—as well as perhaps for European institutions more broadly—the fact that the Polish government was no longer controlled by a party openly hostile to its core values was enough to pave the way to RRF and cohesion funding. In this regard, the episode was suggestive of how rule-of-law conditionality, when combined with robust resource mobilisation, could help to advance efforts to construct a genuinely rather than merely 'as if' constitutional EU.[324] As far as RRF implementation was concerned, apart from partial payment issues, only rule-of-law relevant questions were salient enough to reach the political level in a way that could lead to significant withholding of funds.

D. Substantive Outcomes: The Struggles of the RRF in Action

We turn, finally, to a substantive assessment of the RRF in action, looking at a range of outcomes and what they suggest about the nature of the programme. This final section is essential to completing the task we set for ourselves at the outset of this chapter: to critically examine—rather than simply assume—whether the RRF has had a positive 'integration effect'.[325]

The national plans negotiated by the Member States and the Commission under the RRF have had a broad substantive reach. The planning process 'turned out to be a truly systemic, transversal initiative' touching on 'a very wide array of policy areas: environmental policy, energy, digitalization, but also housing, employment and

[320] Ibid. For more details on the adoption of the Ukraine Facility, see Chapter Five, Section B.1.
[321] European Commission (2024f).
[322] European Commission (2024g).
[323] Jaraczewski (2025).
[324] Lindseth and Fasone (2020). See also Baraggia and Bonelli (2022).
[325] de Witte (2023, pp 233–34). See this chapter above, n 2 and accompanying text.

social policy, public administration and the organization of the State, education and health'.[326] The significant substantive breadth could be expected from the range of domains encompassed under the 'six pillars' of Article 3 of the RRF Regulation, which collectively constituted the 'policy areas of European relevance' at the heart of the RRF.[327] Additionally, the RRF Regulation built on the European Semester, and more particularly the CSR process, which ranged across areas that were both pertinent to coordinating economic policy as well as beyond, including in the area of judicial structures and the rule of law, as we saw in the discussion of Poland and Hungary in the last section.

As will be clear from the discussion below, the investments and reforms in the NRRPs often fell into areas previously thought to be primarily or even exclusively within national competence.[328] Two factors arguably combined to make the plans' reach into national domains even more extensive than the points noted above might suggest. The first was the seemingly 'transactional'[329] (or 'contractual')[330] character of the RRF planning and spending model, which shifted the focus away from EU competence per se to the Member States' willingness to accept EU funding for projects within their own authority.[331] The second was the method of 'financing not linked to costs',[332] which the RRF Regulation explicitly incorporated into its 'performance-based' model.[333] FNLC allowed the EU to offer funding as a pure incentive, sometimes simply for reforms with no evident costs attached to them, or otherwise for the completion of investment projects irrespective of costs. Either way, the method obviated the need to consider whether or where on the spectrum of national or supranational authority the various milestones and targets actually fell. Instead, the only focus was the Member State's 'performance' in achieving those milestones and targets, whose assessment was a task belonging almost entirely to the Commission.[334]

Together these factors helped pave the way for the EU to project its (potential or real) influence in national systems irrespective of the competence structure in the Treaties. That structure, at least formally, could be traced to debates over the Constitutional Treaty two decades prior, the key results of which were then eventually carried over into the Treaty of Lisbon signed in 2007 and entered into force in 2009.[335] Those earlier debates may now seem a world away, when the challenges

[326] See also Dermine (2024, p 980).The national plans themselves can be found on the 'Country Pages' on the European Commission's RRF website, as well as through the Recovery and Resilience Scoreboard. See European Commission (2025f), (2025c).

[327] Regulation (EU) 2021/241 [RRF], art 3.

[328] See Articles 4–6 TFEU.

[329] See Chapter Three, nn 143–45 and accompanying text.

[330] See Chapter Two, nn 235–36 and accompanying text.

[331] See Fasone and Simoncini (2025, p 1164). For further discussion, see this chapter below, nn 521–48 and accompanying text.

[332] Regulation (EU, Euratom) 2018/1046 [FR], art 125(1). See Chapter Two, 263–73 and accompanying text.

[333] Regulation (EU) 2021/241 [RRF], recital (18).

[334] See this chapter above, nn 200–11 and accompanying text.

[335] See generally arts 2–6 TFEU.

facing the EU seemed less existential. Nonetheless, the competence system that these debates engendered—redefining the realms of exclusive, shared, and supportive EU competence relative to the Member States—are thought, at least in principle, to still be a key part of the EU public law landscape. The national domain, which the EU was expected to 'respect in the exercise of its competence',[336] was generally understood to include:

> *Fundamental structures and essential functions of a Member* State e.g., (a) political and constitutional structure, including regional and local self-government...
> *Basic public policy choices and social values of a Member State* e.g., (a) policy for distribution of income; (b) imposition and collection of personal taxes; (c) system of social welfare benefits; (d) educational system; (e) public health care system; (f) cultural preservation and development... [emphasis in original].[337]

While our discussion below does not focus on issues of competence per se, we shall see that the NRRPs nonetheless reached into nearly all these policy areas. This suggests that the old vision of a protected national sphere has been significantly curtailed through a series of putatively voluntary, bilateral, and transactional deals that were 'carried out in conditions of strict confidentiality'.[338]

To structure our analysis, we will focus on a series of substantive struggles that roughly track the six pillars of the RRF itself. Although the RRF was formally structured around these six pillars, in its actual operation the programme ultimately reflected little coherent strategy apart from identifying areas of spending to support national budgets and, hence, perhaps, to serve the ends of macroeconomic stabilisation at a moment of severe dislocation.

1. Green Transition as a National Public Good

Climate change is, by definition, a transnational challenge that requires cross-border action. The governance design of the RRF did not, however, support Europe-wide green transition. If that were the case, much of the money would have gone to supporting a genuine European energy policy, strengthening grids within and between Member States, instead of national subsidies to renewables generation. In its legal design, the RRF made no effort to build on explicit EU competence in trans-European networks in the energy and environmental space,[339] nor did it provide procedures

[336] European Convention, Working Group V (2002, p 10). For assurances precisely along these lines after the adoption of the Treaty of Lisbon, from a member of the Commission Legal Service writing in a personal capacity for a German audience, see Ladenburger (2011).
[337] European Convention, Working Group V (2002, p 11).
[338] European Commission (2022b).
[339] Articles 4(2)(h), 170–71, and 177 TFEU.

that would enable the planning of transnational projects in these areas. The plans, being prepared and owned nationally, were overwhelmingly about national projects, with little cross-border dimension, much less cross-border impact.[340]

The RRF Regulation includes no obligation to pursue cross-border projects, though it did ask that the plans indicate 'whether the measures included in the plan comprise cross-border, or multi-country projects'.[341] But, as the Commission guidance on NRRP drafting noted, the Member State contemplating a cross-border initiative would need to 'coordinate the preparation of their plans with the Member States that would be affected by the cross-border or multi-country project'.[342] The projects would then require 'specific bilateral or multilateral implementation mechanisms' or they could build on 'EU-level instruments [such as] Important Projects of Common European Interest (IPCEI)'.[343] Either way, given their additional planning and administrative burdens, as well as the RRF's more general emphasis on national ownership, cross-border projects were relatively rare.

The European Parliament found that, in the green space, the published number of such projects was both an 'overestimation' and 'misleading': many purely national projects were listed as cross-border projects solely because they had energy saving or energy reducing elements.[344] Purely national solar and wind energy projects were routinely categorised as cross-border projects, on the same grounds.[345] In the end, the nearly €300 billion allocation in the RRF for 'green' projects ended up financing a great deal of solar panels, electric vehicles, as well as broader (and questionable) initiatives like the Italian Superbonus (about which more in a moment). But the funding was largely distributed on an ad hoc basis, making almost no contribution towards a well-planned, integrated European energy system.[346]

The RRF Regulation identified green transition, along with digital transformation, as the first two pillars of the programme and treated them quite symmetrically. The regulation in fact spoke of the 'green and digital transition' as a linked pair.[347] The RRF Regulation then assigned each pillar significant minimum shares of total spending (37% and 20% respectively), together accounting for more than half of the planned spending under the programme.

340 Corti et al (2022a, p 35). Perhaps cognisant of this criticism, in its October 2025 report to the EP and Council on the implementation of the RRF, the Commission asserted that, despite the overwhelmingly national nature of most projects, '[s]pillover effects account for around 40% of the RRF's total economic impact'. European Commission (2025g, p 33).

341 Regulation (EU) 2021/241 [RRF], art 15(3)(cc).

342 European Commission (2021d, p 21).

343 Ibid, p 22. On IPCEIs, see European Commission (2021e). Germany and France, for example, included three IPCEIs in their plans. See Bundesministerium der Finanzen (2021, p 4, Teil 1).

344 European Parliament (2024b, para 277).

345 See, eg, European Commission (2024h, p 16).

346 Leino-Sandberg (2025e).

347 See, eg, Regulation (EU) 2021/241 [RRF], recitals (32), (42), (48); see also recital (7) (referring to 'green and digital technologies'). This harked back to the European Green Deal of 2019, which spoke of the two domains as a 'twin challenge', and 'digital transformation' as 'a key enabler for reaching the Green Deal objectives'. European Commission (2019d).

The RRF Regulation provided some loose guidelines on what should count as 'green', few of which explicitly encompassed cross-border projects.[348] Moreover, those guidelines left a great deal of room for discretion, proving expansive enough to reach a broad range of initiatives. These included, for example, legislation to improve waste management in the construction and demolition sector (Slovakia); streamlining and digitising the licensing framework for renewables (Greece); higher taxes on greenhouse gas emission/deductions for green investments (Denmark);[349] as well as the entry into force of a revised National Strategy for Green Public Procurement (Portugal).[350] Lower-beneficiary states, in particular, seemed to direct a larger proportion of their NRRPs to the green transition. The Danish NRRP, for example, reportedly devoted 60% to this pillar,[351] the Austrian 59%,[352] the Finnish 50%,[353] and the Swedish 44.4%.[354] But so too did certain higher-beneficiary states, like Germany (the fourth largest grant recipient in absolute terms after Spain, Italy, and France), which planned to invest around 40.4% of its funding to support initiatives combatting climate change and supporting energy transition.[355]

These headline percentages, however, could be misleading. One early study, for example, raised questions about whether green elements of the NRRPs would have 'lasting impact'.[356] This was a key assessment criterion under the RRF Regulation,[357] but also one logically essential to furthering a green *transition*, which obviously suggests a degree of permanence. Another more comprehensive study, published in 2022 by two German climate policy research bodies (the Wuppertal Institute and E3G), raised questions about the extent to which various NRRPs even met the 37% threshold for green measures at all.[358] It found that the target was met by only four Member States (Belgium, Finland, Germany, and Hungary), whereas four were between 30–34% (Austria, Estonia, Slovakia, and Spain), five were between 25–29% (Bulgaria, Czechia, France, Latvia, and Poland), and two were between 20–24% (Romania and Slovenia). The remaining countries, and the biggest laggards, were Portugal (17%), Italy (16%), and Greece (14%).[359]

Céline Gauer, the head of the RECOVER task force in the Commission, acknowledged in an interview that there were 'different methodologies to define what is green and what is not', but she was 'very comfortable with what we have' because the RRF Regulation 'set the methodology for us'.[360] When pressed about the scope

[348] See, eg, Regulation (EU) 2021/241 [RRF], recital (11), arts 4 and 18(4)(e), and Annex V.
[349] European Commission (2023k, p 40).
[350] European Commission (2023l).
[351] Holtze (2022, p 3).
[352] Vinzenz (2022, pp 3–4).
[353] Hiilesniemi (2022, p 2).
[354] Iossa (2022, p 4).
[355] Hacker (2022, p 3).
[356] See generally Hindriks et al (2022).
[357] Regulation (EU) 2021/241 [RRF], art 19(3)(g) and Annex V, sec 2.5.
[358] Mölter et al (2022).
[359] Ibid, Figure 1.
[360] Pinster and Witteman (2022).

of the Commission's discretion under that methodology, she replied: 'You are absolutely right that some things are obviously green, renewables, for instance, and some things are clearly unacceptable, such as fossil fuel schemes. And then there's everything in between'.[361] It was the 'in between' where the discretion of the small group of national and supranational officials at the heart of the NRRP process was 'carried out in conditions of strict confidentiality'.[362] In keeping with the Commission's restrictive approach to transparency generally, Gauer pointed her interviewers to the curated picture in the publicly disclosed NRRPs and related documents: 'You will find very detailed descriptions for projects in each and every plan. We had to look at each individual investment in great detail. For example, if you want to renovate a house to have a better energy efficiency performance, that qualifies—but only if you do it in a way that saves energy'.[363]

Among the national reforms approved by the Commission under the green pillar—one that became notorious for its deep flaws in design and implementation—was the so-called 'Superbonus' scheme in Italy. This entire episode demonstrates how Commission oversight and Member State peer scrutiny were in no way guarantees of reform quality. As described in the Italian NRRP, the Superbonus entailed 'a tax deduction of 110 % for expenditure incurred for energy efficiency improvements, such as thermal insulation of buildings and the replacement of winter heating systems, as well as the reduction in the seismic risk of buildings'.[364] The deduction operated as a tax credit that homeowners could claim 'directly against their taxes, have contractors claim them against invoices, or sell them to banks. These credits became a kind of fiscal currency—a parallel financial instrument that functioned as off-the-books debt'.[365]

Originally the Superbonus was supposed to cost €35 billion over fifteen years but, by mid-2024, the estimated total price tag reached nearly €220 billion, a massive overshoot.[366] Because the Superbonus led to significant inflation in renovation costs (exacerbated by fraud and abuse),[367] its 'environmental benefits came at an astronomical cost', well in excess of the total grant to Italy under the RRF.[368] Estimates suggested that '[o]nly 495,717 dwellings [were] renovated—meaning the average cost of the program was around €320,000 per home ... [A]ny calculation [of the total costs] will yield far north of €1,000 per ton of carbon saved'. Consequently, per Luis Garicano, an economist and former MEP, '[w]hile the Superbonus was presented as a major operation of energy efficiency and reduction of greenhouse gas emissions, it was the largest single instance of greenwashing of our time'.[369]

[361] Ibid.
[362] European Commission (2022b).
[363] Pinster and Witteman (2022).
[364] Italian NRRP (2021, p 87).
[365] Garicano (2024), citing Capone and Stagnaro (2024). See also Capone and Stagnaro (2025).
[366] Balmer and Fonte (2024).
[367] Cf EPPO (2024b, p 68).
[368] Garicano (2024).
[369] Ibid.

The implication of the Wuppertal-E3G study noted earlier was that a significant portion of projects deemed 'green' in the NRRPs (and approved as such by the Commission) actually fell outside that category[370]—or, in other words, may well have been instances of greenwashing too.[371] Moreover, the Wuppertal-E3G study found that a significant portion of the planned projects could in fact turn out to have a *negative* climate impact, thus potentially violating the 'do no significant harm' obligation in the RRF Regulation.[372] Consequently, the study maintained that close monitoring was essential 'to strengthen the climate and, at the same time, to constantly implement the do-no-significant-harm principle'.[373]

Over the course of subsequent years, however, it was unclear whether this sort of monitoring was being carried out effectively. In 2024, for example, Tony Murphy, President of the ECA, expressed his concern in the press about the lack of adequate checks to determine whether particular elements in an NRRP actually entailed a green expenditure: 'Flexibility is important of course, but the Commission and the member states [must] also have a reasonable measure of accountability'.[374] The ECA itself found both 'shortcomings in the design' and 'inconsistencies in the implementation' of the purported green measures:

> In particular, we noted that tracking climate expenditure involves a high level of approximation and some coefficients were leading to potential overestimations. We found weak indications on how the implementation of RRF measures contributes to the green transition, and also found that the contribution towards the EU climate objectives and targets is not assessed, as this is not required by the [RRF Regulation]. In addition, we found that the reporting on climate spending and green transition is disconnected from actual costs and results, limiting its relevance for stakeholders.[375]

In short, even if the funding might, at 'a high level of approximation', seem to advance the aims of the green pillar, if one examined the implementation of the NRRPs closely, there was no attempt made to assure that the funding was directed to projects that would be most useful from the perspective of the EU's energy, environmental, or climate aims.

[370] Mölter et al (2022, Figure 1).

[371] See Rubio (2022, p 10) for a concrete example from the French NRRP involving the use of RRF funds to extend 'Ma Prime Renov' (MPR), a grant scheme to support insulation, heating, ventilation, or energy audit works on private dwellings (Component 1, Investment 1). Rubio notes that the definition of the target in the plan as well as the Operational Arrangement does not require the French government to provide any proof of the improvement in terms of energy savings obtained with the MPR grants.

[372] Regulation (EU) 2021/241 [RRF], art 5(2).

[373] Mölter et al (2022, p 13 of the unpaginated pdf).

[374] Murphy (2023b).

[375] European Court of Auditors (2024a, p 4).

2. Questionable Additionality and Disguised Budgetary Support: Digitalisation and Beyond

A significant portion of digital spending under the RRF's second pillar has gone to modernising public services.[376] The EU arguably has some explicit, though narrow, competence in this space under Article 197(2) TFEU, but only as long as the digital funding is used to 'support the efforts of Member States to improve their administrative capacity to implement Union law'.[377] However, there has often been a great deal of difficulty in discerning any genuinely European dimension in these initiatives. Slovakia's NRRP included, for example, 'Creating eGovernment solutions for priority life situations', which were selected based on their frequency, severity, or 'the importance and administrative burden they represent[ed] for people or businesses (e.g. starting a business, buying residential property, marriage and birth)'.[378] Portugal's plan included a reform entitled 'Digital, simple, inclusive and secure public services for citizens and businesses', aimed at implementing the 'digital by definition' paradigm and the 'once-only principle' to make digitally available to users (individuals and businesses) one hundred of the most important public service 'bundles'.[379] Estonia—broadly considered a leader in digital initiatives—included an investment on 'Reconfiguration of basic digital services and safe transition to cloud infrastructure', supporting the migration of public IT systems to a private cloud by the end of 2024. Luxembourg's plan included investments to support the deployment of a mobile app 'allowing users to scan documents with their mobile phone ... convert photos to PDF documents', and complete 'administrative procedures and exchanges with the public administration'.[380] Many NRRPs also contained 'measures targeting the digitalisation of national healthcare and justice systems',[381] most prominently, in the latter category, the large-scale investments in Italy 'to streamline trials ... by enhancing digitisation and the human capital of the Italian judicial system in order to accelerate the backlog of cases'.[382]

The EU's ambitions with digital transformation, in line with its new Digital Decade Policy adopted in December 2022, have stretched well beyond improving administrative, health, and judicial capacities.[383] This policy built specifically on the NRRP process (in addition to various other acts and strategies adopted during the past years).[384]

[376] Lilyanova (2024b).
[377] See Chapter Three, nn 126–37 and accompanying text.
[378] Lilyanova (2024b, p 6).
[379] Ibid, p 5.
[380] Ibid, p 9.
[381] Ibid, p 3.
[382] Italian NRRP (2021, p 23).
[383] Decision (EU) 2022/2481 [Digital Decade].
[384] For a succinct but thorough overview of the digital dimension of the NRRPs, see Lilyanova (2022). The Commission proposal on the Digital Decade Policy, in addition to the 'the minimum 20% earmarking for digital transition of the Recovery and Resilience Facility', also mentioned alignment with 'existing policy proposals (e.g. the Data Governance Act, the Digital Services Act, the Digital Markets Act and those under

It identified four 'digital targets'—skill formation, digital infrastructures, the digital transformation of businesses, as well as digitalisation of public services—which were all in fact well reflected in the NRRPs and thus gave a good sense of how the EU has understood the digital pillar under the RRF more generally. No doubt, digital skill formation and infrastructures, along with digital transformation of businesses and public services—all key goals of the second pillar—are worthy and demanding objectives. But in what ways, and to what extent, were they goals best pursued via RRF funding and steering?

In a report to the European Parliament, the French economist Charles Wyplosz tried to answer precisely this question.[385] Wyplosz suggested that an EU-financed 'digital transition [is] not properly justified' in economic terms.[386] Looking at the four targets specifically, Wyplosz observed:

> The first objective [skill formation] may be seen as education, a public good best delivered at the national level. The second [digital infrastructures] concerns infrastructures that are privately developed, without the need for public intervention as long as they are subject to effective competition. The third [digital transformation of business] refers to private business actions while the last [digitalisation of public services] concerns national level administrations.[387]

Wyplosz did not see any genuine European public goods on this list, at least according to the criteria he applied. The only possible exception was improving the security of digital infrastructures, but he believed that security could probably be better achieved through regulation rather than collective financing or delivery at the EU level.[388]

Given this strong overlap with existing national spending priorities (and public goods), there is a heightened risk that, even if the EU were to pursue funding in this space, it would simply substitute for national or private spending that was already planned or was likely to take place without EU support. There is a word in German to describe this sort of redundant spending—the *Mitnahmeeffekt*—which we might translate as the 'windfall effect',[389] referring to EU money provided for things that the Member States were already planning to carry out on their own. A windfall like this implicates the 'additionality' requirement for EU funding, which applies not just in the digital space but under all pillars of the RRF.[390] In principle, the additionality

the Cybersecurity Strategy), and Union budget instruments (e.g. Cohesion programmes, the Technical Support Instrument, the Digital Europe Programme 15, Horizon Europe and InvestEU)' as well as 'Security Union Strategy, the Skills Agenda of the EU, the Digital Education Action Plan, and builds on the 2021 Strategic Foresight Report, which underpins EU's global leadership on the path towards 2050'. European Commission (2021f) (citations omitted).

385 Wyplosz (2024).

386 Ibid, p 28.

387 Ibid, p 20.

388 Ibid, p 20.

389 Wuppertal Institut and Arepo (2023, p 8).

390 For a brief history of the role of additionality in EU funding debates, see Corti et al (2022a, pp 9–10); see also Corti et al (2022b, pp 17–19).

requirement means that EU funding should not substitute for national funding already in place. However, the RRF Regulation takes an artificially narrow view of additionality, only prohibiting EU funding that would 'substitute [for] *recurring* national budgetary expenditure' (emphasis added).[391] That limited prohibition is intentionally myopic, excising out whole swaths of EU spending that would substitute for already planned but *non-recurring* budgetary items,[392] which would clearly lack the policy impact that one would hope for in genuinely additional spending in the broadest sense. In these circumstances, the likely purpose of the windfall to the Member State is not to incentivise digitalisation or any other purported policy purpose; instead, it is simply disguised budgetary support.

Sympathetic commentators have maintained that the RRF's 'overall macroeconomic benefits cannot be measured by the additionality criterion, but rather by the additional fiscal space it creates for Member States'.[393] The Commission has offered a similar macroeconomic justification:

> [T]he additionality of the RRF relates to the scale of financial support, which is unprecedented in the Union's history. The announcement of the RRF ... contributed to reducing sovereign bond spreads in the EU at the time of the COVID shock, which in turn helped mitigating risks of financial fragmentation and supporting the recovery.[394]

These were undoubtedly crucial political and economic goals. But to achieve them, the EU needed to pursue a legal strategy that masked this financial support as 'performance-based' incentives to achieve goals in certain 'policy areas of European relevance', that is, the 'six pillars'.[395] In reality, the purpose of the RRF was 'alleviating national budgets in times of economic strain'.[396] As a less sympathetic commentator put it, the RRF has served primarily as 'an artifice to expand the financial leeway of the member states by way of debt without this debt appearing in the national accounts or in the budget statistics of the member states'.[397]

To gain a sense of how this artifice has operated under the digital pillar, consider this exchange at a hearing of the EP's Committee of Budgetary Control in 2023. In a question to the Directors-General of RECOVER and ECFIN, Viola von Cramon-Taubadel, a German MEP, expressed scepticism about RRF-funded purchases and distribution of digital devices (laptops and tablets) in schools in Czechia. Referring directly to the *Mitnahmeeffekt*, von Cramon-Taubadel said: 'My bar is not as low as yours' but given the likely substitution of EU funding for national or even private funding, it was difficult to see how these purchases reflected a coherent 'strategy for

391 Regulation (EU) 2021/241 [RRF], art 5(1).
392 Leino-Sandberg and Ruffert (2022, p 443).
393 Corti et al (2022b, p 29). See also Alcidi et al (2020, p 4).
394 European Commission (2024b, p 78).
395 Regulation (EU) 2021/241 [RRF], art 3.
396 European Commission (2023g).
397 Buettner (2023, p 172).

digital transformation'.[398] Céline Gauer, Director-General of RECOVER, defended the programme by first noting that most digital spending in NRRPs had focused on public administration, though she then acknowledged that many plans did indeed include such purchases.[399] Nevertheless, she argued that, even if such purchases might seem like 'a bit of a gift', they were 'extremely beneficial' to promoting distance learning during the lockdown.[400]

There are reasonably strong indicators that this form of 'gift' (or windfall) has operated fairly widely under the digital pillar, particularly but not exclusively in the educational domain. In Austria, for example, 53% of its NRRP was devoted to digitalisation, including a programme to provide digital devices to all Austrian high school students.[401] The Austrian Court of Auditors (*Rechnungshof Österreich*) discovered that those purchases were already planned prior to the RRF, and so the *Rechnungshof* specifically characterised the EU financing as an example of the *Mitnahmeeffekt*.[402] Similarly, in Germany, the European Court of Auditors took note of a digitalisation programme for teachers in North Rhine-Westphalia, which was 'retroactively included in the German RRP', even though 'regional authorities had already decided to finance the [programme] from the regional budget'.[403] Thus, ECA found 'no intrinsic added value of EU financing through the RRF in such a case'.[404]

While these anecdotes are limited to the education context, other studies suggested that windfall effects could be found in other parts of the digital pillar. One researcher concluded, for example, that the Polish NRRP reflected 'the government's priorities over the previous years' and included 'many measures already in the pipeline, especially digitalisation and new technologies'.[405] In a study for the European Parliament on the impact of the RRF on digitalisation of small- and medium-sized enterprises (SMEs), the authors found it 'challenging to assess [whether] the RRF has delivered EU added value' given that many NNRPs in this space simply used EU funds to replace national funds in pre-existing programmes.[406] One might justify this windfall because of 'the very tight time constraints to design RRPs',[407] or perhaps because they were the most urgent and made the most sense. Moreover, 'including reforms and

[398] Committee on Budgetary Control (2023, min 11:34:00–11:34:55) (question of Viola von Cramon-Taubadel, MEP).

[399] Portugal, eg, planned to spend €600 million to purchase 600,000 laptops. The thematic analysis on the Recovery and Resilience Scoreboard for December 2024 (European Commission, 2024i) mentioned device purchases in the education sector in Austria, Germany, Hungary, Ireland, Netherlands and Spain, and equipment purchases additionally in Bulgaria, Cyprus, Czechia, Latvia, Portugal, Slovakia, and Romania. Von Cramon-Taubadel's specific question, however, related to the purchase of 74,000 digital devices (mainly laptops) in Czechia.

[400] Committee on Budgetary Control (2023, min 11:45:27–11:47:12) (response of Céline Gauer, Director-General of RECOVER).

[401] Vinzenz (2022, pp 3–4).

[402] Rechnungshof Österreich (2024, p 11).

[403] European Court of Auditors (2023c, p 50).

[404] Ibid.

[405] Pilati (2021, p 19).

[406] Godlovitch and Bodin (2022, p 30).

[407] Pilati (2021, p 19).

investments that had already been planned for some time' improved the prospects that the Member State would later 'receive the Commission disbursement on schedule and in full. To put it bluntly', this study concluded, Member States were 'incentivised to game the system'.[408]

For this reason, windfall effects are broadly present in other policy domains, as other external studies have found: 'Examples include the French production tax cut, some public transport projects in Belgium and Poland's Clean Air programme'.[409] But other examples abounded, including the German NRRP supporting climate protection research and electric vehicle purchases that were 'both already regularly financed since respectively 2016 and 2015', as well as the Austrian NRRP continuing to finance 'replacement of oil and gas heating systems, which the government announced—already before the RRF—that it intended to continue and expand'.[410] The Commission itself acknowledged that, '[i]n the case of Germany, more than 80% of the investments included in [its total] RRP were already included in the June 2020 [national] *Konjunkturprogramm*' prepared to address the dislocations of Covid.[411] Indeed, the European Court of Auditors even found instances of RRF funding also substituting for *recurring* national expenditures in direct violation of the RRF Regulation.[412]

Some countries receiving relatively large RRF allocations, such as Portugal, Croatia, or Italy—consistent with the aim of additionality—were found to accelerate the rate of their public investments.[413] But in others there was apparently 'no acceleration in investments discernible ... for instance in Poland or Cyprus which also benefit[ted] from considerable RRF injections'.[414] This study concluded that RRF funding was, as a general matter, 'at least partly used by EU Member States to replace national investment spending' across all the RRF pillars.[415] This is consistent with the intuition expressed by the European Parliament in 2023, that RRF funding has been used to replace national expenditure in a number of Member States, thus raising concerns about whether RRF funding 'has been truly additional'.[416] Other studies have provided further support for this concern.[417]

The Commission's own staff working document estimated the number of milestones or targets completed before the actual approval of their Member State's NRRP at 13%.[418] As another study put it, 'the RRF Regulation allowed for the inclusion of

[408] Corti and Ruiz de la Ossa (2023, p 1); see also Corti et al (2022b, p 28).

[409] Pilati (2021, p 19).

[410] ECORYS et al (2023, p 173).

[411] European Commission (2024b, p 67), citing Corti et al (2022a). The original source of this 80% figure was the German Council of Economic Experts (2021, p 5).

[412] European Court of Auditors (2023d, p 347, Box 11.2); European Court of Auditors (2023d, p 360, para 11.63(d)).

[413] Corti et al (2022a, p 28); see also Corti et al (2022b, p 29) ('the RRF has fast-forwarded the implementation of social investments, which would have remained merely on paper, especially in countries with limited fiscal capacity').

[414] Corti et al (2022a, p 28).

[415] Ibid.

[416] European Parliament (2023a, para 184) (discharge of the 2021 budget).

[417] ECORYS et al (2023, pp 16, 185, 187, 219), Bańkowski et al (2024, p 40).

[418] European Commission (2024b, p 68).

programmes that began as early as February 2020', suggesting the Member States were strategically able to select targets that were easy to meet'.[419] Building on already planned measures could of course contribute to greater coherence with national initiatives,[420] and it could also indicate the quality of the measures, since Member States would have been willing to fund them from their own budget. However, it remains unclear what the EU's contribution actually was, beyond offering money.

3. The Quest for (Structural) Reforms via the RRF

The third pillar of the RRF planning process—'smart, sustainable and inclusive growth, including economic cohesion, jobs, productivity, competitiveness, research, development and innovation, and a well-functioning internal market with strong SMEs'—went to the heart of economic policy challenges that had confronted Europe over many decades. How would it be possible to make Europe more competitive, innovative, and productive while promoting 'economic cohesion'—expansively redefined[421]—and also assuring that growth be 'sustainable and inclusive ... with strong SMEs'? As the third pillar's extended title suggested, Europe was groping towards a method of achieving multiple (potentially conflicting) goals all at once, under the broader rubric of 'reforms'. According to the Commission:

> Reforms are typically designed to have an enabling effect for both public and private investments, by setting the right framework conditions, removing absorption bottlenecks, addressing labour market mismatches and skills shortages, and improving the overall business environment. Reforms typically do not carry a large budgetary cost, but they must also be delivered by the Member States.[422]

The system of positive incentives in the RRF was born of the belief that Commission-enforced rules and exhortations (in the form of country-specific recommendations (CSRs) under the European Semester) were not good enough to bring about the necessary economic reforms in the Member States. By making RRF funding contingent on CSR implementation, the RRF seemingly provided EU political leadership the tool to provide financial incentives 'to push [the Member States] towards the implementation of politically costly structural reforms, namely those that have been demanded by the Council under the European Semester'.[423] The problem, however, was that these

[419] Darvas and Weslau (2023, p 22).
[420] ECORYS et al (2023, pp 15, 171, 173, 218).
[421] See Chapter Three, nn 321–27 and accompanying text.
[422] European Commission (2023g).
[423] Lebre de Freitas (2023, p 14). Under the RRF Regulation, NRRPs had to 'be consistent with the relevant country-specific challenges and priorities identified in the context of the European Semester'. Regulation (EU) 2021/241 [RRF], art 17(3). For the initial plans, this obligation included 'the full set of country-specific recommendations ... under the 201 and 2020 Semester cycles'. European Commission (2021d, p 8).

CSRs were often few in number and quite generally worded and hence difficult to evaluate.[424] And yet the RRF Regulation obligated the Commission to assess whether an NRRP was 'expected to contribute to effectively addressing all or a significant subset of challenges identified in [these] recommendations'.[425]

In its actual assessments of the NRRPs, the Commission opted to give all NRRPs an 'A' grade along this dimension,[426] an approach that would prove puzzling to for many reasons. Under the RRF as compared to prior years, the official position was that 'the implementation of the 2019 CSRs observable in actual data [was] higher than a counterfactual featuring the disappointing dynamics of CSR implementation in the pre-RRF period'.[427] Others found that the average implementation rate for 2019–2020 CSRs increased little.[428] Moreover, where the rate of implementation did increase, 'it was mainly attributable to easier fiscal recommendations' adopted during the pandemic.[429] The European Court of Auditors later found notable gaps in the incorporation of the CSRs into various plans.[430] Along similar lines, an outside report to the European Parliament found 'a considerable heterogeneity in the quality of the proposed reforms … so well and ambitiously designed in some RRPs and so vaguely described in others'.[431] Consequently, the 'lack of cross-country differences in [CSR] ratings', as another report to the European Parliament put it, 'raise[d] doubts regarding the objectivity of [Commission] assessments' from the perspective of the CSRs and the European Semester (the authors speculated that the Commission simply did not wish to reject any plans based on this criterion).[432]

If we turn from assessment to implementation of the NRRPs, doubts about the impact of the RRF on reforms persist. First, there is the basic difficulty of applying the performance-based disbursement model in the context of reforms.[433] Reforms 'are inherently difficult to measure using numerical indicators'[434] and hence tend to evade objective measurement. This is something well demonstrated by a key feature of the Italian NRRP: justice reform.[435] The Italian plan includes a comprehensive collection

[424] This was why the European Court of Auditors surmised that the Commission's 'common indicators' include none that corresponded to structural reforms. European Court of Auditors (2023b, p 24, para 45). For further discussion, see this chapter above, n 206 and accompanying text.

[425] Regulation (EU) 2021/241 [RRF], art 19(3)(b).

[426] Regulation (EU) 2021/241 [RRF], Annex V, sec 2.2. The Commission also gave a uniform 'A' grade on Member States' control systems, which might also be regarded as puzzling because, in many Member States, 'at the time of the assessment [many required control systems] were partly not yet in place'. European Court of Auditors (2022a, p 47, para 11). The control systems were included as milestones and hence non-completion could be a basis for non-disbursement of funding.

[427] Bańkowski et al (2024, p 35).

[428] Darvas (2024, p 2).

[429] Ibid. For a different read on the data from an institutional perspective, see European Commission (2024d, p 11, sec 2.2).

[430] European Court of Auditors (2022a, pp 24–25, paras 50–53).

[431] Lebre de Freitas (2023, p 55).

[432] Darvas and Weslau (2023, p 25).

[433] Relatedly, see this chapter above, n 206 and accompanying text, discussing the lack of common indicators for structural reforms.

[434] European Court of Auditors (2023b, p 24, para 46).

[435] Italian NRRP (2021).

of reform measures, from criminal and civil law to insolvency and tax courts, as well as digitalisation and recruitment procedures of the justice system. Looking at the milestones and targets for these reforms, they do include a number of quantitative targets that look very appropriate: there is, for example, a target for the reduction of pending cases both in the Civil Ordinary Court (M1C1-47) and in the Civil Court of Appeal (M1C1-48) by a whopping 90% by Q2 2026,[436] and somewhat less demanding numerical targets for other courts as well. The problem is that such objective, results-oriented targets only come at the very end of the programme. For the first several years, money is paid out on the basis of purely procedural milestones such as the entry into force of certain pieces of legislation, the entry into force of the necessary delegated acts, and the start (and two years later, the conclusion) of the recruitment process.[437] By the time the plan gets to the actual deliverables, most of the money has already been paid out. If, at that point, it is found out that, for one reason or another, the case backlog did not shorten as expected, then there is little the Union can do beyond withholding whatever insignificant amount of money may still remain undisbursed or, more likely, to renegotiate less stringent targets.

The Spanish labour market reform (C23) offers another example of a hard-to-quantify reform.[438] Again, it is a comprehensive package of sub-reforms, with its most contentious parts covered by reforms dealing with types of employment contracts, active labour market policies, public support for temporary layoffs, collective bargaining, and labour rights in subcontracted companies. This package of measures was intended to tackle and, frankly, overturn some of the most disliked features of an earlier 2012 labour reform, then designed by the Troika and enforced on Spain as part of its ESM programme.[439] As such, it is an interesting 'example of the role Europe can play in influencing national policies via funding conditionality'.[440] For these reforms, however, there is no obvious attempt to come up with truly performance-oriented targets, apart from the adoption of the reforms themselves. Disbursements are linked purely to procedural milestones, specifically to the entry into force of the relevant pieces of legislation.

As to the content of those legal acts, the Council Implementing Decision, the only legally binding document in the implementation of a recovery plan, is exceedingly vague.[441] Exacerbating the vagueness is the fact that every key milestone is prefaced with the phrase '[r]especting social dialogue and as part of a comprehensive approach balancing the need for flexibility and security in the labour market . . .'.[442] In their confidential negotiations, the Commission may well have had a sense of the substantive

[436] Council of the European Union (2021a, pp 74–75).
[437] For an overview, see Italian NRRP (2021, pp 55–60) (sec 3. Organizational Innovation of Justice).
[438] Council of the European Union (2021b, pp 207–12, 216–18).
[439] For a brief discussion, see Chapter Two, n 34.
[440] Aranguiz (2022); see also Miró et al (2024).
[441] Council of the European Union (2021b, pp 207–12, 216–18).
[442] Ibid, pp 216–18, R4–6, 8.

content it had in mind, but the Council Implementing Decision contains few traces of what that might be, aside from outputs.[443] As the European Court of Auditors concluded in a recent review: 'The absence of suitable indicators' beyond mere outputs 'significantly limits the possibility of assessing the result or impact of RRF labour market reforms. Although the RRF Regulation does not explicitly require member states to set up specific result indicators, we consider them essential for assessing performance'.[444]

One of the common expectations early in the life of the RRF was that, by linking reforms to funding, there would be the 'hardening' of the notoriously soft CSRs in the face of national resistance.[445] These hopes proved difficult to realise. While the prospect of funding may have helped put 'long-awaited reforms onto the member states' policy agenda',[446] 'the financial incentives offered by the RRF have not resulted in a substantial increase in [reform] implementation rates'.[447] An ECB paper found that, despite the frontloading of reforms in many NRRPS, by the end of 2024 'the percentage of reform-related milestones and targets already classified as fulfilled by the European Commission [was] well below 50% in many euro area countries'.[448] The same paper found 'a risk that the RRF's effectiveness will be diminished by incomplete or ineffective implementation' by the 2026 deadline, noting in particular a fear that Member States might '"rush through" some reforms and pursue an opportunistic "box-ticking" approach (in which deliverables are formally achieved but the measures are insufficient for the intended economic impact to fully materialise)'.[449] If current trends were to continue, the pre-RRF explanations for mediocre CSR implementation rates ('the inherent difficulty in influencing national policy decisions, the lack of coherence with [party] programmes[,] and limited involvement of national parliaments in the CSR process')[450] would still seem to explain the unrealised hopes for 'hardening' under the RRF.

When we focus on structural reforms specifically, we get a sense of why those explanations still have traction. Structural reforms inevitably involve 'the messier world of politics, parliaments and implementation'.[451] As a consequence, 'difficult structural reforms, including the labour market, governance and taxation' saw essentially no improvement in their already low implementation rates.[452] The European Court of Auditors, in a March 2025 report specifically on labour market reforms, also found

[443] See this chapter above, nn 200–11 and accompanying text, discussing European Court of Auditors (2023b).
[444] European Court of Auditors (2025b, p 44, para 93).
[445] See, eg, Vanhercke and Verdun (2022), Bongardt and Torres (2022), Nguyen and Redeker (2022).
[446] Lebre de Freitas (2023, p 13).
[447] Darvas (2024, p 6). Again, for the alternative, curated picture, see European Commission (2024d, p 11, sec 2.2).
[448] Bańkowski et al (2024, pp 39–40).
[449] Ibid, p 41.
[450] Darvas (2024, p 1) (citations omitted).
[451] Bokhorst (2023, p 37).
[452] Darvas (2024, p 6).

that, in cases where 'important elements of the CSRs remained unaddressed', these typically 'related to recurring structural challenges'.[453] Despite commitments in the NRRPs to implement these difficult structural reforms, the plans' negotiators simply could not control whether or what the political process would actually deliver, especially given the limited ownership of the plans and the non-existent role of parliaments in their preparation.[454] Structural reforms are deeply political in their nature, and it was hardly unexpected that they could—and indeed should—generate political debate and even contestation and resistance. The Commission has always needed to walk a delicate line, because experience showed that, when it overtly applied political pressure in national politics, the result was often to undermine the policy reform in question (indeed, even the legitimacy of the EU more broadly).[455]

A suggestive example came from the French effort to reform its pension system to unify disparate regimes and raise the retirement age from 62 to 64 years old. Reform of the pension system had been on the domestic agenda in France for decades, but its impact was especially profound and destabilising in recent years, particularly after the French government forced through a reform in 2023 using a special (and, many argue, undemocratic) constitutional procedure.[456] The effort at reform was largely attributed to Emmanuel Macron, though opposition figures also tried to link it to EU pressure (Marine Le Pen spoke of 'blackmail' by Brussels).[457] A 2019 CSR had indeed recommended: 'Reform the pension system to progressively unify the rules of the different pension regimes, with the view to enhance their fairness and sustainability'.[458] However, the battle lines on pension reform were already well drawn when that CSR was handed down. It its NRRP in 2021, while taking note of that CSR,[459] the French government did not include pension reform as an actual milestone or target or provide a time frame for its completion. This meant that French RRF funding would not be dependent on a successful reform or, perhaps more importantly, it would not raise the prospect of a potential claw-back if the French government were forced to backtrack on reform (which is hardly out of the question, given the fraught state of French national politics).[460]

In this sense, France followed the strategy that many other Member States followed, limiting its milestones and targets to attainable projects to assure future disbursements of RRF funding.[461] The Commission was critical of France's plan that 'the reform of the pension system [was] not accompanied by milestones and target[s] for the implementation of the reform'.[462] The Commission, however, approved the overall

[453] European Court of Auditors (2025a, p 22, para 40).
[454] See this chapter above, nn 78–82 and accompanying text.
[455] Bokhorst (2022, pp 113–14);
[456] French Constitution, art 49(3). For an overview of the surrounding political upheaval, see, eg Drake (2023), Rouxel and Yon (2023).
[457] Sénécat (2023).
[458] European Commission (2019e).
[459] French NRRP (2021, pp 26, 35, 741, 797–98).
[460] Le Monde (2025).
[461] Corti and Ruiz de la Ossa (2023, p 1).
[462] European Commission (2021g, p 47).

plan as 'a comprehensive package of reforms and investments directed at addressing the challenges identified in the country-specific recommendations, with a few gaps that are partially tackled via measures outside the Facility'.[463]

Insofar as pension reform was concerned, the French government filled the gap in the NRRP through its 2023 reform law. That law formally cast the reform as a 'rectification' of the prior year's social security budget (despite its long-term financial impact), which allowed the law to bypass the ordinary legislative procedure by engaging the confidence of the government, leading to the reform's adoption without a vote but subjecting the government to votes of no confidence.[464] The tactic was controversial because elements of this procedure had been used in the past but never in combination to adopt such a momentous piece of legislation.[465] While the Constitutional Council found the chosen process for the most part in conformity with the constitution,[466] the solution provoked an upheaval in French politics from which, as of this writing, it has yet to recover.

What does this episode teach us about structural reforms and European integration? It suggests that, as we get closer to the essence of genuinely constitutional authority—that is, the mobilisation of scarce resources implicating fundamental questions of values and legitimacy in a polity—the essential locus of politics remains national. This sort of robustly constitutional politics is 'no straightforward, purely technocratic exercise'[467] of the type the Commission has mastered (or for which the European Parliament is a helpful adjunct).[468] This explains why the Commission has faced an uphill battle against the Member States in terms of economic policy coordination, at least as measured by CSR implementation rates and structural reforms.[469]

If current trends do continue, Europe will need to face an uncomfortable reality: even *with* the RRF financial incentives, the EU (and certainly the Commission) lacks the ability to mobilise the necessary 'legitimacy resources', much less the actual authority, to fully steer national policy in the face of ground-up resistance mediated through national politics.[470] Consequently, even under the RRF, the power-legitimacy nexus still seems to have been operating in important ways, even with the increased funding leverage. It should also be kept in mind that the reforms that are included in national plans range from broad societal reform agendas to small sectoral projects with little permanent mark. The links to CSRs remain limited in comparison to the massive list of investments and reforms contained in the plans. Moreover, the Union will have spent billions without a possibility 'to assess, based on their final milestones

463 Ibid.
464 French Constitution, art 49(3).
465 Fasone (2024).
466 Décision n° 2023-849 (2023).
467 Bokhorst (2023, p 37).
468 Cf Stie (2012).
469 See generally Miró et al (2024).
470 On the concept of legitimacy resources and its impact on European integration, see Lindseth (2010, pp 11, 52–53, 186, 224, 227–28, 249, 265, 275) See also Leino-Sandberg and Saarenheimo (2018, p 645), as well as Chapter Two n 72 and accompanying text.

or targets alone, whether those measures had been successfully completed and whether the expected outputs and results had been achieved'.[471]

4. Ratcheting, Absorption, and the Eclipse of Traditional Cohesion

We introduced what we are calling the 'ratcheting strategy' in Chapter Two,[472] and we further identified it as a key feature of the legal design of the RRF Regulation in Chapter Three.[473] Ratcheting, as we have been using the term, refers to a strategic effort over two decades to blur the boundaries of cohesion, with the aim of redirecting actions towards broadly macroeconomic needs that are distinct from cohesion's original (and more specific) regional-developmental aims.[474] This subsection moves beyond the question of legal design to the broader systemic effects of this ratcheting strategy.

From early on under the RRF, there was considerable evidence that a major systemic effect of ratcheting was the effective collapse of traditional cohesion policy itself. This was reflected, first, in the marginal place of traditional cohesion in the NRRPs. The fourth pillar, where one would expect to find such policies, 'account[ed] for only about 10.2% of the total RRF resources (i.e. some €50 billion)'[475]—this in a programme that looked to the cohesion flexibility clause as its exclusive legal basis. NRRPs also listed the fourth pillar as the secondary objective on an additional 34.4% of spending, but this was not comforting to many cohesion specialists, reflecting the sort of definitional ratcheting that we were discussing above. As John Bachtler and Viktoriya Dozhdeva put it in late 2021:

> Although economic, social and territorial cohesion are explicitly in the scope and objectives of the RRF, *cohesion does not appear to be a significant objective of NRRPs* [emphasis in original] ... While cohesion is in many cases (broadly) mentioned among the general objectives / expected impacts of the NRRPs, there is often a lack of detail on how this will be delivered ...[476]

Given the RRF's 'peculiar nature and sheer size', one could expect that the programme's operation would be of 'strategic importance for the current implementation and, even more, for the future evolution' of traditional cohesion policy.[477] As the RRF began

[471] European Court of Auditors (2025b, p 15, para 29).
[472] See Chapter Two, nn 204–62 and accompanying text.
[473] See Chapter Three, nn 321–27 and accompanying text.
[474] See also Díez Sánchez (2025).
[475] Sapala (2024, p 4).
[476] Bachtler and Dozhdeva (2021).
[477] ECORYS et al (2023, p 277) (discussing 'a lively debate on the compatibility of this new instrument with Cohesion policy').

to monopolise political attention and administrative resources over the course of 2021, traditional cohesion policy had trouble laying the necessary groundwork for even a modicum of success during the 2021–2027 programming period. Traditional cohesion was beset by delays both in the adoption of a new Common Provisions Regulation as well as in entering into and finalising new Partnership Agreements with various Member States.[478] Cohesion experts also expressed concerns about how Member States were incentivised to shift projects away from traditional cohesion to the RRF. An obvious reason for doing so was avoiding the co-financing obligations that applied to traditional cohesion, thus reducing pressure on 'national budgets in times of economic strain'.[479] Similarly, 'the pressure [for] quick implementation [and] absorption' also favoured the shift to the RRF.[480] Finally, the duplication of goals between the two programmes (green and digital transitions, infrastructure, innovation, etc) made it difficult to demarcate the line between the RRF and traditional cohesion, thus opening the way to substitute RRF funding for traditional cohesion where possible.[481]

Differences in governance between the RRF and traditional cohesion also incentivised these substitution effects, given that, under the RRF, national 'ministries could exercise control of implementation and guarantee compliance with the agreed targets and deadlines', leading to 'the de facto exclusion of sub-national actors' whose involvement traditional cohesion typically required.[482] The external study for the RRF's mid-term evaluation confirmed the existence of these substitution effects,[483] which raised further questions about the RRF's additionality and its incentivising impact on reforms or investments under the rubric of cohesion. Again, one fair implication was that the purpose of the RRF was primarily 'budgetary support' and only secondarily incentivising new actions.[484]

The influx of funding under RRF, when combined with traditional cohesion funding for the 2021–2027 period, had another, even broader systemic effect: it placed considerable downward pressure on absorption rates across both programmes. As the European Court of Auditors documented, 'inflation or supply shortages' undermined RRF absorption, as did 'underestimation of the time needed to implement measures, uncertainties regarding specific RRF implementation rules (such as the "do no significant harm" principle) and challenges related to the administrative capacity of member states'.[485] Absorption rates for traditional cohesion

478 Núñez Ferrer and Ruiz de la Ossa (2022, pp 118, 122).

479 European Commission (2023g).

480 Ferry and Kah (2021, p 37).

481 As ECORYS et al (2023, pp 166–70) makes clear, the effort to demarcate the boundary between cohesion and the RRF was a major challenge, at both the drafting/approval and implementation/disbursement stages.

482 Corti et al (2022b, p 28).

483 ECORYS et al (2023, pp 177–78); see also European Commission (2024b, pp 63–64).

484 Alcidi et al (2020, p 4).

485 European Court of Auditors (2024b, p 4).

funding, however, dropped even more precipitously,[486] and the RRF itself was clearly the cause.[487]

In addition to the reasons mentioned above, there was the sheer scale of RRF funding. In higher-beneficiary states, RRF funding equalled or exceeded the amount of traditional cohesion funding both in absolute terms and as a percentage of GDP. The Court of Auditors later found that there were fourteen countries receiving at least twice as much funding for the 2021–2027 period as they did for 2014–2020.[488] The ECA further concluded that 'for those member states in which cohesion funding already accounted for a significant share of public investments, absorbing significantly more EU funds in the 2021-2027 period with the introduction of the RRF would be particularly challenging'.[489] As Tony Murphy, President of the ECA, stated in an interview regarding Italy, it was 'supposed to spend almost three-and-a-half times as much in 2021-2027 as it had to absorb in 2014-2020. That is a lot of money, and a lot of pressure on public authorities'.[490] The amount of money conferred on Italy under the RRF vastly exceeded the capacity of the Italian government to spend effectively, if at all.[491]

These absorption problems were not only predictable but predicted.[492] They also had potentially significant institutional consequences for traditional cohesion policy as a distinct programmatic field (apart from the ratchetted version of cohesion under the RRF). Given the 'weak position' of traditional cohesion vis-à-vis the RRF,[493] a debate ensued over the course of the early- and mid-2020s on the future of traditional cohesion policy beyond 2027, up to and including whether cohesion could or should survive as a separate programme. For the strongest adherents of traditional cohesion, the threat was perceived as existential, with the RRF serving as 'an alternative centralised and performance-based' model that, if generalised or rendered permanent, would undermine key aspects of traditional cohesion policy.[494] As we will see in Chapter Six, these existential fears proved to be well founded, as later developments would show.[495]

[486] Over the prior two programming periods (2007–2013 and 2014–2020), cohesion funding has been able to reach roughly 60% at the end of seven years and roughly 90% after an additional three years. But in the current cycle, by 2024 or three years in, only 5.1% of available funds had been absorbed. Schwab (2024, p 288).

[487] Ibid, citing Núñez Ferrer and Ruiz de la Ossa (2022).

[488] European Court of Auditors (2024b, p 27, para 43).

[489] ibid, p 29, para 44.

[490] Murphy (2023a).

[491] Di Mascio and Natalini (2023).

[492] See, eg, Alcidi et al (2020, p 4); European Court of Auditors (2023e, p 41, para 53).

[493] Bachtler et al (2024, p v).

[494] Bachtler and Mendez (2023, p 38); see also Molica (2022), Molica et al (2024), Committee of the Regions (2024).

[495] See Chapter Six, n 4 and accompanying text, discussing European Commission (2025h, p 1), (2025i, p 2), (2025j, p 3).

5. 'Resilience': An All-Purpose Justification for EU Spending in Areas of National Competence

The concept of 'resilience', as noted in Chapter Three, has been integral to the expansive use of Article 175(3) TFEU as a legal basis.[496] In practice, this seemingly 'neutral, technical term',[497] whose meaning is 'neither transparent nor objectively determined',[498] could 'be twisted and shaped into all kinds of different forms'.[499] This concept not only figures in the name of the RRF itself but has also served as a sort of catch-all justification for funding a wide range of initiatives that fall almost entirely under national competence. The RRF's final two pillars are cases in point: 'health, and economic, social and institutional resilience, with the aim of, inter alia, increasing crisis preparedness and crisis response capacity' and 'policies for the next generation, children and the youth, such as education and skills'. Both pillars have an open-ended quality, referring to domains (health and education, in particular) that fall squarely within national competence. In many respects these two pillars are simply window dressing for the core purpose of the RRF to distribute nearly €800 billion in budgetary support to the Member States, first for 'recovery' from Covid, but then, more openendedly, to support the overarching aim of 'resilience', which in the end could effectively mean essentially anything at all.

One of the central aims of the RRF's fifth pillar was to reinforce the public health system after Covid. But 'the wide range of policy areas' that also fell under the label 'resilience' under this pillar—'effectiveness of the public administration; long-term care; crisis preparedness; effectiveness of judicial systems; tax measures; fiscal policy and fiscal governance; fraud prevention, to mention but a few'[500]—reflects the protean and, in many ways, substantively boundless quality of that concept. The EU has shared competence under Article 4 TFEU for 'common safety concerns in public health matters'. However, the EU's competence for the broader aspects of 'protection and improvement of human health' is, under Article 6 TFEU, limited to 'support[ing], coordinat[ing] or supplement[ing] the actions of the Member States'. This competence allocation roughly corresponds to the distinction between European and national public goods in the health space. As Charles Wyplosz has observed, 'collection and exchange of information, procurement of medicines and vaccines, and the provision of treatment during unexpected emergencies' are clearly European public goods (as Covid well demonstrated).[501] But 'the provision of health services, the bulk of health policies, are national public goods'.[502] In pillar five, a great deal of what the EU

[496] See Chapter Three, nn 321–27 and accompanying text.
[497] Joseph and Juncos (2024, p 380).
[498] Grove (2018, p 49).
[499] Joseph and Juncos (2024, p 380).
[500] Lilyanova (2023b, p 3).
[501] Wyplosz (2024, p 8, see also p 19).
[502] Ibid.

has funded under the rubric of health measures fell into the second category—for example, improving access to health care, addressing shortages in health staff, and increasing investment in the health care sector.[503] As the Commission summarised the achievements of the RRF in 2024: 'Healthcare capacity has been increased, including in hospitals, clinics, outpatient care centres and specialised care centres. By the end of 2023, thanks to the Recovery and Resilience Facility, up to 45.8 million people annually could benefit from a new or modernised healthcare facility'.[504]

Before NGEU, under the European Semester, access to health care had been a standard focus of many CSRs, but the efforts to implement them needed to be financed nationally. The RRF led to a fundamental change, in which the EU would now take on a role in financing social and health care services in many Member States, at least on a temporary basis. Approximately half of the Belgian NRRP's elements, for example, related to fifth pillar initiatives, with 'measures for the health and social systems of the Flanders and Wallonia regions, which differ substantially from one another'.[505] Finland's plan sought 'to complement a recent social and healthcare system reform that aimed to improve cost efficiency and equal access to services'.[506] Latvia dedicated 10% of its total RRF funding to health, focusing 'on the development of new models for the delivery of effective integrated health services ...; improving human resources management and upskilling ...; and establishing a service laboratory system for testing and evaluating different service models'.[507] Many milestones and targets in the NRRPs under this pillar, however, were quite general, referring to initiatives that only required a certain degree of political commitment rather than concrete legislative measures, such as a National Strategy (for mental health, as in the case of Bulgaria); a National Programme (for oncology, as in the case of Czechia), a report (assessing stocks of critical drugs by the Danish Medicines Agency); or funding guidelines (for establishing new primary health care units in Austria).[508] Many of these were not even 'outputs' under the RRF's misguided sense of 'performance', as ECA argued above,[509] but merely inputs that would hopefully yield a worthwhile positive output in the future.

The range of initiatives that could be placed under the fifth pillar, however, included not just health care but also disparate initiatives that loosely related to 'economic, social and institutional resilience' in the very broadest sense. To get a taste, one could look at Hungary's NRRP.[510] A factsheet issued by the Commission following the plan's approval touted not just 'support for upgraded healthcare infrastructure and equipment' or 'developing primary and preventive care' under this pillar, but also 'gradual

503 Lilyanova (2023b, p 4).
504 European Commission (2024j, p 16).
505 Lilyanova (2023b, p 5).
506 Ibid, p 6.
507 Ibid, p 7.
508 European Commission (2023k, pp 60–61).
509 See this chapter above, nn 201–02 and accompanying text.
510 European Commission (2022l).

wage increases' for teachers, and 'improving access to mainstream education for disadvantaged students and for those with special needs'. But also included under this pillar were rule-of-law 'super milestones' in the area of anti-corruption and judicial independence,[511] as well as 'reforms promoting the medium and long-term sustainability of the Hungarian pension system ... combatting aggressive tax planning, [and] simplifying the tax system'.[512] This gave a sense of the catch-all range to which the concept of 'resilience' could be stretched.

Distributed across multiple pillars have been initiatives relating to housing, one of the strategic priorities of the second van der Leyen Commission. In the Recovery and Resilience Scoreboard, the Commission admitted that housing is not the EU's 'direct competence'[513]—a term unknown to the EU Treaty structure—but that nonetheless the RRF played a 'prominent role' in channelling EU resources in this space.[514] Under the RRF, €19.6 billion was allocated to housing projects, with Italy, Spain, Portugal, France, and Greece as the greatest beneficiaries.[515] While the seriousness of the housing crisis is clear, what remains unclear is the EU's role in addressing it beyond offering money. The Commission stressed the 'variety of policies' in the Member States, operating along a 'complex' continuum responding fundamentally to local conditions.[516] Aside from wishing to appear active in this space, the scoreboard discussion begged the question (essential to the always-applicable principle of subsidiarity): what can the EU do better than the Member States, and why would such measures be better funded from Brussels?

The range of the RRF's final pillar—'policies for the next generation, children and the youth, such as education and skills'—also falls squarely within what had traditionally been regarded as a core national competence. In economic terms, as Charles Wyplosz has shown, education is a national and not a European public good and thus 'best delivered [and funded] at the national level'.[517] To that end, Article 6 TFEU limits EU competence in the domain of 'education, vocational training, youth and sport' to 'support[ing], coordinat[ing] or supplemen[ing]t the actions of the Member States'.[518] One might well say that funding nationally proposed initiatives under the NRRP model falls within this limited competence because Article 6 TFEU does not (on its face, at least) preclude the EU from providing incentives to promote matters within national competence. But there are risks associated with that funding strategy. Given the dominance of Member States in this space, funding could well end up substituting for already planned, indeed *recurring*, national spending in violation of the additionality requirement of Article 5(1) of the RRF Regulation.[519] Concomitantly, the risk of

511 See this chapter above, nn 306–07 and accompanying text.
512 European Commission (2022l).
513 European Commission (2025k, p 4, first para).
514 European Commission (2025k, p 4, second para).
515 Ibid, p 8, table: 'Total housing expenditure in the recovery and resilience plans').
516 Ibid, p 3, last para.
517 Wyplosz (2024, p 20). See this chapter above, nn 387–88 and accompanying text.
518 See also Articles 165–66 TFEU, further delineating these supportive powers.
519 Regulation (EU) 2021/241 [RRF], art 5(1). See this chapter above, nn 390–91 and accompanying text.

the EU funding merely serving as a disguised subsidy to national budgets, without any 'coordinating' (ie incentivising) effect within EU competence, is high.[520] Moreover, there is the question of unequal treatment: why should the EU be able to provide laptops to students in some countries but not in others, or contribute to better quality childcare for some EU citizens but not for others?

6. Avoiding Competence Limitations Through 'Transactional' Funding? The Hamilton–Madison Debate Comes to Europe

One response to these concerns would be to stress the transactional character of the RRF and of NGEU more generally. It is broadly assumed, as noted by Cristina Fasone and Marta Simoncini, that 'the transactional nature of policy implementation [under the NRRPs] confers on the EU flexible tools to negotiate beyond the competence restrictions set in the Treaties'.[521] This claim raises, however, the deeper question of whether the EU is competent to achieve goals *by funding* that it could not achieve *by regulation*.

Alexander Hamilton held a similar view in the United States in the 1790s, in a famous debate with James Madison over the scope and effect of Federal spending power in the first decade of the newly adopted United States Constitution.[522] But in contrast with those advocating a similar position for the EU today, Hamilton based his expansive interpretation on the express commitment in Article I, Section 8, Clause 1 of the US Constitution, which specifically authorises spending 'for the … general Welfare'. This phrasing clearly supports the existence of a spending power autonomous and distinct from the regulatory authority enumerated elsewhere in the US Constitution.[523] James Madison, by contrast, argued for a more restrictive reading, in which the spending authority 'amounted to no more than a reference to the other powers enumerated in the subsequent clauses' of Article I, and spending should be limited 'to the enumerated legislative fields committed to the' Federal Government under the Constitution.[524] The spending power, in Madison's view, could not serve as an alternative means of achieving regulatory goals that the US would not have the authority to achieve directly by way of its enumerated regulatory competence.

In the US constitutional doctrine, the Hamiltonian view of an autonomous spending power 'for the … general Welfare' has prevailed, albeit within certain Madisonian limits.[525] Those limits relate to the regulatory conditions that Congress

[520] See this chapter above, nn 395–96 and accompanying text.
[521] Fasone and Simoncini (2025, p 1164).
[522] For an overview, see the seminal decision of the United States Supreme Court in *United States v Butler*, 297 US 1, 65–66 (1936), which upheld the Hamiltonian view on the basis of the wording of US Constitution, art I, sec 8, cl 1.
[523] See generally 297 US at 64–66.
[524] Ibid, 65.
[525] Again, see ibid, 65–66.

may constitutionally attach to spending consistent with federalism.[526] The prevailing case law in the US, along Hamiltonian lines, gives Congress broad deference on whether the spending is 'for the ... general Welfare', subject only to a 'cursory' inspection of whether 'the condition imposed [is] reasonably related to the purpose for which the funds are expended'.[527] The more demanding analysis—clearly in a Madisonian vein—turns on whether 'the financial inducement offered by Congress might be so coercive as to pass the point at which pressure turns into compulsion'.[528] It is within the power of Congress 'to create incentives for States to act in accordance with federal policies', but Congress cannot, consistent with federalism, use those incentives 'to require the States to regulate'.[529] The core concern in this context is political accountability, in which Congress in effect forces 'state officials [to] bear the brunt of public disapproval, while the federal officials who devised the regulatory program may remain insulated from the electoral ramifications of their decision'.[530] As the US Supreme Court elaborated, 'this danger is heightened when Congress acts under the Spending Clause, because Congress can use that power to implement federal policy it could not impose directly under its enumerated powers'.[531]

The differences between the EU and the US are many, and most obviously, the EU is not a federation and relies instead on conferred powers. Moreover, the EU Treaties contain no explicit general spending provision akin to Article I, Section 8, Clause 1 of the US Constitution, and certainly not one that creates power autonomous and distinct from the regulatory authority enumerated in the remainder of the Treaties. In EU law, EU spending has followed competence.[532] Consistent with this settled understanding of EU spending power, the German FCC, in its ORD ruling of 2022, ruled that any borrowed funds under NGEU must be 'used for the exercise of competences conferred upon the European Union and, to that end, are from the outset strictly assigned to such specific purposes'.[533] The claim that the EU now enjoys an implicit general spending power with an autonomous regulatory power attached to it (in a

526 See *South Dakota v Dole*, 483 US 203 (1987).

527 Ibid, 213 (O'Connor, J, dissenting).

528 Ibid, 211 (internal citation and quotation omitted).

529 *Nat'l Fed'n of Indep Bus v Sebelius*, 567 US 519, 577–78 (2012) (internal citation and quotation omitted).

530 ibid, 578 (internal citation and quotation omitted).

531 Ibid.

532 When the EU has wished to fund something, this has required not only adding the relevant entry in the budget but also approving a basic act on the matter, which requires a legal basis in the EU Treaties. According to the European Court of Justice: 'The requirement that a basic act must be adopted before an appropriation is implemented derives directly from the scheme of the Treaty, in accordance with which the conditions governing the exercise of legislative powers and budgetary powers are not the same'. Case C-106/96, *UK v Commission* (1998), para 28. See also Case 242/87, *Commission v Council* (1989), paras 16–18. The EU's Financial Regulation repeats the same principle: 'Appropriations entered in the budget for any Union action shall only be used if a basic act has been adopted'. Regulation (EU, Euratom) 2024/2509 [Financial Regulation], art 58(1). The Financial Regulation defines a 'basic act' as a provision of the TEU, TFEU, or Euratom Treaty that 'provides a legal basis for an action and for the implementation of the corresponding expenditure entered in the budget'. Regulation (EU, Euratom) 2024/2509 [Financial Regulation], art 2(4).

533 BVerfG (2022), para 171. See also Chapter Three, nn 280-284 and accompanying text.

Hamiltonian sense) derives from the expansive reinterpretation of the cohesion flexibility clause in Article 175(3) TFEU.[534] The institution behind this reinterpretation—the Legal Service of the European Commission—has never sought to explain it, much less defend it, in a publicly disclosed legal opinion.

That is a poor basis on which to build, in effect, a Hamiltonian system in which a general spending power becomes the backdoor means to steer Member State policy-making. To permit such a move in the EU—particularly on the unprecedented scale of spending under the NGEU model[535]—would simply allow utterly opaque executive-technocratic transactions as well as the misaligned incentives of 'integration through funding' to accelerate and intensify the breakdown in the competence structure in the Treaties.[536] This is taking place in a system without a similar textual basis or any real constraints on regulation through spending unlike in the US. From the perspective of comparative federalism, the Commission's expansive policy-steering claims are in fact extraordinary.[537] In the United States, where the federal and state governments are both understood to enjoy robust democratic and constitutional legitimacy (something not true in the EU), the federal government has no power to steer states' exercise of their core powers in a similar way. Indeed, even attempts by the federal government to interfere in core state powers through spending conditionality is subject to considerable constitutional scrutiny.[538]

The EU Treaties do include various legal bases that refer explicitly to using EU funds to promote a policy goal (such as Article 40(3) TFEU on agricultural guidance and guarantee funds, or Article 162 TFEU on the European Social Fund), or where the idea of funding is implicit but clearly a part of the envisaged EU toolkit (such as development cooperation; economic, financial, and technical cooperation; or humanitarian aid). Where the EU has competence to work directly through funding rather than the adoption of legislative or regulatory rules—traditional cohesion being a prime example—the accompanying legislative framework has historically operated as a means of directing or allocating the funding on a cost basis to certain national projects with a view of promoting the enumerated Treaty objective in question (in the case of cohesion, 'reducing disparities between the levels of development of the various regions and the backwardness of the least favoured regions').[539]

The general law of cohesion spending, however, has not been understood to entail the power to work around competence limitations elsewhere in the Treaties,[540] to bring policy-making otherwise under national competence in line with a uniform

534 See Chapter Three, Sections A and D.

535 See Conclusion, n 73 and accompanying text; see also Chapter One, nn 63–68 and accompanying text.

536 For more on those misaligned incentives, see this chapter below, Section E, and Conclusion, Section C.

537 For an examination of the EU compared to several mature federal systems, see Leino-Sandberg and Saarenheimo (2018, pp 631–35).

538 See, eg, *Nat'l Fed'n of Indep Bus v Sebelius*, 567 US 519 (2012); see also *West Virginia v US Dep't of the Treasury*, 59 F 4th 1124 (11th Cir 2023).

539 Article 174(2) TFEU.

540 Indeed, Article 175(3) TFEU specifically includes the proviso 'without prejudice to the measures decided upon within the framework of the other Union policies'.

EU model. That view would violate a well-settled principle in the case law of the EU: 'Other articles of the Treaty may not ... be used as a legal basis in order to circumvent the express exclusion of' competence elsewhere in the Treaty.[541] Moreover, as a shared competence, the EU's cohesion authority is subject to the principles of subsidiarity and proportionality under Article 5 TEU, as is the EU's even more restrictive competence merely to 'support, coordinate or supplement the actions of the Member States, without thereby superseding their competence in these areas'.[542] This would suggest that a general spending power 'for the general Welfare', one that purportedly 'confers on the EU flexible tools to [steer policy] beyond the competence restrictions set in the Treaties',[543] would be antithetical to this carefully calibrated competence structure.

In the EU case, the concern expressed by the US Supreme Court over diluted political accountability in regulation by spending is especially strong under the RRF and the NGEU model more generally. As the analysis in this chapter noted at multiple junctures, the opaque and technocratic character of the RRF's planning and spending model makes it nearly impossible to trace the political 'authorship' of numerous spending/regulatory actions (drawing on the apt terminology of Dermine), thus further undermining political accountability in the EU case.[544] Moreover, the use of spending incentives based on the 'financing not linked to costs' model, as well as the vagaries of measuring 'performance', buries responsibility for the spending/regulatory actions still further into the realm of opaque and technocratic negotiations.[545]

These problems of diluted political accountability exist regardless of whether the RRF's planning and spending model is more transactional than coercive. But even the idea that the Member States were somehow (non-coercively) free to refuse to participate in the programme's planning and spending process is itself deeply questionable.[546] That assertion may have been true *formally*, but the claim depends on bracketing out the realities of massive economic dislocation to which NGEU (and hence the RRF) were meant to respond. The functional pressures on the Member States, particularly those lacking their own fiscal space to adopt counter-cyclical measures, were significant. These realities ensured that national policy makers would not only participate but also that they felt 'induced and pressured to comply with the commitments made in their plans'.[547] As a leading member of the RRF governance structure within the Commission put it: 'This is not a free lunch'.[548]

[541] Case C-376/98, *Germany v. Parliament and Council* (Tobacco Advertising) (2000), para 79, referring specifically to the power to harmonise 'laid down in Article 129(4) of the Treaty'; cf also Case C-19/23, *Denmark v Parliament and Council* (Alternative Minimum Wages) (2025), Opinion of Advocate General Emiliou, paras 133–34.

[542] Article 2(5) TFEU; see also Article 6 TFEU.

[543] Fasone and Simoncini (2025, p 1164).

[544] See this chapter above, nn 90–91, 102–03, 123–26, 150–60, and 165–70 and accompanying text. See also Dermine (2024, pp 980–82).

[545] See this chapter above, nn 52–67, 120–30, 196–230 and accompanying text.

[546] See this chapter above, nn 329–31 and accompanying text.

[547] Dermine (2024, p 981); see also Patrin (2023a).

[548] Pinster and Witteman (2022) (interview with Céline Gauer).

No doubt, that compulsion had its limits—or perhaps better, the socio-political realities went both ways. The Commission, as the EU's key agent here, was also forced to accept that expanded supranational power via funding would necessarily operate against the backdrop of the persistently polycentric and *demoi*-cratic character of European integration. In practical terms, this meant the Commission needed to accept investments and reforms in the NRRPs that had a strongly, even overwhelmingly, national quality to them,[549] no more so than under the fifth and sixth pillars. Indeed, in the quest to augment its institutional position, the Commission may well have been *incentivised* to promote this national orientation of the programme, a topic we take up in the next section. This may be one of the main reasons that the European added value of the investments and reforms, apart from the stimulus itself, was usually missing throughout the RRF.[550] After all, what is the value added of EU action if it merely provides funding for policies or projects that are geared to producing national public goods?

E. 'The Commission Should be Proud of its Success': Debt Overhang and Elusive European Added Value

In the first half of 2025, in bus stops all around Europe, colourful advertisements began to appear to celebrate the achievements of NGEU. They were part of 'a new EU-wide campaign across Member States', the Commission's website explained, which 'focus[ed] on improved strength and resilience' flowing from NGEU 'in the areas of education and skills, business and healthcare in particular'.[551] The campaign spanned twenty-one Member States and used various channels—'out-of-home advertising (OOH), online ads, and print media insertions in national and some regional publications'—costing just under €26 million.[552] The advertisements built on local campaigns that had been under way since February 2024, the date of the Commission's mid-term review of the RRF, 'to show to citizens the positive impact that NextGenerationEU-funded projects have had on local communities'.[553] As the Commission's mid-term review itself had put it, the RRF's 'reform and investment agenda [had] help[ed] to create a more modern, prosperous, inclusive, climate-neutral, and sustainable EU that is resilient and better prepared for future opportunities and challenges'.[554] The minutes of

549 Leino-Sandberg (2023b).
550 See, eg, this chapter above, nn 404 and 406 and accompanying text.
551 European Commission (2025l). The advertisements showed photos of a hospital nurse/university student/laboratory researcher/precision manufacturing worker next to a declaration in large type in all capital letters 'Reinforcing Health in Europe'/'Modernising Education in Europe'/'Updating Skills in Europe'/'Strengthening Companies in Europe', which appeared the common tagline 'NextGenerationEU makes us stronger' and the Commission's 'NextGenEU' logo.
552 Europe Direct (2025b).
553 European Commission (2025l).
554 European Commission (2024d, p 18).

the meeting of the College of Commissioners that approved the mid-term review recounted how then-Vice President Dombrovskis explained: '[T]he NextGenerationEU recovery plan was now delivering the expected results and helping to achieve the political objectives for which it was conceived'.[555] The minutes then recorded Paolo Gentiloni pointing out how, 'on the whole, the NextGenerationEU recovery plan had strengthened the Commission's institutional role, as the implementation of major reforms on sensitive issues for the Member States, such as taxation, was now linked to the disbursement of the Facility's funds'.[556] For her part, the Commission President concluded by stressing 'the enormous progress that had been made thanks to NextGenerationEU' and how the performance-based approach to managing the funds has 'proved effective in practice'.[557] The advertising campaigns of 2024 and 2025 were designed, it seems, to implement her call that 'the Commission should be proud of its success and communicate this to citizens'.[558]

The idea that the RRF had 'proven' the value of the performance-based model by 'linking disbursements to the gradual implementation of reforms and investments through agreed milestones and targets' has become a cardinal of faith within the Commission.[559] But as the European Court of Auditors has repeatedly stressed, the reality is otherwise. In its 2025 review of 'the weaknesses of the RRF', ECA reminded us that the programme simply could not be regarded as performance-based because:

- milestones and targets provide information on progress in the implementation of RRF-funded measures but focus on outputs rather than results, vary in ambition, sometimes lack clarity and do not always cover a measure's key implementation stages, including completion;
- common indicators mainly refer to output, cover the six pillars to only a limited extent, and are not well aligned with the EU objectives in the relevant policy areas (e.g. the green and digital transitions). Neither baselines nor expected targets were set for these common indicators;
- the efficiency of resource use, and therefore value for money, cannot be assessed given that the Commission does not collect or use information on actual costs.[560]

The reality was—and still is—that it was far too early to assess the RRF except in terms of how much money has been funnelled to national budgets.

While assessing performance may be out of the question at this stage, there are still a number of empirical and practical observations that, by way of conclusion to this

555 European Commission (2024k, p 20).
556 Ibid, p 21.
557 Ibid, p 23.
558 Ibid.
559 Ibid, p 6.
560 European Court of Auditors (2025b, p 7) (cross-references to other paras in the review omitted).

chapter, we can make regarding the RRF's 'integration effect'.[561] The major one arises out of a central paradox of the RRF in action. On the one hand, the RRF has almost completely sidelined EU competence limitations by developing a transactional model to influence, through financial incentives, Member State action in areas of national competence. In the process, the cohesion flexibility clause of Article 175(3) TFEU has transformed into a general spending power[562]—albeit with little attempt to prioritise, generally considered a useful guarantee of prudent government spending—while in turn undermining traditional cohesion's focus on disadvantaged regions.[563] On the other hand, despite the expansion in EU power, the RRF has left much to be desired in terms of aligning national policies into a coherent programme at the EU level. The RRF tried to avoid the fate of the European Semester by emphasising 'national ownership'. But in practical terms, ownership typically meant national projects in national siloes, under supervision from the Commission that ultimately did little to gear them towards European public goods. As a result of explicit choices made when designing its governance structures, cross-border projects (for which EU funding would make much sense) were few.[564] The RRF Regulation provided some highly general—and, with their minimum percentages, spuriously accurate—policy objectives, such as 'green' or 'digital' transition. But a closer look at spending in those domains raise serious concerns that those labels have masked either a considerable degree of greenwashing,[565] or support to national budgets without any real impact on advancing the goal of digitalisation (eg the paradigmatic purchases of 'laptops for school kids').[566] In its October 2025 annual RRF report, the best that the Commission could do was to stress purported 'spillover effects' of national projects, claiming these 'account[ed] for around 40% of the RRF's total economic impact'.[567]

There is then the range of democratic concerns about the operation of the RRF, particularly at the interface (or lack thereof) with national parliaments and other stakeholders. As this chapter recounted, the Commission's argumentation on this point has ultimately been troubling and evasive. On RRF document access requests, the Commission has suggested that its decision-making should be understood as outside of democratic politics, better to prevent 'open[ing] the door to undue external pressure' and thus ensuring its 'independence and objectivity'.[568] Its approach was in direct conflict with the one recommended by the European Ombudsman, in collaboration with the Organization for Economic Cooperation and Development (OECD), whose 'good practice principles for government transparency in the use of recovery funds'[569]

[561] See de Witte (2023, pp 233–34), discussed in this chapter above, n 2 and accompanying text.
[562] Lindseth and Leino-Sandberg (2024b).
[563] See this chapter above, nn 472–94 and accompanying text.
[564] See this chapter above, nn 339–43 and accompanying text.
[565] See this chapter above, nn 369–71 and accompanying text.
[566] See this chapter above, nn 398–404 and accompanying text.
[567] European Commission (2025g, p 33).
[568] European Commission (2022e, p 14). See this chapter above, nn 161–63 and accompanying text.
[569] OECD and European Ombudsman (2022).

called for 'a whole-of-society approach'.[570] The Ombudsman's proposed alternative approach would put 'collaboration with key stakeholders and citizens' at the heart of RRF governance, 'coupled with the joint efforts of the European Commission and Member States to ensure transparency, social accountability, and oversight of public decision making'.[571] In this restrictive effort on transparency, the Commission was unfortunately supported by the General Court.[572]

The European Ombudsman, the European Court of Auditors, and the European Parliament all made counter-efforts—which we have discussed at length throughout this chapter—to move past the limited and curated transparency authorised by the RRF Regulation. But these efforts proved to have a primarily informational rather than political impact, though developments in July 2025—both the first motion of censure against the von der Leyen Commission, as well as the broad critique of the process and substance of the new MFF proposals—may portend a modest political shift.[573] But for most of the life of NGEU, hierarchical oversight, such as it was, was supposed to be the primary responsibility of the Council. But that body's role, at least at the approval stage of the plans, proved deeply time-constrained, doing little to displace the Commission's leading position as the guardian of useful information flows. Moreover, at the implementation and disbursement stage, the task of oversight was delegated to the EFC, which was equally time-constrained and dependent on information from the Commission. As a device to promote cross-national political scrutiny of the Member States, the EFC's role ultimately proved to be something of a formality.

Finally, there have been struggles associated with the scale of the RRF planning and model. 'More' has indeed proven to be 'different'.[574] The challenges ranged from the analytical demands on the Commission to evaluate thousands of investment and reform projects across twenty-seven Member States;[575] to the capacity of the Member States to absorb the unprecedented amount of money to be distributed;[576] to the national-supranational complexities of control, audit, and combatting fraud.[577] Adding further complexity was the financing model of funding not related to costs. Because this meant funding with no relation to the actual costs (if any) of the milestones or targets, their 'value' was based on a discretionary assessment of the Commission flowing primarily from confidential negotiations with the Member State.[578] This lacked transparency and also reduced the opportunities to enforce financial accountability on how the funds were used. Additionally, it created incentives

570 Ibid, p 6.
571 Ibid.
572 Case T-77/22, *Asesores Comunitarios* (2023). See this chapter above, nn 171–79 and accompanying text.
573 See Chapter Six, Section B.2.
574 See Chapter One, nn 63–68 and accompanying text.
575 See this chapter above, nn 41–67 and accompanying text.
576 See this chapter above, nn 485–492 and accompanying text.
577 See this chapter above, nn 256–90 and accompanying text.
578 European Court of Auditors (2022a, p 51, para 118; see also pp 31–32, paras 73–75). See this chapter above, nn 63–64 and accompanying text.

for Member States to 'game the system' by including in their NRRPs a large number of already planned projects to maximise chances of completion/disbursement (hence undermining the additionality of the funding and European added value of the programme).[579] The EU's role boiled down to providing funding.

Performance-based funding may have its uses. It may operate well under clearly defined objectives and reasonably measurable results that can be properly evaluated for their impact.[580] This is too often not the case with the RRF, at least not for a significant part of it. Half of the RRF is its reforms, and they tend to evade objective measurement.[581] Many reforms might very well be highly justifiable—that is not the issue. In the absence of actual results-oriented indicators, much of European taxpayers' money is distributed on purely procedural, output-oriented bases. The Commission may choose to call this performance-based but, in substance, it has little to do with performance.

As of this writing, the Member States were scrambling to complete the many remaining investments and reforms while the Commission was hurrying to make disbursements on instalment requests before the facility expires in 2026. In its October 2025 annual RRF report (the last before this book was submitted for publication), the Commission was still reporting that only 55% of RRF funds had been disbursed as of 31 August 2025 (though the Commission also pointed out more hopefully that more than 60% of RRF grant funding had been disbursed).[582] The European Court of Auditors had warned in September 2024 that the 'risk that not all planned measures will be completed in time' was real.[583] ECA stressed that from 'past experience … spending the money as quickly as possible [did] not bode well' because it could lead to 'more spending mistakes': 'Unlike regular EU budget spending, where the Commission exercise[d] greater control and oversight, RRF funds [were] subject to less scrutiny and more self-policing. This increase[d] the risk of irregularities and even fraud'.[584] Moreover, as an ECB paper points out, the push to meet the 2026 deadline could lead Member States to '"rush through" some reforms and pursue an opportunistic "box-ticking" approach (in which deliverables are formally achieved but the measures are insufficient for the intended economic impact to fully materialise)'.[585]

The Commission's response to these concerns was, in effect, to try to move in two directions at once. On the one hand, it tried to simplify procedures governing Member State revision of NRRPs, in order to 'address implementation bottlenecks', while also 'streamlin[ing]' Member State reporting requirements.[586] On the other hand, it tried to accelerate/beef up its independent auditing of Member State spending, pointing to

579 See this chapter above, n 408 and accompanying text.
580 European Court of Auditors (2023b). See this chapter above, nn 200–11 and accompanying text.
581 European Court of Auditors (2023b, p 24, para 46). See this chapter above, nn 433–34 and accompanying text.
582 European Commission (2025g, p 7).
583 European Court of Auditors (2024c).
584 Ibid.
585 Bańkowski et al (2024, p 41). See this chapter above, nn 448–49 and accompanying text.
586 European Commission (2024l).

seventeen 'risk-based ex-post audits ... on the satisfactory fulfilment of milestones and targets' and 'four system audits of national control systems' over the September 2023–August 2024 period. All the while, the Union continued to accumulate debt that needed to be paid back. Compared with the typically scarce discretionary allocations available in the national budget, RRF injected massive amounts of new money into the European economy, particularly in high-beneficiary Member States. And during the time when EU money appeared abundant and free, there was arguably insufficient pressure, much less controls, to ensure that the funding was well spent. This funding misdirection was not merely a product of poor execution but of the RRF's design, which was meant to operate both as a stimulus package and as a mechanism to buy EU leverage in national politics, doing so without the messy process of Treaty reform. The NGEU, via the RRF, no doubt served its purpose in 2020–2021 of pacifying the markets at a point when fragilities were high and risks very real. But when one actually reads the NRRPs, their often overwhelmingly national character raises understandable concerns about why the EU would want to create a massive debt overhang to fund many of these projects.[587]

In June 2025, in its 'road to 2026' communication on the homestretch of the RRF, the European Commission (as always reflecting the 'political culture of total optimism' that Giandomenico Majone noted over a decade ago),[588] insisted that the programme was 'showing tangible results', 'leading to long-lasting growth effects', and 'driv[ing] structural change'.[589] The phrasing was intentionally loose and the back-up evidence anecdotal and patchy, for good reason. The RRF's short-term impact was increasingly looking quite modest, at least in terms of GDP.[590] Moreover, the medium-term GDP impact remained 'a great unknown',[591] with much depending on absorption of the RRF funding. This would in turn depend on whether the Member States would achieve their milestones and targets as planned.[592]

Given the way many of the milestones and targets were formulated, genuine performance assessment may never be possible. All that remains are output measures, and the main ones that could be cited on behalf of the RRF were the amounts of money allocated and disbursed, which were considerable. While the precise allocation numbers continue to shift at the margins, the overall picture had become reasonably clear by the spring of 2025. The RRF allocated 60% of its funding to just three states: Italy, Spain, and Greece (€393 billion of the €650 billion committed).[593] This diverged from the allocations set out in the RRF Regulation, granting them about

587 Leino-Sandberg (2023b).

588 See, eg, Majone (2014) (Chapter 2: A political culture of total optimism: its rise and fall).

589 See European Commission (2025m, pp 2, 4).

590 An ECB paper in 2024, eg, estimated that the impact on GDP for the euro area by the end of 2023 had been 'between 0.1% and 0.2% annually to the GDP level of the euro area, compared with around 0.5% initially expected'. Bańkowski et al (2024, p 4).

591 Martínez Turégano (2025).

592 Bańkowski et al (2024, p 42).

593 See European Commission (2025n) (for total commitment), and European Commission (2025f) (for country allocations).

45%,[594] caused in large part by an imbalanced loan take-up that ultimately altered the nature of the Facility.[595] Despite the 'six pillars', the complex and extended NRRP process, the 'performance-based' framing, etc, the RRF became, over time, primarily a straightforward fiscal transfer to high beneficiary states.

But even as a fiscal transfer mechanism, the programme raised serious questions. Six months out from the beginning of the RRF's final year, '[t]he current pace of implementation [was] not sufficient to ensure the completion of all milestones and targets by August 2026 and the disbursement of the full RRF allocation by the end of the Facility in 2026'.[596] The main way that the Commission proposed to address the problem was, to put it mildly, extraordinary. It advised Member States to revise their plans

> to ensure all milestones and targets can be implemented by the 31 August 2026 deadline. Only measures that are certain to be fully implemented by this deadline should remain in the plans. Measures for which this cannot be guaranteed should be removed to avoid the decommitment of large amounts of RRF funds. Priority should be given to securing the grants allocation.[597]

The next months witnessed the renegotiation of various national plans, highlighting how the interest of Member States in the EFC and Council has focused on securing their own share of RRF funding rather than ensuring that EU funds are directed at justified causes and properly scrutinised. The obvious alternative to 'securing the grants allocation' at all costs would be to save the money and reduce the subsequent NGEU debt overhang.

The risk of eventual backlash is real. Citizens in lower-beneficiary Member States, in particular, may wonder why the EU would, in one country, contribute to household renovations via tradeable tax credits at 110% of the renovation costs, whereas in other states leave the full cost of renovations to the individual citizens themselves. The advertising campaign undertaken by the Commission in spring 2025 conveniently glossed over these concerns, giving the impression that the benefits of NGEU (via the RRF) in the areas of European health care, education, research, and business—all core national domains—were somehow evenly distributed. They were not, and could not be, at least in the sense implied by that campaign, for the simple reason that the real purpose was to address the uneven distribution of fiscal space among Member States and to calm the markets.

594 Regulation (EU) 2021/241 [RRF], Annex IV.

595 More creditworthy Member States were able to borrow from the credit markets on terms more favorable than what the EU was offering via the RRF. Under Regulation (EU) 2021/241 [RRF], art 14(5): 'The maximum volume of the loan support for each Member State shall not exceed 6,8 % of its 2019 GNI in current prices'.

596 European Commission (2025m, p 6).

597 Ibid, pp 8–9.

That well may have been (and may well be) a European policy objective very much worth pursuing. But in the constitutional borderlands in which the EU found (and still finds) itself under NGEU, the EU needed to hide this general-interest spending behind an elaborate 'performance-based' system under the rubric of cohesion, funding a range of national projects in 'policy areas of European relevance structured in six pillars'.[598] In doing so, it drove the EU deep into the domain of national competence, fundamentally blurring the boundary between national and European public goods.[599] The obvious outcome is that, in doing so, NGEU distracted attention away from the sort of European public goods that were genuinely worthy of EU financing. The pressures for spending on real European public goods, in particular defence and security, would only increase as the 2020s progressed, highlighting opportunity costs, a topic we take up in Chapter Five.

598 Regulation (EU) 2021/241 [RRF], art 3.

599 By touting purported transnational 'spillover effects' of those national public goods, the Commission simply has tried to blur that boundary still further. See European Commission (2025g, p 33).

Chapter Five
The Emergence of the NGEU Model
Extensions and Deviations

NextGenerationEU, at its inception, was billed as 'an exceptional response to ... temporary but extreme circumstances', 'clearly limited in size, duration and scope'.[1] Along with the use of the emergency procedures of Article 122 TFEU as a legal basis for the EURI Regulation, this framing was essential to keeping the frugal Member States politically onboard at the outset. The recitals to the EURI Regulation, after reiterating the exceptional and temporary character of the NGEU, specified that its support 'should only be made available for the purposes of addressing the adverse economic consequences of the COVID-19 crisis or the immediate funding needs to avoid a re-emergence of the COVID-19 crisis'.[2] The 2020 ORD included similar assurances: Article 4 set out a general prohibition that '[t]he Union shall not use funds borrowed on capital markets for the financing of operational expenditure'.[3] It then set forth a limited exception to that prohibition as a 'derogation' from Article 4: the collective borrowing destined for grants to the Member States could be used for expenditure but *only for* 'the sole purpose of addressing the consequences of the COVID-19 crisis' through the EURI and its referenced sectoral legislation.[4] Additionally, the 2020 ORD stated: 'The Commission shall manage the borrowing ... so that no new net borrowing takes place after 2026'.[5]

The evident implication of these various assurances was that, once the Covid emergency had passed and all the proceeds of the collective borrowing were distributed via the programmes contemplated by the EURI, normal budgetary practices would return and the exceptional debt would be paid back over time. But as experienced observers of EU politics have long understood, little occurs in the integration project without establishing a precedent.[6] '[W]hat can be done once can be done again', wrote Martin Sandbu in *The Financial Times* soon after the European Council announced the political agreement over NGEU in July 2020. Official insistence of the exceptional or temporary nature of NGEU did not quell calls, often from leading EU officials, to

1 European Council (2020, p 3, para A4).
2 Council Regulation 2020/2094 [EURI], recital (6).
3 Council Decision 2020/2053 [ORD], art 4.
4 Ibid, art 5(1)(b); see also art 2(2)(a)(ii) (allocating 'up to EUR 312 500 million in 2018 prices for a programme financing recovery and economic and social resilience via support to reforms and investments').
5 Ibid, art 5(1), third para.
6 Sandbu (2020).

European Integration in the Constitutional Borderlands. Päivi Leino-Sandberg and Peter L. Lindseth,
Oxford University Press.
DOI: 10.1093/oso/9780198949527.003.0006

make the nascent collective borrowing and spending capacity a permanent feature of EU governance.[7]

The Commission, in particular, found it difficult to maintain the official characterisation of NGEU as a one-off instrument given how tempting it was to take credit for such an objectively momentous step. In May 2021, for example, while debates over the 2020 ORD were still pending in concerned national parliaments, Valdis Dombrovskis, the Executive Vice President in the first von der Leyen Commission, told the European Parliament that the 'more successful we are in the implementation of [the RRF] the more scope there will be for discussions on having a permanent instrument, probably of a similar nature'.[8] Yet the next day, anticipating a tight vote in the Finnish Parliament over the ORD, Dombrovskis tweeted in Finnish: 'It is clear to the Commission that the #NextGenerationEU instrument is a one-off, unique and strictly limited in time'.[9]

With the advent of collective borrowing for grants under the RRF, the debates over whether Europe had finally achieved its 'Hamiltonian moment' now only intensified.[10] Much of the Hamiltonian talk actually reflected a historical misunderstanding. Observers often equated Hamilton's major achievement in the early history of the United States with collective borrowing or assumption of state debts while, in fact, 'the true Hamiltonian innovation ... was the conferral of taxing authority on the federal government in the US Constitution'.[11] This was a step not taken under the NGEU.[12] And insofar as collective borrowing was concerned, the Continental Congress exercised that power as early as 1775.[13] So, if one were seeking an analogue in US history for the integration project post-NGEU, the 'pre-constitutional' regime under the Articles of Confederation was the better choice; at that time, 'the "confederal" level, such as it was, remained entirely dependent on the polycentric legitimacy of its constituent states to mobilise resources on the confederation's behalf'.[14] In the constitutional borderlands in which the EU still found itself under the NGEU, crossing the Rubicon of autonomous taxing power was largely out of the question. The Member States have in fact shown little enthusiasm for adopting

[7] See, eg, Lagarde (2020) ('We should discuss the possibility of [NGEU] remaining in the European toolbox so it could be used again if similar circumstances arise'); Regling (2020) ('a permanent facility ... would be useful. It would expand the fiscal space of a country in a downturn beyond the national fiscal buffers').

[8] Strupczewski (2021).

[9] Dombrovskis (2021) ('*Komissiolle on selvä asia, että #NextGenerationEU -väline on kertaluonteinen, ainutlaatuinen ja se on tiukasti ajallisesti rajattu*') (Leino-Sandberg translation).

[10] For an overview, see Georgiou (2022). See also Buettner (2023).

[11] Lindseth (2023, p 209), citing Edling (2003).

[12] For a succinct analysis, see Buettner (2023, pp 169–71). Cf also Mayer (2024, p 174) ('There was no Hamiltonian or constitutional moment').

[13] Georgiou (2022, pp 139–40). Under the Constitution of 1787 in the United States, it was 'the new fiscal regime based on federal taxation' that paved the way for the other elements of Hamilton's strategic vision: 'the restructuring of the revolutionary war debt stock, the federal assumption of state debts, the creation of a quasi-central bank (the Bank of the United States) and the promotion of a national banking system and securities markets'. Ibid, p 140.

[14] Lindseth (2023, pp 209–10).

the various new own resources politically agreed at the time of NGEU's approval. All of these new own resources would have required amendment to the 2020 ORD, which never happened.[15] As of this writing, the only prospect for such new own resources is via the Commission's proposal for a new ORD as part of the MFF package in July 2025.[16]

None of this should detract from the historical significance of NGEU along the more limited dimensions of borrowing, planning, and spending under the RRF. Those elements of the NGEU model quickly shed their official veneer as exceptional and temporary, emerging as a baseline for multiple extensions of, as well as deviations from, the NGEU model in subsequent years. These extensions and deviations in the development of the NGEU model are the focus of this chapter. The functional pressures for extending and modifying the NGEU model only grew with the Russian war on Ukraine and the ensuing energy crisis (unsurprising given how, in the history of the formation and evolution of states, war and related security threats had long served as key drivers in capacity expansion and constitutional change).[17] Adding further momentum to this process was the increasingly competitive and protectionist stance of the United States, first under the Biden administration via the Inflation Reduction Act of 2022,[18] and then much more aggressively under the second Trump administration via hostile tariff and trade policies and threats of withdrawing the US security umbrella from Europe. The result was an intensified focus by European leaders on rebuilding the continent's competitiveness and autonomous strategic and defence capabilities in the face of deep uncertainties about the geopolitical and international trade situation going forward.[19]

What this meant in terms of altering Europe's constitutional or legal infrastructure, however, was often ambiguous. In the early years of NGEU, some initiatives were made—in the European Parliament and in the Conference on the Future of Europe in particular—to consider amendments to the Treaties, but these proposals failed to gain traction and soon faded from sight.[20] Nor were amendments really considered to the primary legal foundations of the NGEU—the EURI Regulation or the 2020 ORD—whose original versions remained intact over the 2020s. Reform efforts instead focused on the RRF Regulation and the MFF, which found themselves twice amended to cover new emergencies, albeit in ways that were difficult to square with the Covid focus of both the ORD and the EURI.[21] Regardless of how strong the original constraints on the use of NGEU funds may have seemed, their political half-life was short-lived. The funds allocated to the RRF quickly became a generic and readily

[15] See this chapter below, nn 264–79 and accompanying text.
[16] See Chapter Six, Section B.2.
[17] See, most famously, Tilly (1975), (1992); see also Kaspersen and Strandsbjerg (2017).
[18] Pub L 117–69; 136 Stat. 1818; Dermine (2023, p 142).
[19] Dermine (2023, pp 142–43).
[20] See, eg, Conference on the Future of Europe (2022), Group of Twelve (2023), European Parliament (2023c).
[21] See this chapter above, nn 2–5 and accompanying text.

available pot of money that could easily be repurposed with little or no additional political or financial cost.

As we shall see in Section A, amending the RRF would be central to two key extensions of NGEU: the first, via REPowerEU, designed in the wake of the Russian invasion of Ukraine in February 2022 to end the EU's dependence on Russian fossil fuels (oil, coal and gas);[22] and the second, via the Strategic Technologies for Europe Platform (STEP), which repurposed funding from several EU programmes including the RRF to subsidise 'critical technologies' to counteract the protectionist incentives under the US Inflation Reduction Act and other national initiatives.[23] In Section B, we then move beyond amendment of the RRF to the extension of NGEU's planning and 'performance-based' incentives model to other contexts—macro-financial assistance (MFA) programmes, the Social Climate Fund, and the new Economic Governance Framework under the Stability and Growth Pact. In Section C, we examine what the European Court of Auditors has aptly called the 'patchwork construction' of the EU's 'financial landscape' post-NGEU,[24] whether in terms of its complex budgetary mechanics, its financing mechanisms, or its scrutiny and accountability provisions. Section C will consider the mounting pressures on the EU budget flowing from inflation, the need to support Ukraine in the face of Russian aggression, and increasing competitive pressures from the United States and elsewhere. Section C concludes with reflections on what the EU's evolving financial landscape, more particularly the EU's emergence as a so-called 'sovereign-style issuer' of debt, suggests about the continuing 'as if'-constitutional character of the integration project post-NGEU.

A. Amending the RRF: Recycling Funding to New Purposes Beyond Covid

1. REPowerEU: Ending the EU's Dependence on Russian Fossil Fuels

The collapse of Russian fossil fuel deliveries following Putin's invasion of Ukraine in February 2022 triggered a sharp increase in energy prices in Europe, prompting the Union to take several emergency actions falling under the rubric of 'REPowerEU', all aimed at reducing Europe's dependence on Russian fossil fuel imports.[25] By its terms, REPowerEU would build 'on national energy and climate plans and their updates, existing Recovery and Resilience Plans (RRPs), cohesion policy operational programmes and any other relevant plans and climate resilience needs'.[26] It quickly

22 See European Commission (2022m); Regulation (EU) 2023/435 [REPowerEU].
23 European Commission (2023m, p 2); Regulation (EU) 2024/795 [STEP], recital (2).
24 European Court of Auditors (2023g).
25 European Commission (2023m).
26 Ibid.

became clear that amending the RRF would be 'at the heart of the REPowerEU Plan, supporting coordinated planning and financing of cross-border and national infrastructure as well as energy projects and reforms'.[27]

Before turning to that amendment, it is worth noting other emergency measures that the Commission adopted in the following months, generally on the legal basis of Article 122 TFEU.[28] As discussed in Chapter Three, Article 122(1) TFEU specifically empowers the Council, on a proposal by the Commission, to 'decide, in a spirit of solidarity between Member States' to adopt 'measures appropriate to the economic situation' in cases of 'severe difficulties arise in the supply of certain products, notably in the area of energy'.[29] This specific mention of difficulties in energy supplies made Article 122(1) TFEU the obvious choice to ground multiple emergency actions over the course of 2022. Among the more controversial—one indicative of the challenges that the EU faced as it grappled with the limitations of its own fiscal mobilisation powers—was a regulation requiring Member States to establish a 'temporary solidarity contribution' to be applied to the 'surplus profits' of businesses active in the oil, gas, coal and refinery sectors.[30] The regulation further instructed the Member States to use any proceeds to 'mitigate the effects of high prices', in particular on vulnerable households or energy-intensive companies.[31] Though this measure looked very much like tax harmonisation (which would require unanimity in the Council),[32] the contribution was framed as a 'cap on market revenues' to avoid that requirement.[33] This choice of Treaty basis (quite exceptionally) gave rise to considerable litigation challenging the legality of the regulation, which as of this writing is still largely unresolved.[34]

The more secure way to finance other elements of REPowerEU was to amend the RRF, as a means of redirecting a portion of its planning and spending process towards the new needs. Initially proposed in May 2022 and formally adopted in February 2023, the amended RRF Regulation allowed the Member States to incorporate REPowerEU chapters into their NRRPs.[35] The RRF was particularly attractive as a source of financing because, given that only seven Member States had requested loans under the programme, this left up to €220 billion available for REPowerEU.[36]

[27] European Commission (2022n).

[28] See, eg, Council Regulation (EU) 2022/2576; Council Regulation (EU) 2022/2578; Council Regulation (EU) 2022/2577; Council Regulation (EU) 2022/2372; Council Regulation (EU) 2022/1854; Council Regulation (EU) 2022/1369.

[29] See Chapter Three, nn 213–16 and accompanying text.

[30] Council Regulation (EU) 2022/1854, art 14.

[31] Council Regulation (EU) 2022/1854, art 17.

[32] Articles 114(2) and 115 TFEU.

[33] Council Regulation (EU) 2022/1854, art 1.

[34] See, eg, Case C-533/24 *Vermilion Energy Ireland and Others* (2024) (preliminary reference asking, inter alia, whether using Article 122 TFEU as a legal basis for Council Regulation (EU) 2022/1854 was 'in contravention of the requirement for unanimity of voting within the EU Council for the adoption of measures concerning direct taxation and/or fiscal measures?'); Ostaszewska (2025) (analysing the ruling of the ICSID panel in *Klesch Group & Raffinerie Heide v Germany* under the Energy Charter Treaty, suspending the claimants' obligation to pay the contribution until the end of the arbitration).

[35] Regulation (EU) 2023/435 [REPowerEU].

[36] European Court of Auditors (2022b, p 11, para 29).

To justify the inclusion of REPowerEU into the RRF, the new regulation's first recital argued that 'Russia's war of aggression against Ukraine' not only 'direct[ly] and indirect[ly] aggravate[ed] the consequences of the COVID-19 crisis', but it also 'considerably affected the Union's society and economy, its people and its economic, social and territorial cohesion'.[37] The recitals further asserted that 'the Union's energy security and energy independence' was 'indispensable for a successful, sustainable, and inclusive recovery from the COVID-19 crisis, as they are also major factors contributing to the resilience of the Union's economy'.[38] The recitals thus concluded that the RRF was 'an instrument well suited to contribute to the Union's response to those emerging challenges',[39] particularly given that the RRF could also contribute 'to energy affordability and strengthening the strategic autonomy of the Union alongside an open economy'.[40]

The REPowerEU Regulation, however, built on a broader set of legal bases than the original RRF did, mentioning not merely Article 175(3) TFEU but also Articles 177(1), 192(1), 194(2), and 322(1) TFEU.[41] These various other legal bases were presumably considered necessary to support the additional financing mechanisms on which the REPowerEU Regulation sought to draw. Nonetheless, an expansive reinterpretation of the cohesion flexibility clause in Article 175(3) TFEU remained the keystone of the REPowerEU programme. The Commission proposal argued that recourse to Article 175(3) TFEU was justified because the 'current geopolitical situation has highlighted the significant differences between Member States and regions regarding the dependency on fossil fuels and especially on the ones imported from Russia'.[42] This assertion was no doubt true, but it rang a bit hollow given that Germany's advanced economy was by far the largest importer of Russian fossil fuels. As such, the 'differences between Member States' to which the Commission referred had no necessary connection to the levels of development of the various regions and the backwardness of the least favoured regions in a traditional cohesion sense.[43] The same observation could be made about REPowerEU's recourse to Article 177(1) TFEU as a legal basis, which was invoked in view of 'the flexibility [needed] to make transfers from cohesion policy funds', which the Regulation sought to effectuate.[44] These transfers may well have had 'an impact on the organisation of the Structural Funds' necessitating Article 177(1) TFEU as a legal basis,[45] but transfers were designed to benefit the broader European economy, not the 'least favoured regions' in a traditional cohesion sense.[46]

37 Regulation (EU) 2023/435 [REPowerEU], recital (1).
38 Ibid.
39 Ibid, recital (2).
40 Ibid, recital (4).
41 Ibid, preamble.
42 European Commission (2022o) (sec 2, first bullet point 'Legal Basis').
43 Article 174 TFEU.
44 European Commission (2022o) (sec 2, first bullet point 'Legal Basis').
45 Ibid.
46 The environmental and energy policy legal bases—Articles 192(1) and 194(2)—were similarly needed because the REPowerEU Regulation 'aim[ed] at introducing changes to the system for greenhouse gas emission allowance trading within the Union in order to contribute to ensuring security of energy supply in the Union'. Ibid. Article 322 TFEU was required since the 'regulation sets out financial rules for the

Aside from its reliance on loans, the REPowerEU Regulation increased the financial envelope for grants under the RRF by €20 billion.[47] This amount was financed through the sale of emissions trading system (ETS) allowances, the proceeds of which would then be allocated to the RRF as 'external assigned revenue'.[48] The REPowerEU Regulation also authorised Member States to transfer 'all or part' of their allocation from the Brexit Adjustment Reserve,[49] as well as up to 10% of the amounts allocated to certain cohesion funding for SMEs under the 2013 CPR,[50] along with up to 7.5% of the amounts allocated to cohesion funding under the 2021 CPR[51]— which together exceeded another €20 billion.[52] In this sense, 'REPowerEU represent[ed] yet another instrument in the Union's evolving budgetary system while, at the same time, targeting [existing] EU funds towards objectives other than the ones previously earmarked'.[53] But as ECA pointed out, with the exception of the ETS allowances, all the financing sources were actually outside of the Commission's control. Rather, they depended on Member States transferring funds from other policy areas in order to reach the estimated €210 billion needed for REPowerEU.[54]

Although the recycled funding under the REPowerEU Regulation generally followed pre-existing allocation criteria in the RRF, the revenue from the ETS was allocated on the basis of factors set out in a new Annex IVa of the RRF Regulation.[55] This new allocation key, however, did not squarely factor in 'the relative degree of dependence on Russian fossil fuels or the degree of exposure to the consequences of the war'.[56] The reason—as the Council Legal Service noted in a legal opinion subsequently made public—was that '[t]hose circumstances seem[ed] difficult to be framed in the context of the COVID-19 crisis' and hence 'raise[d] serious legal concerns'.[57] As the Council Legal Service stressed, the RRF remained part of NGEU and, as such, it was still subject to the requirements of the EURI Regulation. This meant that any

implementation of the budget, by introducing rules on the provision of appropriations with regard to the new revenue'. Ibid.

47 Regulation (EU) 2023/435 [REPowerEU], art 1 and Annex 1 (inserting new arts 21a and Annex IVa into Regulation (EU) 2021/241 [RRF]).

48 Regulation (EU) 2023/435 [REPowerEU], art 5 (inserting new Article 10e into ETS Directive 2003/87/EC); see also Regulation (EU) 2023/435 [REPowerEU], art 1(8) (inserting new Article 21a(1) into Regulation (EU) 2021/241 [RRF]). For further discussion, see below this chapter, Section C.2.

49 Regulation (EU) 2023/435 [REPowerEU], art 4 (inserting new Article 4a into Regulation (EU) 2021/1755).

50 Regulation (EU) 2023/435 [REPowerEU], art 2 (inserting new Article 25b into Regulation (EU) No 1303/2013).

51 Regulation (EU) 2023/435 [REPowerEU], art 3 (inserting new Article 26a into Regulation (EU) 2021/1060).

52 Schramm and Terranova (2024, p 955).

53 Ibid, p 957.

54 European Court of Auditors (2022b, p 9, para 19).

55 This new annex added, most importantly, 'share of fossil fuels in gross inland energy consumption' as an element in the calculation of the allocation. Regulation (EU) 2023/435 [REPowerEU], Annex 1 (inserting new Annex IVa into Regulation (EU) 2021/241 [RRF]).

56 Council Legal Service (2022, p 9, para 23).

57 Ibid.

funding under the RRF, including the new funding contemplated by the REPowerEU Regulation, was part of 'an exceptional, temporary and coordinated programme of economic and social support for the recovery and aftermath of the COVID-19 crisis, which shall only be made available for those purposes'.[58] The Council Legal Service argued that allocation criteria for REPowerEU could not 'drift' from those objectives in a way that would transform the RRF into 'a sort of general crisis management instrument, for which it was neither designed nor set up'.[59]

To meet these general requirements, the Council Legal Service articulated two conditions drawn not from the Covid-focused demands of the EURI Regulation but from the looser objectives of the RRF. According to the Council Legal Service, the allocation key must remain 'cohesion related' and also be 'consistent with the RRF general objectives and system'.[60] The primary way of satisfying the conditions was by holding unchanged the three main criteria of the RRF's original allocation key (based on the population, the inverse of the GDP per capita, and the relative unemployment rate of each Member State), which together, the Council Legal Service determined, adequately 'respond[ed] to the requirements of Article 175(3) TFEU'.[61] In this way, the REPowerEU Regulation would be able to allocate funding, *not* to disadvantaged regions, but to each Member States as a whole. The recipient Member States, even if disadvantaged in the aggregate, could then distribute the funding in any way they saw fit, including to the capital region or in or around other cities, which were not themselves disadvantaged relative to EU averages.[62]

Viewed from the perspective of traditional cohesion, the Council Legal Service's opinion was further evidence of how far NGEU had moved beyond cohesion's original regional-developmental purposes. The Council Legal Service argued that 'the criterion based on the inverse of the GDP per capita' was enough to meet 'cohesion's objective to reduce the disparities between the levels of development of the least favoured regions'.[63] And yet, by the Council Legal Service's own admission, all that particular condition did was to 'tak[e] account of *the relative degree of prosperity of Member States*' (emphasis added).[64] This approach simply further facilitated precisely the sort of 'drift' that the Council Legal Service argued should be avoided, transforming the RRF in effect into a 'general crisis management instrument'.[65]

58 Ibid, p 3, para 6, citing Council Regulation 2020/2094 [EURI], art 1 and recital (6). See this chapter above, n 2 and accompanying text.

59 Council Legal Service (2022, p 9, para 23).

60 Ibid, p 5, para 13.

61 Ibid, p 6, para 14.

62 Conversely, as with the RRF, because REPowerEU would be implemented through measures put forward by the Member States, this raised the risk, as the ECA noted in its REPowerEU opinion, of an excessive 'attention to the priorities of individual Member States rather than those of the Union as a whole'. European Court of Auditors (2022b, p 5, para 7).

63 Council Legal Service (2022, p 6, para 14), citing Council Legal Service (2019a, paras 36 and 37).

64 Council Legal Service (2022, p 6, para 15), citing Council Legal Service (2019b, para 33). For a discussion of the role of these factors supporting the allocation key of the RRF's predecessor instruments under the euro area budget, see Chapter Three, nn 151–56 and accompanying text.

65 Cf Council Legal Service (2022, p 9, para 23).

However, from a purely functionalist perspective, this recycling funding from the RRF to REPowerEU was not at all difficult to understand, at least from a policy standpoint if not a legal one. Intense time pressures as well as a general reluctance of Member States to adopt another large collective debt instrument meant that, at this point in EU politics, it was unlikely that anything more ambitious could be adopted, leading instead to reworking existing Union instruments and shifting resources.[66] As such, REPowerEU not only built upon, but also re-directed and extended, 'a budgetary tool that was created just one year before in a different context and for supposedly different purposes'.[67] REPowerEU confirmed how plans originally designed to address the pandemic could now be deployed 'to achieve virtually any other public objective'.[68] It further showed how the RRF had become 'the preferential mechanism to be used to finance investments and reforms in the Member States',[69] whether to achieve the RRF's original goals or those new ones subsequently added.

Nonetheless, by formally integrating REPowerEU into the RRF and NGEU, the new regulation also expanded the substantive scope of both to meet the needs of a new crisis of a geopolitical and energy nature.[70] In so doing, REPowerEU also confirmed the definitive emergence of cohesion as 'the foundation of a veritable EU economic and industrial policy, this time in service of European energy transition, security and autonomy'.[71] This shift was clearly in tension with the ruling of the German Federal Constitutional Court in 2022,[72] which had held that NGEU must remain 'strictly limited to the historically exceptional case of "support[ing] the recovery in the aftermath of the COVID-19 crisis" (Art. 1(1) of the EURI Regulation) and "tackl[ing] the adverse economic consequences of the COVID-19 crisis" (Art. 1(2) EURI Regulation)'.[73] As commentators noted at the time, it was questionable whether REPowerEU, if it were ever challenged before the FCC, could fulfil this criterion.[74]

2. STEP: The Strategic Technologies for Europe Platform

In February 2024, as part of a broader package we will explore later,[75] the Union legislator shifted the NGEU model even further away from its original purpose, amending the RRF as part of the effort to create the Strategic Technologies for Europe Platform.[76]

[66] Schramm and Terranova (2024, p 954).
[67] Ibid, p 943.
[68] Panascì (2024, p 32).
[69] de Bellis (2024, p 1142).
[70] Dermine (2023, p 141).
[71] Ibid, p 142; see also Panascì (2024, p 32), viewing REPowerEU as 'illustrative of the potential of cohesion policy to deliver on the aspirations of a quasi-federal fiscal union beyond the mere (negative) economic policy coordination competence of the EU'.
[72] BVerfG (2022).
[73] Ibid, para 186.
[74] Nguyen and van den Brink (2022).
[75] See this chapter below, nn 437–42 and accompanying text.
[76] Regulation (EU) 2024/795 [STEP].

The STEP Regulation authorised Member States to revise their NRRPs to include measures which support STEP objectives.[77] The key objective of the new programme had essentially nothing to do with Covid; its purpose was to increase financial incentives 'to prevent relocation, to transfer production facilities of critical technologies back from third countries, and to attract new facilities to prevent strategic dependencies'.[78] The STEP Regulation did allude to post-Covid supply-chain disruptions but that was seen merely as one factor among many supporting the Regulation, which included '[h]igh inflation, labour shortages ... Russia's war of aggression against Ukraine, rising interest rates, and increases in energy costs and input prices' that together were now 'weighing on the competitiveness of the Union's industry'.[79] These factors highlighted the desire of the EU 'to secure its open strategic autonomy and reduce its strategic dependence on third countries in various sectors'.[80]

Unlike the original RRF Regulation but like REPowerEU, STEP also relied on a broad combination of legal bases—Articles 164, 173, 175(3), 176, 177, 178, 182(1), and 192(1) TFEU[81]— all deemed 'relevant' to supporting the amendment of the various instruments needed to provide sufficient funding for the new technology subsidy programme.[82] In this way, via STEP, the RRF planning process and its associated funding were further repurposed to the ends of this new programme alongside multiple other instruments.[83] According to the Commission's proposal in June 2023, STEP aimed to fulfil three interrelated goals: providing flexibility in, reinforcing the firepower of, and creating synergies among these existing funding instruments.[84] In this search for flexibility, however, traditional cohesion was once again the main source of funding targeted for repurposing. As the Commission argued in its proposal:

> Cohesion funds represent the largest single EU policy financed through the EU budget. To incentivise Member States, the Commission proposes a new priority across all major funds. The Commission also proposes to open up those funds for large companies in less developed and transition regions, as well as in more developed regions of Member States with a GDP per capita below the EU average, to unleash greater investments in the target areas of the STEP. By providing financial incentives in the form of higher prefinancing and EU financing, Member States are encouraged to reprioritise their programmes.[85]

77 Ibid, art 19, inserting a new art 21(1a) into Regulation (EU) 2021/241 [RRF].
78 Ibid, recital (2).
79 Ibid.
80 Ibid.
81 Ibid, preamble; European Commission (2023m, p 4).
82 European Commission (2023m, pp 12–13).
83 These included the Cohesion Fund, the Common Provisions Regulation, Digital Europe, the European Defence Fund, the European Regional Development Fund, European Social Fund Plus, Horizon Europe, the Innovation Fund, and InvestEU in combination with lending guarantees to the European Investment Bank.
84 European Commission (2023m, p 4).
85 Ibid, pp 4–5.

In the process of setting up the STEP programme in late 2023 and early 2024, few political actors voiced reservations about using RRF funds for purposes unrelated to the pandemic. The uniqueness of NGEU had, by then, largely lost its political salience in the Member States, and the financial envelope it created had become just another convenient source of financing to meet new expediencies. Moreover, amending the RRF Regulation for new purposes only required the ordinary legislative procedure, involving no new money, which meant that, politically, the legal implications of the change gained little scrutiny. The STEP's adoption in February 2024 was part of a broader package that would include, most prominently, the Ukraine Facility and an MFF revision.[86] On the eve of that adoption, the European Council—which three and a half years earlier had negotiated intensively over four days and nights in July 2020 to define the exceptionality of NGEU—now welcomed its repurposing:

> The European Union needs to ensure its sovereignty and competitiveness in strategic sectors by strengthening its resilience and productivity, mobilising financing, reducing its strategic dependencies, investing in the skills of the future and making its economic, industrial and technological base fit for the green and digital transitions, safeguarding cohesion and the level playing field in the Single Market. The European Council welcomes the leveraging of existing EU funding instruments to quickly deploy financial support for investments in critical technologies.[87]

This repurposing, however, had certain broad limits. While the Member States were given greater flexibility to reallocate their own funding shares to new purposes, the size of their individual shares did not change. Nor did the division between grants and loans, which remained unamended in the 2020 ORD.[88] Therefore, irrespective of the emergence of new crises requiring a joint response, the actual spending under the repurposed RRF took place in national siloes just as it always had.

B. National Planning and Performance-Based Incentives as Generalised Tools of EU Governance

Much of the structure of NGEU, and more particularly the RRF's planning model and use of 'performance-based' incentives, were aimed at harnessing national ownership as a tool of EU policy-making. But that is not all that the new structure entailed. It also sought, through the planning process, to facilitate an unprecedented flow of information across the national-supranational divide, whether about national priorities,

[86] See this chapter below, nn 436–44 and accompanying text.
[87] European Council (2024, p 4, para 12).
[88] Council Decision 2020/2053 [ORD], art 5(1)(b): 'up to EUR 360 000 million in 2018 prices of the funds borrowed may be used for providing loans and, by way of derogation from Article 4, up to EUR 390 000 million in 2018 prices of the funds borrowed may be used for expenditure'.

their funding needs, as well as their alignment with EU priorities across numerous domains (including a large number within areas of primarily national competence). The planning process then linked outputs to some kind of incentive, most importantly in terms of actual funding on the RRF model or, in the absence of funding, via other incentives such as the extensions of the fiscal adjustment period under the new Economic Governance Framework (EGF), as we shall discuss later.[89]

As we saw in Chapter Two, the quest for national ownership itself could be traced back to the aspirations of IMF and World Bank lending models that provided the initial inspiration for the economic adjustment programmes during the euro crisis in the first half of the 2010s.[90] But importantly, these programmes were intended only to serve as short- to medium-term incentivising tools from which countries would eventually graduate. They were never understood as permanent tools of economic governance. The same could be said, at least initially, of the RRF itself, which was in principle meant to be 'exceptional' and 'temporary' like everything else adopted under the rubric of the EURI.[91] And whatever the systemic and institutional downsides of the RRF model—and there were many, as Chapter Four detailed—they might be tolerated on an 'exceptional' and 'temporary' basis. But if, through repetition and institutional lock-in, they were to become permanent features of a new governance model in the EU, they would become less tolerable, particularly without the necessary democratic and constitutional deliberation that, for example, Treaty change would entail.

In subsequent years, the planning and performance-based incentives model was indeed extended to multiple other contexts, suggesting its increasing normalisation as a mode of EU governance. This section focuses on the EU's macro-financial assistance and other foreign aid programmes extending support to partner countries (most ambitiously, the Ukraine Facility and the Reform and Growth Facility for the Western Balkans) and the Social Climate Fund. The EU's reformed EGF under the Stability and Growth Pact also builds on model of broad national plans but given its lack of funding it is also unconnected to the performance-based funding model in the Financial Regulation. Even with this aberration from the general pattern, the key features of the NGEU model represent a broader trend in EU governance that has manifested itself in domains as diverse as EU Research Policy and the Common Agricultural Policy.[92] For example, as the Commission explained in its annual report for 2023:

> [Under the reformed Common Agricultural Policy,] plans prepared by Member States and approved by the Commission have succeeded in bringing under one single umbrella funding for income support, rural development, and market measures. The new common agricultural policy has become more strategic: 10 specific

[89] See this chapter below, nn 159–235 and accompanying text.
[90] Chapter Two, nn 32–33 and accompanying text.
[91] See this chapter above, nn 1–2 and accompanying text.
[92] European Commission (2024m, p 71).

> objectives have been set at the EU level, while leaving Member States the choice of interventions to best fulfil them in their strategic plans. This has allowed the policy to move closer to a performance-based delivery model, whereby all interventions are planned ex ante and linked with output indicators.[93]

The European Parliament's Committee on Budgetary Control expressed the hope that this overall trend toward performance-based planning and spending suggested the emergence of 'a profound culture of "result orientation" aimed at optimising the use of funds' across numerous programmes.[94]

This trend, however, came with risks. Even if the model was labelled 'performance-based', the hoped-for impact (in terms of greater efficiency, economic dynamism and growth) would take so long to appear that, in practice, the Commission needed to settle for more proximate goals (such as the adoption of regulatory acts) that did not measure actual performance. Moreover, the shift to planning and output incentives risked generalising the opaque and technocratic national-supranational negotiations, as well as lack of clarity around 'authorship' and accountability for outcomes, which we noted in Chapter Four.[95] The normalisation of the planning model also raised questions about a basic aspiration of EU governance already present in earlier stages of EMU development, i.e., that 'democratic control and accountability should occur at the level at which the decisions are taken'.[96] Under the emergent planning and incentives model, it was often not clear 'at which [level] the decisions [were] taken',[97] much less what should be appropriate oversight and control mechanisms, whether national or supranational, legislative or judicial, or perhaps something else.

1. The Ukraine Facility and the Western Balkans Facility

Performance-based spending has long been an element of EU foreign aid programmes, most prominently those providing macro-financial assistance to countries experiencing balance-of-payments crises.[98] As the Commission website puts it:

> MFA funds are released in tranches strictly tied to the fulfilment of conditions aimed at strengthening macro-economic and financial stability. These conditions tend to focus on public finance management and fiscal reform, but may also touch upon other areas such as trade, enterprise restructuring and business environment, or financial sector reform. These conditions are listed in a Memorandum of Understanding signed between the EU and the beneficiary country.[99]

[93] Ibid, p 10.
[94] European Parliament (2022d).
[95] See Chapter Four, Section A.
[96] Four Presidents Report (2012, p 16).
[97] See Dermine (2024, pp 980–82).
[98] See generally European Commission (2025o).
[99] Ibid.

With a legal infrastructure built on Memoranda of Understanding and the associated funding conditionality, MFA programmes, in terms of governance, have generally followed a model drawn from the IMF, which euro-crisis economic adjustment programmes also used. However, while their aims and temporary character made them closer to the traditional development-programme model, they nonetheless shared some common features with other RRF derivatives. A prime example was the 'MFA+' instrument adopted for Ukraine in December 2022.[100] The label was a reference to the programme's threefold aim, which included not just macro-financial stability but also the 'rehabilitation of critical functions and infrastructure and relief for people in need' as well as, perhaps most importantly, 'a reform agenda gearing towards … strengthening Ukraine's institutions, reforming and reinforcing the effectiveness of public administration as well as transparency, structural reforms and good governance at all levels'.[101]

There were, however, two more ambitious instruments involving aid to partner countries—the Ukraine Facility[102] and the Reform and Growth Facility for the Western Balkans[103]—which, in terms of overall governance, drew even more explicitly from the RRF model. The Ukraine Facility built on the MFA+ model, whereas the Western Balkans Facility contained RFF planning and spending elements (though it did not involve emergency lending in an MFA sense). We examine each of these instruments in turn.

The Ukraine Facility was adopted in February 2024 to provide up to €50 billion in stable and predictable financial support to Ukraine, including grants, loans, and loan guarantees 'to attract and mobilise public and private investments for Ukraine's recovery and reconstruction'.[104] In its basic features, the legal design of the Ukraine Facility reflected the strong influence of the RRF model, particularly the centrality of the so-called Ukraine Plan, which was to define 'the reform and investment agenda of Ukraine, integrated in an economic and fiscal policy framework, towards the achievement of the general and specific objectives set out in' the Ukraine Facility Regulation.[105] To promote national ownership,[106] the Regulation charged the government of Ukraine,[107] in the first instance, with preparing the Ukraine Plan, 'as a coherent, comprehensive and adequately balanced response to rebuilding and modernising Ukraine, supporting its economic, social and environmental recovery, sustainable development and its progress towards accession to the Union'.[108] Moreover, the Ukraine Plan was supposed to be 'results and impact based' using performance

[100] Regulation (EU) 2022/2463 [Dec 2022 Ukraine MFA+].
[101] Ibid, art 2(2).
[102] Regulation (EU) 2024/792 [Ukraine Facility].
[103] Regulation (EU) 2024/1449 [Western Balkans Facility].
[104] European Commission (2025p).
[105] Regulation (EU) 2024/792 [Ukraine Facility], art 16(1).
[106] Ibid, recitals (19), (28), (67), and art 4(1).
[107] Ibid, art 14(2).
[108] Ibid, recital (67); see also art 14(1).

indicators to assess achievement of the general and specific objectives of the Ukraine Facility Regulation.[109]

As under the RRF, the Ukraine Facility charged the Commission with determining the instalments schedule included in the Council implementing decision.[110] The Commission was also given the lead role in assessing Ukraine's 'satisfactory fulfilment' of the conditions set out in both the Regulation and the Plan sufficient to warrant disbursement of instalments (though, unlike the RRF, the ultimate decision on disbursements was made through an implementing decision of the Council rather than of the Commission).[111] The Commission's assessment and proposals for disbursement of funding were also to be performance-based, particularly as to the fulfilment of 'essential requirements, such as the maintenance of economic and financial stability, budget oversight and public financial management, and conditions related to the implementation of the reforms and investments set out in the Ukraine Plan'.[112] The Regulation also contemplated extensive arrangements for the management, control, supervision, monitoring, evaluation, reporting, and audit of funds via both a Framework Agreement focused on these elements,[113] as well as the establishment of an Audit Board operating in conjunction with, but 'without prejudice to', the oversight functions of the Commission, OLAF, the European Court of Auditors, and the EPPO.[114]

Throughout the drafting and assessment stage of the Ukraine Facility, consistent with the RRF model, the Ukraine Facility Regulation obligated the Commission to 'act in close cooperation with Ukraine'.[115] The government of Ukraine was to prepare the Plan 'in close consultation with the Commission', which would then be endorsed by the Council via an implementing decision.[116] But a key point of difference between the RRF and the Ukraine Facility was how the latter explicitly contemplated much greater involvement of the national parliament of Ukraine—the Verkhovna Rada—throughout the planning process. Thus, for example, under the Ukraine Facility Regulation, the government of Ukraine was required to prepare its plan 'with due involvement of the Verkhovna Rada in accordance with the constitutional order of Ukraine'.[117] The Regulation also obligated the *European Commission* to 'strive to ensure, as appropriate, democratic scrutiny in the form of consultation by the Ukrainian government of the Verkhovna Rada in accordance with the constitutional order of Ukraine'.[118] The legal obligation to involve the Verkhovna Rada also carried over

[109] Ibid, art 17(2).
[110] Ibid, art 19(2)(c).
[111] Ibid, art 26(3)–(4).
[112] Ibid, art 16(2).
[113] Ibid, art 9.
[114] Ibid, art 36.
[115] Ibid, art 18(1) (referring both to the assessment and the drafting stage); compare Regulation (EU) 2021/241 [RRF], art 19(1).
[116] European Commission (2023n) (Explanatory Memorandum, Section 1, first bullet point 'Reasons for and objectives of the proposal').
[117] Regulation (EU) 2024/792 [Ukraine Facility], art 14(2); see also art 17(1)(i).
[118] Ibid, art 4(6).

explicitly to the implementation stage: 'Ukraine shall ensure that the Verkhovna Rada plays its role in the implementation of the Ukraine Plan in a duly informed way, in line with its prerogatives, including its authority to legislate, approve the state budget and oversee its execution, and oversee the executive branch'.[119] This obligation again extended to the Commission, which not only needed to ensure the inclusion of the Verkhovna Rada but also that of 'local and regional authorities, social partners and civil society, including vulnerable groups, so as to allow them to participate in shaping the design and implementation of activities eligible for funding under the Facility and in the related monitoring, scrutiny and evaluation processes, as relevant'.[120]

No similar legal obligations for the national government or the Commission to involve the national parliament were included in the RRF Regulation. The latter encouraged, but did not require, consultation with local or regional authorities and other stakeholders,[121] but the RRF was designed in a way that de facto made their substantive involvement nearly impossible. In the case of the Ukraine Facility, it was apparently the European Parliament that was most sensitive to the poor optics of using a model that excluded the national parliaments as did the RRF, and thus the EP insisted on revising the Commission's proposal to reinforce the democratic role of the Ukrainian national parliament in the country's constitutional system.[122] Upholding and respecting effective democratic mechanisms, including a multi-party parliamentary system, was a standard precondition for all MFA lending.[123] To exclude the Verkhovna Rada from deeper involvement in the Ukraine Plan process under the Ukraine Facility would thus have been anomalous, to put it mildly (indeed, it was unclear why it was not equally anomalous to exclude the national parliaments of the Member States under the RRF).

The Reform and Growth Facility for the Western Balkans,[124] adopted just a few months after the Ukraine Facility, also referred to giving national parliaments and other stakeholders 'a meaningful role during the design and implementation of programmes and the related monitoring processes' under the Facility.[125] But the actual legal obligations on this point in the Western Balkans Facility were rather weak and ultimately looked more like the RRF.[126] The Western Balkans Facility used slightly different nomenclature—the plans were called 'Reform Agendas' and the recipient countries were called 'beneficiaries'—but the basic features of the RRF model were otherwise retained, including 'ownership of development priorities by the beneficiaries' and 'a focus on clear conditionality and tangible results'.[127] The Reform

[119] Ibid, art 14(4); see also art 17(1)(e).

[120] Ibid.

[121] Regulation (EU) 2021/241 [RRF], art 18(4)(q). See Chapter Four, nn 83–84 and accompanying text.

[122] European Parliament (2023d), (2024c); see also Peters (2024), Peters and Przetacznik (2024).

[123] Decision (EU) 2022/313 [Feb 2022 Ukraine MFA], art 2(1); Decision (EU) 2022/1201 [Jul 2022 Ukraine MFA], art 2(1); Decision (EU) 2022/1628 [Sept 2022 Ukraine MFA], art 2(1); and Regulation (EU) 2022/2463 [Dec 2022 Ukraine MFA+], art 8(1).

[124] Regulation (EU) 2024/1449 [Western Balkans Facility].

[125] Ibid, recital (16); see also recital (34).

[126] Ibid, art 13(1)(m); compare Regulation (EU) 2021/241 [RRF], art 18(4)(q).

[127] Regulation (EU) 2024/1449 [Western Balkans Facility], art 4(1).

Agendas were also required to be 'results-based' and to include indicators for assessing achievement of the Facility's general and specific objectives.[128] The Commission was not only given the lead role in negotiating and assessing the Reform Agendas, it was also given the autonomous role in deciding on the implementing decision (subject to a committee oversight procedure).[129]

The European Court of Auditors was asked to provide an opinion as part of the legislative process for both the proposed Ukraine and Western Balkans Facility Regulations.[130] Key points raised by ECA echoed some of the concerns it had earlier noted regarding the RRF, particularly with regard to the disbursement model: while the planning process 'certainly enhance[d] ... ownership' of reforms in the recipient country, the opaque negotiation and drafting process left 'considerable leeway ... to design the conditions for disbursement'.[131] Moreover, as regards the disbursement conditions, there was the risk that the plans 'will not be ambitious enough and that the underlying indicators will not be sufficiently clear and measurable'.[132] Finally, as with any policy instrument seeking to steer policy outcomes through funding incentives, there was the difficult challenge of the 'sustainability of reforms' once the funding is delivered, as well as the lack of clarity on 'how the Commission intend[ed] to ensure that this risk will be mitigated'.[133]

2. The Social Climate Fund

The EU also extended the RRF planning and incentives model to core questions of social security via the Social Climate Fund.[134] The SCF is part of the Fit for 55 legislative package aimed at reducing EU greenhouse gas emissions by at least 55% by 2030, thus putting the EU on the path to achieve climate neutrality by 2050.[135] The general objective of the SCF is 'to contribute to a socially fair transition towards climate neutrality'.[136] The specific objectives are more granular:

> to support vulnerable households, vulnerable micro-enterprises and vulnerable transport users, through temporary direct income support and through measures and investments intended to increase energy efficiency of buildings, decarbonisation of heating and cooling of buildings, including the integration and storage in

[128] Ibid, art 13(2).
[129] Ibid, arts 14(1) and 15(1).
[130] European Court of Auditors (2023h), (2024d).
[131] European Court of Auditors (2023h, p 15, para 32), (2024d, p 14, para 31).
[132] European Court of Auditors (2023h, p 15, para 32).
[133] Ibid, p 16, para 34, (2024d, p 15, para 33).
[134] Regulation (EU) 2023/955 [SCF].
[135] A succinct overview of the Fit for 55 package can be found on the Council's website. See Council of the European Union (2025a). For further discussion, see this chapter below, nn 264–72 and accompanying text.
[136] Regulation (EU) 2023/955 [SCF], art 3(1).

> buildings of energy from renewable sources, and granting improved access to zero- and low-emission mobility and transport.[137]

In pursuing these objectives, the SCF is again supposed to be 'performance-based'.[138] And the tools for incentivising performance are drawn directly from the RRF model: Social Climate Plans,[139] and EU financial support to Member States in their implementation.[140] The SCF Regulation also gave the Commission the central role in negotiating, approving, and disbursing money under the plans.[141] Following the RRF model, the SCF Regulation included no provisions mandating consultation with national parliaments, though it did actually obligate (rather than merely encourage) that Member State governments consult 'local and regional authorities, representatives of economic and social partners, relevant civil society organisations, youth organisations and other stakeholders'.[142]

For its substantive legal bases, the SCF relied on Article 91(1)(d) TFEU (transport policy), Article 192(1) TFEU (environmental policy), and Article 194(2) TFEU (energy policy). From a substantive viewpoint, however, the envisioned expenditures look very much like social policy. The SCF Regulation spoke in terms of reducing 'energy poverty and transport poverty',[143] including via direct income support. These aims seemed to place the SCF at the heart of social policy, a domain long understood to fall under national competence, in which EU competence was primarily supportive.[144] The SCF navigated around this traditional limitation by again adopting a transactional framing. An official who participated in the SCF negotiations described the transactional logic this way:

> The Regulation includes no detailed legislative obligations. The Regulation establishes the main objectives and general obligations. The Member States make national plans to provide for means that concretise these objectives. This is the structure of both the Social Climate Fund and the RRF Regulation. Instead of approving a directive that is incorporated in national legislation, the EU adopts a binding framework. The Commission justified the extension to social policy by arguing that it is not the EU that offers direct income support through the Fund, but merely provides an opportunity for Member States to provide such support. It is up to the Member State to decide.[145]

137 Ibid, art 3(2).

138 Ibid, recital (40).

139 Ibid, arts 4, 6, 8.

140 Ibid, art 7. As under the RRF, the SCF support was supposed to be 'additional and shall not substitute recurring national budgetary expenditure'. Ibid, art 13(2). This requirement was also in tension with the allowance that the plans may include both 'existing or new national measures and investments'. Ibid, art 4(1).

141 Ibid, recital (19) and arts 16(1) and 17(1).

142 Ibid, art 5(1).

143 Ibid, recital (8).

144 See art 153 TFEU.

145 Leino-Sandberg and Ollikainen (2025) (interview number 3) (Leino-Sandberg translation).

This transactional framing, however, was, as we saw with the RRF,[146] in tension with functional realities of supranational funding, particularly the potentially outsized role it gave to the Commission in steering policy through negotiating, approving, and disbursing money under the plans. These features sought to maximise supranational influence over this area of national competence, though to an extent—given the confidentiality surrounding the process—it may never be possible to properly assess. Regardless, the SCF provided substance to the long-sought but under-realised 'social pillar' of European integration,[147] which had been largely limited previously to subsidiary aspects of free movement, employment questions and labour markets.

During the negotiations of the SCF within the Council, however, a number of national delegations raised concerns over whether the proposed legal bases were sufficient to provide for temporary direct income support.[148] For several other Member States, however, the possibility of direct income support was politically the most attractive element of the SCF Regulation.[149] The Council Legal Service rejected concerns over the legal basis,[150] concluding that the whole regulation could be based on Articles 191 and 192(1) TFEU because the 'the primary objective' of the SCF was 'the reduction of emissions and thus combating climate change in accordance with' the environmental focus of those articles.[151] However, the same frugal Member States that had been cautious about NGEU in the first place (Sweden, Germany, Austria, Denmark, the Netherlands, and Finland) were—despite their relatively high climate ambitions—apparently also most hesitant about the SCF.[152] These countries were concerned about the SCF's budgetary and financial architecture, particularly whether its size would trigger a reopening of the 2021–2027 MFF,[153] but they ultimately accepted it as a part of the overall package to meet the EU's climate obligations.

The European Court of Auditors, for its part, issued an opinion expressing a range of concerns about how the SCF would again replicate the deficiencies of the RRF, notably 'the risk of replacing existing national expenditure',[154] 'insufficient attention to performance and value for money',[155] the 'potential weak link between payments and the Fund's objectives, milestones and targets',[156] 'assurance and accountability gaps',[157] and 'indicators, milestones and targets [that did] not effectively assess performance'.[158] Doubts about the adequacy of the model in ensuring that EU funds are

[146] See Chapter Four, Sections A, B, and D.
[147] See European Commission (2021b), (2017d). For further discussion see Chapter Two, nn 41–43 and accompanying text.
[148] Council of the European Union (2021c, p 26).
[149] Ympäristöministeriö (2022, p 4) (the document is a report of the Finnish Ministry of the Environment on the course of the negotiations).
[150] Ibid, p 8.
[151] Ibid.
[152] Leino-Sandberg and Ollikainen (2025) (interview number 3).
[153] Council of the European Union (2022a, p 4); see also Ympäristöministeriö (2022, p 3).
[154] European Court of Auditors (2022c, pp 7–8, para 12).
[155] Ibid, p 16, para 36.
[156] Ibid.
[157] Ibid, p 17, para 36.
[158] Ibid.

well spent have persisted, particularly in the face of the Commission's reluctance to give these concerns serious consideration or to make adjustments to strengthen the model against the criticism.

3. The Reformed Economic Governance Framework

a. The Basic Contours of the Reform

NGEU, and more particularly the RRF, also provided the key source of inspiration for the Union's new Economic Governance Framework as part of a reformed Stability and Growth Pact, adopted in 2024.[159] As a former Commission official has described, the NGEU's influence over the new EGF was reflected in its two broad orientations.[160] The first was implicit, in effect a kind of national ownership, by making nationally decided budgetary trajectories the centre of the new fiscal architecture.[161] Those trajectories would then be embodied in so-called national medium-term fiscal-structural plans (MTFSPs) prepared by each Member State,[162] using guidance from, and subject to the assessment of, the Commission.[163] The second was explicit. Instead of money, there is an incentive in the form of greater (short-term) leeway for the budgetary targets, but this requires reform and investment commitments that are 'sufficiently detailed, front-loaded, time-bound and verifiable',[164] and seek to fulfil the specified criteria of the new EGF.

As Chapter Two explained, dissatisfaction with the economic coordination and surveillance regime under the old SGP—primarily rules- and sanctions-based rather than incentives-based ('all stick and no carrot')—was long standing.[165] The Commission launched a review of the regime in early February 2020,[166] right on the eve of the Covid crisis. This meant that the process of EGF reform was overtaken by the pandemic, the adoption of NGEU, and the need to establish the planning and spending process under the RRF.[167] The Commission relaunched the EGF review until November 2022;[168] this time in a form that bore the distinct imprint of the RRF model.

The Commission's relaunch identified three interrelated aims: 'Improving national ownership, simplifying the framework and moving towards a greater medium-term focus, combined with stronger and more coherent enforcement'.[169] Given that the

[159] See Regulation (EU) 2024/1263 [EGF].
[160] Pench (2024, p 8). Pench is a former Director for macroeconomic policies at DG ECFIN.
[161] Ibid.
[162] Regulation (EU) 2024/1263 [EGF], art 1(2) et seq.
[163] Ibid, arts 9 and 16(1).
[164] Ibid, art 14(3).
[165] See Chapter Two, nn 65–70 and accompanying text.
[166] European Commission (2020c).
[167] See Chapters Three and Four.
[168] European Commission (2022p).
[169] Ibid (1. Introduction).

EGF regulates a Member State's use of its own tax revenues, national ownership is even more pertinent than in the allocation of EU funds. However, as one academic commentator, Alicia Hinarejos, observed 'radical simplification this is not'.[170] The proposed reform involved, in Hinarejos's view, a significant broadening of the role of the Commission, calling on it to assess each Member State's non-fiscal reforms and public investment in exchange for leniency in their debt adjustment paths. All of this would 'require the Commission to make qualitative, value judgments and exercise a high degree of discretion, bringing us—once again—to the question of political legitimacy' at the heart of complaints about the old system.[171]

b. The Challenge of Legitimacy, Transparency, and Accountability

With a nudge from the European Council to advance the negotiations more quickly towards completion,[172] the Council, in March 2023, agreed on a set of EGF reform orientations of its own.[173] The Council highlighted in particular national ownership as an essential element of the future EGF.[174] The Council stressed the convergence among the Member States on several key points, in particular the need for flexibility on the fiscal adjustment period 'if a member state commits to an eligible set of reforms and investments that enhances growth-prospects or resilience, strengthens public finances and thereby their long-term sustainability, and addresses EU strategic priorities'.[175] The Council demanded that the Commission assessment of national plans be done 'in a fully transparent manner', based on common assessment principles and multilateral scrutiny/endorsement by the Council.[176] The Council also asked that the planning process 'be aligned, upon request, with the national electoral cycle' and 'revised with the accession of new governments', not merely 'updated in objective circumstances'.[177] This was a lesson learned from the RRF context, where the Commission had proved inflexible on this point.[178] The EGF Regulation, as adopted, made the demanded change.[179]

Other features of the Regulation bearing on democratic legitimacy, transparency, and accountability were, however, of ambiguous value. Like the NRRPs under the RRF, the bulk of the expected democratic legitimacy and accountability provisions emphasise the role of the European Parliament,[180] but even these, as commentators observed, were generally 'very restricted', involving primarily 'ex post querying' rather than real *ex ante* influence on decision making.[181] As adopted, the Regulation

170 Hinarejos (2022, p 732).
171 Ibid. See Chapter Two, Section A.
172 European Council (2023, p 8, para 18).
173 Council of the European Union (2023).
174 Ibid, para 4.
175 Ibid, para 5(e).
176 Ibid, para 5(d).
177 Ibid.
178 See Chapter Four, nn 193–95 and accompanying text.
179 Regulation (EU) 2024/1263 [EGF], art 15(2).
180 Ibid, arts 27–28, 30.
181 Amtenbrink and de Haan (2023, p 428).

instead envisions that the national MTFSPs would be produced primarily through confidential exchanges between Member State governments and the Commission (referred to as 'technical dialogue').[182] The MTFSP only becomes public once it has actually been submitted[183] Planning under the EGF is thus likely to replicate the executive-technocratic process of the RRF, in which political influence is limited to core national ministers and members of the Commission; the role of national parliaments is likely to remain formal and peer scrutiny by other Member States nominal.[184]

An analysis of the actual provisions of the EGF Regulation supports this hypothesis. The recitals to the Regulation speak of 'ensuring national ownership' and 'transparent and inclusive policy-making' in terms of 'involvement of national parliaments, social partners, civil society organisations and other relevant stakeholders'.[185] However, the Regulation itself is unspecific about how much or what sort of information needs to be shared with any of these entities or groups before the MTFSP is finalised and approved, and refers it to applicable national legal frameworks that settle how 'a consultation of civil society, social partners, regional authorities and other relevant stakeholders' is to be organised.[186] This needs to happen prior to the submission of the plan without specification as to when, in what way, or on what topics.[187] Moreover, Member States are permitted ('may')—but are not obligated ('shall')—to debate its draft national medium-term fiscal-structural plan with its national parliament.[188] This is problematic given that the plans touch on matters that go to the core of national democracy, making national debates vital. The Regulation only requires that the Member State's proposed plan should explain how the consultation was arranged.[189]

The Regulation also contemplates enhancing national ownership in another way, through the advisory role of independent fiscal institutions (IFIs), that is, technocratic bodies created during the euro crisis to promote disciplined fiscal policy at the national level.[190] The Regulation gives IFIs the right, if asked by the Member State government, to opine on the key components of the initial guidance to the Member State from the Commissioner—'the macroeconomic forecast and the macroeconomic assumptions underpinning the net expenditure path'—which then forms the basis of the Member State's preparation of the plan.[191] The idea is to provide opportunities for informed debate on the sustainability of government plans and their possible alternatives.

182 Regulation (EU) 2024/1263 [EGF], art 12.
183 Ibid, art 11(5).
184 See Leino-Sandberg and Raunio (2023).
185 Regulation (EU) 2024/1263 [EGF], recital (4).
186 Ibid, art 11(3).
187 Ibid.
188 Ibid, art 11(4).
189 Ibid, art 13(g)(vi). See also recital (23).
190 Ibid, recitals (37) and (42).
191 Ibid, art 11(2); see also art 9(1).

c. The Difficult Balance Between More Investment and Credible Debt Reduction

The new EGF seeks to strike a difficult balance between the 'Member States investing more in key sectors while simultaneously establishing a more credible and enforceable regime for debt reduction'.[192] For those Member States whose debt exceeds 60% of GDP or the general government deficit exceeds 3% of GDP, the Regulation requires the Commission to provide a reference trajectory that would define a path for government spending over the medium term to bring debt and deficits within the Treaty thresholds.[193] The reference trajectory establishes, in effect, a baseline for plan assessment as well as a metric for carrying out annual fiscal surveillance for each Member State. Once the Member State submits the plan, the Commission is to determine 'whether [its] net expenditure path complies with the requirements to put or keep general government debt on a plausibly downward path' towards the Treaty thresholds.[194] If the plan includes a higher net expenditure path than in the Commission's reference trajectory, the Member State must provide 'sound and data-driven economic arguments explaining the difference'.[195] The Regulation also allows the Member State to deviate from its net expenditure path, if so authorised by a Council decision taken on a Commission recommendation.[196] These features seek to 'better take into account the increased heterogeneity of fiscal positions, public debt and economic challenges, as well as other vulnerabilities across Member States', while also 'address[ing] the medium- and long-term challenges facing the Union'.[197]

As under the old system, the Member State's plan should explain how they ensure the delivery of reforms and investments to deal with the main challenges identified in the context of the European Semester and CSRs.[198] Additionally, the plan should explain how it addresses 'common priorities of the Union', including 'fair green and digital transition' and climate neutrality objectives; 'social and economic resilience, including the European Pillar of Social Rights'; 'energy security'; and 'where necessary, the build-up of defence capabilities'.[199] But the obligation to 'explain' does not entail an obligation to 'deliver' these various reforms and investments unless the Member State sought an extension of the adjustment period.[200]

The coordination of economic and fiscal policies is clearly within EU competence,[201] but these provisions in the Regulation suggest an effort to influence a whole range of policy domains well beyond that coordination. The old European Semester

[192] Oraheimo and Paasikallio (2024, p 1552).
[193] Regulation (EU) 2024/1263 [EGF], art 5.
[194] Ibid, art 16(2).
[195] Ibid, art 13(b).
[196] Ibid, art 26 (national escape clauses); see also art 25 (general escape clause).
[197] Council Regulation (EU) 2024/1264 [amended EDP], recital (5).
[198] Regulation (EU) 2024/1263 [EGF], art 13(c).
[199] Ibid.
[200] Ibid, art 14(1).
[201] See art 121 TFEU.

system had already done much the same in the aftermath of the Eurozone crisis.[202] But the Commission had sedimented an even broader conception of economic governance during the Covid crisis, arguing in 2021 that '[e]conomic policy coordination has gradually shifted to laying the foundations for a transformational and inclusive recovery and stronger resilience'.[203] As in the RRF, the scope of investments and reforms eligible for the MTFSPs is essentially unlimited and only weakly guided by the country-specific recommendations (which also reach far beyond EU competence). As Dermine has summarised:

> [T]he 2024 reform of the SGP takes a holistic approach to economic and fiscal policymaking. Most tellingly, national fiscal plans, the central tools of the new framework, are to set the entire economic agenda of Member States for the upcoming legislature, covering not only budgetary matters, but also their entire investment and reform strategy. As a result, the new SGP version, and most notably, its new preventive arm, not only serve strictly budgetary objectives but are also closely intertwined with the Union's other policy goals and priorities, and therefore include a number of provisions designed to ensure consistency and synergy with neighbouring policies.[204]

The MTFSPs are thus, as a matter of principle, all-compassing documents covering nearly every sector of national policy-making. The Commission, after assessing this extraordinarily broad range of commitments in the plan, makes a recommendation to the Council. The Council, in turn, is required, within six weeks, to decide on that recommendation as well as endorse the reforms and investments underpinning the possible extension of an adjustment period. Basically, the Council's only option is to accept or reject the Commission's proposal; if the Council is inclined to reject, it can, however, recommend that the Member State submits a revised MTFSP.[205] *In extremis*, in cases where a Member State refuses to comply, the Council can, on a recommendation of the Commission, impose the Commission's recommended 'reference trajectory' as the net expenditure path of the Member State.[206] Moreover, if a Member State with an extension of its adjustment period fails to satisfactorily comply with its set of reform and investment commitments, the Council can, again on a recommendation of the Council, impose a shorter adjustment period.[207] However, it needs to be noted, this is the only and the ultimate remedy, and in practice difficult to enforce, as the remedy applies to the adjustment period as a whole. In the case of non-performance by the Member State of individual investments and reforms, the MTFSPs are a far less

[202] Patrin (2023a, p 18); Dermine (2022, p 114ff).
[203] European Commission (2021h).
[204] Dermine (2025, p 53).
[205] Regulation (EU) 2024/1263 [EGF], art 18.
[206] Ibid, art 19.
[207] Ibid, art 20.

sophisticated tool for the EU than the RRPs, and a shortened adjustment period is not likely to make reaching them any more likely.

In a formal sense, the new EGF, like the RRF before it, reserves ultimate decision-making power to the Council, consistent with the requirements of Article 121 TFEU on the EU's economic policy coordination competence. But these formalities should not disguise how the Commission, in a practical sense, is in the policy-making driver's seat, together with the national officials who serve as its principal interlocutors. It is the Commission that is responsible for negotiating and overseeing the Member States throughout the EGF planning process—from initial technical analysis and guidance, through consultation and formulation of the plans, to their assessment, implementation, and monitoring. The breadth of the topics covered by the plans, as well as the countless exchanges of information contemplated in their formulation—suggest that only a tiny fraction of this information will ever make it to the Council. Consequently, the same sort of information asymmetries that also reinforced the role of the Commission under the RRF will operate here as well.[208]

Nonetheless, one also wonders whether the small Commission teams really possess the necessary expertise and local knowledge to assess such all-compassing documents covering nearly every sector of national policy-making in a responsible and satisfactory manner. DG EFCIN coordinates the assessment of the plans. According to the Commission, 'a precise estimate of the number of officials involved in the assessment of any specific medium-term fiscal-structural plan, or their respective nationalities, is challenging'.[209] The Commission continues:

> [W]ithin DG ECFIN, two 'horizontal' units are consistently involved in the evaluation of all [MTFSPs]: the 'Fiscal Policy & Surveillance' unit and the 'Sustainability of Public Finances and Public Expenditure Trends' unit. These units comprise a total of 27 individuals representing 14 EU nationalities. The ECFIN 'country desks' comprise, on average, 6-7 colleagues. While these are also of mixed nationalities, they would usually include some staff members with the nationality of the Member State concerned (to ensure linguistic, cultural and institutional knowledge).[210]

Thus, the assessment of a particular Member State plan will 'usually' (though not always) involve only one of its nationals on a country desk, supplemented (maybe) by another from one of the horizontal units. It might be argued that any concern over the lack of local knowledge on the teams is somewhat diminished in the context of the MTFSPs because what is at issue, ultimately, is the Member State's use of its own money; thus, the Commission's role is more broad-brush, focusing on the general merits and plausibility of the totality of the plan rather than on each individual project. Still, the limits in the Commission's capacities remain a cause of concern. The

208 See Chapter Four, nn 29–34 and accompanying text.
209 Europe Direct (2025c).
210 Ibid.

Commission's description of the process reaffirms its opaque and technocratic character, in which 'DG ECFIN coordinates the assessment … amongst various services [such as] the Directorate-General for Employment, Social Affairs and Inclusion (DG EMPL) concerning labour market reforms'.[211] Ultimate decision-making is diffused and buried. The information asymmetries between these negotiating units and oversight bodies beyond the Commission necessarily remain high.

Like the RRF before it, to mitigate those information asymmetries, the EGF Regulation establishes structured dialogue, reporting, and information rights for the EP on the model of the RRF Regulation.[212] The EGF also looks to the Economic and Financial Committee at multiple junctures,[213] drawing on its role under Article 134 TFEU to contribute to the preparation of the work of the Council in, inter alia, economic policy coordination under Article 121 TFEU.[214] As far as implementation is concerned, however, the entirety of the monitoring obligations under the Regulation, in all their complexity, fall to the Commission, not the Council.[215]

Upon the entry into force of the new EGF in April 2024, the Commission hailed it as 'the most ambitious and comprehensive reform of the EU's economic governance rules since the aftermath of the economic and financial crisis'.[216] It would, the Commission asserted, help 'to make the EU more competitive and better prepared for future challenges by supporting progress towards a green, digital, inclusive and resilient economy'.[217] Sympathetic external legal commentary concurred, seeing the EGF as a new stage in the evolution of the integration process for giving high-debt Member States 'more options, time and a hospitable environment to bring their fiscal and economic policy back on track'.[218] At the centre of both the RRF and the new EGF is an outsized role of the Commission in exercising discretion in the negotiation, approval, and implementation of national plans. That discretion, however, is deeply context-dependent, exercised in a confidential setting that makes its impact impossible to evaluate from outside. The Commission role is further magnified by its retention of considerable discretion under the corrective arm of the EGF, most importantly in triggering any excessive deficit procedure (EDP) under Article 126 TFEU.[219] The Commission must 'take into account all the relevant factors as indicated in [Article 126(3) TFEU], in so far as they significantly affect the assessment of compliance with the deficit and debt criteria by the Member State concerned.[220] More specifically, the Regulation stated:

211 Ibid.
212 Regulation (EU) 2024/1263 [EGF], arts 27–28 and recitals (21), (29)–(30).
213 Ibid, arts 5, 9, 15(4), 28(2) and recital (43).
214 See Article 134(2) TFEU, third indent.
215 Regulation (EU) 2024/1263 [EGF], art 22.
216 European Commission (2024n).
217 Ibid.
218 Gortsos and Perakis (2024, p 21).
219 For a succinct overview, see Oraheimo and Paasikallio (2024, pp 1560–67); see generally Council Regulation (EU) 2024/1264 [amended EDP].
220 Regulation (EU) 2024/1264 [amended EDP], art 1(1), inserting, inter alia, new art 2(3).

> The Commission shall give due and express consideration to any other factors which, in the opinion of the Member State concerned, are relevant in order to comprehensively assess compliance with the deficit and debt criteria and which the Member State has put forward to the Council and the Commission. In that context, particular consideration shall be given to financial contributions to foster international solidarity and achieve the common priorities of the Union referred to in Article 13, point (c), of Regulation (EU) 2024/1263.[221]

Instead of categorical exclusions of certain kinds of spending from the calculation of a Member State's deficit and debt thresholds—for example, in defence, green transition, or research and development (the so-called 'golden rule' approach)—the new EGF opted for the planning model based on the MTFSPs.[222] But it is not at all clear how the planning approach will avoid the key drawback of categorical exclusions, that is, the difficulty in identifying (and accurately defining) 'good' investments in a way that avoids the 'moral hazard which would result from labelling too many expenditures as exceptions'.[223] The experience of the RRF, with its overwhelming emphasis on spending for ultimately national public goods in national siloes, is hardly encouraging in that regard.[224] Nor is the ultimately formalistic way in which cross-national scrutiny has evolved under the RRF.[225]

The Council publishes its decision on the existence of an excessive deficit in accordance with Article 126(6) TFEU, along the recommendations given. But otherwise the main features of the old EDP remain unchanged, raising questions about whether enforcement under the proposed framework will be fundamentally strengthened.[226] It remains to be seen whether Member States will feel comfortable placing each other in a negative light. There are strong counter-incentives, particularly because 'a vote against a profligate colleague is like providing a public good: all other ministers benefit from it, while the cost falls on the minister that casts the negative vote'.[227] The experience of cross-national scrutiny under the RRF is hardly encouraging.[228]

d. 'A Drift Towards Bilateralism'

At the time of this writing, the first set of MTFSPs have been assessed as part of the 2025 European Semester spring package,[229] marking the conclusion of the first annual cycle of macroeconomic surveillance under the new EGF. Just as we saw under the RRF, however, it is quite difficult for anyone without access to the confidential discussions between the Commission and the individual Member State to have an

221 Ibid, art 1(1), inserting, inter alia, new art 2(3).
222 Oraheimo and Paasikallio (2024, pp 1552–53).
223 Ibid, p 1553.
224 See Chapter Four, Section E.
225 See Chapter Four, Section B.2.
226 Amtenbrink and de Haan (2023, p 442).
227 Ibid, quoting Thygesen et al (2022).
228 See Chapter Four, n 255 and accompanying text, citing Gambetta and Origgi (2013).
229 European Commission (2025q).

informed opinion on the merits of any particular MTFSP or the conclusions that the Commission has reached in its assessments. In its annual report for 2025, the European Fiscal Board (EFB)—the independent advisory body of the Commission on fiscal governance—lamented what it saw as the 'drift towards bilateralism' in the new EGF.[230] As the EFB elaborated:

> Instead of the multilateral scrutiny as envisaged by the Treaty, the process was dominated by confidential bilateral exchanges, which paved the way to some leniency towards optimistic national medium-term assumptions compared to the Commission prior guidance. Furthermore, new types of discretion were applied in the excessive deficit procedure. The overall limited involvement of independent fiscal institutions eroded external checks. Together, these steps and actions reduced transparency and predictability.[231]

An analysis for the European Parliament on early experiences with the EGF planning process underlined the crucial role of the technical dialogue between the Commission and the Member State, while also raising 'questions about the overall level of transparency of this exercise'.[232] The study cited, as an example, the Commission's positive assessment of France's national medium-term fiscal-structural plan, which the new government wished to update just prior to the plan's final approval given its new budgetary orientations. None of the exchanges between the French authorities and the Commission were made public until after their green light by the Council. Similarly, in the cases of Cyprus, Croatia, and Hungary, further adjustments in the national MTSFPs were made following updated technical guidance provided by the Commission, none of which was published until after the approval of the plans.[233]

With the MTFSPs, however, the biggest transparency gap is at the national level, constraining significant parts of national decision-making through commitments made in confidential negotiations without national democratic scrutiny. A survey of the first MTSFPs conducted by the network of independent fiscal institutions in the Member States illuminated this crucial gap:

> [O]nly a minority of Member States engaged pro-actively with national stakeholders, including IFIs, while preparing their [plans]. Engagement with national parliaments was limited and largely confined to informal discussions rather than formal approval processes. Only nine countries officially submitted the [plan] to their parliament, and just three obtained formal parliamentary approval before submitting to the EU. Only ten Member States involved civil and social partners in

[230] European Fiscal Board (2025, p 36).
[231] Ibid, p 7.
[232] de Lemos, et al (2025, p 7).
[233] Ibid, pp 7–8.

> discussions, and these consultations typically occurred after the government had already approved the document.[234]

The IFIs study emphasised the need for 'more comprehensive analysis, greater stakeholder involvement, and sufficient information both at the national and EU level to assess the fiscal trajectory', as well as 'more transparent exchange of information at the EU level and a more detailed quantification of budgetary measures in the [plans]'.[235]

In short, the executive-technocratic planning process from the RRF—almost entirely opaque to outsiders until the final results are produced—seems alive and well, having been successfully transferred to the new EGF.

C. The 'Patchwork Construction' of the EU's Financial Model

Over the course of the crises of the 2010s, as Chapter Two described, the European Union's public finances became increasingly complex.[236] Over the course of the crises of the 2020s, the EU's financial model became even more complex still, almost entirely due to the emergence of the NGEU model and its extensions and deviations that are the focus of this chapter.

A useful point of entry into this complexity is a 2023 report of the European Court of Auditors—The EU's Financial Landscape: A Patchwork Construction Requiring Further Simplification and Accountability[237]—whose title well captures the emergent reality. Just two years after the adoption of the RRF, it had become quite clear how far the EU had travelled from a point where it was still possible to claim that debt-financing and 'external assigned revenues' and the like were somehow exceptional and temporary. ECA's emphasis on the 'piecemeal' and 'patchwork' nature of the EU's financial model suggests that changes had been the product of functionalist pressures rather than any deliberate plan, built in response 'to emerging policy challenges' as well as 'legal or practical constraints'.[238] Three dimensions of this functionalist process are of particular interest to us here:

- the struggle for new own resources that are aligned with the EU's expanding policy goals but also sufficient to meet the EU's growing financial needs (not least flowing from servicing NGEU debt);

[234] European Independent Financial Institutions (2025, p 2).
[235] Ibid.
[236] See also, generally, Crowe (2017).
[237] European Court of Auditors (2023g).
[238] Ibid, p 42, paras 93–94.

- the expansion of the category of external assigned revenue as a necessary budgetary and financial workaround in the face of obstacles of the Member States' failure to reach a consensus on new own resources; and
- financial pressures to respond, via further debt-financing, to an expanding list of geopolitical and macroeconomic challenges, manifest in the EU's steadfast commitment to support Ukraine in the face of the Russian war of aggression starting in February 2022.

In the subsections that follow, we take up each of these dimensions in turn. As is often the case with functionalist dynamics, the piecemeal and patchwork evolution of the EU's financial and budgetary architecture, at least initially, paid little attention to concerns of a more normative nature. As a study for the European Parliament in 2022 put it, the evolution of the EU's public finances 'have occurred both rapidly and without taking sufficiently into account the importance of revisiting how new instruments are decided upon, monitored and controlled'.[239] As we shall see later, the new instruments in question often ignored or discounted issues of public accountability and democratic scrutiny, whether in terms of audit or parliamentary oversight, at both national and supranational levels.[240] Moreover, the legal and practical constraints to which the functionalist construction responded have consistently implicated the EU's ultimate dependence on the mobilisation capacities of the Member States rather than the EU's own autonomous mobilisation capacities. In the end, this was something that in turn shaped both the complex legal and financial engineering of the EU's support for Ukraine as well as the EU's ambiguous character as a 'quasi' but not fully sovereign issuer of debt[241]—a topic we take up in the final subsection of this chapter.[242]

1. The Struggle for New Own Resources from the Member States: The 'Fit for 55' Saga

Introducing new own resources from the Member States aligned with the EU's policy goals, as we discussed in Chapter Two, has been on the EU agenda for much of the last decade. The aim can be traced at least back to the Monti Report in 2016, and it was also a key topic of discussion in the (pre-Covid) negotiations between 2018 and 2020 of the upcoming 2021–2027 MFF.[243] Those advocating greater EU financial autonomy have often tied new own resources to the objective of a larger Union budget; the two objectives are thus 'distinct but interrelated'.[244] Moreover, this larger budget's

[239] Begg et al (2022, p 65).
[240] European Court of Auditors (2023g, p 43, para 96).
[241] On the notion of the EU as a 'quasi-sovereign issuer' of debt instruments, see Christie et al (2021, pp 11–16).
[242] See this chapter below, nn 458–61 and accompanying text.
[243] See Chapter Two, nn 119–35 and accompanying text. See also European Commission (2023o).
[244] Neumeier (2023, p 323).

alignment with Union policies has also been crucial: linking own resources to politically popular aims (such as incentivising plastic waste recycling) has been key to increasing EU revenues (at least in the short term, until the levy depresses the use of plastic waste and thus yields less revenue).[245] The alignment of new resources with these sorts of policy goals has 'provide[d] a political argument without altering the primarily fiscal character of the own resource'.[246]

As a part of the overall political decision on NGEU in July 2020, the European Council had agreed to seek reform of the own resources system and to use the proceeds for repayment of NGEU borrowing.[247] The interinstitutional agreement of 2020 on budgetary matters, approved as a part of the NGEU package, included a so-called Roadmap for the introduction of new own resources.[248] The preamble to the Roadmap emphasised that the Commission's authorisation to borrow funds was limited to 'the sole purpose of addressing the consequences of the COVID-19 crisis',[249] and that the funds would need to be repaid by the Union's general budget by December 2058.[250] The document stressed, moreover, that new own resources were necessary to avoid 'an undue reduction in programme expenditure or investment instruments under the MFF' and that efforts should be made 'to mitigate the increases in the GNI-based own resource for the Member States'.[251] The preamble to the Roadmap thus concluded:

> [I]n order to enhance the credibility and sustainability of the [NGEU] repayment plan, the Institutions will work towards introducing sufficient new own resources with a view to covering an amount corresponding to the expected expenditure related to the repayment. In accordance with the principle of universality, this would not imply an earmarking or assignment of any particular own resource to cover a specific type of expenditure.[252]

As noted in Chapter One, the 2020 ORD in fact established only one new own resource, which would be paid out of Member States' budgets and calculated on the basis of each Member State's non-recycled plastic packaging waste.[253] The measure was designed to incentivise Member States to recycle more plastic;[254] thus, the Member State would need to pay the levy regardless of their economic condition—the only way to lower the amount due was to reduce non-recycled plastic waste. How a Member State went about achieving that goal was largely its own concern; neither the ORD nor the

245 European Commission (2017e, pp 28–29).
246 Neumeier (2023, p 329).
247 European Council (2020, p 8, para A29; Annex, pp 63–65, paras 140–53).
248 Interinstitutional Agreement (2020), Annex II, Interinstitutional Cooperation on a Roadmap towards the Introduction of New Own Resources.
249 Ibid, Annex II, preamble point C.
250 Ibid, Annex II, preamble point D.
251 Ibid, Annex II, preamble point E.
252 Ibid, Annex II, preamble point F.
253 Council Decision 2020/2053 [ORD], art 2(1); see also recital (7).
254 Council Regulation (EU, Euratom) 2021/770.

implementing legislation obligated Member States 'to impose a levy that places the fiscal burden for the new contribution on private actors responsible for the consumption of non-recycled plastic waste'.[255] Consequently, the Member States remained free to pay the contribution from their own general budget if they so chose.[256]

This new own resource was never understood, standing alone, as sufficient to meet the needs of servicing NGEU debt going forward.[257] In line with the European Council Conclusions of July 2020,[258] the 2020 ORD further contemplated—but did not in fact establish—additional own resources (eg a carbon border adjustment mechanism, a digital levy, revenues from the EU Emissions Trading System, as well as, potentially, a Financial Transaction Tax).[259] The Roadmap contained in the 2020 interinstitutional agreement similarly served as a commitment in principle by the Commission, the Council, and the EP to seek 'fresh money',[260] which would be 'sufficient to cover the level of overall expected expenditure for the repayment of the principal and the interest of the funds borrowed to be used for expenditure' under NGEU.[261]

The power to mobilise those fiscal resources—in the sense of actual tax collection—remained national. Moreover, whether any resulting proceeds would be directed to EU coffers, instead of remaining at the national level, would require an amendment to the ORD. And therein lay the challenge before the EU as a still 'as if' constitutional entity without 'true tax autonomy'.[262] While the EU legislature can adopt secondary legislation on the technical details of these resources, it cannot mobilise them, as it would in a genuinely constitutional polity. Rather, consistent with the polycentric and *demoi*-cratic character of integration more generally, the power belonged to the unanimous action of national governments in the Council, only in 'consultation' with the European Parliament, and was then subject to the unanimous ratification of national parliaments.[263]

The interplay between secondary legislation and the new ORD was central to the complicated story behind the Commission's 'Fit for 55' legislative package proposed in July 2021.[264] The Commission's Fit for 55 proposal presupposed that two new own resources would eventually be adopted. The first was an expanded Emissions Trading System (known as ETS2), aimed at helping reduce net greenhouse gas emissions in the EU by at least 55% by 2030, directing 30% of the revenues from emissions trading to the EU budget. The second was a new carbon border adjustment mechanism

255 Neumeier (2023, p 328).
256 Ibid.
257 In 2023, revenue from this own resource amounted to €7.2 billion, or 4.0% of the EU's total revenue. European Court of Auditors (2024e, p 6, para 4). However, ECA found implementation was hampered by a lack preparation at both the Member State and the Commission level.
258 European Council (2020).
259 Council Decision 2020/2053 [ORD], recital (8).
260 Interinstitutional Agreement (2020), Annex II, preamble point I.
261 Ibid, Annex II, Part A(2)(a).
262 Buettner (2023, p 171).
263 Article 311 TFEU.
264 European Commission (2021i). For an overview of the operation of these two proposals as own resources, see Hadjiyianni (2024).

(CBAM), which would apply to any product imported from a country outside of the EU that did not have a system to price carbon; that proposal would direct 75% of what EU countries collect under CBAM to the EU budget. As noted earlier, the Fit for 55 package also added new costs to the EU budget, most importantly the Social Climate Fund.[265] The SCF was supposed to be financed by the ETS2 own resource; that is, one of the funding streams that the European Council had agreed in July 2020 should be used to repay the collective borrowing under NGEU.

Following the Commission Fit for 55 proposal, legislative negotiations on the package advanced in the Council working groups and the EP's sectoral committees. But the corresponding amendments to the 2020 ORD were delayed, first by the Commission itself, then by the Council. Rather than packaging the ETS2 and CBAM legislative proposals with the needed ORD amendments, the Commission held off on the latter until nearly the end of 2021.[266] This allowed the legislative process to focus exclusively on Fit for 55 alone, in some sense downplaying any potential problems with the ORD. The Commission's eventual ORD amendment proposal, submitted in December 2021, included own resources drawn from a 25% share of ETS2 revenues, a 75% share from CBAM revenues, as well as a 15% share of any revenues accruing to Member States under a possible multilateral corporate tax reform that had been proposed by the OECD/G-20.[267] The Commission also proposed a targeted amendment of the MFF Regulation, which would allow repayment of the borrowing for NextGenerationEU to begin during the current MFF; that amendment would also increase the relevant MFF expenditure ceilings for 2025–2027 to accommodate part of the additional expenditure under the new Social Climate Fund.[268]

With this proposal, the Commission stated it would 'now work hand in hand with the European Parliament and the Council towards swift implementation of the package within the timelines set in the interinstitutional agreement' of 2020.[269] While the proposed amendment to the 2020 ORD received the EP's support,[270] it never advanced in the Council. Initially, the Council insisted that consideration of how to allocate revenue shares in an amended ORD could 'only begin after the underlying sectoral regulations [were] adopted'.[271] That excuse was removed by the adoption of the Fit for 55 package in May 2023,[272] which was accompanied by a resolution of the

[265] See this chapter above, nn 134–58 and accompanying text.

[266] See European Commission (2021j).

[267] European Commission (2021k). The proposal involved a new own resource based on 'reallocated profits' under the OECD's Base Erosion and Profit Shifting (BEPS) initiative. For further background, see Buettner (2023, pp 170–71).

[268] European Commission (2021k), (2021l).

[269] European Commission (2021k).

[270] European Parliament legislative resolution of 23 November 2022 on the proposal for a Council decision amending Decision (EU, Euratom) 2020/2053.

[271] Council of the European Union (2022b, p 3).

[272] Regulation (EU) 2023/955 [SCF]; Regulation (EU) 2023/956 [CBAM]; Regulation (EU) 2023/957 [ETS2]; Directive (EU) 2023/958 [amending ETS Directive 2003/87/EC]; Directive (EU) 2023/959 [amending ETS Directive 2003/87/EC].

European Parliament urging the Council to move forward with amendment to the 2020 ORD.[273] But the Council did not do so, likely for two main reasons. First, and most importantly, the unanimity requirement in the Council for an ORD had the effect of empowering countries like Hungary to seek, in exchange for its vote, financial concessions relating to release of RRF funding withheld for rule-of-law noncompliance.[274] Second, the Commission proposal had included own resources related to the OECD/G-20 multilateral corporate tax reform that touched on domains in which the Member States already had existing regimes of national taxation, thus making the proposal politically delicate in several countries.

In the face of Council reluctance, the Commission in June 2023 submitted an adjusted package for the next generation of own resources.[275] Because the Social Climate Fund, as adopted, would initially be financed through a form of external assigned revenue (about which more in the next subsection),[276] the Commission proposed postponing the introduction of the own resource based on ETS2 from 2027 to 2028, after the start of the new MFF. The Commission also proposed a small increase in the own-resources share of existing ETS revenues, while leaving the share of CBAM unchanged. But the Commission dropped the proposed own resource based on the OECD/G-20 corporate tax reform pending further legislative action on that initiative. In its place, the Commission proposed a statistical own resource (not unlike the existing statistical own resources derived from the VAT base or GNI), which would be based on 'a harmonised indicator that roughly approximate[d] company profits: gross operating surplus'.[277] The Commission hastened to add that this was 'not a tax on companies, nor [did] it increase companies' compliance costs: it would be a national contribution calculated on the basis of statistics from national accounts under the European system of accounts (ESA)'.[278] The Commission expressed the hope that the package of new own resources could now be 'negotiated immediately' and called on the Council to 'accelerate the negotiations'.[279]

However, based on the documents in the Council's public register, there was little internal work within the Council on this proposal. This suggests that negotiations among the Member States not only did not accelerate, but they largely stalled. The question of new own resources has now become a topic of negotiation in the forthcoming MFF for 2028–2034.[280]

[273] European Parliament (2023e).

[274] Just as it would do later in 2023 in connection with Ukraine funding. See Chapter Four, nn 318–20 and accompanying text.

[275] European Commission (2023p).

[276] See this chapter below, nn 283–88, 306–15 and accompanying text.

[277] European Commission (2023p) (sec 3. A basket complemented with a temporary statistical based own resource on company profits).

[278] Ibid (sec 3. A basket complemented with a temporary statistical based own resource on company profits).

[279] Ibid (sec 4. An adjusted package to accelerate negotiations).

[280] See Chapter Six, Section B.2.

2. External Assigned Revenue as a Quasi-Autonomous Workaround: The Social Climate Fund Revisited

The Council's failure to amend the 2020 ORD created both a long- and short-term funding problem. The long-term problem involved figuring out a way to pay back NGEU debt, a task for which the EU most definitely would either need new own resources or increased GNI-based contributions from the Member States. As the Draghi Report of September 2024 put it:

> [I]n the absence of a decision on new own resources, effective spending power at the EU level would be mechanically reduced by interest and principal payments. Member States would have to increase their GNI-based contributions to maintain current levels of spending or spending cuts would have to be applied to programmes under the next MFF.[281]

The short-term problem related to the Social Climate Fund, now in force as part of the Fit for 55 package.[282] The SCF was supposed to derive its funding from new own resources in an amended ORD and thus needed replacement funding to operate.

The Union legislator located that replacement in one of the more obscure features of the NGEU model: the category of external assigned revenue under Article 21 of the Financial Regulation.[283] Pending ETS2 revenues being established as an own resource under a future ORD, the SCF Regulation provided that the Fund would be 'temporarily and exceptionally financed by external assigned revenue generated from allowances of the emission trading system'.[284] The ETS Directive, also amended as part of the Fit for 55 package, allocated revenues from the auctioning of 50 million allowances to the SCF and specified that those revenues 'shall constitute external assigned revenue'.[285] This allocation was in derogation of the general rule under the ETS Directive that the 'Member States shall determine the use of revenues generated from the auctioning of allowances ... except for the revenues established as own resources in accordance with Article 311, third paragraph, TFEU and entered in the Union budget'.[286] The recitals to the amended ETS Directive further stated that, when the ORD is finally adopted, 'the same revenue should cease to be externally assigned when

[281] Draghi Report (2024b, p 289).
[282] Regulation (EU) 2023/955 [SCF].
[283] Regulation (EU, Euratom) 2018/1046 [Financial Regulation], art 21.
[284] Regulation (EU) 2023/955 [SCF], art 27(4). The Regulation specifies that any financial support received from the sale of allowances under the ETS Directive 'shall constitute external assigned revenue for the purposes of Article 21(5)' of the Financial Regulation. Regulation (EU) 2023/955 [SCF], art 10(1); see also recitals (30) and (32).
[285] Directive (EU) 2023/959 [amending ETS Directive 2003/87/EC], art 1(13)(i) (inserting art 10a (8b) into ETS Directive 2003/87/EC).
[286] Directive (EU) 2023/958 [amending ETS Directive 2003/87/EC], art 1(3)(d) (replacing art 3d(4) of ETS Directive 2003/87/EC).

such a decision enters into force'.[287] In that event, the Commission was called upon to propose the necessary amendment to the SCF Regulation, all 'without prejudice to the outcome of the post-2027 Multiannual Financial Framework negotiations'.[288]

As discussed in Chapter Three, the category of external assigned revenue, or EAR, ultimately derives from an oblique reference in Article 311(2) TFEU: 'Without prejudice to *other revenue*, the budget shall be financed wholly from own resources' (emphasis added). As we also noted in Chapter Three, before the adoption of NGEU, the category of 'other revenue' was relatively small,[289] encompassing such things as 'revenue accruing from the administrative operation of the institutions, contributions and refunds in connection with Union agreements and programmes, interest on late payments and fines, revenue from borrowing and lending operations, and miscellaneous revenue—as well as surpluses from previous years'.[290] As a further subset of 'other revenue', external assigned revenue was an even more discreet category still. It historically included such things as contributions to EU programmes from candidates or other third countries, or contributions by Member States to programmes not funded by the EU budget (often special spending programmes in the area of external action).[291]

Under NGEU, external assigned revenue massively expanded as a category within the EU's financial landscape, most importantly because it was at the centre of the 'accounting trick'[292] essential to the operation of NGEU itself: all the borrowing proceeds for grants under RRF, via the EURI, were categorised as EAR, thus placing those funds outside the EU budget so as avoid throwing it wildly out of balance in violation of Article 310(1) TFEU.[293] With the SCF, the Union legislator took another step in transforming the EAR category beyond its originally marginal role. The SCF made recourse to EAR precisely because 'the necessary unanimity [in the Council] could not be obtained' for a new ORD.[294] In other words, recourse to EAR as a budgeting category was used to avoid the complicated unanimity politics under Article 311 TFEU. This EAR workaround allowed for qualified-majority voting under the ordinary legislative procedure via a 'basic act', which the Financial Regulation specified was all that was needed to recategorise revenue as EAR.[295] This explains the role served by the designation of 'external assigned revenue', discussed earlier, in both the SCF Regulation and the amended ETS Directive under the Fit for 55 package.[296]

287 Directive (EU) 2023/959 [amending ETS Directive 2003/87/EC], recital (84).
288 Ibid.
289 See Chapter Three, nn 253–54 and accompanying text.
290 European Commission (2023q, p 6).
291 See Begg, et al (2022, p 29).
292 Dermine (2020, p 349).
293 See Chapter Three, nn 249–74 and accompanying text.
294 Crowe (2024, p 52).
295 Regulation (EU, Euratom) 2018/1046 [Financial Regulation], art 21(5). This requirement is unchanged in the Financial Regulation in its current version. See Regulation (EU, Euratom) 2024/2509 [Financial Regulation], art 21(5).
296 Regulation (EU) 2023/955 [SCF]; Directive (EU) 2023/959 [amending ETS Directive 2003/87/EC].

But this use of EAR as an ORD workaround was also legally delicate. As the Council Legal Service stressed in its legal opinion of June 2020 on NGEU:

> Such assigned revenue ... cannot become a generalised means for financing Union needs that would circumvent and replace the usual budgetary procedures ... External assigned revenue must, therefore, remain additional or complementary in nature in order to avoid deconstructing the system of own resources and the regular budgetary mechanisms, in circumvention of the applicable procedures.[297]

Similarly, the German Federal Constitutional Court held in its December 2022 ruling on the 2020 ORD that the category of 'other revenue' (including EAR) must 'remain the exception in relation to own resources'; otherwise there was a risk of 'changing the financial system of the EU "through the backdoor"'.[298]

The effect of the workaround in the case of the SCF was potentially to give the Union legislator a form of autonomous fiscal mobilisation power based on the sale of ETS allowances which the EU otherwise lacked without an amended ORD. As is often the case in situations of stealth change of a potentially fundamental nature, this recourse to EAR was not entirely without precedent: the Innovation Fund, created in 2019 to support the development of low-carbon technologies, had also designated the sale of ETS allowances as EAR in a similar way.[299] But there were distinctions to be drawn between the Innovation Fund and the SCF. Prior to the Innovation Fund, as the Monti Report of 2016 had noted, proceeds from ETS auctioning were envisioned as a possible category of other revenue that might in the future be used 'more systematically', even 'at the stage of policy design'.[300] A briefing for the European Parliament in 2017 had raised the possibility of using EAR in these types of situations but only if it remained 'marginal compared to own resources'.[301]

This was precisely what the Innovation Fund arguably did by designating ETS proceeds as EAR. It was the product of a Commission Delegated Regulation implementing a 2018 amendment to the ETS Directive calling for the establishment of the Fund. The financing mechanism was in line with the purposes of the ETS Directive and, as such, was better seen as an 'intervention measure' for which an ORD amendment was not 'compulsory ... merely because the measure entails the collection of revenue'.[302] In addition to own resources, the Union has well-established competence to collect levies that regulate private-party conduct under the EU's general regulatory competence in that space. The only requirement is that the 'intervention measure' be 'part of

[297] Council Legal Service (2020a, pp 25–26, paras 59 and 62).
[298] BVerfG (2022, para 195) (citations omitted).
[299] See Commission Delegated Regulation (EU) 2019/856, art 19(3), adopted pursuant to Directive (EU) 2018/410, art 1(14)(h), amending ETS Directive 2003/87/EC, art 10a(8).
[300] Monti Report (2016, p 71).
[301] Mathis (2017, p 6).
[302] Case 265/87, *Hermann Schräder HS Kraftfutter GmbH*, para 11.

a common policy'.[303] In such cases, no ORD amendment is considered necessary because the measure does not involve revenue 'intended to finance the [Union]'s general budget'.[304] These levies are treated as 'other revenue' within the meaning of Article 311 TFEU.[305]

How the SCF's financing mechanism fits into this framework is a bit murky. The broader context leading to its adoption includes:

- the interinstitutional agreement expressing the explicit intention of the Institutions to create new own resources for the EU's general budget;[306]
- the Commission's subsequent proposal, which also contemplated own resources as a general funding source, as well as its revision in the face of the failure to adopt the amended ORD;[307] and finally
- the language in both the SCF Regulation and the amended ETS Directive making clear that recourse to EAR here was an ORD workaround that 'should cease ... when such a decision enters into force'.[308]

To borrow the language from the Council Legal Service opinion of June 2020,[309] the use of EAR here was clearly meant to 'circumvent' the ORD process. Nonetheless, it is hard to say that it sought to 'replace' it. It would also be hard to say, drawing on the language of the German Federal Constitutional Court in December 2022, that this use of EAR sought to 'chang[e] the financial system of the EU "through the backdoor"'.[310] Rather, drawing language again from the Council Legal Service opinion of June 2020, one could argue that the purpose was 'additional or complementary' to the standard system of own resources.[311]

Part of the analytical problem here is that the CJEU case law on this point is no longer really useful. It suggests that there is a reasonably clear distinction between an 'intervention measure part of a common policy' and 'revenue intended for the general budget', when that distinction is now much more fluid. There are at least two reasons for this. First, the ambition to align own resources with EU policy goals means that own resources (*qua* 'revenue intended for the general budget') are also increasingly, by definition, 'intervention measure[s] part of a common policy'. Second, there is the issue of scale. Even when some measures may first be established to pursue a policy (like selling ETS allowances to combat climate change), they may grow into such a potentially large and versatile source of revenue that they become a good candidate for a new category of own resources.

303 Ibid, para 11.
304 Ibid, paras 8–10.
305 See Neumeier (2023, p 336).
306 See this chapter above, nn 248–52 and accompanying text.
307 See this chapter above, nn 266–79 and accompanying text.
308 See this chapter above, nn 284–87 and accompanying text.
309 See this chapter above, n 297 and accompanying text.
310 See this chapter above, n 298 and accompanying text.
311 See this chapter above, n 297 and accompanying text.

Both of these factors are clearly present in the legal construction of the SCF. The financing mechanism of the SCF, even if drawing upon ETS revenues intended for the general budget, was clearly part of a common policy bound up in a complex package deal to keep Central and Eastern European Member States onboard with the Fit for 55 programme as a whole.[312] Perhaps that is why the Union legislator felt the need to stress, under the SCF Regulation, that ETS allowances were being used as EAR simply as a 'temporary and exceptional' measure,[313] pending the establishment of 'an own resource in accordance with Article 311(3) TFEU'.[314] The aim was to cast EAR in 'a temporary bridging role until the more complex ORD [was] fully in place'.[315]

The fact that this alternative labelling existed for an otherwise unchanged source of revenue is an indication of the blurred legal boundaries that characterise the constitutional borderlands in which the EU now finds itself. From a purely functionalist perspective, recourse to EAR could be justified as way to 'strengthen the EU's financial autonomy' while also 'contribut[ing] to EU policies' and 'mak[ing] the EU budget more flexible'.[316] But from a more political-cultural perspective, the increasing revenue potential of ETS allowances could also be seen as part of an effort to create a new kind of fiscal mobilisation capacity. For critics of the EU's inability to amend the 2020 ORD—in this case Richard Crowe from the Parliament's Legal Service—'[t]he Council's hesitant approach to the implementation of the 'Roadmap' for the introduction of new own resources that was agreed as part of the NGEU package ... suggests that the Member States are still not prepared to take own resources seriously'.[317] For Crowe, 'it is striking that more than 50 years after the adoption of the first Own Resources Decision, the Union still lacks the budgetary autonomy that was intended for it by the authors of the Treaties, as a complement to the autonomy of its legal order'.[318]

Whether the authors of the Treaties actually had that intention, or whether such an intention would have been considered compatible with national constitutions even if they had it, is a highly debatable proposition. The German Federal Constitutional Court would certainly have strong views on the topic. As it stated in its ruling on the ORD in 2022:

> The Member States have refrained from conferring upon the European Union direct taxation or levying powers ... [T]he allocation of own resources to the European Union not only requires a unanimous Council decision, but must also be approved by the Member States in accordance with their respective constitutional requirements. Thus, the Member States have the final say over the resources allocated to

312 See generally Leino-Sandberg and Ollikainen (2025).
313 Regulation (EU) 2023/955 [SCF], recital (32).
314 See also Regulation (EU) 2023/955 [SCF], art 27(4).
315 Kubeková et al (2024, p 55).
316 Ibid, p 7.
317 Crowe (2024, p 70.
318 Ibid.

> the European Union. This reservation is imperative from a constitutional perspective – under the Basic Law it is prescribed by Art. 20(1) and (2) GG in in conjunction with Art. 79(3) GG – in order to safeguard the budgetary autonomy of national parliaments.[319]

Regardless of the legal debates, however, what is important here is that, socio-politically and socio-historically, the recourse to EAR—using QMV to adopt the necessary 'basic act' via the ordinary legislative procedure[320]—suggests the extent to which the EU has been, and still is, struggling to develop an autonomous fiscal mobilisation capacity no longer fully mediated through the Member States.[321]

As with NGEU before it, the recourse to this quasi-autonomous capacity was enabled by the unprecedented scale of 'other revenue' now flowing through EU public finances and otherwise available for EAR redesignation via a 'basic act'. And therein might lie the seed of a risk for a broader based transformation of 'the financial system of the EU "through the backdoor"'.[322] According to a 2024 study for the European Parliament,[323] the share of other revenue as a percentage of total EU revenue increased from 11.7% in 2019 to 39.8% by 2023.[324] And within that latter number, nearly all of it (92.6%) was assigned; moreover, the overwhelming proportion of that assigned revenue was in fact EAR.[325] Neither NGEU nor the SCF would have been possible without this transformative development, demonstrating that 'more' is indeed 'different',[326] given that scale also enables potentially unexpected institutional and systemic effects, not least circumventing the requirements for an ORD through the EAR workaround.

EAR has quickly developed into 'an accepted and arguably necessary component of EU budgetary arrangements'.[327] From the Innovation Fund to NGEU, and from REPowerEU to the SCF, the category of external assigned revenue seems well on its way to becoming an established and permanent feature of the EU budgetary practice.[328] EAR, in other words, should now be seen as a basic feature of the broader NGEU model. Its use has both positive and negative dimensions, at least from the perspective of accountability and oversight. On the positive side, recourse to EAR improves the visibility of off-budget funds (OBFs), something well demonstrated by

319 BVerfG (2022, para 166) (citations omitted).

320 Regulation (EU, Euratom) 2018/1046 [Financial Regulation], art 21(5); Regulation (EU, Euratom) 2024/2509 [Financial Regulation], art 21(5).

321 Cf Lindner and Nguyen (2024, p 93).

322 See this chapter above, n 298 and accompanying text.

323 Kubeková et al (2024).

324 Ibid, p 17.

325 Ibid, p 24.

326 See Chapter One, nn 63–68 and accompanying text.

327 Begg et al (2022, p 65).

328 Even SURE—the EU's emergency borrowing and lending programme adopted in the run-up to NGEU to support depleted national unemployment insurance schemes—uses EAR as a backup feature to cover any payments made by Member States in response to calls on their guarantees in case of default (hopefully an unlikely occurrence). Council Regulation (EU) 2020/672 [SURE], art 11(6).

comparing the Innovation Fund to its counterpart instrument, the Modernisation Fund, established by the same amendment to the ETS Directive in 2018.[329] Both instruments provide non-repayable support financed by auctioning ETS allowances. But the Innovation Fund is integrated into the EU budget (via an EAR line item) and is further under the control of the Commission. The Modernisation Fund is fully off-budget and controlled by an investment committee composed of representatives from the Member States, to which the EIB and the Commission appoint one representative each.[330] One practical consequence of these differences is that ECA lacks audit rights for the Modernisation Fund and, because its spending does not count against MFF own-resource ceilings, the EP lacks any real possibilities of input as well. The Modernisation Fund, according to ECA, is the prime example of the EU's financial 'patchwork' undermining public accountability and legislative oversight;[331] hence ECA's recommendation to integrate it into the EU budget in the next MFF.[332]

While EAR is 'an improvement over the use of off-budget instruments' in this way, on the negative side it is still an exception to the normal budgetary procedure.[333] It is neither included in the MFF expenditure headings nor is it negotiated annually by the Council and EP under the annual budget procedure.[334] This weakens the role of the Parliament as a budgetary authority, with EP scrutiny only coming, if at all, 'at the discharge stage, when the accounts are closed (i.e. with a lag of two years)'.[335] However, the EP has also successfully demanded ongoing scrutiny rights in this space, both under the interinstitutional agreement of 2020 on budgetary matters as well as the incorporation of structured Commission-EP 'dialogues' into various instruments under the NGEU model (most prominently the RRF and the new EGF).[336] Moreover, because, under the Financial Regulation, the use of EAR as a funding instrument requires the authorisation via a prior 'basic act',[337] the adoption of which has typically *augmented* the EP's involvement, up to and including all the rights guaranteed by the ordinary legislative procedure as was the case under the RRF, REPowerEU, and the SCF. Thus, the EP's interest is arguably more aligned with reforming and expanding EAR's role rather than eliminating it.[338] Any further reform of EAR, if it comes, will need to await the negotiations of the post-2027 MFF, in which all the necessary (and

[329] See Directive (EU) 2018/410, art 1(14)(h), amending ETS Directive 2003/87/EC, art 10a(8) (authorising the Innovation Fund), and Directive (EU) 2018/410, art 1(16), inserting new Article 10d into ETS Directive 2003/87/EC (authorising the Modernisation Fund).

[330] For an overview, see European Court of Auditors (2023g, p 24, Box 4).

[331] See Ibid, pp 30–32, Figure 6 and paras 59–61; Figure 7 and para 63; see also p 43, para 97.

[332] Ibid, p 44, Recommendation 3, para 99.

[333] Ibid, p 34, paras 70–71.

[334] Ibid, pp 34–35, para 71.

[335] Begg et al (2022, p 26).

[336] See, eg, Chapter Four, nn 108–09 and accompanying text, and this chapter above, n 212 and accompanying text.

[337] Regulation (EU, Euratom) 2018/1046 [Financial Regulation], art 21(5); see also Regulation (EU, Euratom) 2024/2509 [Financial Regulation].

[338] This is the main thrust of Begg et al (2022, pp 68–70, sec 7.2. Reforms of the governance of EAR).

likely complex) trade-offs can be negotiated across the full range of revenue and expenditures.

3. The EU's Continuing Dependence on Fiscal Mobilisation in the Member States

As stressed at the outset of this chapter, all EU measures enacted to address the Covid pandemic in 2020 and 2021 were, in principle, temporary and exceptional. At the same time, the collective borrowing at the heart of the Covid response, first under SURE and then under NGEU, offered a policy template and legal model that could be used to address new crises.

SURE continued the pattern in which ORD headroom above the MFF ceilings, if inadequate to support collective borrowing, could be supplemented by the Member States through guarantees. NGEU demonstrated that the EU could use collective borrowing to redistribute money through non-repayable grants (at least in part), thus rupturing 'two deeply entrenched taboos at once': that 'there would be neither financing of expenditure through joint debt issuance nor new solidarity transfers between states'.[339] Nonetheless, as we stressed in Chapter One, even under the NGEU model the collective borrowing (and hence redistribution) still ultimately depended on the underlying creditworthiness and legal commitments of the EU's strongest Member States.[340]

When new spending needs have arisen that might be addressed through common debt, moreover, certain basic Treaty limitations still apply even post-NGEU. Most importantly, the collective borrowing must comply with Article 310(4) TFEU, which prohibits any act 'likely to have appreciable implications for the budget without providing an assurance that the expenditure arising from such an act is capable of being financed within the limit of the Union's own resources'.[341] Regardless of the workarounds of the 'balance' requirement in Article 310(1) TFEU on which NGEU depended,[342] the prohibition of Article 310(4) TFEU still means that 'the budgetary ceilings impose constraints on the extent to which the Union can engage in borrowing'.[343] As long as the EU operates within the limits of the commitments of the Member States under the MFF and the ORD, the EU has room for manoeuvre on the debt front[344]—something

[339] Pisani-Ferry (2020).
[340] See Chapter One, nn 47–56 and accompanying text.
[341] Article 310(4) TFEU.
[342] See Chapter Three, nn 249–74 and accompanying text.
[343] Crowe (2024, p 41).
[344] Council Legal Service (2020a, p 18, para 40) (footnote omitted): 'Borrowing by the Union would be budgetarily neutral if the resulting debt is matched by a claim allowing the Union to cover the principal, interests and costs associated with that borrowing and where sufficient assets are dedicated for that purpose. That claim would constitute the "assurance" for the financing of expenditure to which Article 310(4) TFEU refers and would be essential to guarantee the future annual repayments of the debt, and hence to ensure the budgetary balance throughout the repayment period . . . .'

that even the German Federal Constitutional Court accepted in its 2022 ruling.[345] But if collective borrowing, *qua* 'other revenue', exceeds Member State commitments to provide own resources over the life of an MFF and ORD, there would be a violation of EU (as well as German constitutional) law.[346]

Given the constraining effect of the relationship between 'own resources' and 'other revenue' (including borrowing), it should perhaps be unsurprising that some enterprising legal commentators have floated the idea of recasting collective borrowing as a new kind of 'own resource', with the aim, in effect, of freeing it from this 'other revenue' restriction.[347] We reserve addressing that proposal until the final subsection of this chapter, when we explore more deeply the EU's ambiguous character as a 'sovereign-style' rather than fully 'sovereign' issuer of debt.[348] For the moment, suffice it to say that the very existence of such proposals—regardless of their merits—is an indication of the continuing intensity of the pressures facing EU finances in the constitutional borderlands, which have only grown in the aftermath of the Russian invasion of Ukraine in February 2022.

a. Inflation, Financing Costs, and the 'Cascade Mechanism'

The need to extend broad-based support to Ukraine—eventually in the form of loans backed by the non-NGEU headroom above the MFF ceilings, with additional guarantees from the Member States—served as the major driver of two revisions of the 2021–2027 MFF, the first in December 2022,[349] and the second in February 2024.[350] We trace this process in greater detail in the next subsection.[351] Before turning to that discussion, we must first examine the extent to which support for Ukraine effectively 'pushed the resources of the EU budget to the point of exhaustion'.[352] As the Commission summarised in its June 2023 communication on the second MFF revision, the Russian war on Ukraine brought in its wake 'new and unexpected challenges' just as the EU thought it was emerging from the Covid crisis.[353] These included the energy crisis and the pick-up of migration, while the combination of generous fiscal support and covid closures resulted in high inflation. This subsection focuses on the impact of that inflation on the EU budget, particularly as it related to NGEU. As we shall see in the discussion later, how this impact was ultimately managed is again a reminder of the foundational role of the Member States in the EU financial system.

345 See above this chapter, n 298 and accompanying text.
346 See Grund and Steinbach (2023, p 5).
347 For detailed exploration of this idea, see ibid, pp 1008–16). See also Crowe (2024, p 65).
348 See this chapter below, nn 458–516 and accompanying text.
349 Council Regulation (EU, Euratom) 2022/2496 [Dec 2022 MFF Revision], amending Council Regulation (EU, Euratom) 2020/2093 [MFF 2021–2027].
350 Council Regulation (EU, Euratom) 2024/765 [Feb 2024 MFF Revision], amending Council Regulation (EU, Euratom) 2020/2093 [MFF 2021–2027].
351 See this chapter below, nn 391–451 and accompanying text.
352 European Commission (2023r) (sec 1. Introduction).
353 Ibid.

Driven by the spike in energy prices and a further breakdown in supply chains following the Russian invasion, inflation peaked in October 2022 at 10.6% for the euro area and 11.5% for the EU as a whole. The average annual inflation rate for 2022 was in excess of 8%, declining only modestly to around 6% in 2023. Persistently high inflation, in turn, led to a rapid rise in interest rates and, hence, higher funding costs for NGEU debt. As the Commission noted in its June 2023 call for a mid-term revision of the MFF:

> Since 2022, financial markets experienced a sharp rise in interest rates as a result of tighter monetary policies to curb inflation. Funding costs substantially increased for all bond issuers, including for the EU. The 10-year EU bonds interest rate increased from about zero at the time of the first bond issuance for NextGenerationEU in 2021 to more than 3%. As a result, the full 2021-2027 envelope of EUR 14.9 billion to cover the financing costs [was] expected to be used by the summer of 2023.[354]

'Facing a lofty invoice', as a news report would later describe, the Commission asked the Member States 'to add €18.9 billion to [a revised MFF], an amount that immediately raised eyebrows'.[355]

The Commission was no doubt correct that, in this environment, '[f]unding costs substantially increased for all bond issuers, including for the EU'.[356] Nonetheless, the EU's costs arguably increased *more* than one might have expected given the AAA ratings that NGEU debt had initially received from credit-rating agencies.[357] The spreads between EU bonds and the German Bund suggested that investors viewed the credit risk of new EU debt (SURE and NGEU) closer to that of France or even Spain than the traditional 'safe-debt issuers such as Germany and the Netherlands'.[358] As two economists observed in December 2022, the then-existing spread relative to the Bund was even 'higher than that of the safest (AAA) European corporate issuers and similar to the spread of less safe (single A) corporate issuers. This is not, by any means, the yield of a safe asset'.[359]

As these spreads (and concomitantly higher funding costs) persisted, a good deal of economic and financial commentary sought to identify possible causes of the market's perception of a heightened EU credit risk.[360] Among the possible factors cited were the large increase in the supply of the EU bonds, the temporary nature of NGEU and

[354] Ibid (Technical adjustments to the new economic realities: (I) A sustainable solution for NextGenerationEU funding costs).

[355] Liboreiro (2024).

[356] European Commission (2023r) (Technical adjustments to the new economic realities: (I) A sustainable solution for NextGenerationEU funding costs).

[357] As discussed in Chapter One, n 47 and accompanying text, NGEU bonds have been consistently rated AAA/Aaa/AAA (outlook stable) by most leading CRAs—Fitch, Moody's, and DBRS—and as AA+ (outlook stable) by S&P.

[358] Bonfanti and Garicano (2022).

[359] Ibid.

[360] In addition to Bonfanti and Garicano (2022), see, eg, Bletzinger et al (2023b), Kraemer (2023), Claeys et al (2023), Janse (2023), Born et al (2024), Darvas and McCaffrey (2024).

SURE or questions about the EU's repayment capacity; other factors were more technical, like the absence of bond futures for EU bonds or the lack of repo markets for European supranational issuers.[361] Regardless of the explanation, there was a sense taking hold that investors now believed 'the EU's triple A ratings [did] not reflect its underlying credit characteristics' and 'trade[d] its securities accordingly'.[362]

The near exhaustion of the MFF's full 2021–2027 envelope for financing costs by the summer of 2023 was, in the Commission's eyes, simply one species of a broader problem: the MFF's 'limited built-in flexibilities' as currently designed.[363] As the Commission noted in its call for a broader mid-term revision:

> While the multiannual nature of the EU budget provides stability and predictability, it has limited capacity to respond to major unexpected events, and its flexibilities are being depleted. 90% of the EU budget and NextGenerationEU are already pre-allocated for specific purposes, programmes or national programmes. Already 75% of the initial unallocated margins for the period 2021-2027 (which were only EUR 5.5 billion, or 0.45% of the total expenditure) have already been used or ear-marked to adapt to new needs and respond to unexpected crises.[364]

Even the MFF's existing Flexibility Instrument, designed to provide 'some limited additional flexibility over and above the ceilings of the Multiannual Financial Framework for approximately EUR 1 billion per year', had been fully used.[365] The Commission thus needed to make '[e]xtensive use of redeployments and reprogramming, on top of existing budgetary flexibilities'—chief among them cohesion funding,[366] the usual target of redeployment in crisis circumstances.[367] The Commission also cited as an example how REPowerEU had also been financed by redeploying and repurposing of other funds.[368] In these circumstance, the Commission argued that, if the EU wished to meet all its objectives, 'urgent and traditional', through 2027, there was 'no alternative [but] a targeted revision' of the 2021–2027 MFF.[369]

'Targeted' may well have been the apt term to justify the narrower December 2022 revision (as we shall see in the next subsection).[370] But it seemed distinctly out of place to justify the second revision, whose objectives were quite broad, including, inter alia, '[u]nwavering and long-term support to Ukraine via the new Ukraine Facility', '[p]romoting long-term competitiveness on critical technologies via [STEP]',

[361] This summary is drawn from Darvas and McCaffrey (2024, pp 10–12).
[362] Kraemer (2023).
[363] European Commission (2023r) (sec 1. Introduction).
[364] Ibid (sec 2. Budget Under Pressure).
[365] Ibid. For the actual proposal to amend the MFF, see European Commission (2023s).
[366] European Commission (2023r) (sec 2. Budget Under Pressure).
[367] See this chapter above, n 85 and accompanying text. See also Chapter Two, nn 257–62 and accompanying text, citing European Court of Auditors (2023a, p 42).
[368] European Commission (2023r) (sec 2. Budget Under Pressure).
[369] Ibid.
[370] See this chapter below, n 427 and accompanying text.

a 'sustainable solution for NextGenerationEU funding costs', and '[e]quipping the EU budget with flexibility for unforeseen needs', among several other pressing needs.[371] The political negotiations over the mid-term revision were intense, as battles over money tend to be. Only the €50 billion proposed for the Ukraine Facility emerged unscathed.[372] The Flexibility Instrument was topped up by €2 billion, a billion less than what the Commission sought. The €10 billion sought for STEP was reduced to €1.5 billion of new funding, which would be funnelled through the European Defence Fund.[373] Most importantly, to cover increased financing costs for NGEU due to rising interest rates, the Commission received a commitment for ... *exactly zero additional euros*. Instead, the revised MFF established the so-called 'cascade mechanism',[374] involving three steps.[375] As a journalist succinctly summarised:

> First, money will come from the existing provisions within the [EURI]. If this is not enough, [the Commission] will draw funds from programmes that are underperforming and [from] the Flexibility Instrument. If this is *still* not enough [emphasis in original], the third step will kick in and create an instrument financed by 'decommitments', financial envelopes that were unspent or cancelled.[376]

Only after exhausting these three steps—none of which involved any new money (with the exception of the Flexibility Instrument)—could the Commission resort to the 'backstop' of asking the Member States for additional funding to cover increased financing costs.[377] The cascade mechanism did not even leave the Commission free to resort to that backstop after the three steps were exhausted. Instead, the Commission's request was subject to further gatekeeping, first by the Council (which could 'invite the Commission to reassess its proposal')[378] and second by an individual Member State (which, if it had 'serious concerns', could elevate the matter to the European Council).[379]

b. The Road to Two MFF Revisions: Ukraine, Collective Borrowing, and Member State Guarantees

Living up to the promise of the EU providing '[u]nwavering and long-term support to Ukraine' would also depend on Member State support, whether bilaterally (something that has proved highly uneven) or through EU channels. A threshold example comes from Article 41(2) TEU, a provision in the Treaty on European Union governing

[371] European Commission (2023r) (sec 3. A targeted and balanced adjustment of the BUDGET to respond to new challenges).
[372] The numbers in this paragraph are drawn from European Council (2024) and Liboreiro (2024).
[373] European Council (2024, p 9, para 30).
[374] Ibid, p 4, para 15.
[375] Ibid, p 5, para 16.
[376] Liboreiro (2024).
[377] European Council (2024, p 5, para 16).
[378] Ibid, p 6, para 17.
[379] Ibid, p 6, para 18.

the EU's Common Foreign and Security Policy (CFSP). Article 41(2) TEU prohibits charging the EU budget for any expenditures 'arising from operations having military or defence implications'.[380] Expenditures falling into this category must instead be charged directly to the Member States under a contribution key based on relative GNI. A prime example is the European Peace Facility (EPF),[381] established in 2021 explicitly as an off-budget instrument with Member States contributing based on GNI in compliance with Article 41(2) TEU.

The EPF's aim was (and is) to 'strengthen the ability of partner countries to prevent and respond to crises, and contribute to their resilience, in order to enable them to protect their populations'.[382] The EPF contemplated that the EU might eventually supply a recipient country with lethal weapons (subject to contribution abstentions by neutral Member States),[383] though that would have been unprecedented for the EU. And yet, following the Russian attack on Ukraine, the Council quickly adopted a CFSP decision to supply lethal weapons to Ukraine via the EPF—an EU first.[384] As Josep Borrell, then the EU High Representative for Foreign Affairs and Security Policy, stated at the time: 'Another taboo has fallen. The taboo that the European Union was not providing arms in a war. Yes, we are doing it. Because this war requires our engagement to support the Ukrainian army'.[385] Between 2022 and 2024, the EU used the EPF as a financing mechanism for €6.1 billion of EU grants to Ukraine, funding 'lethal and non-lethal military equipment and supplies, such as personal protective equipment, first aid kits, fuel, ammunition and missiles'.[386]

Another instrument adopted in the spring of 2021—the European Defence Fund (EDF)—was designed to finance transnational defence research and development projects.[387] While the EDF itself would not finance any direct provision of military aid to Ukraine, the EDF could provide funding to the European defence industry and technological base, which in turn could indirectly benefit Ukraine by increasing the EU's capacity to produce and supply defence equipment. The EDF, however, demonstrated the sort of workarounds needed to put this sort of military spending on-budget. An MEP noted in a parliamentary question during the legislative process that 'the Commission proposes that EU monies should be used for the [EDF] "in accordance with the Treaties"', which raised the question of 'what monies (from which sources and for what purposes) can or clearly cannot be used for the Defence Fund' under Article 41(2) TEU?[388] The Commission responded that, in the case of the EDF, Articles 173 TFEU (on fostering R&D in EU industry) and 182 TFEU (on

380 For further background, Leino-Sandberg (2021a, pp 66–67), Leino-Sandberg and Ojanen (2022). To get a sense of the legal complications that art 41(2) TEU in the foreign aid context, see, eg, Hautala (2017).

381 Council Decision (CFSP) 2021/509 [EPF].

382 Ibid, recital (18).

383 Ibid, arts 5(3), 26(7), 57(3), 59(5).

384 Council Decision (CFSP) 2022/338.

385 Borrell (2022). For a detailed analysis, see Bartoloni (2022).

386 Council of the European Union (2025b) (under 'EU support to Ukraine').

387 Regulation (EU) 2021/697 [EDF].

388 European Parliament (2017).

programmes for research, technological development, and space) were available as legal bases. This avoided—'as a consequence of Article 41(2) [TEU]'—the prohibition against on-budget military 'expenditure arising from operations under the common foreign and security policy'.[389] The presence of the word 'implications' in Article 41(2) TEU might seem to foreclose this standard centre-of-gravity approach. 'Implications' can be small but still exist, after all. But no matter: using other legal bases as a work-around opened up some interesting avenues for on-budget expenditures with obvious defence 'implications'.[390]

Following the Russian invasion in February 2022 and prior to the adoption of the Ukraine Facility in February 2024, aid to Ukraine primarily took the form of MFA loans, sometimes combined with small grants for interest rate subsidies and coverage of administrative costs.[391] These loans presented their own legal and financial challenges under a series of progressively more ambitious MFA decisions in February, July, and September 2022, culminating in the MFA+ Regulation in December 2022.[392] The problem was that, because the Ukrainian economy and public finances had deteriorated so dramatically following the Russian invasion, there was a strong likelihood that any loans would not be paid back on time or at all. This necessitated additional protections in the lending process to account for the heightened risk. In turn, those additional protections—eventually in the form of further guarantees from the Member States to support EU lending—were among the key drivers that put the EU on the path to the MFF revisions in December 2022, with the adoption of the MFA+ Regulation,[393] and again February 2024, with the adoption of the Ukraine Facility.[394]

Article 212 TFEU enables the EU to 'carry out economic, financial and technical cooperation measures, including assistance, in particular financial assistance, with third countries' based on instruments adopted by the ordinary legislative procedure. When the instruments involve lending, they have historically been in the form of back-to-back loans or loan guarantees to the third country.[395] The Financial

[389] European Commission (2017f).

[390] For example, the drafters of the STEP Regulation—which amended the EDF Regulation by adding (a modest) €1.5 billion to its envelope—could claim the EDF was 'the leading programme for enhancing the competitiveness, innovation, efficiency and technological autonomy of the Union's defence industry'. Regulation (EU) 2024/795 [STEP], recital (31). In order to amend the RRF Regulation, the STEP Regulation was itself based in part on Article 175(3) TFEU (see this chapter above, nn 81–82 and accompanying text.), thus demonstrating how far the cohesion flexibility clause, in a quite buried way, had been stretched through a complex network of legal and financing instruments serving unrelated purposes.

[391] Decision (EU) 2022/1201 [July 2022 Ukraine MFA], art 5(2); Decision (EU) 2022/1628 [Sept 2022 Ukraine MFA], art 6(1).

[392] Decision (EU) 2022/313 [Feb 2022 Ukraine MFA]; Decision (EU) 2022/1201 [Jul 2022 Ukraine MFA]; Decision (EU) 2022/1628 [Sept 2022 Ukraine MFA]; and Regulation (EU) 2022/2463 [Dec 2022 Ukraine MFA+]. For an overview of EU macro-financial assistance to Ukraine, see EUR-Lex (2025).

[393] Council Regulation (EU, Euratom) 2022/2496 [Dec 2022 MFF Revision]; Regulation (EU) 2022/2463 [Dec 2022 Ukraine MFA+].

[394] Council Regulation (EU, Euratom) 2024/765 [Feb 2024 MFF Revision]; Regulation (EU) 2024/792 [Ukraine Facility].

[395] In 2023, the Commission would broadly shift from back-to-back lending, in which the proceeds of specific debt issues were restricted to funding further loans to specified borrowers, to a 'unified funding approach' with the proceeds of debt issues going into a common pool that would fund multiple programmes. For more detail, see this chapter below, nn 466–94 and accompanying text.

Regulation further required that lending or guarantees of this type include a 'provisioning rate as a percentage of the amount of the financial liability authorised'.[396] The provisioning rate is a 'fraction of the capital amount of that loan or guarantee' that must be held in reserve in the EU budget to prudently cover the risk of the instrument.[397] That reserve—known as the Common Provisioning Fund (CPF)[398]—must normally be provisioned by paid-in money, and for that reason, the amount in the EU budget for provisioning 'determine[d] the overall amount of possible lending or guaranteeing' in which the EU may engage at any given time.[399] The standard provisioning rate for MFA loans to third-countries is 9% under what is known as the EU's External Action Guarantee (EAG), which normally applies to such lending.[400] However, the Union legislator is empowered, in a particular instrument, to deviate from the EAG standard rate according to the heightened risks in that case.

The EU's first 'emergency' MFA decision in February 2022 involved €1.2 billion of back-to-back loans to Ukraine.[401] The lending was provisioned in the standard way under the EAG, at 9% paid into the CPF,[402] 'consistent with the budgetary appropriations provided for in the multiannual financial framework'.[403] The second decision of July 2022 involved a further €1 billion of 'exceptional' MFA loans.[404] At this point, however, the Commission was growing increasingly concerned about the deteriorating economic and financial state of Ukraine. Consequently, it raised the provisioning rate to the extraordinarily high level of 70%,[405] 'reflect[ing] the more acute risks of losses on this loan compared to traditional MFA assistance to countries addressing a balance-of-payment crisis'.[406]

One observer commented that this provisioning rate 'all but turn[ed] [the] loans into grants',[407] but this really reflected the economic reality that the loans were not expected to be repaid. Initially, the €700 million provisioning required under the July 2022 decision was to be 'covered separately from other financial liabilities under the External Action Guarantee and the provisioning set aside in the common provisioning fund in respect of the Union's macro-financial assistance [to Ukraine] under this Decision shall be used solely for the financial liabilities derived' from EU loan funding the support to Ukraine.[408] But the 70% provisioning rate placed considerable

[396] Regulation (EU, Euratom) 2018/1046 [Financial Regulation], art 211; Regulation (EU, Euratom) 2024/2509 [Financial Regulation], art 211.
[397] European Commission (2002, p 2).
[398] Regulation (EU, Euratom) 2018/1046 [Financial Regulation], art 212; Regulation (EU, Euratom) 2024/2509 [Financial Regulation], art 212.
[399] European Commission (2002, p 2).
[400] Regulation (EU) 2021/947 [NDICI], art 31(5).
[401] Decision (EU) 2022/313 [Feb 2022 Ukraine MFA], art 1 and recitals (7), (10), (24).
[402] European Commission (2022q) (sec 4. Budgetary Implications).
[403] Decision (EU) 2022/313 [Feb 2022 Ukraine MFA], recital (20).
[404] Decision (EU) 2022/1201 [July 2022 Ukraine MFA], art 1(1).
[405] Ibid, art 7(1).
[406] European Commission (2022r) (sec 4. Budgetary Implications).
[407] Spielberger (2024).
[408] Decision (EU) 2022/1201 [Jul 2022 Ukraine MFA], art 7(2).

strain on the capacity of the EAG and the CPF, hence also the lending capacity of the EU, necessitating relief and/or reinforcement at some point.

That point came quickly, with a new MFA decision in September 2022 on a further €5 billion in loans to Ukraine.[409] The 70% provisioning rate was retained but its sources were restructured to relieve the pressure on the budget. Only the first tranche of 9% provisioning was covered by the EAG and the CPF in the standard way.[410] The second tranche—the remaining 61%—would be covered by new Member State guarantees, which meant no additional paid-in money to the CPF.[411] Moreover, the Member State guarantees would be used to provision not just the €5 billion loans under the September MFA decision but also the €1 billion authorised in the July decision.[412] Moreover, the new provisioning also extended to €1.59 billion in EU-guaranteed loans from the EIB under its External Lending Mandate (ELM) (pursuant to a different Commission action in July 2022, these ELM loans had been 'repurposed' to support Ukraine).[413]

Under the September 2022 MFA decision, the Member State guarantees to support the Ukraine lending would be deemed 'voluntary'.[414] An individual Member State's guarantee contribution would be based on its relative share of the total EU gross national income in 2022.[415] To make the support as palatable to Member States as possible, the guarantees neither required paid-in capital nor could they be called, under the terms of the decision, until after the first 9% EAG-CPF tranche had been exhausted and not replenished.[416] Once made, the guarantee would involve 'irrevocable, unconditional and on-demand guarantees through a guarantee agreement to be concluded with the Commission'.[417] The Commission, however, remained quite secretive about the timing and content of these agreements. In response to a Europe Direct request, the Commission acknowledged only that it 'has progressively concluded guarantee agreements with all 27 Member States', but otherwise '[t]he Commission does not make the guarantee agreements publicly available'.[418] It has been difficult to obtain copies of the guarantee agreements (only the Irish agreement was discoverable online).[419]

In any case, the increasing MFA lending to Ukraine over the course of 2022 would have been impossible without the Member States providing the additional budgetary coverage.[420] This step then paved the way for taking the guarantee structure to a whole

409 Decision (EU) 2022/1628 [Sept 2022 Ukraine MFA], art 1(1).
410 Ibid, art 11(1).
411 Ibid, art 9.
412 Ibid, art 9(1).
413 Ibid, art 11(1) and recital (24).
414 Ibid, recital (16).
415 Ibid, art 9(3).
416 Ibid, art 10(a).
417 Ibid, art 9(2).
418 Europe Direct (2025d).
419 See Electronic Irish Statute Book (2022). In Finland, the only publicly available reference is in the Government Proposal to Parliament on Supplementing the 2023 Budget. See Valtioneuvosto (2022).
420 European Commission (2022s) (sec 2b. Need to establish the required budgetary cover through Member State guarantees).

new level in the MFA+ Regulation adopted in December 2022. The instrument contemplated a new round of €18 billion in concessional loans to help Ukraine meet its short-term funding needs through 2023.[421] The concessional nature was further enhanced by granting a ten-year grace period with no repayment of the principal before 2033, longer loan maturity (up to thirty-five years), and a commitment by the EU to cover the interest rate costs.[422] These provisions, too, might seem to have 'all but turn[ed] [the] loans into grants',[423] particularly given the often unstated assumption that some degree of debt forgiveness for Ukraine would be likely in the end.[424] The MFA+ Regulation explicitly excluded use of the EAG or provisioning under the CPF[425] but relied on the headroom above the MFF ceilings to back the loans, supplemented by Member State guarantees.[426]

This approach also required the December 2022 revision of the MFF ceilings.[427] In effect, what had been established was a new round of collective borrowing. However, the pressures of the moment and the need to move quickly to support Ukraine likely prevented any deeper reflection about the systemic and institutional effects of the move.[428] The process of establishing the Member State guarantees was very rushed, taking place over a matter of a few months. The recitals to both the September 2022 MFA Decision and the MFA+ Regulation stressed the urgency of the moment in nearly identical language: 'It is important that Member States complete the applicable national procedures to provide the guarantees as a matter of the utmost priority'.[429]

It was not entirely clear whether anyone outside a small group of 'financial technocrats' fully appreciated what had transpired.[430] As one researcher has described: 'Given the widespread political consensus in favour of supporting Ukraine', the new guarantee structure was perceived as largely a 'technical change' that effectively buried 'the financial and political risks ... deep in the EU budget'.[431] Among the frugal countries, the Swedish government acknowledged that it was 'generally critical of joint borrowing above the expenditure ceiling', at least when used to support 'other Member States' operating costs'.[432] But breaching the MFF ceilings was justified for Ukraine because it was facing an 'urgent and extraordinary situation' requiring 'exceptional solutions'.[433] Another researcher in Finland raised questions about whether Finnish

[421] European Commission (2023t, p 5).
[422] Ibid.
[423] See Spielberger (2024).
[424] Ibid.
[425] Regulation (EU) 2022/2463 [Dec 2022 Ukraine MFA+], art 16(3) and recital (29).
[426] Ibid, art 5.
[427] Council Regulation (EU, Euratom) 2022/2496 [Dec 2022 MFF Revision], art 1, amending Council Regulation (EU, Euratom) 2020/2093 [MFF 2021–2027], art 2(3).
[428] On the lack of 'deeper reflection' in the Covid crisis, cf Dermine (2020, p 8). See Chapter Three, n 11 and accompanying text.
[429] Regulation (EU) 2022/2463 [Dec 2022 Ukraine MFA+], recital (32). See also Decision (EU) 2022/1628 [Sept 2022 Ukraine MFA], recital (21).
[430] See this chapter below, nn 474–94 and accompanying text.
[431] Spielberger (2024).
[432] Regeringskansliet (2022, p 7).
[433] Ibid.

political leadership, both before or after the April 2023 parliamentary election, understood how, via the MFA loan packages of 2022, the EU effectively had undertaken another round of collective borrowing.[434] This confusion has arguably remained in the years since.[435]

The Ukraine lending packages of 2022 suggested a continuing role for additional Member State guarantees in supporting EU borrowing. But their use was transitional, not unlike how Member States guarantees under SURE served as a transitional step to NGEU. The Ukraine Facility—first proposed in June 2023[436] and then adopted in February 2024,[437] along with the second revision to the MFF[438]—did not use them. The Ukraine Facility offered resources up to €50 billion for 2024–2027, spread across loans (€33 billion) as well as loan guarantees and outright grants (€17 billion). On the lending side, like the MFA+ Regulation before it, the Ukraine Facility explicitly excluded use of the EAG or provisioning by the CPF.[439] However, unlike the MFA+ Regulation, the Ukraine Facility did not rely on supplemental Member State guarantees, instead backing the loans solely with ORD headroom above the MFF ceilings. The MFF revision of February 2024 provided the authorisation by extending until 2027 the existing Union budget guarantee to cover the financial assistance under the Ukraine Facility.[440] On the grants and guarantees side, funding came from the EU budget via a new instrument, the Ukraine Reserve,[441] which the MFF revision of February 2024 also authorised,[442] and a newly created dedicated guarantee capacity, the Ukraine Guarantee,[443] provisioned at 70%,[444] provided the backing for the grants and loan guarantees, again funded directly out of the EU Budget.

In its reliance on direct EU budget guarantees, the Ukraine Facility reflected a growing confidence within the institutions that they could now engineer significant collective borrowing without the support of explicit additional Member State guarantees. Although the Ukraine Facility did not completely eliminate the need for Member State contributions in extreme scenarios—their guarantees via the ORD remained—the design of the Facility emphasised the EU budget's role as the primary guarantor. This evolution thus suggests that collective borrowing has lost its salience as a legal question and increasingly become a political one.[445] Helping in this regard was that these arrangements were created to pursue an indisputably European public

[434] Ronkainen (2024).
[435] Juga (2025) (interviewing Päivi Leino-Sandberg about the need for broader discussion in Finland about the legal and political dimensions of collective borrowing in the EU).
[436] European Commission (2023n).
[437] Regulation (EU) 2024/792 [Ukraine Facility].
[438] Council Regulation (EU, Euratom) 2024/765 [Feb 2024 MFF Revision].
[439] Regulation (EU) 2024/792 [Ukraine Facility], art 22(3)–(4).
[440] Council Regulation (EU, Euratom) 2024/765 [Feb 2024 MFF Revision], recital (8) and art 1(b).
[441] Regulation (EU) 2024/792 [Ukraine Facility], art 6(1).
[442] Council Regulation (EU, Euratom) 2024/765 [Feb 2024 MFF Revision], art 1(6), inserting new Article 10b into the 2021–2027 MFF.
[443] Regulation (EU) 2024/792 [Ukraine Facility], art 31.
[444] Regulation (EU) 2024/792 [Ukraine Facility], art 32(1).
[445] Juga (2025) (interview with Päivi Leino-Sandberg).

good—security and defence—by supporting the resilience of a partner state under attack by a geopolitical adversary. In this sense, the Ukraine Facility might also be suggestive of where the EU might best direct its nascent fiscal capacities in the future, as it continues to traverse the constitutional borderlands. However, it is crucial to remember that, while these pressures on the EU budget to pursue genuine European public goods were increasing, the EU was still locked into the funding commitments of NGEU, with their strong national orientations. These conflicting goals increasingly raised the question of opportunity costs, in which the debt overhang from NGEU might inhibit the ability of the EU to pursue strategically more important priorities going forward.

As it faced this multiplicity of pressures, the EU also sought to make use of funding sources outside its own resources—as it did, pending the adoption of a new ORD, with the use of ETS allowances as external assigned revenues to temporarily fund the Social Climate fund.[446] An example is the EU's participation in the G7's 'Extraordinary Revenue Acceleration Loans for Ukraine' (ERA) initiative.[447] This programme involves a series of bilateral loans to the Ukraine from G7 countries along with a €35 billion MFA loan from the EU. These loans are serviced through a levy on revenues accrued to Euroclear from its holdings of cash from matured Russian Central Bank assets, immobilised by the EU as part of a G7 initiative. These revenues will be used to repay the loans and the associated interest costs, without any recourse to the Ukraine at all. The EU established and operates the mechanism through which the loan servicing will occur, the Ukraine Loan Cooperation Mechanism (ULCM).[448] The revenues levied from Euroclear are directed into the ULCM as external assigned revenue,[449] with the effect of converting the loans to Ukraine into non-repayable grants.[450] The Commission made the first disbursement to Ukraine under the programme (€3 billion) in January 2025.[451] In some sense, the availability of this revenue was a one-off. But on a more general level, this instrument was further evidence of the EU's need to be creative, in the constitutional borderlands, in locating funding sources unmediated through the Member States to support its own autonomous fiscal needs.

4. 'A Sovereign-Style Issuer': The Benefits, Risks, and Limits of 'As If' Constitutionalism in EU Debt-Financing

The legal engineering of the Ukraine loan packages, as one legal scholar put it, 'highlights the legacy of the NGEU model and suggests a trend toward consolidating a

[446] See this chapter above, nn 284–88 and accompanying text.
[447] For a succinct overview, see Dobreva and Vozovych (2024). See also Council of the European Union (2024b); Regulation (EU) 2024/2773 [UCLM]; Council Implementing Decision (CFSP) 2024/2760.
[448] Regulation (EU) 2024/2773 [UCLM].
[449] Ibid, art 4(1).
[450] Ibid, art 5(1).
[451] European Commission (2025r).

centralized fiscal capacity at the EU level of government'.[452] With the exception of the 'of government' tag at the end of this quotation—about which more in a moment—there is some truth to this statement. Key aspects of the NGEU model involving national plans and performance-based financing had existed in the MFA, but now became mainstream in EU funding. In addition, the NGEU model built on but also further developed two significant aspects: MFF authorisation to borrow against the headroom and funding through the unified funding approach. The collective borrowing that began under NGEU and continued through the support for Ukraine in the face of Russian aggression has undoubtedly represented an effort by the Commission to consolidate 'a centralized fiscal capacity at the EU level'. That fiscal capacity nonetheless remained incomplete, limited only to borrowing rather than taxing power, hence necessarily backed by constitutional mobilisation capacity at the national level.

The 'of government' tag at the end of the quotation is more aspirational, a statement about how European integration *should be*, or at least how the changes since the inception of NGEU *should be interpreted*. It is a reminder of how 'as if' constitutionalism—the sense that the EU is trending towards, or indeed has already become, a robustly constitutional level of government in its own right—pervades much of the legal scholarship on the integration project.[453] The view reflects an historical teleology, in which the development of EU fiscal capacities is not merely functionally advantageous—something on which many would agree—but also historically inevitable. The claim is also ultimately normative, meant to stake out a position in the messy political process of legal and institutional change—in which the functionally most advantageous outcomes do not always prevail. Indeed, some who take this position go so far as to suggest that constraints on those outcomes are, in effect, 'reactionary' and in opposition to 'the trajectory of history'.[454] That position is historiographically contestable precisely because it brackets out the messy and complex process of socio-political, legal, and institutional change in favour of a simplification based on a sense of historical inevitability.[455]

Even from a purely descriptive standpoint, however, it is necessary to take account of the ever-present 'as if'-constitutional arguments in policy-political debates. This is especially so in debates over EU debt-financing, whose conceptual categories force us to confront the nature of the integration project in a fundamental way. In the global bond markets, there is a well-established distinction between 'supranationals', the category within which the EU is placed (both by credit-rating agencies and bond indexes), and 'sovereigns', the category to which the EU hopes one day to belong. The first category is ultimately grounded in the administrative character of the integration project, whereas the second reflects the EU's aspiration to be regarded as robustly constitutional in its own right.[456] This categorisation question can be understood as the

452 Fabbrini (2024, p 178).
453 See Chapter One, nn 28–29, 57–105 and accompanying text.
454 Panascì (2024, p 54).
455 See Chapter One, nn 93–105 and accompanying text.
456 See Chapter One, nn 54–56 and accompanying text.

financial version of the classic debate over whether the EU is an 'international organisation' or a 'state', only this time the issue is not merely academic but has real financial consequences, particularly in terms of the EU's financing costs.[457]

The Commission's strategy, from nearly the inception of NGEU, has been to claim the mantel of, if not a fully sovereign issuer, then a 'sovereign-style issuer'.[458] The term is very much in the 'as if'-constitutional vein, meant to reassure the markets that the EU's creditworthiness is like that of a sovereign issuer, and its debt instruments can thus be relied upon as a safe and stable store of value. In line with that strategy, the EU is developing both a strategy (the 'Diversified Funding Strategy') and an approach (the 'Unified Funding Approach') that 'draw on best practices of'[459] and are 'similar to'[460] and 'much like'[461] those used by sovereign issuers. We explore the implications of both the strategy and the approach in greater detail in the following subsection.

a. From the Diversified Funding Strategy to the Unified Funding Approach

The Diversified Funding Strategy uses multiple funding instruments (EU-Bonds with varying maturities as well as short-term debt instruments called EU-Bills) and techniques (syndication, auctions, private placements), as well as a primary dealer network to execute and support those techniques. Taken together, these three elements seek to support liquidity in secondary markets and ensure the 'placement of EU debt with the widest possible investor base'.[462] In 2024, the Commission launched a Repurchase Agreement (Repo) facility to further support the market activity of its primary dealers.[463] In April 2025, the creation of a futures market for EU bonds was announced, with a target launch date in September 2025, again to 'strengthen the liquidity in EU bond markets and support the position of the EU as a major issuer in the European and global capital markets'.[464]

There are clear functional benefits of the strategy. Its overarching aim, first with regard to NGEU but carried through the Ukraine loan packages, was squarely focused on scale. As the Commission elaborated in a policy brief in 2022:

> NGEU required a funding strategy that: (i) enabled the significant scaling up of issuances in a very short amount of time (NGEU required the Commission to become an issuer comparable in activity to large EU Member States, with issuance of on

[457] See this chapter above, 356–62 and accompanying text.

[458] This is the label that Christian Engelen, Head of Unit, Borrowing and Lending, in DG Budget at the European Commission, used in a presentation to investors in 2022. Engelen (2022, at 19:50 min); see also Spielberger et al (2025, p 1197). The Commission has also used the label, as have members of the specialised press covering the Commission's evolving funding strategy. European Commission (2023u); see also, eg, Lee (2023), EU Reporter (2024).

[459] Commission Decision (EU, Euratom) 2021/625, recital (6).

[460] European Commission (2021m) (sec 2. Eight Success Factors for the NGEU Issuance Programme).

[461] European Commission (2022t, p 7).

[462] European Commission (2025s).

[463] European Commission (2024o), EU Reporter (2024).

[464] Eurex (2025).

average roughly EUR 150 billion per year); and (ii) provided the necessary tools to manage issuances in a way that met complex disbursements of loans and grants to Member States (with disbursements having to take place at speed, high frequency and uncertain timings given their dependence on the implementation of related plans).[465]

The pressures of increasing scale were similarly felt in the Ukraine MFA loan packages, whose trajectory started small (at €1.2 and €1 billion respectively in February and July 2022), then jumped to €5 billion in September and grew to €18 billion under MFA+ in December 2022. The level would then jump again in 2024, reaching €33 billion under the Ukraine Facility and €35 billion under the MFA loan which was part of the G7's ERA initiative.

It is no coincidence that the dramatic jump in the scale of Ukraine issuances started in December 2022 with the MFA+ programme; both it and the Unified Funding Approach were adopted together as a matter of urgency for precisely that purpose.[466] The aim was to extend the toolbox developed for NextGenerationEU—that is, the Diversified Funding Strategy—to all EU issuances, most importantly those for Ukraine.[467] As the Commission elaborated:

> Under this approach, the Commission will be issuing single branded 'EU-Bonds', rather than separately denominated bonds for individual programmes such as NextGenerationEU, SURE and Macro-Financial Assistance (MFA). The Commission will be collecting all proceeds in a central funding pool and internally allocating them to various policy programmes funded through bond issuances. This will avoid the fragmentation of EU issuances and support a more homogenous secondary market for EU-Bonds.[468]

The advent of a central funding pool suggested the partial realisation of a long-held aspiration of the EU, stretching back at least to the Five President's Report of 2015, to establish an EU Treasury with far-reaching economic, fiscal, and budgeting powers.[469] The Five President's Report saw this as part of a 'a genuine Fiscal Union' involving 'more joint decision-making on fiscal policy', subject to 'democratic accountability and legitimacy' at the EU level.[470]

Before reaching that macro-institutional (and ultimately socio-political) question, it is worth considering first the micro-level risks of extending the Unified Funding

465 European Commission (2022t, p 6).
466 Regulation (EU, Euratom) 2022/2434 [Unified Funding Approach]; Regulation (EU) 2022/2463 [Dec 2022 Ukraine MFA+].
467 European Commission (2022u).
468 Ibid.
469 Five Presidents' Report (2015, p 17). Indeed, calls for an EU Treasury could also be found in the Four Presidents' Report (2012, p 12) and European Commission (2012, pp 30–33) (A blueprint for a deep and genuine economic and monetary union).
470 Five Presidents' Report (2015, p 17).

Approach outside the context of NGEU. What this extension meant in practice was the abandonment of back-to-back lending as a funding technique, rooted in the idea that, for every tranche of debt, the EU must hold a directly corresponding asset on its books and 'each single borrowing transaction is linked to a single disbursement'.[471] In terms of risk management, each back-to-back loan had been separately guaranteed and provisioned (eg via the EAG and the CPF); moreover, the provisioning requirement—by requiring actual cash in hand in the current budget—acted as a further limit on the amount of debt that the EU could take on.[472] In this sense, back-to-back was primarily an accounting practice, intended to keep borrowing strictly in check. But it also meant that EU borrowing was dispersed across a large number of individual small bond issuances with limited liquidity and poor secondary markets, instead of concentrating into a few benchmark bonds.[473] Importantly, though, back-to-back lending did not create bankruptcy-remote SPVs. Ultimately, all debt issued before the UFA was still Union debt and guaranteed by the full faith and credit of the Union. So, from a risk management purpose, the difference was limited.

As the Commission would later explain, back-to-back lending 'proved successful in addressing smaller funding needs' but it could not handle 'bigger and more complex' issuances.[474] Extending the Diversified Funding Strategy to all borrowing would 'decouple the funding transactions from the programme's immediate funding needs, providing more flexibility in the execution of borrowing operations'.[475] In short, traditional provisioning requirements—and the cap on debt that they functionally entailed—had to be abandoned precisely because the EU now needed to borrow at a new and unprecedented scale. This is understandable from a functional perspective but there were also clear risks. The European Court of Auditors captured their essence when reflecting on the exclusion of standard loan provisioning in the context of MFA+ loans to Ukraine:

> Up until now, the relevant assets have been set aside as a provision to honour any calls relating to guarantee of [the] loans . . . [Without such provisioning] the related risks of possible defaulted payments are transferred to the future. This could potentially put pressure on future budgets and payment needs . . . Currently, there are no plans to increase the size of the headroom correspondingly.[476]

It is perfectly legitimate to make a choice in favour of transferring risks to the future, as long as the choice is presented openly and discussed thoroughly, both in national

[471] European Court of Auditors (2022d, p 7, paras 15–17).
[472] See this chapter above, nn 395–400 and accompanying text.
[473] This did not mean that each bond issuance was secured by different collateral and hence had different credit quality. All debt issued by the EU was always ultimately backed up by the same pool of wealth, first the whole EU budget and then through access to Member State's financing obligations through the ORD.
[474] European Commission (2022u).
[475] Ibid.
[476] European Court of Auditors (2022d, p 7, paras 15–17).

and supranational fora. But that is not what happened with the extension of the Diversified Funding Strategy beyond the NGEU context. Rather, the decision was the product of an extremely rushed process in November-December 2022 together with the €18 billion in MFA+ loans to support Ukraine.

The timeline of that process is illuminating. On 9 November 2022, the Commission submitted the proposal to amend the Financial Regulation to establish a diversified funding strategy as a general borrowing method (what would become the Unified Funding Approach Regulation).[477] The Commission's explanatory memorandum was sparse. Its arguments boiled down to '[t]he funding needs for Ukraine require mobilisation and disbursement in a cost-effective flexible and financially sound manner'; '[t]he diversified funding strategy has been introduced for NGEU borrowing and has proven successful so far in that context'; and the 'proposal should be adopted as a matter of urgency'.[478] Perhaps more importantly, in terms of budget implications, the Commission stated: 'The proposal has no direct implications for the level of appropriations in the Union budget',[479] which was not exactly true: it reduced allocations by eliminating current loan provisioning and ignored the potential implications for *future* budgets given the absence of that same loan provisioning.

The European Court of Auditors submitted its opinion on 22 November 2022.[480] Beyond its reservations about the impact on future budgets noted earlier, it also questioned the Commission's use of an 'exceptional fast track procedure', pointing out that 'the diversified funding strategy is a long term measure', and that the Union legislature has had 'limited time and supporting analyses to consider this proposed long-term change'.[481] ECA's opinion was largely ignored. Just two days later, on 24 November 2022, the European Parliament adopted its position at first reading not to amend the Commission proposal. On 28 November, the Council decided, in view of 'the urgency of the matter' to agree to shorten 'the eight-week period ... on the role of national Parliaments' to review the legislation under the early-warning mechanism.[482] The regulation was adopted on 6 December,[483] less than a month after it was proposed by the Commission. Requests to both the Commission and the Council for the documents containing the legal advice relating to this change were unavailing; both institutions claimed no such documents exist.[484]

In national administrations, there typically is a separation of debt issuance function from the finance ministry into a dedicated debt office, which takes care of bond issuance under some main risk tolerance parameters. Following a similar pattern, the new Unified Funding Approach Regulation leaves it almost entirely to the Commission

477 European Commission (2022v).
478 Ibid.
479 Ibid.
480 European Court of Auditors (2022d).
481 Ibid, p 5, para 8.
482 Council of the European Union (2022c).
483 Regulation (EU, Euratom) 2022/2434 [Unified Funding Approach].
484 European Commission (2025t, p 2) ('no such documents ... are held by the Commission'); Council of the European Union (2025c) ('the Council was not able to find [such] documents').

to 'establish the necessary arrangements for the implementation of the diversified funding strategy' across all categories of EU debt.[485] The Commission stated that it would 'apply a uniform robust risk, compliance and governance framework to all borrowing operations',[486] including oversight by the independent Chief Risk Officer (CRO).[487] The next version of the CRO's High Level Risk and Compliance Policy in July 2023 (updated again in July 2024) indicated:

> The headroom provides a guarantee for contingent liabilities arising from financial assistance to Member States [under NGEU] and for financial assistance to Ukraine under the MFA+ instrument and under the Ukraine Facility... For contingent liabilities that are backed by the Common Provisioning Fund (CPF) and fall under the scope of this policy, the CPF holds the provisions protecting the EU budget against losses which may arise. Availabilities under the relevant expenditure ceiling allow for the necessary replenishment of the CPF in case of need.[488]

In September 2024, a new version of the Financial Regulation was adopted.[489] One of its aims was 'to better reflect the specific nature and functioning of the provisioning of financial liabilities and of the budgetary guarantees'.[490] However, the new version retained aspects of the 2018 version that suggested loan provisioning 'applied to all budgetary guarantees', language that could be understood to reach headroom guarantees.[491] In practice, however, headroom guarantees and CPF provisioning remained distinct. The latter category applies only to an increasingly small category, such as the recent traditional MFA loans to Egypt and Jordan,[492] that is, a tiny percentage of the EU's current borrowing operations. The purpose of provisioning—'to deliver leverage while ensuring an adequate level of protection against financial liabilities'—while still in principle recognised under the 2024 version of the Financial Regulation,[493] was pushed to the margins of the EU's financial landscape. Instead,

[485] Regulation (EU, Euratom) 2022/2434 [Unified Funding Approach], art 1(2), inserting new art 220a into Regulation (EU, Euratom) 2018/1046 [Financial Regulation].
[486] European Commission (2022u).
[487] European Commission (2022t, p 9). ECA was critical, however, of the structure and resourcing of the CRO position and recommended reinforcement; see European Court of Auditors (2023i, p 45, Recommendation 2 and para 93). The European Commission (2023v, pp 2–3) accepted the recommendation and committed to adopting a 'charter explaining the operational management tasks of the CRO, in their capacity as Deputy Director-General of DG Budget'—see Commission Decision (EU, Euratom) 2025/369 [CRO]—as well as reinforcing the CRO team 'with a view to strengthening and optimising its operational capacity and aligning its organisation, so it becomes commensurate with the tasks assigned to the CRO'.
[488] This quotation comes from the July 2024 version of the policy. See European Commission (2024p, p 7). The passage from the July 2023 version is identical, except for the reference to the Ukraine Facility, which had not yet been adopted. See European Commission (2023w, pp 6–7).
[489] Regulation (EU, Euratom) 2024/2509 [Financial Regulation].
[490] Ibid, recital (7).
[491] Regulation (EU, Euratom) 2024/2509 [Financial Regulation], recital (247); see also art 214.
[492] This is made clear in the Commission proposals on the two loans. See European Commission (2024q), (2024r) (sec 4. Budgetary Implications).
[493] Regulation (EU, Euratom) 2024/2509 [Financial Regulation], recital (250).

traditional '[b]ack-to-back lending has been replaced by active debt management' by the Commission.[494]

The scholarly literature has raised general concerns about 'accountability gaps' in EU borrowing,[495] pointing in particular to how 'the EP [was] kept at arm's length from Commission borrowing instruments until relatively recently'.[496] The Unified Funding Approach Regulation now explicitly requires the Commission to 'regularly and comprehensively inform the European Parliament and the Council about all aspects of its borrowing and debt management strategy'.[497] The Commission meets this obligation in two ways, first, by submitting its annual borrowing decisions and funding plans to the EP and Council; and second, by 'report[ing] twice per year on all aspects of its borrowing, debt management and liquidity management strategy'.[498]

The situation is quite different for national parliaments, of course, who enjoy few informational rights at the EU level (the Early-Warning Mechanism being the prime example, which was overridden in the adoption of the Unified Funding Approach Regulation).[499] But insofar as the technical management of sovereign debt is concerned, their role has often been limited even on the national level,[500] thus perhaps accounting for their 'patchy' interest or role in EU borrowing.[501] Instead, the primary national accountability mechanism operates through the Council, in practice via the EFC and its Sub-Committee on Sovereign Debt Markets.

b. Market Hesitance and Constitutional Politics on the Shores of the Rubicon

Over the last several years, the Commission has taken numerous steps that have sought to move the EU, in a credible way, towards becoming something like a sovereign issuer. Academic observers have often applauded these moves. Nonetheless, the markets themselves—as evidenced by the persistent spreads between EU bonds and the German Bund—have been more hesitant in their judgement.[502]

From a purely functional perspective, the Diversified Funding Strategy and the Unified Funding Approach, supplemented more recently by the creation of a repo facility and the announcement of a futures market,[503] have all been designed to add scale, depth, and liquidity to the market for EU bonds. These efforts, which have responded directly to suggestions from market actors,[504] have been particularly

494 Spielberger et al (2025, p 1209).
495 Hodson et al (2025, p 698).
496 Ibid, p 714.
497 Regulation (EU, Euratom) 2022/2434 [Unified Funding Approach], art 1(2), inserting new art 220a into Regulation (EU, Euratom) 2018/1046 [Financial Regulation]; see Regulation (EU, Euratom) 2024/2509 [Financial Regulation], art 224(2).
498 Commission Implementing Decision (EU, Euratom) 2023/2825, arts 3(6), 4(5), and 13.
499 See this chapter above, n 482 and accompanying text.
500 Spielberger et al (2025, p 1119), citing Trampusch and Gross (2021).
501 Hodson et al (2025, p 714).
502 See this chapter above, nn 357–62 and accompanying text.
503 See this chapter above, nn 463–64 and accompanying text.
504 European Commission (2023x).

important recently, 'at a time when American policy is creating global economic upheaval', and investors have been looking more 'warily' at US Treasuries.[505] The emergence of EU bonds as a potential safe asset comparable to a high-quality sovereign bond would have multiple potential benefits, not least for the Euro as a global currency. These include, among others, further developing European capital markets and reinforcing the European banking union by helping to break the 'doom loop' between Member State public finances and domestic banks holding their bonds.[506] To aid that latter process, in December 2022 the European Central Bank announced that it would begin treating EU bonds in the same way as European Government Bonds (EGBs) as collateral in its financing operations for banks.[507]

While the Commission has worked diligently over the last several years to 'adopt many of the trappings of a sovereign issuer', it has nonetheless 'struggled to shift its supranational tag'.[508] The major indexes have continued to place EU bonds in the category of Supranationals, Sub-Sovereigns, and Agencies (SSAs) rather than that of EGBs. Over the last several years, the Commission has undertaken a concerted campaign[509]—to this point unsuccessful[510]—to change its indexing category.[511] Inclusion in EGB indexes would increase the structural demand for EU bonds and almost certainly reduce borrowing costs.[512] That benefit, in itself, could prompt officials in Member States that are otherwise hesitant to view the EU as autonomously 'sovereign' (or 'constitutional'), to favour the index recategorisation on these instrumental grounds alone.[513]

The difficulty for the Commission is that inclusion in the sovereign-bond indexes ultimately turns on a complex interplay of policy action and market response.[514] The factors for success include ones that the Commission can sometimes control (eg creating a repo facility),[515] as well as others that it can politically pursue in the short-to-medium term (eg establishing a more permanent borrowing capacity post-NGEU

[505] Dolan (2025). See also Ritchie (2025).

[506] See Chapter Two, nn 171–72 and accompanying text.

[507] European Central Bank (2022).

[508] Fleming and Stubbington (2023).

[509] Pronina and Ritchie (2023); Khadbai (2024a).

[510] McDougall (2024), Ritchie (2024), Khadbai (2024b).

[511] The Commission also tries to blur the distinction between the EU as a supranational versus the EU as a (near) sovereign in its presentations to investors. See, eg, European Commission (2025u) (slide 3: The EU: A unique union of sovereign states; slide 6: How EU debt (*sic*): a direct and unconditional obligation of the EU; slide 42: EU as an issuer: Institutional structure unlike a typical supranational; slide 43: EU Bonds seen increasingly as substitutes for core area EGBs; slide 44: EU-Bond market increasingly like market of large, liquid EGBs).

[512] Khadbai (2024c) ('If the EU joins a government bond index, it will have a certain weighting of bonds held in that index so investors who link their portfolios to that index will also have the same exposure. Sovereign index inclusion will also open up the possibility to allow other investors who only buy government bonds to start investing in EU bonds').

[513] Kowalcze and Ritchie (2024), quoting Tammo Diemer, co-director of the German Finance Agency: 'We have an interest in the EU financing itself as cheaply as possible, because the EU's costs are also the costs of the member states. So we support and approve [the EU's attempt to reclassify the bloc's debt]'.

[514] Ibid ('it is ultimately up to markets to decide whether a bond segment is considered a government bond or not').

[515] See this chapter above, nn 463–64 and accompanying text.

to meet pressing needs like defence and security). But other factors involve changes over which the Commission has no ultimate control (eg fully supranationalising the ORD, shifting its adoption to qualified-majority voting, or, even more ambitiously, establishing an autonomous taxing power at the EU level—all of which involve complex unanimity politics and, at least formally and more demandingly, Treaty change). This last factor has been particularly crucial in explaining not just the persistence of spreads but also the difficulties of including EU bonds in the sovereign indexes:

> [E]ven though the EU has some features of a sovereign, with a legislative branch and a judicial branch, it misses a key feature of the usual definition of sovereignty which is taxation power. Even if the EU can access indirectly member states' resources through GNI-based contributions to the EU budget, it also signals to markets that the EU is fully reliant for its financing on its members and difficult negotiations between them, and is thus different from a sovereign that can resort to taxation very easily and quickly.[516]

Put another way, the EU's ultimate status as a sovereign issuer 'depends on market actors accepting the EU's stance as [a] solvent and liquid market participant, an assessment which, in the absence of genuine EU taxing power, remains linked to Member States' willingness (and legal obligation) to provide the necessary financial backing'[517] (or indeed their ultimate willingness to remain Members of the European Union).

In short, the question of sovereign indexing, as a matter of constitutional politics, necessarily implicates the Rubicon of autonomous fiscal mobilisation—undoubtedly the most daunting obstacle that the EU must transcend as it navigates the constitutional borderlands in which it currently finds itself. For those observers of an openly 'as if'-constitutional bent, the fact that the EU has yet to cross this fiscal Rubicon is an anomaly that simply shows how economic and fiscal integration are out of sync with the autonomy that the EU enjoys in its legal order. As Grund and Steinbach have put it, '[t]he EU has transformed from an international organization to an autonomous legal regime with supremacy and direct effect. However, in economic terms, the Union never fully emancipated—it remains dependent on Member States in securing funding to fulfil its objectives.'[518]

Short of the power to tax, which the EU does not autonomously possess,[519] there is the question of the nature and scope of the EU's power to borrow. In its standard presentation to investors, the Commission makes the unqualified claim that '[t]he European Commission is empowered by the EU Treaties to borrow from international capital markets on behalf of the European Union'.[520] No doubt, once a

[516] Claeys et al (2023) (emphasis omitted).
[517] Grund and Steinbach (2024, p 1018).
[518] Ibid, p 993 (Abstract); see also Crowe (2024, p 70). See this chapter above, n 318 and accompanying text.
[519] Contra the claim of Fabbrini (2020, p 25), made to the Department of Finance of Ireland, that NGEU 'endows the EU with a fiscal capacity *independent from state transfers*, and suitable to invest on EU programs to promote EU public goods' (emphasis added). See also Crowe (2024, p 65).
[520] European Commission (2025u, slide 6) (emphasis omitted).

political decision is made under the ORD to authorise borrowing, the Commission is the institution to create the Treasury arrangements to implement that empowerment. Nonetheless, the Treaties do not create any explicit independent empowerment to borrow. Indeed, as the German FCC noted in its ruling on the 2020 ORD in December 2022: 'The EU institutions themselves ... assume that the Treaties give rise to a general prohibition on borrowing ... as was confirmed by a representative of the European Commission in the oral hearing' before the Court.[521] Aside from that oral confirmation, the Court cited the Commission's June 2020 Q&A, as well as the Council Legal Service's conclusion in its own June 2020 opinion.[522] Of course, the Commission may have since changed its views, just as it did for the purposes of Covid, reversing its earlier position that the 'balance' requirement in Article 310(1) TFEU prohibited any debt-financing, without Treaty change.[523] However, given the confirmations to the FCC, which it then cited as a basis for its ruling, a further shift in position may now be more difficult to do.

As Chapter Six discusses in detail, the EU's funding needs up to and beyond 2027 will remain intense, something that is figuring prominently in the negotiations over the new MFF for 2028–2034. The ongoing MFF negotiations are necessarily confronting head on the debt burden from NGEU as well as its broader impact on the budget. If NGEU is understood as a temporary front-loading of future EU spending, then the grant-related debt service under NGEU should crowd out other EU spending,[524] forcing difficult reprioritisations in the overall budget—the 'cascade mechanism' on steroids—and the likely target will once again be traditional cohesion funding.[525] The alternative is a bigger budget, which is favoured by the Commission and the EP, but that would require more own resources from the Member States, which to date they have been reluctant to do.

Under current law, the relationship between 'own resources' and 'other revenue' (including borrowing) also imposes clear limits on the amount of borrowing the EU can undertake.[526] Grund and Steinbach have argued, however, that 'creating debt as a new type of own resource seems to be a "legally workable" solution',[527] one that would act to free borrowing from these limits on 'other revenue'. Crowe has also suggested that the same option is open.[528] We consider such a step deeply unlikely. Even Grund and Steinbach, who have offered the most detailed explanation of the

[521] BVerfG (2022, para 152).

[522] European Commission (2020a) [Q&A]; Council Legal Service (2020a, p 24, n 39).

[523] European Commission (2015) ('[t]he Treaty establishes the principle of a balanced budget for the EU. Filling a gap between revenue and expenditure by issuing public debt is therefore not possible ... The Commission is at this stage not envisaging submitting proposals to modify the Treaty [to overcome this limitation].'). See Chapter Two, nn 166–67 and accompanying text; see also Chapter Three, nn 248–50 and accompanying text.

[524] Darvas and McCaffrey (2024, p 3).

[525] See Chapter Six, n 4 and accompanying text, discussing European Commission (2025h, p 1), (2025i, p 2), (2025j, p 3).

[526] See this chapter above, nn 341–46 and accompanying text.

[527] Grund and Steinbach (2024, p 1015).

[528] Crowe (2024, p 65).

debt-as-own-resources proposal, have recognised a whole series of complications.[529] They have conceded, most importantly, that this new debt-financing could not, under the current Treaties, be used to roll over earlier debt:

> [D]ebt cannot be repaid with debt, and must ultimately be shouldered by the Member States through permanent contributions to the Union budget. Another impediment hampering the economic effect of debt financing is that revolving debt is precluded – the EU cannot take on new debt in order to service outstanding liabilities.[530]

How these discussions will end remains to be seen. But even if the debt-as-own-resources proposal were to be adopted, that would leave the EU financial model in an odd place, in which the still-polycentric and *demoi*-cratic nature of the integration project would have a continuing and significant impact on the EU's financing options. The EU may be increasingly sovereign-'like' but it will never be fully sovereign unless and until the European peoples choose to 'constitute' it as a genuinely federal level of government (not governance) over and above the Member States. To take that step requires more than mere Treaty reinterpretation. For those who want the EU 'to breathe more freely and autonomously with both its legislative and budgetary lungs',[531] the answer is not more 'as if' constitutionalism. The answer is to recognise that '[t]ransitioning to a fully-fledged fiscal Union would render Treaty amendments indispensable'.[532]

[529] They stress, eg, that unlike debt as 'other revenues', debt as 'own resources' would need to respect the principle of universality, Grund and Steinbach (2024, p 1013), but then they suggest various ways in which it could or should deviate from that principle. See ibid, p 1017); see also Grund and Steinbach (2023, pp 12–13).

[530] Grund and Steinbach (2024, p 1016).

[531] Crowe (2024, p 71).

[532] Grund and Steinbach (2024, p 1018).

PART THREE

TAKING STOCK OF ‘WHERE WE ARE AND WHITHER WE ARE TENDING’

Chapter Six
The NGEU Model Made Permanent?

Our aim in this chapter is to cover developments in the period from the Draghi Report of September 2024 through the announcement of the Commission's new MFF and ORD proposals in July 2025 as well as the subsequent few months. The two key developments of this chapter's coverage—the Draghi Report and the Commission's MFF proposals—might be regarded as the (so far) ultimate extensions of the NGEU model, looking to planning and spending as the means of solidifying what has been a deep transformation in EU governance. This proposed transformation would likely impact both the governance of legacy programmes (such as CAP and cohesion) as well as the design of new programmes to address Europe's profound challenges in terms of competitiveness and defence/security.

While these two developments are chronologically the culmination of this volume, they are merely the next step in the EU's effort to address the unrelenting functional demands of the last half-decade, a process that will no doubt continue into the future. These functional pressures have been, and will remain, real, and we believe that the goals of the many actors who have tried to develop various Treaty workarounds to reach this point have often been noble. But in the face of the functional demands pushing towards greater centralisation of power at the EU level—more particularly in the hands of the Commission—there have also been persistent difficulties derived from integration's deeply polycentric and *demoi*-cratic character, torquing the NGEU model in other, more national directions. The result is a governance system that is sub-optimal in multiple ways—on the one hand, it is technocratic and opaque, characterised by increasing Commission power at the expense of other institutions and levels of governance; on the other hand, it produces outcomes that are poorly geared towards delivering the sort of European public goods and cross-border projects commensurate with the geopolitical and macroeconomic demands of the moment.

We begin in Section A with a discussion of the functionalist logic in the Draghi Report and its carry-over into the first nine months of the second von der Leyen Commission. The chapter then turns in Section B to the aspirations surrounding the next MFF, first as reflected in the high ambitions of the Draghi Report itself and then in the initial outlines of the MFF from the Commission in February 2025, before turning to the hard realities of budgetary politics that manifested themselves quite quickly with the Commission's proposal of the new MFF and ORD in July 2025. The chapter concludes in Section C with a brief set of reflections on what these developments suggest about the state of the NGEU model and European democracy more generally, which will set the stage for the Conclusion that follows.

European Integration in the Constitutional Borderlands. Päivi Leino-Sandberg and Peter L. Lindseth,
Oxford University Press.
DOI: 10.1093/oso/9780198949527.003.0007

A. Unconstrained Functionalism: Bypassing the Treaties Through 'Targeted Adjustments'

As we noted in Chapter Five, 'targeted' is a word the Commission tends to fall back on when justifying fundamental legal changes to make them sound more limited or technical than they actually are.[1] 'Targeted' gives the sense that the change in question is somehow close to, or perhaps even falls within the meaning of, the instrument being altered. The implicit message is 'all that is needed are just a few tweaks' to meet the demands of the moment. In this chapter we encounter several additional examples of this rhetorical strategy in action.

Most notoriously, the Draghi Report called for 'a small number of overarching, targeted institutional changes ... without the need for Treaty change',[2] as well as 'targeted adjustments without the need for such a change'.[3] Additionally, the Commission's proposals in April 2025 on redirecting cohesion funding towards defence and security projects—a major stretch of the cohesion concept from its original regional-developmental goals—also talked of 'targeted amendments' of existing cohesion funding instruments.[4] Finally, the Commission's proposal for the new ORD for 2028–2034 called for a 'targeted tool',[5] involving establishing a permanent collective borrowing capacity to fund loans to Member States on an emergency basis. What these examples suggest is the extent to which 'targeted' has become a rhetorical contrivance to obscure broader systemic and institutional shifts, often with profound impact on fidelity to the law as it stands. In this environment, as Mark Dawson has rightly pointed out, law becomes 'less a system of "uniform application" of rules with sanctions for breach than a negotiation framework where discretion abounds, and rules are never broken but rather "adjusted"'.[6]

1. The Vision of EU Governance in the Draghi Report

The Draghi Report is the lead example of the many current expressions of this mindset. Based on its proposed 'targeted adjustments', the Report in fact sought a deep and comprehensive transformation of European economy and society in order to address the EU's competitiveness shortfalls.[7] 'Until the consensus for Treaty changes is in place', the Report maintained, the task is to 'refocus the work of the EU'

1 See Chapter Five, nn 369–71 and accompanying text.
2 Draghi Report (2024a, p 18).
3 Draghi Report (2024b, p 307).
4 European Commission (2025h, p 1), (2025i, p 2), (2025j, p 3).
5 European Commission (2025v, p 4, recital (21)).
6 Dawson (2024, p 747). See also Koskenniemi (2007, p 11), discussed in the Conclusion, n 30 and accompanying text.
7 Draghi Report (2024a, p 5) ('Foreword' by Mario Draghi).

on the comprehensive challenge of 'accelerating EU action' and 'simplifying rules'[8]—concepts that, when used in the governance context, pointed to changes of a systemic character in deep tension with the sense that 'targeted' typically conveys.

The key driver behind the Draghi Report was the quest for improved access to investment capital. Most importantly, this aim meant 'building on the model of NGEU … to issue common debt instruments, which would be used to finance joint investment projects that will increase the EU's competitiveness and security'.[9] From Mario Draghi's Foreword onward, the Report stressed the need for 'the issuance of common safe assets. To maximise productivity, some joint funding for investment in key European public goods, such as breakthrough innovation, will be necessary.'[10] Permanent forms of debt-financing—together with efforts to facilitate private funding, most importantly through the completion of the long-sought Capital Markets Union—would then be mobilised to support reforms and investments across numerous sectors, including energy, automotive, defence, space, pharma, advanced technology, and transport, to name a few that the Report highlighted. This would also involve numerous 'horizontal' (ie cross-sectoral) reforms aimed at 'accelerating innovation', 'closing the skills gap', 'sustaining investment', 'revamping competition', and 'strengthening governance'.

The headline price tag to for this transformative programme over the coming five years was approximately €800 billion *annually*, in both public and private funding. The contemplated reforms and investments would likely require considerable compromises in each of the Member States in terms of their social model—something about which both the Draghi Report and the Commission were effectively silent. To accomplish this goal, the Draghi Report planned to follow the lead of the NGEU model, in which a planning and spending mechanism, with the Commission at its core, would be used to try to incentivise the Member States to make different ('better') choices more conducive to the overarching goal of European competitiveness. However, in terms of substance, the trade-offs would be significant and deeply political and, judging from the NGEU model in action, it would not always be obvious that Commission involvement would lead to better outcomes. The whole setup seems predicated on the assumption that, rather than the absence of the right framework conditions or resources, the main obstacle to better policies and economic dynamism in Member States is the lack of political will, and hence the remedy is to roundtrip money through Brussels and bring it back to the Member States with conditions attached.

Governance impacts would likely be as profound as those of policy substance. The changes in governance contemplated by the Draghi Report only seem 'small [in] number' because the Report's description of them was so sparse and vague, occupying

[8] Ibid, p 67.

[9] Ibid, p 66, (2024b, p 296).

[10] Draghi Report (2024a, p 9) ('Foreword' by Mario Draghi); see also ibid, pp 18, 64–66), (2024b, pp 290, 296).

portions of 12 out of 397 pages across a two-volume report.[11] Just a moment of deeper reflection suggests how the contemplated changes would in fact hardly be 'targeted' at all. They would be aimed at 'accelerating' (another favourite word of the Report) a transformation of the power relations and modes of governance between EU institutions, the Member States, and the private sector.[12] At the summit of the new system would be EU Competitiveness Priorities established by the European Council, which would in turn be embodied within a new Competitiveness Coordination Framework, from which Competitiveness Action Plans for each strategic priority would be produced.[13] All of this would be carved out of the European Semester process (ie the new European Governance Framework), the remainder of which would henceforth only focus on fiscal surveillance,[14] instead of the myriad other domains now shoehorned into it.[15]

Under NGEU and the RRF, the national–supranational planning process was both technocratic and opaque, as well as riddled with complexities involving twenty-seven NRRPs across all Member States. The Draghi Report, however, would take this technocratic and opaque planning model to a whole new level of complexity:

> Multiple Action Plans would be needed to achieve the goals outlined in the Competitiveness Priorities. The involvement of all relevant stakeholders, Member States, experts, the private sector, EU institutions and agencies is essential to define and use the most agile and efficient model of governance, depending on the area concerned. For example, the European Commission should have a mandate for exclusive EU competences and horizontal actions, such as revamping competition policy and reducing regulatory and administrative burdens (as discussed, two priorities for 'scaling up'). Instead, for shared competences like closing the skills gap and accelerating innovation, the Commission would provide guidelines but share the institutional set-up to implement the proposals with national structures and experts, as discussed in the relevant chapters of this report. In specific sectors of the economy, a new set-up bringing the Commission together with industry experts and Member States, as well as relevant sectoral agencies where they exist, could be in the lead in defining and implementing the Action Plans.[16]

Once again, the Commission is placed in the central policy-making node in the system—certainly in areas of exclusive EU competence, but also in areas where EU

[11] Draghi Report (2024a, pp 67–68), (2024b, pp 307–16).
[12] The following draws from, but also supplements, the discussion in Lindseth and Leino-Steinberg (2024a).
[13] Draghi Report (2024a, p 67).
[14] Draghi Report (2024b, p 311).
[15] See Chapter Five, Section B.3.
[16] Draghi Report (2024b, p 312).

competence is more limited. The Report glosses over the fact that much of that competence falls into areas where the EU's authority is not shared but merely *supportive* of the Member States, such as skills formation.[17]

The Draghi Report's governance vision also has a heavily technocratic air to it, all in the search for 'the most agile and efficient model of governance'.[18] The Report makes references to the inclusion of relevant stakeholders, experts, and the private sector,[19] without mentioning here, of course, national parliaments or the European Parliament. But as the NGEU model in action demonstrated, when policy-making and implementation are the product of confidential planning between the Commission and Member State governments, there is little practical room for stakeholder or parliamentary consultations, which tend to get 'streamlined' out rather than opening up the process to further questions, complications, and potential delays. Moreover, under the Draghi Report, the role of national parliaments would be limited to enforcing subsidiarity in the EU legislative process under the Early-Warning System—more actively, the Report hoped[20]—to ensure that the EU focuses only on supranational priorities and the production of European public goods. This is an important goal,[21] but it also expresses a quite marginalised vision for national parliaments (ie national elected legislative representatives). All the concerns raised in Chapter Four regarding the RRF and the NRRP process, in which plans effectively imposed faits accomplis on national parliaments,[22] would likely be reproduced here.

As foreseen in the Draghi Report, the Competitiveness Action Plans would be multiple and thematic, initially including separate action plans for Innovation, Energy, Education and Skills, Digital and Defence.[23] But the Report also contemplated 'financial incentives for Member States to coordinate national policies and engage in regulatory adjustments and reforms',[24] which would necessitate national sub-plans on the NRRP model. The combination of planning and incentives-based spending would, in turn, implicate all the many issues regarding the effectiveness of the NRRP planning model in promoting structural reforms, as Chapter Four outlined.[25] It would also implicate all the many difficulties in measuring the quality of performance under the plans rather than focusing merely on outputs, a point stressed repeatedly by ECA.[26]

Taken as a whole, the Draghi Report contemplated transforming governance in essentially all policy domains, whether supranational or national, via a new system

[17] See Chapter Four, Section D.5–6.

[18] By opening up the planning process to this broader range of players, the model contemplated by the Draghi Report could lead to normative power being effectively exercised by a range of entities beyond the Commission—including the private sector—which raises constitutional concerns of its own.

[19] Draghi Report (2024b, p 312).

[20] Ibid, pp 310–11.

[21] See this chapter below, nn 123–28 and accompanying text.

[22] See Chapter Four, nn 79, 188–95 and accompanying text.

[23] Draghi Report (2024b, pp 313–14).

[24] Ibid, p 312.

[25] See Chapter Four, Section D.3.

[26] See this chapter below, nn 143–48 and accompanying text; see also Chapter Four, Section B.1.

of opaque and technocratic, multi-pronged and multi-level planning, all of which was supposed to be accomplished without Treaty change. The drafters of the Draghi Report did recognize that, in an ideal world, '[s]trengthening the EU requires Treaty changes'.[27] But more typically, the Draghi Report cast the Treaties as an impediment rather than as a legitimising basis for ambitious and needed action. The Report's drafters, in effect, sought to exploit what commentators have called 'the softness of [the EU's] constitutional rules', which permit key players to 'bend the EU framework or sidestep it'.[28] The Report argued that, rather than 'focusing all minds and energies on [such a] long and burdensome process',[29] Treaty change was 'not a precondition for Europe to move forward: much can be done with targeted adjustments'.[30] In contrast with the attitude that prevailed during the height of the euro crisis—for example, the Commission's 2012 Blueprint on deepening and completing the EMU, which mentioned the need for Treaty change thirty-nine times in a fifty-one page document[31]—twelve years later the Draghi Report mentioned it only six times on four pages (always paired with references to 'targeted adjustments' or the like)—this, again, in a two-volume report comprising a total of 397 pages.[32]

The overwhelming focus of the Draghi Report was detailing the necessary substantive policy changes, both national and supranational, to address Europe's severe competitiveness shortfalls across essentially all sectors of the economy, as well as in the horizontal (ie cross-sectoral) reform areas. In view of its overwhelming policy focus, it was a stretch to claim the Draghi Report merely envisioned the coordination of Member State economic policies in the sense of Article 121 TFEU.[33] In exchange for implementing EU-steered policies, the Member States would receive financial incentives to be defined in the next MFF.[34] This was not coordination but the transactional model taken to a new and comprehensive level, overtly circumventing Article 121 TFEU. The Report further envisioned building its programme around various kinds of partnerships[35]—whether public-private, or between the EU and Member States—to reinforce the transactional feel. The talk of partnerships again blurred traditional divisions of national and supranational competence (or the lack of supranational competence at all), 'undermin[ing] the capacity of EU law to draw effective limits' on exercises of authority within this new world of governance in the constitutional borderlands.[36]

27 Draghi Report (2024a, p 67).
28 White (2023, pp 784–85).
29 Draghi Report (2024a, p 18).
30 Ibid, p 67.
31 See Conclusion, nn 10–18 and accompanying text.
32 Draghi Report (2024a, pp 18, 67), (2024b, pp 307, 316).
33 Draghi Report (2024a, p 67, n 2), (2024b, p 311, n 5).
34 Draghi Report (2024b, p 312).
35 Draghi Report (2024a, pp 7, 17, 18, 52, 67, 68), (2024b, pp 307, 312, and numerous other points).
36 Bornemann (2025, p 16).

To support this all-encompassing system of borderlands governance, the Draghi Report looked to a range of unspecified legal bases that would need to be reinterpreted in order to implement the ambitious plans the Report envisioned.[37] Presumably these would include cohesion, which the Report mentioned at a few key junctures,[38] along with two instruments based on cohesion in whole or in part: the RRF and STEP.[39] But there would also need to be reinterpretations of many other (unmentioned) substantive legal bases to accommodate the manifold and complex nature of the competitiveness programme. As for the legal bases that the Report chose to specify, these were typically procedural, aimed at the overarching task of '[a]ccelerating the work of the EU'.[40] The Report mentioned expanded use of qualified-majority voting under the *passerelle* clause in Article 48(7) TEU, which enables the European Council to authorise the Council to act by qualified majority instead of unanimity,[41] as well as enhanced cooperation under Articles 20 TEU and 329 TFEU.[42] Finally, 'in the clear absence of the required conditions' for enhanced cooperation, the Report proposed reliance on intergovernmental cooperation on the model of the Fiscal Compact.[43] Either way, the plan would rely on 'coalitions of the willing' to build new 'concentric circles' in the integration project,[44] enhancing its transactional feel.

The emergency powers provisions of Article 122 TFEU figured prominently in the Draghi Report's otherwise brief governance discussion, emerging as the preferred means of working around Treaty limitations and constraints. In a somewhat convoluted paragraph, the Report contemplated a non-Treaty-based reform of the operation of Article 122 TFEU, currently dominated by the Council and Commission, as a means of involving the EP to a greater extent. The aim was, above all, '[t]o avoid Treaty changes'; hence the envisioned redefinition of the EP's role via an interinstitutional arrangement at the beginning of each legislature, which 'would allow the codification of past successful practices, and the establishment in advance of clear "rules of the game" to deal with emergency situations'.[45] The use of interinstitutional agreements (IIAs) to engage, in effect, in 'Treaty rewriting' has a long history and is rightly regarded as suspect (at least rhetorically).[46] Article 295 TFEU, which now specifically authorises the use of IIAs, adds beseechingly that they must be 'in compliance with the Treaties' rather than rewriting it. It is thus well established (again, at least at the rhetorical level) that such agreements 'cannot grant institutions powers which are not

[37] Draghi Report (2024a, pp 65–66), (2024b, pp 312–14).
[38] Draghi Report (2024a, pp 19, 52, 64), (2024b, pp 161, 200, 212, 205, 218–19, 235, 245, 289, 312).
[39] Draghi Report (2024b, pp 101, 125, 200, 266–67, 312).
[40] Ibid, p 315.
[41] Draghi Report (2024a, p 68), (2024b, p 315).
[42] Draghi Report (2024a, p 68), (2024b, pp 254, 308–09, 315, 326).
[43] Draghi Report (2024b, p 315).
[44] Ibid, pp 308–09, 315.
[45] Ibid, p 316.
[46] Weiler (2011).

conferred on them' by the Treaties themselves.[47] Nonetheless, these agreements often exist to fudge the boundaries of those very same limits, and the Draghi Report's discussion of a possible interinstitutional agreement here is very much in keeping with this tradition.

The Report recognised that Article 122 TFEU had allowed the EU to adopt necessary measures to deal with emergency situations and that recent practices —that is, the Interinstitutional Agreement on budgetary matters of December 2020[48]—'have managed to ensure the involvement of the European Parliament to a certain degree'.[49] The Report, however, also recognised that, 'if the EU would have the ambition of accelerating its action using this article, it would be necessary to clarify the emergency procedure in EU law'.[50] The Report was effectively alluding here to ongoing debates around Article 122 TFEU, whose use by the Commission and Council, the Report noted, could gain more 'democratic legitimacy by involving the European Parliament' to some unspecified greater degree.[51] This portion of the Report—presumably drafted by officials from the Commission itself—was only able to imagine an EP role 'in triggering a state of emergency, and entailing strict deadlines once set', although this statement was prefaced by a precatory 'at least'.[52] What greater EP role would emerge beyond that point was left to the imagination, or, more precisely, future political contestation and negotiation.

The prominence of Article 122 TFEU in the governance section of the Draghi Report—and more particularly the allusion to 'accelerating [EU] action using this article'—raises the obvious concern that all European politics (or certainly at least competitiveness politics, which amount to pretty much the same thing) are now emergency politics.[53] That expansive category is no longer limited to addressing acute crises like pandemics or wars but also chronic problems like investment deficits stretching back decades. Mario Draghi, in the foreword to the Report, stressed the all-encompassing nature of the competitiveness challenge: 'We have reached the point where, without action, we will have to either compromise our welfare, our environment or our freedom'.[54] As the Report itself further stated, drawing a comparison to the Covid crisis that gave rise to NGEU and extensive common borrowing: 'The present circumstances are equally serious';[55] in fact, they constitute 'an existential challenge'.[56]

[47] Council Legal Service (2017, p 7, para 18).
[48] See Chapter Four, n 107 and accompanying text.
[49] Draghi Report (2024b, p 316), citing Calleja et al (2024).
[50] Draghi Report (2024b, p 316).
[51] Ibid.
[52] Ibid.
[53] The literature on emergency politics in the EU is vast, For recent overviews of that literature from a legal and constitutional perspective, see Bornemann (2025), Dawson (2024), White (2023), (2019). See also Calleja et al (2024, p 558, n 202 and sources cited), as well as Kreuder-Sonnen and White (2022), Schmidt (2022).
[54] Draghi Report (2024a, p 9).
[55] Ibid, p 65, (2024b, p 290).
[56] Draghi Report (2024a, p 5).

2. Von der Leyen 2.0, Article 122 TFEU, and the Challenge of Democratic Legitimation Under the NGEU Model

The Draghi Report was always intended to serve as the foundation for the political programme of the second von der Leyen Commission: the Commission President signalled this in her Political Guidelines in July 2024, even before the Report was published.[57] Once installed in January 2025, as one of its first major actions, the new Commission announced its so-called Competitiveness Compass[58] to provide the framework for various sectoral action plans as well as a (vaguely described but far-reaching) Competitiveness Coordination Tool (CCT) 'to align industrial and research policies and investments at the EU and the national levels' and 'to deliver new major initiatives and/or cross-border projects with European added value, for structural economic transformation, productivity, [and] long-term growth'.[59] What the new CCT exactly is, and what it would add to the existing frameworks, remains unclear. The financial incentives for the implementation of coordinated investments would come from a new Competitiveness Fund to be established in the next MFF[60] (about which more below).[61]

In terms of European democracy, however, one could ask: how strong is the electoral mandate for all this? In other words, how well were European voters informed about, and consulted on, these far-reaching plans in the lead-up to the June 2024 EP elections? The election manifesto for von der Leyen's own political group, the European People's Party (EPP), had stressed the importance of maintaining and improving European competitiveness,[62] alluding to 'an investment plan … bringing European added value'.[63] But that was it. As for what this plan meant for European governance, the manifesto was almost entirely mute, speaking in vague generalities. The document offered no normative observations about the NGEU model as such, stating only—in a passage on making the social market economy 'fit for new challenges'— that, '[i]n response to the COVID pandemic, we launched the NextGenerationEU, the largest stimulus package ever financed in Europe'.[64] The manifesto stressed, moreover, that 'the Welfare State' would remain 'in the hands of the Member States' and that Europe's role was simply supportive, to help establish 'the conditions for economic growth and prosperity' so that social programmes could be properly financed.[65] The manifesto

[57] von der Leyen (2024, p 6) (presenting her Political Guidelines as a 'new plan for Europe's sustainable prosperity and competitiveness', which would specifically draw on the then-'upcoming report by Mario Draghi').
[58] European Commission (2025w).
[59] Ibid, p 23.
[60] Ibid, p 24.
[61] See this chapter below, nn 159–60 and accompanying text.
[62] European People's Party (2024, pp 1, 9).
[63] Ibid, p 10.
[64] Ibid, p 8.
[65] Ibid, p 17.

acknowledged that 'the EU must also improve its institutions. We want to make the EU more capable of acting, more efficient, stronger and more democratic.'[66] But then it immediately added that 'the Member States will continue to have the right to decide which competences the EU should have and which ones could possibly be transferred back'.[67] In this regard, the manifesto vaguely suggested 'a European convention in the coming years to discuss and decide on possible improvements to the Treaties.'[68]

Von der Leyen's Political Guidelines of July 2024, like the EPP manifesto and the Draghi Report, also made passing reference to Treaty change: 'I believe we need Treaty change where it can improve our Union.'[69] But even that sole mention of Treaty change was telling: the Political Guidelines supported this step only where it was *functionally beneficial*, saying nothing about where it was *legally necessary* or even *politically useful* to strengthening the democratic legitimacy of Union action. By not elaborating further, von der Leyen implied she could proceed on the assumption that the existing Treaties were adequate for pursuing the competitiveness programme. And yet, very much in line with the ambition of the Draghi Report to 'accelerat[e] EU action' without Treaty change,[70] the Commission President wrote: 'We will put forward proposals to *enhance Europe's capacity to act* [emphasis in original], looking at new formats and decision-making processes',[71] but again, all without Treaty change.

The Political Guidelines acknowledged that future recourse to Article 122 TFEU might be a potential source of conflict with the EP. Von der Leyen committed to revising the Interinstitutional Agreement of December 2020[72] to 'increase the flow of information and ensure greater transparency' and thereby 'help strengthen our joint political responsibility, [and] strengthen our dialogue'.[73] She acknowledged EP concerns about the use of Article 122 TFEU as a legal basis, which the EP had reiterated on 16 July 2024, the first day of the new EP term, just two days prior to the publication of the Guidelines.[74] That day, the Parliament's new rules of procedure came into force, including a new Rule 138 regarding any legislative proposal based on Article 122 TFEU. Aside from setting up an internal review process for such proposals (about which more below),[75] the rule directed the EP President to seek a statement from the Commission President 'explaining the reasons for the choice of that legal basis, as well as outlining the main objectives and elements of the proposal'.[76] In a later agreement with the EP President, Roberta Metsola, on the principles guiding the renegotiation of the Interinstitutional Agreement, President von der Leyen further committed to

[66] Ibid, p 22.
[67] Ibid.
[68] Ibid.
[69] von der Leyen (2024, p 30) (emphasis omitted).
[70] Draghi Report (2024a, p 67).
[71] von der Leyen (2024, p 30).
[72] Interinstitutional Agreement (2020).
[73] von der Leyen (2024, p 30).
[74] Mańko (2024, p 1).
[75] See this chapter below, nn 101–03 and accompanying text.
[76] Rule 138, Rules of Procedure of the European Parliament (2025).

'comprehensive justification and information on the exceptional cases where the proposals by the Commission are based on Article 122 TFEU'.[77]

Also in dispute, however, was the substantive scope of Article 122 TFEU. Although we do not have access to the Commission's internal advice on the matter, we do have a 2024 article co-authored by the then-Director-General of the Commission Legal Service, Daniel Calleja.[78] While the article was formally published only in a personal capacity, it nonetheless provides a direct window onto just how expansive the prevailing view of Article 122 TFEU was and is within the Commission.[79] According to Calleja and his co-authors, Article 122 TFEU 'is a primary law provision, granting extraordinary powers for the attainment of the Union's objectives in emergency situations'.[80] Calleja and his co-authors emphatically rejected the view that enacting measures using Article 122 TFEU 'may lead to "competence-creep", "bending the law", or "reinterpreting the Treaties"'.[81] The authors claimed, instead, that the use of this provision was subject to 'strict conditions'.[82] However, when one looks at the conditions Calleja and his co-authors identified, it becomes evident that they were not particularly strict at all.

The first was that, given the wording and inclusion of Article 122 TFEU in the chapter on economic policy, the measures 'must be of an economic nature'.[83] Economic here, however, had a broad meaning, including an 'emergency of a non-economic nature [with] significant economic consequences … In those situations, measures appropriate to deal with the economic situation often require addressing non-economic emergency situations'.[84] The second condition was that the measures 'must generally be limited in time', which the co-authors claimed 'act[ed] as an important check to the far-reaching powers that this provision entrusts upon the Council and preserves institutional balance'.[85] In elaborating, however, Calleja and his co-authors were willing to accept *proactive* mechanisms 'to deal with emergencies, whereby the respective emergency powers and requirements are triggered only when certain conditions materialize'.[86] Calleja and his co-authors argued that, 'in order to respect the required temporal limitation, these [proactive] measures must be specifically designed to be activated on a temporary basis, and their activation to address a given emergency

[77] European Parliament (2024d, Annex, point 3).
[78] Calleja et al (2024). On many crucial points, this piece is aligned with the similarly expansive views of Chamon (2023a), (2023b), (2024), noted in Chapter One, n 83 and accompanying text; Chapter Two, n 27 and accompanying text; and Chapter Three, n 228 and accompanying text.
[79] In this regard, this article is reminiscent of the academic writing of Leo Flynn presenting the Commission's expansive interpretation of the cohesion flexibility clause in Article 175(3) TFEU. See Flynn (2019); see also Chapter Three, nn 171–75 and accompanying text.
[80] Calleja et al (2024, p 549).
[81] Ibid, quoting, respectively, Demine (2020, p 347), Kreuder-Sonnen and White (2022, p 956), and Leino-Sandberg and Ruffert (2022, p 439).
[82] Calleja et al (2024, p 549), quoting, respectively, Demine (2020, p 347), Kreuder-Sonnen and White (2022, p 956), and Leino-Sandberg and Ruffert (2022, p 439).
[83] Calleja et al (2024, p 554).
[84] Ibid.
[85] Ibid, p 553.
[86] Ibid.

situation must necessarily be limited in time'.[87] Such proactive measures, however, seemed to violate the holding of the CJEU in *Pringle* (2012) that Article 122(2) TFEU only provided a legal basis for non-permanent, reactive measures in situations of severe difficulties.[88]

Overall, Calleja and his co-authors seemed to be looking to the open-endedness of the term 'exceptional occurrences' in Article 122(2) TFEU, which, in their estimation, 'covers exceptional economic, financial, military, or geopolitical occurrences'.[89] Moreover, they relied heavily on the wide margin of appreciation of the institutions that 'may be used to take into account, *inter alia*, the broad economic context and long-term economic challenges faced by the Union in order to guarantee the effectiveness of the measures adopted under Article 122 TFEU'.[90] The only requirements were that (i) the future assistance satisfy the required causal link under Article 122(2) TFEU that the Member State find itself 'in difficulties' or 'seriously threatened by severe difficulties'; and (ii) the assistance be made 'under certain conditions', hence satisfying the conditionality requirement of the *Pringle* judgment to avoid violating the no bail-out clause in Article 125 TFEU.[91] That financial assistance could, in their view, also include collective borrowing by the EU directly based on Article 122 TFEU.[92]

The moment of direct conflict with the EP over Article 122 TFEU came soon enough, in the form of the Security Action for Europe (SAFE) Instrument, a €150 billion loan programme to the Member States for joint procurement and investment in European defence capabilities, which the Commission proposed in March 2025 and the Council adopted two months later.[93] The EU would have almost certainly been focusing on defence capacities and strategic autonomy regardless of political developments in the United States;[94] nonetheless, the increasingly hostile attitude of the new US administration was crucial in giving impetus to these efforts.[95] In a letter to the European Council in advance of its special summit on 6 March 2025 on European defence and security, Ursula von der Leyen spoke of 'a clear and present danger on a scale that none of us have seen in our adult lifetime'.[96] The European Council conclusions to that summit stressed that 'Europe must become more sovereign, more responsible for its own defence and better equipped to act and deal autonomously with immediate and future challenges and threats'.[97]

[87] Ibid.
[88] Case C-370/12, *Pringle* (2012), paras 65 and 105 et seq. See Chapter Two, nn 22–28 and accompanying text.
[89] Calleja et al (2024, p 530).
[90] Ibid, p 552.
[91] Ibid, p 531.
[92] Council Legal Service (2020a, p 37, para 92). See also Calleja et al (2024, pp 556–57).
[93] European Commission (2025x), Council Regulation (EU) 2025/1106 [SAFE].
[94] Defence and security were central, for example, both to the Political Guidelines of Commission President von der Leyen in July 2024 as well as the Commission's work programme for 2025. von der Leyen (2024, pp 13–14); European Commission (2025y).
[95] See, eg, Vance (2025); see also Hegseth (2025).
[96] von der Leyen (2025b).
[97] European Council (2025).

Von der Leyen's letter outlined a series of proposals, initially labelled 'ReArm Europe' and later developed into 'Readiness 2030', to 'mobilise close to EUR 800 billion for a safe and resilient Europe'.[98] The programme, broadly endorsed by the European Council, was built on multiple pillars, the first and most urgent of which was the €150 billion loan programme to the Member States that would become the SAFE Instrument. While SAFE would not provide performance-based funding or require reforms, it still incorporated the planning element of the NGEU model in the form of 'European defence industry investment plans'. The other major pillar of ReArm Europe/Readiness 2030—also suggestive of a continuing and important evolution of the NGEU model—was a call to use the mid-term review of cohesion programmes to reprioritise defence spending via the EU budget, allowing Member States to use cohesion funding for defence and security purposes.[99] This last element demonstrated how far cohesion was now being stretched to accommodate goals almost completely unrelated to supporting disadvantaged regions or population sectors. The subsequent communication from the Commission on this point outlined an intention to propose 'targeted amendments to the regulatory framework of the cohesion policy funds'.[100]

The Commission's explanatory memorandum on the SAFE proposal provided formal justification for the use of Article 122 TFEU as a unified legal basis, without distinguishing between its two subparagraphs:

> Article 122 TFEU is the appropriate legal basis for financial assistance responding to crisis or exceptional event and is not confined to crises of a financial or financial stability nature. The Council has a broad margin of discretion for assessing whether it is necessary to have recourse to that instrument in a context of emergency. In the past, it has used this provision to provide financial assistance to Member States experiencing sudden and exceptional increases in public expenditure, such as during the COVID-19 pandemic, where it helped preserve employment (SURE Instrument). Similarly, the Council is entitled to invoke this provision in the current exceptional security context to provide financial assistance, through the SAFE instrument, to Member States that need to make urgent and massive investments in the EU's defence manufacturing capacities, through collaborative procurement, hence enhancing their military capabilities.

This justification fits comfortably within the scope of Article 122 TFEU as interpreted by Calleja and his co-authors above. The programme is cast as primarily an emergency response, and hence reactive; nonetheless, there is a strong proactive element as well, in that a key aim is to benefit 'the EU's defence manufacturing capacities'.

98 von der Leyen (2025c).

99 For the remaining pillars, see von der Leyen (2025c); see also European Commission (2025z, pp 16–18).

100 European Commission (2025h, p 1), See also European Commission (2025i, p 2), (2025j, p 3), discussed this chapter above, n 4 and accompanying text.

Given the legal basis in Article 122 TFEU, the SAFE proposal triggered Rule 138 of the EP's new rules of procedure, which meant referral of the matter to the committee on legal affairs (JURI) for 'verification of the legal basis'.[101] On 23 April, JURI decided unanimously that Article 122 TFEU was not appropriate (albeit in an *in camera* meeting, without disclosing the advice of the Parliament's Legal Service on the issue).[102] Reporting to the plenary,[103] the JURI chair stated the Commission had failed to explain how SAFE could be justified without differentiating between the two subsections of Article 122 TFEU, and it did not explain why other possible legal bases were discarded, among which was Article 173(3) TFEU on industrial policy that had previously been used for the European Defence Fund.[104] However, the Commission President asserted—according to news reports—that the measure is 'fully justified' as an 'exceptional and temporary response to an urgent and existential challenge'.[105] On that basis, the Council adopted the proposed regulation at the end of May.[106] In August 2025, the EP commenced an action for annulment of the SAFE Regulation before the CJEU.[107]

Critics within the EP (at least among the pro-European parties) were always careful to stress that they supported the substance of the SAFE Regulation, and that their problem was with process and explanation.[108] Consistent with its own 'as if'-constitutional mindset, however, the EP's critique suggests that use of Article 122 TFEU was fundamentally about 'sidelining democratic control',[109] which necessarily equates the EP with being the primary, indeed exclusive, source of such control under the NGEU model. If one looks at the issue from the perspective of the power-legitimacy nexus, however, the nature and meaning of this dispute is altered. From this perspective, one could argue that Article 122 TFEU appropriately gives authority over decisions like SAFE to the Council, comprised of Member State leaders who, in principle, are

[101] Rule 138(1)–(2), Rules of Procedure of the European Parliament (2025).

[102] European Parliament (European Parliament, 2025c, p 5, item 17).

[103] European Parliament (2025d).

[104] See Chapter Five, nn 387–90 and accompanying text.

[105] de La Feld (2025).

[106] Council Regulation (EU) 2025/1106 [SAFE].

[107] See Case C-560/25, *Parliament v Council* (2025) (making two pleas: first, 'the contested act is incorrectly based on Article 122 TFEU [and] concerns instead the development of the Union's industrial policy in the field of defence pursuant to Article 173 TFEU'; and second, 'the Council has failed, in violation of Article 296 TFEU, to adequately state the reasons justifying the choice of the legal basis'). The EP's complaint did not address a third potential illegality of SAFE, that it involves the use of the EU budget (in this case for loan guarantees) for 'operations having military or defence implications' in violation of Article 41(2) TEU. See Chapter Five, nn 380–81 and accompanying text. The official position of the Commission, as reflected in a 'Q&A' it published with the proposal, was highly formalistic: 'The new instrument will provide loans to Member States to strengthen Europe's defence industry. The loans will not implement the Common Foreign and Security Policy (CFSP), and do not constitute expenditure arising from CFSP operations having military or defence implications within the meaning of Article 41(2) TEU'. European Commission (2025aa, pp 3–4). See also Knoll et al (2025, p 11), citing opinions of the Council Legal Service which, to our knowledge, have not been released to the public.

[108] Neubert and Ionta (2025) (quoting the EP press release); see also Deyl (2025a) ('The Parliament's ire centres on procedure, not policy').

[109] S&D Press Release (2025).

backed by the democratic and constitutional legitimacy of their national parliamentary systems.

This episode may simply be a reminder that, as Alan Milward long ago taught, in key moments of crisis the EU must be able to draw on these deeper wells of (national) legitimacy to exercise more ambitious forms of (supranational) power.[110] However, the issue is really, as this book has stressed at numerous junctures, whether the NGEU model is properly drawing on methods of democratic legitimation at *both* the national and supranational level. Unfortunately, more often than not, given the highly opaque and technocratic character of the emergent model governance in the constitutional borderlands, the necessary democratic oversight and control may often be lacking at both levels.

B. Negotiating the New MFF: High Ambition, Hard Realities

1. From the Draghi Report to the Commission's Initial Vision

There was one silver lining in the political cloud cast by the new Trump Administration that descended on the integration project in the first half of 2025. There could no longer be any doubt—at least among broadly pro-European forces—that the EU should be focusing its organisational, regulatory, and financial capacities on facilitating and supporting investment in European public goods. Defence and security were in the first rank among them.

This was, in fact, a key take-away of the Draghi Report: 'Under the next EU budget, a "Competitiveness Pillar" would direct EU funding towards EU public goods and multi-country industrial projects, as defined under the Competitiveness Coordination Framework.'[111] The particular focus should be on public goods 'that will be undersupplied without common action and funding'.[112] Among the possibilities were not only investments in defence (eg joint procurement and defence R&D)[113] but also in transport (infrastructure development and resilience, regulatory structures to support an integrated and intermodal market),[114] energy (eg grids, interconnectors,

[110] As Milward described the establishment of the European Council in the tumultuous aftermath of the oil crisis of the mid-1970s: 'rather than reversing the process of European integration [as some federalists argued]', the establishment of the European Council outside the formal integration framework 'actually signifie[d] a wish to extend [supranational] decision-making to new areas in response to changes in national policy objectives arising from the fundamental change in economic circumstances of the western European countries after 1974'. Milward and Sørensen (1993, pp 24–25); see also Lindseth (2010, pp 129–30).

[111] Draghi Report (2024b, p 294; see also p 312).

[112] Ibid, p 290.

[113] Ibid.

[114] Ibid, p 218.

pipelines, storage),[115] or aspects of digitalisation (eg high-speed broadband networks, cloud computing capabilities, infrastructures to embed AI across sectors).[116]

Embedded in the urgent challenges that the Draghi Report articulated, however, was also a dilemma. The challenges required both a major financial and regulatory mobilisation, on the one hand, as well as a political and (dare we say it) constitutional mobilisation, on the other. But as Mario Draghi would later stress on the first anniversary of his Report in September 2025, reforms in the political and constitutional domains 'will take time—time we may not have'.[117] So instead of pressing for them, he called for intensified technocratic solutions and creative legal engineering, with the Commission taking the lead on both. This was the only way, he suggested, to address 'how slowly the EU moves' or how national governments—and presumably, behind them, national electorates—'have not grasped the gravity of the moment'. He worried that too many Europeans were prepared to excuse the EU's standard slowness/inertia as 'simply how the EU is built' or worse, to justify it as 'the 'rule of law' in action.[118]

In our view, Draghi is rightly worried about the EU's inability to move quickly but his proposed solution does not target one of the root causes of the problem: the Commission's own failure, under the NGEU model, to prioritise European public goods on a consistent basis.[119] When reading the Draghi Report's call for more provision of EU public goods, one could be excused for forgetting that NGEU, and more particularly the RRF, had just allocated nearly 40% of its envelope to green transition and another 20% to digitalisation, each of which were central to the EU public goods that the Draghi Report sought to pursue with even greater intensity. Nonetheless, all the talk in the Draghi Report about intensified cross-border cooperation could be taken as a (barely veiled) critique of the Commission's failure to make much (or even any) progress in yielding genuine European public goods of this type, most especially in the energy domain.[120] The Draghi Report hardly mentioned the EU funds already spent or committed in this area, nor did it analyse how far NGEU funding had helped advance the EU towards a proper energy union. While the Commission itself has never openly acknowledged this design failure and has continued to insist on perpetuating the NGEU model into the future, the Draghi Report called for much greater effort to '[l]aunch multi-country industrial projects', perhaps supported by 'pre-allocated envelopes' in the next MFF.[121]

As a consequence, relying on supranational technocratic solutions and legal engineering without mechanisms to ensure greater discipline at the supranational level strikes us as a recipe for stasis or indeed failure. The Commission must be compelled

[115] Ibid, pp 34, 290.
[116] Ibid, pp 67, 290.
[117] Draghi (2025b).
[118] Ibid.
[119] For a discussion of the misaligned incentives under the NGEU model that favoured this outcome, see Chapter Four, Section E, and Conclusion, Section C.
[120] See Chapter Four, Section D.1 and Section E.
[121] Draghi Report (2024b, p 312). This could include, in particular, a reform of Important Projects of Common European Interest (IPCEIs), to create, in effect, a 'Competitiveness ICPEI'. Ibid, p 305.

to heed the admonition in the Draghi Report to avoid enmeshing itself in the production of national public goods at the expense of European public goods.[122] The Draghi Report was well aware of the challenge and, in response, suggested more vigorous application of the principle of subsidiarity,[123] either by national parliaments under the existing 'yellow card procedure' or, failing that, by the Commission exercising more 'self-restraint'. The Report also acknowledged, however, the weakness of these controls even under the old regime of 'integration through law'.[124] The Commission has historically treated subsidiarity as a flexible and technical procedure whose demands can be easily avoided where it concludes, 'by reason of the scale or effects', that the proposed action can 'be better achieved at Union level'.[125] Subsidiarity becomes, from this perspective, just a procedural step with little substantive constraint.[126] Moreover, the procedure itself can be avoided in cases of urgency.[127] It would seem rather quixotic, therefore, to expect any significant improvement in the application of the subsidiarity principle solely by providing the Member States additional funding 'to reinforce the administrative capacity and role of national parliaments and Member States in their control over EU legislative activity'.[128]

Meeting the challenge of refocusing on European public goods would not only require a legal framework to enforce greater spending discipline—not to mention, also, an understanding that subsidiarity should apply to funding decisions—but also a commensurately ambitious reform of the EU budget. The pressures on the budget, as the Draghi Report recognised, came from multiple directions. They included not just the need to address new strategic priorities but also the burden of legacy spending commitments (notably, according to the Report's own estimates, cohesion and CAP—30.5% and 30.9% of the budget, respectively), as well as the need to repay NGEU debt (€30 billion per year starting in 2028) and the lack of agreement on new own resources.[129] Without new own resources, the Report stressed, effective spending power at the EU level would be 'mechanically reduced' by interest and principal payments, and Member States would need to increase their GNI-based contributions 'to maintain current levels of spending or spending cuts would have to be applied to programmes under the next MFF'.[130]

According to the Draghi Report, the need for reform in the budget flowed from its combination of 'fragmentation, complexity and rigidity':

122 See this chapter above, nn 111–16 and accompanying text.
123 Draghi Report (2024a, pp 18, 68), (2024b, p 310).
124 Draghi Report (2024b, p 310).
125 Article 5(3) TEU.
126 While the Subsidiarity Protocol defines an eight-week stay of EU legislative action while national parliaments review (and possibly object to) the proposed action, their arguments rarely convince the Commission.
127 TFEU Protocol (No 1) on the Role of National Parliaments in the European Union, art 4. See, eg, Chapter Five, nn 477–83 and accompanying text.
128 Draghi Report (2024a, p 68).
129 Draghi Report (2024b, p 289).
130 Ibid.

> First, financing instruments are fragmented and lack focus on strategic priorities. The EU has close to 50 spending programmes which prevents the EU budget from reaching sufficient scale for larger projects at pan-European level ... Second, access to EU public financing is complex and overly bureaucratic for private actors ... Third, the EU budget is much more rigid than national budgets. The MFF is proposed more than two years before implementation and sets the Union budget for seven years ... In addition, the MFF delineates specific spending over key categories and transfers between different headings or different programmes are difficult, offering limited room to accommodate new policy priorities or respond to unforeseen developments.[131]

Rigidity, of course, is partly an institutional choice. The Treaties already permit the MFF to be approved for a shorter period (five years instead of seven, according to Article 312 TFEU), and a reform in that direction would align with the mandate period of the European Commission and the Parliament. A five-year MFF could facilitate greater debate on EU funding priorities in EP elections and in the preparation of the Commission programme, even if the lengthy negotiations would in practice be difficult to fit within the electoral cycle. Proposals along these lines, however, rarely gain traction in the institutions. The critique of the Draghi Report echoed the Commission's own understanding, going back to the June 2023 proposal to revise the 2021–2027 MFF, seeking a budget that would further expand Commission discretion.[132] In her Political Guidelines of July 2024, Ursula von der Leyen stressed 'the need for simplicity and flexibility, speed and strategic focus in our spending', which in her view was currently 'spread over too many overlapping programmes—many of which fund the same things but with different requirements and difficulties to combine funding effectively'. Hence, 'I will propose a new long-term budget ... targeted to where EU action is most needed in a flexible way. I want a policy-based budget, not a programme-based budget'.[133]

Maximising discretion—under the rubric of combatting budgetary fragmentation, complexity, and rigidity—was also a central theme of the Commission's February 2025 communication, 'The road to the next multiannual financial framework'.[134] At the interface of all three features were the numerous nationally pre-allocated funds that have required 'separate planning and programming efforts' creating 'administrative burden for managing authorities and project promoters', flowing from different eligibility rules, application processes, co-financing rates (if any), management verifications, auditing requirements, etc.[135] Left unstated, however, was how many

[131] Ibid.
[132] See Chapter Five, Section 3.C.
[133] von der Leyen (2024, p 29) (emphasis omitted).
[134] European Commission (2025ab).
[135] Ibid, pp 6–7. The funds include the Cohesion Fund, the European Regional Development Fund, the European Social Fund+, the Just Transition Fund, the Recovery and Resilience Facility, the European Agricultural Guarantee Fund, the European Agricultural Fund for Rural Development, the European

of these requirements exist to make the use of the funds more accountable and focused on Treaty-based objectives.[136] In a story we began to tell in Chapter Four,[137] the adoption of NGEU and the RRF was deeply disruptive for several of these other funds (notably in the cohesion space, effectively eclipsing traditional cohesion), making them ripe for the sort of 'modernisation' and 'targeted amendments'—that is, redirection, repurposing, and redeployment to other purposes—that we discussed earlier.[138]

The Commission also celebrated performance-based planning as an effective way of aligning EU policy objectives and EU spending, moving away 'from payments based on the reimbursement of costs to delivery models that are more focused on objectives and results to be achieved'.[139] The Commission also noted how the FNLC model had been used 'to improve the performance of EU spending'.[140] The Commission's vision reflected barely a trace of concern about the flaws in the RRF's planning and spending model, particularly as repeatedly stressed by the European Court of Auditors.[141] The Commission's February 2025 communication on the next MFF only alluded to how ECA has identified areas with scope for improvement, citing two 2023 reports,[142] without acknowledging—much less engaging with—the more fundamental nature of their critique.

In mid-June, ECA presented a review that sought to present its prior critiques of the RRF—all familiar from Chapters Four and Five—in the most constructive light, casting them as a series of 'opportunities' for the Commission. The new MFF gave the Commission the chance to: design a new performance measuring framework 'more focused on results and data reliability';[143] agree how EU added value could be defined and systematically taken into account in funding decisions;[144] ensure simplification while maintaining accountability (not least by a general streamlining of the EU's financial landscape);[145] examine how flexibility could be reconciled with predictability;[146] and finally, strengthen the link between EU funding and structural reforms.[147] This latter point necessarily involved revisiting the many problems relating to how money had been spent under the RRF: 'the focus on performance, the funding of zero-cost measures, the definition of payment and eligibility conditions, the need

Maritime, Fisheries and Aquaculture Fund, the Brexit Adjustment Reserve, and—outside the EU budget or the multiannual financial framework—the Social Climate Fund (from 2026) and the Modernisation Fund.

136 Cf Mashaw (1996, p 415) (accountability is 'wonderfully bureaucratizing').

137 See Chapter Four, Section D.4.

138 See this chapter above, nn 4, 100 and accompanying text.

139 European Commission (2025ab, p 8) (emphasis omitted).

140 Ibid, p 9 (noting FNLC as a mechanism 'to improve the performance of EU spending').

141 See Chapter Four, Section B.1.

142 European Commission (2025ab, p 9), citing European Court of Auditors (2023f), (2023b).

143 European Court of Auditors (2025c, p 3, para 03).

144 Ibid, p 3, para 03.

145 Ibid, p 3, para 04.

146 Ibid, p 3, para 05.

147 Ibid, p 4, para 06.

for clear supervision and control responsibilities and the protection of the financial interest of the EU including compliance with EU and national rules.'[148]

And then, of course, there was the question of the NGEU debt overhang. The Commission noted in its February 2025 communication that, going forward, the €25–30 billion annual estimated interested payments would be '*almost 20% of the current annual budget*' (emphasis in original), twice the total amount of the budget for security and defence under the old MFF.[149] In practice, the only options to address this debt overhang would be spending cuts, increased own resources, or further debt-financing. As to the first option, the February 2025 communication was evasive, speaking in vague terms of focusing spending 'on common challenges where spending at European level brings the highest added value' and suggesting that some goals would be better advanced 'by mobilising private investments' or 'through national budgets'.[150] As to debt-financing as an integral feature of EU budgeting going forward, the February 2025 communication was silent, limiting itself to lauding how 'the EU is now the fifth largest issuer in the European capital market, with high credit rating'.[151]

2. The Commission's MFF Proposals: Backlash From All Sides

The new MFF proposals were always going to entail difficult negotiations. The Commission's proposals of 16 July 2025 for a new MFF Regulation and an ORD were the start of a complex political and legal process ultimately requiring unanimity in the Council as well as sign-off by the European Parliament (for the MFF), followed by unanimous national approval (for the new ORD). Thus, it would be impossible, as of this writing, to predict the final outcome over the subsequent two years. Nonetheless, certain basic observations about the politics surrounding the Commission's proposals could be made from the moment they were announced, particularly as to what they suggest about future directions of the NGEU model. We begin with the planning and spending side of the proposals, before turning to the revenue side, that is, new own resources and potentially new collective borrowing.

a. Planning and Spending: A Commission 'Trust' Deficit?

As the discussion in the last subsection suggests, the Commission hoped to broaden significantly its discretion in the new MFF proposals. Nonetheless, in the lead up to the announcement of the new MFF proposals themselves, the Commission was, at the same time, already quite 'beleaguered'.[152] Far-right and hard-right parties had

[148] Ibid.
[149] European Commission (2025ab, p 12).
[150] Ibid, p 2 (emphasis omitted).
[151] Ibid, p 5 (emphasis omitted).
[152] Griera et al (2025).

gathered sufficient signatures to file a censure motion in the European Parliament, the first in eleven years against a Commission.[153] Even if there was little risk of the motion carrying, its very existence created negotiating leverage for pro-European parties—the Commission's putative allies—to seek concessions in exchange for avoiding embarrassing defections or abstentions. Faced with a threat from the S&D to abstain, for example, von der Leyen needed to agree to preserve the European Social Fund (ESF+) as a separate programme in the new MFF.[154] Earlier, pressed by centrist MEPs, von der Leyen reportedly had to agree to continue distributing cohesion funding to regional and local authorities as opposed to national governments.[155]

The Commission's eventual MFF proposal called for an overall budget of €1.98 trillion for the 2028–2034 period, equivalent to 1.26% of EU GNI, an increase over the 1.13% in the 2021–2027 period (excluding NGEU). As part of 'a thorough simplification of the EU budget architecture',[156] the Commission reduced the number of MFF headings from seven to four[157] including, most relevantly for our purposes, a general heading (€1.06 trillion), primarily for National and Regional Partnership Plans (NRPPs) subsuming most legacy spending programmes, such as CAP and cohesion, but also including NGEU repayment. The Commission's proposal would further reduce the number of specific funding programmes from fifty-two to sixteen.[158] The allocations under the general heading going to NRPPs, however, would still be based on pre-fixed national envelopes, in the style of NGEU. Thus, the added flexibility in the budget under this heading did not mean flexibility to move funds from one national envelope to another but only between different purposes in the same national envelope.[159] The proposal also included, however, a new competitiveness heading (€590 billion), encompassing a new European Competitiveness Fund (ECF) that would be directly managed by the Commission without pre-fixed national envelopes, operating along the traditional lines of European research funding. The MFF proposals nonetheless envisioned coordination between the ECF and NRPPs via the Competitiveness Coordination Tool introduced in January 2025.[160]

Over the life of the NGEU programme, the need for budgetary flexibility had become more pronounced, with EU funds being repeatedly redirected within the 2021–2027 MFF (through REPowerEU, STEP and the redirection of cohesion funds, for example). In the new proposed MFF, flexibility was sought through larger programme packages, more non-programmed funding in the financial programmes, a new

[153] See Introduction, nn 57–60 and accompanying text.
[154] Griera et al (2025).
[155] Ibid.
[156] European Commission (2025ac, p 2).
[157] Ibid, pp 30–31, Annex.
[158] Ibid, p 2.
[159] Even that flexibility would be constrained. The largest allocation for each Member State NRPP would be 'general' but there would also be smaller specified allocations for 'migration, security and home affairs' as well as for the Social Climate Fund. See European Commission (2025ae). Additionally, income support for farmers would be ringfenced and there would also be a mandatory minimum for less developed regions.
[160] See this chapter above, nn 59–61 and accompanying text.

flexibility instrument (of questionable necessity, one could argue),[161] and a separate crisis borrowing mechanism (about which more below).[162] For the Commission, the emphasis on flexibility aimed to 'make it easier to redeploy resources that are not pre-programmed within and across programmes'.[163] The drive for increased flexibility also aimed to reduce the scope for earmarking funds for particular purposes and again increasing Commission discretion. Under the prior MFF, the Commission regularly complained about the scarcity of resources and the resulting inability to respond to new challenges, even as it distributed money under the RRF to numerous projects that were often trivial in terms of European added value. The result, unfortunately, was a debt burden that European taxpayers will bear for decades—an experience that did little to inspire confidence in the Commission's ability to prioritise the use of funds going forward in the best possible way.

This overall flexibility in the new MFF was meant to synergise with (and be enabled by) a vastly expanded and now generalised planning process, whether in legacy domains like CAP or ESF+ or in the new domains associated with bolstering European competitiveness. The aim was to 'combine EU funds implemented by Member States and regions into a coherent, tailored planning process—fully aligned with the Union's common priorities'.[164] There was no acknowledgement of how difficult the process of such alignment had proven to be under NGEU. Instead, the Commission simply stated:

> The plans will respond to the main priorities and challenges identified, including through the European Semester. They will be owned and designed in partnership with national and regional authorities. The new delivery system will accommodate the diversity of the Member States, offering them flexibility to develop national, sectoral and, where relevant, regional and territorial chapters, as under current rules, depending on each Member State's constitutional structures and traditions.[165]

The Commission believed that, through the planning process, legacy programmes could also expand the range of spending targets, particularly towards investments and reforms in the area of Union defence capabilities and security projects.[166] Its proposal reiterated the plan for a 'strengthened and modernised' cohesion policy that—while paradoxically purporting to maintain 'regions at its core'[167]—would continue the

[161] European Commission (2025af) [Proposed MFF Regulation], art 8. The need for a separate flexibility instrument could arguably be avoided by setting the own resources ceiling sufficiently high so that the margin between it and the financial framework ceiling would enable the EU to respond flexibly to changing situations and enable the adoption of new funding instruments relying on the appropriate substantive legal basis when the need is concretised.

[162] See this chapter below, nn 214–28 and accompanying text.

[163] European Commission (2025ad, pp 21–22).

[164] Ibid, p 3.

[165] Ibid, p 4.

[166] Ibid, p 11.

[167] Ibid, p 5.

effort of directing cohesion funds to Union-wide or global priorities rather than regional development goals.

Calling the NRPPs in legacy domains like cohesion 'national *and regional* partnership plans' (emphasis added) was undoubtedly a recognition of the general unhappiness of the regions about being effectively treated as bystanders in the preparation and implementation of the National Recovery and Resilience Plans under the RRF. In its proposed regulation on the new NRPPs, the Commission introduced the idea of 'comprehensive partnerships' to 'foster ownership at all levels, with a multi-level governance and a strong regional dimension, based on shared management and the partnership principle', with 'balanced representation' of 'regional, local, urban, rural and other public authorities or associations'; 'economic and social partners, including farmers, fishers and their organisations'; 'relevant bodies representing civil society'; and 'research organisations and universities'.[168] These partners are then to be involved in the preparation of the NRPPs and throughout the preparation, implementation, and evaluation of its chapters. One wonders how such procedures, in the view of the Commission, are meant to cure the democratic and participatory problems involved in the RRF, in particular given the total absence of national parliaments. In the Comission's model of democratic participation, the modalities are dictated by the EU, reflecting indifference to (or ignorance about) how national decision-making works, in particular regarding national parliaments.

Along a different dimension, however, the Commission seems to have heard the criticism that funding targets under the RRF were almost entirely national in nature and contained little or no cross-border elements; hence the numerous references to 'EU priorities' and 'EU value added' in the proposed MFF, in line with the language in the Draghi Report. Nonetheless, it was difficult not to notice that 'regional' and 'EU value added' were often in tension with each other, making it a challenge to pursue both at the same time. Similarly, the underlying rational of planning—stronger 'national ownership', again with its strong RRF pedigree—seemed to be at cross purposes with 'EU priorities'. The creation of a separate ECF under direct management by the Commission and hence unmediated through the Member States (though apparently operating in coordination with the NRPPs) suggests an unwillingness to extend the NGEU model to these domains. Instead, as noted earlier, they will apparently operate along the traditional lines of European research funding but at a vastly expanded scale.

One of the key lessons of the NGEU model, however, was that the EU had great difficulty prioritising where European money should best be directed as well as to what ends. The Commission instead sought to buy output legitimacy in the Member States by offering EU money to fund national public goods such as health care, housing,

[168] European Commission (2025aj, pp 3, 41) (quoting Explanatory Memorandum and proposed art 6(1)). Under Articles 54 to 56, every Member State is to set up monitoring and coordinating committees, according to the same principles of 'balanced representation'. These committees are then assigned the task of approving the relevant chapters of the plan and to monitor progress in their implementation. Ibid, pp 87–88, proposed arts 54–56.

or social security costs. One thus might fairly ask: instead of expanding the use of that model, why should the money be circulated through the EU bureaucracy at all, if the EU added value remains limited? Unless and until the EU 'agree[s] on a definition of EU added value and … take[s] account of it systematically in funding decisions', as ECA argued,[169] it would seem more efficient to leave the money with the Member States and let them bear the costs of their own operations, without channelling it through the EU. The generalised planning and spending process is, according to the Commission, supposed to be 'results-based'.[170] The focus will purportedly be on 'deliver[ing] funding and results faster and more efficiently'.[171] To that end, the Commission offered a technocratic discussion of a 'single expenditure and performance monitoring system [that] will apply to all relevant programmes, allowing for a comprehensive overview of where EU funds are allocated and what they deliver',[172] suggesting it was in line with recommendations from the European Court of Auditors.[173] The Commission also proposed a dedicated regulation to define the new performance framework,[174] with the aim of being 'simpler, less burdensome and more consistent, thereby strengthening a results-driven approach and providing greater transparency and accountability'.[175]

Combining all the various reporting systems into a single framework undoubtedly aimed to reduce the administrative burden. Nonetheless, it was less clear how the framework would actually 'support the delivery of EU policy priorities'.[176] Presumably, this was the job of Article 8 of the proposed regulation, which sets out the basic elements of the tracking and performance framework. According to Article 8, performance was to be measured by how much a particular EU policy would contribute to one of four 'intervention fields' (designated broadly as 'climate change mitigation', 'climate change adaptation and resilience', 'environment', and 'social') based on a set of fixed coefficients in an attached annex. The coefficients, however, are unexplained and often quite arbitrary.[177] Taken as a whole, the annex gives little impression of an underlying coherent European plan to direct the investments, coming across instead as a low-ambition box-ticking exercise rather than a serious attempt to promote European priorities. The challenge of assessing performance was all the greater

169 European Court of Auditors (2025c, p 3, para 03).
170 European Commission (2025ad, pp 6, 24).
171 Ibid, p 6.
172 Ibid, p 25.
173 Ibid, citing European Court of Auditors (2025c).
174 European Commission (2025ag).
175 European Commission (2025ah, p 23).
176 European Commission (2025ad, p 25).
177 For example, any measure falling into the intervention field 'targeted support to farmers' income' would always make a 40% contribution to climate change mitigation and adaptation and a similar contribution to the Union's environmental priorities but no contribution to the Union's social priorities, regardless of the details of the measure. European Commission (2025ai, p 1). Correspondingly, an investment in 'transmission of electricity' would always count as a 100% contribution to climate change mitigation but would make no contribution to other priorities, regardless of what is the at the other end of the power line or whether it in a sensible way fits into the rest of electricity infrastructure to create a functioning European grid. European Commission (2025ai, p 31).

given the Commission's aspiration to make more widespread use of simplified cost options and FNLC in the new MFF.[178] The Commission's default position appears to be centralisation of more power in itself, enabling more opaque and technocratic negotiations under the guise of 'planning' and 'flexibility', which results in more discretionary power for the Commission.[179]

The backlash to this approach emerged quickly with the announcement of the Commission's proposals on 16 July 2025. The roll-out was broadly described variously as 'chaotic',[180] 'messy, confused and secretive',[181] and 'a communications train wreck',[182] in which, behind the scenes, there was 'rebellion'[183] and 'revolt' within the College of Commissioners itself.[184] Key aspects of the package were prepared in the President's cabinet, leaving members of the College in the dark concerning the final figures of the funding in their own sectors.[185] The consolidation of programmes entailed, moreover, absorbing previously dedicated spending lines into broader targets, like 'climate and environment'.[186] A similar approach to the consolidation of CAP funding prompted the leader of a leading agricultural lobby to speak of 'dismantling 70 years of European history' and a 'declaration of war' on farmers (although Ursula von der Leyen insisted '[a]griculture will be strengthened').[187] The President of the Committee of the Regions spoke of a 'monster plan that aims to swallow cohesion policy and crack its backbone by nationalizing and centralizing' behind 'the smokescreen of simplification'.[188]

In the European Parliament, views were broadly critical but varied. Some MEPs critiqued the fivefold increase in defence spending while agriculture would shrink by over 20%, whereas others (particularly on the far-right) criticised the amounts destined for Ukraine.[189] Among the leading centre-right and centre-left pro-European parties (EPP and S&D) there was concern that a budget of just 1.26% of GNI, including 0.11% of GNI for NGEU debt repayments, would be, after taking into account inflation, a budget that was simply 'standing still'.[190] Siegfried Mureşan, from von der Leyen's own EPP and co-rapporteur for the MFF, was particularly critical of the expansive incorporation of the NGEU planning and spending model into the EU budget: 'A stronger EU budget cannot be built on the mistakes of the past ... We will not approve a budget that promotes fragmented national plans with no link to European objectives. Europe needs a shared vision—not 27 separate shopping lists'.[191] A joint

[178] European Commission (2025ad, p 24).
[179] Andor (2025).
[180] Foy et al (2025); Wulff Wold (2025).
[181] Sorgi (2025).
[182] Wax (2025a).
[183] Wulff Wold (2025).
[184] Foy et al (2025).
[185] Ibid.
[186] POLITICO (2025).
[187] Brzeziński et al (2025).
[188] Bortoletto (2025).
[189] Deyl (2025b).
[190] European Parliament (2025e).
[191] Ibid.

statement from leading EPP and S&D MEPs stressed that 'any new performance-based mechanism for member states to access funds must include robust parliamentary oversight and cannot circumvent democratic scrutiny of EU spending'.[192] As our research suggests, however, the technocratic and opaque nature of the NGEU planning and spending model will likely undermine the EP's ability to serve this role.

b. Own Resources and Common Borrowing: More Legal Engineering at the Frontiers of Legitimacy

In terms of pushback against the Commission's proposals, the most important criticisms were those of the Member States, which would be in the frontline of budgetary negotiations with the Commission over the following two years. In the two months following the announcement in late July 2025, the Commission reportedly received 3,000 written questions from Member States about the MFF proposals, which observers took as a signal of inadequate advance consultations.[193] These queries were especially important regarding the revenue side of the new MFF, including new own resources and, potentially, new collective borrowing.

On the day of the Commission's announcement in mid-July, the German and French finance ministers published a joint op-ed in *Handelsblatt* and *Les Echos* calling for, among other things, an exploration of 'how European public goods can increasingly be funded using genuine EU own resources. This will make EU funding more autonomous.'[194] The German government, the EU's key paymaster, however, rejected the Commission's expenditure and revenue proposals just hours after they were announced in Brussels. While Chancellor Friedrich Merz was said to support Ursula von der Leyen's plans to modernise the budget and put a bigger emphasis on defence and innovation, the headline number on the spending side was 'simply too big'.[195] In that regard, Germany was likely expressing the sentiments of all or most net-contributor Member States, although many also looked favourably on increased common defence spending.[196] Moreover, the Commission's package of proposals did little to address a key driver behind the overall size of the budget—the NGEU debt-overhang—which will undoubtedly remain an irritant in post-NGEU politics in the years to come.

As foreseen from the inception of NGEU, that debt-overhang would require new own resources. As part of its MFF announcement, the Commission proposed a new ORD that included a package of new own resources to cover increased expenditure, particularly for repayment of NGEU debt but also to reduce the EU's dependence on GNI-based contributions from the Member States.[197] The proposed ORD included a version of both the ETS and CBAM own resources proposed previously,[198] as well

[192] Ibid.
[193] Wax (2025b).
[194] Klingbeil and Lombard (2025).
[195] Nienaber et al (2025).
[196] Tamma (2025).
[197] European Commission (2025v, p 1).
[198] See Chapter Five, Section C.1.

as three additional new own resources: first, a levy calculated on the basis of non-collected waste of electrical and electronic equipment, second, a tobacco excise duty, and third, the so-called 'Corporate Resource for Europe' (CORE). The CORE would create an obligation for corporate entities with a net annual turnover above €100 million to make a payment to the Member States, which would then pay that money over to the EU budget.[199]

How the proposed own resources would ultimately be designed or implemented—if they were to survive at all—was, as of this writing, an open question. Of particular interest in this regard is the CORE. The German government quickly criticised it as sending 'the wrong signal' given that Germany and Europe were trying to increase investment (indeed, even the tobacco excise appeared unlikely to garner German support).[200] Over the subsequent two months criticisms intensified, to the point that there was serious doubt about the political future of both the CORE and the tobacco levy.[201] The reaction was a reminder that new own resources are not 'free money' to the EU—they are paid by somebody and, more importantly, have implications for how Member States are able to finance their own national budgets. From a purely European perspective, the aim of these levies was 'robust, reliable and resilient financing of the Union budget' which in turn 'requires a diversified and enlarged set of own resources' to 'improv[e] the fiscal equilibrium between the Union and its Member States'.[202] But when the EU seeks to increase the financial burden of own resources on private actors and companies, the Member States' ability to collect taxes and levies from the same companies decreases. At least fourteen countries, including Italy, Greece, Austria, Sweden, Portugal, and Romania, criticised the tobacco levy for its adverse impact on similar national levies. The opposition to CORE was apparently even more widespread.[203]

The CORE proposal, in particular, suggested an ambition on the part of the Commission to test the line between traditional own resources collected by and from Member States as opposed to EU taxes collected directly from private entities. On the one hand, the ORD would create a duty to pay that would belong to the corporate entity, referring to 'annual contributions from companies' and '[t]he annual contribution from each company'.[204] On the other hand, the proposed ORD specified that '[t]he Member States shall collect' the contribution;[205] the proposed ORD did not contemplate the creation of an autonomous EU tax administration, 'wearing the EU badge', so to speak, with the power and legitimacy to collect the EU 'tax'.[206] Rather,

[199] European Commission (2025v, pp 7, 11, arts 3(1)(b) and 11(2)).
[200] Reuters (2025a).
[201] Wulff Wold and Michalopoulos (2025). On 30 October 2025, the Finnish government announced its opposition to the CORE as a tax on companies that could not be based on Article 311 TFEU. Valtioneuvosto (2025).
[202] European Parliament (2023e, para 3).
[203] Wulff Wold and Michalopoulos (2025).
[204] European Commission (2025v, p 7, art 3(1)(b)).
[205] Ibid, p 11, art 11(2).
[206] See Chapter One, nn 39–40 and accompanying text.

both the power and legitimacy to collect this mandatory contribution were to be mediated through the Member States, just as with traditional own resources like customs duties and tariffs.[207] The transition to a genuine sort of EU tax, if one can call it that, would raise a myriad of issues that, as of this writing, had yet to be concretised but would eventually need to be addressed to develop a fully 'autonomous' instrument on the revenue side of the budget.[208]

In terms of new collective borrowing, the Commission's proposal specified that '[t]he Union shall not use funds borrowed on capital markets for the financing of operational expenditure'.[209] But this did not mean that the Commission envisioned no role for further collective borrowing; it just refrained from proposing borrowing-for-spending on the NGEU model.[210] Aside from borrowing for Ukraine (under an as-yet-unspecified portion of the new Ukraine Reserve), all borrowing would instead be used to finance loans to the Member States. Several Member States, not least Germany, had made clear in advance that grants were out of the question (whereas initially only the Netherlands opposed new joint debt entirely,[211] later apparently joined by Finland).[212]

The Commission envisioned two such borrowing-for-lending vehicles. The first, 'Catalyst Europe', €150 billion facility, was not technically part of the MFF and ORD proposals but the Commission alluded to it in its press materials. The borrowing was apparently to be backed by the headroom under the new MFF as proposed (no raising required). The EU would then lend the proceeds to 'Member States who want for favourable [borrowing] conditions … to invest in European objectives', such as 'defence industry or energy infrastructure or strategic technologies and others'.[213] In effect, it would be a reprise of SAFE but with a slightly broader focus, although the precise contours (eg legal basis, role of the EP) were left for future determination (and contestation).

The second borrowing instrument, contained in the proposed ORD itself, was 'a new limited, extraordinary and targeted tool' valued at €400 billion 'to respond solely to severe crises, severe hardship or serious threat thereof'.[214] The borrowing would be backed by a dedicated increase of the MFF ceiling of 0.25% 'for the sole purpose of covering all liabilities of the Union resulting from the borrowing' under this tool.[215] The tool would be actually activated (and governed) by a future Council Regulation, under a prompt from the European Council, which the Commission says should provide 'the necessary impetus … in defining the general political directions and

207 European Commission (2025v, p 11, art 11(2)). The sole difference is that the Member States are entitled to 'retain, by way of collection costs, 10 % of the' customs duties, though apparently not of the CORE contributions. Ibid, p 12, art 11(3).
208 For further exploration, see van der Vlugt (2025); see also Caziero (2024).
209 European Commission (2025v, p 10, art 5).
210 See Chapter Five, nn 3–4 and accompanying text.
211 Tamma (2025).
212 Valtioneuvosto (2025).
213 von der Leyen (2025d).
214 European Commission (2025v, p 4, recital (21)).
215 Ibid, p 11, art 8.

priorities including in times of crises, hardships or threats thereof'.[216] The new tool, however, 'should not be activated where Union programmes already adequately address the consequences of the situation'.[217]

Given all the talk of 'exceptional', 'extraordinary', 'temporary', and 'targeted' measures, one might have expected that the legal basis for this Council Regulation would be Article 122 TFEU, just as with the 'several ad-hoc and temporary instruments' (namely NGEU, SURE, and SAFE) that purportedly inspired this new tool.[218] But the Commission proposed instead that the governing Council Regulation would be adopted 'in accordance with the procedure set out in Article 311(4) TFEU, after obtaining the consent of the European Parliament'.[219] Article 311(4) TFEU establishes a special legislative procedure intended for laying down 'implementing measures for the Union's own resources system in so far as this is provided for' in the ORD. Until now, Article 311(4) TFEU had been used for Council regulations defining the technical details of ORD implementation, including the calculation and budgeting of the balance, or control and supervision measures such as inspections and combating fraud.[220]

When we compare this proposal to the 2020 ORD, we see that the earlier ORD authorised debt-financing for specific purposes (even as the funds were, in practice, used far beyond those specifications). By contrast, the purposes of the borrowing authorisation in the new ORD, apart from the limitation to financing loans only, are much more general and unspecific ('severe crises, severe hardship or serious threat thereof'). In effect, the power to approve the specification of those purposes would shift away from national parliaments under Article 311(3) TFEU to the Council under Article 311(4) TFEU, with democratic legitimation now provided by the EP via consent. The new tool could be understood as a further step in 'integration by stealth',[221] in which important powers heretofore belonging to national bodies were now being supranationalised. One might argue that this simply tracks the actual practice under the NGEU model, in which funds were redirected to other purposes through the amendment of the RRF Regulation, with no role for national parliaments at all. The role of the European Parliament, however, would also be adversely impacted. While the new tool appeared to augment the role of the EP relative to other emergency procedures under Article 122 TFEU, it weakened that role relative to the actual practice under NGEU. The de facto NGEU model gave the EP a co-equal role under the ordinary legislative procedure in the adoption and amendment of the RRF Regulation; now that role would be limited to consent under Article 311(4) TFEU.

The new borrowing mechanism—repeatedly characterised by the Commission as 'limited, extraordinary and targeted'[222]—is one, in fact, that any future ORD could

[216] Ibid, p 5, recital (22).
[217] Ibid, p 5, recital (21).
[218] Ibid, p 4, recital (20).
[219] Ibid, p 5, recital (22).
[220] See, eg, Council Regulation (EU, Euratom) 2021/768; Council Regulation (EU, Euratom) No 608/2014.
[221] Majone (2005).
[222] See, eg, European Commission (2025v, p 4, recital (21)).

easily replicate and could thus mark the advent of a permanent borrowing capacity for Union governance, without Treaty change.[223] In her presentation of the new MFF and ORD to the press on 16 July 2025, Ursula von der Leyen characterised the new tool as simply a 'shortcut to enable funding for a crisis'.[224] She added, however, that 'crises are no longer the exception, they are the norm, and we have learnt the lesson'.[225] The EU had thus travelled far from December 2022 when the Commission had assured the German Federal Constitutional Court that the Treaties included 'a general prohibition on borrowing'.[226] The new tool responded to the functionalist concerns of those who view unanimity among national parliaments as 'cumbersome ... every time the EU wants to increase spending or borrow money',[227] even if the maximum level of the ceilings, and thus Member States' obligations to contribute to the EU budget, are still defined in the ORD. This exercise in legal engineering would also likely be welcomed by those who have argued—or at least hoped—that the ongoing atmosphere of crisis might (or should) lead to a gradual setting aside of unanimity rules applicable to various stages in the EU budgetary procedures.[228]

C. Navigating Beyond the Constitutional Borderlands?

This new borrowing tool in the proposed ORD was further evidence of how far into the constitutional borderlands the EU had navigated since the advent of the Covid crisis and the adoption of NGEU. But the proposed new borrowing mechanism (along with the borrowing contemplated in 'Catalyst Europe') was also evidence of the extent to which the EU was still struggling to find a way to cross the constitutional Rubicon of fiscal autonomy with the limited tools at hand. Travelling through the borderlands to this point had required reinterpretation of multiple Treaty provisions (the cohesion flexibility clause of Article 175(3) TFEU, the emergency powers of Article 122 TFEU, and now perhaps also Article 311(4) TFEU). To create any semblance of a governance system for the constitutional borderlands, these reinterpretations would need to be combined with interinstitutional agreements and (the hoped-for) jerry-rigged system based on *passerelle* clauses, enhanced cooperation mechanisms, and intergovernmental cooperation outside the Treaties. The tenuousness and evident creakiness of the proposed governance system simply reiterated the point made in the

[223] Again, apparently, only the Netherlands was opposed. Per Dutch Finance Minister Eelco Heinen, 'As far as the Netherlands is concerned, new instruments for joint debt are ... not on the table'. Reuters (2025b).

[224] von der Leyen (2025e).

[225] von der Leyen (2025d).

[226] BVerfG (2022, para 152). See Chapter Five, nn 521–22 and accompanying text.

[227] Fabbrini (2024, p 181).

[228] de Witte (2021, p 681). See also European Parliament (2023f, Annex to the Motion, Amendment 247, re Article 311 TFEU) (proposal of the European Parliament's Committee on Constitutional Affairs—Rapporteurs: Guy Verhofstadt, et al—to empower the Union legislator to adopt an ORD without the approval of the Member States).

preface of this book: the EU as it stands today simply was 'not built to operate in this environment'.[229]

In view of this reality, one might fairly ask: what lessons do the Commission's MFF and ORD proposals draw from the NGEU experience? What shortcomings do they correct? What mistakes do they perpetuate? And, perhaps most importantly for the purposes of this book, what new trails do they blaze further into the constitutional borderlands in which the EU today finds itself? One certainty regarding the negotiations of the next two years is that the MFF and ORD that will emerge out of the process will differ in numerous ways from the Commission's proposals. Indeed, it is also possible that the current proposals may not survive in-depth political scrutiny, and the Commission will need to return to the drafting board.

Regardless of what develops, one could nonetheless draw several conclusions about how the Commission understands the legacy of the NGEU model on which it has sought to build the new MFF and ORD. The Commission appears to be convinced that NGEU (and more particularly the RRF) were a resounding success (or, conceivably, the Commission knew that admitting anything else would be political suicide). Either way, the Commission clearly looks to the key elements of the NGEU model (national plans and ownership, broad area of application, performance-based financing) as the foundations for national and regional partnership plans that it hopes will take over much of what used to be common agricultural and cohesion policies, as well as providing the framework for new competitiveness initiatives. In this sense, the Commission has now 'succeeded in setting the terms of the debate. With Europe in the clutch of so many crises—and found wanting on so many fronts—aligning behind a vision for a competitive continent that can withstand existential economic and security threats is a must'.[230]

From the legal-constitutional viewpoint, the MFF and ORD proposals are a mixed bag. They consolidate certain key elements of the NGEU, take timid steps beyond others, but also refrain from trying to replicate some of NGEU's most audacious elements (notably, in effect, borrowing-for-spending). The consolidation is evident in the (hoped for) generalisation of the planning process, with a vastly expanded scope, ratcheting cohesion even further afield from its regional-developmental anchor. It is further evidenced in the Commission's commitment—despite cogent criticisms of ECA—to its particular understanding of performance-based funding. The ORD would also take another step in the direction of borrowing as a standard part of the EU financial system, even if limited only to funding loans. In doing so, the Commission's proposals may move beyond the reliance on Article 122 TFEU and perhaps seeks to ground the borrowing system in Article 311(4) TFEU. It further seeks to transcend the limits of the NGEU model by moving in the direction of EU taxation through CORE. However, the Commission understood that it could not risk extending 'flexibility' to

[229] Wyplosz (2024, p 9). See Preface and Acknowledgments, n 8 and accompanying text.
[230] Wulff Wold (2025).

anything that would suggest a reduction or circumvention of Member State funding commitments, given how far the EU actually is from developing its own autonomous sources of income. Hence, the proposed ORD makes clear that, contrary to the de facto reality of the NGEU model, borrowing should not be used 'for the financing of operational expenditure'.[231]

The question, then, is whether it is possible to make this emergent system of borderlands financing and governance work better going forward. This is the question we take up in the Conclusion to this book. Suffice it to say here that the NGEU model, which has served as the EU's vehicle for navigating the borderlands to this point, emerged at precisely the moment when the biggest challenges facing the EU (the Russian war on Ukraine, the ensuing energy crisis, the threat of withdrawal of the US security umbrella) have all required increasing focus on the production of European (not national) public goods. The NGEU model's shortcomings for *that* purpose, as this book has sought to show, are increasingly evident. The Commission's July 2025 MFF proposals nonetheless sought to generalise that model, once again harnessing 'national ownership' in the delicate task of both reducing legacy spending in areas like CAP and cohesion (along with their fundamentally '*juste retour*' logic) while also increasing spending on European public goods in the area of competitiveness and defence. But rather than dealing with the many trade-offs between these goals in the open, the Commission again sought to largely displace the difficult politics into an opaque and technocratic process of 'transactional' negotiation, combined with further legal engineering by institutional lawyers operating outside of the public eye. This combination does not bode well for the future of European democracy, both national and supranational.

[231] European Commission (2025v, p 10, art 5). See this chapter above, n 209 and accompanying text.

Conclusion
Democratic Politics and the Fate of the NGEU Model

The task we set for ourselves in this book was to assess the historical origins, current trajectories, and potential future implications of the NGEU model for European policy and governance. Our framing metaphor—constitutional borderlands—was meant to emphasise the liminal condition in which the integration project currently finds itself. Among many EU legal professionals, the idea that the EU already possesses a constitutional character has a long pedigree, even as that claim also reflects a fundamental category mistake. The integration project no doubt has had major constitutional *implications*, not least for Member States. But without fiscal mobilisation capacities of its own—most importantly with regard to taxation—the EU has fallen well short of possessing an autonomously constitutional *character* in its own right. During the five years of NGEU we have studied, the EU has found various new ways of spending money, often primarily on national rather than European public goods. Finding ways to finance its new spending has proved much more difficult. The EU's constitutional autonomy remains limited.

Viewing the integration project 'as if' it were already constitutional was always more of an ideological imaginary[1]—an exercise in epistemic empowerment[2]—in the effort to construct an autonomous legal order, not a description of an actual socio-political reality in a robust sense.[3] Europe is now struggling to make that description real in a way it never could before, navigating its way through the borderlands between the sub-constitutional domain of mere regulatory power ('integration through law') and the constitutional domain of autonomous mobilisation of fiscal resources ('integration through funding'). The NGEU model, both in its original incarnation as well as its subsequent extensions and deviations, is playing a crucial role in that struggle. But given the deeper historical character of integration itself—which the NGEU model has arguably only perpetuated rather than fundamentally altered—this struggle has had an overwhelmingly executive and technocratic orientation, doing a poor job of mobilising parliaments or the broader public in the political task of constitutional transformation.

[1] Komárek (2023).
[2] Isiksel (2015, pp 5–6).
[3] Lindseth (2023).

European Integration in the Constitutional Borderlands. Päivi Leino-Sandberg and Peter L. Lindseth, Oxford University Press.
DOI: 10.1093/oso/9780198949527.003.0008

The NGEU model was developed to circumvent problems with competence limitations, giving the supranational encroachment of national competences a seemingly 'transactional' quality. But it has had the unfortunate side-effect of moving the EU away from where it could have provided most value added: the pursuit of genuine European public goods. The Commission's recent MFF proposals try to generalise the planning model, relying on a series of basic assumptions: that the EU is better positioned than national authorities to shape policy (now through spending); that it possesses the legitimacy and means to raise and distribute the funds needed to finance projects and service any debts; and that it has the ability to manage the risks involved while ensuring that taxpayers' money is spent well. At the time of this writing, all these assumptions are in doubt. Moreover, the Commission has done its best to keep the flow of information about the planning and spending process strictly limited and curated, making it very difficult for the broader public (and indeed, many insiders) to understand, much less analyse, what the process actually entails.

One thing, however, is clear. Against anticipation, NGEU (both as a programme and model) did not trigger a Hamiltonian moment in terms of fiscal mobilisation capacity. In fact, there was little observable progress in the direction of fiscal federalism even at the level of political rhetoric (though there was a highly questionable Hamiltonian move towards trying to expand EU regulatory power through spending, as we discussed in Chapter Four).[4] From the viewpoint of fiscal mobilisation, given the cost of debt servicing, NGEU left the Union in a more difficult position and will make the MFF and ORD negotiations more challenging. Instead of deepening integration, NGEU developed primarily into a tool for budgetary transfers, with pre-allocated national envelopes demonstrating the EU's fundamental incapacity to prioritise. If this choice were openly explained and justified to voters, we suppose it could have been a legitimate way of proceeding. But as the NGEU model evolved, it in fact drifted considerably from the original explanations and justifications at the time of the programme's adoption, ultimately becoming a tool to spend money primarily in national siloes on essentially any and all things. It was striking how little attempt was made to ensure that Europe would actually get the best possible value out of its investment. The legal background work supporting this move, not to mention the buried interpretive and political choices, have had massive distributive consequences as well as a fundamental impact on the functioning of democracy and its future direction. One of our core purposes in this book has been to bring these various dimensions of NGEU to light, especially its legal dimension.

A. *Necessitas Non Habet Legem*: The Decline of Legal Constraint under Perpetual Crisis?

The five years of the NGEU model in action, whatever else it accomplished, has had one indisputable impact: it led to a paradigm shift in how the limits of EU law are

[4] See Chapter Four, Section D.6.

understood. The old language of European integration and Treaty requirements was overtaken by an unconstrained functionalist logic, in which talk of competence limitations and governance rules—much less democratic legitimacy—increasingly merited little more than desultory consideration.[5]

To be clear, among EU legal professionals, law has rarely been seen as establishing or upholding absolute constraints. Law has long been understood, rather, as fundamentally intertwined with the political objective of an 'ever closer Union', serving as the means to pursue that overarching objective.[6] Law has nonetheless provided the arguments these legal professionals have needed to anchor EU actions in the Treaties, even if tenuously, or at least anchor them in the perceived broader purposes of the Treaties. This anchoring has been important because overt disregard for Treaty constraints could grow into a political obstacle for the final approval and implementation of measures. This is especially so given the emphasis that one of the most powerful Member State apex courts—the German Federal Constitutional Court—has placed on 'the principle of conferral and the constitutional responsibility with regard to European integration of the individual Member State'.[7] Consistent with basic conceptions of lawful delegation of regulatory power to administrative bodies, the German Court has required that the nature and scope of the conferral to the EU be reasonably foreseeable, because '[o]nly such foreseeability can provide sufficient democratic legitimation' to the supranational delegation of powers as a matter of national constitutional law.[8] This understanding of the legal underpinnings of the integration process stands in contrast to more open-ended conceptions of the Treaties as a 'living constitution' now dominant among EU legal professionals.[9]

If we think back to just over a decade ago, to the aftermath of the global financial crisis and the ensuing euro crisis, we can get a sense of how the role of Treaty constraint has changed in EU policy and political discussions. We should again recall the Commission's 'Blueprint for a deep and genuine economic and monetary union' of 2012.[10] The Blueprint acknowledged very specifically that some of the instruments it envisioned would 'require modifications of the current Treaties and new competences for the Union'.[11] In retrospect, these instruments (if not the need for Treaty change) look prescient. The Commission envisaged a debt redemption fund which, in exchange for fiscal discipline and a programme of structural reforms, would mutualise part of Member States' debt.[12] It also envisaged creating 'a corresponding, dedicated budgetary and own resources procedure'; 'new taxation power at the EU level, or a power to raise revenue by indebting itself on the markets (presently barred by Articles

[5] Leino-Sandberg (2025c).
[6] Leino-Sandberg (2025d).
[7] BVerfG, 2 BvE 2/08 (2009) [German Lisbon Judgment], para 238.
[8] Ibid, para 318. For further analysis, see Lindseth (2010, pp 182–83).
[9] de Gregorio Merino (2024, p 162). See also Chapter One, n 82 and accompanying text.
[10] European Commission (2012). See Chapter Two, nn 91–93 and accompanying text; see also Chapter Six, n 31 and accompanying text.
[11] European Commission (2012, p 12).
[12] Ibid, pp 28–29.

310 and 311 TFEU)'; as well 'an EMU Treasury within the Commission'.[13] It again fully acknowledged: 'Major Treaty reform will be required on this path.'[14] Moreover, any Treaty changes would also need to include 'adaptations to the EU's model of democratic legitimacy'.[15] While not necessarily reflecting the 'original intent'[16] of Treaties, these statements were reflective of what might be called 'framework originalism' that 'requires fidelity to the semantic meanings of the words in the text at the time of adoption, including generally recognized terms of art'.[17]

Fast forward to 2025, the year that the post-euro crisis reports like the Commission's Blueprint (or the Four Presidents' Report) hoped would mark the attainment of the final stage of 'a deep and genuine' EMU. Looking back, it would not be an exaggeration to say that much of what was envisaged in 2012 as requiring Treaty change has indeed been achieved by 2025 without it. This may well be a tribute to the intensity of the functional demands over the course of the last fifteen years, and more particularly in the last half decade. Technical solutions continued to evolve but the crucial elements of a new regime are now in place—most importantly, large-scale issuance of joint debt and its mutualisation, financial incentives to Member States to undertake structural reforms, and the establishment of a de facto EMU Treasury in embryo—not just for euro-area members but for the EU27 as a whole. And it was all accomplished through a succession of intersecting and unprecedented crises, the functional demands of which have been both relentless and existential, on a scale much greater than even contemplated during the euro crisis itself. As Ursula van der Leyen noted, '[n]one of this—none—would have been explicitly foreseen in the Treaties, but it was possible. And we did it together—because Europeans expected their Union to step up'.[18]

The Europeans to whom von der Leyen alludes here, however, arguably know very little about how this transformation took place and what its actual effects have been. The guiding impulse behind the NGEU experiment has been what Majone called 'the EU political culture of total optimism' among EU elites,[19] a culture that simply 'push[es] ahead with European integration without worrying too much about public support or democratic legitimacy'.[20] What constitutes success 'is determined by the decision makers themselves—by the very fact that they agreed on that particular decision—rather than by those who will be affected by the actual results it will eventually produce'.[21] This has been the animating spirit behind the NGEU model on which the Draghi Report has explicitly sought to build,[22] and it also underlies the

[13] Ibid, p 33.
[14] Ibid, p 30.
[15] Ibid, p 36.
[16] For the classic rejection of the 'original intent' argument in the US context, along with the defence of the idea of the 'living constitution', see Marshall (1987).
[17] Balkin (2012, p 1132).
[18] von der Leyen (2022).
[19] See Majone (2015).
[20] Ibid, p 3.
[21] Ibid.
[22] Draghi Report (2024a, p 66).

political guidelines of Ursula van der Leyen's second Commission,[23] as well as the MFF package presented in July 2025.[24]

This is hardly the first time in history where important changes in a governing regime have involved stretching and straining legality, both substantively and procedurally, even to the point of outright illegality.[25] Indeed, one might say that the very essence of functionalism as a theory (and justification) of legal change is that, at certain points in time, the demands of necessity overwhelm prior legal constraint—*necessitas non habet legem*—necessity knows no law, as the venerable saying goes. Nearly two decades ago, Alexander Somek identified the roots of this line of thinking in the EU in what he called the 'normativity of distress', in which the law is overtaken by the sense 'that "something must be done", regardless by whom and how'.[26] As he elaborated:

> The poignant exhortative tone reveals a built-in preference for quick action over deliberation ... Since the justification for action lies in its responsiveness to exigency it would not even make sense for it to stay within pre-established constraints. Wherever jurisdictional boundaries exist—be they officially classified as emergency powers or not—they are likely to be extended and transgressed.[27]

In the constitutional borderlands in which the EU finds itself, the EU professional legal elite has now taken such claims out of the realm of the exceptional and proceeded to normalise them as the standard operating procedure of the EU under conditions of seemingly perpetual crisis.[28] Formalism—fidelity to law—risks becoming in these circumstance almost an obscenity,[29] in which seemingly outdated Treaty rules require workarounds because they no longer offer a way of managing the intense demands of today's Europe. As a result, '[w]hat little is left of formal law is reduced to a frame for negotiation and adjustment', while broad principles such as solidarity, resilience, and cohesion 'pay homage to functional discretion'.[30]

From this perspective, as we saw in Chapter One, an 'evolutive' and 'teleological' interpretation of the Treaties is easily justified as 'necessary to avoid a stasis that could compromise the very future of the EU project', which in turn justifies 'a continuous exercise of constitutional audacity'—to use the words of the new Director-General of the Commission Legal Service.[31] This is the sense in which the EU Treaties became, as his immediate predecessor argued, 'living instruments' animated by the 'political will of the institutions working together in order to respond to the urgent

[23] von der Leyen (2024).
[24] European Commission (2025ad).
[25] See, eg, Ackerman (1991), Kay (2014); see also Lindseth (2021b).
[26] Somek (2008, p 233).
[27] Ibid, pp 233–34.
[28] See Chapter One, nn 81–89 and accompanying text.
[29] See Koskenniemi (2007).
[30] Ibid, p 11.
[31] de Gregorio Merino (2024, p 162).

nature of the [EU's] challenges', leading, in turn, to the '[e]volution of the EU's institutional system through "constitutional practice" '.[32] As Ursula von der Leyen herself stated in her 'solemn undertaking' before the Court of Justice at the investiture of her new Commission in January 2025: 'Today we vow to be the Guardian of the Treaties ... *filling them with life*' (emphasis added).[33] That life-giving impulse has required numerous (often revolutionary) reinterpretations of the Treaty, developed and implemented without public debate. In this process, there was no consideration of the democratic and distributive implications of such changes—certainly not publicly—nor does there appear to have been much consideration of possible alternatives or who should be held accountable for them. This is the dark side of the instrumentalism towards law in the EU institutions and more particularly in the European Commission. As Martti Koskenniemi has described:

> A legal technique that reaches directly to law's purposes is either compelled to think that it can access the right purpose in some politics-independent fashion ... or it transforms to a licence to those powers in position to realise their own purposes to do precisely that. Instrumentalism inculcates a heroic mindset: we can do it! It is the mindset of well-placed, powerful actors, confident in their possessing the 'right' purpose ... But the instrumentalist mindset creates a consistent bias in favour of dominant actors with many policy-alternatives from which to choose and sufficient resources to carry out their objectives.[34]

In short, the 'constitutional audacity' of the Commission has inevitably had the character of an 'elite construction', as Bruce Ackerman has put it, in which constitutional change has occurred without popular participation or even much 'self-conscious consideration' of the change by citizens.[35]

B. Living Constitutionalism—'Anything Goes'?

This brings us, then, to what might be called the 'anything goes' problem with so-called living constitutionalism in the EU (which, in its features of epistemic empowerment, is really just another name for 'as if' constitutionalism).[36] The 'anything goes' mentality risks turning living constitutionalism into 'an invitation to the people in power to do what they want'.[37] As one articulate advocate of the approach has

[32] European Commission Legal Service (2022, pp 383, 387) (chapter on 'The Future of European Union Law' by Daniel Calleja and Clemens Ladenburger, respectively the Director and Deputy Director of the Commission Legal Service).
[33] von der Leyen (2025f).
[34] Koskenniemi (2024, p 37).
[35] Ackerman (2019, pp 6, 22–23) (referring explicitly to the conclusion of the Lisbon Treaty).
[36] See this chapter above, nn 1–3 and accompanying text.
[37] Strauss (2010, p 139).

acknowledged: 'A living constitution is, surely, a manipulable constitution. If the Constitution is not constant—if it changes from time to time—then someone is changing it. And that someone is changing it according to his or her own ideas about what the Constitution should look like.'[38]

Michelle Everson and Julie Eisner asked the right question about this approach almost twenty years ago: 'how [do] the lawyers, who are creating a European constitution "outside" conventional political process, sift through a multitude of competing European ideologies, establish authoritative constitutional values, and, subsequently, reconnect with the popular sentiments and aspirations that are prevalent within European society'?[39] As this book's extended analysis suggests, the transformation under NGEU appears to have been an attempt to dress up, in 'living' (ie 'as if') constitutionalist terms, a form of executive-technocratic governance to invade quite deeply into the legislative realm of mobilising and redistributing fiscal resources.

Ackerman articulates what should be, for all of us, the crucial check on this 'anything goes' propensity in EU living constitutionalism: 'The aim of interpretation is to understand the constitutional commitments that have actually been made by the … people in history, not the commitments that one or another [member of the legal elite] thinks they should have made.'[40] The idea of anchoring interpretation in actual historical commitments brings us to a crucial distinction between the American and European versions of living constitutionalism. On the US side, the advocates of living constitutionalism can rest assured that what they are interpreting is indeed a constitution, in both form and substance. It is not just that there is, in the US case, a positive enactment called a 'constitution'. This potentially trivial point is supplemented, in crucial substance, by a fact that the constitution reflects the transition of the old regime of the Articles of Confederation to a new regime of genuine *constitutional* power in the most robust sense. As Article I, Section 8, Clause 1 provides: 'Congress shall have Power To lay and collect Taxes … and provide for the … general Welfare of the United States.'[41]

In the US, in other words, the system of government was carried across the constitutional Rubicon by a foundational *Gesamtakt* of positive law,[42] that is, by a collective enactment of 'We the People'. It is upon this secure foundation that a living constitutionalism can emerge as 'an attribute of a mature society'.[43] The need for such a *Gesamtakt* is not in service to some kind of crude originalism; we fully agree that constitutional interpretations should respond to societal evolution.[44] But constitutions nonetheless need to be grounded in actual historical commitments, and a *Gesamtakt*

38 Ibid, p 2.
39 Everson and Eisner (2007, p 5).
40 Ackerman (2007, p 1754).
41 US Const, Art I, sec 8, cl 1.
42 Cf Lindseth (2016a, p 701), discussing Köck (1978).
43 Strauss (2010, p 117).
44 Ackerman (2007, p 1809).

of positive law is the very best evidence of that choice, most importantly regarding the very essence of constitutional authority: fiscal (and human) mobilisation powers. As David Strauss has argued, living constitutionalism can operate 'only within certain limits and only in ways that are rooted in the past'.[45] This prevents those in power from 'simply manipulat[ing] [the living-constitutionalist claim] to fit their own ideas'.[46] The demands of constitutional clarity and definitiveness, we would maintain, are heightened with regard to powers of legitimate compulsory mobilisation of the most fundamental type; hence the need for such a *Gesamtakt*.

On the EU side, by contrast, there has been no such *Gesamtakt*. Living constitutionalism is, instead, a profoundly elite project, attached to a set of instruments (the EU Treaties) whose purported constitutional character is the product of interpretive ratcheting by that same legal elite. The peoples of Europe, when asked, have refused even to label the Treaties a 'constitution', much less to look to them as instruments of autonomous fiscal mobilisation capacity in a constitutional sense. Without that 'constitutional commitment by the people in history', advocates of living constitutionalism in the EU seek to carry the integration project across the constitutional Rubicon on the basis of heroic legal interpretation alone, 'as if' the EU Treaties were, according to the CJEU's bootstrapping terminology, a 'constitutional charter of a Community based on the rule of law'.[47] This ratcheting of the Treaties into the purported domain of constitutional empowerment took place 'far away from political constituencies', relegating 'the world-creating and distributive aspects of institutional power to men and women whose experiences and normative expectations are geared' towards their own epistemic empowerment (even as they claim their legal expertise is neutral).[48]

The problem with this approach, socio-politically speaking, is that the EU cannot be rendered constitutional simply because a legal elite declares it to be so. It can only be rendered constitutional through a historical process of profoundly democratic politics, in which a political community confers on the governance structure the essential attributes of constitutional sovereignty, notably the capacity to extract and mobilise resources from society in a legitimate and compulsory manner (most importantly, through taxation) and then to redirect those resources to public ends.[49] The European peoples have never given the EU that power; it has remained, rather, exclusively mediated through the Member States, where the necessary democratic and constitutional legitimacy (and hence power) continues to reside. This is a fundamental expression of the 'power-legitimacy nexus' in EU public law.[50]

[45] Strauss (2010, p 3).
[46] Ibid.
[47] Case 294/83, *Parti écologiste 'Les Verts'* v *European Parliament* (1986), para 23.
[48] See Koskenniemi (2022, p 40); see also Leino-Sandberg (2025c), (2025d).
[49] See generally Lindseth (2021a).
[50] See Chapter One, nn 41–43 and accompanying text, as well as Chapter Two, Section A. For additional background, see, eg, Lindseth (2023), (2020a), (2016a).

It is, for this reason, well beyond the remit of a professional legal elite, through the act of Treaty (re-)interpretation, to short-circuit the democratic-constitutional process and declare, in effect, that all the important questions have already been answered. Europe's living (again, 'as if') constitutionalists cling to the example of 'integration through law' in which legal interpretation served—in a much lower-stakes environment—as the vehicle to transform the EU 'from an international organization to an autonomous legal regime with supremacy and direct effect'.[51] A judge of the European Court of Justice long ago justified this transformation, in an extra-judicial writing, by claiming it reflected a purported 'preference for Europe' built into 'the genetic code' of European integration.[52] The current President of the CJEU, also writing extra-judicially, has updated this justification by arguing that the 'true functional matrix of integration' and 'the very DNA of the Union' is found in the principle of solidarity.[53] From this perspective, NGEU is 'completely fundamental to deepening the bonds of solidarity woven between Member States and all their citizens, on the way to a Union more resilient in the face of crises and the challenges of globalization'.[54] The claim ignores, however, that most key redistributive policies in the European context—such as social security, health, and education—remain explicitly under Member State competence and cannot be subject to legislative harmonisation measures at EU level. Given that 'competences not conferred upon the Union in the Treaties remain with the Member States' (Article 4(1) TEU), it is difficult to treat these gaps as if they were mere 'silences of the Constitution' that can be filled in to 'improve and complete the constitutional project'.[55]

As we noted in Chapter Five,[56] in the domain of fiscal mobilisation capacity, constitutionalists of the 'living' sort lament how 'the Union [was] never fully emancipated' from its national constitutional foundations, as it had been in the legal and regulatory realm under 'integration through law'.[57] Nonetheless, an autonomous fiscal capacity was, according to this view, still 'intended for by the authors of the Treaties, as a complement to the autonomy of its legal order',[58] a claim made on the basis of the thinnest historical conjecture. The idea of the EU as not yet fully 'emancipated' (and hence now acting contrary to the previously obscured intent of the Treaties) may be a powerful rhetorical device—as is the idea of 'solidarity'. But these statements presuppose the existence of a constitutional commitment that has not been made by the European peoples in history, that fiscal autonomy is the telos of integration on par with legal autonomy. These statements, taken to their logical conclusion, reflect a mindset (or

[51] Grund and Steinbach (2024, p 993) (Abstract).
[52] Mancini and Keeling (1994, p 186).
[53] Lenaerts and Adam (2021, p 417) (authors' translation).
[54] Ibid.
[55] See Loughlin (2018, p 923).
[56] See Chapter Five, n 518 and accompanying text.
[57] Grund and Steinbach (2024, p 993) (Abstract).
[58] Crowe (2024, p 70).

set of presumptions) that are both radical but nonetheless deeply recognisable in the history of European integration. They suggest that it is the role of the EU professional legal elite—just as in the halcyon days of 'integration through law'—to emancipate the EU through reinterpreting the Treaties so that it may pursue its true intent and telos of solidarity.

This captures what we might call the ideal-type of 'as if' constitutionalism transferred into the fiscal domain. This ideal-type, operating under the guise of living constitutionalism, assumes that the EU is *already* robustly constitutional but is now being prevented from living up to its true character by some unnamed apostates (normally read: Member State governments) who have successfully diverted the integration project from its true path.[59] From this perspective, while Treaty change might be helpful, there is no actual need for it, because purposive (evolutive and teleological) interpretation of the existing Treaties can do most of the work.[60] 'A revision of the Treaties would certainly open up new possibilities' one might say, but 'the wide margin of discretion that the current Treaties already afford the institutions in the design of the Union's budgetary system should not be overlooked'.[61] 'Treaty changes [are] not a precondition for Europe to move forward: much can be done with targeted adjustments.'[62] '[T]he EU Treaties are a living instrument, whose interpretation can be adjusted in light of changing circumstances ... [O]ne could conceive of Article 175 TFEU as a self-standing legal basis to enact another fiscal stimulus programme at EU level.'[63] And so on.

There is, in other words, no need to engage in the hard work of democratic-constitutional politics *today* about what kind of Europe is needed *now and in the future*, because the important questions were already (mostly) answered *in the past*—and if they were not, the law itself (read: EU legal professionals) can provide the answers simply by turning to the tool of 'living' ('as if') constitutionalism. An *already* constitutional EU could thus be justified, without Treaty change but through the simple act of reinterpretation, to override the public meaning of the Treaties as established by nearly seven decades of institutional practice and democratic politics[64]—that is, real living constitutionalism in action—according to which the EU 'remains dependent on Member States in securing funding to fulfil its objectives'.[65]

59 Cf Baquero Cruz (2018).

60 For example, because 'the Treaty authorizes Member States to create new types of own resources[,] ... creating debt as a new type of own resource seems to be a "legally workable" solution'. Grund and Steinbach (2024, p 1015). See also (2024b, p 307).

61 Crowe (2024, p 70).

62 Draghi Report (2024a, p 67); see also Draghi Report (2024b, p 307) ('much is already possible with targeted adjustments without the need for [Treaty] change').

63 Fabbrini (2022a, p 61); see also Panascì (2024, p 45, n 95).

64 See, eg, the discussion of including debt-financing in the category of new 'own resources' in Chapter Five, nn 527–28 and accompanying text.

65 Grund and Steinbach (2024, p 993) (Abstract).

C. Testing the Boundaries: EU Taxes, New Common Borrowing, and Regulation by Spending in Areas of National Competence

The NGEU model has arguably brought integration to the edge of the constitutional Rubicon of autonomous fiscal mobilisation and has raised hopes for many that a decisive move beyond those constitutional limits is in the offing. These hopes were, at least partly, dashed by the Commission's MFF and ORD proposals of July 2025, which, while seeking to generalise the planning and spending model, marked a retreat towards the traditional constitutional terrain in terms of borrowing-for-lending rather than borrowing-for-spending. For the moment at least, a decisive Hamiltonian transition seems to have been put off until some unknown point in the future.

Nonetheless, in other more subtle ways, the Commission's MFF and ORD proposals were still testing constitutional boundaries. As we saw in Chapter Six, the Commission's proposal for a Corporate Resource for Europe (CORE)—if it survives (and there is doubt on that score)—could well test the line between a traditional own resource and an outright European tax, raising numerous questions of design and implementation as well as legality.[66] On the debt-financing side, the Commission's proposed 'targeted' tool to serve as a 'shortcut to enable [common borrowing] for a crisis'[67] is also testing multiple boundaries, between unanimity and QMV, and, more subtly, between own resources and collective borrowing. The tool looks to the ORD adopted by unanimity under Article 311(3) TFEU to define the general parameters of any future emergency borrowing, and yet it contemplates triggering emergency borrowing in specific cases via QMV under Article 311(4) TFEU. In doing so, the new tool arguably sediments a potentially transgressive legal claim:[68] that common borrowing is now so thoroughly related to the 'the Union's own resources system'—the key scope language in Article 311(4) TFEU—that grounding specific instances of borrowing on this provision becomes justified. In this sense, while the new tool may not have overtly declared debt-financing to be a new category of own resources as some commentators had advocated,[69] it comes as close as possible by exploiting this language of Article 311(4) TFEU. Indeed, the Commission's proposal draws on the logic of those debt-as-own-resources advocates by arguing the 'Union needs to continue to provide itself with the means to attain its objectives',[70] drawing on the language of Article 311 TFEU.

The line that the Commission is testing most vigorously, however, is the one between spending and regulation. By seeking to generalise the transactional model of

[66] See Chapter Six, Section B.2.

[67] von der Leyen (2025e).

[68] On the notion of 'sedimentation' in legal argumentation, see Tuori (2013).

[69] See Chapter Five, nn 527–28 and accompanying text.

[70] European Commission (2025v, p 4, recital (20)). Compare Grund and Steinbach (2024, pp 1008–09); see also Crowe (2024, p 65).

NGEU across large sections of the new MFF, the Commission's proposals seek to augment, through the funding channel, its steering capacities in numerous domains, including several belonging to national competence over which the EU lacks competence to regulate directly. As the NGEU model has demonstrated, the incentives for both the Member States and the Commission are often seriously misaligned in this regard. The prospect of increased EU funding to national budgets has often led Member States (as well as political actors within Member States) to welcome increased Commission policy steering as the price of budgetary support. Because the Commission has desired to augment its institutional position, it has seemed more than happy to involve itself in these essentially national matters, thus diverting its attention away from matters of greater European importance.[71] Cross-national scrutiny mechanisms under the NGEU and RRF did essentially nothing to counteract these misaligned incentives, allowing them to operate unchecked. They were on full display in Ursula von der Leyen's State of the Union speech in September 2025, which included calls for a 'European Affordable Housing Plan' and a 'European Anti-Poverty Strategy'—both policy domains squarely in national competence.[72] Von der Leyen's operating slogan—'If it matters to Europeans, it matters to Europe'—aptly expressed the incentive structure that 'integration through funding' now seems to entail. It also demonstrated the inability of the Commission to focus on matters where the EU can actually be useful.

One might fairly ask: what is wrong with Europe being responsive to political hopes in this way? The problem is not that the policy goals are not worthy—most would agree they are. The problem is that the Union's resources are limited—*very* limited—and housing and anti-poverty work are both expensive and involve little or no European added value. It is purely a question of opportunity costs. The Commission devoting resources (including its own time and attention) to areas best left to the Member States means that it is taking resources away from European public goods that will otherwise be underproduced without concerted efforts at the EU level. As discussed in earlier chapters, the performance of NGEU and more particularly the RRF in this regard offers a cautionary tale, by creating burdensome debt-service obligations that continue to syphon scarce resources away from more pressing needs in European security, defence, and competitiveness.

The misaligned incentives of the NGEU model have been reinforced at multiple junctures by the elasticity of many of the justifications typically advanced to justify the EU's steering role ('solidarity', 'resilience', and above all 'cohesion'). At the highest level of abstraction, who could possibly oppose such laudable goals? The problem is that, on a more granular level, they are ultimately boundless, imposing no limits on spending whatsoever. This boundlessness has contributed to the sense that a European interest could be found for any spending, even if it would have little or no impact on the production of public goods with high European added value. As we discussed in detail in Chapters Three and Four, the ratcheting of cohesion in particular—with a dose of

[71] See Chapter Four, Section E.
[72] von der Leyen (2025g).

solidarity and resilience thrown in as needed—has had the effect of breaking down the EU's competence structure almost entirely. This is particularly the case given the scale of money now flowing through the cohesion channel. 'More' truly has become 'different',[73] transforming the nature of the integration project, albeit not in ways that conduce to meeting the challenges now facing Europe as a whole. To produce European public goods in the future, substantive constraints on EU spending must entail more discipline than 'cohesion', 'solidarity', or 'resilience' can provide.

The misaligned incentives of the NGEU model have also arguably led the EU to adopt, in effect, a legally untenable position in what we called above the 'Hamilton-Madison debate' on the relationship between spending and regulatory powers, drawn from the constitutional history of the United States.[74] As we noted in Chapter Four, many EU lawyers and legal scholars now assume that 'the transactional nature of policy implementation [under the NGEU model] confers on the EU flexible tools to negotiate beyond the competence restrictions set in the Treaties'.[75] In the end, the claim that the transactional NGEU model has provided a new channel for the EU to exert authority beyond the competence limitations in the Treaties—even if true as a socio-political matter—should be regarded as unacceptable in normative-legal terms. The similar claim in US law at least has some basic grounding in foundational *Gesamtakt* of positive law: Article I, Section 8, Clause 1 of the United States Constitution. Moreover, that claim in the US is subject to limits flowing from broader constitutional commitments to federalism.[76] In the EU, the claim lacks any grounding in the Treaties (beyond 'cohesion' in the broadest sense, detached from its historic meaning); moreover, it operates apparently free from *controlimiti* derived from the autonomously sovereign nature of the Member States. Creating a transactional frame to obscure political responsibility for often unpopular structural reforms are features, not bugs, in the NGEU model. As such, they reflect precisely the sort of 'anything goes'/'living'/'as if' constitutionalism that should be avoided, not embraced, in defining the path forward in the integration process.

D. Technocracy, Democratic Politics, and European Public Goods

Debates about the future of the integration project already suffer from a number of limitations. Most importantly, they rarely command public attention beyond a specialised circle of EU geeks and a limited group of EU-focused media outlets. Equally problematic is the underlying assumption often operating in these debates—that it is not really possible, even if it were desirable, to engage the broader public on

[73] See Chapter One, nn 63–68 and accompanying text.
[74] See Chapter Four, Section D.6.
[75] Fasone and Simoncini (2025, p 1164).
[76] *South Dakota v Dole*, 483 US 203 (1987); *Nat'l Fed'n of Indep Bus v Sebelius*, 567 US 519 (2012).

European questions. Treaty change often offers the best route for broad-based democratic engagement, but among pro-European forces that option is now apparently assumed to be out of the question. This assumption reflects the fear that, if subjected to broader debate, needed reforms might not gather sufficient support. Deepening this concern is the increasing electoral success of populist parties as well as the presence of authoritarian governments around the EU negotiation table, who do not hesitate to hijack reform negotiations for other political purposes. This is a serious concern that we also share.

In view of these assumptions and fears, the EU feels compelled to fall back on its standard modus operandi, disguising fundamentally political questions as matters of legal expertise or technocratic decision-making.[77] While that strategy may have been sustainable when the EU's function was primarily regulatory (under a system of 'integration through law'), the functional demands of the last half decade (under an emergent system of 'integration through funding') have placed the EU's legitimacy resources under considerable strain. The temptation to shift important political questions into a fragmented, opaque, and technocratic planning and spending process may be understandable ('something must be done', 'we can do it!'). Nonetheless, avoiding a broader public debate about what Europe's needs are, as well as how its objectives should be reached (notably through expanded collective borrowing), simply gives the impression that Europe is resigned to stick to its traditional model of transformation through elite constitutionalism rather than democratic politics.

Because of the reliance on technocracy, little attempt has been made to devise legal constraints on the Commission's discretion within this fragmented and opaque planning and spending process. Nor would such constraints likely be effective, given that beyond questions of formal procedure, the von der Leyen Commission does not seem to think that legal constraints prevent it from doing what it thinks needs to be done. What the integration project needs, however, is more *political* mobilisation across EU institutions (the Commission, the Council, and the Parliament) as well as in the EU's polycentric and *demoi*-cratic power centres (that is, national governments, national parliaments, as well as regional and local institutions) around a shared understanding of what a new system of 'integration through funding' is best for. In this regard, the NGEU model should serve as a cautionary tale, particularly in view of its misaligned incentives or its ultimately undisciplined spending under elastic conceptions of cohesion, solidarity, and resilience.

Emphasising the key role of political mobilisation is not meant to suggest that there is no role for legal reforms going forward, including in the Treaties themselves. Article 122 TFEU could benefit from revision to specify both its substantive and temporal scope as well as its role as a legislative procedure, which requires further specification of EP involvement. Additionally, the likely continued role of external assigned revenues as part of the EU's financial landscape should mean incorporating EAR within

[77] This practice in fact has deep roots in the history of European integration. See, eg, Lindseth (2010, p 107).

the EU's formal budgetary and auditing processes. Moreover, the EU's increasing role in defence should lead to a reform of Article 41 TEU. But finally, we also think that the reinterpretation of the cohesion flexibility clause of Article 175(3) TFEU as a general spending legal basis (especially when combined with the 'financing not linked to costs' model) should be reversed—precisely because it is an invitation to spend in an undisciplined and ad hoc way.

Recourse to the open-ended cohesion flexibility clause of Article 175(3) TFEU is in fact unnecessary. The reality is that the EU *already* has competence, under Part Three of the TFEU, to pursue numerous crucial European public goods (relating to the environment, energy, industry, trans-European networks, research and technological development, migration, cross-border dimensions of public health, disaster response, defence, and many others). Indeed, the scope of these specified competences are so extensive that it is difficult to think of a European public good that would not already be covered by strong EU competences. This should not come as a surprise, given that it is the logical consequence of the way the Treaties have been written to promote the joint handling of transnational issues that require European-wide problem solving. Legal framing matters. There is no competence-related reason why the NGEU's environmental and climate objectives could not have been regulated based on explicit legal bases, rather than creating a 'green pillar' within a cohesion policy measure and then requiring that at least 37% of the recovery and resilience plan's total allocation be devoted to the green transition. As Chapter Four demonstrated, while the NGEU model created enormous flexibility to allocate the funds in national envelopes, it resulted in highly inefficient policy measures from the environmental and climate perspectives.[78] In order to ensure greater focus, the EU needs more detailed legislative frameworks building on EU competences, but also political debate and control of how its scarce resources are to be used under these existing dedicated legal bases. Rather than trying to buy its way into national competence spheres, the Commission should rediscover its own function in the properly European competence sphere.

Another area for reform relates to the transparency in the way the Commission operates. The institutional mindset in the Commission is geared to minimising the possibilities for outsiders to question its choices, which is best ensured by limiting transparency. Despite its Treaty obligation to act 'as openly as possible',[79] the Commission is rarely proactive in making available a complete documentary record of any actions relating to legislation, planning, spending, borrowing, or policy analysis (including legal analysis) in the implementation of the EU's strategic priorities. While the Court has scrutinised the Commission's understanding of its transparency obligations to a limited extent, the Ombudsman investigations have highlighted how the Commission seldom sees transparency as a possibility, and even less an obligation, let alone as something that could actually enhance the acceptability of its own actions and support it in ensuring the proper use of Union funds.

[78] See Chapter Four, Section D.1.
[79] Article 15(1) TFEU.

At this point in time, it seems unclear what 'integration through funding' actually means. Under the RRF, it arguably did not really mean integration at all—it simply referred to a model in which the EU funded national policies based on national plans under deeply constrained EU scrutiny. In a world of unlimited EU funds this might work but, from a 'value for money' perspective, it was far from an ideal choice, considerably reducing the EU's opportunities to fund objectives that have real European relevance. Moreover, strengthening the steering capacity of EU institutions in these policy areas would require more than just money—it would require EU institutions with democratic mandates, supported by the emergence of a European public sphere engaged in critical debate about Europe's strategic priorities. To make progress along this dimension, it is crucial to address the information asymmetries that have restricted robust oversight of the Commission as the key player in the 'transactional' NGEU model. Too often under NGEU, particularly in the final stretch of the 'road to 2026', the Commission gave the impression that the real purpose of the programme was simply to spend the allocated money in full and—as an important by-product—augment its institutional position, with little regard to the actual value added of the spending.[80]

The opaque and technocratic character of the planning, borrowing, and spending process under NGEU further allowed the Commission to control the flow of information, maintaining a highly curated picture of the system in action. As the European Court of Auditors found, there was little attempt by the Commission to make its underlying policy decisions 'traceable'.[81] Indeed, it often seemed determined to do exactly the opposite, despite the availability of advanced forms of information technology that would enable timely retention of relevant documents as well as disclosure to other EU institutions or the public in appropriate circumstances. Given the ambitiousness of the planning and spending model contemplated by the July 2025 MFF and ORD proposals, the Commission needs to move towards what the European Ombudsman, together with the OECD, earlier described as 'a whole-of-society approach', in which 'transparency, social accountability, and oversight of public decision making' must be assured to the greatest extent possible.[82]

Strengthening transparency must also entail making the *legal* choices visible, as well the justifications on which they are based. Making legal advice publicly available, regardless of form, enables the public to debate its quality or contest its conclusions against alternative readings and their consequences. The case law has consistently recognised the importance of disclosing legal interpretations despite the persistent opposition of the institutional legal services. The Court has underlined the need to enable 'citizens to participate more closely in the decision-making process', which in turn 'guarantees that the administration enjoys greater legitimacy and is more effective and more accountable to the citizen in a democratic system'.[83] This requires,

[80] See Chapter Four, Section E.
[81] European Court of Auditors (2022a, p 18).
[82] OECD and European Ombudsman (2022, p 6). See Chapter Four, Section A.2.
[83] Joined Cases C-39/05 P and C-52/05 P, *Sweden and Turco v Council* (2008), para 45.

above all, the ability to 'scrutinise all the information which has formed the basis for a legislative act', including legal advice, as a 'precondition for the effective exercise of their democratic rights'.[84]

These basic principles are obviously uncomfortable for EU institutions, as our own experience seeking access to their advice outlined in this book makes clear.[85] But rather than giving in to the temptation of non-transparency, the institutions need to recognise that the 'lack of information and debate' is worse, because it gives 'rise to doubts in the minds of citizens, not only as regards the legitimacy of an isolated act, but also as regards the legitimacy of the decision-making process as a whole'.[86] The Commission, in particular, seems to be intent on moving in the opposite direction, doing its utmost to frustrate the work of researchers and investigative journalists who have tried to provide a critical analysis of its work. Reinforcing this trend are the Commission's recently reformed Rules of Procedure, which create a new presumption of secrecy for all its legal advice, 'unless the applicant demonstrates an overriding public interest'.[87] The Commission apparently does not want to allow prying eyes to watch it 'filling [the Treaties] with life',[88] in the fear of being subjected to 'undue external pressure'.[89] Yet it is precisely that pressure that is a cornerstone of, and indeed breathes life into, a modern democratic system.[90]

When it comes to accessing legal advice specifically, the unit that most empathically seeks to limit public scrutiny has been the Commission Legal Service,[91] whose lawyers are also among the most vocal advocates of a 'living constitution'. The development of the legal underpinnings of the NGEU model took place in an entirely secret negotiation process between Council and Commission officials, apparently grounded in key respects on 'one or two [PowerPoint] slides' which the Commission Legal Service has refused to produce.[92] To be truly 'alive', rather than merely an elite construction, a living constitution depends on healthy democratic exchange and an informed citizenry, which in turn depends on public institutions living up to their obligations of transparency, participation, and explanation. If the Commission Legal Service believes in a democratic and constitutional Europe, 'living' or otherwise, it should embrace the right of the public to call power-holders to account—including its lawyers, who serve a vital public service function in interpreting the law—even when this feels inconvenient and risks inefficiencies in the short term. '[O]ne or two [PowerPoint] slides' cannot substitute for that necessary democratic process, particularly given that the Commission Legal Service still today, several years after the

[84] Ibid, para 46; see also Case C-57/16 P *ClientEarth v Commission* (2018), para 75.
[85] See Introduction, Section C.
[86] Joined Cases C-39/05 P and C-52/05 P, *Sweden and Turco v Council* (2008), para 59; see also C-506/08 P, *Sweden v MyTravel and Commission* (2011), para 113.
[87] Commission Decision (EU) 2024/3080, art 4(2)(c).
[88] von der Leyen (2025f).
[89] European Commission (2022e, p 14).
[90] See Chapter Four, nn 162–63 and accompanying text.
[91] See this Conclusion above, nn 9, 31–32 and accompanying text.
[92] See Chapter Three, 130–32 and accompanying text.

transformation took place, refuses to disclose, debate, and defend its legal reasoning in public.

Beyond these fundamental obligations, the legal services of European institutions also need to do their part, on a more prosaic level, to reconsider what the European interest actually means beyond just enhancing the power of the supranational level more generally. A broader understanding of the European interest should mean bringing questions of subsidiarity and national competences more directly into legal analysis. We agree with the Draghi Report that increased attention to subsidiarity is essential to the pursuit of European public goods; but we disagree that the only option is either increased capacity of national parliaments or Commission 'self-restraint' (something that has not been abundant supply within the Commission during the RRF experiment).[93] Subsidiarity is, or should be, a substantive legal imperative for the Commission rather than a procedural step treated as a box-ticking exercise. Subsidiarity and European added value are the flip sides of the same coin; greater emphasis on subsidiarity would, as a necessary byproduct, also help sharpen the Commission's focus on European public goods and European added value.

In addition to addressing the legal aspects of subsidiarity, the institutional legal services should highlight any undue encroachments on domains belonging to Member States under the Treaties. During the research for this book, we found exactly one legal opinion (from the Council Legal Service in March 2020, on cross-border administrative cooperation) expressing concerns about the EU trespassing on national competence under the cohesion flexibility clause in Article 175(3) TFEU.[94] All the opinions pertinent to the construction of the NGEU or its earlier incarnations sought to justify the envisaged measures through an expansive reinterpretation of that provision with little regard to the established competence structure in the Treaties, or the existing case law on the scope of EU power under the cohesion flexibility clause.[95] The impact of the resulting measures on the functions of national parliaments or democratic decision-making simply was not raised, much less explored.[96]

The failure to consider the democratic implications of the reinterpretation reflected a set of presumptions that lawyers in the legal services had come to accept more or less unconsciously. No doubt, it has often fallen to EU lawyers, at the behest of political leaders, to find a way to respond to some very real challenges in the absence of Treaty change, enabling the EU to do a number of unprecedented things. Nonetheless, this legal ingenuity has also led to the capture of Treaty interpretation by a professional elite whose biases and blind spots are hidden behind an impenetrable idiomatic language, not to mention nondisclosure pure and simple. The result is a governance model that undermines democratic accountability and control at both EU and

[93] See Chapter Six, n 123 and accompanying text, discussing Draghi Report (2024b, p 310).

[94] See Council Legal Service (2020c).

[95] See Chapter Three, Section A. The only contexts in which national budgetary sovereignty was considered related to ratification of ORDs, as well as to the possibility of concluding an intergovernmental agreement to complement one of the euro-area budget instruments.

[96] European Commission (2020a) [Q&A].

national levels. The impact on legal debate has been particularly unfortunate: when instrumentalist legal interpretation becomes the baseline against which all other interpretations of the Treaties are measured, any defence of established readings of the law, regardless of their rigour or aims, becomes suspect as disguised (or 'reactionary') opposition to the political project of integration as a whole.[97] What is lost in these circumstances is not merely the stability of law but any semblance of means-end rationality or sense of cost-benefit trade-offs involved in legal choice.

Europeans of all stripes should be cautious not to lapse into the view that there is only one 'right' way to think about integration, one purportedly 'required by the Treaties', one that is dictated by the 'trajectory of history', or simply one that is just legally 'true'. The obscurity of the political choices buried under these claims is a serious democratic problem for Europe. It treats the European constitution not as truly 'living' but as a rhetorical instrument of elite empowerment whose variability and susceptibility to shifting political demands contradicts its core purpose of memorialising enduring constitutional commitments. A constitution must undoubtedly be 'sufficiently flexible and sufficiently rigid', as de Witte has rightly argued.[98] It must adapt to new circumstances but it cannot live like there is no tomorrow (or no yesterday, for that matter). A constitution that lives too hard and beyond its means risks turning into a dead constitution. To live and age gracefully, a constitution must remain faithful to the will of 'We the People' expressed at particular historical moments, as Ackerman has maintained.[99]

No such 'constitutional moment' has yet occurred in Europe, at least not in the most robust sense of genuine fiscal capacities. That moment may yet come in the future, and we would certainly welcome its arrival. It would suggest that a European 'people' has emerged to confer on the EU the power and legitimacy to mobilise human and fiscal resources ('blood and treasure'), which is the essence of genuine constitutional authority. The integration project increasingly needs such mobilisation. But short of the equally necessary constitutional transformation to make it happen, Europe will remain mired in the borderlands in which it currently finds itself, with tools limited to technocratic solutions and legal engineering that are inadequate to the challenges before it. In these circumstances, claims of 'living' constitutionalism will continue to ring hollow, remaining simply a variant of 'as if' constitutionalism destined to disappoint.

97 Cf Panascì (2024, p 54).
98 de Witte (2009).
99 Ackerman (1991).

Bibliography

Cases

[alphabetical by jurisdiction and case name, then reverse chronological]

European Union

Case T-77/22, *Asesores Comunitarios, SL v the European Commission*, Judgment (General Court), 15 February 2023, ECLI:EU:T:2023:69.

Case C-57/16 P, *ClientEarth v Commission*, Judgment (Grand Chamber), 4 September 2018, ECLI:EU:C:2018:660.

Case 242/87, *Commission v Council*, Judgment, 30 May 1989, ECLI:EU:C:1989:217.

Case C-408/21 P, *Council v Laurent Pech*, Judgment, 8 June 2023, ECLI:EU:C:2023:461.

Case T-146/25, *De Capitani and Others v Commission*, action brought on 28 February 2025, https://curia.europa.eu/juris/document/document.jsf?text=&docid=298621&pageIndex=0&doclang=EN&mode=req&dir=&occ=first&part=1&cid=3793890

Case C-19/23, *Denmark v Parliament and Council* (Alternative Minimum Wages), Opinion of Advocate General Emiliou, 14 January 2025, ECLI:EU:C:2025:11.

Case C-62/14, *Gauweiler and others*, Judgment (Grand Chamber), 16 June 2015, ECLI:EU:C:2015:400.

Case C-376/98, *Germany v Parliament and Council* (Tobacco Advertising), Judgment, 5 October 2000, ECLI:EU:C:2000:544.

Case 265/87, *Hermann Schräder HS Kraftfutter GmbH & Co KG v Hauptzollamt Gronau*, Judgment, 11 July 1989, ECLI:EU:C:1989:303.

Case C-156/21, *Hungary v Parliament and Council*, Judgment (Full Court), 16 February 2022, ECLI:EU:C:2022:97.

Case C-156/21, *Hungary v Parliament and Council*, Opinion of Advocate General Campos Sánchez-Bordona of 2 December 2021, ECLI:EU:C:2021:974.

Case C-135/11 P, *IFAW Internationaler Tierschutz-Fonds v Commission*, Judgment of 21 June 2012, ECLI:EU:C:2012:376.

Case T-356/24, *Lithuania v Commission*, action brought on 16 July 2024 to annul Commission Implementing Decision C(2024) 3171 final on the reduction of the amount of the first instalment of the non-repayable support for Lithuania, 2024 OJ C/2024/5424 https://eur-lex.europa.eu/legal-content/EN/TXT/HTML/?uri=OJ%3AC_202405424&.

Case C-130/10, *Parliament v Council*, Judgment (Grand Chamber), 19 July 2012, ECLI:EU:C:2012:472.

Case C-166/07, *Parliament v Council (International Fund for Ireland)*, Judgment, 3 September 2009, ECLI:EU:C:2009:499.

Case C-166/07, *Parliament v Council (International Fund for Ireland)*, Opinion of Advocate General Bot, 2 April 2009, ECLI: ECLI:EU:C:2009:213.

Case 294/83, *Parti écologiste 'Les Verts' v European Parliament*, Judgment, 23 April 1986, ECLI:EU:C:1986:166.

Case C-157/21 *Poland v Parliament and Council*, Judgment (Full Court), 16 February 2022, ECLI:EU:C:2021:978.

Case C-157/21, *Poland v Parliament and Council*, Judgment (Full Court), 16 February 2022, ECLI:EU:C:2022:98.

Case C-370/12, *Pringle v Government of Ireland and others*, Judgment (Full Court), 27 November 2012, ECLI:EU:C:2012:756.

Case C-265/87, *Schräder v Hauptzollamt Gronau*, Judgment, 11 July 1989, ECLI:EU:C:1989:303.

Case T-669/11, *Spirlea v Commission*, Judgment (General Court), 25 September 2014, ECLI:EU:T:2014:814.

Case T-36/23, *Stevi and The New York Times v Commission*, Judgment (General Court, Grand Chamber), 14 May 2025, ECLI:EU:T:2025:483.

C-506/08 P, *Sweden v MyTravel and Commission*, Judgment, 21 July 2011, ECLI:EU:C:2011:496.

Joined Cases C-39/05 P and C-52/05 P, *Sweden and Turco v Council*, Judgment (Grand Chamber), 1 July 2008, ECLI:EU:C:2008:374.

Case C-106/96, *UK v Commission*, Judgment, 12 May 1998, ECLI:EU:C:1998:218.

Case C-493/17, *Weiss and others*, Judgment (Grand Chamber), 11 December 2018, ECLI:EU:C:2018:1000.

Case C-533/24, *Vermilion Energy Ireland and Others*: Reference for a preliminary ruling from High Court (Ireland) made on 1 August 2024—*Vermilion Energy Ireland Ltd, Vermilion Exploration and Production Ireland Ltd, Vermilion Energy Corrib Ireland Ltd v The Minister for the Environment, Climate and Communications, Ireland, The Attorney General*, 2024 OJ C/2024/6632, https://eur-lex.europa.eu/eli/C/2024/6632/oj/eng.

France

Décision n° 2023-849 DC du 14 avril 2023, Loi de financement rectificative de la sécurité sociale pour 2023, https://www.conseil-constitutionnel.fr/decision/2023/2023849DC.htm.

Germany

BVerfG, 2 BvR 547/21 and 2 BvR 798/21, Judgment of the Second Senate of 6 December 2022 (Act Ratifying the EU Own Resources Decision—Next Generation EU) [official English translation] https://www.bundesverfassungsgericht.de/SharedDocs/Entscheidungen/EN/2022/12/rs20221206_2bvr054721en.html;jsessionid=649F325E661BF8E4DF380E6815764405.internet961.

BVerfG, Judgment of the Second Senate of 30 June 2009 [Treaty of Lisbon], 2 BvE 2/08, 2 BvE 5/08, 2 BvR 1010/08, 2 BvR 1022/08, 2 BvR 1259/08, 2 BvR 182/09 [Official English Translation] https://www.bundesverfassungsgericht.de/SharedDocs/Entscheidungen/EN/2009/06/es20090630_2bve000208en.html.

Brunner v European Union Treaty, Cases 2 BvR 2134/92 and 2159/92 of 12 October 1993, BVerfGE 89, 155, translated at 33 ILM 388 (1994).

United States

Nat'l Fed'n of Indep Bus v Sebelius, 567 US 519 (2012).

United States v Butler, 297 US 1 (1936).

West Virginia v US Dep't of the Treasury, 59 F 4th 1124 (11th Cir 2023).

Legislative Acts and Other Instruments

[alphabetical by instrument type, then reverse chronological]

Commission Decision (EU, Euratom) 2025/369 of 21 February 2025 establishing the role of the Chief Risk Officer overseeing the financial risks arising from the Union's financial operations, 2025 OJ L, 2025/369.

Commission Decision (EU) 2024/3080 of 4 December 2024 establishing the Rules of Procedure of the Commission and amending Decision C(2000) 3614, 2024 OJ L, 2024/3080.

Commission Decision (EU, Euratom) 2021/625 of 14 April 2021 on the establishment of the primary dealer network and the definition of eligibility criteria for lead and co-lead mandates for syndicated transactions for the purposes of the borrowing activities by the Commission on behalf of the Union and of the European Atomic Energy Community, 2021 OJ L 131/170.

Commission Delegated Regulation (EU) 2021/2106 of 28 September 2021 on supplementing Regulation (EU) 2021/241 of the European Parliament and of the Council establishing the Recovery and Resilience Facility by setting out the common indicators and the detailed elements of the recovery and resilience scoreboard, 2021 OJ L 429/83.

Commission Delegated Regulation (EU) 2019/856 of 26 February 2019 supplementing Directive 2003/87/EC of the European Parliament and of the Council with regard to the operation of the Innovation Fund (Text with EEA relevance), 2019 OJ L 140/6.

Commission Delegated Regulation (EU) 2019/694 of 15 February 2019 supplementing Regulation (EU) 1303/2013 of the European Parliament and of the Council with regard to the form of financing which is not linked to costs of the relevant operations, 2019 OJ L 118/4.

Commission Implementing Decision (EU, Euratom) 2023/2825 of 12 December 2023 establishing the arrangements for the administration and implementation of the Union borrowing and debt management operations under the diversified funding strategy and related lending operations, 2023 OJ L 2023/2825.

Council Decision (EU) 2022/1026 of 21 June 2022 on the position to be adopted, on behalf of the European Union, within the EEA Joint Committee concerning the amendment of Protocol 31 on cooperation in specific fields outside the four freedoms and Protocol 32 on financial modalities for implementation of Article 82, annexed to the EEA Agreement (InvestEU) (Text with EEA relevance), ST/9349/2022/INIT, 2022 OJ L 172/13.

Council Decision (CFSP) 2022/338 of 28 February 2022 on an assistance measure under the European Peace Facility for the supply to the Ukrainian Armed Forces of military equipment, and platforms, designed to deliver lethal force, 2022 OJ L 60/1.

Council Decision (CFSP) 2021/509 of 22 March 2021 establishing a European Peace Facility, and repealing Decision (CFSP) 2015/528, 2021 OJ L 102/14.

Council Decision (EU, Euratom) 2020/2053 of 14 December 2020 on the system of own resources of the European Union and repealing Decision 2014/335/EU, Euratom, 2020 OJ L 424/1.

Council Decision (EU) 2015/900 of 8 June 2015 on the position to be adopted, on behalf of the European Union, within the EEA Joint Committee concerning an amendment to Protocol 31 to the EEA Agreement, on cooperation in specific fields outside the four freedoms (EaSI), 2015 OJ L 147/19.

Council Decision (EU) 2015/632 of 20 April 2015 repealing Council Decision 77/706/EEC on the setting of a Community target for a reduction in the consumption of primary sources of energy in the event of difficulties in the supply of crude oil and petroleum products and Commission Decision 79/639/EEC laying down detailed rules for the implementation of Council Decision 77/706/EEC, 2015 OJ L 104/12.

Council Decision 2014/348/EU of 5 June 2014 on the position to be adopted, on behalf of the European Union, within the EEA Joint Committee concerning an amendment to Protocol 31 to the EEA Agreement, on cooperation in specific fields outside the four freedoms, 2014 OJ L 174/40.

Council Directive 2009/119/EC of 14 September 2009 imposing an obligation on Member States to maintain minimum stocks of crude oil and/or petroleum products, 2009 OJ L 265/9.

Council Implementing Decision (CFSP) 2024/2760 of 24 October 2024 implementing Decision 2014/512/CFSP concerning restrictive measures in view of Russia's actions destabilising the situation in Ukraine, 2024 OJ L 2024/2760.

Council Regulation (EU) 2024/1264 of 29 April 2024 amending Regulation (EC) No 1467/97 on speeding up and clarifying the implementation of the excessive deficit procedure, 2024 OJ L 2024/1264.

Council Regulation (EU, Euratom) 2024/765 of 29 February 2024 amending Regulation (EU, Euratom) 2020/2093 laying down the multiannual financial framework for the years 2021 to 2027, 2024 OJ L 2024/765.

Council Regulation (EU) 2022/2578 of 22 December 2022 establishing a market correction mechanism to protect Union citizens and the economy against excessively high prices, 2022 OJ L 335/45.

Council Regulation (EU) 2022/2577 of 22 December 2022 laying down a framework to accelerate the deployment of renewable energy, 2022 OJ L 335/36.

Council Regulation (EU) 2022/2576 of 19 December 2022 enhancing solidarity through better coordination of gas purchases, reliable price benchmarks and exchanges of gas across borders, 2022 OJ L 335/1.

Council Regulation (EU, Euratom) 2022/2496 of 15 December 2022 amending Regulation (EU, Euratom) 2020/2093 laying down the multiannual financial framework for the years 2021 to 2027, 2022 OJ L 325/11.

Council Regulation (EU) 2022/2372 of 24 October 2022 on a framework of measures for ensuring the supply of crisis-relevant medical countermeasures in the event of a public health emergency at Union level, 2022 OJ L 314/64.

Council Regulation (EU) 2022/1854 of 6 October 2022 on an emergency intervention to address high energy prices, 2022 OJ L 261I/1.

Council Regulation (EU) 2022/257 of 22 December 2022 laying down a framework to accelerate the deployment of renewable energy, 2022 OJ L 335/36.

Council Regulation (EU) 2022/1369 of 5 August 2022 on coordinated demand-reduction measures for gas, 2022 OJ L 206/1.

Council Regulation (EU, Euratom) 2021/770 of 30 April 2021 on the calculation of the own resource based on plastic packaging waste that is not recycled, on the methods and procedure for making available that own resource, on the measures to meet cash requirements, and on certain aspects of the own resource based on gross national income, 2021 OJ L 165/15.

Council Regulation (EU, Euratom) 2020/2093 of 17 December 2020 laying down the multiannual financial framework for the years 2021 to 2027, 2020 OJ LI 433/11.

Council Regulation 2020/2094 of 14 December 2020, establishing a European Union Recovery Instrument to support the recovery in the aftermath of the COVID-19 crisis, 2020 OJ LI 433/23.

Council Regulation (EU) 2020/672 of 19 May 2020 on the establishment of a European instrument for temporary support to mitigate unemployment risks in an emergency (SURE) following the COVID-19 outbreak, 2020 OJ L 159/1.

Council Regulation (EU) 2020/521 of 14 April 2020 activating the emergency support under Regulation (EU) 2016/369, and amending its provisions taking into account the COVID-19 outbreak, 2020 OJ L 117/3.

Council Regulation (EU) 2017/1939 of 12 October 2017 implementing enhanced cooperation on the establishment of the European Public Prosecutor's Office ('the EPPO'), 2017 OJ L 283/1.

Council Regulation (EU, Euratom) No 609/2014 of 26 May 2014 on the methods and procedure for making available the traditional, VAT and GNI-based own resources and on the measures to meet cash requirements, 2014 OJ L 168/3.

Council Regulation (EU) 407/2010 of 11 May 2010 establishing a European financial stabilisation mechanism, 2010 OJ L 118/1.

Council Regulation (EC) No 1083/2006 of 11 July 2006 laying down general provisions on the European Regional Development Fund, the European Social Fund and the Cohesion Fund and repealing Regulation (EC) No 1260/1999, 2006 OJ L 210/25.

Council Regulation (EC) No 1084/2006 of 11 July 2006 establishing a Cohesion Fund and repealing Regulation (EC) No 1164/94.

Council Regulation (EC) No 2012/2002 of 11 November 2002 establishing the European Union Solidarity Fund, 2002 OJ L 311/3.

Council Regulation (EC) No 1164/94 of 16 May 1994 establishing a Cohesion Fund, 1994 OJ L 130/1.

Decision (EU) 2022/2481 of the European Parliament and of the Council of 14 December 2022 establishing the Digital Decade Policy Programme 2030, 2022 OJ L 323/4.

Decision (EU) 2022/1628 of the European Parliament and of the Council of 20 September 2022 providing exceptional macro-financial assistance to Ukraine, reinforcing the common provisioning fund by guarantees by Member States and by specific provisioning for some financial liabilities related to Ukraine guaranteed under Decision No 466/2014/EU, and amending Decision (EU) 2022/1201, 2022 OJ L 245/1.

Decision (EU) 2022/1201 of the European Parliament and of the Council of 12 July 2022 providing exceptional macro-financial assistance to Ukraine, 2022 OJ L 186/1.

Decision (EU) 2022/313 of the European Parliament and of the Council of 24 February 2022 providing macro-financial assistance to Ukraine, 2022 OJ L 55/4.

Directive (EU) 2023/959 of the European Parliament and of the Council of 10 May 2023 amending Directive 2003/87/EC establishing a system for greenhouse gas emission allowance trading within the Union and Decision (EU) 2015/1814 concerning the establishment and operation of a market stability reserve for the Union greenhouse gas emission trading system (Text with EEA relevance), 2023 OJ L 130/134.

Directive (EU) 2023/958 of the European Parliament and of the Council of 10 May 2023 amending Directive 2003/87/EC as regards aviation's contribution to the Union's economy-wide emission reduction target and the appropriate implementation of a global market-based measure (Text with EEA relevance), 2023 OJ L 130/115.

Directive (EU) 2018/410 of the European Parliament and of the Council of 14 March 2018 amending Directive 2003/87/EC to enhance cost-effective emission reductions and low-carbon investments, and Decision (EU) 2015/1814 (Text with EEA relevance), 2018 OJ L 76/3.

Directive 2003/87/EC of the European Parliament and of the Council of 13 October 2003 establishing a scheme for greenhouse gas emission allowance trading within the Community and amending Council Directive 96/61/EC (Text with EEA relevance), 2003 OJ L 275/32.

European Parliament legislative resolution of 23 November 2022 on the proposal for a Council decision amending Decision (EU, Euratom) 2020/2053 on the system of own resources of the European Union (COM(2021)0570—C9-0034/2022—2021/0430(CNS)). P9_TA(2022)0404. System of own resources of the European Union (Special legislative procedure—consultation). 2021 OJ C 167/162.

Interinstitutional Agreement of 16 December 2020 between the European Parliament, the Council of the European Union and the European Commission on budgetary discipline, on cooperation in budgetary matters and on sound financial management, as well as on new own resources, including a roadmap towards the introduction of new own resources, 2020 OJ L 433I/28.

Regulation (EU) 2024/2773 of the European Parliament and of the Council of 24 October 2024 establishing the Ukraine Loan Cooperation Mechanism and providing exceptional macro-financial assistance to Ukraine, 2024 OJ L 2024/2773.

Regulation (EU, Euratom) 2024/2509 of the European Parliament and of the Council of 23 September 2024 on the financial rules applicable to the general budget of the Union (recast), 2024 OJ L, 2024/2509.

Regulation (EU) 2024/1449 of the European Parliament and of the Council of 14 May 2024 on establishing the Reform and Growth Facility for the Western Balkans, 2024 OJ L 2024/1449.

Regulation (EU) 2024/1263 of the European Parliament and of the Council of 29 April 2024 on the effective coordination of economic policies and on multilateral budgetary surveillance and repealing Council Regulation (EC) No 1466/97, 2024 OJ L 2024/1263.

Regulation (EU) 2024/795 of the European Parliament and of the Council of 29 February 2024 establishing the Strategic Technologies for Europe Platform (STEP), and amending

Directive 2003/87/EC and Regulations (EU) 2021/1058, (EU) 2021/1056, (EU) 2021/1057, (EU) No 1303/2013, (EU) No 223/2014, (EU) 2021/1060, (EU) 2021/523, (EU) 2021/695, (EU) 2021/697 and (EU) 2021/241, 2024 OJ L 2024/795.

Regulation (EU) 2024/792 of the European Parliament and of the Council of 29 February 2024 establishing the Ukraine Facility, 2024 OJ L 2024/792.

Regulation (EU) 2023/957 of the European Parliament and of the Council of 10 May 2023 amending Regulation (EU) 2015/757 in order to provide for the inclusion of maritime transport activities in the EU Emissions Trading System and for the monitoring, reporting and verification of emissions of additional greenhouse gases and emissions from additional ship types (Text with EEA relevance), 2023 OJ L 130/105.

Regulation (EU) 2023/956 of the European Parliament and of the Council of 10 May 2023 establishing a carbon border adjustment mechanism (Text with EEA relevance), 2023 OJ L 130/52.

Regulation (EU) 2023/955 of the European Parliament and of the Council of 10 May 2023 establishing a Social Climate Fund and amending Regulation (EU) 2021/1060, 2023 OJ L 130/1.

Regulation (EU) 2023/435 of the European Parliament and of the Council of 27 February 2023 amending Regulation (EU) 2021/241 as regards REPowerEU chapters in recovery and resilience plans and amending Regulations (EU) No 1303/2013, (EU) 2021/1060 and (EU) 2021/1755, and Directive 2003/87/EC, 2023 OJ L 63/1.

Regulation (EU) 2022/2463 of the European Parliament and of the Council of 14 December 2022 establishing an instrument for providing support to Ukraine for 2023 (macro-financial assistance +), 2022 OJ L 322/1.

Regulation (EU, Euratom) 2022/2434 of the European Parliament and of the Council of 6 December 2022 amending Regulation (EU, Euratom) 2018/1046 as regards the establishment of a diversified funding strategy as a general borrowing method, 2022 OJ L 319/1.

Regulation (EU) 2021/1755 of the European Parliament and of the Council of 6 October 2021 establishing the Brexit Adjustment Reserve, 2021 OJ L 357/1.

Regulation (EU) 2021/1060 of the European Parliament and of the Council of 24 June 2021 laying down common provisions on the European Regional Development Fund, the European Social Fund Plus, the Cohesion Fund, the Just Transition Fund and the European Maritime, Fisheries and Aquaculture Fund and financial rules for those and for the Asylum, Migration and Integration Fund, the Internal Security Fund and the Instrument for Financial Support for Border Management and Visa Policy, 2021 OJ L 231/159.

Regulation (EU) 2021/947 of the European Parliament and of the Council of 9 June 2021 establishing the Neighbourhood, Development and International Cooperation Instrument—Global Europe, amending and repealing Decision No 466/2014/EU of the European Parliament and of the Council and repealing Regulation (EU) 2017/1601 of the European Parliament and of the Council and Council Regulation (EC, Euratom) No 480/2009 (Text with EEA relevance), 2021 OJ L 209/1.

Regulation (EU) 2021/783 of the European Parliament and of the Council of 29 April 2021 establishing a Programme for the Environment and Climate Action (LIFE), and repealing Regulation (EU) No 1293/2013, 2021 OJ L 172/53.

Regulation (EU) 2021/697 of the European Parliament and of the Council of 29 April 2021 establishing the European Defence Fund and repealing Regulation (EU) 2018/1092 (Text with EEA relevance), 2021 OJ L 170/149.

Regulation (EU) 2021/691 of the European Parliament and of the Council of 28 April 2021 on the European Globalisation Adjustment Fund for Displaced Workers (EGF) and repealing Regulation (EU) No 1309/2013, 2021 OJ L 153/48.

Regulation (EU) 2021/241 of the European Parliament and of the Council of 12 February 2021 establishing the Recovery and Resilience Facility, 2021 OJ L 57/17.

Regulation (EU) 2021/240 of the European Parliament and of the Council of 10 February 2021 establishing a Technical Support Instrument, 2021 OJ L 57/1.
Regulation (EU) 2020/2221 of the European Parliament and of the Council of 23 December 2020 amending Regulation (EU) No 1303/2013 as regards additional resources and implementing arrangements to provide assistance for fostering crisis repair in the context of the COVID-19 pandemic and its social consequences and for preparing a green, digital and resilient recovery of the economy (REACT-EU), 2020 OJ L 437/30.
Regulation (EU, Euratom) 2020/2092 of the European Parliament and of the Council of 16 December 2020 on a general regime of conditionality for the protection of the Union budget, 2020 OJ L 433 I/1.
Regulation (EU) 2020/558 of 23 April 2020 amending Regulations (EU) No 1301/2013 and (EU) No 1303/2013 as regards specific measures to provide exceptional flexibility for the use of the European Structural and Investments Funds in response to the COVID-19 outbreak, 2020 OJ L 130/1.
Regulation (EU) 2020/461 of the European Parliament and of the Council of 30 March 2020 amending Council Regulation (EC) No 2012/2002 in order to provide financial assistance to Member States and to countries negotiating their accession to the Union that are seriously affected by a major public health emergency, 2020 OJ L 99/9.
Regulation (EU) 2020/460 of the European Parliament and of the Council of 30 March 2020 amending Regulations (EU) No 1301/2013, (EU) No 1303/2013 and (EU) No 508/2014 as regards specific measures to mobilise investments in the healthcare systems of Member States and in other sectors of their economies in response to the COVID-19 outbreak (Coronavirus Response Investment Initiative), 2020 OJ L 99/5.
Regulation (EU) 2019/1796 of the European Parliament and of the Council of 24 October 2019 amending Regulation (EU) No 1309/2013 on the European Globalisation Adjustment Fund (2014-2020), 2019 OJ LI 279/4.
Regulation (EU) 2018/1671 of the European Parliament and of the Council of 23 October 2018 amending Regulation (EU) 2017/825 to increase the financial envelope of the Structural Reform Support Programme and adapt its general objective, 2018 OJ L 284/3.
Regulation (EU, Euratom) 2018/1046 of the European Parliament and of the Council of 18 July 2018 on the financial rules applicable to the general budget of the Union, amending Regulations (EU) No 1296/2013, (EU) No 1301/2013, (EU) No 1303/2013, (EU) No 1304/2013, (EU) No 1309/2013, (EU) No 1316/2013, (EU) No 223/2014, (EU) No 283/2014, and Decision No 541/2014/EU and repealing Regulation (EU, Euratom) No 966/2012, 2018 OJ L 193/1.
Regulation (EU) 2017/2396 of the European Parliament and of the Council of 13 December 2017 amending Regulations (EU) No 1316/2013 and (EU) 2015/1017 as regards the extension of the duration of the European Fund for Strategic Investments as well as the introduction of technical enhancements for that Fund and the European Investment Advisory Hub, 2017 OJ L 345/34.
Regulation (EU) 2017/1199 of the European Parliament and of the Council of 4 July 2017 amending Regulation (EU) No 1303/2013 as regards specific measures to provide additional assistance to Member States affected by natural disasters, 2017 OJ L 176/1.
Regulation (EU) 2017/825 of the European Parliament and of the Council of 17 May 2017 on the establishment of the Structural Reform Support Programme for the period 2017 to 2020 and amending Regulations (EU) No 1303/2013 and (EU) No 1305/2013, 2017 OJ L 129/1.
Regulation (EU) 2016/2135 of 23 November 2016 amending Regulation (EU) No 1303/2013 as regards certain provisions relating to financial management for certain Member States experiencing or threatened with serious difficulties with respect to their financial stability, 2016 OJ L 338/34.

Regulation (EU) 2015/1839 of the European Parliament and of the Council of 14 October 2015 amending Regulation (EU) No 1303/2013 as regards specific measures for Greece, 2015 OJ L 270/1.

Regulation (EU) 2015/1017 of the European Parliament and of the Council of 25 June 2015 on the European Fund for Strategic Investments, the European Investment Advisory Hub and the European Investment Project Portal and amending Regulations (EU) No 1291/2013 and (EU) No 1316/2013—the European Fund for Strategic Investments, 2015 OJ L 169/1.

Regulation (EU) 661/2014 of the European Parliament and of the Council of 15 May 2014 amending Council Regulation (EC) No 2012/2002 establishing the European Union Solidarity Fund, 2014 OJ L 189) 143.

Regulation (EU) No 223/2014 of the European Parliament and of the Council of 11 March 2014 on the Fund for European Aid to the Most Deprived, 2014 OJ L 72/1.

Regulation (EU) No 1309/2013 of the European Parliament and of the Council of 17 December 2013 on the European Globalisation Adjustment Fund (2014-2020) and repealing Regulation (EC) No 1927/2006, 2013 OJ L 347) 855.

Regulation (EU) No 1302/2013 of the European Parliament and of the Council of 17 December 2013 amending Regulation (EC) No 1082/2006 on a European grouping of territorial co-operation (EGTC) as regards the clarification, simplification and improvement of the establishment and functioning of such groupings, 2013 OJ L 347/303.

Regulation (EU) No 1303/2013 of the European Parliament and of the Council of 17 December 2013 laying down common provisions on the European Regional Development Fund, the European Social Fund, the Cohesion Fund, the European Agricultural Fund for Rural Development and the European Maritime and Fisheries Fund and laying down general provisions on the European Regional Development Fund, the European Social Fund, the Cohesion Fund and the European Maritime and Fisheries Fund and repealing Council Regulation (EC) No 1083/2006, 2013 OJ L 347/320.

Regulation (EC) No 1927/2006 of the European Parliament and of the Council of 20 December 2006 on establishing the European Globalisation Adjustment Fund, 2006 OJ L 406/1.

Regulation (EC) No 1082/2006 of the European Parliament and of the Council of 5 July 2006 on a European grouping of territorial cooperation (EGTC), 2006 OJ L 210/19.

Regulation (EC) No 1367/2006 of the European Parliament and of the Council of 6 September 2006 on the application of the provisions of the Aarhus Convention on Access to Information, Public Participation in Decision-making and Access to Justice in Environmental Matters to Community institutions and bodies, 2006 OJ L 264/13, as amended 2021 OJ L 356/1.

Regulation (EC) No 1049/2001 of the European Parliament and of the Council of 30 May 2001 regarding public access to European Parliament, Council and Commission documents, 2001 OJ L 145/43.

Regulation (EEC) No 724/75 of the Council of 18 March 1975 establishing a European Regional Development Fund, 1975 OJ L 73/1.

Regulation No 31 (EEC), 11 (EAEC), laying down the Staff Regulations of Officials and the Conditions of Employment of Other Servants of the European Economic Community and the European Atomic Energy Community [consolidated text as of 13 May 2025] https://eur-lex.europa.eu/eli/reg/1962/31(1)/2025-05-13.

References

[alphabetical by author, then reverse chronological]

Abbasov, R, 2025. The Effectiveness of Performance-Based Budgeting in the Public Sector: An Empirical Analysis and Policy Implications. *iBusiness* 17, 56–76, https://doi.org/10.4236/ib.2025.171003.

Ackerman, B, 2019. *Revolutionary Constitutions: Charismatic Leadership and the Rule of Law.* Belknap Press: An Imprint of Harvard University Press, Cambridge, Massachusetts.

Ackerman, B, 2007. The Living Constitution. 2006 Oliver Wendell Holmes Lectures. *Harvard Law Review* 120, 1737–812.

Ackerman, BA, 1991. *We the People: Foundations.* Harvard University Press.

Ahner, D, 2009. What do you really know about European cohesion policy? Institut Jacques Delors. https://institutdelors.eu/wp-content/uploads/2018/01/ecp_rational_and_objectives.pdf.

Albuquerque Matos, N, 2025. The Transformation of EU Economic Union: How Enhanced Central Fiscal Capacity Sows the Seeds for the Future. *Legal Issues of Economic Integration* 52, 45–66.

Alcidi, C and Gros, D, 2017. Research Report No 2017/15. How to strengthen the European Semester? CEPS.https://www.ceps.eu/wp-content/uploads/2017/12/RR2017_15_CAandDG_EuropeanSemester.pdf.

Alcidi, C, Gros, D, and Corti, F, 2020. PI2020-25. Who will really benefit from the Next Generation EU funds? CEPS Policy Insight. October 2020. https://www.ceps.eu/wp-content/uploads/2020/10/PI2020-25_Next-Generation-EU_funds.pdf.

Amtenbrink, F and de Haan, J, 2023. The European Commission's approach to a reform of the EU fiscal framework: A legal and economic appraisal. *European Law Review* 48, 422–42, https://doi.org/10.3316/agispt.20231014097024.

Anderson, PW, 1972. More is Different: Broken Symmetry and the Nature of the Hierarchical Structure of Science. *Science* 177, 393–96, https://doi.org/10.1126/science.177.4047.393.

Andor, L, 2025. Ursula von der Leyen in the MFF porcelain shop. Substack. 19 July 2025. https://substack.com/@laszloandoreu/note/c-136923963

AP News, 2023. Trump's vow to only be a dictator on 'day one' follows growing worry over his authoritarian rhetoric. 7 December 2023. AP News. https://apnews.com/article/trump-hannity-dictator-authoritarian-presidential-election-f27e7e9d7c13fabbe3ae7dd7f1235c72.

Aranguiz, A, 2022. Spain's labour reform: less transience, more balance. Social Europe. 6 January 2022. https://www.socialeurope.eu/spains-labour-reform-less-temporary-work-more-balance.

Augenstein, D. (ed), 2012. *'Integration through Law' Revisited: The Making of the European Polity*, 1st edn, Routledge.

Bachtler, J and Dozhdeva, V, 2021. The Recovery & Resilience Fund: An Economic Stimulus at the Expense of Territorial Cohesion? EPRC Blog. June 2021, https://prc-strath.org/the-recovery-resilience-fund-an-economic-stimulus-at-the-expense-of-territorial-cohesion/.

Bachtler, J and Mendez, C, 2023. Navigating Stormy Waters: Crises and Cohesion Policy Beyond 2027. EoRPA Report 23/3, European Regional Policy Research Consortium. University of Strathclyde Publishing, https://eprc-strath.org/wp-content/uploads/2023/12/Cohesion-Policy-EoRPA-report-23_3-ISBN.pdf.

Bachtler, J and Mendez, C, 2020. Cohesion and the EU's Budget: Is Conditionality Undermining Solidarity?, in: Coman, R, Crespy, A, and Schmidt, VA (eds), *Governance and Politics in the Post-Crisis European Union.* Cambridge University Press, pp 121–39.

Bachtler, J, Mendez, C, and Downes, R, 2024. Charting a New Course for Cohesion Policy After 2027. EoRPA Report 24/3, European Regional Policy Research Consortium. University of Strathclyde Publishing, https://pure.strath.ac.uk/ws/portalfiles/portal/246984750/Bachtler-etal-EPRC-2024-Charting-a-New-Course-for-EU-Cohesion-Policy-After-2027.pdf.

Bachtler, J, Mendez, C, and Wishlade, F, 2013. *EU Cohesion Policy and European Integration: The Dynamics of EU Budget and Regional Policy Reform.* Routledge.

Balkin, JM, 2012. The Roots of the Living Constitution. *Boston University Law Review* 92, 1129–60.

Balmer, C and Fonte, G, 2024. Explainer: Why Italy's Superbonus blew a hole in state accounts. Reuters, https://www.reuters.com/world/europe/why-italys-superbonus-blew-hole-state-accounts-2024-04-09/.

Bańkowski, K, Benalal, N, Bouabdallah, O, Stefani, RD, Dorrucci, E, Huber, C, Jacquinot, P, Modery, W, Nerlich, C, Rodríguez Vives, M, Szörfi, B, Zorell, N, and Zwick, C, 2024. Four Years into NextGenerationEU: What Impact on the Euro Area Economy. ECB Occasional Paper No 2024/362, https://papers.ssrn.com/abstract=5050897.

Baquero Cruz, J, 2018. *What's Left of the Law of Integration?: Decay and Resistance in European Union Law*. Oxford University Press.

Baraggia, A and Bonelli, M, 2022. Linking Money to Values: The New Rule of Law Conditionality Regulation and Its Constitutional Challenges. *German Law Journal* 23, 131–56, https://doi.org/10.1017/glj.2022.17.

Barca Report, 2009. An Agenda for a Reformed Cohesion Policy: A place-based approach to meeting European Union challenges and expectations. Independent Report prepared at the request of Danuta Hübner, Commissioner for Regional Policy by Fabrizio Barca, https://ec.europa.eu/migrant-integration/sites/default/files/2010-12/docl_17396_240404999.pdf.

Bartolini, S, 2005. *Restructuring Europe: Centre Formation, System Building, and Political Structuring between the Nation State and the European Union*. Oxford University Press.

Bartoloni, ME, 2022. First-Ever EU Funding of Lethal Weapons: 'Another Taboo Has (Lawfully) Fallen'. *European Papers—A Journal on Law and Integration* 7, 379–83, https://doi.org/10.15166/2499-8249/569.

Bast, J and Bogdandy, A von, 2024. The Constitutional Core of the Union: On the CJEU's New, Principled Constitutionalism. *Common Market Law Review* 61, 1471–500.

Becker, P, 2019. The Reform of European Cohesion Policy or How to Couple the Streams Successfully. *Journal of European Integration* 41, 147–68, https://doi.org/10.1080/07036337.2018.1553964.

Becker, P, 2012. Lost in Stagnation: The EU's Next Multiannual Financial Framework (2014–2020) and the Power of the Status Quo. SWP Research Paper, RP 14. Stiftung Wissenschaft und Politik (SWP), German Institute for International and Security Affairs, https://ideas.repec.org/p/zbw/swprps/rp142012.html.

Begg, I, Benedetto, G, Belicka, D, Corti, F, Nuñez Ferrer, J, and Rubio, E, 2022. PE 721.500. The Next Revision of the Financial Regulation and the EU Budget Galaxy: How to Safeguard and Strengthen Budgetary Principles and Parliamentary Oversight. Study requested by the BUDG committee, European Parliament. Policy Department for Budgetary Affairs, Directorate-General for Internal Policies. March 2022. https://www.europarl.europa.eu/RegData/etudes/STUD/2022/721500/IPOL_STU(2022)721500_EN.pdf.

Beraldo, S, 2024. Stability or Sovereignty? Italy's Challenging Relationship with the European Stability Mechanism. IREF Europe, https://en.irefeurope.org/publications/online-articles/article/stability-or-sovereignty-italys-challenging-relationship-with-the-european-stability-mechanism/.

Binder, EW, Bonacci, P, Bunevičiūtė, R, Dias Pinheiro, B, Pikiotienė, A, Zoppè, A, and Zsitnak, A, 2022. PE 699.524. Survey on the Role of National Parliaments in the Implementation of the Recovery and Resilience Facility: Synthetic Presentation of the Results. In-Depth Analysis, European Parliament. Economic Governance Support Unit (EGOV), Directorate-General for Internal Policies, https://www.europarl.europa.eu/RegData/etudes/IDAN/2022/699524/IPOL_IDA(2022)699524_EN.pdf.

Blackhawk, M, 2023. The Supreme Court, 2022 Term—Foreword: The Constitution of American Colonialism. *Harvard Law Review* 137, 1–152.

Bletzinger, T, Greif, W, and Schwaab, B, 2023a. The Safe Asset Potential of EU-Issued Bonds. European Central Bank Research Bulletin No 103, https://www.ecb.europa.eu/pub/economic-research/resbull/2023/html/ecb.rb230116~e55fb14a74.en.html.

Bletzinger, T, Greif, W, and Schwaab, B, 2023b. The Safe Asset Potential of EU-Issued Bonds. VoxEU | CEPR, https://cepr.org/voxeu/columns/safe-asset-potential-eu-issued-bonds.

Bofinger, P, Feld, LP, Franz, W, Schmidt, CM, and Mauro, BW di, 2011. A European Redemption Pact. VoxEU | CEPR, http://www.voxeu.org/index.php?q=node/7253.

Bokhorst, D, 2023. Steering National Social Reforms through the EU's Recovery Plan, in: Vanhercke, B, Sabato, S, and Spasova, S (eds), *Social Policy in the European Union: State of Play 2022, Policymaking in a Permacrisis*. European Trade Union Institute, pp 25–41.

Bokhorst, D, 2022. The Influence of the European Semester: Case Study Analysis and Lessons for its Post-Pandemic Transformation*. *JCMS: Journal of Common Market Studies* 60, 101–17, https://doi.org/10.1111/jcms.13266.

Bokhorst, D and Corti, F, 2024. Governing Europe's Recovery and Resilience Facility: Between Discipline and Discretion. *Government and Opposition* 59, 718–34, https://doi.org/10.1017/gov.2023.14.

Bonelli, M, Claes, M, de Witte, B, and Podstawa, K, 2022. Usual and Unusual Suspect in Protecting EU Values: An Introduction. *European Papers—A Journal on Law and Integration* 7, 641–50, https://doi.org/10.15166/2499-8249/591.

Bonfanti, G and Garicano, L, 2022. Do financial markets consider European common debt a safe asset? Bruegel Blog, https://www.bruegel.org/blog-post/do-financial-markets-consider-european-common-debt-safe-asset.

Bongardt, A and Torres, F, 2022. The European Green Deal: More than an Exit Strategy to the Pandemic Crisis, a Building Block of a Sustainable European Economic Model. *JCMS: Journal of Common Market Studies* 60, 170–85, https://doi.org/10.1111/jcms.13264.

Borger, V, 2020. EU Financial Assistance, in: Amtenbrink, F, Herrmann, C, Repasi, R (eds), *The EU Law of Economic and Monetary Union*. Oxford University Press, https://doi.org/10.1093/oso/9780198793748.003.0039.

Born, A, Lambert, C, Molestina Vivar, L, Sowiński, A, and Simon, JMV, 2024. Do EU SURE and NGEU bonds contribute to financial integration? European Central Bank. Contribution to the Biennial Report on Financial Integration and Structure in the Euro Area. 18 June 2024, https://www.ecb.europa.eu/press/fie/box/html/ecb.fiebox202406_06.en.html.

Bornemann, J, 2025. Legal Legacies of Co-ordinative Europeanisation: EU Crisis Governance Between Political Expedience and Normative Credence. *JCMS: Journal of Common Market Studies* 64(2), 582–602, https://doi.org/10.1111/jcms.13768.

Borrell, J, 2022. Further measures to respond to the Russian invasion of Ukraine: Press statement by High Representative/Vice-President Josep Borrell. 26 February 2022, https://ec.europa.eu/commission/presscorner/detail/en/statement_22_1463.

Bortoletto, F, 2025. European Parliament slams Commission's EU budget proposal: 'It's a joke'. *EU News*. 16 July 2025, https://www.eunews.it/en/2025/07/16/european-parliament-slams-commissions-eu-budget-proposal-its-a-joke/.

Boughton, JM, 2003. Who's in Charge? Ownership and Conditionality in IMF-Supported Programs. IMF Working Papers, WP/03/191, https://www.elibrary.imf.org/view/journals/001/2003/191/article-A001-en.xml.

Bradford, A, Gadinis, S, and Linos, K, 2018. Unintended Agency Problems: How International Bureaucracies Are Built and Empowered. *Virginia Journal of International Law* 57, 159.

Bremer, B, Genschel, P, and Jachtenfuchs, M, 2020. Juncker's Curse? Identity, Interest, and Public Support for the Integration of Core State Powers. *JCMS: Journal of Common Market Studies* 58, 56–75, https://doi.org/10.1111/jcms.12980.

Bressanelli, E, Chelotti, N, and Nebbiai, M, 2023. The Recovery and Resilience Dialogues: Cheap Talk or Effective Oversight? *Politics and Governance* 11, 297–310, https://doi.org/10.17645/pag.v11i4.7344.

Brunnermeier, MK, Garicano, L, Lane, PR, Pagano, M, Reis, R, Santos, T, Thesmar, D, Van Nieuwerburgh, S, and Vayanos, D, 2016a. The Sovereign-Bank Diabolic Loop and ESBies. *American Economic Review* 106, 508–12, https://doi.org/10.1257/aer.p20161107.

Brunnermeier, MK, Garicano, L, Lane, PR, Pagano, M, Reis, R, Santos, T, Thesmar, D, Van Nieuwerburgh, S, and Vayanos, D, 2011. European Safe Bonds (ESBies). euro-nomics.com, https://personal.lse.ac.uk/vayanos/euronomics/esbies.pdf.

Brunnermeier, MK, Langfield, S, Pagano, M, Reis, R, Van Nieuwerburgh, S, and Vayanos, D, 2016b. ESBies: Safety in the tranches. ESRB Working Paper Series No 21, https://www.esrb.europa.eu/pub/pdf/wp/esrbwp21.en.pdf.

Brunsden, J, Fleming, S, and Peel, M, 2020. Crisis in Europe: von der Leyen's audacious bid for new powers. Financial Times, https://www.ft.com/content/775c4db2-4e3d-426f-b937-243f0673cc14.

Brzeziński, B, Mackenzie, L, and Knapp, F, 2025. Brussels slashes the EU farm budget, calls it a win. Farmers call it a declaration of war. POLITICO. 17 July 2025, https://www.politico.eu/article/brussels-slashes-eu-farm-budget-cap-declaration-war-ursula-von-der-leyen-agriculture/.

Brzozowski, A, 2023. EU leaders approve accession talks with Ukraine, Moldova, bypassing Hungary. Euractiv, https://www.euractiv.com/section/europe-s-east/news/eu-leaders-greenlight-opening-accession-talks-with-ukraine-moldova/.

Buettner, T, 2023. Next Generation EU: A Hamiltonian Moment for the Public Finances of the European Union? *FinanzArchiv/Public Finance Analysis* 79, 164–173, https://doi.org/10.1628/fa-2023-0008.

Buiter, W and Rahbari, E, 2012. The European Central Bank as Lender of Last Resort for Sovereigns in the Eurozone. *JCMS: Journal of Common Market Studies* 50, 6–35, https://doi.org/10.1111/j.1468-5965.2012.02275.x.

Bundesministerium der Finanzen, 2021. Deutscher Aufbau-und Resilienzplan (DARP), 27 April 2021, https://bundesfinanzministerium.de/Content/DE/Standardartikel/Themen/Europa/DARP/deutscher-aufbau-und-resilienzplan.html.

Burley, A-M and Mattli, W, 1993. Europe Before the Court: A Political-Theory of Legal Integration. *International Organization* 47, 41–76.

Buti, M, Turrini, A, Van den Noord, P, and Biroli, P, 2008. Defying the 'Juncker Curse': Can Reformist Governments be Re-elected? European Commission Economic Papers No 324, https://ec.europa.eu/economy_finance/publications/pages/publication12586_en.pdf.

Calleja, D, Rusche, TM, and Shipley, T, 2024. EU Emergency—Call 122? On the Possibilities and Limits of Using Article 122 TFEU to Respond to Situations of Crisis. *Columbia Journal of European Law* 29, 520–60.

Capoccia, G, 2015. Critical Junctures and Institutional Change, in: Mahoney, J and Thelen, K (eds), *Advances in Comparative-Historical Analysis*. Cambridge University Press.

Capone, L and Stagnaro, C, 2025. Bad ideas have bad consequences: Italy's Superbonus and the influx of MMT. Mimeo, February 2025.

Capone, L and Stagnaro, C, 2024. *Superbonus. Come fallisce una nazione*. Rubbettino.

Caziero, M, 2024. What Legal Basis for an EU Tax? *Common Market Law Review* 61, 1527–48.

Chamon, M, 2024. The EU's Dormant Economic Policy Competence: Reliance on Article 122 TFEU and Parliament's Misguided Proposal for Treaty Revision. *European Law Review* 49, 166–87.

Chamon, M, 2023a. The rise of Article 122 TFEU: On crisis measures and the paradigm change. Verfassungsblog, https://verfassungsblog.de/the-rise-of-article-122-tfeu/.

Chamon, M, 2023b. PE 753.307. The use of Article 122 TFEU: Institutional implications and impact on democratic accountability. Study, Requested by the AFCO committee, European Parliament. Policy Department for Citizens' Rights and Constitutional Affairs,

Directorate-General for Internal Policies, https://www.europarl.europa.eu/RegData/etudes/STUD/2023/753307/IPOL_STU(2023)753307_EN.pdf.

Charlemagne, 2010. Do Europeans want a dynamic economy? *The Economist*, https://www.economist.com/charlemagne/2010/01/08/do-europeans-want-a-dynamic-economy.

Christie, R, Claeys, G, and Weil, P, 2021. Next Generation EU borrowing: a first assessment. Bruegel Policy Contribution 22/21. 10 November 2021, https://www.bruegel.org/system/files/wp_attachments/PC-22-101121.pdf.

Cipriani, G, 2017. The EU Budget, in: Zahariadis N, and Buonanno, L (eds), *The Routledge Handbook of European Public Policy*. Routledge, pp 142–54.

Claeys, G, 2018a. Are SBBS really the safe asset the euro area is looking for? Bruegel Blog, https://www.bruegel.org/blog-post/are-sbbs-really-safe-asset-euro-area-looking.

Claeys, G, 2018b. Make euro-area sovereign bonds safe again. Bruegel Blog, https://www.bruegel.org/comment/make-euro-area-sovereign-bonds-safe-again.

Claeys, G, McCaffrey, C, and Welslau, L, 2023. The rising cost of European Union borrowing and what to do about it. Bruegel Policy Brief. 31 May 2023, https://www.bruegel.org/policy-brief/rising-cost-european-union-borrowing-and-what-do-about-it.

Common Market Law Review Editorial Comments, 2021. Editorial comments: Compromising (on) the General Conditionality Mechanism and the Rule of Law. *Common Market Law Review* 58, 267–84.

Committee of the Regions, 2024. The top-down management of the EU recovery plan is putting cohesion at risk. COR Press Release. 8 October 2024, https://cor.europa.eu/en/news/top down-management-eu-recovery-plan-putting-cohesion-risk.

Committee on Budgetary Control, 2023. European Parliament, Committee on Budgetary Control, Question of Viola von Cramon-Taubadel, MEP, to Céline Gauer, Director-General, RECOVER, and Maarten Verwey, Director-General, ECFIN. 21 September 2023, https://multimedia.europarl.europa.eu/webstreaming/committee-on-budgetary-control_20230921-0900-COMMITTEE-CONT.

Conference on the Future of Europe, 2022. Report on the Final Outcome, https://wayback.archive-it.org/12090/20220915201021/https://prod-cofe-platform.s3.eu-central-1.amazonaws.com/2po250fn174z62m8g8c9ya9e62m7?response-content-disposition=inline%3B%20filename%3D%22Book_CoFE_Final_Report_EN_full.pdf%22%3B%20filename%2A%3DUTF-8%27%27Book_CoFE_Final_Report_EN_full.pdf&response-content-type=application%2Fpdf&X-Amz-Algorithm=AWS4-HMAC-SHA256&X-Amz-Credential=AKIA3LJJXGZPDFYVOW5V%2F20220915%2Feu-central-1%2Fs3%2Faws4_request&X-Amz-Date=20220915T200910Z&X-Amz-Expires=300&X-Amz-SignedHeaders=host&X-Amz-Signature=9da6e64b707df344c8772d076bc07e818cd0e1e0b662480f30d2f367446042e8.

Corti, F, Gros, D, Liscai, A, Ruiz de la Ossa, T, Kiss-Gálfalvi, T, Fuest, C, Gstrein, D, Herold, E, and Dolls, M, 2022a. PE 699.513. The European added value of the Recovery and Resilience Facility. Study Requested by the ECON Committee, European Parliament. Economic Governance Support Unit (EGOV), Directorate-General for Internal Policies. April 2022, https://www.europarl.europa.eu/RegData/etudes/STUD/2022/699513/IPOL_STU(2022)699513_EN.pdf.

Corti, F, Liscai, A, and Ruiz, T, 2022b. The Recovery and Resilience Facility: Boosting Investment in Social Infrastructure in Europe? *Italian Labour Law e-Journal* 15, 15–30, https://doi.org/10.6092/issn.1561-8048/15706.

Corti, F and Ruiz de la Ossa, T, 2023. The Recovery and Resilience Facility: What are we really monitoring with a performance-based approach? CEPS Explainer 2023-01. 10 January 2023, https://cdn.ceps.eu/wp-content/uploads/2023/01/CEPS-Explainer-2023-01_Limits-of-the-RRF-performance.pdf.

COSAC, 2021. 35th Bi-annual Report: Developments in European Union Procedures and Practices Relevant to Parliamentary Scrutiny. Prepared by the COSAC Secretariat and presented to: LXV Conference of Parliamentary Committees for Union Affairs of Parliaments of the European Union. Lisbon. 31 May–1 June 2021, https://secure.ipex.eu/IPEXL-WEB/download/file/8a8629a879787ca101797ba09dff0398/35th%20Bi-annual%20Report%20of%20COSAC%20EN.pdf.

Costamagna, F and Goldmann, M, 2020. Constitutional Innovation, Democratic Stagnation? Verfassungsblog, https://verfassungsblog.de/constitutional-innovation-democratic-stagnation/.

Council Legal Service, 2022. 12660/22. Contribution of the Legal Service. To: Financial Counsellors. Subject: Proposal for a Regulation of the European Parliament and of the Council amending Regulation (EU) 2021/241 as regards REPowerEU chapters in recovery and resilience plans and amending Regulation (EU) 2021/1060, Regulation (EU) 2021/2115, Directive 2003/87/EC and Decision (EU) 2015/1814. Article 21(2) - Allocation key for the new revenue. 21 September 2022, https://data.consilium.europa.eu/doc/document/ST-12660-2022-INIT/en/pdf.

Council Legal Service, 2020a. 9062/20. Council of the European Union, Opinion of the Legal Service, 24 June 2020. Subject: Proposals on Next Generation EU—Compatibility of the package with the Union's principles of budgetary balance and discipline under Article 310 TFEU - Compatibility of the package with the integrity of the system of own resources (Article 311 TFEU) - Suitability of Article 122 TFEU as legal basis for the Recovery Instrument proposal - Compatibility of the package with Article 125(1) TFEU (no bail-out clause), https://data.consilium.europa.eu/doc/document/ST-9062-2020-INIT/en/pdf.

Council Legal Service, 2020b. 5483/20. Council of the European Union. Opinion of the Legal Service, 23 January 2020. Subject: Proposal for a Regulation of the European Parliament and of the Council on the establishment of the Reform Support Programme—BICC—compatibility of the proposed allocation method with the cohesion legal basis (art 175, 3rd para, TFEU) [on file with authors].

Council Legal Service, 2020c. 6009/20. Council of the European Union. Opinion of the Legal Service, 2 March 2020. Subject: Proposal for a Regulation of the European Parliament and of the Council on a mechanism to resolve legal and administrative obstacles in a cross-border context—Choice of the legal basis—Compatibility with the Treaties—Choice of the legal instrument and voluntary nature [on file with authors].

Council Legal Service, 2019a. 5347/19. Council of the European Union. Opinion of the Legal Service, 15 January 2019. Subject: Proposal for a Regulation of the European Parliament and of the Council on the establishment of a European Investment Stabilisation Function—choice of legal basis—restriction of the group of Member States entitled to receive financial assistance financing in accordance with an intergovernmental instrument [on file with authors].

Council Legal Service, 2019b. 6582/19. Council of the European Union. Opinion of the Legal Service, 19 February 2019. Subject: Proposal for a Regulation of the European Parliament and of the Council on the establishment of the Reform Support Programme—'choice of legal basis'—'restricted geographical scope of application' [on file with authors].

Council Legal Service, 2017. 5151/1/17. Opinion of the Legal Service. From: Legal Service, To: Working Party on General Affairs, Subject: Commission Proposal for an Inter-Institutional Agreement on a Mandatory Transparency Register—Legal analysis. 10 February 2017, https://www.europarl.europa.eu/cmsdata/216435/ST_5151_2017_REV_1_EN.pdf.

Council of the European Union, 2025a. Fit for 55, https://www.consilium.europa.eu/en/policies/fit-for-55/.

Council of the European Union, 2025b. European Peace Facility, https://www.consilium.europa.eu/en/policies/european-peace-facility/#ukraine.

Council of the European Union, 2025c. Ref. 25/0478, Letter of Fernando Florindo, Head Of Unit, Information Services Unit / Transparency, Directorate Information and Outreach, Directorate-General Communication and Information—COMM, to Päivi Leino-Sandberg, Request made on: 15 February 2025, Registered on: 17 February 2025. 4 March 2025 [on file with authors].

Council of the European Union, 2024a. SGS 24/00010. Letter of 12 April 2024 from Peter Javorcik, Acting Director-General, DG COMM, Council of the European Union, to Päivi Leino-Sandberg. Subject: Your confirmatory application 07/c/01/24. Including as annex: Reply To Confirmatory Application No 07/c/01/24 made by email on 28 February 2024 and registered on the same day [on file with authors].

Council of the European Union, 2024b. Immobilised assets: Council agrees on up to €35 billion in macro-financial assistance to Ukraine and new loan mechanism implementing G7 commitment. 9 October 2024, https://www.consilium.europa.eu/en/press/press-releases/2024/10/09/immobilised-assets-council-agrees-on-up-to-35-billion-in-macro-financial-assistance-to-ukraine-and-new-loan-mechanism-implementing-g7-commitment/.

Council of the European Union, 2023. 6995/1/23. Note From: General Secretariat of the Council, To: Delegations, Subject: Orientations for a reform of the EU economic governance framework - Revised Draft Council Conclusions. 14 March 2023, https://data.consilium.europa.eu/doc/document/ST-6995-2023-REV-1/en/pdf.

Council of the European Union, 2022a. 10685/22. Note From: Presidency, To: Council; No Cion doc. 10920/21 + COR 1 + ADD 1 + ADD 1 COR 1 - COM(2021) 568 final; Subject: 'Fit for 55' package; Proposal for a Regulation of the European Parliament and of the Council on establishing a Social Climate Fund—General approach. 25 June 2022, https://data.consilium.europa.eu/doc/document/ST-10685-2022-INIT/en/pdf.

Council of the European Union, 2022b. 15178/22. Note From: Presidency, To: Delegations, Subject: Presidency report on new own resources. 25 November 2022, https://data.consilium.europa.eu/doc/document/ST-15178-2022-INIT/en/pdf.

Council of the European Union, 2022c. 15225/22. Note, From: General Secretariat of the Council, To: Permanent Representatives Committee/Council, No prev doc: 14474/22, No Cion doc: 14443/22 (COM(2022) 596 final), Subject: Regulation of the European Parliament and of the Council amending Regulation (EU, Euratom) 2018/1046 as regards the establishment of a diversified funding strategy as a general borrowing method (1st reading)—Adoption of the legislative act—Decision to derogate from the eight-week period provided for in Article 4 of Protocol 1 on the role of national parliaments in the EU. 28 November 2022, https://data.consilium.europa.eu/doc/document/ST-15225-2022-INIT/EN/pdf.

Council of the European Union, 2021a. 10160/21. Note, From: General Secretariat of the Council, To: Delegations, Subject: Revised Annex to the Council Implementing Decision on the approval of the assessment of the recovery and resilience plan for Italy. 8 July 2021, https://data.consilium.europa.eu/doc/document/ST-10160-2021-ADD-1-REV-2/en/pdf.

Council of the European Union, 2021b. 10150/21. Note, From: General Secretariat of the Council, To: Delegations, Subject: Revised Annex to the Council Implementing Decision on the approval of the assessment of the recovery and resilience plan for Spain. 7 July 2021, https://data.consilium.europa.eu/doc/document/ST-10150-2021-ADD-1-REV-2/en/pdf.

Council of the European Union, 2021c. 14585/21. Note From: General Secretariat of the Council, To: Permanent Representatives Committee/Council; Subject: Fit for 55 package, a) Revision of Directive (EU) 2003/87/EC establishing a scheme for greenhouse gas emission allowance trading to implement the ambition of the new 2030 climate target and related proposals; b) Revision of Regulation (EU) 2018/842 on binding annual greenhouse gas emission reductions by Member States from 2021 to 2030 contributing to climate action to meet commitments under the Paris Agreement; c) Revision of Regulation (EU) 2018/

841 on the inclusion of greenhouse gas emissions and removals from land use, land use change and forestry in the 2030 climate and energy framework; d) Revision of Regulation (EU) 2019/631 setting CO2 emission performance standards for new passenger cars and for new light commercial vehicles; e) Regulation establishing a Social Climate Fund—Progress report—Policy debate. 6 December 2021, https://data.consilium.europa.eu/doc/document/ST-14585-2021-INIT/en/pdf.

Council of the European Union, 2020. Statement on the Stability and Growth Pact in Light of the Covid-19 Crisis. 23 March 2020, https://www.consilium.europa.eu/en/press/press-releases/2020/03/23/statement-of-eu-ministers-of-finance-on-the-stability-and-growth-pact-in-light-of-the-covid-19-crisis/.

Council of the European Union, 2019a. Explainer on the euro area budgetary instrument, https://www.consilium.europa.eu/en/policies/emu-deepening/bicc-faq/.

Council of the European Union, 2019b. Term Sheet on the Budgetary Instrument for Convergence and Competitiveness (BICC). 10 October 2019, https://www.consilium.europa.eu/en/press/press-releases/2019/10/10/term-sheet-on-the-budgetary-instrument-for-convergence-and-competitiveness-bicc/.

Council of the European Union, 2017. Investment Plan for Europe, https://www.consilium.europa.eu/en/policies/investment-plan/.

Council of the European Union, 2016. Conclusions on Results and New Elements of Cohesion Policy and the European Structural and Investment Funds. 16 November 2016, https://www.consilium.europa.eu/en/press/press-releases/2016/11/16/cohesion-policy-conclusions/.

Craig, P, 2013. Pringle: Legal Reasoning, Text, Purpose and Teleology. *Maastricht Journal of European and Comparative Law* 20, 3–11, https://doi.org/10.1177/1023263X1302000101.

Craviotto, N, Meredith, D, and Prizzon, A, 2023. The European Investment Bank's foreign and development policy: our action points for the soon-to-be President. ODI: Think change, https://odi.org/en/insights/the-european-investment-banks-foreign-and-development-policy-our-action-points-for-the-soon-to-be-president/.

Crespy, A and Vanheuverzwijn, P, 2016. What 'Brussels' means by structural reforms. *Les Cahiers du Cevipol* 5, 58–87.

Crowe, R, 2024. The European Union's Public Finances in Times of Crisis, in: Kilpatrick, C and Scott, J (eds), *New Frontiers of EU Funding: Law, Policy, Politics*. Oxford University Press, pp 23–71.

Crowe, R, 2017. The European Budgetary Galaxy. *European Constitutional Law Review* 13, 428–52, https://doi.org/10.1017/S1574019617000219.

Darvas, Z, 2024. Analysis: Countries are still slow to follow European Union policy recommendations. Bruegel, https://www.bruegel.org/sites/default/files/2024-11/countries-are-still-slow-to-follow-european-union-policy-recommendations-10162_0.pdf.

Darvas, Z and McCaffrey, C, 2024. PE 766.173. Management of debt liabilities in the EU budget under the post-2027 MFF. Briefing Requested by the BUDG Committee. European Parliament, Policy Department for Budgetary Affairs, Directorate-General for Internal Policies. October 2024, https://www.europarl.europa.eu/RegData/etudes/BRIE/2024/766173/IPOL_BRI(2024)766173_EN.pdf.

Darvas, Z and Weslau, L, 2023. PE 741.478. First lessons from the Recovery and Resilience Facility for the EU economic governance framework. Study requested by the ECON committee. European Parliament, Economic Governance and EMU Scrutiny Unit (EGOV), Directorate-General for Internal Policies. In-Depth Analysis, March 2023, https://www.europarl.europa.eu/RegData/etudes/IDAN/2023/741748/IPOL_IDA(2023)741748_EN.pdf.

Dawson, M, 2024. Europe's expanding coordination space. *European Law Open* 3, 746–67, https://doi.org/doi:10.1017/elo.2025.8.

Dawson, M, 2023. The National Case for Reforming the EU Treaties. Verfassungsblog, https://verfassungsblog.de/the-national-case-for-reforming-the-eu-treaties.

Dawson, M and de Witte, F, 2013. Constitutional Balance in the EU after the Euro–Crisis. *Modern Law Review* 76, 817–44.

DBRS, 2022. DBRS Morningstar Confirms the European Union at AAA, Stable Trend. DBRS Morningstar, https://dbrs.morningstar.com/research/394274/dbrs-morningstar-confirms-the-european-union-at-aaa-stable-trend.

DBRS, 2015. Methodology: Rating Supranational Institutions. DBRS Morningstar, https://dbrs.morningstar.com/research/278329/rating-supranational-institutions-archived.

de Bellis, M, 2024. The NGEU and the Energy Crisis: The Shifting Boundaries of Conditionality. *European Papers—A Journal on Law and Integration* 9, 1114–47, https://doi.org/10.15166/2499-8249/802.

de Grauwe, P, 2011. The European Central Bank as a lender of last resort. VoxEU | CEPR, https://cepr.org/voxeu/columns/european-central-bank-lender-last-resort.

de Grauwe, P and Ji, Y, 2013. Self-fulfilling Crises in the Eurozone: An Empirical Test. *Journal of International Money and Finance, The European Sovereign Debt Crisis: Background & Perspective* 34, 15–36, https://doi.org/10.1016/j.jimonfin.2012.11.003.

de Gregorio Merino, A, 2024. The EU Treaties as a Living Constitution of the Union in Times of Crisis. *AJIL Unbound* 118, 162–66, https://doi.org/10.1017/aju.2024.25.

de Gregorio Merino, A, 2021. The Recovery Plan: Solidarity and the Living Constitution. EU Law Live, 6 March 2021, https://eulawlive.com/long-read-the-recovery-plan-solidarity-and-the-living-constitution-by-alberto-de-gregorio-merino/.

de La Feld, S, 2025. EU Parliament pushes to drag Member States before the EU Court over fast-track rearmament plan. EU News, 24 June 2025, https://www.eunews.it/en/2025/06/24/eu-parliament-pushes-to-drag-member-states-before-the-eu-court-over-fast-track-rearmament-plan/.

de Lemos, S, Loi, G, Sangers, B, and Rokos Castillo, A, 2025. PE 764.184. Implementation of the reformed Stability and Growth Pact. In-Depth Analysis. European Parliament. Economic Governance and EMU Scrutiny Unit (EGOV). Directorate-General for Economy, Transformation and Industry. January 2025, https://www.europarl.europa.eu/RegData/etudes/IDAN/2025/764184/ECTI_IDA(2025)764184_EN.pdf.

de Witte, B, 2023. Integration through Funding: The Union's Finances as Policy Instrument, in: Weber, R (ed), *EU Integration through Financial Constitution: Follow the Money?* Hart Publishing, pp 221–36.

de Witte, B, 2022. Guest Editorial: EU Emergency Law and its Impact on the EU Legal Order. *Common Market Law Review* 59, 3–18.

de Witte, B, 2021. The European Union's COVID-19 Recovery Plan: The Legal Engineering of an Economic Policy Shift. *Common Market Law Review* 58, 635–68.

de Witte, B, 2009. The Rules of Change in the European Union: The Lost Balance between Rigidity and Flexibility, in: Moury, C and de Sousa, L (eds), *Institutional Challenges in Post-Constitutional Europe*. Routledge.

Delhomme, V and Hervey, T, 2022. The European Union's Response to the Covid-19 Crisis and (the Legitimacy of) the Union's Legal Order. *Yearbook of European Law* 41, 48–82, https://doi.org/10.1093/yel/yeac011.

Deloitte, 2022. Comparative Analysis of Receipt of the Recovery & Resilience Funds among European Union Member States, https://www2.deloitte.com/content/dam/Deloitte/gr/Documents/about-deloitte/gr_ComparativeAnalysisofRRFproress13OCT2022_ENG_noexp.pdf.

Delors Report, 1989. Report on Economic and Monetary Union in the European Community. Presented 17 April 1989 to the European Council by Committee for the Study of Economic and Monetary Union, chaired by Jacques Delors, President, European Commission, https://ec.europa.eu/economy_finance/publications/pages/publication6161_en.pdf.

Delpla, J and von Weizsäcker, J, 2010. The Blue Bond Proposal. Breugel Policy Brief 2010/03, https://www.bruegel.org/sites/default/files/wp_attachments/1005-PB-Blue_Bonds.pdf.

Dermine, P, 2025. The New EU Economic Governance Framework: Perspectives for Social Europe, in: Sabato, S, Ghailani, D, and Spasova, S (eds), *Social Policy in the European Union: State of Play 2024 - Social Europe amidst the Security and Competitiveness Paradigms*. European Trade Union Institute (ETUI), pp 43–57.

Dermine, P, 2024. The Planning Method: An Inquiry into the constitutional Ramifications of a New EU Governance Technique. *Common Market Law Review* 61, 959–92.

Dermine, P, 2023. Le plan de relance 'Next Generation EU' de l'Union européenne: Analyse constitutionnelle d'une initiative historique. *Larcier-Intersentia*.

Dermine, P, 2022. The New Economic Governance of the Eurozone: A Rule of Law Analysis, Cambridge Studies in European Law and Policy. Cambridge University Press, https://doi.org/10.1017/9781009216630.

Dermine, P, 2020. The EU's Response to the COVID-19 Crisis and the Trajectory of Fiscal Integration in Europe: Between Continuity and Rupture. *Legal Issues of Economic Integration* 47, 337–58.

Deutsche Welle, 2010. Economic unity. Spain, the new holder of the rotating EU presidency, has called for binding goals under a 10-year plan to boost the bloc's economy. Prime Minister Zapatero says penalties are in store for uncooperative members, https://www.dw.com/en/spain-calls-for-binding-eu-economic-goals-and-penalties/a-5098907.

Deyl, D, 2025a. Defence loans spark EU institutional clash as MEPs sue to stay relevant. EU Perspectives. 22 August 2025, https://euperspectives.eu/2025/08/defence-loans-spark-eu-institutional-clash-meps-sue/.

Deyl, D, 2025b. EU next long-term budget: Defence wins, health and farmers fear cuts. EU Perspectives. 16 July 2025, https://euperspectives.eu/2025/07/eu-long-term-budget-defence-health-farmers/.

Di Mascio, F and Natalini, A, 2023. Implementing the NRRP from the Draghi Government to the Government of Giorgia Meloni: Italian Public Administration under the Pressure of Too Large a Volume of Resources. *Contemporary Italian Politics* 15, 237–51, https://doi.org/10.1080/23248823.2023.2190642.

Dias, C, 2022. PE 659.627. Briefing: European Parliament Involvement in Scrutinising the Recovery and Resilience Facility. European Parliament, Economic Governance Support Unit (EGOV). October 2022, https://www.europarl.europa.eu/RegData/etudes/BRIE/2021/659627/IPOL_BRI(2021)659627_EN.pdf.

Díez Sánchez, L, 2025. Why Cohesion Policy is not About Cohesion. *Common Market Law Review* 62, 13–48.

Dobreva, A and Vozovych, A, 2024. PE 767.160. The Ukraine Loan Cooperation Mechanism and exceptional macrofinancial assistance. Briefing, European Parliament. EPRS - European Parliamentary Research Service, Members Research Service. December 2024, https://www.europarl.europa.eu/RegData/etudes/BRIE/2024/767160/EPRS_BRI(2024)767160_EN.pdf.

Dolan, M, 2025. 'Blue' euro bonds to rival Treasuries? Reuters, 9 June 2025, https://www.reuters.com/markets/europe/blue-euro-bonds-rival-treasuries-mike-dolan-2025-06-09/.

Dombrovskis, V, 2021. @VDombrovskis: Komissiolle on selvä asia, että #NextGenerationEU -väline on kertaluonteinen, ainutlaatuinen ja se on tiukasti ajallisesti rajattu. Se on meidän mahdollisuutemme toipua tästä poikkeuksellisesta kriisistä. @EUkomissio. Twitter, 11 May 2021, https://x.com/VDombrovskis/status/1392027720721260546.

Drachenberg, R, 2020a. PE 631.732. Briefing: The European Council and the 2021-27 Multiannual Financial Framework. European Parliament, European Parliamentary

Research Service, European Council Oversight Unit, https://www.europarl.europa.eu/RegData/etudes/BRIE/2020/631732/EPRS_BRI(2020)631732_EN.pdf.

Drachenberg, R, 2020b. PE 642.815. Briefing: Outcome of the special European Council, 20-21 February 2020. European Parliament, Post-European Council Briefing, European Parliamentary Research Service, European Council Oversight Unit, https://www.europarl.europa.eu/RegData/etudes/BRIE/2020/642815/EPRS_BRI(2020)642815_EN.pdf.

Draghi, M, 2025a. I267271. Transcript. European Parliamentary Week 2025: keynote speech by Mario Draghi, former Italian Prime Minister and former President of the European Central Bank. 18 February 2025 [corrected against delivery], https://api.multimedia.europarl.europa.eu/documents/20125/81296251/1739781678112_I267271%5BSD-EN%5D.pdf.

Draghi, M, 2025b. Keynote Speech of Professor Draghi. High Level Conference—One year after the Draghi report: what has been achieved, what has changed. European Commission. 16 September 2025, https://commission.europa.eu/document/download/0951a4ff-cd1a-4ea3-bc1d-f603decc1ed9_en?filename=Draghi_Speech_High_Level_Conference_One_Year_After.pdf.

Draghi, M, 2023. On the path to fiscal union in the euro zone. *The Economist*, https://www.economist.com/by-invitation/2023/09/06/mario-draghi-on-the-path-to-fiscal-union-in-the-euro-zone.

Draghi, M, 2012. Speech by Mario Draghi, President of the European Central Bank at the Global Investment Conference in London. 26 July 2012, https://www.ecb.europa.eu/press/key/date/2012/html/sp120726.en.html.

Draghi Report, 2024a. The Future of European Competitiveness, Part A: A competitiveness strategy for Europe. Report of Mario Draghi for the European Commission, https://commission.europa.eu/document/download/97e481fd-2dc3-412d-be4c-f152a8232961_en?filename=The%20future%20of%20European%20competitiveness%20_%20A%20competitiveness%20strategy%20for%20Europe.pdf.

Draghi Report, 2024b. The Future of European Competitiveness, Part B: In-depth analysis and recommendations. Report of Mario Draghi for the European Commission, https://commission.europa.eu/document/download/ec1409c1-d4b4-4882-8bdd-3519f86bbb92_en?filename=The%20future%20of%20European%20competitiveness_%20In-depth%20analysis%20and%20recommendations_0.pdf.

Drake, H, 2023. Reform or Revolution? French Politics at the Crossroads. *Political Insight* 14, 36–39, https://doi.org/10.1177/20419058231167271.

Dudziak, ML and Volpp, L, 2006. *Legal Borderlands: Law and the Construction of American Borders*. Johns Hopkins University Press, https://doi.org/10.56021/9780801884146.

Dyevre, A, 2022. Theories of European Legal Integration, Social Science Research Network, https://doi.org/10.2139/ssrn.4031808

Eckes, C and Leino-Sandberg, P, 2022. The EU-UK Trade and Cooperation Agreement – Exceptional Circumstances or a new Paradigm for EU External Relations? *Modern Law Review* 85, 164–97, https://doi.org/10.1111/1468-2230.12698.

Economic and Financial Committee, 2025. Economic and Financial Committee—European Union, https://economic-financial-committee.europa.eu/index_en.

Economic and Financial Committee, 2023a. ecfin.cef.cpe(2023)4269533, Economic and Financial Committee, Secretariat, 8 May 2023. Implementation of the Recovery and Resilience Facility—Streamlining the adoption of EFC Opinions on Commission's preliminary assessments—Secretariat Note [on file with authors].

Economic and Financial Committee, 2023b. ecfin.cef.cpe(2023)12917998, Economic and Financial Committee, Secretariat, 22 December 2023. Preparation of the EFC opinions under the Recovery and Resilience Facility—Lessons learnt—January 2024 [on file with authors].

Economic and Financial Committee, 2021. ecfin.cef.cpe(2021)539085, Economic and Financial Committee, Secretariat, 19 August 2021. Implementation of the Recovery and Resilience Facility: Payment requests and the preparation of the EFC opinions—Secretariat issues note [on file with authors].

ECORYS, CEPS, CSIL, NIESR, Wavestone, 2023. Study Supporting the Mid-Term Evaluation of the Recovery and Resilience Facility. Final Report, prepared by ECORYS, CEPS, CSIL, NIESR, and Wavestone for the European Commission, Directorate-General for Economic and Financial Affairs. December 2023, https://commission.europa.eu/document/download/7fff9205-b77a-4a3f-ad85-8a4c88cb6503_en?filename=study-supporting-the-mid-term-evaluation-of-the-recovery-and-resilience-facility_0.pdf.

Edling, MM, 2003. *A Revolution in Favor of Government: Origins of the U.S. Constitution and the Making of the American State*. Ebsco Publishing.

Eichengreen, B, Hausmann, R, and Panizza, U, 2023. Yet it Endures: The Persistence of Original Sin. *Open Economies Review* 34, 1–42, https://doi.org/10.1007/s11079-022-09704-3.

Eisl, A and Tomay, M, 2020. European Debt Mutualisation: Finding a Legitimate Balance Between Solidarity and Responsibility Mechanisms. Notre Europe, Jacques Delors Institute, Policy Paper No 255, https://institutdelors.eu/wp-content/uploads/2020/10/PP255_European-debt-mutualisation_Eisl_EN.pdf.

Electronic Irish Statute Book, 2022. Finance (State Guarantees, International Financial Institution Funds and Miscellaneous Provisions) Act 2024. Guarantee Agreement to be Entered into Between the State and the European Commission Pursuant to Article 10 of Decision 2022/1628 of the European Parliament and of the Council of 20 September 2022, https://www.irishstatutebook.ie/eli/2024/act/3/schedule/3/enacted/en/html.

Engelen, C, 2022. Presentation, Team Europe borrowers seminar: a new era for sovereign debt [Video]. OMFIF. 25 October 2022, https://www.omfif.org/videos/team-europe-borrowers-seminar-a-new-era-for-sovereign-debt/.

EPPO, 2025. EPPO Annual Report 2024. 24 March 2025, https://www.eppo.europa.eu/assets/annual-report-2024/pdfs/EPPO_Annual_Report_2024_en.pdf.

EPPO, 2024a. Investigation 'Resilient Crime': 22 arrests in raid against criminal organisation suspected of €600 million fraud involving NextGenerationEU funds, https://www.eppo.europa.eu/en/news/investigation-resilient-crime-22-arrests-raid-against-criminal-organisation-suspected-eu600.

EPPO, 2024b. EPPO Annual Report 2023. 1 March 2024, https://www.eppo.europa.eu/sites/default/files/2024-03/EPPO_Annual_Report_2023.pdf.

Erce, A and Corsetti, G, 2020. Maturity, seniority and size: Make sure the ESM's pandemic crisis support is fit for purpose! VoxEU | CEPR, https://cepr.org/voxeu/columns/maturity-seniority-and-size-make-sure-esms-pandemic-crisis-support-fit-purpose.

ESM, 2022. Pandemic Crisis Support: Explainer, Timeline and Documents, https://www.esm.europa.eu/content/europe-response-corona-crisis.

ESRB High-Level Task Force on Safe Assets, 2018. Sovereign bond-backed securities: a feasibility study, Volume 1: main findings. January 2018, https://www.esrb.europa.eu/pub/task_force_safe_assets/shared/pdf/esrb.report290118_sbbs_volume_I_mainfindings.en.pdf.

EU Reporter, 2024. Commission launches EU Repurchase Agreement, thereby becoming a sovereign-style issuer on EU capital markets. EU Reporter. 10 October 2024, https://www.eureporter.co/politics/european-commission/2024/10/10/commission-launches-eu-repurchase-agreement-thereby-becoming-a-sovereign-style-issuer-on-eu-capital-markets/.

Eurex, 2025. Eurex to launch futures on EU bonds. Deutsche Börse Group. 23 April 2025, https://www.eurex.com/ex-en/find/news-center/news/Eurex-to-launch-futures-on-EU-bonds--4411966.

EUR-Lex, 2025. Macrofinancial assistance to Ukraine, https://eur-lex.europa.eu/legal-content/EN/TXT/?uri=legissum:4581923.

Euro Summit, 2018. Statement of the Euro Summit. Press Release, 14 December 2018, https://www.consilium.europa.eu/en/press/press-releases/2018/12/14/statement-of-the-euro-summit-14-december-2018/.

Eurogroup, 2020. Report on the comprehensive economic policy response to the COVID-19 pandemic. Press Release, 9 April 2020, https://www.consilium.europa.eu/en/press/press-releases/2020/04/09/report-on-the-comprehensive-economic-policy-response-to-the-covid-19-pandemic/.

Eurogroup, 2019. Term sheet on the budgetary instrument for convergence and competitiveness (BICC). 10 October 2019, https://www.consilium.europa.eu/en/press/press-releases/2019/10/10/term-sheet-on-the-budgetary-instrument-for-convergence-and-competitiveness-bicc/.

Europe Direct, 2025a. Europe Direct Contact Centre—the EU's helpline for citizens, https://european-union.europa.eu/contact-eu/write-us/answering-your-questions_en.

Europe Direct, 2025b. 6012996. Email from Europe Direct Contact Centre, to Päivi Leino-Sandberg. Subject: Your Europe Direct reply no #6012996. 5 June 2025 [on file with authors].

Europe Direct, 2025c. 6345551. Email from Europe Direct Contact Centre, to Päivi Leino-Sandberg. Subject: Your Europe Direct reply no #6345551. 19 August 2025 [on file with the authors].

Europe Direct, 2025d. 5461376. Email from Europe Direct Contact Centre, to Päivi Leino-Sandberg. Subject: Your Europe Direct reply no #5461376. 20 March 2025 [on file with authors].

Europe Direct, 2024. 3766276. Email from Europe Direct Contact Centre, to Päivi Leino-Sandberg. Subject: Your Europe Direct reply no #3766276. 22 April 2024 [on file with authors].

European Central Bank, 2025a. Asset purchase programmes, https://www.ecb.europa.eu/mopo/implement/app/html/index.en.html.

European Central Bank, 2025b. Pandemic emergency purchase programme (PEPP) https://www.ecb.europa.eu/mopo/implement/pepp/html/index.en.html https://www.ecb.europa.eu/mopo/implement/pepp/html/index.en.html.

European Central Bank, 2023. Annual Report 2022, https://www.ecb.europa.eu/press/annual-reports-financial-statements/annual/html/ecb.ar2022~8ae51d163b.en.html.

European Central Bank, 2022. ECB reviews its risk control framework for credit operations. Press Release, 20 December 2022, https://www.ecb.europa.eu/press/pr/date/2022/html/ecb.pr221220_1~ca6ca2cc09.en.html.

European Central Bank, 2016. The Euro Area Fiscal Stance. *Economic Bulletin* 4, https://www.ecb.europa.eu/pub/pdf/other/eb201604_article02.en.pdf.

European Commission, 2025a. Banking Union, https://finance.ec.europa.eu/banking-and-banking-union/banking-union_en.

European Commission, 2025b. Balance of payments (BoP) assistance facility, Information on how the EU offers BoP assistance to EU countries outside the euro area, https://economy-finance.ec.europa.eu/eu-financial-assistance/non-euro-area-countries/balance-payments-bop-assistance-facility_en.

European Commission, 2025c. Recovery and Resilience Scoreboard, https://ec.europa.eu/economy_finance/recovery-and-resilience-scoreboard/index.html?lang=en.

European Commission, 2025d. Commission endorses positive preliminary assessment of Italy's seventh payment request. Press Release. 1 July 2025, https://ec.europa.eu/commission/presscorner/detail/en/ip_25_1696.

European Commission, 2025e. Information provided to the European Parliament or to the Council on the Recovery and Resilience Plans (as of 15 July 2025), https://commission.europa.eu/business-economy-euro/economic-recovery/recovery-and-resilience-facility/information-provided-european-parliament-or-council-recovery-and-resilience-plans_en.

European Commission, 2025f. Country pages, https://commission.europa.eu/business-economy-euro/economic-recovery/recovery-and-resilience-facility/country-pages_en.

European Commission, 2025g. COM(2025) 637 final. Report from the Commission to the European Parliament and the Council on the Implementation of the Recovery and Resilience Facility. 8 October 2025, https://commission.europa.eu/document/download/81dd7c71-7b75-4b2a-8323-fb7b4326fa16_en?filename=COM_2025_637_1_EN_ACT_part1_v4.pdf.

European Commission, 2025h. COM(2025) 163 final. Communication from the Commission to the European Parliament and the Council. A modernised Cohesion policy: The mid-term review. 1 April 2025, https://eur-lex.europa.eu/legal-content/EN/TXT/PDF/?uri=CELEX:52025DC0163.

European Commission, 2025i. COM(2025) 164 final. Proposal for a Regulation of the European Parliament and of the Council amending Regulation (EU) 2021/1057 establishing the European Social Fund + (ESF+) as regards specific measures to address strategic challenges. 1 April 2025, https://eur-lex.europa.eu/legal-content/EN/TXT/PDF/?uri=CELEX:52025PC0164.

European Commission, 2025j. COM(2025) 188 final. Proposal for a Regulation of the European Parliament and of the Council amending Regulations (EU) 2021/694, (EU) 2021/695, (EU) 2021/697, (EU) 2021/1153, (EU) 2023/1525 and 2024/795, as regards incentivising defence-related investments in the EU budget to implement the ReArm Europe Plan. 22 April 2025, https://eur-lex.europa.eu/legal-content/EN/TXT/PDF/?uri=CELEX:52025PC0188.

European Commission, 2025k. Thematic analysis: Housing. Recovery and Resilience Scoreboard, https://ec.europa.eu/economy_finance/recovery-and-resilience-scoreboard/assets/thematic_analysis/scoreboard_thematic_analysis_housing.pdf.

European Commission, 2025l. NextGenerationEU: for a stronger, more resilient Europe, https://next-generation-eu.europa.eu/index_en.

European Commission, 2025m. COM(2025) 310 final/2. Communication from the Commission to the European Parliament and Council. NextGenerationEU—The road to 2026. 4 June 2025, https://commission.europa.eu/document/download/ad5f00c9-4101-41a0-9d8f-e78f06c0c7ed_en?filename=COM_2025_310_1_EN_ACT_part1_v8.pdf.

European Commission, 2025n. Recovery and Resilience Facility, https://commission.europa.eu/business-economy-euro/economic-recovery/recovery-and-resilience-facility_en.

European Commission, 2025o. Macro-Financial Assistance (MFA), https://economy-finance.ec.europa.eu/eu-financial-assistance/macro-financial-assistance-mfa_en.

European Commission, 2025p. Ukraine Facility, https://enlargement.ec.europa.eu/funding-technical-assistance/ukraine-facility_en.

European Commission, 2025q. 2025 European Semester: Spring package, 4 June 2025, https://commission.europa.eu/publications/2025-european-semester-spring-package_en.

European Commission, 2025r. Commission disburses first €3 billion to Ukraine of its part of the G7 loan, to be repaid with proceeds from immobilised Russian assets. Press Release, 9 January 2025, https://ec.europa.eu/commission/presscorner/detail/ro/ip_25_223.

European Commission, 2025s. How EU issuance works, https://commission.europa.eu/strategy-and-policy/eu-budget/eu-borrower-investor-relations/how-eu-issuance-works_en#documents.

European Commission, 2025t. Ref. Ares(2025)2349784 - 24/03/2025. BUDG.01. Letter of Stéphanie Riso, Director-General, DG Budget (BUDG), to Päivi Leino-Sandberg, Subject: Your application for access to documents (2025/0746). 24 March 2025 [on file with authors].

European Commission, 2025u. EU Investor Presentation: Investing in EU-Bonds & EU-Bills. 28 February 2025, https://commission.europa.eu/document/download/eb6d75f1-5936-4526-961d-2ba8178a3549_en?filename=EU%20Investor%20Presentation%2010%20December%202024.pdf.

European Commission, 2025v. COM(2025) 574 final. Proposal for a Council Decision on the system of own resources of the European Union and repealing Decision (EU, Euratom) 2020/2053. 16 July 2025, https://commission.europa.eu/document/download/eb03e969-37ed-4697-98a8-a9709a09a9c4_en?filename=COM_2025_574_1_EN_ACT_part1_v5.pdf.

European Commission, 2025w. COM(2025) 30 final. Communication from the Commission to the European Parliament, the European Council, the Council, the European Economic and Social Committee and the Committee of the Regions. A Competitiveness Compass for the EU. 29 January 2025, https://commission.europa.eu/document/download/10017eb1-4722-4333-add2-e0ed18105a34_en.

European Commission, 2025x. COM(2025) 122 final. Proposal for a Council Regulation establishing the Security Action for Europe (SAFE) through the reinforcement of European defence industry Instrument. 19 March 2025, https://eur-lex.europa.eu/legal-content/EN/TXT/?uri=celex:52025PC0122.

European Commission, 2025y. COM(2025) 45 final. Communication from the Commission to the European Parliament, the Council, the European Economic And Social Committee and the Committee of The Regions. Commission work programme 2025: Moving forward together: A Bolder, Simpler, Faster Union. 11 February 2025, https://eur-lex.europa.eu/legal-content/EN/TXT/?uri=celex:52025DC0045.

European Commission, 2025z. White Paper for European Defence—Readiness 2030. 19 March 2025, https://commission.europa.eu/document/download/e6d5db69-e0ab-4bec-9dc0-3867b4373019_en?filename=White%20paper%20for%20European%20defence%20%E2%80%93%20Readiness%202030.pdf.

European Commission, 2025aa. Questions and answers on ReArm Europe Plan/Readiness 2030. 19 March 2025, https://ec.europa.eu/commission/presscorner/api/files/document/print/en/qanda_25_790/QANDA_25_790_EN.pdf.

European Commission, 2025ab. COM(2025) 46 final. Communication from the Commission to the European Parliament, the European Council, the Council, the European Economic and Social Committee and the Committee of the Regions. The road to the next multiannual financial framework. 11 February 2025, https://eur-lex.europa.eu/legal-content/EN/TXT/?uri=celex:52025DC0046.

European Commission, 2025ac. SWD(2025) 570 final. Commission Staff Working Document Accompanying the document Communication from the Commission to the European Parliament, the European Council, the Council, the European Economic and Social Committee and the Committee of the Regions: A dynamic EU budget for the priorities of the future: the Multiannual Financial Framework 2028-2034. 16 July 2025, https://eur-lex.europa.eu/legal-content/EN/TXT/?uri=CELEX%3A52025SC0570.

European Commission, 2025ad. COM(2025) 570 final. Communication from the Commission to the European Parliament, the European Council, the Council, the European Economic and Social Committee and the Committee of the Regions. A dynamic EU Budget for the priorities of the future - The Multiannual Financial Framework 2028-2034. 16 July 2025, https://eur-lex.europa.eu/legal-content/EN/TXT/PDF/?uri=CELEX:52025DC0570&qid=1753221095089.

European Commission, 2025ae. Europe's Budget: Member States Allocation. MFF 2028-2034 National And Regional Partnership Plans Allocations. July 2025, https://commission.europa.eu/document/download/5868c188-933f-49dc-b7c3-d7fb3c82a064_en?filename=MFF_Member%20States%20allocation_17.07_22h35.pdf.

European Commission, 2025af. COM(2025) 571 final. Proposal for a Council Regulation laying down the multiannual financial framework for the years 2028 to 2034. 16 July 2025, https://eur-lex.europa.eu/legal-content/EN/TXT/HTML/?uri=CELEX:52025PC0571.

European Commission, 2025ag. COM(2025) 545 final. Proposal for a Regulation of the European Parliament and of the Council establishing a budget expenditure tracking and performance framework and other horizontal rules for the Union programmes and activities. 16 July 2025, https://eur-lex.europa.eu/resource.html?uri=cellar:bb24b1ec-62fc-11f0-bf4e-01aa75ed71a1.0001.02/DOC_4&format=PDF.

European Commission, 2025ah. SWD(2025) 570 final/2. Commission Staff Working Document, Accompanying the document Communication from the Commission to the European Parliament, the European Council, the Council, the European Economic and Social Committee and the Committee of the Regions. A dynamic EU budget for the priorities of the future: the Multiannual Financial Framework 2028-2034. 16 July 2025, https://eur-lex.europa.eu/legal-content/EN/TXT/PDF/?uri=CELEX:52025SC0570R(01).

European Commission, 2025ai. COM(2025) 545 final Annex I. Annex to the Proposal for a Regulation of the European Parliament and of the Council establishing a budget expenditure tracking and performance framework and other horizontal rules for the Union programmes and activities. 16 July 2025, https://commission.europa.eu/document/download/e04d25a4-73ed-458b-8ec9-8cf27465510c_en?filename=COM_2025_545_1_EN_annexe_propositi on_part1_v7.pdf.

European Commission, 2025aj. COM(2025) 565 final. Proposal for a Regulation of the European Parliament and of the Council establishing the European Fund for economic, social and territorial cohesion, agriculture and rural, fisheries and maritime, prosperity and security for the period 2028–2034 and amending Regulation (EU) 2023/955 and Regulation (EU, Euratom) 2024/2509. 16 July 2025, https://eur-lex.europa.eu/resource.html?uri=cel lar:0d5ded06-639d-11f0-bf4e-01aa75ed71a1.0001.02/DOC_1&format=PDF.

European Commission, 2024a. C(2024) 3961 final. Decision of the European Commission Pursuant to Article 4 of the Implementing Rules to Regulation (EC) No 1049/2001, addressed to Päivi Leino-Sandberg, 9 June 2024. Subject: Your confirmatory application for access to documents under Regulation (EC) No 1049/2001 - 2023/5187 [on file with authors].

European Commission, 2024b. SWD(2024) 70 final. Commission Staff Working Document: Mid-term evaluation of the Recovery and Resilience Facility. Accompanying the Communication from the Commission to the European Parliament, the Council, the European Economic And Social Committee and the Committee of the Regions: Mid-Term Evaluation of the Recovery and Resilience Facility: Strengthening the EU through ambitious reforms and investments [COM(2024) 82 final]. 21 February 2024, https://commission.europa.eu/document/download/17c82840-518c-4c3d-ba98-7dae436b3a70_en?filename=SWD_2024_70_1_EN_autre_document_travail_service_part1_v4.pdf.

European Commission, 2024c. Ref. Ares(2024)1155817 - 15/02/24. REFORM.A.2.002. Letter of Mario Nava, Director-General, Directorate-General for Structural Reform Support, to Viivi Säiläkivi, dated 13 February 2024. Subject: Your application for access to documents—case 2024/0039, https://www.asktheeu.org/request/information_request_technical_su_2#outgoing-28058.

European Commission, 2024d. COM(2024) 82 final. Communication from the Commission to the European Parliament, the Council, the European Economic And Social Committee and the Committee of the Regions: Mid-Term Evaluation of the Recovery and Resilience Facility: Strengthening the EU through ambitious reforms and investments 21 February 2024, https://commission.europa.eu/document/download/f953f881-5a01-4040-804c-16be479ed3c4_en?filename=COM_2024_82_1_EN_ACT_part1_v5.pdf.

European Commission, 2024e. COM(2024) 318 final. Report from the Commission to the Council and the European Parliament. 35th Annual Report on the Protection of the European Union's financial interests and the Fight against fraud 2023. 25 July 2024, https://anti-fraud.ec.europa.eu/document/download/e600af45-0604-4102-a320-1764987ba220_en?filename=pif-report-2023_en.PDF.
European Commission, 2024f. Positive preliminary assessment of the satisfactory fulfilment of milestones and targets related to the first payment request submitted by Poland on 15 December 2023, transmitted to the Economic and Financial Committee by the European Commission. 29 February 2024, https://commission.europa.eu/document/download/52bd45c7-da37-4ba0-b623-95da8cdad7f9_en?filename=C_2024_1438_1_EN_annexe_acte_autonome_nlw_part1_v1.pdf.
European Commission, 2024g. Press Release. Poland's efforts to restore rule of law pave the way for accessing up to €137 billion in EU funds. Brussels, 29 February 2024, https://ec.europa.eu/commission/presscorner/api/files/document/print/en/ip_24_1222/IP_24_1222_EN.pdf.
European Commission, 2024h. SWD(2024) 197 final/2. Commission Staff Working Document. Analysis of the recovery and resilience plan of Luxembourg. Accompanying the document Proposal for a Council Implementing Decision amending Implementing Decision (EU) (ST 10155/21 INIT; ST 10155/21 ADD 1) of 13 July 2021 on the approval of the assessment of the recovery and resilience plan for Luxembourg. 6 September 2024, https://eur-lex.europa.eu/legal-content/EN/TXT/PDF/?uri=CELEX:52024SC0197R(01).
European Commission, 2024i. Recovery and Resilience Scoreboard, NextGenEU. Thematic Analysis: Digital skills and education. December 2024, https://ec.europa.eu/economy_finance/recovery-and-resilience-scoreboard/assets/thematic_analysis/scoreboard_thematic_analysis_digital_skills.pdf.
European Commission, 2024j. *Annual management and performance report for the EU budget: financial year 2023. Volume I.* Publications Office of the European Union.
European Commission, 2024k. PV(2024)2483. Minutes of the 2483rd meeting of the Commission. Brussels, 21 February 2024, https://ec.europa.eu/transparency/documents-register/detail?ref=PV(2024)2483&lang=en.
European Commission, 2024l. The Recovery and Resilience Facility continues to deliver, Commission third annual report shows. Press Release, 9 October 2024, https://ec.europa.eu/commission/presscorner/detail/en/ip_24_5206.
European Commission, 2024m. *Annual management and performance report for the EU budget: financial year 2023. Volume 2, Annexes.* Publications Office of the European Union.
European Commission, 2024n. New economic governance framework. An economic governance framework fit for the challenges ahead, https://economy-finance.ec.europa.eu/economic-and-fiscal-governance/eu-assessment-and-monitoring-national-economic-policies/evolution-eu-economic-governance/new-economic-governance-framework_en.
European Commission, 2024o. Launch of EU Repo Facility, https://ec.europa.eu/newsroom/budget/items/849939/en.
European Commission, 2024p. High Level Risk and Compliance Policy. July 2024, https://commission.europa.eu/document/download/89c4b6ec-82f1-43fb-8efd-032b54fe886c_en?filename=Risk%20and%20Compliance%20Policy2024.pdf.
European Commission, 2024q. COM(2024) 460 final. Proposal for a Council Decision on providing short-term macro-financial assistance to the Arab Republic of Egypt. 15 March 2024, https://eur-lex.europa.eu/legal-content/EN/TXT/?uri=CELEX%3A52024PC0460.
European Commission, 2024r. COM(2024) 159 final. Proposal for a Decision of the European Parliament and of the Council on providing macro-financial assistance to the Hashemite Kingdom of Jordan. 8 April 2024, https://economy-finance.ec.europa.eu/document/downl

oad/571cca54-c731-4d9f-a98e-6e8e4716fc5d_en?filename=COM_2024_159_1_EN_ACT_part1_v3.pdf.

European Commission, 2024s. C(2024) 3171 final. Commission implementing decision of 6.5.2024 on the reduction of the amount of the first instalment of the non-repayable support for Lithuania, https://commission.europa.eu/document/download/99c6f86a-342d-4a0e-b750-ae9449658828_en?filename=C_2024_3171_1_EN_ACT_part1_v2.pdf.

European Commission, 2023a. C(2023) 5806 final. Decision of the European Commission Pursuant to Article 4 of the Implementing Rules to Regulation (EC) No 1049/2001, addressed to Päivi Leino-Sandberg, 22 August 2023. Subject: Your confirmatory application for access to documents under Regulation (EC) No 1049/2001 – EASE 2023/1806, 2023/1807 and 2023/1808 [on file with authors].

European Commission, 2023b. Ref. Ares(2023)6974568—13/10/2023. Letter of Daniel Calleja, Director-General, Legal Service, to Päivi Leino-Sandberg, 13 October 2023. Subject: Request for access to documents. Ref.: Your requests of 6 September 2023 registered under reference 2023/5187 [on file with authors].

European Commission, 2023c. Study Supporting the Mid-Term Evaluation of the Recovery and Resilience Facility: Final Report, https://commission.europa.eu/document/download/7fff9205-b77a-4a3f-ad85-8a4c88cb6503_en?filename=study-supporting-the-mid-term-evaluation-of-the-recovery-and-resilience-facility_0.pdf.

European Commission, 2023d. COM(2023) 240 final—2023/0138(COD). Proposal for a Regulation of the European Parliament and of the Council on the effective coordination of economic policies and multilateral budgetary surveillance and repealing Council Regulation (EC) No 1466/97. 26 April 2023, https://eur-lex.europa.eu/legal-content/EN/TXT/?uri=celex:52023PC0240.

European Commission, 2023e. EU Funding Programmes 2014-2020, https://commission.europa.eu/strategy-and-policy/eu-budget/long-term-eu-budget/2014-2020/eu-funding-programmes_en.

European Commission, 2023f. COM(2023) 790 final. Amended proposal for a Regulation of the European Parliament and of the Council on a mechanism to resolve legal and administrative obstacles in a cross-border context. 12 December 2023, https://eur-lex.europa.eu/legal-content/EN/TXT/?uri=CELEX%3A52023PC0790.

European Commission, 2023g. COM(2023) 99 final. Recovery and Resilience Facility: Two years on—A unique instrument at the heart of the EU's green and digital transformation. Communication from the Commission to the European Parliament and the Council. 21 February 2023, https://eur-lex.europa.eu/legal-content/EN/TXT/?uri=CELEX:52023DC0099.

European Commission, 2023h. Case SI/6/2021/PVV, Follow-up reply of the European Commission to the European Ombudsman on the transparency and accountability of the Recovery and Resilience Facility. 18 April 2023, https://www.ombudsman.europa.eu/en/doc/correspondence/en/174448.

European Commission, 2023i. Case 1129/2022/SF, Reply by the European Commission to the proposal for a solution on the European Commission's refusal to give public access to documents concerning the French national plan under the Recovery and Resilience Facility. 6 June 2023, https://www.ombudsman.europa.eu/en/doc/correspondence/en/176524.

European Commission, 2023j. Ref Ares(2023)8201233—30/11/2023. REFORM.A.2./RL. Letter of Mario Nava, Director-General, Directorate-General for Structural Reform Support, to Peter Teffer, dated 30 November 2023. Subject: Your application for access to documents—case 2023/6675, https://www.asktheeu.org/en/request/13709/response/50841/attach/2/231129%202023%206675%20Initial%20reply%20refusal.pdf?cookie_passthrough=1.

European Commission, 2023k. COM(2023) 545 final/2. Report from the Commission to the European Parliament and the Council on the Implementation of the Recovery and Resilience

Facility: Moving Forward. 25 September 2023. Corrects document COM(2023) 545 final of 19.09.2023. Correction of formatting errors, no change to the text, https://eur-lex.europa.eu/legal-content/EN/TXT/PDF/?uri=CELEX:52023DC0545R(01).

European Commission, 2023l. C(2023) 9290 final. Commission implementing decision of 22.12.2023 on the authorisation of the disbursement of the third and fourth instalments of the non-repayable support and the third and fourth instalments of the loan support for Portugal, https://commission.europa.eu/document/download/1275a439-95bd-4b60-b860-7e89d0e27819_en?filename=C_2023_9290_1_EN_ACT_part1_v5.pdf.

European Commission, 2023m. COM(2023) 335 final. Proposal for a Regulation of the European Parliament and of the Council establishing the Strategic Technologies for Europe Platform ('STEP') and amending Directive 2003/87/EC, Regulations (EU) 2021/1058, (EU) 2021/1056, (EU) 2021/1057, (EU) No 1303/2013, (EU) No 223/2014, (EU) 2021/1060, (EU) 2021/523, (EU) 2021/695, (EU) 2021/697 and (EU) 2021/241. 20 June 2023, https://commission.europa.eu/system/files/2023-06/COM_2023_335_1_EN_ACT_part1_v11.pdf.

European Commission, 2023n. COM(2023) 338 final—2023/0200(COD). Proposal for a Regulation of the European Parliament and of the Council on establishing the Ukraine Facility. 20 June 2023, https://eur-lex.europa.eu/legal-content/EN/TXT/?uri=celex:52023PC0338.

European Commission, 2023o. The next generation of EU own resources, https://commission.europa.eu/strategy-and-policy/eu-budget/long-term-eu-budget/2021-2027/revenue/next-generation-eu-own-resources_en.

European Commission, 2023p. COM(2023) 330 final. Communication from the Commission to the European Parliament, the Council, the European Economic And Social Committee and the Committee of the Regions. An adjusted package for the next generation of own resources. 20 June 2023, https://eur-lex.europa.eu/legal-content/EN/TXT/?uri=celex:52023DC0330.

European Commission, 2023q. SWD(2023) 218 final. Commission Staff Working Document Accompanying the Document: Report from the Commission to the European Parliament and the Council. Long-term forecast of future inflows and outflows of the EU budget (2024-2028). 20 June 2023, https://eur-lex.europa.eu/legal-content/EN/TXT/PDF/?uri=CELEX:52023SC0218.

European Commission, 2023r. COM(2023) 336 final. Communication from the Commission to the European Parliament, the European Council, the Council, the European Economic and Social Committee and the Committee of the Regions. Mid-term revision of the Multiannual Financial Framework 2021–2027. 20 June 2023, https://eur-lex.europa.eu/legal-content/EN/TXT/?uri=COM%3A2023%3A336%3AFIN.

European Commission, 2023s. COM(2023) 337 final. Proposal for a Council Regulation amending Regulation (EU, Euratom) 2020/2093 laying down the multiannual financial framework for the years 2021 to 2027. 20 June 2023, https://eur-lex.europa.eu/legal-content/EN/TXT/?uri=CELEX%3A52023PC0337.

European Commission, 2023t. SWD(2023) 264 final. Commission Staff Working Document. First review of the 70% provisioning rate for Macro-financial Assistance (MFA) and certain EIB loan disbursements covered by the External Lending Mandate (ELM) to Ukraine Staff Working Document. 18 July 2023, https://data.consilium.europa.eu/doc/document/ST-12008-2023-INIT/en/pdf.

European Commission, 2023u. EU as a borrower: European Commission to issue €40 billion in long-term EU-Bonds in the second half of 2023. Press Release, 26 June 2023, https://ec.europa.eu/commission/presscorner/detail/en/ip_23_3494.

European Commission, 2023v. Replies of the European Commission to the European Court of Auditors' Special Report [16/2023] on NGEU debt management at the Commission: An encouraging start, but further alignment with best practice needed. 12 June 2023, https://www.eca.europa.eu/Lists/ECAReplies/COM-Replies-SR-2023-16/COM-Replies-SR-2023-16_EN.pdf.

European Commission, 2023w. High Level Risk and Compliance Policy. July 2023, https://commission.europa.eu/document/download/ba794e0f-5637-40b4-891d-688ee9632450_en?filename=High%20Level%20Risk%20and%20Compliance%20Policy%20Report.pdf.

European Commission, 2023x. EU Inaugural Investor Survey: Overview of results. 29 September 2023, https://ec.europa.eu/newsroom/budget/items/800643/en.

European Commission, 2022a. Replies of the European Commission to the European Court of Auditors' Special Report [21/2022], 'The Commission's Assessment of National Recovery and Resilience Plans', https://www.eca.europa.eu/Lists/ECAReplies/COM-Replies-SR-22-21/COM-Replies-SR-22-21_EN.pdf.

European Commission, 2022b. C(2022) 6154 final. Decision of the European Commission Pursuant to Article 4 of the Implementing Rules to Regulation (EC) No 1049/2001, addressed to Peter Teffer, 22 June 2022. Subject: Your confirmatory application for access to documents under Regulation (EC) No 1049/2001 - GESTDEM 2021/7168 and 2022/654 [on file with authors].

European Commission, 2022c. COM(2022) 383 final. Review Report on the implementation of the Recovery and Resilience Facility. Report from the Commission to the European Parliament and the Council. 29 July 2022, https://eur-lex.europa.eu/legal-content/EN/TXT/?uri=CELEX:52022DC0383.

European Commission, 2022d. Case SI/6/2021/PVV, Reply of the European Commission to the European Ombudsman on the transparency and accountability of the Recovery and Resilience Facility. 30 June 2022, https://www.ombudsman.europa.eu/en/doc/correspondence/en/158511.

European Commission, 2022e. C(2022) 3797 final. Decision of the European Commission Pursuant to Article 4 of the Implementing Rules to Regulation (EC) No 1049/2001, addressed to Jean Comte, 2 June 2022. Subject: Your confirmatory application for access to documents under Regulation (EC) No 1049/2001—GESTDEM 2021/2929 [on file with authors].

European Commission, 2022f. Ref. Ares(2022)7706144 - 08/11/2022. REFORM.A.2.002. Letter of Mario Nava, Director-General, Directorate-General for Structural Reform Support, to Carlotta Indiano, dated 7 November 2022. Subject: Your application for access to documents—case 2022/5596, https://www.asktheeu.org/en/request/11892/response/40637/attach/html/3/221107%202022%205596%20initial%20reply%20final.pdf.html.

European Commission, 2022g. Ref Ares(2022)2991252–12/04/2022. SG.RECOVER.A.1/VPP. Letter of Eric von Breska, Director - Recovery & Resilience I, Recovery & Resilience Task Force, to Jarno Liski, 12 April 2022. Subject: Your application for access to documents—GESTDEM 2021/7331 [on file with authors].

European Commission, 2022h. NextGenerationEU: European Commission endorses Poland's €35.4 billion recovery and resilience plan. Press Release, 31 May 2022, https://ec.europa.eu/commission/presscorner/detail/en/ip_22_3375.

European Commission, 2022i. PV(2022) 2420 final. Minutes of the 2420th meeting of the Commission. Brussels, 1 June 2022, https://ec.europa.eu/transparency/documents-register/detail?ref=PV(2022)2420&lang=en.

European Commission, 2022j. C(2022)7157. Commission Implementing Decision of 6 October 2022 approving the programme 'European Funds for Eastern Poland 2021-2027' for support from the European Regional Development Fund under the Investment for jobs and growth goal for the regions Lubelski, Mazowiecki regional, Podkarpacki, Podlaski, Świętokrzyski and Warmińsko-Mazurski in Poland CCI 2021PL16RFPR003, https://ec.europa.eu/transparency/documents-register/detail?ref=C(2022)7157&lang=en.

European Commission, 2022k. PV(2022) 2439 final. Minutes of the 2439th meeting of the Commission. Brussels, 30 November 2022, https://ec.europa.eu/transparency/documents-register/detail?ref=PV(2022)2439&lang=en.

European Commission, 2022l. Factsheet: Laying the foundations for recovery: Hungary. 29 November 2022, https://ec.europa.eu/commission/presscorner/detail/sk/fs_22_7270.

European Commission, 2022m. COM(2022) 108 final. Communication from the Commission to the European Parliament, the European Council, the Council, the European Economic and Social Committee and the Committee of the Regions. REPowerEU: Joint European Action for more affordable, secure and sustainable energy. 8 March 2022, https://eur-lex.europa.eu/legal-content/EN/TXT/?uri=celex:52022DC0108.

European Commission, 2022n. REPowerEU: A plan to rapidly reduce dependence on Russian fossil fuels and fast forward the green transition. Press Release, 17 May 2022, https://ec.europa.eu/commission/presscorner/detail/en/ip_22_3131.

European Commission, 2022o. COM(2022) 231 final - 2022/0164(COD). Proposal for a Regulation of the European Parliament and of the Council amending Regulation (EU) 2021/241 as regards REPowerEU chapters in recovery and resilience plans and amending Regulation (EU) 2021/1060, Regulation (EU) 2021/2115, Directive 2003/87/EC and Decision (EU) 2015/1814. 18 May 2022, https://eur-lex.europa.eu/legal-content/EN/TXT/?uri=celex%3A52022PC0231.

European Commission, 2022p. COM(2022) 583 final. Communication from the Commission to the European Parliament, the Council, the European Central Bank, the European Economic and Social Committee and the Committee of the Regions. Communication on orientations for a reform of the EU economic governance framework. 9 November 2022, https://eur-lex.europa.eu/legal-content/EN/TXT/?uri=celex:52022DC0583.

European Commission, 2022q. COM(2022) 37 final. Proposal for a Decision of the European Parliament and of the Council on providing macro-financial assistance to Ukraine. 1 February 2022, https://eur-lex.europa.eu/legal-content/EN/TXT/?uri=celex%3A52022PC0037.

European Commission, 2022r. COM(2022) 450 final. Proposal for a Decision of the European Parliament and of the Council Providing exceptional macro-financial assistance to Ukraine. 1 July 2022, https://eur-lex.europa.eu/legal-content/EN/TXT/?uri=celex%3A52022PC0450.

European Commission, 2022s. COM(2022) 557 final. Proposal for a Decision of the European Parliament and of the Council providing exceptional macro-financial assistance to Ukraine, reinforcing the Common Provisioning Fund by guarantees by the Member States and by specific provisioning for some financial liabilities related to Ukraine guaranteed under Decision No 466/2014/EU, and amending Decision (EU) 2022/1201. 7 September 2022, https://eur-lex.europa.eu/legal-content/EN/ALL/?uri=COM:2022:0557:FIN.

European Commission, 2022t. EU Budget Policy Brief: The EU as an issuer—the NextGenerationEU transformation. #3. July 2022, https://op.europa.eu/en/publication-detail/-/publication/accacfb6-0966-11ed-b11c-01aa75ed71a1/language-en.

European Commission, 2022u. Questions and Answers: Unified funding approach to EU borrowing. 18 December 2022, https://ec.europa.eu/commission/presscorner/detail/en/qanda_22_7789.

European Commission, 2022v. COM(2022) 596 final. Proposal for a Regulation of the European Parliament and of the Council amending Regulation (EU, Euratom) 2018/1046 as regards the establishment of a diversified funding strategy as a general borrowing method, 9 November 2022, https://eur-lex.europa.eu/legal-content/EN/TXT/?uri=celex%3A52022PC0596.

European Commission, 2021a. COM(2021) 577 final - 2021/0294(NLE). Proposal for a Council Regulation on a framework of measures for ensuring the supply of crisis-relevant medical countermeasures in the event of a public health emergency at Union level. 16 September 2021, https://eur-lex.europa.eu/legal-content/EN/TXT/?uri=CELEX%3A52021PC0577.

European Commission, 2021b. COM(2021) 102 final. Communication from the Commission to the European Parliament, the Council, the European Economic and Social Committee and the Committee of The Regions. The European Pillar of Social Rights Action Plan. 4 March 2021, https://eur-lex.europa.eu/legal-content/EN/TXT/?uri=celex:52021DC0102.

European Commission, 2021c. Commission welcomes European Parliament's approval of Recovery and Resilience Facility. Press Release, 10 February 2021, https://ec.europa.eu/commission/presscorner/detail/en/ip_21_423.

European Commission, 2021d. SWD(2021) 12 final, Part 1/2. Commission Staff Working Document, Guidance to Member States Recovery and Resilience Plans. 22 January 2021, https://commission.europa.eu/document/download/7c55aadf-6b8d-4d9c-a930-bc7ef8656de1_en?filename=document_travail_service_part1_v2_en.pdf.

European Commission, 2021e. C/2021/8481. Communication from the Commission Criteria for the analysis of the compatibility with the internal market of State aid to promote the execution of important projects of common European interest. 30 December 2021, https://eur-lex.europa.eu/legal-content/EN/TXT/?uri=uriserv%3AOJ.C_.2021.528.01.0010.01.ENG&toc=OJ%3AC%3A2021%3A528%3ATOC.

European Commission, 2021f. COM(2021) 574 final. Proposal for a Decision of the European Parliament and of the Council establishing the 2030 Policy Programme 'Path to the Digital Decade'. 15 September 2021, https://eur-lex.europa.eu/legal-content/EN/TXT/?uri=celex%3A52021PC0574.

European Commission, 2021g. SWD(2021) 173 final. Commission Staff Working Document, Analysis of the recovery and resilience plan of France, Accompanying the document Proposal for a Council Implementing Decision on the approval of the assessment of the recovery and resilience plan for France {COM(2021) 351 final}, 23 June 2021, https://eur-lex.europa.eu/legal-content/EN/TXT/PDF/?uri=CELEX:52021SC0173.

European Commission, 2021h. COM(2021) 740 final. Communication from the Commission to the European Parliament, the European Council, the Council, the European Central Bank, the European Economic and Social Committee, the Committee of the Regions and the European Investment Bank. Annual Sustainable Growth Survey 2022. 24 November 2021, https://eur-lex.europa.eu/legal-content/EN/TXT/?uri=CELEX:52021DC0740.

European Commission, 2021i. COM(2021) 550 final. Communication from the Commission to the European Parliament, the Council, the European Economic and Social Committee and the Committee of the Regions. 'Fit for 55': delivering the EU's 2030 Climate Target on the way to climate neutrality. 14 July 2021, https://eur-lex.europa.eu/legal-content/EN/TXT/?uri=celex:52021DC0550.

European Commission, 2021j. COM(2021) 570 final. Proposal for a Council Decision amending Decision (EU, Euratom) 2020/2053 on the system of own resources of the European Union. 22 December 2021, https://eur-lex.europa.eu/legal-content/EN/TXT/?uri=celex:52021PC0570.

European Commission, 2021k. The Commission proposes the next generation of EU own resources. Press Release, 21 December 2021, https://ec.europa.eu/commission/presscorner/detail/en/ip_21_7025.

European Commission, 2021l. COM(2021) 569 final. Proposal for a Council Regulation amending Regulation (EU, Euratom) 2020/2093 laying down the multiannual financial framework for the years 2021 to 2027. 22 December 2021, https://eur-lex.europa.eu/legal-content/EN/TXT/?uri=CELEX%3A52021PC0569.

European Commission, 2021m. COM(2021) 250 final. Communication from the Commission to the European Parliament and the Council on a new funding strategy to finance NextGenerationEU. 14 April 2021, https://eur-lex.europa.eu/legal-content/EN/ALL/?uri=COM:2021:250:FIN.

European Commission, 2020a. Q&A: Next Generation EU—Legal Construction. 8 June 2020, https://ec.europa.eu/commission/presscorner/detail/en/qanda_20_1024.

European Commission, 2020b. COM(2020) 408 final—2020/0104(COD). Proposal for a Regulation of the European Parliament and of the Council establishing a Recovery and Resilience Facility, https://eur-lex.europa.eu/legal-content/EN/TXT/?uri=CELEX%3A52020PC0408.

European Commission, 2020c. COM(2020) 55 final. Economic Governance Review: Report on the Application of Regulations (EU) No 1173/2011, 1174/2011, 1175/2011, 1176/2011, 1177/2011, 472/2013 and 473/2013 and on the suitability of Council Directive 2011/85/EU. 5 February 2020, https://eur-lex.europa.eu/legal-content/EN/TXT/?uri=CELEX%3A52020DC0055.

European Commission, 2020d. Europe's Moment: Repair and Prepare for the Next Generation. Press Release, 26 May 2020, https://ec.europa.eu/commission/presscorner/detail/en/ip_20_940.

European Commission, 2020e. COM(2020) 409 final. Proposal for a Regulation of the European Parliament and of the Council establishing a Technical Support Instrument. 28 May 2020, https://eur-lex.europa.eu/legal-content/EN/TXT/?uri=celex%3A52020PC0409.

European Commission, 2020f. COM(2020) 123 final. Communication to the Council on the Activation of the General Escape Clause of the Stability and Growth Pact. 20 March 2020, https://eur-lex.europa.eu/legal-content/EN/TXT/?uri=CELEX%3A52020DC0123.

European Commission, 2020g. 2020 OJ C91/1. Communication [on the] Temporary framework for State aid measures to support the economy in the current COVID-10 outbreak. 20 March 2020, https://eur-lex.europa.eu/legal-content/EN/TXT/?uri=OJ%3AJOC_2020_091_I_0001.

European Commission, 2020h. COVID-19: Commission sets out European coordinated response to counter the economic impact of the Coronavirus. Press Release, 12 March 2020, https://ec.europa.eu/commission/presscorner/detail/en/ip_20_459.

European Commission, 2020i. COM(2020) 139 final—2020/0057(NLE). Proposal for a Council Regulation on the establishment of a European instrument for temporary support to mitigate unemployment risks in an emergency (SURE) following the COVID-19 outbreak. 2 April 2020, https://eur-lex.europa.eu/legal-content/EN/TXT/?uri=COM%3A2020%3A0139%3AFIN.

European Commission, 2019a. COM(2019) 354 final—2019/0161(COD). Proposal for a Regulation of the European Parliament and of the Council on a governance framework for the budgetary instrument for convergence and competitiveness for the euro area. 24 July 2019, https://eur-lex.europa.eu/legal-content/EN/TXT/?uri=CELEX:52019PC0354.

European Commission, 2019b. Vade Mecum on the Stability and Growth Pact. 2019 Edition. European Economy Institutional Paper 101. DG ECFIN. April 2019, https://economy-finance.ec.europa.eu/document/download/f5e4d0a2-9363-4563-a656-c7de43b8d9a3_en?filename=ip101_en.pdf.

European Commission, 2019c. Sovereign Bond-Backed Securities (SBBS), https://finance.ec.europa.eu/banking-and-banking-union/banking-union/sovereign-bond-backed-securities-sbbs_en.

European Commission, 2019d. COM(2019) 640 final. Communication from the Commission: the European Green Deal. 11 December 2019, https://eur-lex.europa.eu/legal-content/EN/TXT/?uri=CELEX:52019DC0640.

European Commission, 2019e. Recommendation for a Council Recommendation on the 2019 National Reform Programme of France and delivering a Council opinion on the 2019 Stability Programme of France. 5 June 2019, https://eur-lex.europa.eu/legal-content/EN/TXT/HTML/?uri=CELEX:52019DC0510&from=EN.

European Commission, 2018a. COM(2018) 391 final—2018/0213(COD). Proposal for a Regulation of the European Parliament and of the Council on the establishment of the Reform Support Programme. 31 May 2018, https://eur-lex.europa.eu/legal-content/EN/ALL/?uri=COM%3A2018%3A391%3AFIN.

European Commission, 2018b. COM(2018) 387 final—2018/0212(COD). Proposal for a Regulation of the European Parliament and of the Council on the establishment of a European Investment Stabilisation Function. 31 May 2018, https://eur-lex.europa.eu/legal-content/EN/TXT/?uri=COM:2018:387:FIN.

European Commission, 2018c. COM(2018) 321 final. Communication to the European Parliament, the European Council, the Council, the European Economic and Social Committee and the Committee of the Regions. A Modern Budget for a Union that Protects, Empowers and Defends: the Multiannual Financial Framework for 2021-2027. 2 May 2018, https://eur-lex.europa.eu/resource.html?uri=cellar:c2bc7dbd-4fc3-11e8-be1d-01aa75ed71a1.0023.01/DOC_1&format=DOC.

European Commission, 2018d. COM/2018/339 final. Proposal for a Regulation of the European Parliament and of the Council on sovereign bond-backed securities, 2018/0171(COD), (Text with EEA relevance). 24 May 2018, https://eur-lex.europa.eu/legal-content/EN/TXT/?uri=CELEX%3A52018PC0339.

European Commission, 2018e. The Reform Support Programme and the European Investment Stabilisation Function explained. 30 May 2018, https://ec.europa.eu/commission/presscorner/detail/en/MEMO_18_3971.

European Commission, 2018f. COM(2018) 373 final, 2018/0198(COD). Proposal for a Regulation of the European Parliament and of the Council on a mechanism to resolve legal and administrative obstacles in a cross-border context. 29 May 2018, https://eur-lex.europa.eu/legal-content/EN/TXT/?uri=CELEX%3A52018PC0373.

European Commission, 2017a. COM(2017)2025. White Paper on the Future of Europe: Reflections and Scenarios for the EU27 by 2025. 1 March 2017, https://commission.europa.eu/document/download/b2e60d06-37c6-4943-820f-d82ec197d966_en?filename=white_paper_on_the_future_of_europe_en.pdf.

European Commission, 2017b. Reflection Paper on the Future of EU Finances. Publications Office of the European Union, https://data.europa.eu/doi/10.2775/94244.

European Commission, 2017c. COM(2017) 650 final. Communication from the Commission to the European Parliament, the Council, the European Economic and Social Committee and the Committee Of The Regions. Commission Work Programme 2018: An agenda for a more united, stronger and more democratic Europe, https://commission.europa.eu/document/download/3719f3cc-1529-41eb-b06e-38553f01d5cf_en?filename=cwp_2018_en.pdf.

European Commission, 2017d. COM(2017) 250 final. Communication from the Commission to the European Parliament, the Council, the European Economic and Social Committee and the Committee of the Regions. Establishing a European Pillar of Social Rights. 26 April 2017, https://eur-lex.europa.eu/legal-content/EN/TXT/?uri=celex%3A52017DC0250.

European Commission, 2017e. COM(2017) 358. Reflection Paper on the Future of EU Finances, 28 June 2017, https://op.europa.eu/en/publication-detail/-/publication/5f9c0e27-6519-11e7-b2f2-01aa75ed71a1.

European Commission, 2017f. Parliamentary question, European Parliament - E-003113/2017(ASW). Answer given by Ms Bieńkowska on behalf of the Commission, 10 October 2017, https://www.europarl.europa.eu/doceo/document/E-8-2017-003113-ASW_EN.html.

European Commission, 2015. Parliamentary question, European Parliament—E-001662/2015(ASW). Answer given by Vice-President Georgieva on behalf of the Commission, 23 March 2015, https://www.europarl.europa.eu/doceo/document/E-8-2015-001662-ASW_EN.html.

European Commission, 2014. 6th Report on Economic, Social and Territorial Cohesion, https://ec.europa.eu/regional_policy/information-sources/publications/reports/2014/6th-report-on-economic-social-and-territorial-cohesion_en.

European Commission, 2013a. COM(2013) 166 final. Communication from the Commission to the European Parliament and the Council: Towards a Deep and Genuine Economic and Monetary Union—Ex ante coordination of plans for major economic policy reforms. 20 March 2013, https://eur-lex.europa.eu/legal-content/EN/TXT/PDF/?uri=CELEX:52013DC0166.

European Commission, 2013b. COM(2013) 165 final. Communication from the Commission to the European Parliament and the Council: Towards a Deep and Genuine Economic and Monetary Union—The introduction of a Convergence and Competitiveness Instrument. 20 March 2013, https://eur-lex.europa.eu/legal-content/EN/TXT/PDF/?uri=CELEX:52013DC0165.

European Commission, 2012. COM(2012) 777 final. Communication from the Commission. A blueprint for a deep and genuine economic and monetary union: Launching a European Debate. 28 November 2012, https://eur-lex.europa.eu/legal-content/EN/TXT/?uri=celex:52012DC0777.

European Commission, 2002. COM(2002) 20 final. Communication from the Commission to the Council and the European Parliament. EC/EURATOM Lending and Guarantee Capacity for External Actions. 21 January 2002, https://www.europarl.europa.eu/meetdocs/committees/cont/20020709/20-02EN.pdf.

European Commission Legal Service, 2022. *70 Years of EU Law: A Union for Its Citizens*. Publications Office of the European Union.

European Convention, Working Group V, 2002. CONV 375/1/02, REV 1, WG V 14. Final report of Working Group V, from Chairman of Working Group V, 'Complementary Competencies', to Members of the Convention. European Convention. 4 November 2002, https://wayback.archive-it.org/org-1495/20200226195305/http://european-convention.europa.eu/pdf/reg/en/02/cv00/cv00375-re01.en02.pdf.

European Council, 2025. European Council conclusions on European defence, 6 March 2025, https://www.consilium.europa.eu/en/press/press-releases/2025/03/06/european-council-conclusions-on-european-defence/.

European Council, 2024. EUCO 2/24. Note. From: General Secretariat of the Council; To: Delegations; Subject: Special meeting of the European Council (1 February 2024) – Conclusions, https://www.consilium.europa.eu/media/69874/20240201-special-euco-conclusions-en.pdf.

European Council, 2023. EUCO 1/23. Note From: General Secretariat of the Council, To: Delegations, Subject: Special meeting of the European Council (9 February 2023)—Conclusions, https://data.consilium.europa.eu/doc/document/ST-1-2023-INIT/en/pdf.

European Council, 2020. EUCO 10/20. Note from General Secretariat of the Council to Delegations. Subject: Special meeting of the European Council (17, 18, 19, 20 and 21 July 2020)—Conclusions, https://www.consilium.europa.eu/media/45109/210720-euco-final-conclusions-en.pdf.

European Council, 2000. Lisbon European Council, 23-24 March 2000. Conclusions of the Presidency, https://aei.pitt.edu/43340/1/Lisbon_1999.pdf.

European Court of Auditors, 2025a. Special report 10/2025: Labour market reforms in the national recovery and resilience plans: Some results, but not sufficient to address structural challenges. 26 March 2025, http://www.eca.europa.eu/en/publications/sr-2025-10.

European Court of Auditors, 2025b. Review 02/2025: Performance-orientation, accountability and transparency—lessons to be learned from the weaknesses of the RRF, 6 May 2025, https://www.eca.europa.eu/ECAPublications/RV-2025-02/RV-2025-02_EN.pdf.

European Court of Auditors, 2025c. Review 03/2025: Opportunities for the post-2027 Multiannual Financial Framework. 16 June 2025, https://www.eca.europa.eu/ECAPublications/RV-2025-03/RV-2025-03_EN.pdf.

European Court of Auditors, 2024a. Special report 14/2024: Green transition—Unclear contribution from the Recovery and Resilience Facility. 11 September 2024, http://www.eca.europa.eu/en/publications/sr-2024-14.

European Court of Auditors, 2024b. Special report 13/2024: Absorption of funds from the Recovery and Resilience Facility: Progressing with delays and risks remain regarding the completion of measures and therefore the achievement of RRF objectives. 2 September 2024, http://www.eca.europa.eu/en/publications/sr-2024-13.

European Court of Auditors, 2024c. COVID recovery money trickles more slowly than planned into the real economy, http://www.eca.europa.eu/en/news/news-sr-2024-13.

European Court of Auditors, 2024d. Opinion 01/2024 concerning the proposal for a Regulation of the European Parliament and of the Council on establishing the Reform and Growth Facility for the Western Balkans. 7 February 2024, http://www.eca.europa.eu/en/publications/op-2024-01.

European Court of Auditors, 2024e. Special report 16/2024: EU revenue based on non-recycled plastic packaging waste. 16 September 2024, https://www.eca.europa.eu/ECAPublications/SR-2024-16/SR-2024-16_EN.pdf.

European Court of Auditors, 2023a. Special report 02/2023: Adapting cohesion policy rules to respond to COVID-19: funds used more flexibly, but reflection needed on cohesion policy as a crisis response tool, https://www.eca.europa.eu/Lists/ECADocuments/SR23_02/SR_Covid_II-ReACT_EU_EN.pdf.

European Court of Auditors, 2023b. Special report 26/2023: The Recovery and Resilience Facility's performance monitoring framework—Measuring implementation progress but not sufficient to capture performance. 24 October 2023, https://www.eca.europa.eu/en/publications?ref=SR-2023-26.

European Court of Auditors, 2023c. Special report 11/2023. EU support for the digitalisation of schools: Significant investments, but a lack of strategic focus in the use of EU financing by member states. 24 April 2023, http://www.eca.europa.eu/en/publications/sr-2023-11.

European Court of Auditors, 2023d. Annual reports concerning the financial year 2022. 4 October 2023, https://www.eca.europa.eu/en/publications/AR-2022.

European Court of Auditors, 2023e. Review 01/2023: EU financing through cohesion policy and the Recovery and Resilience Facility: A comparative analysis. 19 January 2023, https://www.eca.europa.eu/lists/ecadocuments/rw23_01/rw_rff_and_cohesion_funds_en.pdf.

European Court of Auditors, 2023f. Special report 07/2023: Design of the Commission's control system for the RRF. 8 March 2023, http://www.eca.europa.eu/en/publications/sr-2023-07.

European Court of Auditors, 2023g. Special report 05/2023: The EU's financial landscape—A patchwork construction requiring further simplification and accountability. 1 March 2023, https://www.eca.europa.eu/en/publications?did=63502.

European Court of Auditors, 2023h. Opinion 03/2023 concerning the proposal for a Regulation of the European Parliament and of the Council on establishing the Ukraine Facility. 5 October 2023, https://www.eca.europa.eu/en/publications/OP-2023-03.

European Court of Auditors, 2023i. Special report 16/2023: NGEU debt management at the Commission. 12 June 2023, http://www.eca.europa.eu/en/publications/sr-2023-16.

European Court of Auditors, 2022a. Special report 21/2022: The Commission's assessment of national recovery and resilience plans—Overall appropriate but implementation risks remain, http://www.eca.europa.eu/en/publications/sr22_21.

European Court of Auditors, 2022b. Opinion 04/2022 concerning the proposal for a Regulation of the European Parliament and of the Council amending Regulation (EU) 2021/241 as regards REPowerEU chapters in recovery and resilience plans and amending Regulation (EU) 2021/1060, Regulation (EU) 2021/2115, Directive 2003/87/EC and Decision (EU) 2015/1814 [2022/0164 (COD)]. 26 July 2022, https://www.eca.europa.eu/Lists/ECADocuments/OP22_04/OP_REPowerEU_EN.pdf.

European Court of Auditors, 2022c. Opinion 08/2022 (pursuant to Article 322(1), TFEU) concerning the proposal for a Regulation of the European Parliament and of the Council establishing a Social Climate Fund as revised by the Council. 16 December 2022, http://www.eca.europa.eu/en/publications/op22_08.

European Court of Auditors, 2022d. Opinion 07/2022 concerning the proposal for a Regulation of the European Parliament and of the Council amending Regulation (EU, Euratom) 2018/1046 as regards the establishment of a diversified funding strategy as a general borrowing method. 22 November 2022, https://www.eca.europa.eu/en/publications?did=62737.

European Court of Auditors, 2021. Special report 24/2021: Performance-based financing in Cohesion policy: worthy ambitions, but obstacles remained in the 2014-2020 period, http://www.eca.europa.eu/en/Pages/Report.aspx?did=59899&TermStoreId=8935807f-8495-4a93-a302-f4b76776d8ea&TermSetId=49e662c4-f172-43ae-8a5e-7276133de92c&TermId=5f6589a2-5a2e-4ae8-8cc6-e05bf544b71f.

European Court of Auditors, 2017. Special report No 15/2017: Ex ante conditionalities and performance reserve in Cohesion: innovative but not yet effective instruments, https://www.eca.europa.eu/Lists/ECADocuments/SR17_15/SR_PARTNERSHIP_EN.pdf.

European Economic and Social Committee, 2013. 2013/C 271/08. Opinion of the European Economic and Social Committee on the 'Communication from the Commission to the European Parliament and the Council—Towards a Deep and Genuine Economic and Monetary Union—The introduction of a Convergence and Competitiveness Instrument' COM(2013) 165 final and on the 'Communication from the Commission to the European Parliament and the Council—Towards a Deep and Genuine Economic and Monetary Union—Ex-ante coordination of plans for major economic policy reforms' COM(2013) 166 final. 19 September 2013, https://eur-lex.europa.eu/legal-content/EN/TXT/?uri=CELEX%3A52013AE3043.

European Fiscal Board, 2025. Annual Report, https://commission.europa.eu/document/download/aa49a920-7b0b-465d-ae49-0b311dc904dd_en?filename=EFB%202025%20Annual%20Report.pdf.

European Independent Fiscal Institutions, 2025. The first round of Medium-term fiscal-structural plans. 10 March 2025, https://www.euifis.eu/publications/40.

European Ombudsman, 2025. Case 2498/2023/SF. Decision on how the European Commission handled a request for public access to documents concerning legal advice issued during the preparatory stages of three legislative proposals. 2 April 2025, https://www.ombudsman.europa.eu/en/decision/en/202005.

European Ombudsman, 2024a. Case 2498/2023/SF. Letter of Emily O'Reilly, European Ombudsman, to Ursula von der Leyen, President, European Commission, 18 March 2024. Complaint 2498/2023/SF, Subject: Proposal for a solution in the above case on how the European Commission handled a request for public access to documents concerning legal advice issued during the preparatory stages of three legislative proposals [your reference: EASE 2023/5181] [on file with authors].

European Ombudsman, 2024b. Case 409/2023/OAM. How the European Commission dealt with a request for public access to documents concerning the Dutch national plan under the Recovery and Resilience Facility. 13 November 2024, https://www.ombudsman.europa.eu/en/case/en/63458.

European Ombudsman, 2024c. Case 409/2023/OAM. Decision on how the European Commission dealt with a request for public access to documents concerning the Dutch national plan under the Recovery and Resilience Facility. 13 November 2024. European Ombudsman, https://www.ombudsman.europa.eu/en/decision/en/195509.

European Ombudsman, 2023a. Case OI/2/2022/OAM. Special Report of the European Ombudsman in her strategic inquiry concerning the time the European Commission takes to deal with requests for public access to documents, https://www.ombudsman.europa.eu/en/special-report/en/175425.

European Ombudsman, 2023b. Case SI/6/2021/PVV. Closing note on the Strategic Initiative concerning the transparency and accountability of the Recovery and Resilience Facility, 11 September 2023, https://www.ombudsman.europa.eu/en/doc/correspondence/en/175056.

European Ombudsman, 2023c. Case 1443/2023/SF. Decision on the European Commission's failure to take a final decision within the applicable time limit on requests for public access to documents concerning legal opinions on three legislative proposals. Email of Rosita Hickey, Director of Inquiries, European Ombudsman, to Päivi Leino-Sandberg, 6 September 2023 [on file with authors].

European Ombudsman, 2023d. Case 1129/2022/SF. Decision on the European Commission's refusal to give public access to documents concerning the French national plan under the Recovery and Resilience Facility. 27 October 2023, https://www.ombudsman.europa.eu/en/decision/en/177073.

European Ombudsman, 2023e. Case 2186/2022/SF. How the European Commission dealt with a request for public access to messages sent by Commissioners to the Commission President concerning Poland's national plan under the Recovery and Resilience Facility. 17 July 2023, https://www.ombudsman.europa.eu/en/case/en/62960.

European Ombudsman, 2022. Case 925/2022/LDS, Decision on how the European Commission dealt with two requests for public access to documents concerning the Swedish and Danish Recovery and Resilience Plans. 29 November 2022, https://www.ombudsman.europa.eu/en/decision/en/163529.

European Ombudsman, 2021. Case 1410/2021/MIG. How the European Commission dealt with a request for public access to documents concerning Germany's recovery and resilience plan under the Recovery and Resilience Facility (RRF) (your reference: GestDem 2021/4558). Letter of Emily O'Reilly, European Ombudsman to Commission President Ursula von der Leyen, dated 23 August 2021, https://www.ombudsman.europa.eu/en/doc/correspondence/en/145914.

European Parliament, 2025a. B10-0319/2025. Motion of Censure on the Commission (2025/2140(RSP)). 3 July 2025, https://www.europarl.europa.eu/doceo/document/B-10-2025-0319_EN.html.

European Parliament, 2025b. MEPs reject motion of censure against the European Commission. Press Release. 10 July 2025, https://www.europarl.europa.eu/news/en/press-room/20250704IPR29455/meps-reject-motion-of-censure-against-the-european-commission.

European Parliament, 2025c. JURI_PV(2025)0423_1. Minutes, Meeting of 23 April 2025, 09.00-12.30 and 14.30-18.00. Committee on Legal Affairs. 23 April 2025, https://www.europarl.europa.eu/doceo/document/JURI-PV-2025-04-23-1_EN.pdf.

European Parliament, 2025d. Verbatim report of proceedings—Announcement by the President (Rule 138(2)). 5 May 2025, https://www.europarl.europa.eu/doceo/document/CRE-10-2025-05-05-ITM-005_EN.html.

European Parliament, 2025e. Budget proposal 'simply not enough' to meet Europe's challenges, lead MEPs say. Joint Press Release from Siegfried Mureşan (EPP, RO), Carla Tavares (S&D, PT), Sandra Gómez López (S&D, ES), Danuše Nerudová (EPP, CZ). 16 July 2025, https://www.europarl.europa.eu/news/en/press-room/20250714IPR29630/budget-proposal-simply-not-enough-to-meet-europe-s-challenges-lead-meps-say.

European Parliament, 2024a. Scrutiny of the Recovery and Resilience Facility (RRF) [though April 2024), https://www.europarl.europa.eu/cmsdata/284704/Overview%20RRF%20scrutiny.pdf.

European Parliament, 2024b. European Parliament resolution of 11 April 2024 with observations forming an integral part of the decisions on discharge in respect of the implementation of the general budget of the European Union for the financial year 2022, Section III – Commission and executive agencies (2023/2129(DEC)), https://www.europarl.europa.eu/doceo/document/TA-9-2024-0228_EN.html#title9.

European Parliament, 2024c. Provisional Agreement Resulting from Interinstitutional Negotiations, submitted to the Committee on Foreign Affairs and the Committee on Budgets. Subject: Proposal for a regulation of the European Parliament and of the Council on establishing the Ukraine (COM(2023)0338—C9-0210/2023—2023/0200(COD)). 15 February 2024, https://www.europarl.europa.eu/meetdocs/2014_2019/plmrep/COMMITTEES/CJ15/AG/2024/02-22/1296877EN.pdf.

European Parliament, 2024d. European Parliament and European Commission agree on strengthening cooperation. Press Release. 21 October 2024, https://www.europarl.europa.eu/news/en/press-room/20241021IPR24772/european-parliament-and-european-commission-agree-on-strengthening-cooperation.

European Parliament, 2023a. European Parliament resolution of 10 May 2023 with observations forming an integral part of the decisions on discharge in respect of the implementation of the general budget of the European Union for the financial year 2021, Section III—Commission and executive agencies (2022/2081(DEC)), https://www.europarl.europa.eu/doceo/document/TA-9-2023-0137_EN.html#title10.

European Parliament, 2023b. Protection of EU funds: EU should do more to detect, prevent and recover frauds. Committee on Budgetary Control, European Parliament. Press Release, 5 December 2023, https://www.europarl.europa.eu/news/en/press-room/20231204IPR15632/protection-of-eu-funds-eu-should-do-more-to-detect-prevent-and-recover-frauds.

European Parliament, 2023c. P9_TA(2023)0427, A9-0337/2023. European Parliament resolution of 22 November 2023 on proposals of the European Parliament for the amendment of the Treaties (2022/2051(INL), https://www.europarl.europa.eu/doceo/document/TA-9-2023-0427_EN.html.

European Parliament, 2023d. Texts adopted—Establishing the Ukraine Facility—Tuesday, 17 October 2023, Amendments adopted by the European Parliament on 17 October 2023 on the proposal for a regulation of the European Parliament and of the Council on establishing the Ukraine Facility (COM(2023)0338–C9-0210/2023–2023/0200(COD)), https://www.europarl.europa.eu/doceo/document/TA-9-2023-0363_EN.html.

European Parliament, 2023e. P9_TA(2023)0195, A9-0155/2023. European Parliament resolution of 10 May 2023 on own resources: a new start for EU finances, a new start for Europe (2022/2172(INI)), https://www.europarl.europa.eu/doceo/document/TA-9-2023-0195_EN.html.

European Parliament, 2023f. A9-0337/2023, 2022/2051(INL). Report on proposals of the European Parliament for the amendment of the Treaties, Committee on Constitutional Affairs. Rapporteurs: Guy Verhofstadt, Sven Simon, Gabriele Bischoff, Daniel Freund, Helmut Scholz. 7 November 2023, https://www.europarl.europa.eu/doceo/document/A-9-2023-0337_EN.html.

European Parliament, 2022a. Verbatim report of proceedings. Speech by the Prime Minister of Italy, Mario Draghi. 3 May 2022, https://www.europarl.europa.eu/doceo/document/CRE-9-2022-05-03-ITM-005_EN.html.

European Parliament, 2022b. Working Document on ECA Special Report 21/2022 - The Commission's assessment of national recovery and resilience plans. Committee on

Budgetary Control, Rapporteur: Monika Hohlmeier. 7 December 2022, https://www.europarl.europa.eu/doceo/document/CONT-DT-736630_EN.pdf.

European Parliament, 2022c. European Parliament resolution of 9 June 2022 on the rule of law and the potential approval of the Polish national recovery plan (RRF) (2022/2703(RSP)), https://www.europarl.europa.eu/doceo/document/TA-9-2022-0240_EN.html.

European Parliament, 2022d. A9-0241/2022. Report on the Council position on the draft general budget of the European Union for the financial year 2023. Part 1: Motion for a resolution, Committee on Budgets. Rapporteurs: Nicolae Ştefănuţă (Section III – Commission), Niclas Herbst (Other Sections).12 October 2022, https://www.europarl.europa.eu/doceo/document/A-9-2022-0241_EN.html.

European Parliament, 2021. P8_TA(2019)0373. Sovereign bond-backed securities ***I European Parliament legislative resolution of 16 April 2019 on the proposal for a regulation of the European Parliament and of the Council on sovereign bond-backed securities (COM(2018)0339—C8-0206/2018—2018/0171(COD)) P8_TC1-COD(2018)0171 Position of the European Parliament adopted at first reading on 16 April 2019 with a view to the adoption of Regulation (EU) 2019/ . . . f of the European Parliament and of the Council on sovereign bond-backed securities (Text with EEA relevance). 30 April 2021, https://eur-lex.europa.eu/legal-content/EN/TXT/?uri=CELEX%3A52019AP0373&qid=1685636869593.

European Parliament, 2020. A9-0214/2020. Report on the proposal for a regulation of the European Parliament and of the Council establishing a Recovery and Resilience Facility. Committee on Budgets, Committee on Economic and Monetary, Affairs. Rapporteurs: Eider Gardiazabal, Siegfried Muresan, Dragos Pîslaru. 10 November 2020, https://www.europarl.europa.eu/doceo/document/A-9-2020-0214_EN.html.

European Parliament, 2017. Parliamentary question. Article 41(2) of the Treaty on European Union. Question for written answer E-003113/2017 to the Commission. Rule 130. Sabine Lösing (GUE/NGL). 3 May 2017, https://www.europarl.europa.eu/doceo/document/E-8-2017-003113_EN.html.

European Parliament, 2011. Comparative Study on the Visions and Options for Cohesion Policy after 2013. Directorate General for Internal Policies, Policy Department B: Structural and Cohesion Policies, Regional Development. Authors: Carlos Mendez, John Bachtler, Fiona Wishlade. 31 August 2011, https://www.europarl.europa.eu/RegData/etudes/etudes/join/2011/460062/IPOL-REGI_ET(2011)460062_EN.pdf.

European People's Party, 2024. EPP 2024 Manifesto: Our Europe, a safe and good home for the people, https://www.epp.eu/files/uploads/2024/03/Manifesto_2024.pdf.

European Stability Mechanism, 2025a. ESM legal documents and policies, https://www.esm.europa.eu/about-us/transparency/esm-policies-documents.

European Stability Mechanism, 2025b. ESM Treaty Reform—Explainer, https://www.esm.europa.eu/about-us/esm-reform/esm-treaty-reform-explainer.

European Systemic Risk Board, 2016. *High-Level Task Force on Safe Assets*, https://www.esrb.europa.eu/pub/task_force_safe_assets/html/index.en.html.

Eurostat, 2021. Guidance Note on the Statistical Recording of the Recovery and Resilience Facility. Methodological Note, Revised September 2021 (original from November 2020, no longer available online), https://ec.europa.eu/eurostat/documents/10186/10693286/GFS-guidance-note-statistical-recording-recovery-resilience-facility.pdf.

Everson, M and Eisner, J, 2007. *The Making of a European Constitution: Judges and Law Beyond Constitutive Power*. Routledge-Cavendish, Abingdon, UK; New York.

Fabbrini, F, 2025. The Recovery and Resilience Facility as a New Legal Technology of European Governance. *Journal of European Integration* 47, 85–103, https://doi.org/10.1080/07036337.2024.2361830.

Fabbrini, F, 2024. From the Pandemic to the War: The EU Fiscal Response to Russia's Aggression of Ukraine, the Legacy of NGEU, and the Challenge to 'Promote the General Welfare' *AJIL Unbound* 118, 177–81, https://doi.org/10.1017/aju.2024.28.

Fabbrini, F, 2022a. Next Generation EU: Legal Structure and Constitutional Consequences. *Cambridge Yearbook of European Legal Studies* 24, 45–66, https://doi.org/10.1017/cel.2022.2.

Fabbrini, F, 2022b. *EU Fiscal Capacity: Legal Integration After Covid-19 and the War in Ukraine*. Oxford University Press.

Fabbrini, F, 2022c. The Legal Architecture of the Economic Responses to COVID-19: EMU beyond the Pandemic. *JCMS: Journal of Common Market Studies* 60, 186–203, https://doi.org/10.1111/jcms.13271.

Fabbrini, F, 2022d. Italy's National Recovery and Resilience Plan: Context, Content and Challenges. *Journal of Modern Italian Studies* 27, 658–76.

Fabbrini, F, 2020. Europe's Economic & Monetary Union Beyond Covid-19. Department of Finance. Government of Ireland. September 2020; revised December 2020, https://gov.ie/en/department-of-finance/publications/europes-economic-monetary-union-beyond-covid-19/.

Fasone, C, 2024. Constitutional Courts as Part of the Separation of Powers' Arrangement in the Member States: From the Euro Crisis to the NGEU, in: Eckes, C, Leino-Sandberg, P, and Ghavanini, A (eds), *The Dynamics of Powers in the European Union*. Hart Publishing, pp 185–204.

Fasone, C and Lupo, N, 2024. Learning from the Euro Crisis: A New Method of Government for the European Union's Economic Policy Coordination after the Pandemic. *International Journal of Constitutional Law* 22, 882–904, https://doi.org/10.1093/icon/moae064.

Fasone, C and Simoncini, M, 2025. Next Generation EU and Governance by Conditionality: A Transformation of the European Economic Constitution? *European Papers—A Journal on Law and Integration 2024* 9, 1148–79, https://doi.org/10.15166/2499-8249/803.

Ferry, M and Kah, S, 2021. Pursuing Positive Interactions—within Structural Funds and with the RRF. European Policies Research Centre. Report to the 50th IQ-Net Conference (Online), 23 June 2021, https://eprc-strath.org/wp-content/uploads/2023/12/IQ-Net-Thematic_Paper_update.pdf.

Fitch, 2022a. Fitch Affirms European Union and Euratom at 'AAA'; Outlook Stable. FitchRatings, https://www.fitchratings.com/sovereigns/fitch-affirms-european-union-euratom-at-aaa-outlook-stable-18-02-2022.

Fitch, 2022b. Supranationals Rating Criteria. FitchRatings, https://www.fitchratings.com/research/sovereigns/supranationals-rating-criteria-11-04-2022.

Fitch, 2021. EU Debt Can Aid Recovery, Adds to Sovereign Contingent Liabilities. FitchRatings, https://www.fitchratings.com/research/sovereigns/eu-debt-can-aid-recovery-adds-to-sovereign-contingent-liabilities-20-09-2021.

Fitch, 2015. Supranationals Rating Criteria—Effective from 29 May 2015 to 27 July 2016. FitchRatings, https://www.fitchratings.com/research/sovereigns/supranationals-rating-criteria-effective-from-29-may-2015-to-27-july-2016-29-05-2015.

Five Presidents' Report, 2015. Completing Europe's Economic and Monetary Union. Report of 1 July 2015 by: Jean-Claude Juncker in close cooperation with Donald Tusk, Jeroen Dijsselbloem, Mario Draghi, and Martin Schulz. European Commission, https://commission.europa.eu/system/files/2016-03/5-presidents-report_en.pdf.

Fleming, S and Stubbington, T, 2023. EU debt suffers under competition with sovereign borrowers. *Financial Times*. 24 January 2023, https://www.ft.com/content/9ca73db9-9773-483b-b4bc-e4e2c7646726.

Flynn, L, 2019. Greater convergence, more resilience?—Cohesion Policy and the deepening of the Economic and Monetary Union, in: Fromage, D and de Witte, B (eds), *Recent Evolutions in the Economic and Monetary Union and the European Banking Union: A Reflection*. Maastricht Law Faculty of Law Working Paper Series 2019/03.

Fonte, G and Amante, A, 2023. Italy parliament rejects ESM reform, irking Brussels. Reuters, 21 December 2023, https://www.reuters.com/world/europe/italian-coalition-parties-vote-against-esm-reform-partl-committee-2023-12-21/.

Four Presidents Report, 2012. Towards a Genuine Economic and Monetary Union. By: Herman Van Rompuy, President of the European Council, in close collaboration with: José Manuel Barroso, President of the European Commission; Jean-Claude Juncker, President of the Eurogroup; and Mario Draghi, President of the European Central Bank. 5 December 2012, https://www.consilium.europa.eu/media/23818/134069.pdf.

Foy, H, Moens, B, and Tamma, P, 2025. Von der Leyen's €2tn EU budget proposal hit by chaotic infighting. *Financial Times*. 16 July 2025, https://www.ft.com/content/c88eae41-24b7-47a9-bdf5-543770c6c8eb.

Frankel, J, 2012. Could Eurobonds be the answer to the Eurozone crisis? VoxEU | CEPR, https://cepr.org/voxeu/columns/could-eurobonds-be-answer-eurozone-crisis.

French NRRP, 2021. Gouvernement Français. France Relance. Plan National de Relance et de Résilience 2021, https://www.economie.gouv.fr/files/files/directions_services/plan-de-relance/PNRR%20Francais.pdf.

Fruzzetti, M, Gariano, G, Palazzo, G, and Scalia, A, 2021. From SMP to PEPP: A Further Look at the Risk Endogeneity of the Central Bank (Approfondimenti: Mercati, infrastrutture, sistemi di pagamento No 11). Banca d'Italia—Eurosistema.

Galli, G, 2020. The Reform of the ESM and Why it is so Controversial in Italy. *Capital Markets Law Journal* 15, 262–76, https://doi.org/10.1093/cmlj/kmaa011.

Gambetta, D and Origgi, G, 2013. The LL Game: The Curious Preference for Low Quality and its Norms. *Politics, Philosophy & Economics* 12, 3–23.

Garicano, L, 2024. How to torch 220 billion euros. Silicon Continent, https://www.siliconcontinent.com/p/how-to-incinerate-220-billion-euros.

Genschel, P and Jachtenfuchs, M, 2018. From Market Integration to Core State Powers: The Eurozone Crisis, the Refugee Crisis and Integration Theory. *JCMS: Journal of Common Market Studies* 56, 178–96, https://doi.org/10.1111/jcms.12654.

Genschel, P and Jachtenfuchs, M, 2016. More Integration, Less Federation: The European Integration of Core State Powers. *Journal of European Public Policy* 23, 42–59, https://doi.org/10.1080/13501763.2015.1055782.

Genschel, P and Jachtenfuchs, M (eds), 2014. *Beyond the Regulatory Polity?: The European Integration of Core State Powers*. Oxford University Press.

Georgiou, C, 2022. Europe's 'Hamiltonian moment'? On the Political Uses and Explanatory Usefulness of a Recurrent Historical Comparison. *Economy and Society* 51, 138–59, https://doi.org/10.1080/03085147.2021.1968676.

German Council of Economic Experts, 2021. Sachverständigenrat zur Begutachtung der wirtschaftlichen Entwicklung, Stellungnahme des Sachverständigenrates zum DARP, Annex 2: Stellungnahme Nationaler Ausschuss für Produktivität [German Council of Economic Experts, Statement of the German Council of Economic Experts on the DARP, Annex 2: Statement of the National Productivity Committee]. 30 March 2021, https://www.bundesfinanzministerium.de/Content/DE/Standardartikel/Themen/Europa/DARP/5-annex-2-stellungnahme-nationaler-ausschuss-fuer-produktivitaet.pdf?__blob=publicationFile&v=4.

Giovannini Group, 2000. Co-Ordinated Public Debt Issuance in the Euro Area, https://ec.europa.eu/economy_finance/publications/pages/publication6372_en.pdf.

Godlovitch, I and Bodin, C, 2022. PE 733.734. Addressing the challenges of the digital transition in national RRF plans: Measures to support digitisation of SMEs. Study requested by the ECON committee. European Parliament, Economic Governance Support Unit (EGOV), Directorate-General for Internal Policies. November 2022, https://www.europarl.europa.eu/RegData/etudes/STUD/2022/733734/IPOL_STU(2022)733734_EN.pdf.

Goldmann, M, 2023. Langfristige Bindungen: Zum Urteil des BVerfG vom 6.12.2022 – NextGenEU – 2 BvR 547/21 und 2 BvR 798/21. *Neue Zeitschrift für Verwaltungsrecht* 791–98.

Gortsos, CV and Perakis, ME, 2024. On the Reform of the EU Stability and Growth Pact. *EuZ—Zeitschrift für Europarecht* 05, 1–22.

Government of Ireland, 2025. Ireland submits its third payment request under EU's Recovery and Resilience Facility (RRF), with a value of €240 million. Press Release. 12 August 2025, https://gov.ie/en/department-of-public-expenditure-infrastructure-public-service-reform-and-digitalisation/press-releases/ireland-submits-its-third-payment-request-under-eus-recovery-and-resilience-facility-rrf-with-a-value-of-240-million/.

Griera, M, Sorgi, G, and Mathiesen, K, 2025. Socialists to support von der Leyen in no-confidence vote after she backs down on EU budget. POLITICO. 9 July 2025, https://www.politico.eu/article/socialist-ursula-von-der-leyen-eu-budget-seven-year-commission-president/.

Group of Twelve, 2023. Sailing on the High Seas: Reforming and Enlarging the EU for the 21st Century. Report of the Franco-German Working Group on EU Institutional Reform. 18 September 2023, https://www.auswaertiges-amt.de/resource/blob/2617322/4d0e0010ffcd8c0079e21329bbbb3332/230919-rfaa-deu-fra-bericht-data.pdf.

Grove, K, 2018. *Resilience*. Routledge.

Grund, S and Steinbach, A, 2024. Debt-Financing the EU. *Common Market Law Review* 61, 993–1018.

Grund, S and Steinbach, A, 2023. European Union Debt Financing: Leeway and Barriers from a Legal Perspective. Bruegel Working Paper 15/2023. 12 September 2023, https://www.bruegel.org/sites/default/files/private/2023-09/WP%2015.pdf.

Hacker, B, 2022. National Recovery and Resilience Plan: Germany. *Italian Labour Law e-Journal* 15, Special issue 1, 1–17, https://doi.org/10.6092/issn.1561-8048/15651.

Hadjiyianni, I, 2024. The Emergence of New Own Resources to Strengthen the EU Budget and Achieve Green Policy Objectives: A Win-win or a Difficult Fit? EUI Academy of European Law Working Paper, AEL 2024/15, https://cadmus.eui.eu/server/api/core/bitstreams/2839d09e-4b00-518f-90c7-eb9bb9b7083a/content.

Hadoulis, J, 2017. AFP: Greece takes home foreclosures online to avoid protests. *Yahoo News*, https://sg.news.yahoo.com/greece-takes-home-foreclosures-online-avoid-protests-033341406.html.

Hakahuhta, A, 2021. Ylen tiedot: Suomi kysyi EU:lta elvytyspaketin hylkäämisestä – mainehaitta ja poliittinen paine arvioitiin ennennäkemättömäksi [Yle Exclusive: Finland asked EU about rejection of the stimulus package - told reputational damage and political pressure would be unprecedented]. Yle Uutiset (Helsinki), https://yle.fi/a/3-11902316.

Hautala, H, 2017. Europe's legal U-turn on militarising development policy. Euractiv. 3 July 2017, https://www.euractiv.com/section/development-policy/opinion/europes-legal-u-turn-on-militarising-development-policy/.

Hegedus, D, 2023. Same, Same but Different?: The Pitfalls in Unfreezing EU Funds. 21 December 2023. Verfassungsblog, https://verfassungsblog.de/same-same-but-different/.

Hegseth, P, 2025. Opening Remarks by Secretary of Defense Pete Hegseth at Ukraine Defense Contact Group (As Delivered). 12 February 2025, https://www.defense.gov/News/Speeches/Speech/article/4064113/opening-remarks-by-secretary-of-defense-pete-hegseth-at-ukraine-defense-contact/.

Henley, J and Oltermann, P, 2020. Italy records its deadliest day of coronavirus outbreak with 475 deaths. *The Guardian*, 18 March 2020, https://www.theguardian.com/world/2020/mar/18/coronavirus-lockdown-eu-belgium-germany-adopt-measures.

Hiilesniemi, S, 2022. National Recovery and Resilience Plan: Finland. *Italian Labour Law e-Journal* 15, Special issue 1, 1–14, https://doi.org/10.6092/issn.1561-8048/15697.

Hinarejos, A, 2022. The Commission's Proposed Path to Reform of the European Fiscal Framework. *European Law Review* 47, 731–32, https://doi.org/10.3316/agispt.20230113081926.

Hinarejos, A, 2015. *The Euro Area Crisis in Constitutional Perspective, Oxford Studies in European Law*. Oxford University Press.

Hindriks, I, Schlemmer, L, Rodrigues, M, and Belicka, D, 2022. PE 733.735. Addressing the challenges of the Green Transition in National Recovery and Resilience Plans: a preliminary assessment. Study requested by the ECON committee. European Parliament, Economic Governance Support Unit (EGOV), Directorate-General for Internal Policies. November 2022, https://www.europarl.europa.eu/RegData/etudes/STUD/2022/733735/IPOL_STU(2022)733735_EN.pdf.

Hirschl, R and Shachar, A, 2018. Competing Orders? The Challenge of Religion to Modern Constitutionalism. *University of Chicago Law Review* 85, 425–55.

Hodson, D, Howarth, D, Mugnai, I, and Spielberger, L, 2025. Accountability in Pan-European Borrowing: Mind the Gap. *West European Politics* 48, 696–722, https://doi.org/10.1080/01402382.2024.2321559.

Holtze, B, 2022. National Recovery and Resilience Plan: Denmark. *Italian Labour Law e-Journal* 15, Special issue 1, 1–11, https://doi.org/10.6092/issn.1561-8048/15647.

Horn, S, Meyer, J, Trebesch, C, 2020. European Community Bonds since the Oil crisis: Lessons for today? Kiel Policy Brief 136.

International Monetary Fund, 2024. Technical Assistance, https://www.imf.org/external/about/techasst.htm.

International Monetary Fund, 2018. Assessing Fiscal Space: An Update and Stocktaking. IMF Policy Paper, https://www.imf.org/en/Publications/Policy-Papers/Issues/2018/06/15/pp041118assessing-fiscal-space.

International Monetary Fund, 2001a. Strengthening Country Ownership of Fund-Supported Programs. IMF Policy Development and Review Department, https://www.imf.org/external/np/pdr/cond/2001/eng/strength/120501.htm.

International Monetary Fund, 2001b. IMF Reviews Strengthening Country Ownership of Fund-Supported Programs. IMF Public Information Notice, https://www.imf.org/en/News/Articles/2015/09/28/04/53/pn01125.

Ioannidis, M, 2020. Between Responsibility and Solidarity: COVID-19 and the Future of the European Economic Order. Max Planck Institute for Comparative Public Law & International Law (MPIL) Research Paper No 2020-39, https://papers.ssrn.com/sol3/papers.cfm?abstract_id=3725458#.

Ioannidis, M, 2016. Europe's New Transformations: How the EU Economic Constitution Changed during the Eurozone Crisis. *Common Market Law Review* 53, 1237–82.

Iossa, A, 2022. National Recovery and Resilience Plan: Sweden. *Italian Labour Law e-Journal* 15, https://doi.org/10.6092/issn.1561-8048/15700.

Isiksel, T, 2016. *Europe's Functional Constitution: A Theory of Constitutionalism Beyond the State*. Oxford University Press.

Isiksel, T, 2015. Functional Constitutionalism in the European Union, EUSA Biannual Meeting, Boston. 5 March 2015, https://eustudies.org/conference/papers/download/196.

ISMERI Europa, WIIW, 2018. Final Report to the European Commission: Support of ESI Funds to the Implementation of the Country Specific Recommendations and to Structural Reforms in Member States, https://op.europa.eu/en/publication-detail/-/publication/de79c16e-6eb4-11e8-9483-01aa75ed71a1/language-en.

Italian NRRP, 2021. Recovery and Resilience Plan #NextGenerationItalia. Approved by the Council of Ministers 21 January 2021, https://www.mef.gov.it/export/sites/MEF/en/focus/documents/PNRR-NEXT-GENERATION-ITALIA_ENG_09022021.pdf.

Janse, K.A, 2023. Developing European Safe Assets. *Intereconomics* 58, 315–19, https://doi.org/10.2478/ie-2023-0065.

Jaraczewski, J, 2025. Poland's ongoing rule-of-law crisis explained. Notes From Poland, https://notesfrompoland.com/2025/03/17/polands-ongoing-rule-of-law-crisis-explained/.

Joseph, J and Juncos, AE, 2024. Conceptual Politics and Resilience-at-Work in the European Union. *Review of International Studies* 50, 373–92, https://doi.org/10.1017/S0260210523000463.

Joseph, J and Juncos, AE, 2019. Resilience as an Emergent European Project? The EU's Place in the Resilience Turn. *JCMS: Journal of Common Market Studies* 57, 995–1011, https://doi.org/10.1111/jcms.12881.

Jouen, M, 2009. The Barca Report: a spring clean for Europe's cohesion policy. Notre Europe. May 2009, https://institutdelors.eu/wp-content/uploads/2018/01/mjouen-rapportbarca-en.pdf.

Juga, T, 2025. Yhteisvelasta tulikin hyväksyttävää, kun kyse on puolustuksesta – näin komission uusi esitys eroaa kiistellystä koronaelvytyspaketista [Joint debt became acceptable when it comes to defense - this is how the Commission's new proposal differs from the controversial corona recovery package] Suomen Kuvalehti, 16 June 2025, https://suomenkuvalehti.fi/paajutut/yhteisvelasta-tulikin-hyvaksyttavaa-kun-kyse-on-puolustuksesta-nain-komission-uusi-esitys-eroaa-kiistellysta-koronaelvytyspaketista/.

Juncker, J-C, 2017. President Jean-Claude Juncker's State of the Union Address 2017. European Commission, https://ec.europa.eu/commission/presscorner/detail/en/SPEECH_17_3165.

Juncker, J C, 2016. Speech at the Annual General Meeting of the Hellenic Federation of Enterprises (SEV). European Commission, https://ec.europa.eu/commission/presscorner/detail/en/SPEECH_16_2293.

Juncker, J-C and Timmermans, F, 2017. State of the Union 2017: Letter of Intent to President Antonio Tajani and to Prime Minister Jüri Ratas. European Commission, https://asvis.it/public/asvis/files/letter-of-intent-2017_en_1_.pdf.

Karagyozov, K, 2025. Bulgaria's Second Payment Request under Recovery, Resilience Facility to Be Refused, Deputy PM Donchev Says. Bulgarian News Agency. 26 February 2025, https://www.bta.bg/en/news/bulgaria/841075-bulgaria-s-second-payment-request-under-recovery-resilience-facility-to-be-refu.

Kaspersen, LB and Strandsbjerg, J (eds), 2017. *Does War Make States?: Investigations of Charles Tilly's Historical Sociology*. Cambridge University Press.

Kay, RS, 2019. Updating the Constitution: Amending, Tinkering, Interpreting. *Drake Law Review* 67, 887–907.

Kay, RS, 2014. *The Glorious Revolution and the Continuity of Law*. CUA Press.

Kazmin, A, 2023. Italy at odds with Brussels over using EU money for football stadium, *Financial Times*, 28 March 2023, https://www.ft.com/content/7640e7bc-6006-47d9-bf66-ae3033338618.

Kelemen, RD and McNamara, KR, 2022. State-building and the European Union: Markets, War, and Europe's Uneven Political Development. *Comparative Political Studies* 55, 963–91, https://doi.org/10.1177/00104140211047393.

Kelemen, RD and Pavone, T, 2023. Where Have the Guardians Gone? Law Enforcement and the Politics of Supranational Forbearance in the European Union. *World Politics* 75, 779–825.

Keppenne, J-P, 2020a. Non-Fiscal Surveillance of the Member States, in: Amtenbrink, F, Herrmann, C, and Repasi, R (eds), *The EU Law of Economic and Monetary Union*. Oxford University Press, pp 850–77, https://doi.org/10.1093/oso/9780198793748.003.0035.

Keppenne, J-P, 2020b. Economic Policy Coordination: Foundations, Structures, and Objectives, in: Amtenbrink, F, Herrmann, C, and Repasi, R (eds), *The EU Law of Economic and Monetary Union*. Oxford University Press, pp 787–812, https://doi.org/10.1093/oso/9780198793748.003.0035.

Khadbai, B, 2024a. Commissioner Hahn: EU bonds moving closer to sovereign status. OMFIF. 1 May 2024, https://www.omfif.org/2024/05/commissioner-hahn-eu-bonds-moving-into-the-market-for-sovereign-bonds/.

Khadbai, B, 2024b. EU's sovereign ambition in capital markets suffers setback ... for now. OMFIF. 9 August 2024, https://www.omfif.org/2024/08/eus-sovereign-ambition-in-capital-markets-suffers-setback-for-now/.

Khadbai, B, 2024c. Sovereign index inclusion will be a 'game-changer' for EU bonds. OMFIF. 11 September 2024, https://www.omfif.org/2024/09/sovereign-index-inclusion-will-be-a-game-changer-for-eu-bonds/.

Khosla, M and Tushnet, M, 2022. Courts, Constitutionalism, and State Capacity: A Preliminary Inquiry. *American Journal of Comparative Law* 70, 95–138, https://doi.org/10.1093/ajcl/avac009.

Klingbeil, L and Lombard, É, 2025. Getting Europe on track in a new geo-economic era. Bundesministerium der Finanzen. Op-ed by Lars Klingbeil and Éric Lombard in the Handelsblatt and Les Echos. 16 July 2025, https://www.bundesfinanzministerium.de/Content/EN/Standardartikel/Press_Room/Guest-Article/2025-07-16-klingbeil-lombard-europe-on-track.html.

Knoll, B, Alester, L, Rehbein, L, Zick, C, Claus, S, Sommerfeld, E, Bognitz, J, Wigand, R, Philippe, H, and Franz, A, 2025. EuDoX 55/2025. EU-Sachstand. Zukunft der Europäischen Verteidigung. Deutscher Bundestag. Europa-Dokumentation. Referat EU 2, Referat EU 3. 30 April 2025, https://www.politico.eu/wp-content/uploads/2025/06/20/Dokument_EuDoX_55_2025_EU-Sachstand-Verteidigung.pdf.

Köck, HF, 1978. *Der Gesamtakt der deutschen Integrationslehre*. Duncker & Humblot.

Komárek, J (ed), 2023. *European Constitutional Imaginaries: Between Ideology and Utopia*. Oxford University Press.

Körner, K, 2020. EUR 750 bn EU Recovery Fund: Deal! Deutsche Bank Research. EU Monitor, European Integration. 21 July 2020, https://www.dbresearch.de/PROD/RPS_DE-PROD/PROD0000000000510497/EUR750bn_EU_Recovery_Fund%3A_Deal!.PDF?undefined&realload=4dPl~HFCRLn6Yi82Gs~SsoPW1L7xBORNiGs9ob/TM7xB0qR2B8cEHTLLMhq1XdoN.

Koskenniemi, M, 2024. What Is International Law For?, in: Evans, M (ed), *International Law*. Oxford University Press, pp 28–50, https://doi.org/10.1093/he/9780192848642.003.0002.

Koskenniemi, M, 2022. Performing Legal Expertise: Reflections on the Construction of Transnational Authority, in: Korkea-aho, E and Leino-Sandberg, P (eds), *Law, Legal Expertise and EU Policy-Making*. Cambridge University Press, pp 19–42.

Koskenniemi, M, 2007. Formalism, Fragmentation, Freedom: Kantian Themes in Today's International Law. *No foundations: Journal of Extreme Legal Positivism* 4, 7–28.

Kowalcze, K. and Ritchie, G, 2024. German Finance Agency Backs EU Bid to Issue Sovereign Debt. Bloomberg. 17 December 2024, https://www.bloomberg.com/news/articles/2024-12-17/german-finance-agency-backs-eu-bid-to-issue-sovereign-debt.

Kraemer, M, 2023. EU bonds have not lived up to high expectations. *Financial Times*. 18 April 2023, https://www.ft.com/content/dc82d584-4961-4af3-ab32-eb504bb3e375.

Kreuder-Sonnen, C and White, J, 2022. Europe and the Transnational Politics of Emergency. *Journal of European Public Policy* 29, 953–65, https://doi.org/10.1080/13501763.2021.1916059.

Kubeková, V, Sanz, M, Schmoigl, L, Schratzenstaller, M, Sutrich, A, and Heimberger, P, 2024. PE 768.313. Mapping the current structure and discovering the potential of 'other revenue'.

Study Requested by the BUDG Committee, European Parliament. Budgetary Support Unit, Directorate-General for Budgetary Affairs. December 2024, https://www.europarl.europa.eu/RegData/etudes/STUD/2025/768313/BUDG_STU(2025)768313_EN.pdf.

Lamer, E, 2026. How Tax Reform Triggered an EU Funding Freeze, TaxNotes. 8 January 2026, https://www.taxnotes.com/tax-notes-today-international/corporate-taxation/how-tax-reform-triggered-eu-funding-freeze/2026/01/08/7tvh5.

Ladenburger, C, 2011. Anmerkungen zu Kompetenzordnung und Subsidiarität nach dem Vertrag von Lissabon. *Zeitschrift für Europarechtliche Studien* 14, 389–408.

Laffan, B and De Feo, A (eds), 2020. *EU Financing for Next Decade: Beyond the MFF 2021-2027 and the Next Generation EU*. European University Institute.

Lagarde, C, 2020. Interview with Le Monde. Interview with Christine Lagarde, President of the ECB, conducted by Marie Charrel and Eric Albert. 19 October 2020, https://www.ecb.europa.eu/press/inter/date/2020/html/ecb.in201019~45f5cf8040.en.html.

Langevoort, DC, 2018. Behavioral Ethics, Behavioral Compliance, in: Arlen, J (ed), *Research Handbook on Corporate Crime and Financial Misdealing*. Edward Elgar, pp 263–81.

Le Monde, 2025. French PM Bayrou survives no-confidence motion. Le Monde, 1 July 2025, https://www.lemonde.fr/en/france/article/2025/07/01/french-pm-survives-no-confidence-motion_6742917_7.html.

Lebre de Freitas, M, 2023. PE 699.557. Addressing the challenges of smart, sustainable, and inclusive growth in national Recovery and Resilience Plans: Italy, Spain, Portugal, and Cyprus. Study requested by the ECON committee, European Parliament. Economic Governance and EMU scrutiny Unit (EGOV), Directorate-General for Internal Policies. May 2023, https://www.cde.ual.es/wp-content/uploads/2023/05/addressing-the-challenges-of-smart-sustainable-and-QA0323135ENN.pdf.

Lee, G, 2023. EU insists transition to 'sovereign-style' issuer on track despite funding cut. GlobalCapital. 30 June 2023, https://www.globalcapital.com/article/2bv05i5gudj71yjp8k1ds/ssa/eu-insists-transition-to-sovereign-style-issuer-on-track-despite-funding-cut.

Lehner, S, 2020. The Dual Nature of the EU Multiannual Financial Framework, in: Laffan, B, De Feo, A (eds), *EU Financing for Next Decade: Beyond the MFF 2021-2027 and the Next Generation EU*. European University Institute.

Leino-Sandberg, P, 2025a. What Can Non Judicial (Legal) Data Tell about the Politics of EU Law?, in: Šadl, U, Naurin, D, and Zglinski, J (eds), *Empirical Legal Studies in EU Law*. Cambridge University Press.

Leino-Sandberg, P, 2025b. WARNING. Confidential documents. Not to be disclosed to anyone (Part 2). EU Law Analysis. 26 June 2025, https://eulawanalysis.blogspot.com/2025/06/warning-confidential-documents-not-to_26.html.

Leino-Sandberg, P, 2025c. The Secret Life of the EU Treaties: NGEU and the Politics of the EU's 'Living Constitution'. *European Law Open*, [first view] 1–26 https://doi.org/10.1017/elo.2025.10055.

Leino-Sandberg, P, 2025d. '70 Years of EU Law'—The Politics of a Professional Language. Helsinki Legal Studies Research Paper No 89. Social Science Research Network. 4 February 2025 (forthcoming *Heidelberg Journal of International Law*), https://papers.ssrn.com/abstract=5128043.

Leino-Sandberg, P, 2025e. Leaked and Loaded: Why the NGEU Model is Ill-Suited for Responding to the EU's Current Geopolitical Challenges. Verfassungsblog. 18 March 2025, https://verfassungsblog.de/mff_ngeu_leaked-and-loaded/.

Leino-Sandberg, P, 2024a. In the Dark: How the Commission Deals with Access to Documents Requests relating to Europe's Recovery Transformation. Verfassungsblog, https://verfassungsblog.de/in-the-dark/.

Leino-Sandberg, P, 2024b. Cohesion Policy and the Principle of Subsidiarity—A Legal Analysis. ZEW Discussion Paper No 24-042, Mannheim, https://www.zew.de/en/publications/cohesion-policy-and-the-principle-of-subsidiarity-a-legal-analysis-1.

Leino-Sandberg, P, 2024c. 'Very Tight Control': On (the Absence of) Member State Scrutiny of the EU's Recovery Spending. 22 April 2024. Verfassungsblog, https://verfassungsblog.de/very-tight-control/.

Leino-Sandberg, P, 2023a. Constitutional Imaginaries of Solidarity: Framing Fiscal Integration Post-NGEU, in: Weber, R (ed), *EU Integration through Financial Constitution: Follow the Money?* Hart Publishing, pp 161–88.

Leino-Sandberg, P, 2023b. Recovery and Resilience Facility two years after—quo vadis EU money? Verfassungsblog, https://verfassungsblog.de/recovery-and-resilience-facility-two-years-after-quo-vadis-eu-money/.

Leino-Sandberg, P, 2022. Enchantment and critical distance in EU legal scholarship: what role for institutional lawyers? *European Law Open* 1, 231–56, https://doi.org/10.1017/elo.2022.17.

Leino-Sandberg, P, 2021a. *The Politics of Legal Expertise in EU Policy-Making.* Cambridge University Press.

Leino-Sandberg, P, 2021b. Next Generation EU—A Constitutional Change without Constitutional Change. RECONNECT, https://reconnect-europe.eu/blog/new-generation-eu-a-constitutional-change-without-constitutional-change/.

Leino-Sandberg, P, 2020. Constitutional Constraints meet Political Pressure: Finland's precarious participation in the COVID-19 solidarity measures. Verfassungsblog, https://verfassungsblog.de/constitutional-constraints-meet-political-pressure/.

Leino-Sandberg, P and Lindseth, P, 2023. How Cohesion Became the EU's Vehicle for Economic Policy: Tracing the Hidden History of Article 175(3) TFEU. Verfassungsblog, https://verfassungsblog.de/how-cohesion-became-the-eus-vehicle-for-economic-policy/.

Leino-Sandberg, P and Losada Fraga, F, 2020. How to make the European Semester more effective and legitimate?: euro area scrutiny. Directorate-General for Internal Policies of the Union (European Parliament), Publications Office of the European Union.

Leino-Sandberg, P and Ojanen, H, 2022. Time for Military Integration in the EU? Armed aggression and the scope of Article 42 TEU. Verfassungsblog. 3 March 2022, https://verfassungsblog.de/time-for-military-integration-in-the-eu/.

Leino-Sandberg, P and Raunio, T, 2023. From Bad to Worse: The Continuous Dilemma Facing Parliaments in European Economic and Fiscal Governance. Government and Opposition 1–18, https://doi.org/10.1017/gov.2023.29.

Leino-Sandberg, P and Ruffert, M, 2022. Next Generation EU and its Constitutional Ramifications: A Critical Assessment. *Common Market Law Review* 59, 433–72.

Leino-Sandberg, P and Saarenheimo, T, 2019. Discretion, Economic Governance and the (New) Political Commission, in: Mendes, J (ed), *EU Executive Discretion and the Limits of Law*. Oxford University Press, pp 132–54.

Leino-Sandberg, P and Saarenheimo, T, 2018. Fiscal Stabilisation for EMU: Managing Incompleteness. *European Law Review* 43, 623–47.

Leino-Sandberg, P and Saarenheimo, T, 2017. Sovereignty and Subordination: On the Limits of EU Economic Policy Coordination. *European Law Review* 42, 166–89.

Lenaerts, K and Adam, S, 2021. La solidarité, valeur commune aux États membres et principe fédératif de l'Union européenne. *Cahiers de droit européen* 307–417.

Levinson, S, 1991. Accounting for Constitutional Change (Or, How Many Times Has the United States Constitution Been Amended? (A) <26; (B) 26; (C) >26; (D) All of the Above). *Constitutional Commentary* 8(2), 409–31.

Liboreiro, J, 2024. The truth behind the €64.6-billion budget deal agreed by EU leaders. Euronews. 3 Feburary 2024, https://www.euronews.com/my-europe/2024/02/03/the-truth-behind-the-646-billion-budget-deal-agreed-by-eu-leaders.

Lilyanova, V, 2024a. PE 762.322. The 100 largest recipients of Recovery and Resilience Facility funds. Briefing: Next Generation EU (NGEU) delivery—Governance. European Pariliament, EPRS: European Parliamentary Research Service, Members' Research Service. June 2024, https://www.europarl.europa.eu/RegData/etudes/BRIE/2024/762322/EPRS_BRI(2024)762322_EN.pdf.

Lilyanova, V, 2024b. PE 762.367. Recovery and Resilience Facility implementation: Digital public services. Briefing, Next Generation EU (NGEU) delivery—Sectoral focus, European Parliament. EPRS: European Parliamentary Research Service, Members' Research Service. July 2024, https://www.europarl.europa.eu/RegData/etudes/BRIE/2024/762367/EPRS_BRI(2024)762367_EN.pdf.

Lilyanova, V., and Schollaert, L., 2024. PE 762.407, Partial payments under the Recovery and Resilience Facility: An overview. Briefing, European Parliament. Next Generation EU (NGEU) delivery – Governance. EPRS - European Parliamentary Research Service, Members' Research Service. September 2024, https://www.europarl.europa.eu/RegData/etudes/BRIE/2024/762407/EPRS_BRI(2024)762407_EN.pdf.

Lilyanova, V, 2023a. PE 747.883. Governance and oversight of the Recovery and Resilience Facility. Briefing: Next Generation EU (NGEU) delivery - Governance. European Parliament, EPRS: European Parliamentary Research Service, NGEU Monitoring Service, Members' Research Service. May 2023, https://www.europarl.europa.eu/RegData/etudes/BRIE/2023/747883/EPRS_BRI(2023)747883_EN.pdf.

Lilyanova, V, 2023b. PE 753.932, Health related measures in the national recovery and resilience plans. Briefing, European Parliament. Next Generation EU (NGEU) delivery – Sectoral focus. EPRS—European Parliamentary Research Service. September 2023, https://www.europarl.europa.eu/RegData/etudes/BRIE/2023/753932/EPRS_BRI(2023)753932_EN.pdf.

Lilyanova, V, 2022. PE 733.606. The digital dimension of the National Recovery and Resilience Plans. Briefing, Next Generation EU (NGEU) delivery—Sectoral focus. European Parliament, EPRS: European Parliamentary Research Service. July 2022, https://www.europarl.europa.eu/RegData/etudes/BRIE/2022/733606/EPRS_BRI(2022)733606_EN.pdf.

Lincoln, A, 1953. 'A House Divided': Speech at Springfield, Illinois, June 16, 1858, in: Basler, RP (ed), *Collected Works of Abraham Lincoln*. Rutgers University Press.

Lindner, J and Nguyen, T, 2024. The Politics of European Union Funding: Time for Treaty Change?, in: Kilpatrick, C and Scott, J. (eds), *New Frontiers of EU Funding: Law, Policy, Politics*. Oxford University Press, https://doi.org/10.1093/oso/9780198940319.003.0003.

Lindseth, PL, 2023. The Constitutional Imaginary and the Metabolic Realities of European Integration, in: Komárek, J (ed), *European Constitutional Imaginaries: Between Ideology and Utopia*. Oxford University Press.

Lindseth, PL, 2021a. Evolutionary Public Law: Constituting and Administering Human Ultra-Sociality, in: Cane, P, Hofmann, HCH, Ip, EC, and Lindseth, PL (eds), *The Oxford Handbook of Comparative Administrative Law*. Oxford University Press.

Lindseth, PL, 2021b. Institutional Change and the Continuity of Law. *Connecticut Law Review* 55, 1473–95.

Lindseth, PL, 2020a. The Democratic Disconnect, the Power-Legitimacy Nexus, and the Future of EU Governance, in: Bignami, F (ed), *EU Law in Populist Times: Crises and Prospects*. Cambridge University Press.

Lindseth, PL, 2020b. Theorizing Backlash: Supranational Governance and International Investment Law and Arbitration in Comparative Perspective. *Journal of World Investment & Trade* 21, 34–70, https://doi.org/10.1163/22119000-12340167.

Lindseth, PL, 2018. The Metabolic Constitution and the Limits of EU Legal Pluralism, in: Davies, G and Avbelj, M (eds), *Research Handbook in Legal Pluralism in EU Law*. Edward Elgar Publishing, pp 223–42.

Lindseth, PL, 2017. Between the 'Real' and the 'Right': Explorations Along the Institutional-Constitutional Frontier, in: Adams, M, Ballin, EH, Meuwese, A (eds), *Constitutionalism and the Rule of Law: Bridging Idealism and Realism*. Cambridge University Press, pp 60–93.

Lindseth, PL, 2016a. The Perils of 'As If' European Constitutionalism. *European Law Journal* 22, 696–718.

Lindseth, PL, 2016b. Supranational Organizations, in: Hurd, I, Johnstone, I, and Cogan, JK (eds), *Oxford Handbook of International Organizations*. Oxford University Press.

Lindseth, PL, 2015. Transatlantic Functionalism: New Deal Models and European Integration. *Critical Analysis of Law* 2, 83–105.

Lindseth, PL, 2014. Equilibrium, Demoi-cracy, and Delegation in the Crisis of European Integration. *German Law Journal* 15, 529–67.

Lindseth, PL, 2012a. Of the People: Democracy, the Eurozone, and Lincoln's Threshold Criterion. *Berlin Journal* 22, 4–7.

Lindseth, PL, 2012. The Critical Promise of the New History of European Law. *Contemporary European History* 21, 457–75, https://doi.org/10.1017/S096077731200029X.

Lindseth, PL, 2012b. Author's Reply: 'Outstripping', or the Question of 'Legitimate for What?' in EU Governance. *European Constitutional Law Review* 8, 153–64.

Lindseth, PL, 2010. *Power and Legitimacy: Reconciling Europe and the Nation-State*. Oxford University Press.

Lindseth, PL, 1999. Democratic Legitimacy and the Administrative Character of Supranationalism: The Example of the European Community. *Columbia Law Review* 99, 628–738.

Lindseth, PL and Fasone, C, 2020. Rule-of-Law Conditionality and Resource Mobilization – the Foundations of a Genuinely 'Constitutional' EU? Verfassungsblog, https://verfassungsblog.de/rule-of-law-conditionality-and-resource-mobilization-the-foundations-of-a-genuinely-constitutional-eu/.

Lindseth, PL and Leino-Sandberg, P, 2024a. Democratizing Draghi: Why the 'Competitiveness Report' Demands Treaty Reform. Verfassungsblog, https://verfassungsblog.de/draghi-report-investment-eu-competition-treaty-reform/.

Lindseth, PL and Leino-Sandberg, P, 2024b. Crisis, Reinterpretation, and the Rule of Law: Repurposing 'Cohesion' as a General EU Spending Power. *Hague Journal on the Rule of Law* 16, 587–610.

Liski, J, 2021. Marin ja virkamiehet mykkäkoulussa EU-uhkauksesta—vain toinen Ylen väitteistä vahvistetaan [Marin and officials mute about EU threat—only one of Yle's claims is confirmed]. Iltalehti (Helsinki), https://www.iltalehti.fi/politiikka/a/f1f3261b-888c-49db-8302-ff00e41d9038.

Löfven, S, 2020. 'Frugal four' warn pandemic spending must be responsible. *Financial Times*. 16 June 2020, https://www.ft.com/content/7c47fa9d-6d54-4bde-a1da-2c407a52e471.

Loughlin, M, 2018. The Silences of Constitutions. International Journal of Constitutional Law 16, 922–35, https://doi.org/10.1093/icon/moy064.

Lupo, N, 2023. PNRR e cicli politico-elettorali, tra Unione europea e Stati membri. Editoriale di Nicola Lupo. Numero 28. 29 November 2023. Federalismi.it: Rivista di diritto pubblico italiano, comparato ed europeo, https://www.federalismi.it/nv14/editoriale.cfm?eid=689&content=&content_auth=.

Magnus, M, Loi, G, De Lemos Peixoto, S, and Lehofer, W, 2024. PE 755.725. Recovery and Resilience Dialogue with the European Commission, BUDG-ECON Committee meeting on 5 February 2024. In-Depth Analysis, European Parliament, Economic Governance and EMU Scrutiny Unit (EGOV), https://www.europarl.europa.eu/RegData/etudes/IDAN/2024/755725/IPOL_IDA(2024)755725_EN.pdf.

Magnus, M, Loi, G, Hanina, K, and Lehofer, W, 2024. PE 760.236. Recovery and Resilience Dialogue with the European Commission: BUDG-ECON Committee meeting on 16

September 2024. In-Depth Analysis, European Parliament, Economic Governance and EMU Scrutiny Unit (EGOV), Directorate-General for Internal Policies, https://www.europarl.europa.eu/RegData/etudes/IDAN/2024/760236/IPOL_IDA(2024)760236_EN.pdf.

Majone, G, 2015. The Deeper Euro-Crisis or: The Collapse of the EU Political Culture of Total Optimism, https://cadmus.eui.eu/server/api/core/bitstreams/8bbf7ce7-da35-5474-aa6b-519ff93a8af2/content.

Majone, G, 2014. *Rethinking the Union of Europe Post-Crisis: Has Integration Gone Too Far?* Cambridge University Press.

Majone, G, 2005. *Dilemmas of European Integration: The Ambiguities and Pitfalls of Integration by Stealth*. Oxford University Press.

Majone, G, 2001. Two Logics of Delegation: Agency and Fiduciary Relations in EU Governance. *European Union Politics* 2, 103–22.

Majone, G, 1996. Temporal Consistency and Policy Credibility: Why Democracies Need Non-Majoritarian Institutions. European University Institute, Working Paper RSC No 96/57, https://www.eui.eu/Documents/RSCAS/Publications/WorkingPapers/9657.pdf.

Majone, G, 1994. The European Community: An 'Independent Fourth Branch of Government?,' in: Brüggemeier, G (ed), *Verfassungen Für Ein Ziviles Europa*. Nomos, pp 23–44.

Majone, G, 1993. The European Community Between Social Policy and Social Regulation. *JCMS: Journal of Common Market Studies* 31, 153–70, https://doi.org/10.1111/j.1468-5965.1993.tb00455.x.

Mancini, GF and Keeling, DT, 1994. Democracy and the European Court of Justice. *Modern Law Review* 57, 175–90.

Mańko, R, 2024. PE 762.396. The European Parliament's new Rules of Procedure: Parliament 2024 reforms. Briefing, European Parliament. EPRS: European Parliamentary Research Service, Members' Research Service. September 2024, https://www.europarl.europa.eu/RegData/etudes/BRIE/2024/762396/EPRS_BRI(2024)762396_EN.pdf#:~:text=The%20European%20Parliament's%20new%20Rules%20of%20Procedure,control%20and%20improve%20scrutiny%20of%20the%20Commission.

Marin, S, 2020. Minutes item PTK 109 /2020 vp. Pääministerin ilmoitus EU:n monivuotisesta rahoituskehyksestä ja elpymiskokonaisuudesta [Prime Minister's announcement on the EU's multiannual financial framework and recovery package]. Finnish Parliament, Plenary. 9 September 2020, https://www.eduskunta.fi/FI/vaski/PoytakirjaAsiakohta/Sivut/PTK_109+2020+3.aspx.

Marján, A, 2009. Some of the Present and Future Challenges of EU Regional Policy. *Society and Economy* 30, 293–302, https://doi.org/10.1556/socec.30.2008.2.9.

Marshall, T, 1987. The Constitution: A Living Document. *Howard Law Journal* 30, 915–20.

Martínez Turégano, D, 2025. NGEU funds: what can we say about their impact and future challenges?. CaixaBank Research. Economics & Markets: Public Sector. 18 March 2025, https://www.caixabankresearch.com/en/economics-markets/public-sector/ngeu-funds-what-can-we-say-about-their-impact-and-future-challenges.

Mashaw, JL, 1996. Reinventing Government and Regulatory Reform: Studies in the Neglect and Abuse of Administrative Law. *University of Pittsburgh Law Review* 57, 405–41.

Mathis, A, 2017. PE 603.810. 'Other Revenue' in the European Union Budget. Briefing, European Parliament, Policy Department D - Budgetary Affairs. November 2017, https://www.europarl.europa.eu/RegData/etudes/BRIE/2017/603810/IPOL_BRI(2017)603810_EN.pdf.

Mattarella, S, 2020. Nota del Presidente della Repubblica Sergio Mattarella, Roma, 12 March 2020, https://www.quirinale.it/elementi/46574.

Mayer, FC, 2024. NextGenerationEU and the Future of European Integration: Foreseeing the Unforeseeable. *AJIL Unbound* 118, 172–76, https://doi.org/10.1017/aju.2024.27.

McDougall, M, 2024. EU bonds fall after MSCI declines to include them in sovereign debt indices. *Financial Times*. 13 June 2024, https://www.ft.com/content/a86a51e6-cf64-4b7c-80b4-d63dc4ce09de.

Mendez, C, 2011. The Lisbonization of EU Cohesion Policy: A Successful Case of Experimentalist Governance? *European Planning Studies* 19, 519–37, https://doi.org/10.1080/09654313.2011.548368.

Meseberg Declaration, 2018. Declaration of France and Germany on Renewing Europe's promises of security and prosperity, https://www.elysee.fr/en/emmanuel-macron/2018/06/19/meseberg-declaration-renewing-europes-promises-of-security-and-prosperity.

Meyer, J, Trebesch, C, and Horn, S, 2020. Coronabonds: The forgotten history of European Community debt. VoxEU | CEPR, https://cepr.org/voxeu/columns/coronabonds-forgotten-history-european-community-debt.

Milward, AS, 2000. *The European Rescue of the Nation-State*, 2nd edn, Routledge.

Milward, AS and Sørensen, V, 1993. Interdependence or Integration? A National Choice, in: Milward, AS, Lynch, FMB, Ranieri, R, Romero, F, and Sørensen, V (eds), *The Frontier of National Sovereignty: History and Theory, 1945-1992*. Routledge.

Miró, J, Natili, M, and Schelkle, W, 2024. Money Makes the World Go Round: How Much Difference Do Recovery and Resilience Plans Make to EU Reform Governance? *JCMS: Journal of Common Market Studies* 62, 1615–32, https://doi.org/10.1111/jcms.13558.

Mody, A, Vallee, S, and Claessens, S, 2012. Making sense of Eurobond proposals. VoxEU | CEPR, https://cepr.org/voxeu/columns/making-sense-eurobond-proposals.

Moesen, W and de Grauwe, P, 2009. Gains for All: A proposal for a common Eurobond. CEPS Policy Brief, https://www.ceps.eu/ceps-publications/gains-all-proposal-common-eurobond/.

Molica, F, 2022. The lack of high-level debate on cohesion policy poses a risk to its survival. Regional Studies Association, https://www.regionalstudies.org/rsa-blog/blog-21030/.

Molica, F, de Renzis, A, and Bourdin, S, 2024. Between re-renationalisation and hyper-Lisbonisation: the long goodbye to the EU Cohesion Policy original goals. Discussion Paper No.2024-10, Gran Sasso Science Institute, Discussion Paper Series in Regional Science & Economic Geography. May 2024, revised October 2024, https://www.gssi.it/images/discussion%20papers%20rseg/2024/DPRSEG_2024-10.pdf.

Moller-Nielsen, T, 2024. EU auditors warn of 'irregularity or even corruption' in bloc's pandemic recovery fund. 20 March 2024. Euractiv. https://www.euractiv.com/section/economy-jobs/news/eu-auditors-warn-of-irregularity-or-even-corruption-in-blocs-pandemic-recovery-fund/.

Mölter, H, Lehne, J, Wehnert, T, and Klingen, J, 2022. Summary Report of the Green Recovery Tracker: Tracking the contribution of national covid-19 recovery efforts towards a climate neutral EU. Written in collaboration between the Wuppertal Institute and E3G as part of the Green Recovery Tracker project, funded by the European Climate Initiative, https://epub.wupperinst.org/frontdoor/deliver/index/docId/7935/file/7935_Green_Recovery_Tracker.pdf.

Monti Report, 2016. Future Financing of the EU: Final Report and Recommendations of the High Level Group on Own Resources, Mario Monti (Chairman), Daniel Dăianu, Clemens Fuest, Kristalina Georgieva, Ivailo Kalfin, Alain Lamassoure, Pierre Moscovici, Ingrida Šimonytė, Frans Timmermans, Guy Verhofstadt. European Commission, https://commission.europa.eu/publications/future-financing-eu_en.

Moody's, 2022. Ratings Action: Moody's affirms the European Union's (EU) Aaa rating, maintains stable outlook. Moody's Investors Service, https://www.moodys.com/research/Moodys-affirms-the-European-Unions-EU-Aaa-rating-maintains-stable-Rating-Action--PR_463445.

Moody's, 2013. Rating Methodology: Multilateral Development Banks and Other Supranational Entities. Moody's Investors Service, https://www.moodys.com/research/doc--PBC_161372?WT.mc_id=RateSov.

Moynihan, DP and Beazley, I, 2016. Toward next-generation performance budgeting: lessons from the experiences of seven reforming countries. World Bank, https://documents1.worldbank.org/curated/en/356081478497402740/pdf/109808-PUB-Box396311B-PUBLIC-DOCDATE-11-1-16.pdf.

Munta, M, Pircher, B, and Bekker, S, 2024. Ownership of National Recovery Plans: Next Generation EU and Democratic Legitimacy. *Journal of European Public Policy* 31, 3787–811, https://doi.org/10.1080/13501763.2023.2248202.

Murphy, T, 2023a. Tony Murphy, President of the European Court of Auditors, believes that Rome's spending issues are due to an excess of available funds. Translation of interview in Il Sole 24 Ore (Italy), https://www.linkedin.com/pulse/tony-murphy-president-european-court-auditors-romes-murphy-fcca-/.

Murphy, T, 2023b. European Court of Auditors finds shortcomings in the EU's recovery programme. Translation of interview originally appearing Frankfurter Allgemeine Zeitung (FAZ), 22 September 2023, https://www.linkedin.com/pulse/european-court-auditors-finds-shortcomings-eus-tony-murphy-fcca-/.

Navarro, V, 2014. Spain's labour market and social reforms have exacerbated the country's unemployment problem. LSE EUROPP Blog, https://blogs.lse.ac.uk/europpblog/2014/04/09/spains-labour-market-and-social-reforms-have-exacerbated-the-countrys-unemployment-problem/.

Neubert, K and Ionta, N, 2025. European Parliament sues Council over €150 billion defence loan scheme. Euractiv. 20 August 2025, https://www.euractiv.com/section/defence/news/european-parliament-sues-council-over-e150-billion-defence-loan-scheme/.

Neumeier, C, 2023. Political Own Resources: Towards a legal framework. *Common Market Law Review* 60, 319–44.

Nguyen, T and Redeker, N, 2022. How to make the marriage work: Wedding the Recovery and Resilience Facility and European Semester. Hertie School, Jacques Delors Centre, Policy Brief, https://www.delorscentre.eu/en/publications/detail/publication/how-to-make-the-marriage-work.

Nguyen, T and van den Brink, M, 2022. An early Christmas Gift from Karlsruhe?: The Bundesverfassungsgericht's NextGenerationEU Ruling. Verfassungsblog, https://verfassungsblog.de/an-early-christmas-gift-from-karlsruhe/.

Nicolaïdis, K, 2013. European Demoicracy and Its Crisis. *JCMS: Journal of Common Market Studies* 51, 351–69.

Nicolaïdis, K, 2012. The Idea of European Demoicracy, in: Dickson, J and Eleftheriadis, P (eds), *Philosophical Foundations of European Union Law*. Oxford University Press, pp 247–74.

Nicolaïdis, K, 2011. Germany as Europe: How the Constitutional Court Unwittingly Embraced EU Demoi-cracy: A Comment on Franz Mayer. *International Journal of Constitutional Law* 9, 786–92.

Nicolaïdis, K, 2004. The New Constitution as European 'Demoi-cracy'? *Critical Review of International Social and Political Philosophy* 7, 76–93.

Nienaber, M, Valero, J, and Kowalcze, K, 2025. Germany Rejects EU Plan for Beefed-Up €2 Trillion Budget. Bloomberg.com. 17 July 2025, https://www.bloomberg.com/news/articles/2025-07-17/germany-rejects-eu-s-2-trillion-budget-plan-as-maneuvers-begin.

Nikolov, K, 2024. Brussels halts EU recovery plan payment for Bulgaria. Euractiv. 2 December 2024, https://www.euractiv.com/section/politics/news/brussels-halts-eu-recovery-plan-payment-for-bulgaria/.

Núñez Ferrer, J, Musmeci, R, Rinaldi, D, and Polli, O, 2018. *The EU Budget and Its Conditionalities: An Assessment of Their Contribution to Performance and Reforms*. CEPS, https://cdn.ceps.eu/wp-content/uploads/2020/06/The-EU-Budget-and-its-Conditionalities.pdf.

Núñez Ferrer, J and Ruiz de la Ossa, T, 2022. Substitution effects, delays, constraints and administrative capacity risk considerably reducing actual investments under cohesion policy and NGEU/RRF. ECA Journal 2/2022, 'The EU Recovery and Resilience Facility: a jump to a resilient Europe?', pp 118–24, https://www.eca.europa.eu/Lists/ECADocuments/JOURNAL22_02/Journal22_02.pdf.

OECD, European Ombudsman, 2022. Towards good practice principles for government transparency in the use of recovery funds. OECD Public Governance Policy Paper. 15 November 2022, https://www.ombudsman.europa.eu/en/publication/en/163019.

OLAF, 2022. OLAF in 2021: Exposing and preventing fraud. Press Release No 7/2022, OLAF Report 2021. 8 June 2022, https://anti-fraud.ec.europa.eu/media-corner/news/olaf-2021-exposing-and-preventing-fraud-2022-06-08_en.

Ollikainen, P and Leino-Sandberg, P, 2025. EU-oikeuden kielestä legalismiin—Suomen oikeudelliset argumentit ennallistamisasetuksen ja sosiaalisen ilmastorahaston käsittelyssä *Lakimies* 123, 679–708.

Oraheimo, H and Paasikallio, K, 2024. Reforming the Stability and Growth Pact: Debt reduction versus sustainable and inclusive growth. *Common Market Law Review* 61, 1549–74.

Orefice, M, 2022. Implementation of the National Recovery and Resilience Plan: Assessment by the Italian Court of Auditors. ECA Journal 2/2022, 'The EU Recovery and Resilience Facility: a jump to a resilient Europe?', pp 98–103, https://www.eca.europa.eu/Lists/ECADocuments/JOURNAL22_02/Journal22_02.pdf.

Ostaszewska, O, 2025. Legality of the solidarity contribution under international law – Klesch Group & Raffinerie Heide v. Germany. International Bureau of Fiscal Documentation (IBFD), 28 March 2025, https://www.ibfd.org/sites/default/files/2025-04/Legality%20of%20the%20solidarity%20contribution%20under.pdf.

Panascì, MA, 2024. Unravelling Next Generation EU As A Transformative Moment: From Market Integration To Redistribution. *Common Market Law Review* 61, 13–54, https://doi.org/10.54648/cola2024002.

Patrin, M, 2023a. Governance by Funding: NGEU, Solidarity and the EU Institutional Balance. REBUILD Centre Working Paper 4. Italian PRIN 2020 project REACT—Re-shaping the EU integration Agenda after the COVID Turmoil. February 2023, https://rebuildcentre.eu/publication/governance-by-funding-ngeu-solidarity-and-the-eu-institutional-balance/.

Patrin, M, 2023b. *Collegiality in the European Commission: Legal Substance and Institutional Practice*. Oxford University Press.

Pench, LR, 2024. The New Stability and Growth Pact: Innovation and Continuity in the Light of Next Generation EU. REBUILD Centre Working Paper No 14. 11 January 2024. Forthcoming in Fabbrini, F and Petit, C (eds), *Research Handbook on Post-Pandemic EU Economic Governance and NGEU Law* (Elgar 2024), https://papers.ssrn.com/abstract=4691440.

Peters, T, 2024. PE 759.582. At a Glance: Plenary, February II 2024. European Parliament. Establishing the Ukraine Facility. EPRS - European Parliamentary Research Service, Members' Research Service, February 2024, https://www.europarl.europa.eu/RegData/etudes/ATAG/2024/759582/EPRS_ATA(2024)759582_EN.pdf.

Peters, T and Przetacznik, J, 2024. Establishing the Ukraine Facility. Legislative Train Schedule, European Parliament. Members' Research Service. 15 December 2024, https://www.europarl.europa.eu/legislative-train/theme-a-stronger-europe-in-the-world/file-ukraine-facility.

Pilati, M, 2021. National Recovery and Resilience Plans: Empowering the green and digital transitions? Discussion paper. Joint project between the European Office of the

Konrad-Adenauer-Stiftung (KAS) and the European Policy Centre (EPC). April 2021, https://aei.pitt.edu/103764/1/National_RRPs_DiscussionPaper.pdf.

Pinster, J and Witteman, L, 2022. RRF boss Céline Gauer: 'We shouldn't approve recovery plans made in ivory towers'. Follow the Money, https://www.ftm.eu/articles/eu-celine-gauer-power-in-the-name-of-recovery.

Pisani-Ferry, J, 2020. La postérité du plan de relance européen sera une affaire d'exécution. 20 June 2020. *Le Monde,* https://www.lemonde.fr/idees/article/2020/06/20/jean-pisani-ferry-la-posterite-du-plan-de-relance-europeen-sera-une-affaire-d-execution_6043532_3232.html.

POLITICO, 2025. EU budget: The winners and losers. POLITICO. 17 July 2025, https://www.politico.eu/article/european-commission-budget-ursula-von-der-leyen-ukraine-research-defense-technology-agriculture/.

Popli, N, 2025. What Trump Says He Will Do on Day One, 13 January 2025. TIME, https://time.com/7206595/donald-trump-day-one-promises-pardons-border-executive-order/.

Portugal.gov.pt, 2023. European Commission approves 2.6-billion-euro RRF payment. Press Release. 12 December 2023, https://www.portugal.gov.pt/en/gc23/communication/news-item?i=european-commission-approves-26-billion-euro-rrf-payment.

Pronina, L and Ritchie, G, 2023. EU to Start Talks on Adding Its Debt to Sovereign Indexes. Bloomberg. 5 October 2023, https://www.bloomberg.com/news/articles/2023-10-05/eu-to-start-talks-soon-on-adding-its-debt-to-sovereign-indexes.

Rechnungshof Österreich, 2024. 8 Punkte Plan für eine digitale Schule. Bericht des Rechnungshofes. Reihe Bund 2024/29; Reihe Kärnten 2024/3; Reihe Niederösterreich 2024/6, https://www.parlament.gv.at/dokument/XXVII/III/1233/imfname_1657251.pdf.

Rega, C and Bonifazi, A, 2020. The Rise of Resilience in Spatial Planning: A Journey through Disciplinary Boundaries and Contested Practices. *Sustainability* 12, 7277, https://doi.org/10.3390/su12187277.

Regeringskansliet, 2022. Faktapromemoria 2022/23:FPM23. Lagstiftningspaket om stöd till Ukraina under 2023. 2022/23:FPM23. Finansdepartementet. 30 November 2022, https://www.regeringen.se/contentassets/13977cc7d4504af5bd7a30420e9a6b31/lagstiftningspaket-om-stod-till-ukraina-under-2023-202223fpm23.pdf.

Regling, K, 2020. Europe's response to Covid-19. Speech by Klaus Regling, ESM Managing Director, UniCredit European Conference Online. 21 October 2020, https://www.esm.europa.eu/speeches-and-presentations/europes-response-covid-19-speech-klaus-regling.

Reuters, 2025a. Taxation in EU budget proposal sends 'wrong signal', German minister says. Reuters. 17 July 2025, https://www.reuters.com/markets/europe/taxation-eu-budget-proposal-sends-wrong-signal-german-minister-says-2025-07-17/.

Reuters, 2025b. Reactions to the European Commission's new EU budget proposal. Reuters. 16 July 2025, https://www.reuters.com/sustainability/climate-energy/reactions-european-commissions-new-eu-budget-proposal-2025-07-16/.

Ritchie, G, 2025. BlackRock's Hildebrand Calls for EU Bonds to Rival Treasuries. Bloomberg.com. 5 June 2025, https://www.bloomberg.com/news/articles/2025-06-05/blackrock-s-hildebrand-calls-for-eu-bonds-to-rival-treasuries.

Ritchie, G, 2024. ICE Rejects Proposal to Include EU Debt in Sovereign Indexes. Bloomberg. 5 August 2024, https://www.bloomberg.com/news/articles/2024-08-05/ice-rejects-proposal-to-include-eu-bonds-in-sovereign-indexes.

Roche, D, 2025. Von der Leyen's defiance: a lost chance for transparency and reform. EUalive. 15 July 2025, https://eualive.net/von-der-leyens-defiance-a-lost-chance-for-transparency-and-reform/.

Rodríguez Muñoz, L and Buti, M, 2016. Why we need a positive fiscal stance for the Eurozone and what it means. VoxEU | CEPR, https://cepr.org/voxeu/columns/why-we-need-positive-fiscal-stance-eurozone-and-what-it-means.

Ronkainen, A, 2024. Eivätkö Orpo, Purra ja Saarikko tiedä hyväksyneensä uuden yhteisvelan Ukrainan tukemiseksi? Blogit vallan mahotonta!, https://suomenkuvalehti.fi/vallan-mahotonta/eivatko-orpo-purra-ja-saarikko-tieda-hyvaksyneensa-uuden-yhteisvelan-ukrainan-tukemiseksi/.

Ronkainen, A, Ghavanini, AW, and Leino-Sandberg, P, 2024. The House Always Wins. A Systematic Analysis of CJEU Case Law Relating to the Economic and Monetary Union (2010-2020). *European Papers* 9, 876–909, https://doi.org/10.15166/2499-8249/790.

Rouxel, P and Yon, K, 2023. From Pension Reform to Regime Crisis: The Social Movement of 2023 in France. *Global Labour Journal* 14, 185–88 https://doi.org/10.15173/glj.v14i2.5519.

RRF Financing Agreement [Bulgaria], 2022. Recovery and Resilience Facility Financing Agreement between the Commission and the Republic of Bulgaria, https://www.minfin.bg/upload/52702/BG+RRF+FA+1+countersigned.pdf.

RRF Financing Agreement [Greece], 2021. Recovery and Resilience Facility Financing Agreement between the Commission and the Hellenic Republic, https://greece20.gov.gr/en/useful-documents/.

RRF Financing Agreement [Spain], 2021. Recovery and Resilience Facility Financing Agreement between the Commission and the Kingdom of Spain, https://planderecuperacion.gob.es/sites/default/files/2021-12/ES_RRF_Financing_Agreement.pdf.

Rubio, E, 2022. From words to action: Analysing possible scenarios and political dynamics in the process of disbursing the European Recovery and Resilience Facility funds. Institut Jacques Delors. Economy & Finance Policy Paper No 274. February 2022, https://institutdelors.eu/en/publications/from-words-to-action/.

Rutte, M, 2020. Tweede Kamer, 14 juli 2020. Debat over de Europese Top van 17 en 18 juli 2020, https://www.tweedekamer.nl/debat_en_vergadering/plenaire_vergaderingen/details/activiteit?id=2020A03073, quoted in Bokhorst (2023, p 28).

Sacriste, G and Vauchez, A, 2023. European plans: between market and democratic planning. Groupe d'études géopolitiques. Working Paper, June 2023, https://geopolitique.eu/wp-content/uploads/2023/06/Note-de-travail-EN.pdf.

Sadurski, W, 2022. The European Commission Cedes its Crucial Leverage vis-à-vis the Rule of Law in Poland. 6 June 2022. Verfassungsblog, https://verfassungsblog.de/the-european-commission-cedes-its-crucial-leverage-vis-a-vis-the-rule-of-law-in-poland.

Sandbu, M, 2020. EU crosses the Rubicon with its emergency recovery fund. *Financial Times*, 22 July 2020, https://www.ft.com/content/bd570dde-3095-4074-bd37-18003f2bd3c2.

Santos, I, 2009. Is structural spending on solid foundations? Bruegel Policy Brief 2008/02. 27 August 2009, https://www.bruegel.org/policy-brief/structural-spending-solid-foundations.

Sapala, M, 2024. PE 757.590. Social and territorial cohesion in the Recovery and Resilience Facility. Briefing, Next Generation EU (NGEU) delivery, Sectoral focus. European Parliament. EPRS—European Parliamentary Research Service. January 2024, https://www.europarl.europa.eu/RegData/etudes/BRIE/2024/757590/EPRS_BRI(2024)757590_EN.pdf.

Scheppele, KL and Morijn, J, 2023a. Frozen: How the EU is Blocking Funds to Hungary and Poland Using a Multitude of Conditionalities. Verfassungsblog, https://verfassungsblog.de/frozen/.

Scheppele, KL and Morijn, J, 2023b. What Price Rule of Law?, in: Södersten, A and Hercock, E (eds), *The Rule of Law in the EU: Crisis and Solutions*. Swedish Institute for European Policy Studies, pp 39–45.

Schick, A, 2014. The Metamorphoses of Performance Budgeting. *OECD Journal on Budgeting* 13, 49–79.

Schlosser, P, 2018. *Europe's New Fiscal Union*. Springer.

Schmidt, VA, 2022. European emergency politics and the question of legitimacy. *Journal of European Public Policy* 29, 979–93, https://doi.org/10.1080/13501763.2021.1916061

Schramm, L and Terranova, C, 2024. From NGEU to REPowerEU: policy steering and budgetary innovation in the EU. *Journal of European Integration* 46, 943–61, https://doi.org/10.1080/07036337.2024.2353791.

Schramm, L, Krotz, U, and de Witte, B, 2022. Building 'Next Generation' after the Pandemic: The Implementation and Implications of the EU Covid Recovery Plan. *JCMS: Journal of Common Market Studies* 60, 114–24, https://doi.org/10.1111/jcms.13375.

Schutze, R, 2020. Models of Demoicracy: Some Preliminary Thoughts, https://papers.ssrn.com/abstract=3658493.

Schwab, T, 2024. Quo Vadis, Cohesion Policy? European Regional Development at a Crossroads. *Intereconomics Review of European Economic Policy* 59, 284–92.

Schwarcz, A, 2023. PE 741.581. Rule of law-related 'super milestones' in the recovery and resilience plans of Hungary and Poland. Briefing requested by the CONT Committee, European Parliament. Policy Department for Directorate-General for Internal Policies. January 2023, https://www.europarl.europa.eu/RegData/etudes/BRIE/2023/741581/IPOL_BRI(2023)741581_EN.pdf.

S&D Press Release, 2025. European Parliament votes to take legal action after being excluded from decision-making process of EU defence funding. Press Release. Socialists and Democrats. 24 June 2025, https://www.socialistsanddemocrats.eu/newsroom/european-parliament-votes-take-legal-action-after-being-excluded-decision-making-process.

Sénécat, A, 2023. Is the French pension reform dictated by Brussels? *Le Monde*, 13 January 2023, https://www.lemonde.fr/en/les-decodeurs/article/2023/01/13/is-the-french-pension-reform-dictated-by-brussels_6011446_8.html.

Smeets, S and Beach, D, 2023. New Institutional Leadership Goes Viral: EU Crisis Reforms and the Coming about of the Covid Recovery Fund. *European Journal of Political Research* 62, 377–96, https://doi.org/10.1111/1475-6765.12508.

Snyder, F, 1999. EMU Revisited: Are we Making a Constitution? What Constitution are we Making?, in: Craig, P and Burca, G de (eds), *The Evolution of EU Law*. Oxford University Press.

Somek, A, 2008. *Individualism: An Essay on the Authority of the European Union*. Oxford University Press.

Sorgi, G, 2025. The muddled €1.8 trillion EU budget launch that exposes von der Leyen's weaknesses. POLITICO. 16 July 2025, https://www.politico.eu/article/ursula-von-der-leyen-eu-budget/.

S&P, 2022. Supranationals Special Edition 2022. S&P Global Ratings, https://www.spglobal.com/ratings/en/research/pdf-articles/221011-supranationals-special-edition-2022-101567466.

S&P, 2019. Supranationals Special Edition 2019. S&P Global Ratings, https://www.spglobal.com/_assets/documents/ratings/research/spgr_supranationals_2019_final_corrected.pdf.

Spieker, LD, 2024. Trust the Treaties! Protecting EU Values Does Not Require Treaty Change. *Heidelberg Journal of International Law (ZaöRV)* 84, 745–59, https://doi.org/10.17104/0044-2348-2024-4-745.

Spielberger, L, 2024. Financial Power Europe? The Challenges of EU Financial Assistance to Ukraine. CSDS Policy Brief, 27/2024. Brussels School of Governance, Centre for Security, Diplomacy, and Strategy. 7 October 2024, https://csds.vub.be/publication/financial-power-europe-the-challenges-of-eu-financial-assistance-to-ukraine/.

Spielberger, L, Hodson, D, Howarth, D, and Mugnai, I, 2025. Building a European Union 'Treasury': Explaining the European Commission's New Approach to Debt Issuance and Management. *JCMS: Journal of Common Market Studies* 63, 1197–16, https://doi.org/10.1111/jcms.13696.

Stamouli, N, 2024. Fraud-busters swoop on Greek contracts involving €2.5B of EU recovery funds. POLITICO, 10 April 2024, https://www.politico.eu/article/fraud-busters-swoop-greece-contract-involve-e2-5-billion-eu-recovery-fund-cosmote-vodafone-nova/.

Stie, AE, 2012. *Democratic Decision-making in the EU: Technocracy in Disguise?* Routledge.

Strauss, DA, 2010. *The Living Constitution*. Oxford University Press.

Strupczewski, J, 2021. EU Recovery Fund success could the pave way for a repeat: EU Commission. *Reuters*, 10 May 2021, https://www.reuters.com/article/us-eu-recovery-idUSKBN2CR1D9/ppr

Tamma, P, 2025. Brussels to seek more joint debt in EU budget plan. *Financial Times*. 3 July 2025, https://www.ft.com/content/2f12781a-c087-4884-a6ae-92479fa20a3d.

Tamma, P, 2023. OLAF probes potential fraud involving EU recovery funds. POLITICO, 28 April 2023, https://www.politico.eu/article/olaf-investigates-potential-fraud-involving-eu-recovery-funds/

Tesche, T, 2023. Keep it Complex! Prodi's Curse and the EU Fiscal Governance Regime Complex. *New Political Economy* 28, 29–41, https://doi.org/10.1080/13563467.2022.2061436.

The Economist, 2020. The European Union is having a bad crisis. *The Economist*. 14 May 2020, https://www.economist.com/leaders/2020/05/14/the-european-union-is-having-a-bad-crisis.

Thygesen, N, Szczurek, M, Bordignon, M, Debrun, X, and Beetsma, R, 2022. Making the EU and national budgetary frameworks work together. VoxEU | CEPR, https://cepr.org/voxeu/columns/making-eu-and-national-budgetary-frameworks-work-together.

Tilly, C, 1992. *Coercion, Capital and European States, A.D. 990 - 1992*, Revised edn. Wiley-Blackwell.

Tilly, C, 1975. Reflections on the History of European State-Making, in: Tilly, C (ed), *The Formation of National States in Western Europe*. Princeton University Press.

Tooze, A, 2020. *The Death of the Central Bank Myth*. Foreign Policy, 13 May 2020, https://foreignpolicy.com/2020/05/13/european-central-bank-myth-monetary-policy-german-court-ruling/.

Trampusch, C and Gross, P, 2021. Do Parliaments Have Control over Sovereign Debt Management? *West European Politics* 44, 299–326, https://doi.org/10.1080/01402382.2019.1680513.

Tsoukala, P, 2020. Post-Crisis Economic and Social Policy: Some Thoughts on Structural Reforms 2.0, in: Bignami, F (ed), *EU Law in Populist Times: Crises and Prospects*. Cambridge University Press.

Tuori, K, 2015. *European Constitutionalism*. Cambridge University Press.

Tuori, K, 2013. *Ratio and Voluntas: The Tension Between Reason and Will in Law*. Ashgate Publishing, Ltd.

Tuori, K and Tuori, K, 2014. *The Eurozone Crisis: A Constitutional Analysis, Cambridge Studies in European Law and Policy*. Cambridge University Press, https://doi.org/10.1017/CBO9781107297289.

Valtioneuvosto, 2025. Valtioneuvoston U-kirjelmä U 48/2025 vp. 30 October 2025, https://www.eduskunta.fi/FI/vaski/Kirjelma/Sivut/U_48+2025.aspx.

Valtioneuvosto, 2022. Hallituksen Esitys Eduskunnalle Vuoden 2023 Talousarvioesityksen (HE 154/2022 Vp) täydentämisestä, HE 277/2022 vp, 17 November 2022, https://www.eduskunta.fi/FI/vaski/HallituksenEsitys/Documents/HE_277+2022.pdf.

van der Vlugt, S, 2025. Can The EU Levy Its Own Taxes? A 'Corporate Resource for Europe' (Re)enters A Legal Minefield. Verfassungsblog. 28 July 2025, https://verfassungsblog.de/can-the-eu-levy-its-own-taxes/.

Vance, J, 2025. Speech by JD Vance, in: Franke, B (ed), *Munich Security Conference 2025: Speech by JD Vance and Selected Reactions, Selected Speeches Held at the Munich Security Conference*. Munich Security Conference.

Vanhercke, B and Verdun, A, 2022. The European Semester as Goldilocks: Macroeconomic Policy Coordination and the Recovery and Resilience Facility. *JCMS: Journal of Common Market Studies* 60, 204–23, https://doi.org/10.1111/jcms.13267.

Vauchez, A and White, J, 2025. The Crisis of Long-Termism: Time and Independence in the European Union. *West European Politics*, [advance view] 1–25, https://doi.org/10.1080/01402382.2025.2521595.

Vinzenz, V, 2022. National Recovery and Resilience Plan: Austria. *Italian Labour Law e-Journal* 15, https://doi.org/10.6092/issn.1561-8048/15683.

von der Leyen, U, 2025a. Speech by President von der Leyen at the EP plenary debate on the motion of censure of the Commission. 7 July 2025, https://ec.europa.eu/commission/presscorner/detail/en/speech_25_1758.

von der Leyen, U, 2025b. Letter of Ursula von der Leyen to the European Council. 4 March 2025, https://ec.europa.eu/commission/presscorner/api/files/attachment/880628/Letter%20by%20President%20von%20der%20Leyen%20on%20defence.pdf.

von der Leyen, U, 2025c. Press statement by the President on the defence package. European Commission. 3 March 2025, https://ec.europa.eu/commission/presscorner/detail/et/statement_25_673.

von der Leyen, U, 2025d. Statement by the President: next long-term EU budget. 15 July 2025, https://ec.europa.eu/commission/presscorner/detail/et/statement_25_1851.

von der Leyen, U, 2025e. When Crisis Strikes Again: Europe's Emergency Plan Explained by Von der Leyen. EU Debates | eudebates.tv. 16 July 2025, https://www.youtube.com/watch?v=FqAmsVwsVL4.

von der Leyen, U, 2025f. Speech by President von der Leyen at the solemn undertaking of the College of Commissioners before the European Court of Justice. European Commission. 26 January 2025, https://ec.europa.eu/commission/presscorner/detail/en/speech_25_330.

von der Leyen, U, 2025g. 2025 State of the Union Address by President von der Leyen. European Commission. 9 September 2025, https://ec.europa.eu/commission/presscorner/detail/ov/SPEECH_25_2053.

von der Leyen, U, 2024. Europe's Choice: Political Guidelines for the Next European Commission 2024-2029. 18 July 2024, https://commission.europa.eu/document/download/e6cd4328-673c-4e7a-8683-f63ffb2cf648_en?filename=Political%20Guidelines%202024-2029_EN.pdf.

von der Leyen, U, 2022. Speech by President von der Leyen at the closing event of the Conference on the Future of Europe. European Commission. 8 May 2022, https://ec.europa.eu/commission/presscorner/detail/en/SPEECH_22_2944.

von der Leyen, U, 2021. Case 1410/2021/MIG. The European Commission's Reply to the European Ombudsman's Letter on How the Commission Dealt with a Request for Public Access to Documents Concerning Germany's Recovery and Resilience Plan under the Recovery and Resilience Facility. Letter of Ursula von der Leyen. 14 October 2021, https://www.ombudsman.europa.eu/en/doc/correspondence/en/148333.

von der Leyen, U, 2020. Speech by President von der Leyen on the Recovery Plan and Resilience at the Fundação Champalimaud. 29 September 2020, https://ec.europa.eu/commission/presscorner/detail/en/SPEECH_20_1772.

Walby, K and Larsen, M, 2012. Access to Information and Freedom of Information Requests: Neglected Means of Data Production in the Social Sciences. *Qualitative Inquiry* 18, 31–42, https://doi.org/10.1177/1077800411427844.

Wanat, Z, Bayer, L, and Tamma, P, 2022. EU gives Poland route to pandemic recovery cash. POLITICO, 1 June 2022, https://www.politico.eu/article/eu-vows-deal-to-unlock-poland-pandemic-cash-hinges-recovery-fund-covid-19-on-reforms/.

Wax, E, 2025a. Dead on arrival. Euractiv. 17 July 2025, https://www.euractiv.com/section/politics/news/the-capitals-dead-on-arrival/.

Wax, E, 2025b. Rapporteur: EUCO under attack; Moldova tilts West as Sandu poised for decisive victory; Fico's illiberal constitution; Commission gets 3,000 budget questions; etc.

Euractiv. 29 September 2025, https://www.euractiv.com/news/rapporteur-euco-under-attack/.

Weiler, J, 2011. Dispatch from the Euro Titanic: And the Orchestra Played On [EJIL Editorial]. EJIL: Talk! https://www.ejiltalk.org/dispatch-from-the-euro-titanic-and-the-orchestra-played-on-ejil-editorial/.

White, J, 2023. Constitutionalizing the EU in an Age of Emergencies. *JCMS: Journal of Common Market Studies* 61, 781–96, https://doi.org/10.1111/jcms.13415.

White, J, 2019. *Politics of Last Resort: Governing by Emergency in the European Union*. Oxford University Press, https://doi.org/10.1093/oso/9780198791720.001.0001.

Wulff Wold, J, 2025. The Brief—Von der Leyen's big budget moment ends in chaos. Euractiv. 16 July 2025, https://www.euractiv.com/section/economy-jobs/opinion/the-brief-von-der-leyens-big-budget-moment-ends-in-chaos/.

Wulff Wold, J, and Michalopoulos, S, 2025. EXCLUSIVE: EU capitals move to spike Commission's new corporate, tobacco levies. Euractiv. 22 September 2025, https://www.euractiv.com/news/for-editing-exclusive-commissions-new-corporate-tobacco-levvies-under-heavy-fire-from-eu-countries/.

Wuppertal Institut, Arepo, 2023. Evaluation of the KfW funding programs 'EBS NWG' in the funding year 2020. Study conducted on behalf of the Federal Ministry of Economics and Climate Protection (BMWK). 14 April 2023, https://www.bmwk.de/Redaktion/DE/Downloads/E/Evaluation-Kfw-Foerderprogramme-ebs-nwg/evaluation-of-the-kfw-funding-programs-ebs-nwg-in-the-funding-year-2022-summary.pdf?__blob=publicationFile&v=4.

Wutscher, C, 2023. When Size Matters: On the Legality of the Recovery Instrument 'Next Generation EU' in Light of Its Unprecedented Volume, in: Weber, R (ed), *EU Integration through Financial Constitution: Follow the Money?* Hart Publishing.

Wyplosz, C, 2024. PE 755.722. Which European Public Goods? In-Depth Analysis Requested by the ECON committee. European Parliament, Economic Governance and EMU Scrutiny Unit (EGOV) Directorate-General for Internal Policies. March 2024, https://www.europarl.europa.eu/RegData/etudes/IDAN/2024/755722/IPOL_IDA(2024)755722_EN.pdf.

Wyplosz, C, 2010. The failure of the Lisbon strategy. VoxEU | CEPR, https://cepr.org/voxeu/columns/failure-lisbon-strategy.

Ympäristöministeriö, 2022. U 61/2021 vp. Ympäristöministeriö Perusmuistio YM2022-00106. Asia: Komission ehdotus ilmastotoimia koskevan sosiaalirahaston perustamisesta; Kokous; U/E/UTP-tunnus: U 61/2021 vp. 25.05.2022 [Ministry of the Environment Memorandum YM2022-00106. Subject: Commission proposal on the establishment of a social fund for climate action; Meeting; U/E/UTP code: U 61/2021 vp. 25 May 2022], https://www.eduskunta.fi/FI/vaski/Liiteasiakirja/Documents/EDK-2022-AK-29410.pdf.

Zeitlin, J, Bokhorst, D, and Eihmanis, E, 2024. Governing the European Union's recovery and resilience facility: National ownership and performance-based financing in theory and practice. *Regulation & Governance*, 19(3), 864–84. https://doi.org/10.1111/rego.12619.

Zeitlin, J, Bokhorst, D, and Eihmanis, E, 2023. Governing the RRF: Drafting, Implementing, and Monitoring National Recovery and Resilience Plans as an Interactive Multilevel Process. Recovery Watch Policy Study, https://feps-europe.eu/publication/governing-the-rrf/.

Zeitlin, J and Vanhercke, B, 2018. Socializing the European Semester: EU Social and Economic Policy Co-Ordination in Crisis and Beyond. *Journal of European Public Policy* 25, 149–174.

ZEW, 2024. Scientific Sympoisum: The Future of Cohesion Policy 2028-2034 from a Fiscal Policy Perspective. Brussels. July 2024, https://www.zew.de/en/events-and-professional-training/detail/the-future-of-cohesion-policy-2028-2034-from-a-fiscal-policy-perspective-1/4427?cHash=a479fc792925574402b8d2fe9ac4e403.

Index

For the benefit of digital users, indexed terms that span two pages (e.g., 52–53) may, on occasion, appear on only one of those pages.